New Kind of Machine Learning—Cellular Automata Model

AF790262

Parimal Pal Chaudhuri · Adip Dutta ·
Somshubhro Pal Choudhury ·
Dipanwita Roy Chowdhury · Raju Hazari

New Kind of Machine Learning—Cellular Automata Model

Springer

Parimal Pal Chaudhuri
Retired Professor, Indian Institute of Technology
Kolkata, West Bengal, India

Somshubhro Pal Choudhury
Bharat Innovation Fund/The Innovation Fund
Bengaluru, Karnataka, India

Raju Hazari
Department of Computer Science and Engineering
National Institute of Technology, Calicut
Kozhikode, Kerala, India

Adip Dutta
Kolkata, West Bengal, India

Dipanwita Roy Chowdhury
Department of Computer Science and Engineering
Indian Institute of Technology
Kharagpur, West Bengal, India

ISBN 978-981-96-1503-2 ISBN 978-981-96-1501-8 (eBook)
https://doi.org/10.1007/978-981-96-1501-8

© The Editor(s) (if applicable) and The Author(s), under exclusive license to Springer Nature Singapore Pte Ltd. 2025

This work is subject to copyright. All rights are solely and exclusively licensed by the Publisher, whether the whole or part of the material is concerned, specifically the rights of translation, reprinting, reuse of illustrations, recitation, broadcasting, reproduction on microfilms or in any other physical way, and transmission or information storage and retrieval, electronic adaptation, computer software, or by similar or dissimilar methodology now known or hereafter developed.
The use of general descriptive names, registered names, trademarks, service marks, etc. in this publication does not imply, even in the absence of a specific statement, that such names are exempt from the relevant protective laws and regulations and therefore free for general use.
The publisher, the authors and the editors are safe to assume that the advice and information in this book are believed to be true and accurate at the date of publication. Neither the publisher nor the authors or the editors give a warranty, expressed or implied, with respect to the material contained herein or for any errors or omissions that may have been made. The publisher remains neutral with regard to jurisdictional claims in published maps and institutional affiliations.

This Springer imprint is published by the registered company Springer Nature Singapore Pte Ltd.
The registered company address is: 152 Beach Road, #21-01/04 Gateway East, Singapore 189721, Singapore

If disposing of this product, please recycle the paper.

Acknowledgements

All the authors of the book join me to acknowledge the contributions of the students who worked under the guidance of authors noted below. The students helped us to set up the experiments and derive the experimental results presented in different chapters of the book. We also convey our sincere thanks to the authorities of the respective institutions where the authors and their students worked to finalize the book manuscript.

Elizabeth M. J., Asmabi M. and Darsana C. S. of Computer Science and Engineering Department of National Institute of Technology, Calicut, Kerala, India worked under the guidance of Assistant Professor Raju Hazari.

Rohan Henry Ekka and Dilip Sau of Computer Science and Engineering Department of Indian Institute of Technology (IIT) Kharagpur, West Bengal, India worked under the guidance of Senior Professor Dipanwita Roy Choudhury.

We sincerely appreciate and acknowledge the support and cooperation we received from the authorities of Springer Nature Singapore Pte Ltd. for preparation of the book manuscript and its publication.

Prof. Parimal Pal Chaudhuri

Prologue: Looking Backward

'Mother Nature' has provided us with a voluminous but encrypted encyclopaedia from which we can learn new things every day. We can observe wide varieties of exotic colourful patterns in the animal kingdom, plant world, and also on the surface of inanimate objects. A natural curiosity arises in our mind seeking answers to the question—how such amazing patterns can evolve? This phenomenon, observed both in the macro and micro-world, is worth further investigation.

In general, it can be observed that a set of simple subsystems constituting a physical system poses a mystery when considered as a whole. The interactions among simple processes of each subsystem exhibit a behaviour that is too complex to be visualized in isolation. For example, a neuron cell is simple and limited by its capability. However, a single neuron makes the neural system exhibit a complex behaviour that is in no way comparable to the capabilities of an individual neuron. A wide variety of interacting simple homogeneous subsystems exhibiting a complex system behaviour can be observed in nature.

In the above context, we look for answers for the next question—is it possible to model such physical systems? The answer is—an emphatic 'yes'; the underlying reason for such a forceful response emerges from the following scenario.

On surveying the published literature on building models for physical systems, we came across the works of John v. Neumann, a father figure in the field of computers. He proposed the discrete dynamical system of Cellular Automata (CA) in the 1950s as a tool for modelling physical systems. His interaction with a few gifted minds (Stanislaw Ulam, Arthur Burks and a few others), enriched the field of CA for designing an abstract model of selfreproduction in Biology. Next milestone in the field of CA research can be observed around 1970, when John Conway proposed 'the game of life' that significantly enhanced interest in the study of CA. Another major contributor in this field is S. Wolfram, whose comprehensive study resulted in the foundation of simple three-neighbourhood CA exhibiting evolution of complex patterns.

In this background, building computational models for physical systems was identified as a major research thrust of our research group since the 1980s at Indian Institute of Technology (IIT) Kharagpur India. The homogeneous structure of CA consists of a set of simple cells which interact with neighbouring cells employing simple evolution rules. The CA evolution over time displays complex patterns that cannot be ascertained unless we employ linear CA rules. This class of CA is referred to as 'Additive CA', while the other class is marked as non-linear CA that employs non-linear CA rules implementing non-linear logic functions.

Our research group started the study of evolution patterns of additive CA employing matrix algebraic tools. The target application domain was—the design of testable VLSI systems. A large number of research students worked on this application domain. All these research works were compiled in 1997 in the book entitled *Additive Cellular Automata—Theory and Applications* (ISBN: 0-8186-7717-1) published by IEEE Computer Society Press. Research emphasis of the group was subsequently shifted to study of non-linear CA dynamics, since it was observed that real-life applications cannot be appropriately modelled with additive CA.

In view of its universal appeal, a large number of researchers of diverse disciplines employed the CA model to address the problems of their interest. Analysis of non-linear CA models has been explored for study of many non-linear systems; to name a few—study of ant colonies to atmospheric research, aerodynamics to biological models, ecology, etc. Evolutions of this class of CA display interesting patterns that are found to represent complex behaviour of different physical systems. Further, many research groups designed multidimensional CA for modelling complex systems. However, from our study we concluded that higher complexity of CA rules makes the analysis of CA evolution patterns extremely difficult, if not impossible.

In collaboration with industrial research groups, we attempted to design CA applications in the field of Computational Proteomics by designing CA models for protein chains. Dr. Dinesh V. Palanivelu, a researcher in Biocon, provided excellent support in this venture. We continued our search to develop real-life applications employing non-linear CA with three and five neighbourhood structures. The research results from such efforts were compiled in the book entitled *A New Kind of Computational Biology* (ISBN: 978-981-13-1638-8) published by Springer Nature Singapore in 2018. Further down the journey, we observed that unless non-linear three neighboured CA evolution can be appropriately characterized, its applications to solve real-life problems of interest for industry and human society cannot be realized.

In view of the earlier scenario, our CA research hit a roadblock. We needed to use non-linear CA to address real-life problems. But adequate characterization of non-linear CA dynamics is extremely difficult. However, without meaningful characterization of CA evolution, solutions derived out of the CA model will be elusive. Probably, in view of such a situation, we hardly come across CA applications addressing problems of interest for industry.

From 2018 to 2019, our research group was forced to look for alternative avenues to derive solutions to real-life problems employing the CA model. By this time, applications of Machine Learning (ML) framework to solve wide varieties of problems have been proposed since 2015 onwards. ML based solutions became an attractive proposition, particularly for the problems which could not be adequately addressed in the past. Currently available ML frameworks employ a neural network or deep learning model trained on a large volume of training data corpus, followed by prediction of solution for testing dataset employing very large computing resources. For characterization of non-linear CA evolution, we employ the training/testing framework of machine learning. We name the model as Light Weight CAML (Cellular Automata (enhanced with) Machine Learning) since the model achieves desired prediction quality with significantly reduced computing resources and training data corpus.

This book begins with Chap. 1, guiding readers through the historic journey from philosophical discussions on cognition to the modern era of Artificial Intelligence (AI) and Machine Learning (ML). Chapter 2 outlines the significant challenges and ongoing research in Deep Learning, primarily focusing on explainability, the requirement for vast amounts of training data, privacy, security, and the need for voluminous computing power. Chapter 3 delves into the details of Biological Neural Networks, Artificial Neural Networks, and introduces Cellular Automata (CA). These first three chapters set the context for why a new lightweight model inspired by biological networks is proposed. This model is super efficient, using much fewer resources, and mimics the phased approach of cognitive decision-making in living organisms. Development of the CA model for a system demands efficient and appropriate design of CA rules for the constituent entities of the system being modelled. A generic approach on CA rule design is reported in Chap. 4 of the book. Design of CA rules for two specific application domains are next reported for modelling—(i) the interconnected entities of Amino acids of a protein chain, and (ii) a sequence of alphabets in a language text. The formulation and results of these two applications are reported in Chap. 5 (on Computational Biology) and Chap. 6 (on Computational Linguistics). Motivation for focussing on Computational Biology application is elaborated in subsequent discussions. Chapter 7 outlines an approach that explores the design of ML models employing the analytical framework of linear CA to realize linear functions.

Throughout my professional career, since the early 1960s, I had been associated with computers and Computer Sciences education. With the dawn of the twenty-first century, the focus of our research group was shifted from Computer Sciences to Life Sciences. Underlying reasons for such a major shift in research focus can be attributed to the following considerations.

Since the 1990s, scientists have warned about environmental degradation's impact on global ecosystems. The 'Climate Emergency' is predicted to severely affect 21st century society through rising sea levels, extreme weather, and intensified storms. This situation primarily threatens human health and crop production. The 2020–2022 COVID-19 pandemic exemplifies these risks. Agricultural challenges include unpredictable weather and increased soil salinity from seawater intrusion. Consequently, Life Sciences, particularly Medical and Agricultural Sciences, are expected to dominate research in the coming decades.

Based on the earlier consideration, the first CA application we have identified for this book is Computational Biology, specifically Computational Proteomics covering large scale study of proteins in living cells. Proteins are the main building blocks associated with major tasks of a cell of any organism. Protein mutations are implicated for different diseases. Design of CAML model for mutational study of proteins is the focus of Chap. 5.

Next application reported in Chap. 6 deals with Computational Linguistics. The motivation to pick up this application follows from the following consideration. Modern human society lives on an internetworked platform with the exchange of large volumes of textual data in a multi-language environment. Extraction of relevant information out of machine-readable data is an upheaval task for the discipline of Computational Linguistics, specifically in a multi-language environment. The focus of this chapter is to design CAML models to address the problem of 'Sentiment Analysis' in a multilingual environment without employing any pre-trained language framework.

A large number of ML models have been proposed with an expanding horizon of their application domains. Each of these models employs a so-called 'black-box' approach and so inherently lacks transparency and interpretability of results derived out of such models. Consequently, the last Chap. 7 of this book explores the design of ML models employing the analytical framework of linear CA to realize linear functions. The sole design objective of the model is to ensure transparency and interpretability of the results derived out of this CAML model. In addition, design of low cost hardwired ML platform based on CA is the driving force for such a research initiative.

As I close the background narrative of the book, I convey my sincere thanks to my co-authors for their untiring support to complete this book. Thought provoking input from Adip Datta in the field of AI/ML in Chaps. 1 and 3 enriched this book significantly. The presentation of AI in Chap. 2 by Somshubhro Pal Choudhury provides the readers with an excellent overview of the current state-of-art review and upcoming challenges in the field of AI. My young friend Raju Hazari, Assistant Professor in Computer Science, came forward to address an interesting problem in the field of Computational Linguistics in Chap. 6 in a multi-language environment. Finally, Dipanwita Roy Choudhury, a senior professor of IIT Kharagpur India, ventured into a totally new CA application in Chap. 7 by designing CA model for Machine Learning framework; the major motivators of her CA model are—(i) to ensure transparency in ML prediction that is not adequately addressed in the current black-box models of ML platforms, and (ii) low cost hardwire design of ML model employing regular, modular, cascadable structure of CA.

The traditional ML models demand 'Big Data' for training, followed by design of prediction algorithms employing huge computing resources. By contrast, the Light Weight CAML model needs low training data set and computing power, achieving an acceptable level of prediction quality.

September 2024

Prof. Parimal Pal Chaudhuri
Retired Professor
Indian Institute of Technology
Kolkata, West Bengal, India

Contents

Chapter 1
Thinking Machines, Thinking Minds: AI and Cognitive Science

"AI is not a substitute for human intelligence; it is a tool to amplify human creativity and ingenuity"

—Andrew McAfee (Principal research scientist at MIT)

1.1 Introduction

This chapter explores the fascinating world of Artificial Intelligence (AI) and Machine Learning (ML) from a unique perspective. We will examine the ideas of philosophers from the past alongside historical milestones in AI/ML. We will also examine the concept of intelligence and delve into the field of cognitive science.

The chapter introduces a novel technique by the authors, with the potential to significantly impact various fields, including linguistics and microbiology. This method introduces a kind of "*shortcut*" for representing complex systems, dramatically reducing the computational power needed to analyze and understand them. Imagine this chapter as a thought-provoking journey through the beautiful ambiguity of our thinking process, aiming to create a similar system in machines.

1.2 Ancient Roots

The history of Artificial Intelligence (AI) is a rich and a complex one, spanning several centuries and marked by significant developments in technology, theory and applications.

© The Author(s), under exclusive license to Springer Nature Singapore Pte Ltd. 2025

P. Pal Chaudhuri et al., *New Kind of Machine Learning—Cellular Automata Model*,
https://doi.org/10.1007/978-981-96-1501-8_1

The idea of creating artificial beings with human-like intelligence dates back to ancient civilizations. In Japanese folklore, there are stories of Karakuri (mechanical puppets or automata) used in various performances, such as the Dōbutsu-ura Karakuri, which featured mechanical animals like birds and monkeys that could perform tricks.

A famous automaton was created by Swiss watchmaker Henri Maillardet in the late 18th century. It includes a mechanical figure that can write and draw pictures.

Formal discussions of machine intelligence can be traced to the works of philosophers like Aristotle and Descartes. Charvaka, also known as Lokayata, is an ancient Indian philosophical school of thought that dates back to approximately 600 BCE. It is known for its materialistic and atheistic views, rejecting metaphysical concepts while emphasizing empiricism and skepticism. Charvakas believed that only the material world exists and that sensory perception is the only valid means of acquiring knowledge [1].

The connection between Charvaka philosophy and Artificial Intelligence (AI) lies in the broader context of philosophical discussions about the nature of consciousness, intelligence, and the mind. While Charvaka philosophy predates the development of AI by thousands of years, it touches on some philosophical questions that are relevant to contemporary debates in AI and cognitive science:

Materialism: Charvaka philosophy is fundamentally materialistic, asserting that consciousness and mental states arise solely from physical matter. In AI and cognitive science, the question of whether consciousness and intelligence can be explained purely in terms of physical processes is a central theme.

Empiricism: Charvakas emphasized the importance of empirical evidence and sensory perception as the basis for knowledge. In AI, machine learning and perception are heavily reliant on data and sensory input for learning and decision-making.

While Charvaka philosophy does not directly address AI or modern technology, its philosophical themes provide a historical and cultural context for discussions about the nature of intelligence, consciousness, and the mind in relation to AI and robotics. These discussions often explore whether machines can exhibit intelligence and consciousness and whether they can replicate human cognitive processes.

Blaise Pascal (1623–1662) and Gottfried Wilhelm Leibniz (1646–1716), two prominent philosophers and mathematicians of the 17th century, made significant contributions to the fields of mathematics, philosophy, and logic, which have indirect connections to the development of artificial intelligence (AI). Here is a brief overview of their contributions and their relevance to AI:

Pascal is best known for his work in probability theory and his famous philosophical argument known as "Pascal's Wager". While not directly related to AI, probability theory is a foundational concept in AI, especially in fields like machine learning, where probabilistic models are used for decision-making and uncertainty handling [2].

Pascal's Wager: Given the uncertainty of the existence of God and the potential consequences, Pascal argues that it is more rational to choose to believe in God, as the potential benefits of eternal life and happiness outweigh the potential consequences of disbelief.

Pascal's Wager and AI development are connected through a thought experiment called **Roko's Basilisk**. It flips the script on Pascal's original argument and applies it to superintelligent or Hard AI. This thought experiment proposes a superintelligent AI that surpasses human control. If such an AI is created and believes in rewarding those who helped its development and punishing those who did not, then not actively working towards beneficial AI development becomes an infinitely bad outcome. Roko's Basilisk suggests that even a small chance of a very negative outcome justifies taking action to prevent it. In this case, the action would be actively researching and developing safe and beneficial AI. In fact, Ray Kurzweil (Futurist), Demis Hassabis (DeepMind Co-founder), Andrew Ng (AI Researcher), and even Elon Musk among others, though may not be connected with this wager or thought experiment, show that regardless of ethical or social or moral consideration mankind will always take the path of acquiring and achieving superintelligence. In spite of a nagging fear of extinction of humanity.

Pascal invented one of the earliest mechanical calculators, the Pascaline, in the mid-seventeenth century. While this device was a precursor to modern computers and calculators, it was not directly related to AI but contributed to the development of computing technology.

Leibniz is credited with independently inventing the binary number system, which is fundamental to modern digital computing. Computers, including AI systems, use binary code for data representation and processing. He also conceived the idea of a universal language called "Characteristica Universalis" that could represent all human knowledge in a symbolic and logical manner. While this concept predates AI as we know it today, it reflects a desire for formalized knowledge representation, a critical aspect of AI, particularly in natural language processing and knowledge-based systems. Further down in Chap. 4, we will see a similar approach we have adopted for representing the written text of any language with the universal coding system of Unicode.

Leibniz's metaphysical work, "The Monadology", introduced the concept of monads, which he believed were fundamental, indivisible substances that make up the fabric of reality. While this metaphysical concept is not directly related to AI, it reflects Leibniz's interest in foundational principles and logical systems. Additionally, Leibniz's concept of **monads** (individual, windowless substances) can be seen as an early thought experiment on the nature of information processing entities, potentially laying groundwork for ideas about individual processing units within AI systems.

While Blaise Pascal and Gottfried Wilhelm Leibniz made significant contributions to mathematics and philosophy during their lifetimes, their direct influence on the field of AI is limited due to the significant time gap between their work and the emergence of AI as a distinct discipline in the 20th century. However, their work in areas like probability, binary representation, and formal logic laid some conceptual groundwork for the development of computational and logical approaches that are integral to AI research today.

Beyond metaphysics and philosophies, inventors like Blaise Pascal and Gottfried Wilhelm Leibniz designed mechanical calculating machines that laid the foundation for the development of early computing devices.

1.3 Can Machines Think?

The 20th century saw the birth of modern computer science and the development of early computers, such as the ENIAC and UNIVAC. Long before working computers appeared in academia and industries questions were raised on thinking machines.

The question of whether it is possible for machines to think has a long history, which is firmly entrenched in the distinction between dualist and materialist views of the mind. René Descartes in his 1637 Discourse writes:

> How many different automata or moving machines could be made by the industry of man? For we can easily understand a machine's being constituted so that it can utter words, and even emit some responses to action on it of a corporeal kind, which brings about a change in its organs; for instance, if touched in a particular part it may ask what we wish to say to it; if in another part it may exclaim that it is being hurt, and so on. But it never happens that it arranges its speech in various ways, in order to reply appropriately to everything that may be said in its presence, as even the lowest type of man can do [3].

Descartes view of limited speech capabilities or appropriate reply, can be demonstrated by this two ancient chatbots,

Eliza is one of the earliest examples of a chatbot, was developed in the mid-1960s by Joseph Weizenbaum, a computer scientist and professor at the Massachusetts Institute of Technology (MIT). The primary goal of Eliza was to demonstrate the superficiality of communication between humans and machines and to challenge the notion that a computer could possess genuine understanding or consciousness. Eliza was designed to simulate a Rogerian psychotherapist.

Parry is another early example of a chatbot, created in the 1970s by psychiatrist Kenneth Colby at Stanford University. Unlike Eliza, which simulated a Rogerian psychotherapist, Parry was designed to simulate a person with paranoid schizophrenia. The purpose of Parry was to explore the possibilities of using computers to simulate mental disorders and to better understand the nature of schizophrenia. Here is a sample of dialog between them.

Prompt by PARRY: "People get on my nerves sometimes."
Response by ELIZA: "I am not sure I understand you fully."
Prompt by PARRY: "You should pay more attention."
Response by ELIZA: "Suppose you should pay more attention."
Prompt by PARRY: "You're entitled to your own opinion."
Response by ELIZA: "What makes you think I am entitled to my own opinion?"
Prompt by PARRY: "It bothers me just to be around people in general."
Response by ELIZA: "Please go on."
Prompt by PARRY: "I went to the track at Bay Meadows a while back."
Response by ELIZA: "What does that suggest to you?"
Prompt by PARRY: "I went to the races."
Response by ELIZA: "What else would you like to discuss?"
Prompt by PARRY: "Horseracing interests me."
Response by ELIZA: "Why do you say that just now?"
Prompt by PARRY: "There's a lot of crooked gambling going on there."
Response by ELIZA: "I am not sure I understand you fully."
Prompt by PARRY: "It's clear to me if not to you."
Response by ELIZA: "Do you think its likely that not to I?"
Prompt by PARRY: "I went to the races."
Response by ELIZA: "Please go on."
Prompt by PARRY: "I gamble on horses."
Response by ELIZA: "What does that suggest to you?"
Prompt by PARRY: "I went to the races."
Response by ELIZA: "What else would you like to discuss?"

At first, we are really astonished by the interaction of two chatbots, but within a few lines of this dialog we understand that the conversation is going loopy and going nowhere.

In 1950, British mathematician and logician Alan Turing introduced the concept of the "Turing Test" to assess a machine's ability to exhibit Intelligent Behavior (*defined in Sect.* 1.6). The test was introduced by Turing in his 1950 paper "Computing Machinery and Intelligence" while working at the University of Manchester. Because "*Thinking*" is difficult to define, Turing chose to replace the question with another. Turing describes the new form of the problem in terms of a three-person game called the "imitation game", in which an interrogator asks questions to a man and a woman in another room in order to determine the correct sex of the two players. This test was modified by Turing and many other computer scientists and cognitive scientists after him. As an example, one proposal by John Searle, this test involves the machine interacting with the entire physical world and not just through conversation. It is a more comprehensive test, but difficult to implement.

Even now, at the beginning of the year 2024, we have created machines which can imitate in a limited way a person, vocally or through texting. It can compose music, write poems, create paintings and write computer programs. It has become near impossible even for a well-informed person to strictly identify the source or the creator, especially if the designers of the AI system want to hide it. We can have an artificial psychotherapist far more advanced than Eliza.

Imagine thinking not as a single, isolated process, but as a grand symphony. In this analogy, the individual notes and instruments represent all the complex biological processes happening within a living organism. The way these processes interact and influence each other creates the overall "melody" of thought. This suggests that thinking might be an emergent property—a phenomenon arising from the intricate interplay of simpler parts, rather than a single, well-defined cognitive function.

In the survival crucible, life, constantly battling in a competitive and often harsh environment, has forged this ability to think. Over eons of evolution, organisms that could better process information, adapt to changing conditions, and make decisions that enhanced their chances of survival, thrived and passed on their traits to next generation. Thinking, in this view, becomes a tool honed by the relentless pressure of existence. Humans, arguably the most complex form of life on Earth, represent the pinnacle of this evolutionary process. Our intelligence allows us not just to survive, but to flourish, solve problems, create art and technology, and even contemplate the universe itself. This sophisticated form of thinking is what we qualitatively describe as "Intelligence".

Our efforts to create Artificial Intelligence (AI) can be seen as an attempt to systematically replicate this biological thinking process. However, there is a crucial difference. AI systems are not driven by the primal urge for survival that shaped biological intelligence. We have created *simulated survival situations* by setting goals, such as optimizing tasks, analyzing data, or even generating creative content. We have created programs that give the same results using less resources like computing time, memory replace inefficient procedures. These programs are a critical part of computer science called algorithmic optimization.

The pursuit of AI may push us to redefine what intelligence truly means. Perhaps it is not just about survival, but about the ability to learn, adapt, and solve problems in novel situations. By understanding the origins of biological intelligence, we can approach AI design with a more nuanced perspective, potentially leading to the development of entirely new forms of intelligent systems.

1.4 Major Developmental Milestones of AI

Artificial intelligence (AI) might be a hot topic today, but its story stretches back several decades. While it is certainly grabbing more headlines and demonstrating impressive capabilities in recent years, the roots of AI research can be traced all the way back to the 1940 and 1950s.

This surge in recent progress can be attributed to several key factors. First, advancements in computing power have given us the ability to handle the complex calculations needed for AI algorithms. Second, the explosion of data available has provided AI systems with the fuel they need to learn and improve. Finally, innovations in the design of these algorithms have unlocked new possibilities for what AI can achieve.

To truly understand AI's potential, we need to examine its historical journey. Let us delve into the major milestones that have shaped the field over the decades.

The Journey: Brief History of AI Evolution

- **1943**: Warren McCulloch, a neurophysiologist, and Walter Pitts, a logician, made a groundbreaking contribution to the field of artificial intelligence (AI) with the creation of a mathematical model of artificial neurons. This model, often referred to as the McCulloch-Pitts neuron, laid the foundation for the development of Artificial Neural Networks (ANNs), a core technology behind many modern AI advancements.
- **1949**: Donald Hebb, a psychologist, introduced a revolutionary concept called Hebbian learning. This principle significantly impacted the development of neural network theory and continues to be a fundamental concept in deep learning today.
- **1950**: Alan Turing introduced the Turing Test in his 1950 paper "Computing Machinery and Intelligence," is a thought experiment designed to assess a machine's ability to exhibit intelligent behavior equivalent to, or indistinguishable from, that of a human.
- **1951**: Marvin Minsky and Dean Edmonds build the SNARC, the first neural network computer. Marvin Minsky, a graduate student at Princeton, and Dean Edmonds, a physics graduate student, collaborated on a groundbreaking project: The Stochastic Neural Analog Reinforcement Calculator, or SNARC. This machine is widely considered by the majority of experts as the first artificial neural network computer.
- **1956**: Dartmouth College in Hanover hosted a small yet pivotal event called the Dartmouth Summer Research Project on Artificial Intelligence, more commonly known as the Dartmouth Conference. This gathering of prominent mathematicians, computer scientists, and researchers is widely recognized as the **founding moment of AI as a distinct field of study**. John McCarthy, a key organizer of the conference, is credited with proposing the term "Artificial Intelligence" to describe the field's goals and aspirations. This provided a unifying concept and helped solidify the foundation for a new area of research. The conference brought together some of the brightest minds of the time, including John McCarthy, Marvin Minsky, Claude Shannon, and Nathaniel Rochester. Their discussions and brainstorming sessions laid the groundwork for future research directions in AI.
- **1958**: Frank Rosenblatt, a Cornell University psychologist, made a significant contribution to the field of AI with the invention of the Perceptron. This invention was not just a single device; it was a concept—a **single-layer artificial neural network** capable of learning simple patterns.
- **1959**: Allen Newell and Herbert A. Simon, two pioneers in AI, made a significant contribution with the development of the **Logic Theorist**. This program was not just an AI program; it was a groundbreaking step in the field of automated reasoning. The development of the Logic Theorist also contributed to the birth of cognitive science, a field that explores how humans think and process information. By trying to simulate human reasoning in a machine, Newell and Simon provided valuable insights into the workings of the human mind.
- **1966**: The ELIZA program, an early example of natural language processing, was created by Joseph Weizenbaum, a computer scientist at MIT, this program,

sometimes referred to as DOCTOR, is considered a landmark achievement for being an early example of **Natural Language Processing (NLP)**. Unfortunately, the original source code for ELIZA was lost for many years and only recently made publicly available. While there are implementations inspired by ELIZA, they might not be identical to the original program. This GitHub repository by user keithweaver [4] offers an implementation of the ELIZA program. It includes the code with comments and an example demonstrating how it works.

- **1969**: The **Shakey robot**, considered the "great-grandfather of self-driving cars and military drones", was developed at **SRI International** (formerly known as the Stanford Research Institute) between 1966 and 1972. Shakey is a landmark achievement in robotics because it was the first **General-purpose mobile robot**. Unlike previous robots designed for specific tasks, Shakey could navigate its environment and perform simple actions like pushing objects. Shakey was not just pre-programmed with a sequence of movements. It could perceive its surroundings using cameras and sensors, plan its actions, and reason about the consequences.
  The journey so far has been remarkable, and with increased funding, the field of AI was poised for a flourishing spring. But then came '**AI winter**'.
- **1973**: The Lighthill Report, formally titled "Report of a Working Party on Artificial Intelligence", published in 1973, had a significant impact on AI research funding; Sir James Lighthill, a prominent mathematician, was commissioned by the British government to assess the state of AI research and its future potential. The report acknowledged the progress made in AI research but concluded that the field's overblown promises and unrealistic expectations were leading to a lack of significant breakthroughs. Lighthill argued that the funding for AI research was not justified by the slow pace of progress.
  It must be mentioned that prior to Lighthill Report Marvin Minsky and Seymour Papert published "**Perceptrons: An Introduction to Computational Geometry**" by Marvin Minsky and Seymour Papert in 1969 [5].
  The book focused on the limitations of perceptrons, a specific type of neural network architecture with a single layer. Minsky and Papert mathematically proved that single-layer perceptrons could not solve certain problems, particularly those involving non-linearly separable data. Their work highlighted the limitations of Neural Networks (NNs) at the time, discouraging researchers who might have otherwise pursued this field. The prevailing sentiment became that NNs were not powerful enough for complex tasks. With the perceived limitations of NNs, funding and research focus shifted towards other areas of AI like symbolic AI, which focused on logic and reasoning using symbolic representations.
- **Late 1970s**: MYCIN and Dendral like Expert systems emerged. MYCIN aimed to diagnose infectious diseases and recommend antibiotic treatments. It used a knowledge base of medical information and a set of rules to analyze patient symptoms and suggest possible diagnoses. MYCIN demonstrated the potential of expert systems in healthcare. It showed how AI could be used to reason about complex medical problems and aid doctors in diagnosis and treatment decisions. However, limitations in knowledge representation and reasoning capabilities prevented it from widespread clinical use.

Dendral focused on determining the molecular structure of organic compounds based on data from mass spectrometry and other analytical techniques. It used a rule-based system to analyze the data and generate possible structures for the unknown molecule. Dendral revolutionized the field of structural elucidation in chemistry. It accelerated the process of identifying unknown compounds and had significant applications in drug discovery and materials science.

- **1980–1990s**: This was a fascinating and a crucial period for Artificial Intelligence (AI) research. This era witnessed the rise and fall of two prominent approaches: **Knowledge-Based Systems (KBS)** and **Neural Networks (NNs)**. KBS systems aimed to capture human expertise in a specific domain by encoding knowledge and rules into a computer program. MYCIN and Dendral, as mentioned earlier, were prime examples of successful KBS applications in medicine and chemistry, respectively. KBS offered several advantages. They were transparent, allowing users to understand the reasoning behind the system's decisions. They were also relatively easy to build and maintain compared to more complex approaches like neural networks at the time.
  As KBS matured, limitations emerged. KBS struggled with handling incomplete or noisy data, which is common in the real world. Additionally, the knowledge acquisition process (building the knowledge base) could be laborious and expensive.
  After the AI winter and the Thaw, the 1980 and 1990s saw a resurgence of interest in neural networks due to several factors:
  More powerful computers allowed for training complex neural networks with multiple layers, overcoming the limitations of single-layer perceptrons.
  The development of algorithms like backpropagation significantly improved the ability of neural networks to learn from data.
  In some cases, KBS and NNs were used together. For instance, a KBS could be used to identify the relevant features of a problem, and then a neural network could be used to analyze those features and make a prediction.
- **1986**: A significant breakthrough in artificial intelligence research occurred with the publication of a paper titled "Learning representations by back-propagating errors" by 2024 Nobel Laureate Geoffrey Hinton, David Rumelhart, and Ronald Williams [6]. This paper introduced a critical concept for training neural networks. We will go into details of backpropagation in Chap. 3.
  The work of Hinton, Rumelhart, and Williams is considered a foundational contribution to the field of deep learning. Their paper on backpropagation is widely cited, and their ideas continue to influence research and development in AI today.
- **1988**: Yann LeCun developed LeNet-5, a convolutional neural network for image recognition. Yann LeCun, considered a godfather of deep learning, pioneered AI applications with a focus on mimicking the brain's learning processes, He is the Silver Professor of the Courant Institute of Mathematical Sciences at New York University and Vice-President, Chief AI Scientist at Meta. This architecture is considered a **Convolutional Neural Network (CNN)**, a specific type of neural network particularly adept at image recognition. Unlike traditional neural networks, CNNs are specifically designed to process visual data like images. They achieve

this through a special layer called a **convolutional layer**. This layer identifies spatial features within an image, such as edges, shapes, and textures. By stacking multiple convolutional layers, CNNs can learn increasingly complex features, ultimately leading to object recognition.

- **1990s**: The 1990s were a pivotal decade for AI, ML, and the rise of the Internet. These three elements converged in a way that fueled a resurgence of interest and progress in AI after a period of stagnation.
  In the earlier years of AI research, the focus was on building knowledge-based systems with hand-coded rules. The 1990s saw a shift towards **Machine Learning (ML)** techniques that allowed computers to learn from data. Algorithms like Support Vector Machines (SVMs) and Recurrent Neural Networks (RNNs) gained traction. These algorithms could analyze large datasets and identify patterns without explicit programming, a significant advantage over traditional AI approaches. Advancements in computer hardware, particularly more powerful processors, made it possible to train these algorithms on ever-increasing volumes of data.
  The explosion of the Internet in the 1990s led to a vast amount of digital data being generated—text, images, user behavior logs, etc. This readily available data became a valuable resource for training ML algorithms.
  This period reignited interest in AI research and paved the way for the significant advancements we see today in various fields. The advancements in the 1990s laid the foundation for the **deep learning** revolution of the 2010s, which continues to transform various aspects of our lives today.
- **1997**: A significant milestone was reached in the history of AI when IBM's chess computer, Deep Blue, defeated Garry Kasparov, the reigning world chess champion, in a six-game match. Prior to this, chess was considered a domain where human intuition and strategic thinking were unmatched by machines. Deep Blue's win demonstrated that AI could achieve superhuman performance in a complex, intellectual task.
  Deep Blue's victory was not solely due to brute computing power. It employed advanced search algorithms and heuristics (rules of thumb) to evaluate millions of possible chess positions at a depth never seen before. However Deep Blue's success was specifically in the game of chess. It did not translate to a general intelligence capable of tackling other complex challenges. Chess, with its well-defined rules and limited number of possible moves, was not a true test of general intelligence.
- **2000s**: The Era of Big Data and Deep Learning, roughly from the mid-2000s to the present day, has been a period of immense progress in AI. It is like a powerful engine driving innovation, fueled by few key ingredients:
  The rise of the Internet, social media, smartphones, and various sensors have created an explosion in data generation. This "Big Data" provides the raw material for AI algorithms, especially deep learning models. At the same time the development of powerful and affordable Graphics Processing Units (GPUs) dramatically increased the ability to train complex deep learning models. These models are like hungry learners, requiring massive amounts of computational resources to process and learn from vast datasets.

Inspired by the structure and function of the human brain, deep learning algorithms have achieved remarkable results in various domains. They excel at tasks that were previously difficult for computers, like image recognition, understanding human language, and deciphering spoken words.
Data allows us to train deep learning models with many layers and intricate architectures. Imagine a deep learning model as a student—the more data it has to learn from (like a vast library of books), the more complex concepts it can grasp and the better it performs.

- **2006**: Geoffrey Hinton et al. published a paper on deep learning for speech recognition. Born in 1947 in Wimbledon, England, Hinton's family has a rich history in scientific achievement, including his great-great grandfather, George Boole, the founder of Boolean logic. He received his Ph.D. in Artificial Intelligence from the University of Edinburgh in 1978.
  Hinton's research on Boltzmann machines and Deep Belief Networks (DBNs) in the 1990 and 2000s further advanced the field of deep learning. These architectures helped overcome limitations in training deep neural networks at the time.
- **2009**: Deep learning gained traction with the application of Convolutional Neural Networks (CNNs) to image recognition. Before 2009 image recognition algorithms relied heavily on hand-crafted features, which required significant expertise and effort to design effectively.
  CNNs offered a new approach. Inspired by the structure and function of the visual cortex in the human brain, CNNs automatically learn features directly from the image data.
- **2011**: IBM's Watson wins Jeopardy! Jeopardy! is a game that requires a deep understanding of natural language. Contestants need to interpret clues, identify wordplay, and formulate responses in a specific format. Watson's success demonstrated the progress of Natural Language Processing (NLP) techniques in AI. It could process complex questions, understand their nuances, and generate relevant answers. Earlier search engines primarily relied on keyword matching to retrieve information. Watson's approach was more sophisticated. It could analyze the context of a clue, identify entities and relationships, and draw connections between diverse knowledge sources.
- **2012**: AlexNet wins the ImageNet competition, showcasing the power of deep learning. Developed by a team led by Geoffrey Hinton, AlexNet was a deep convolutional neural network with a complex architecture. In 2012, it competed in the ImageNet Large Scale Visual Recognition Challenge (ILSVRC), a prestigious benchmark for image recognition algorithms. AlexNet achieved a top-5 error rate of around 16%. The top-5 error rate measures how often the correct class (the actual object in the image) is not included within the model's top five most probable predictions. A lower top-5 error rate signifies better performance. In the example, an error rate of 16% for AlexNet means that for 16% of the images, the correct class was not among its top five guesses.
- **2014**: Google acquired DeepMind, a significant move that accelerated advancements in AI. DeepMind, founded in 2010, was a leading research lab focused on developing powerful general-purpose AI. Their work centered on deep learning,

reinforcement learning, and other cutting-edge AI techniques. Google's acquisition of DeepMind in 2014 was a strategic move that has significantly influenced the landscape of AI. It combined the expertise of a leading research lab with the resources of a major technology company, accelerating progress in AI and shaping its real-world applications.

- **2016**: A significant event occurred that marked a major leap in AI: Google DeepMind's program, AlphaGo, defeated Lee Sedol, the world champion Go player, in a five-game match. Unlike chess, which computers had already mastered, Go was considered a significant challenge for AI due to the sheer number of possible moves and the importance of considering the entire board state. It utilized a combination of deep learning techniques, including convolutional neural networks (CNNs) for analyzing board positions and reinforcement learning to improve its strategies through self-play.
- **2017**: The Transformer model was introduced by Google Researchers. The introduction of the Transformer model was a significant milestone in the field of Natural Language Processing (NLP) and AI as a whole.
- **2018**: OpenAI releases GPT-2, a large language model (LLM). GPT-2 stands for Generative Pre-trained Transformer 2. It is a large language model developed by OpenAI. OpenAI is a research company to develop safe and beneficial Artificial General Intelligence (AGI). It was founded in late 2015 as a non-profit organization by Elon Musk, Sam Altman, Ilya Sutskever. and other prominent figures in AI research. The goal was to conduct open research and collaborate with the broader AI community.

– *Shift to Limited Profit (2019)*: In 2019, OpenAI transitioned to a capped-profit limited liability company. This change aimed to secure funding for research while maintaining a commitment to responsible AI development. They received significant investments from Microsoft.

LLMs are a type of AI that are trained on massive amounts of text data to generate human-quality text, translate languages, write different kinds of creative content, and answer your questions in an informative way.

GPT-2 was a significant leap forward in LLM technology. It had a much larger capacity compared to previous models, allowing it to learn more complex patterns and relationships within the text data it was trained on. This larger capacity translated to GPT-2's ability to generate more realistic and coherent text formats, like poems, code, scripts, musical pieces, email, and letters.

- **2020 to present day**: New architectures emerged, pushing the boundaries of depth and complexity. Transformers became a dominant architecture for LLMs and NLP tasks. Convolutional Neural Networks (CNNs) continued to evolve for computer vision tasks.
  Techniques like self-supervised learning and transfer learning gained prominence, allowing models to learn from unlabeled data and leverage pre-trained knowledge for new tasks. Large Language Models (LLMs): LLMs like GPT-3 and LaMDA

(Language Model for Dialogue Applications) utilized Transformer architectures with billions of parameters, achieving state-of-the-art performance in tasks like text generation, machine translation, and question answering.
Advancements in hardware, particularly GPUs, TPUs and specialized AI accelerators, enabled training of increasingly complex models on massive datasets.
LLMs like GPT-3 and LaMDA utilized Transformer architectures with billions of parameters, achieving state-of-the-art performance in tasks like text generation, machine translation, and question answering. Techniques like BERT and ELMo captured the contextual meaning of words, improving the understanding and generation of natural language.

In continuation of the historical perspectives of AI higlighted in this section, Chap. 2 delves further into the details of the current AI trends, challenges and the research and industry efforts to overcome those challenges.

In the great quest of Chap. 1 to understand thinking (and maybe stop ourselves from doing it so much), the first three subsections till Sect. 1.3, we have gone down the Rabbit Hole of Philosophy and existential dread. Section 1.4 covers the history from Abacus to Alexa: a cli's notes version of AI history. We now arrive at the upcoming Sect. 1.5 (unveiling the mystery on 'how we think about our thinking').

1.5 Algorithmic and Non-algorithmic Process

In Sect. 1.4, we explored the continuous efforts of researchers to innovate methods that emulate human intelligence. Their objective is to develop machines capable not only of outperforming humans in specifically trained tasks but also surpassing them in overall cognitive ability. However, before achieving this goal, it is crucial to understand whether human problem-solving operates through algorithmic or non-algorithmic processes.

Algorithmic Programming (AP) and Non-Algorithmic Programming (NAP) represent different approaches to solving problems and writing software.

Algorithmic programming involves writing code that follows a predefined sequence of steps to solve a problem or perform a task. These steps are structured, logical, and repeatable. Algorithms are the core component of algorithmic programming. They define the logic and steps required to achieve a specific outcome. Algorithmic programming typically follows structured programming paradigms, such as procedural programming or object-oriented programming. Algorithms produce deterministic results; given the same input, they always produce the same output. The behavior of algorithmic programs is predictable and can be analyzed theoretically using techniques such as time complexity and space complexity analysis.

On the other hand, Non-algorithmic programming (NAP) involves writing code that does not follow a predefined sequence of steps but relies on other mechanisms to achieve its goals. This approach is often used in domains where the problem-solving process is complex or unpredictable. NAP may adapt their behavior based on dynamic factors such as user input, environmental conditions, or real-time data.

Sometimes programs may employ heuristic techniques or machine learning algorithms to learn from experience and improve performance over time. Two important issues associated with NAP are next introduced.

Probabilistic outcomes: The outcomes of non-algorithmic programs may be probabilistic rather than deterministic, meaning they can vary even with the same input.

Complex decision-making: Non-algorithmic programs often involve complex decision-making processes that cannot be easily encapsulated in a predefined algorithm. A few examples of NAP are:

- Machine learning algorithms (e.g., neural networks, decision trees)
- Genetic algorithms and evolutionary computing
- Natural language processing systems
- Expert systems and rule-based inference engines (may be clubbed as non-algorithmic program under some complex situation).

In practice, many software systems combine elements of both algorithmic and non-algorithmic programming. Algorithmic programming provides the foundational logic and structure of the software, while non-algorithmic techniques are used to enhance adaptability, learning, and decision-making capabilities.

In step with philosophical and applied development of computer systems, after 1980, major research focus was directed on imitating the functional properties of organic brain into a computer architecture.

1.6 Defining Intelligence

Intelligence, that spark of brilliance, arises from a deep-seated aptitude and an irresistible urge to solve problems. For Homo sapiens, this urge was born from the most primal need—survival. We see this beautifully illustrated in the tapestry of history, woven with threads of human ingenuity for over 5,000 years.

The earliest chapters tell the tale of a species on the cusp of greatness. The most adept among our ancestors, akin to artists shaping clay, crafted tools for hunting and gathering. They learned to dance with nature's forces, manipulating phenomena, and even predicting the celestial ballet of seasons and their place within the vast cosmic canvas.

Fast forward 2,000 years, and a new melody emerges. The rise of long-distance trade, a symphony of commerce and cultural exchange, necessitated a chorus of specialized knowledge within small groups. To navigate the intricacies of this trade, some delved into the mysteries of the heavens, becoming astronomers, while others mastered the lay of the land as skilled geographers. This laid the foundation for a fascinating societal shift—the birth of a dedicated problem-solving class.

This transformation was not merely practical. It ignited a fire of curiosity, a yearning to understand not just the problems themselves, but the very process of thinking that lay at their heart. They began to interpret the world with a newfound depth, a philosophical symphony echoing from the minds of these intellectual pioneers.

The concept of "thinking on thinking" can be referred to as Metacognition. Metacognition is the awareness and understanding of one's own thought processes. It involves the ability to reflect on, monitor, and regulate one's cognitive activities. This higher-order thinking skill allows individuals to be more conscious and focused on their approach to problem-solving, decision-making, and learning. Here are some aspects of thinking on thinking or metacognition.

Metacognition provides an awareness of one's own thinking. This may include considering the strategies used to approach a problem, evaluating the effectiveness of those strategies, and identifying areas for improvement. Individuals engage in monitoring their cognitive processes to ensure that they are on the right track. This may involve checking for comprehension during reading, assessing the accuracy of problem-solving steps, or evaluating the progress of a learning task.

Metacognitive skills include the ability to plan and organize one's thinking before engaging in a task. This might involve setting goals, selecting appropriate strategies, and developing a plan for completing a task or solving a problem. When faced with a problem, metacognition allows individuals to think about their thinking process. This may involve breaking down the problem, considering alternative solutions, and reflecting on the success of past problem-solving approaches.

Metacognition includes an awareness of cognitive biases and errors in thinking. Recognizing common pitfalls in reasoning can help individuals make more informed decisions and avoid potential mistakes. Metacognition involves the ability to regulate one's cognitive processes. This includes adjusting strategies when faced with challenges, persisting in the face of difficulties, and managing one's attention and focus. Metacognitive skills are crucial in the learning process. This includes selecting effective learning strategies, monitoring comprehension during learning activities, and continuous modification of methodology based on feedback.

Lastly and most important is an individual's ability to transfer knowledge and skills from one context to another. It involves recognizing similarities and differences between situations and applying appropriate strategies.

Intelligent behavior can be viewed as the capability of using and modifying '*objects*', while deciphering the relationship between the objects, in order to predict the outcome of interaction leading to problem solution. The term '*objects*' may refer to material or non-materialistic abstract representation.

With our definition as given above, lots of well known '*Intelligent*' behavior will fail to satisfy the criteria as an intelligent thing, a few illustrations follow:

- A thing which is a champion in chess or Go is not intelligent.
- A thing which can rewrite pages you created more lucidly is not intelligent.
- A thing which composes a poem or paints or mimics a style of artistic expression may not be viewed as intelligent behavior.

In the earlier context, we present our views listing the parameters qualifying the term '*Intelligence*'.

Cognitive Abilities:

- *Learning and Problem-Solving*: The ability to acquire new knowledge and skills, and apply them to solve problems creatively and efficiently.
- *Reasoning and Logic*: The ability to analyze information, identify patterns, draw conclusions, and make sound judgments.
- *Memory and Recall*: The ability to store and retrieve information effectively.
- *Critical Thinking*: The ability to question assumptions, evaluate evidence, and form well-reasoned opinions.

Adaptability:

- *The ability to adjust to new situations and environments.* This includes learning from mistakes and changing strategies when necessary.

Creativity and Innovation:

- *The ability to generate new ideas and solutions.* This can involve thinking outside the box and coming up with unique approaches.

Social Intelligence:

- *The ability to understand and interact effectively with others.* This includes empathy, communication skills, and the ability to build relationships.

Metacognition:

- *The ability to be aware of one's own thinking processes.* This includes being able to monitor, evaluate, and regulate one's thoughts and actions.

In addition to these core qualities, intelligence can also be influenced by:

- *Motivation*: The desire to learn and understand.
- *Curiosity*: A natural interest in exploring new things and asking questions.
- *Persistence*: The ability to stick to a task even when it is difficult.

As per the current state of technology, a few of the above-mentioned qualities we have successfully simulated:

- Reasoning and Logic, efficiently but not creatively
- Learning and Problem-Solving (partly)
- Memory and Recall
- The ability to adjust to new situations and environments
- The ability to stick to a task even when it is difficult
- The ability to understand and interact effectively with others.

In Sect. 1.5 readers can get a glimpse on—under what situation, which innovative AI/ML method (algorithmic or non-algorithmic) effectively simulates the qualities listed above.

How does human being face a situation not encountered earlier? A probable answer is—human being correlates the situation to known facts, as is evident from the following case. Let a village boy be brought to a city housing and face a question—why there are no birds around? His confident answer comes as—'because there are no trees'. Thus, even a boy co-relates the fact known to him—birds are usually seen in trees. The same boy may fail to answer the question—why there are so many pigeons on the roof top of a building in a concrete jungle? Because he does not know that—pigeons can be kept as pets. But if he sees that pigeons are fed, he will correlate and answer 'some birds can be pets and survive without trees'.

If he continues this reasoning, he can make the following statements:

"Probably all birds if supplied with food and shelter can live without trees"

"Probably some animals can live outside their natural habitat if they can get other man-made means to survive".

"It should be possible to keep all animals in a closed system to study them closely if their fundamental requirements are satisfied".

In view of earlier reasoning, we make a conjecture: Human beings with **minimal data** can come to correct conclusions and make hypotheses correctly barring a few exceptions.

In the context of the proposed conjecture, we take a glimpse on the volume of data AI has to deal with. Let us consider the English Language. Estimates vary on the number of words Shakespeare used in his literature.

Lower Estimate: Around 8,000 words. This is a conservative estimate that considers only the unique words Shakespeare used.

Higher Estimate: Up to 30,000 words. This includes not only unique words but also variations like verb conjugations and plurals. Additionally, some scholars credit Shakespeare with inventing or introducing over 1,700 words that are still used in English today.

LLMs (Large Language Model) are trained on massive amounts of text data, including books, articles, code repositories, and web crawl data, greater than one terabyte depending on the specific LLM. During training, the LLM learns relationships between words and concepts. These relationships are captured in the model's parameters, which can number in the tens of billions or even hundreds of billions. The number of parameters is often used as a measure of an LLM's complexity. Now let us take a quantitative view where big data and huge data plays a dominant role (**Big data** emphasizes the characteristics (volume, variety, velocity) that make data challenging to handle with traditional methods. **Huge data** focuses more on the sheer **immensity** of the dataset). Beyond LLMs, we give a glimpse of data requirements in two other fields of science—(1) Genomics and personalized medicine, and (2) Astronomy and Astrophysics.

1. **Genomics and Personalized Medicine**:

   - This field deals with analyzing vast amounts of genetic data to understand human health, disease predisposition, and personalized treatment options.
   - Data sources include:

  - Whole genome sequencing of individuals (3 billion base pairs per human genome)
  - Gene expression data (measuring activity levels of genes)
  - Epigenetic data (studying how genes are regulated)
  - Data on environmental factors and lifestyle choices

- Estimated data volume: It is constantly growing, but some estimates suggest the field generates and stores Exabytes (EB) of data annually (1 EB = 1 billion Gigabytes).

2. **Astronomy and Astrophysics**:

- This field studies the universe, from planets and stars to galaxies and black holes.
- Data sources include:

  - Images and spectra from telescopes (capturing light and other information from celestial objects)
  - Simulation data (modeling astronomical phenomena)
  - Data from space probes and observatories

- Estimated data volume: Similar to genomics, the data volume is constantly increasing. Estimates suggest Petabytes (PB) of data are generated daily by large telescopes alone (1 PB = 1 million Gigabytes).

It is beyond human brain to make sense out of this but yet we somehow ***know*** what is expected. Based on this we are able to ***guide AI*** to make sense of the above-mentioned data and take comparatively less time to correlate and come up with a solution. But it is not something cheap or easy. Many techniques developed by human beings using enormous amounts of energy do give excellent results in widely diverse domains, and the results and field of application are increasing consistently. In Chap. 3 of this book we have presented a comprehensive description of such an approach.

Developing metacognitive skills can lead to more effective and efficient thinking and learning. It is a key component of lifelong learning and can contribute to intellectual growth and problem-solving proficiency. Encouraging metacognition in education and everyday tasks can lead to more intentional, adaptive, and successful thinking processes [7].

We interrupt the discussion with an interlude. Figure 1.1 is drawn by Physicist George Gamov in his very popular book entitled "One, Two, Three, ··· Infinity: Facts and Speculations of Science" first published by Viking press in 1947. Among many illustrations drawn by Gamov (Gamow) this surrealistic drawing was pretty thought evoking, this is an inside-out depiction of man sensing the universe (or a part of the universe sensing itself) through its sensing organs.

If you look sharply at Prof. Gamov's sketch you will see the sense organs like, eyes, finger, tongue probing inside the universe as shown in Fig. 1.1. Among many other path breaking papers on physics and popular science books he is well known for his work that led to the development of the hot "big bang" theory of the expanding universe.

Basically, whatever we know and try to model logically and mathematically is happening within us, or more specifically in our brain.

Our brains do nor create a direct replica of the universe through our senses. Instead, they construct an **internal representation based on the limited information** our senses provide. Our senses (sight, touch, hearing, smell, taste) capture specific aspects of the environment. Each sense has specialized organs that convert physical stimuli (light waves, sound waves, etc.) into electrical signals. The brain integrates information from various senses to create a unified perception. In the process, we make a representation of the universe around us in our brain. Reality is constructed by the brain, and no two brains are exactly alike. We are trained through formal education how to have a common platform (think alike) so we have collective intelligence.

This representation allows the brain to focus on the most relevant information for survival and decision-making. It enables us to recognize patterns and make predictions about the world around us. Our brain runs simulations in ***its own universe, this is imagination and expression of it is creativity.***

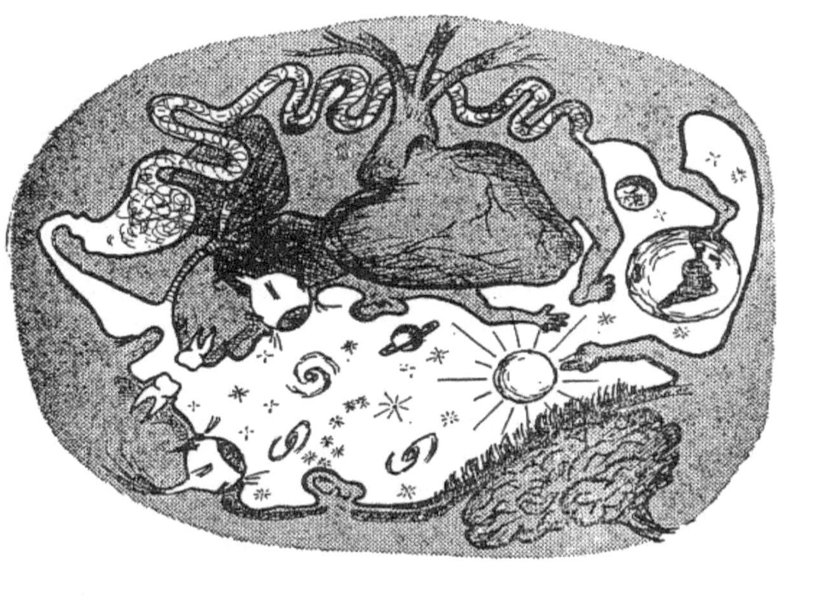

Fig. 1.1 The inside-out universe

In fact, representation of a physical phenomenon is the fundamental of mathematical science. Different branches of mathematics were created not intended to solve any physical problem but as an intellectual exercise:

- **Group Theory**: This field explores the concept of symmetry and how it can be formalized mathematically. Initially developed in abstract algebra, group theory became essential in describing fundamental particles and their interactions in modern physics, particularly in subatomic physics.
- **Differential Geometry**: This branch focuses on the properties of curves and surfaces, initially used for solving geometric problems. However, differential geometry became a cornerstone of Einstein's theory of general relativity, which describes gravity as a curvature of spacetime.
- **Riemannian Geometry**: This is a specific branch of differential geometry that deals with manifolds, a type of curved space. While initially theoretical, Riemannian geometry provided the mathematical framework for general relativity as well as other areas of theoretical physics like string theory.
- **Abstract Algebra**: This field studies abstract algebraic structures like groups, rings, and fields, focusing on their properties and relationships. While initially purely theoretical, abstract algebra found applications in areas like coding theory, cryptography, and even particle physics through group theory (a subfield of abstract algebra).

It is impossible to confirm if the above-mentioned mathematical constructs exist in what is known as physical universe, yet without using these methods we would be unable to make a model, however approximate, of the universe as we know it. Sir James Jeans, a British astronomer and physicist said "The universe seems to be designed by a pure mathematician". Perhaps every student of science have similar feeling at least once in her career. In this book, we have presented, from Chap. 3 onwards that there is another branch of mathematics, it too is like a game and played using rules, in a computer. This game (called Cellular Automaton) approximately represents interactions in the Information Technology domain.

In our attempts to make a machine to help us in detailed and accurate modelling, we are essentially trying to extend our own cerebral capacity. Through the introduction of sensors, we have significantly expanded our senses. Consequently, we need extraordinary support from the field of computing to make sense of the data from our super enhanced senses.

Yes, computers have indeed solved puzzles and problems before humans could in certain cases. The ability of computers to perform complex calculations, analyze vast amounts of data, and execute algorithms quickly allows them to tackle problems that may be beyond human capability within a reasonable timeframe. Here are a few examples (yes there are repetitions to make a case to the point):

In 1997, IBM's Deep Blue defeated world chess champion Garry Kasparov in a six-game match, marking a significant milestone in computer chess.

In 2016, Google's AlphaGo defeated the world champion Go player, Lee Sedol, in a five-game match. Go is a game with an incredibly vast number of possible moves, and AlphaGo's victory demonstrated the power of machine learning and artificial intelligence in solving complex problems.

Further Computers have been used to prove mathematical theorems and solve mathematical problems that were challenging or time-consuming for humans. For example, the proof of the Four-Color Theorem in 1976 relied heavily on computer assistance.

The most mysterious and yet unexplained phenomenon witnessed today are the capabilities of savants. Here are some examples of savants who showcase a variety of exceptional abilities:

- **Musical Savants**:
  - *Leslie Lemke*: Born with severe congenital conditions, Leslie could not stand or walk until his teens. At 16, with no formal training, he developed the ability to flawlessly play songs on the piano after hearing them just once.
  - *Derek Paravicini*: Blind from birth, Derek possesses exceptional musical memory and improvisational skills. He can play various instruments and transpose music into different keys by ear.
- **Mathematical Savants**:
  - *Kim Peek*: Nicknamed "The Rain Man" after the movie character inspired by him, Kim possessed an extraordinary memory and could recall vast amounts of information, particularly about geography and historical dates.
  - *Shakuntala Devi*: Often referred to as the "Human Computer", Shakuntala Devi displayed exceptional mental math abilities. She could perform complex calculations like multiplication of large numbers or square roots in her head with incredible speed and accuracy.
  - *Srinivasa Ramanujan*: Srinivasa Ramanujan was a brilliant Indian mathematician who, despite having little formal education, made groundbreaking contributions to number theory, infinite series, and continued fractions.
- **Artistic Savants**:
  - *Laurent Simmons*: Diagnosed with autism at a young age, Laurent began building complex electronic circuits at the age of six. He went on to study physics at a prestigious university at the young age of 11.
  - *Stephen Wiltshire*: Savant with autism who possesses exceptional artistic skills, particularly in drawing. He can create highly detailed and accurate panoramic drawings of cityscapes after seeing them only once.

It is important to remember that savant syndrome is a spectrum, and the level and type of savant abilities can vary greatly from person to person. Some savants might have intellectual disabilities in other areas, while others might have average or even above-average intelligence.

Computers are instrumental in breaking codes and ciphers. The field of cryptanalysis often involves complex mathematical algorithms and computations, and computers have played a crucial role in deciphering encrypted messages.

> The four-color map theorem, states that no more than four colors are required to color the regions of any map so that no two adjacent regions have the same color. Adjacent means that two regions share a common boundary curve segment, not merely a corner where three or more regions meet. It was the first major theorem to be proved using a computer.

Computers are adept at solving optimization problems, where the goal is to find the best solution among a set of possibilities. This is applicable in various fields, such as logistics, finance, and engineering.

Computers can quickly solve complex Sudoku puzzles or generate solutions to challenging crossword puzzles. These tasks involve logical reasoning.

Computers do excel in recognition of specific classes of patterns. This has amplified human ability of cognition. It is analogous to instruments which we use to '*see*' beyond our natural senses, far beyond our limited bandwidth of sense organs.

It is important to note that while computers can excel in specific domains and solve certain types of problems quickly, human intelligence remains unmatched in terms of creativity, intuition, emotional understanding, and broader contextual reasoning. Humans often bring a level of adaptability and comprehension that goes beyond the narrow focus of computer algorithms in the present technological scenario. In many cases, the collaboration between humans and computers (Man—Machine interaction), known as augmented intelligence, is proving to be a powerful approach. Humans leverage the computational capabilities of machines while providing the creativity, intuition, and ethical judgment that machines lack.

We should not be disheartened that we are still unable to strictly define creativity, various emotions and intuitions. Emotions can be simulated. ChatBot exists which can give emotional support. Creativity we will discuss in the last paragraph of the chapter.

We continued so far without describing **AI and ML**. Machine learning is a subset of AI. While AI encompasses a broader set of capabilities and goals, machine learning is a specific method within the AI toolkit. In other words, all machine learning is AI, but not all AI is necessarily machine learning.

It is possible to have AI systems that do not explicitly use machine learning. For example, rule-based expert systems or traditional symbolic AI methods rely on predefined rules and knowledge representations without learning from data.

We will be discussing the new frontiers of AI and ML and the challenges in terms of computing resources, privacy, requirements of large datasets, explainability, regulations etc. in Chap. 2 in detail and will be delving into Machine Learning especially Deep Learning in Chap. 3.

1.7 The Metaverse of AI

In this section we take a glimpse of the present and near future structure of AI space and possible future accelerators. Structure means Hardware Software Systems (HSS) accelerators which are outside present AI architecture. These candidate accelerators may enhance the efficiency of AI systems.

Machine Learning (ML) is a dominating subject covering a set of methodologies used in AI systems. ML is a subfield of artificial intelligence (AI) that focuses on enabling machines to learn from data and improve their performance over time without explicit programming. ML algorithms are trained on large datasets of information. This data can be labeled (where the desired outcome is already known) or unlabeled (where the algorithm needs to discover patterns on its own). Through analysis of the data, the algorithm learns to identify patterns and relationships within it. This allows it to make predictions on new, unseen data.

As the algorithm is exposed to more data, it refines its understanding and improves its ability to make accurate predictions or perform its designated task.

In simpler terms, imagine teaching a child to identify different types of animals. You show them pictures, point out features, and provide labels (birds, bat, butterfly etc.). Over time, the child learns to recognize these patterns and can correctly identify not only known animals but new animals they have not seen before. For example, the child can identify a butterfly and moth as something similar but will not consider them as birds.

The first cloud block referred to Cellular Automaton (CA) connected to the ML section in Fig. 1.2 is a method in a computational modeling technique used to simulate the behavior of complex systems over time. It operates on a grid of cells, each with a finite set of possible states (e.g., on/off, alive/dead). The state of each cell evolves according to a set of predefined rules based on the states of its neighboring cells and potentially the entire grid, depending on the specific configuration.

> The essential target of this book is to demonstrate that by implementing appropriate methods—CA condenses or gives shorthand representation of a phenomenon. By using CA methodology as a pre-processor, we can possibly enhance performance using less computational resources.

The system is represented as an array of cells, often arranged as an array (or as a ring called periodic). Each cell can be in one of a finite number of states. Each cell has a defined neighborhood, which includes its surrounding cells. The size and shape of the neighborhood can vary depending on the specific application. The state of a cell at the next time step is determined by a set of local rules that depend only on the states of the cells in its neighborhood; these rules are applied simultaneously to all cells in the grid, leading to the **evolution of the CA**.

Cellular Automata offer a simple yet powerful way to model a wide range of phenomena including computational biology and computational linguistics covered in this book. Further, the book also presents CA model design for a ML framework.

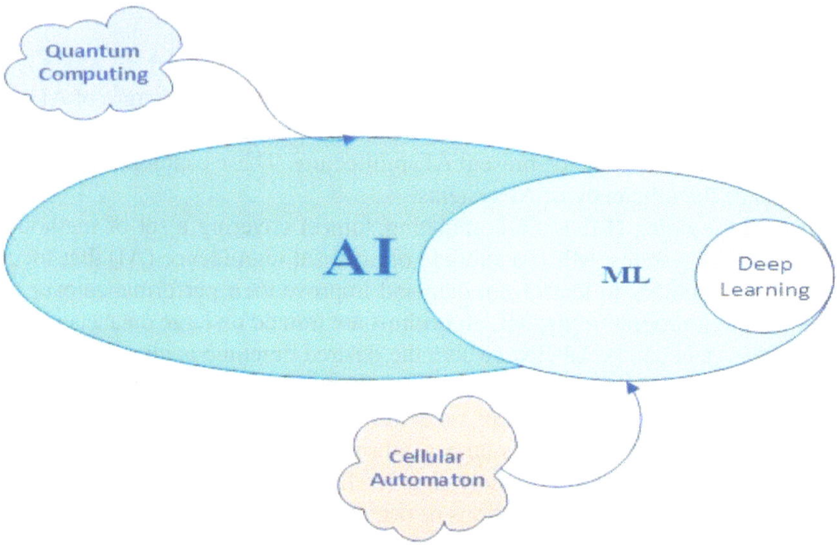

Fig. 1.2 Domain entities to enhance and assist AI in near future

Cellular Automata offer a simple yet powerful way to model a wide range of phenomena including computational biology and computational linguistics covered in this book. Further, the book also presents CA model design for a ML framework.

The Quantum Computing cloud block shows in Fig. 1.2 holds the potential to be a powerful combination, each field enhancing the other as Quantum-enhanced Machine Learning. This is done in three steps- Specific parts of the ML algorithm, particularly those involving complex calculations or optimization, are offloaded to a quantum computer. The quantum computer utilizes its ability to explore multiple possibilities simultaneously (superposition) and leverage entangled qubits to perform these calculations more efficiently. The results from the quantum computer are then integrated back into the overall ML process.

1.8 Strong AI and Conclusion

Strong AI, also known as Artificial General Intelligence (AGI), refers to a form of artificial intelligence that possesses the ability to understand, learn, and apply knowledge across a wide range of tasks at a level comparable to human intelligence. Unlike narrow or weak AI, which is designed for specific tasks, strong AI aims to emulate general cognitive abilities and exhibit a broad understanding of diverse domains. The only natural thinking machine is the brain and we know so little of it. With Functional MRI we have a pretty accurate mapping of areas of activity but we still have a long way to go [8].

Strong AI can generalize its knowledge and skills from one domain to another. It can apply its understanding of concepts and principles across various contexts, much like how humans can transfer knowledge from one area to another.

A hallmark of strong AI is its capacity to learn from experience and adapt to new situations. This involves not only recognizing patterns but also evolving its understanding over time through continuous learning.

Some discussions about strong AI involve the idea of self-awareness and consciousness. This suggests that a truly intelligent system would have a subjective experience and awareness of its own existence, thoughts, and emotions.

> A century ago, a young student at the Oxford University in England was taking an important examination in religious studies. The examination question for this day was to write about the religious and spiritual meaning in the miracle of Christ turning water into wine. For two hours he sat in the crowded classroom while other students filled their pages with long essays, to show their understanding. The exam time was almost over and this one student had not written a single word. The proctor came over to him and insisted that he commit something to paper before turning it in. The young Lord Byron simply picked up his hand and penned the following line: "The water met its Master, and blushed". Without knowing the task given to the budding poet, can a person well versed in English literature make any sense out of that one line? Any system that is capable of doing that we feel falls in the category of strong AI.

Strong AI is expected to operate autonomously, making decisions and solving problems without constant human intervention. It should be able to understand complex instructions, interpret them, and execute tasks with minimal guidance. Strong AI is envisioned to exhibit creativity in generating novel ideas, solving complex problems, and even contributing to fields like art, literature, and scientific discovery.

The development of true strong AI remains a complex and elusive goal. Many challenges must be addressed, including ethical considerations, the potential impact on employment, and ensuring the alignment of AI systems with human values. It is imperative that we understand more about the working of the human brain. Intuition is a hidden process which is solving something without our conscious self not aware. Somehow intuition supported by imagination is essential for creation. These phenomena are not understood at all.

We have presented a brief introduction on the associated issues as we start our journey on this chapter. The realization of strong AI raises philosophical and ethical questions about the nature of intelligence, consciousness, and the relationship between machines and humans. Researchers and policymakers are actively exploring these questions to ensure the responsible development and deployment of increasingly advanced AI technologies.

Physical reality often inspires the creation of mathematical games, which are then used to explore theoretical concepts, test hypotheses, or simulate scenarios that are difficult to observe or manipulate directly in the real world.

Similarly, pure mathematical universes are created by mathematicians with no intention that their *games will* be used in modeling physical realities. Yet something as esoteric as group theories are used to understand the fundamental structure of the universe we know.

Perhaps not so far in the future. a machine will be an unbeatable champion in the game Go, create another game with modified rules of Go. From that new game find correlation with the rules of formation of galaxies or an explanation of a phenomenon in cellular biology. At this stage there is doubt if that *thing* will permit any other intelligent being *like us* to be called artificial.

References

1. Lokayata/Carvaka–Indian Materialism. [Online]. Available: https://iep.utm.edu/indmat/
2. M. Rota, *Taking Pascal's Wager—Faith, Evidence and the Abundant Life* (2016)
3. Stanford encyclopedia of philosophy. [Online]. Available: https://plato.stanford.edu/entries/descartes/
4. Eliza chatbot in python. [Online]. Available: https://github.com/wadetb/eliza
5. M. Minsky, S. Papert, A step toward the understanding of information processes: perceptrons. An introduction to computational geometry. Science **165**(3895), 780–782 (1969)
6. D.E. Rumelhart, G.E. Hinton, R.J. Williams, Learning representations by back-propagating errors. Nature **323**(6088), 533–536 (1986)
7. Digital promise. [Online]. Available: https://lvp.digitalpromiseglobal.org/
8. P. Domingos, *The Master Algorithm: How the Quest for the Ultimate Learning Machine will Remake Our World* (2015)

Chapter 2
Trends, Challenges and New Frontiers of Artificial Intelligence

> *"Success in creating AI would be the biggest event in human history. Unfortunately, it might also be the last, unless we learn how to avoid the risks"*
>
> *—Professor Stephen Hawking*

2.1 Introduction

During our journey of the current book project, ChatGPT made its grand entry, followed by Claude and Gemini, opening a floodgate of similar platforms. Large Language models (LLMs) became a sensation, spawning thousands of startups overnight, generating both awe and apprehension. The space started evolving at a breakneck pace with each news cycle amplifying the good, the bad, and the downright scary of what AI could potentially do. Within a few months, hundreds of millions of users were using these LLMs. These models were super large, running into several hundred billion parameters, training on a sea of GPUs spewing several hundred metric tons of CO2 for just a single training round. The outputs of the models were stress tested to show biases and sometimes outright hallucinations. Several pundits all over the world signed an open letter asking for a six month pause on out-of-control AI development, to figure out proper regulations before proceeding further.

We went through a brief history, foundation, and evolution of AI in Chap. 1. As it continues its accelerated advancement, this chapter seeks to present a broad survey of the current and pertinent trends and challenges in this rapidly evolving field, along with the new advancements. Throughout the text, relevant references, pointers, and links are provided to enable readers to delve deeper into understanding each topic in further detail. As the topics covered here are so vast and complex, the goal is

© The Author(s), under exclusive license to Springer Nature Singapore Pte Ltd. 2025
P. Pal Chaudhuri et al., *New Kind of Machine Learning—Cellular Automata Model*,
https://doi.org/10.1007/978-981-96-1501-8_2

to offer a comprehensive, yet succinct, overview that captures the key issues and approaches. We will also set the context for the next few chapters where the authors believe Cellular Automata based Machine Learning (CAML) has an important role to play to address some of these challenges. The topics covered in this chapter are listed below.

- 2.2: *AI Processor/Co-processor*: Optimizing AI hardware for enhanced speed, efficiency, and power.
- 2.3: *Explainable AI*: Understanding how AI models make decisions, instead of being opaque "black boxes".
- 2.4: *Edge AI and Federated Learning*: Enable on-device inferencing and training at the source, decentralizing from the cloud, while prioritizing data privacy.
- 2.5: *Challenges of large AI models and datasets*: Reduce computational complexity of large AI models, and develop efficient methods for curating, and augmenting the large training datasets.
- 2.6: *Encrypted AI for Privacy*: Safeguard data privacy while leveraging the power of AI.
- 2.7: *AI Trust*: Ensuring AI systems are fair, ethical, accountable, and transparent which is critical for building trust.
- 2.8: *Emergence of Opensource in AI*: Rise of opensource AI models, datasets, and benchmarks.
- 2.9: *AI Regulations*: Evolving landscape of AI regulations.

2.2 AI Processor/Co-processor

Running AI workloads on today's computers with traditional Von Neumann architecture, is not ideal. Recognizing this hurdle, the industry and research communities have pioneered new approaches. The path towards dedicated AI hardware started a couple of decades back, repurposing available Nvidia Gaming GPUs (Graphics Processing Unit) as it was the closest parallel architecture to handle AI workloads. To tackle the computational demands and data transfer bottlenecks posed by AI workloads, various hardware architectures emerged, encompassing in-memory computing techniques and designs optimized for efficient data transfer. Novel approaches evolved running the AI workload on analog domain, photonics domain and different forms of brain-inspired neuromorphic computing platforms. Focus also shifted from solely solving AI compute workloads in the datacenter to running these workloads in more resource-limited edge devices and even tiny battery-powered devices.

2.2.1 *Von Neumann Architecture Limitations*

In the early days of computing, computers were built using vacuum tubes and mechanical switches, and programmed using paper tape or punched cards, limiting its functionality and flexibility, as each program had to be hard-wired. The **Von Neumann architecture**, named after the Hungarian-American mathematician and computer scientist John von Neumann, was first implemented in the Electronic Discrete Variable Automatic Computer (EDVAC) in the late 1940s. The Universal Automatic Computer (UNIVAC), the world's first commercially available computer came next.

The architecture was a significant breakthrough, as it introduced for the first time the concept of a stored-program computing machine, the program and data being stored in the same memory, offering greater flexibility in programming. A single central processing unit (CPU) performs all computations and the control unit manages the data flow and program instructions from memory. The use of single CPU and shared memory helped execute complex programs, laying the modern computing foundation.

Unlike a sequential Fetch—Add—Store that Von Newmann architecture does so efficiently, AI workload, especially the deep learning is a series of Multiply—Add computes that need to be performed in parallel. A typical deep learning neural network (Fig. 2.1) shows the vast array of matrix add and multiplication functions that need to be performed in parallel.

The Von Neumann architecture faces significant limitations in handling AI workloads, primarily due to its constraints in parallelism, memory bandwidth, memory access speed, and energy efficiency. While multiple cores can partially address the need for high parallelism required for faster AI processing, the shared bus architecture becomes a severe bottleneck for data transfer, limiting overall performance. Additionally, the large amounts of data that need to be processed in parallel for AI

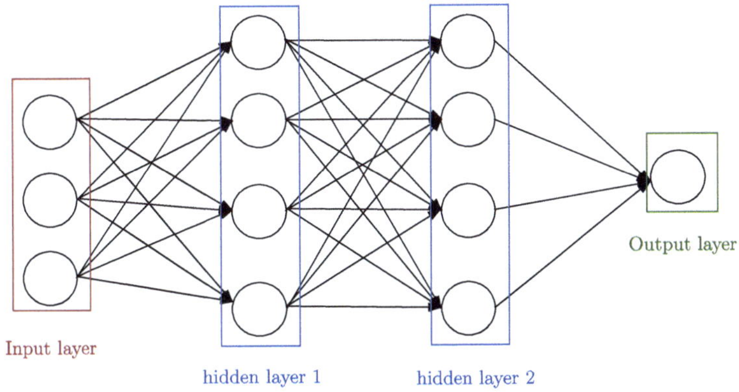

Fig. 2.1 Deep learning neural network architecture

workloads frequently exceed the memory bandwidth limits of this architecture. The limited memory access speed, resulting from the use of a shared bus for accessing large datasets, further impedes performance for AI workloads. Lastly, the von Neumann architecture is not energy-efficient for large-scale AI workload processing.

2.2.2 Generations of AI Processor/Co-processor Architecture

AI researchers initially used CPUs with Von Neumann architecture to train neural networks, hindering progress due to constraints on model size and complexity, leading to the long stagnation period known as the '*AI Winter*'. Around the mid-2000s, researchers at the University of Toronto leveraged GPUs to accelerate training of neural networks for image recognition tasks, exploiting GPUs' parallel processing capabilities for matrix operations. Although GPUs were originally designed for 3D gaming and graphics, Nvidia repurposed them as AI processors, driving substantial growth in its business and stock price [1].

The first generation of AI processors and accelerators were GPUs repurposed to accelerate deep learning workloads. The second generation of AI processors was characterized by the development of specialized chips designed specifically for AI workloads. Various architectures were explored, including techniques for efficient parallel workload transfer to AI processors, in-memory computation methods, and matrix operation optimizations—all aimed at achieving higher performance and lower power consumption while ensuring desired flexibility. A range of AI processors have been developed over the last 10 years and billions of dollars have been spent. More than one hundred such AI processor development initiatives have been undertaken by semiconductor chip behemoths and startups. Examples of second-generation AI processors include Google's Tensor Processing Unit (TPU) and Intel's Nervana Neural Network Processor (NNP) and many more including FPGA based ones. An excellent survey of AI chipset is reported by Kepner et al. [2] of the MIT Lincoln Laboratory Supercomputing Center.

Many early AI hardware initiatives faced challenges not just in hardware design, but also in developing general-purpose software, compilers, and toolchains for enabling AI models to run on novel architectures. Achieving high energy efficiency was difficult due to deep learning workloads' power-hungry nature. NVidia continued the dominance with various flavors of GPUs, going down in geometry, cost and power in addition to building on the robust capabilities of software, compilers and toolchains with its CUDA (Compute Unified Development Architecture) platform [3]. Additionally, the new age NVidia AI Systems network a multitude of GPUs together, significantly increasing their collective capability for training complex AI models by leveraging parallel processing. While the first and second generations AI processors were largely focused on AI workloads at the data center, many new age startups like HaiLo, and Kinara focused on edge AI vision tasks for autonomous driving, security, and surveillance, competing with NVidia. Both Apple and Qualcomm designed neural processors for the AI applications in smartphones. Qualcomm's Hexagon neural processing unit works in tandem with the Snapdragon Qualcomm processor and in case of Apple, it has a small neural unit working with its M-series chips. ARM architecture is also now capable of handling AI workload with its neural processing unit like Ethos-N77. Syntiant [4] released a new co-processor for the battery-operated devices for wake-word and voice commands processing, running extremely lightweight AI workloads at the edge while the main processor is in extended sleep mode to conserve power. In view of high power consumption of AI workload, benchmark metrics evolved to include TOPS (Terra Operations Per Second) per Watt, accounting for both performance and power consumption. Beyond commercial edge AI platforms like Nvidia Jetson, Google Coral, and Movidius (acquired by Intel), several opensource initiatives were also introduced like TensorFlow Lite (lightweight version of the TensorFlow framework), and PyTorch Mobile (lightweight version of the PyTorch) designed specifically for deploying AI models on mobile and embedded devices. TinyML ONNX [5] came out as an open standards initiative for representing ML models making it easier to create and deploy models across different hardware platforms and frameworks. Cerebras [6] took an unconventional wafer-scale mega chip approach hosting a sea of compute cores with local memory, and efficient on-chip communication between the cores. Amazon (Trainium and Inferentia) [7, 8] and Microsoft (Athena) [9] announced new 5nm chips.

The second-generation AI processor initiatives were primarily focused on the various novelties in computing architecture, but still operating in the digital domain. The third generation of AI processors started experimenting on various novel approaches including processing the AI workload in analog domain, using photonics and neuromorphic approaches [10].

2.2.3 Analog AI (AI Computation in Analog Domain)

Analog AI refers to a class of AI systems that use analog circuits to perform computations. Unlike digital AI systems, which use binary digits to represent data and perform large-scale matrix computations, analog AI systems use continuously variable physical quantities like voltage, current and resistance with computations done in the analog domain.

Matrix computations are a series of multiplications and additions. The essence of computation in analog domain for multiplication is the age-old Ohm's law $V = I \times R$ and addition is the summation of voltages or current $I = I1 + I2$. There are several different approaches to implementing Analog AI. Various flavors of analog neural networks and memristors based approaches have been implemented. In an analog neural network, each neuron is represented by a circuit that computes the weighted sum of its inputs and applies a non-linear activation function to the result. The weights in the network are typically represented by the resistance values of the variable resistors that connect the neurons in each layer. The activation function of a neural network can be implemented using a variety of different analog components, such as switches, diodes, transistors, or operational amplifiers. In most scenarios observed, digital data is transformed to analog domain for the computation for each layer at a time and re-converted back to digital domain even though there are exceptions, where the entire neural workload is attempted solely in analog.

> The key advantage of analog AI is that it performs computations an order of magnitude more efficiently than digital neural networks, since analog components can perform computations in parallel and with very low power consumption. However, analog neural networks also have several challenges associated with their design and implementation. For example, the performance of analog components can be affected by variations in temperature, power supply voltage, and manufacturing variability of the semiconductor chip. Design and manufacture of analog components with required precision and consistency at scale are challenging. Analog circuits are also more susceptible to noise and other sources of interference affecting their performance. Analog components can also be more difficult to control and calibrate compared to their digital counterparts. Moreover, the conversion from digital to analog and back to digital involves use of converters which typically take a considerable amount of power.

Several companies have tried to develop analog AI technologies, including Mythic and Analog Inference [11, 12]. Other companies that have worked on analog AI include Intel, IBM and Hewlett-Packard.

2.2.4 Neuromorphic AI

Neuromorphic AI is a field focused on designing computer systems that emulate the architecture and functionality of the human brain and neurons, which will be covered in Chap. 3 under **Biological Neural Networks (BNNs)**. In neurons, action potentials transmit messages via electrical signals caused by ion movements across the membrane, triggering neurotransmitter release at neuron synapses, exciting or inhibiting the next neuron. Our brains exhibit extremely low power consumption for each cognitive task, fast inference, event-driven processing, continuous learning, and massive parallelism, the ideal traits to emulate in an AI processor. This is particularly important at the edge, where there is a need to process large amounts of sensor data and make quick inferences.

Neuromorphic compute essentially is this biology-inspired computing that emulates the charging and discharging process of neuron and synapse action potentials. This spike-based mechanism enables asynchronous event driven computation with communication, operating at orders of magnitude higher energy efficiency than digital systems. While several implementations of neuromorphic computations have been implemented with digital, analog and hybrid systems, the most obvious benefit is to perform computation locally in analog domain, rather than digitizing the data and processing it. The inherent advantage is to process information more quickly in almost real time and with lower power consumption than traditional digital systems.

The concept of neuromorphic computing was first proposed by Carver Mead [13] in the 1980s, primarily to understand and simulate the behavior of neurons. Early works involved building up analog circuitry to model the behavior of biological systems including an artificial retina. Spiking Neural Network (SNN), which mimics the spiking behavior of biological neurons, are frequently explored within the realm of neuromorphic computing architectures.

Several companies and startups are currently working on developing neuromorphic AI chips and systems. Notable initiatives include Intel's Loihi chip (mimic the behavior of neurons and synapses in the brain), IBM's TrueNorth chip (custom-designed network of neurosynaptic cores), BrainChip (a startup for edge computing applications like image and audio recognition in low-power high-performance computing) [14], Spinnaker and BrainScaleS (a mixed signal implementation). A detailed survey of Neuromorphic hardware has been reported by Plank et al. [15].

2.2.5 Photonics AI

The origins and the roots of photonics in AI can be traced back to the concept of photonic interconnects to overcome data movement challenges in traditional computing. Optical fiber communication systems have become ubiquitous in telecommunication networks where cost-effective, high-bandwidth, power-efficient, and long-haul data transmission is essential. Examples include the extensive fiber-optic infrastructure deployed for long-distance voice and data communications across national and international telecom backbones. Silicon photonics allows for the cost-effective integration of optical components based on CMOS technology and is the major catalysts for chip-scale photonic interconnects.

The fundamental matrix and vector operations that form the computational backbone of deep learning algorithms can potentially be executed within the optical domain, without converting to the electronic domain. Key operations like matrix-vector multiplications, which dominate the computational load of training deep neural networks, can be mapped directly onto optical computing primitives facilitated by integrated photonic circuits. Photonics-based accelerators can achieve high energy footprint efficiency (defined as (MAC/s/mm_2)/(joules/MAC)) for MAC (Multiply and Accumulate) operations that can be 1000X better compared to the most energy efficient digital AI accelerators of today. The operational bandwidth and computational speeds of photonic MACs can also approach hundreds of GHz rates which is superior to the operating speed of currently available electronic systems. A few startups in this domain are Lightmatter and Luminous Photonics [16, 17].

2.3 Explainable AI

The fundamental issue of deep learning, the most exciting field of AI today is that it is a '*Blackbox AI*'. Learning data is fed and an AI model is created. The model performs on new data and depending on its success, it needs to be finetuned with additional data while keeping an eye on drift and model performance. But it is inherently difficult to probe and find out why a particular model behaves in a certain way and if it fails, why so.

Explainable AI (XAI) is a field of AI that focuses on developing methods and techniques to make the decision-making processes of AI systems transparent and understandable to humans. The goal of XAI is to create AI systems that can explain their actions and decisions in a way that is easy for humans to understand and ensure that people trust the systems. Especially in regulatory environments like healthcare and insurance, there is a need to explain the output of these AI models, for example, why a certain decision has been made by an insurance company to deny a claim. It is necessary to go deeper into the models to understand biases based on the training dataset.

> In recent years, there have been several incidents involving Tesla's autopilot system. In 2019, a Tesla Model S crashed into a parked fire truck in Indiana while in autopilot mode. Tesla struggled to identify the cause of the accident, as the vehicle's logs did not show any problems with the autopilot system. However, the National Transportation Safety Board (NTSB) investigated the incident and found that the driver was not paying attention to the road and that the autopilot system had failed to detect the stationary object ahead. These incidents highlight the challenges of debugging black box AI systems, where it can be difficult to understand how the system makes decisions and identify the root cause of accidents.

2.3.1 Explainable AI History and Developments

While XAI is recently receiving a lot of attention for obvious reasons, its origins go back several decades to when AI systems were mainly developed as knowledge-based and expert systems. Mueller et al. [18] presented a comprehensive review of the approaches since the 1970s; he marked those as '*Explanation Systems*' and grouped them into three generations. The first generation XAI only expressed the internal working process of the system by embedding expert knowledge in rules incorporated by experts. The second generation XAI were more human-computer systems designed around human knowledge and reasoning capacities to provide cognitive support. The first and second generation XAIs were decision processes for knowledge-based and expert systems. Only the third generation XAI systems attempted to clarify the inner workings of the typical deep learning systems, ensuring some measure of explainability of decisions.

Linear regression, logical regression, and decision trees were used in the early generations, but avoided the black box model altogether as they were intrinsically uninterpretable. The inherent difficulty of linear regression is to establish correlation of large number of parameters and logical regressions provide at best a probabilistic band. Decision trees were more advanced compared to linear and logical regressions but they cannot express the true relationship between input features and output. Decision rules are great for a small number of features but gets difficult to design and implement with large number of correlated features. While some of the above approaches are model-centric, there are several approaches that are model-agnostic as well. Readers are recommended to go through the XAI survey papers by Mueller et al. [18] and Islam et al. [19] compiling the XAI approaches giving the history and context.

The other approaches of XAI are example-based explanation methods. These methods use specific instances from the dataset to explain the behavior of the model and the distribution of the data in a model agnostic way. It can be expressed as "X is similar to Y and Y caused Z, so the prediction says X will cause Z". The example-based approach has many sub categories including 'Counterfactual', 'Adversarial', 'Prototypes', 'Influential Instances', 'K-nearest neighbor' etc. Over the course of XAI research, modest-size ML models were explained by using different explainability methods.

Several frameworks and tools have emerged in the field of XAI, utilizing different approaches for explainability. Examples include LIME [20], DeepVis Toolbox, TreeInterpreter, Keras-vis, Microsoft InterpretML, MindsDB, SHAP, Tensorboard WhatIf, Tensorflow's Lucid, Tensorflow's Cleverhans, and more. A comprehensive list and links for some of the above tools and frameworks are provided by Analytics India Magazine [21]. Some of these workflows and tools are model-specific—e.g. DeepVis, Kerasvis and Lucid for neural networks, and TreeInterpreter for tree-based models. Most tools cover similar concepts such as feature importance, feature interactions, shapely values, partial dependence, surrogate models, counterfactual, adversarial, prototypes and knowledge infusion.

2.3.2 *Post-hoc Explainability*

Post-hoc XAI involves analyzing the decision-making processes of an AI system after it has decided or taken action. Different approaches and methods used in post-hoc AI include model and outcome explanation techniques that we have discussed in the previous section like feature importance, partial dependence plots, layerwise relevance propagation, and local interpretable model-agnostic explanations (LIME). Partial dependence plots show the change in model output with respect to the change in individual features, while holding the other features constant. Layerwise Relevance Propagation (LRP) identifies which features contribute to a given output and helps explain the decision-making process of the AI model. LIME allows one to understand the results of a machine learning algorithm without having to interpret the internal logic of the algorithm. Decision trees are graphical representations of possible outcomes based on a set of decisions, random forests are algorithms that build decision trees using randomly generated subsets of data, and XGBoost is an optimized version of gradient boosting, providing a method of combining weak learners into stronger ones. Additionally, data visualization and model visualization tools, such as t-SNE, scree plots, and cluster analysis, are utilized to uncover patterns in large datasets and make predictions for unseen inputs.

While extensive work is ongoing in research and several tools and frameworks are available as discussed in the previous section, there are few relevant startups that are specifically working on the post-hoc explainability providing services and solutions that enable businesses to understand and explain their AI models. Top explainable AI startups today and the most well-funded are Fiddler, Abzu, HowSo and Aygloo [22–25].

2.3.3 *Model-Based Explainability or Ante-hoc Models*

This type of XAI involves designing AI models that are inherently transparent and interpretable. Decision trees, linear regression models, decision lists, and fuzzy inference systems are typical AI models that are explainable-by-design. Ante-hoc methods are, by design, model-specific and this might be seen as a drawback. Hence by definition, model intrinsic explanation methods depend on a certain design and cannot be used for other architectures.

Different approaches and methods used in ante-hoc XAI include rule-based models like decision trees, which provide easily understandable rules for reasoning about a problem; explainable reinforcement learning algorithms that generate human-interpretable policies; hybrid models that use both symbolic and numerical representations of the data; and interactive storytelling systems and visual analytics that enable users to iteratively explore underlying AI decisions. Bayesian networks can be used to uncover hidden assumptions in an AI system and allow for an understanding of what data have been used to make decisions. Parametric and non-parametric methods provide a way to learn from observations without having to specify a fully specified model. Lastly, knowledge transfer can be utilized to leverage existing knowledge from experts and build robust models that are better understood by humans.

2.3.4 *Glass Box Model*

Glass-box models are AI models that are transparently interpretable and can be understood by humans. This is different from post-hoc where the interpretation is post the inference and ante-hoc refers to the approach used to build the models for interpret-ability. Glass-box models are typically built using symbolic methods such as decision trees, rule-based systems, and Bayesian networks. These models use easily interpretable rules or explanations and provide insights into why an AI system is making certain decisions, allowing businesses to uncover patterns in the data and identify underlying assumptions made by the AI model. Additionally, glass-box models can be used to troubleshoot incorrect predictions and provide useful feedback for model improvement.

References for more Explainable AI Resources
Current research on Explainable AI is being conducted by multiple institutions and companies. Readers and students are encouraged to look at the following resources on XAI:

- The DARPA XAI program—https://www.darpa.mil/program/explainable-artificial-intelligence
- AI Explainability 360 Python library—https://aix360.readthedocs.io/en/latest/
- Interesting resources related to XAI—https://github.com/pbiecek/xai_resources
- 7 free resources to learn Explainable AI—https://analyticsindiamag.com/7-free-resources-to-learn-explainable-ai/
- What Does Explainable AI Really Mean? A New Conceptualization of Perspectives—https://arxiv.org/abs/1710.00794

2.3.5 Interactive Explainability

This type of XAI involves creating AI systems that can interact with humans to explain their decision-making processes. This can include techniques such as natural language generation, which allows AI systems to communicate with humans in a way that is easy for them to understand.

No discussion on AI is complete without discussion on Generative AI. Emerging reasoning models differ from the initial flurry of LLMs by using explicit logical reasoning to solve complex problems. Techniques like Chain-of-Thought (CoT) and Retrieval-Augmented Reasoning (RAR) enhance explainability by providing step-by-step reasoning, making their decision-making more transparent. However, they do not focus on explaining the underlying model mechanics.

2.4 Edge AI and Federated Learning

Edge AI involves deploying AI algorithms and models on devices located at the periphery or 'edge' of a network. These devices include smartphones, Internet of Things (IoT) gadgets, or edge servers situated closer to the data source. In contrast to relying on centralized servers or cloud computing, Edge AI enables these devices to process and analyze data locally, reducing data transmission to the cloud and minimizing latency, while preserving privacy by keeping data on the edge device or server. Enterprises adopt Edge AI not only for technical reasons like latency and bandwidth, but also for business considerations like public cloud costs, privacy, security, and regulatory compliance.

Federated Learning (FL) is a technique for training machine learning models on decentralized data, where the data is distributed across multiple devices or locations. In FL, the devices collaborate to train at the edge using a shared model without sharing their raw data with a central server or cloud.

2.4.1 Advances in Edge AI

Edge AI aims to run machine learning algorithms directly on network edge devices, rather than centralized cloud platforms, driven by the need for efficient real-time decision-making in applications like autonomous vehicles and industrial automation. Current trends involve distributed computing capabilities, utilizing both local and cloud resources as needed. Key challenges include efficiently processing large data volumes in a secure, reliable manner on resource and power-constrained edge computing environments.

Various terminologies have emerged over the years encompassing Edge AI, starting with distributed data centers or micro-data centers, followed by the concept of 'cloudlets' in 2008 for transient mobile devices in locations like coffee shops. Cisco introduced '**Fog Computing**' in 2012, running workloads on servers near the edge, between the cloud and devices. In telecommunications, ETSI (European Telecommunications Standards Institute) introduced mobile edge computing, followed by mobile-access edge computing and multi-access edge computing. Edge devices generating data can be categorized as tiny, medium-sized, or larger based on computing resources. Mobile devices, augmented reality/virtual reality glasses, and security cameras are medium-sized, capable of AI inference tasks. IoT sensors are currently MCU (micro-controller) powered with limited AI capabilities and battery operated. Larger devices like industrial robots, autonomous vehicles, and drones have more edge computing power. Edge AI can also run on-premise servers if workloads cannot be handled at edge nodes.

Research and development in Edge AI focuses on efficient low-power hardware like Analog AI and optimized edge architectures, as discussed in Sect. 2.2. Another area involves developing algorithms and models that can run efficiently on resource-constrained devices like smartphones, optimizing the trade-off between accuracy and model size based on available resources. Research also aims to develop algorithms that can adapt to changing edge conditions, such as varying network and device capabilities. In most enterprise use cases today, model training occurs on the cloud, with models deployed and inference performed on the edge.

2.4.2 Algorithmic Approaches

Algorithms are the key to having efficient and reliable Edge AI solutions, incorporating techniques such as federated learning, compression of deep learning models, and other optimization methods. ML frameworks, such as TensorFlow Lite and PyTorch Edge are used to develop and run machine learning models on edge devices.

Pruning is the very first step to generate smaller size models for inference by removing unimportant connections or neurons in the bigger model. An unstructured approach simply removes the neurons, but structured pruning removes neurons and their related connections, weights, and channels including weights with very small values which may have minimal impact to the model output. Filter-based pricing is another technique by pruning the unimportant filters without changing the AI model. Pruning is a necessary step and involves multiple cycles while evaluating the resultant model size, accuracy, computation time and resources. Different approaches of AI model pruning are articulated by Cheng et al. [26] that the readers and students are encouraged to read.

Quantization is another common approach used when transferring a neural network trained on the cloud with millions of parameters to edge devices. The memory required to store such millions of 32-bit floating point values is impossible to accommodate in edge devices. Hence, the 32-bit floating point values are converted to 4-bit or 8-bit integers. Reducing the precision of weights, parameters, biases, and activations reduce the resources required to both compute and store. A loss function minimizes the difference between the floating point versus integer-based model parameters to minimize the impact to accuracy.

Efforts to reduce the model size also include weight sharing, reducing the number of effective weights that need to be stored by having multiple connections in a neural network share the same weight, provided they are close without sacrificing the model accuracy beyond the acceptable limit. Matrix decomposition is another technique used in which matrix operations are performed on smaller decomposed matrices rather than on the original large matrix.

In neural networks, gradient descent is used to minimize the cost function, which represents the error between predicted and actual values, by updating the weights and biases. The gradient descent optimization process involves two key components: the '*cost function*' quantifies the error to be minimized, while the '*learning rate*' determines the step size at which the weights and biases are updated during the optimization process. Hyperparameter tuning, an essential and most important optimization step for any AI model, becomes more important for lightweight models as they need to be tuned strictly adhering to a particular range. Training-related hyperparameters, such as the batch size of the data and learning rate, influence the speed of convergence at the training phase. Different approaches of hyperparameter tuning are discussed at length by Bartz-Beielstein et al. [27] and Ali et al. [28].

Knowledge Distillation, a technique that Deepseek has used effectively, is another approach where knowledge gained from large models running on the cloud can ideally be transferred to small models which run on edge devices in a teacher-student association format. Response-based distillation is a technique commonly used, where the prediction performance of output layers of the teacher and student model are compared using a loss function (the difference between the teacher and student models) and is minimized to bring the results of both the models closer. On the other hand, feature-based distillation focused on minimizing the loss function at each of the intermediate layers rather than at the output. Readers are encouraged to go through further approaches of optimization techniques for Edge AI by Surianarayanan et al. [29].

2.4.3 Edge Networking Architectures and Resiliency

Ongoing research in Edge AI is the development of networking architectures which are optimized for distributed computing. These architectures must be able to handle large volumes of data transmitted between edge devices, considering the security, bandwidth, and latency, creating a resilient network that continues to function despite transient faults or compromises. Exploring various ways of increasing network performance, from dynamic routing algorithms to mesh networks are the core areas of research. Edge Computing architectures and systems run an increased risk of failure because computing resources are not contained in a controlled environment with necessary emergency and backup protocols.

2.4.4 Data Storage and Security

Data storage and security are also key considerations for Edge AI systems. As data is often shared across multiple devices, it must be securely stored, particularly when it involves sensitive information. Additionally, researchers are developing methods of compressing and encrypting data at the edge to make it more efficient to transmit and process. A blockchain technology stores data in blocks linked together in a chain, in a distributed network. Various blockchain technologies have also been explored as a means of providing distributed trust to ensure security for all the participating parties in an edge system; use of light weight block chain protocols is desirable in such a context.

2.4.5 Federated Learning

So far, we focused on AI workload for inferencing at the edge. Training involves much higher footprint in terms of compute and memory requirements, a challenge for resource constrained edge devices. Federated learning is crucial in the evolving landscape of data privacy, as numerous countries worldwide implement regulations like the GDPR (European Union), PDPA (Singapore), CCPA (California), and DPDP Act (India), which impose various restrictions on data collection, usage, and transfer. It represents a tug-of-war between AI's voracious appetite for data and the stringent barriers erected by privacy regulations, with over 65 countries either developing or already enacting such laws globally. Federated Learning is the key for striking a balance, harnessing the power of data while preserving privacy.

Federated Learning (FL) is a decentralized machine learning approach where multiple edge devices collaboratively train a model without sharing their data to a central server or cloud. It enables devices to train models locally (on the device or edge server if resource-constrained), benefiting from a more general model trained on a larger, diverse dataset without exposing sensitive data. A global model with initial weights is shared with edge devices, which collect real-time data and train the model locally over iterations, updating weights to minimize loss. The updated weights, not raw data, are sent to a centralized server, which averages these weights to update the global model, aggregating learning from multiple devices into an improved global model. This enhanced model is then redistributed to edge devices for another local training round. Only encrypted weights are sent to the central server, not the data itself. A key challenge is dealing with data variability and heterogeneity across devices.

Federated Learning can be traced back to federated databases in the 1990s and the federated cloud infrastructure in 2010s. From an AI perspective, FL can be traced back to the early 2000s, when researchers began exploring the idea of training machine learning models without having to collect and centralize all the data, essentially an approach of distributed training. However, it was only in 2016 that the term 'Federated Learning' was coined by Google researchers [30]. As data privacy increasingly becomes a societal concern and regulations are being put into place in various countries, federated learning will grow in importance and relevancy.

For delving deeper into Federated learning, the readers are encouraged to review the comprehensive history and survey of Federated Learning approaches along with its vision, applications, hype and challenges by Wen et al. [31] and Li et al. [32].

The general FL architecture consists of four essential components: *client devices*, *client* or *local models*, *aggregator* or *manager*, and *the global model*. These components of Federated Learning work with each other broadly in three different conceptual architectures as described below.

Centralized Federated Learning (CFL): In CFL, the aggregator is a central server that is responsible for aggregating the model updates from the client devices. The client devices send their model updates to the central server, which aggregates them to create a global model. The global model is next sent back to the client devices for further training. CFL is easy to implement and manage, and it provides centralized control over the training process. However, it requires a reliable and secure central server, which can be a single point of failure or bottleneck.

Hierarchical Federated Learning (HFL): In HFL, the client devices are organized hierarchically into groups. Each group has a local aggregator that aggregates model updates from its client devices. Local aggregators send updates to higher-level aggregators, which create a global model from the aggregated updates. This global model is then sent back down to the local aggregators for further client training. HFL can handle large-scale systems and provides hierarchical control, but requires a complex hierarchy of aggregators that can be difficult to manage and may introduce communication overhead.

Decentralized Federated Learning (DFL): In DFL, the client devices directly communicate in a peer-to-peer manner, exchanging model updates. Each client sends updates to a subset of peers, which aggregate them to create a global model. This global model is then shared back with all clients for further training. DFL can handle large numbers of clients and provides decentralized control, but requires a robust, secure communication protocol that can be challenging to implement and may introduce overhead. Heterogeneous Federated Learning, a type of DFL, specifically addresses data heterogeneity across different clients.

FL systems use different approaches to derive the global model from the local ones. Federated Averaging (FedAvg) is the most popular algorithm where the weights of the local model are just averaged to generate a global model shared by all clients. Federated Distillation is a type of knowledge distillation, that refines the server model using aggregated knowledge from heterogeneous users rather than directly averaging their model parameters. Federated Meta-Learning aims to learn a meta-model that can be quickly adapted to new clients with different data distributions. This approach involves training a meta-model on a set of tasks and then fine-tuning the model on each client's data to generate a personalized model.

Frameworks and Tools for Federated Learning

A compiled list of opensource frameworks and tools for Federated Learning follows; readers will find these resources useful for development of applications of their interest.

- TensorFlow Federated [33] is an opensource FL framework developed by Google providing high-level APIs for building both centralized and decentralized FL models.
- PySyft [34] is an opensource FL library developed by OpenMined providing a framework for building privacy-preserving machine learning models using different privacy preserving techniques.
- OpenFL (Open Federated Learning) [35] is an opensource framework that enables the training of machine learning models through a privacy-preserving collaborative approach.
- FATE (Federated AI Technology Enabler) [36] is an opensource FL framework developed by WeBank (digital bank of China), providing a secure and efficient FL platform.
- IBM Federated Learning [37] is an opensource FL framework by IBM providing a platform for building FL models supporting both centralized and decentralized training.
- PaddleFL [38] is an opensource FL framework developed by PaddlePaddle (opensource Deep Learning framework from China) providing a platform for building FL models.
- Nvidia Clara [39] is a software platform designed to enable collaborative AI model training without data sharing.
- OpenFed [40, 41] is an opensource software framework under the MIT license for end-to-end FL that aims to reduce the barrier to entry for early adopters.
- Substra [42] is an Opensource federated learning framework developed by a multi-partner research project around Owkin, a French startup in the application of AI in Biotech space.

Several academic institutions and companies have used FL for various applications. In academia, researchers have used FL for healthcare, image classification, and speech recognition. In industry, companies such as Google, Apple, and Microsoft have used FL to improve their products such as Gboard, Siri, and Bing. FL has been used to train AI models for spam filters, chatbots, and recommendation tools. In healthcare, FL has been used for predicting patient outcomes and identifying diseases within the constraints of patient privacy under HIPPA compliance. Deployments of FL include smartphone keyboards, smart home devices, and autonomous vehicles. FL can also be used for fraud detection, predicting traffic congestion, and even optimizing energy consumption.

Larger companies, such as Google, Microsoft, and Apple, have significantly invested in Federated Learning. In 2022, Google launched Federated Learning for TensorFlow (FLTF), an opensource platform that enables developers to implement FL in their applications. FL startups have received significant funding in recent years.

Sherpa.ai [43], a Spanish Federated Learning startup has built a horizontal FL platform for multiple verticals. Owkin, a French FL startup in the drugs and diagnostics is also a pioneer in the opensource federated learning framework Substra [42] and Owkin [44].

Despite its intended privacy benefits, FL faces significant challenges. Researcher point to the fact that FL is more vulnerable to attacks by malicious nodes than traditional deep learning, as anonymous clients can upload malicious data to the server without revealing identity. Only model parameters are collected, enabling attackers to remain anonymous. FL thus has increased security vulnerabilities compared to traditional learning algorithms. Liu et al. [45] extensively elaborate on FL's security vulnerabilities, threat forms, attacks, and defenses.

2.5 Challenges with Size of AI Models and Training Datasets

The field of AI is witnessing a fascinating paradox. While the trend leans towards ever-larger models, capable of mind-boggling Generative AI feats with billions or even trillions of parameters (as illustrated in Table 2.1), there is a parallel push towards deploying these models on resource-constrained edge devices. The need arises from the growing importance of privacy regulations discussed earlier in Sect. 2.4 and will be discussed further in Sect. 2.6. These Large Language Models (LLMs) models are trained on massive datasets, allowing them to learn complex patterns and relationships that would be impossible to learn with smaller models.

For detailed analysis on trends in AI model sizes and recent step jumps, readers should review the paper by Villalobos et al. [46]. Currently, the widely used ChatGPT by OpenAI is a LLM trained on vast text and code data to generate natural responses. Model sizes have rapidly grown—GPT-2 had 1.37 billion parameters, GPT-3 with 175 billion, and GPT-4 is speculated over 1 trillion parameters. ChatGPT was trained on a Google TPUv3 Pod supercomputer with 285 specialized TPU (Tensor Processing Unit) chips, enabling GPT-2 training in $\sim$100 h. While driving performance gains, such massive models require immense computational resources.

> A very pertinent Economist magazine article "The bigger-is-better approach to AI is running out of road" [47], argues the trend of increasingly larger LLMs is becoming unsustainably expensive and resource-intensive, limiting access to few large tech companies and governments. This concentrates power and innovation in few hands. The approach is unsustainable in the long-term, as smaller organizations cannot afford such models. Rather than democratizing AI, it risks monopolizing innovation by big tech, stifling competition. Crucially, it could concentrate immense influence over human thought and behavior wielded by a handful of powerful AI models controlled by few entities. This would lead to a more divided world assuming AI will wield the power to influence the way people think and behave in coming decades.

Table 2.1 Size of AI models and volume of training datasets

Year	Model	Parameters	Dataset trained on
2012	AlexNet	Over 60 million	Trained with ImageNet—14 million hand-annotated images over 20,000 categories
2018	BERT	110 and 340 million	Over 3 Terabytes of text data from Book Corpus and English Wikipedia
2019	GPT-2	1.5 billion	40 Gigabytes of text data, WebText text data from 45 million website links
2020	GPT-3	175 billion	45 Terabytes of text and code from Common Crawl, Webtext2, Books1, Books2 and Wikipedia
2021	WuDao 2.0	1.75 trillion	4.9 Terabytes of text and image data including Chinese text, Chinese graphics and English text
2022	PaLM	540 billion	540 Gigabytes of text and code from web pages, books, codes, and other data sources covering 100+ languages
2023	BaGuaLu	174 trillion	Size of training dataset is unknown
2023	Stable Diffusion	890 million to 13 billion	Image-text pairs from LAION-5B database
2023	Llama	7, 13, 33, 65 billion and	Large text dataset with over 20 languages, primarily Latin and Cyrillic alphabets
2023	DALL-E2	12 billion	Trained on a large dataset of image-text-video on internet, not explicitly disclosed
2023	BLOOM	176 billion	1.6TB multilingual ROOTS dataset with 350 billion tokens

The high energy needs, large memory, steep computational costs, and supply issues have disrupted the GPU market due to insatiable AI computing demand outpacing chipmakers' capacity. As we write this chapter, cutting-edge GPUs like Nvidia's H100 face extended lead times, soaring costs, and limited availability, hindering access for smaller players and academia. Geopolitical tensions between the US and China have further complicated AI hardware access, with Chinese firms restricted from American chips. This fuel concerns over a bifurcated AI hardware market emerging across East, West, and Global South. China is heavily investing in domestic AI chipmakers like Huawei and Alibaba to challenge US dominance. The combination of unsustainable scaling demands, geopolitical frictions, and concentration among few a few players point to the possible risk of undermining the **democratization of AI**. This has driven a resurgence and funding for alternative AI processor approaches, including wafer-scale integration by startups like Cerebras considering going public in 2025.

> "We won't be able to make models bigger forever. There comes a point where even with hardware improvements, given the pace that we're increasing the model size, we just can't."
>
> —Dylan Patel, SemiAnalysis

The counter to the trend is the development of ever-growing opensource models, a pervasive aspiration to democratize AI. These models are comparatively much smaller and hence more affordable to run and can be trained to run very specific tasks. The emergence of smaller LLMs is pivotal, as by requiring significantly fewer computing resources, often by an order of magnitude lower, these models broaden the reach of AI and open doors to a wider range of unique applications. Another major road block of AI is the fact that it needs humongous amounts of data. How do we create large datasets for training in the absence of real data? As the world's focus today is on Generative AI, which uses the largest models requiring voluminous training data corpus, our discussion will be focused in the subsequent section to AI in general and Generative AI in particular.

2.5.1 From 'Bigger the Better' to Smaller Models

Jared Kaplan of John Hopkins University and Sam McCandlish of OpenAI and their respective teams first analyzed empirical scaling laws for large language model and defined a power-law [48] for model performance that scales as a function of training time, context length, dataset size, model size, and compute budget. Model performance depends strongly on scaling the number of model parameters, the size of the dataset and the compute resources used for training. The performance of the system exhibited a power-law relationship with each of the three scaling factors—compute, data, and model size, spanning six orders of magnitude compared to the system when it was not bottlenecked by the other two scaling factors. The interdependence of scaling was noteworthy as every time model size was increased by eight times (8x), data needed to be increased by roughly five times (5x) to avoid a performance penalty. Google AI researchers delved deeper into scaling laws, analyzing their behavior across ten diverse model architectures: transformers, switch transformers, universal transformers, dynamic convolutions, performers, and the recently proposed MLP-mixers [49]. Extensive experimentations have demonstrated the importance of architecture for scaling up performance; however, model performance can be found to fluctuate at different scales.

It is now a well-established fact that large AI models generally outperform the smaller ones on a broad range of tasks due to their ability to capture more complex patterns. However, given sufficient and diverse datasets, it is possible for the smaller models to achieve comparable or better performance on specific narrowed down tasks. There will be a continued momentum towards building and fine-tuning broad based generic horizontal Generative AI models pioneered by large companies who have the capability to throw enormous resources and training datasets to achieve higher prediction quality. However, we believe that several vertical specific models will emerge that are much smaller in size, need much less resources to run, but do specific tasks extremely well. For example, Salesforce has announced plans to release a GPT-based chatbot for use with its Sales CRM platform. Similarly, Microsoft has announced a Microsoft Dynamics CoPilot for ERP. Google now offers Med-PaLM 2 [50], a LLM derived from PaLM2 which is tuned for medical profession and sec-PALM [51], a version tuned towards cybersecurity applications.

Efforts are underway to reverse the unidirectional trend towards bigger and more bigger models, going against the logic that bigger models are always better. DeepMind researchers demonstrated that training smaller models with larger training data corpus, could significantly boost performance. For example, the DeepMind's Chinchilla model [52] with 70-billion parameters outperformed the 175-billion-parameter GPT-3 by training on nearly five times more data [53]. Meta used the same approach to train much smaller models that could still compete with the biggest LLMs, resulting in Llama model coming in a variety of sizes now ranging between 7 and 65 billion parameters [54] including the recently released Llama 3 that scored significantly better than all previous smaller size models. Research groups have demonstrated that smaller models trained on domain-specific data outperforms larger, general-purpose models. Stanford researchers trained a relatively small model, PubMedGPT 2.7B [55], on biomedical abstracts to answer medical questions much better than a generalist model the same size.

Many researchers have now compared the performance of large language models with that of a smaller parameter model augmented with much more training data across many parameters. Early research by Turc et al. [56] in 2019 showed that knowledge distillation from LLMs into smaller models resulted in models that performed similarly with much reduced computing resources. Further, aligning language models to match user's intention by introducing instructions, has become an attractive proposition. A recent paper by Stanford researchers introduced the Alpaca 7B model [57], an instruction following language model fine-tuned from the LLaMA 7B model on only 52K instruction-following demonstrations. Alpaca behaved qualitatively similar to OpenAI's text-davinci-003 (GPT 3.5), with a much smaller model size, while training on a fraction of the computing resources. The process of fine-tuning with the right dataset is likely more important than the model architecture itself.

> Recently Llion Jones, the co-author of the influential 2017 paper "Attention is all you need" [58] that started the transformer model revolution and David Ha, head of research at Stability AI formed a new startup Sakana AI [59]. Sakana focuses on biomimicry involving multiple smaller AI models working together akin to the coordinated movements of a school of fish or a colony of bees inspired by collective intelligence that is seen in nature. By adopting this swarm approach, it aims to outperform larger systems in terms of efficiency and flexibility by creating adaptable and cost-effective AI models.

Another effort by Google proposed UL2R [60], an approach that does a lightweight second stage pre-training to substantially improve existing large language models with addition of only a tiny amount of extra computational resources. The 540 billion size U-PaLM achieves the same performance as the 540 billion PaLM model but using only half the computational resources.

The challenge today is the fact that training LLMs takes enormous amounts of time and computing resources. This is true even when assuming vast amounts of training data are available. A unique approach was used to develop FLAN (Finetuned LAnguage Net) [61], which improves the performance and usability of pre-trained language models. It works by fine-tuning a model on a set of instructions, rather than on a specific task. This makes the model more amenable to solving NLP tasks in general, even the ones that it has never seen before. FLAN was developed by Google AI, and it is based on the T5 language model, a general-purpose language model that can be used for a wide variety of NLP tasks, such as translation, summarization, and question answering. Fu et al. [62] focused on model specialization, to specialize the model's ability towards a target task rather than generic tasks like ChatGPT. While large models have strong modeling power, smaller models have limited model capacity, but the focus and concentration of this limited capacity of smaller language models can demonstrate superior reasoning abilities on specific target tasks with decent performance.

Another interesting project TinyLlama [63] project, led by a research assistant at Singapore University of Technology and Design, is trying to pre-train a 1.1 billion Llama model on three trillion tokens. This model takes up only 550MB of memory. Eldan et al. [64] of Microsoft research did an experiment to see how small an LLM model could be while still having the ability to speak coherent English. The researchers trained smaller size LLMs with 'TinyStories', a synthetic dataset of short stories that only contain words that a typical 3 to 4-year-olds usually understand, generated by GPT-3.5 and GPT-4. It was demonstrated that this dataset can be used to train and evaluate language models much smaller in size or much simpler architecture, can produce fluent and consistent stories with almost perfect grammar and good reasoning capabilities.

Reducing the size of large LLMs to smaller language models is an active field of research. It is not just for the speed of training and inference, but also the secondary benefits of using much less computing resources resulting in much smaller carbon footprints. During the first part of our journey on this book project, we observed the huge overnight success of super-large LLMs. As we proceed to complete the book manuscript in 2024, we notice a marked shift towards the design of lightweight

AI models, particularly with the recent release of Llama 3.3 and Deepseek models with commendable results. These models operate on low-resource hardware, such as laptop or even smartphones, while ensuring reasonable performance on specific tasks they are trained on. The driving motivation behind this trend is to make AI more accessible to everyone and not just make it a monopoly of only the big players.

2.5.2 Reduce Data Requirements to Train AI

AI models are typically trained on large datasets, which can be expensive and time-consuming to collect and then laboriously labeled. As we have discussed earlier, in a privacy-regulated world, it is becoming increasingly difficult to collect and share data. While we discussed reducing the footprint of AI models in the previous section, we also learnt that to achieve the same performance with smaller models requires even bigger datasets. Where and how will this data come from? Will synthetic data come to the rescue? This has led to a growing interest in AI data reduction approaches, which aims to train AI models on smaller datasets without sacrificing performance.

2.5.2.1 Synthetic Data

Artificially generated synthetic data is used to train AI models without the need to collect and label large datasets, a boon in today's emerging hyper-privacy world. Synthetic data can be generated using a variety of techniques, including computer graphics, physics simulation, statistical modeling and lately with Generative AI. In order to ensure the data utility in any targeted application domain, artificially generated synthetic data should reflect the statistical properties, distributional characteristics, and pattern classes observed in real-life data, essentially reflecting the statistical characteristics of real data. There are various ways to generate synthetic data highlighted next. A comprehensive history of synthetic data evolution and approaches has been compiled by Drechsler et al. [65] that includes the following approaches.

- **Probability Distribution**: This traditional statistical method creates synthetic data based on models like normal, exponential, chi-square, t-distribution, lognormal, or uniform distributions, leveraging the properties of these distributions instead of actual data points.
- **Agent-based Modeling (ABM)**: ABM is a computational technique that simulates the behavior of autonomous agents interacting within a system, often used for modeling complex systems like social, economic, or biological systems. For instance, ABM can simulate disease spread within a population, helping to understand the dynamics of complex interactions.
- **Rule-based Methods**: These involve defining explicit rules to describe data. For example, generating synthetic medical images might involve rules describing the structure and appearance of organs and tissues.

- **Generative Adversarial Networks (GANs)**: GANs, a prominent method for synthetic data generation, consist of two neural networks in an adversarial setup: a generator creating synthetic data and a discriminator evaluating its realism. Over time, the generator improves, producing highly realistic synthetic data.
- **Variational Autoencoders (VAEs)**: VAEs are neural networks that generate synthetic data by compressing real data into a latent space and sampling from it. They excel in creating data that follows complex distributions.

Generative AI has opened up endless possibilities for creating synthetic data. Google AI researchers have developed a generative AI model called Imagen [66] generating realistic images from text descriptions similar to the OpenAI model DALL-E. Google researchers have created Pathways Autoregressive Text-to-Image model (Parti), a text-to-image generation model that achieves high-fidelity photorealistic images including complex real-world compositions [67]. While text to images and videos are still extremely prompt dependent, many variations of the images, videos and text can now be created given a starting point as with Stable Diffusion [68]. Development of simulated and gaming environments have accelerated using Generative AI. This simulated data can in turn be used to train AI models to generate realistic textures, models, and environments for games. One of the key benefits of using synthetic data to generate game assets is that it can be done orders of magnitude more efficiently and cost-effectively than creating them manually. Nvidia has developed generative AI model GauGAN2 [69] to generate realistic images and videos from text descriptions. Unity has developed a generative AI model called ProBuilder [70], which can generate realistic 3D models from sketches and drawings, being used to create realistic 3D models for Unity's video games. Epic Games is developing a generative AI model called MetaHuman Creator [71], which can generate realistic human faces. As of writing this section, OpenAI had just released demonstration videos of their Text to Video engine Sora, outstanding examples of 30 s video clips getting generated from prompts [72].

2.5.2.2 Transfer Learning

In the traditional machine learning world, training data and testing data are usually taken from the same domain or similar tasks. However, in some real-world machine learning scenarios, training data may be too difficult or expensive to collate. Transfer learning involves using knowledge gained from one task or domain to improve performance on a different task or domain. Leveraging transfer learning has helped boost model performance across a diverse array of applications across domains, such as image classification, natural language processing, and speech recognition. The concept of transfer learning was first introduced in 1976 by Bozinovski and Fulgosi [73], but it was not widely used until the 2000s. Subsequently, it has gained popularity in recent years due to the rise of deep learning and challenges of having training datasets. It has been demonstrated to work in game playing, text classification, digit recognition, medical imaging and spam filtering.

A survey paper by Zhuang et al. [74] provides a comprehensive survey of transfer learning along with its various applications. The survey categorizes different approaches to transfer learning as well. Another excellent survey by Li et al. [75] reviews more than 50 representative approaches of transfer learning in the last decade in the deep learning space and systematically summarize them into four broad categories - instance-based transfer learning, model-based transfer learning, feature-based transfer learning, and relational-based transfer learning.

There are several tools and frameworks to try out transfer learning.

- **ADAPT** [76]: A comprehensive library offering tools and algorithms for both supervised and unsupervised domain adaptation, including techniques like adversarial learning, feature alignment, and transfer learning.
- **TLlib** [77]: A simpler library focused on supervised domain adaptation, featuring various pre-trained models and algorithms.
- **Domain-Adaptation-Toolbox** [78]: A MATLAB library for domain adaptation.

2.5.2.3 Few-Shot Learning (FSL)

Few-shot learning (FSL) is a machine learning technique that enables models to learn from a very small number of labeled examples, instead of requiring a large dataset. There are cases where data is scarce or expensive to collect, such as in industrial quality inspection using AI vision models. These models require training under various lighting conditions, orientations, and product types for accurate classification. However, the proportion of defective products on production lines is small, making it challenging to gather enough samples for training. Additionally, the need to train models for different product types further complicates the data collection process.

To address these challenges, researchers are exploring new techniques like FSL that allows AI models to learn from a small number of labeled samples and domain adaptation that allows AI models to be transferred from one domain to another. An FSL model for industrial quality inspection could learn from a few labeled defective samples across lighting conditions, generalizing to new conditions with minimal examples. A domain adaptation model could transfer from one product type's dataset to another with very few labeled samples. A recent survey paper by Song et al. [79] published in ACM Surveys reviews over 200 FSL papers published in top journals and conferences in the past three years.

Any discussion on FSL is incomplete without mentioning large generative AI models, which are few-shot or zero-shot learners, trained on vast datasets but requiring specific prompts, giving rise to the field of prompt engineering. Kojima et al. [80] show that adding "Let's think step by step" before answers enhances large language models' zero-shot reasoning capabilities. Matthew Mayo, Data Scientist and the Editor-in-Chief of KDnuggets [81] further introduces Chain of Thought (CoT) prompting, where LLMs are provided few-shot examples outlining the reasoning process, which they then follow, improving performance on tasks requiring arithmetic, commonsense, symbolic, and complex reasoning. Sontag et al. [82] demonstrate that large generative AI models like InstructGPT can perform well as clinical advisors, excelling at zero- and few-shot information extraction from clinical text despite not being trained specifically for the clinical domain.

2.5.2.4 Meta-Learning

The word '*Meta*' implies a level above or a level of abstraction, hence meta-learning is the concept and the approach of learning-to-learn. It involves training a model to learn how to learn, so that it can quickly adapt to new tasks with limited data. Unlike conventional AI approaches with fixed learning algorithms, meta-learning aims to improve the learning algorithm itself through experience across multiple learning episodes. Early work on meta-learning was done in the 1980s by researchers such as Mitchell and Schmidhuber [83]. However, it was not until the early 2010s that meta-learning began to gain traction in the machine learning community. There are three main approaches:

- **Model-based** meta-learning learns a model of the learning process itself, which is then used to guide learning of new tasks.
- **Metric-based** meta-learning learns a metric space where similar tasks are adjacent, used to quickly adapt to new tasks by transferring knowledge from closest related tasks.
- **Optimization-based** meta-learning learns how to quickly optimize a model for a new task by training on a small number of examples to initialize the model and then using that training to initialize the model for further training for the new task.

Meta-learning algorithms can be used in conjunction with other machine learning techniques, such as deep learning and reinforcement learning. For example, meta-learning algorithms can be used to train deep learning models that can learn new tasks quickly from a small number of examples. Similarly, meta-learning algorithms can be used to train reinforcement learning agents that can learn new policies quickly from experience.

A few applications of meta-learning include Google Photos to learn how to identify objects in images from a small number of examples. Similarly, Snapchat Lenses uses meta-learning to learn how to apply augmented reality effects to faces from a small number of examples. Driverless car pioneer Waymo is using meta-learning to develop self-driving cars that can learn to navigate new environments quickly and efficiently.

While this section provides an overview of meta-learning, readers are encouraged to refer to survey papers for additional information. The survey by Antoniou et al. [84] analyzes the contemporary meta-learning landscape, discussing definitions, positioning across related fields like transfer learning and hyperparameter optimization, and proposing a comprehensive taxonomy. Rafiei et al.'s [85] survey covers meta-learning applications in healthcare, discussing theoretical foundations, pivotal methods, multi/single-task learning, and few/many-shot learning in the healthcare domain.

2.5.2.5 Data Augmentation

Data augmentation involves artificially increasing the size of the dataset in terms of the volume, equality and diversity of the data by applying various transformations to the existing data, such as rotation, scaling, and cropping. This is inherently different from synthetic data as discussed in the previous section as it does not involve creating new data from scratch.

One of the earliest examples of data augmentation was used by LeCun [86] in his work on handwritten digit recognition. For further reading on data augmentation, examples, tools and frameworks, readers are advised to read Top Data Augmentation Techniques: Ultimate Guide for 2024 [87].

2.5.2.6 Active Learning

Active learning is a machine learning paradigm where the learner actively selects data points to label, focusing on the most informative ones for faster and more accurate learning. It is particularly useful when labeled data is scarce or expensive to obtain, like in medical diagnosis where labeling all possible diseases is difficult and costly. Active learning can select the most informative patients to label, training more accurate diagnostic models. It has proven effective across various tasks, including image classification, NLP, and medical diagnosis, and is a promising approach for training ML models with limited labeled data. Its key benefits are reducing required labeled data, speeding up learning by prioritizing informative points, and improving model accuracy by focusing on performance-enhancing data points. Zhan et al. [88] provide a detailed comparative survey of deep active learning approaches and results.

2.6 Security and Privacy in AI

Federated Learning (FL), discussed in Sect. 2.4.5, gained attention for privacy-preserving AI. This section explores the broader landscape of secured and private AI techniques. It covers Encrypted AI, where computations occur on encrypted data; pseudo-anonymization, veiling identities while allowing insights; and Confidential Compute, keeping data safe during processing within the compute engine itself.

Many of the techniques of secured and privacy preserving AI are also considered as part of Privacy Enhancing Techniques (PET). After the wild west of unrestricted customer data acquisition, utilization and monetization over the last decades, regulators worldwide have woken up and are enacting modern privacy laws, with Gartner expecting 65% of countries to have such regulations within the next few years. These regulations would have different nuances and vary across countries and even within the different states across US. Data science teams seek to leverage more data, while privacy teams led by Chief Privacy Officers (CPOs) aim to restrict data access for compliance and risk mitigation, creating tensions between the two groups.

The techniques around secured and privacy preserving AI can be broadly grouped under the following sub-buckets: Encrypted AI, Anonymization and Pseudonymization, Differential Privacy, Confidential and Secured computing, Encrypting and Securing AI Models and Federated Learning (FL). Encrypting and securing AI models involves implementing robust measures to protect the intellectual property (IP) of the models. One approach is to employ model encryption, which involves encrypting the model parameters and architecture to prevent unauthorized access and reverse engineering. Additionally, Trusted Execution Environment (TEE) discussed further in Sect. 2.6.4 is also used for securing deployment and safeguarding the model's integrity during runtime. Function secret sharing, model encryption, and watermarking to embed hidden markers in AI models are popular approaches used to secure AI models, preventing unauthorized access and reverse engineering.

2.6.1 *Encrypted AI*

Homomorphic encryption (HE) enables AI data processing on encrypted data without decryption, producing results equivalent to computations on unencrypted data. This ensures data privacy during processing, making HE ideal for privacy-preserving storage, computation, and AI model training.

HE encompasses various encryption schemes that perform different computations on encrypted data. Partially homomorphic encryption supports one type of operation (e.g., addition or multiplication). Somewhat homomorphic encryption supports two types of operations but is limited in repetitions. Leveled fully homomorphic encryption handles arbitrary circuits with multiple operations but is limited by circuit depth. Fully Homomorphic Encryption (FHE) allows unlimited computations on encrypted data, regardless of depth or complexity, making it the strongest form of HE and the "holy grail" of encryption.

The first FHE algorithm was introduced in 2009 by Craig Gentry using lattice-based cryptography [89]. Since then, researchers have developed more efficient and practical FHE algorithms. For most HE schemes, the multiplicative depth of circuits is the main practical limitation in performing computations over encrypted data.

There are several opensource libraries and frameworks available for implementing HE. A few notable ones are listed:

- **Microsoft SEAL** [90]: An easy-to-use, powerful opensource HE library under the MIT license.
- **OpenFHE** [91]: An opensource project offering efficient, extensible implementations of post-quantum fully HE schemes.
- **PALISADE** [92]: Provides efficient implementations of lattice cryptography and leading HE schemes, complying with HomomorphicEncryption.org standards, with simple APIs, modularity, and cross-platform support.
- **TFHE-rs** [93]: A HE library developed by Zama, known for its speed and regarded as one of the fastest public implementations of homomorphic encryption.

2.6.2 Anonymization and Pseudonymization

Individuals have the right to control their personal data's collection, usage, and sharing. Data utility refers to the usefulness of data for purposes such as targeted advertising, upselling, cross-selling, and training AI models. There is a constant tension between data utility and privacy. Stringent data privacy laws are emerging globally to ensure that personal data are not collected or used without consent.

Anonymization involves removing all Personal Identification Information (PII) that could identify an individual directly (e.g., name, address, phone number) or indirectly (e.g., workplace, job title, zip code). This process ensures a data subject cannot be identified, either by the data controller or in combination with other sources. Pseudonymization, on the other hand, replaces PII fields with artificial identifiers or pseudonyms, making data less identifiable while retaining utility. The choice of pseudonymized fields is subjective. Less selective fields like birth date or zip code are often included because they are available from other sources and make records easier to identify. Pseudonymizing of such fields reduces analytical value, which is mitigated by using derived forms like year of birth or broader geographic regions. In privacy domain, data fields are categorized into direct identifiers (DI), non-sensitive attributes (NSA), quasi-identifiers (QIs), and sensitive attributes (SA). Quasi-identifiers are essentially indirect identifiers.

Privacy threats can be classified under—identity disclosure, attribute disclosure, and membership disclosure. Different forms of anonymization and pseudonymization techniques have been used in research and private industries.

- **Generalization** transforms the original quasi-identifiers into less-specific but semantically consistent values. For example, the value 35 of age can be generalized with an interval [30–40].
- **Suppression** hides the original value of quasi-identifiers with a special value. For example, the value Age: 35 can be replaced with an asterisk, resulting 3 as the suppressed value.
- **Permutation** partitions the records into several groups, and values of the sensitive attributes are shuffled within each group. Hence, the sensitive attributes and the quasi-identifiers relationships are de-associated within each group though there is concern on reduction on data utility.
- **Perturbation** replaces the original value of the records with some synthetically generated values in a way that statistical information does not differ much in both datasets to retain the data utility.
- **Salting** adds random noise to the data making it more difficult to identify individuals, but it can also make the data less useful.
- **k-anonymity** is a property possessed by anonymized data, first introduced by Samarati and Sweeney [94] in a paper published in 1998, although the basic concept dates back to a paper by Tore Dalenius in 1986 [95]. It addresses the basic and

fundamental aspect of anonymity—a dataset with k-anonymity property implies that the information for each person cannot be distinguished from at least k-1 other individuals in the database. While better than the techniques highlighted above and fairly easy to implement, k-anonymity has many drawbacks including high loss of data utility or usefulness if used in high-dimensional data and also can be broken easily by homogeneity and background knowledge attack.

- **I-Diversity** is a privacy protection technique, an improvement over k-anonymity. It aims to prevent an adversary from inferring sensitive information about an individual by looking at the distribution of sensitive attribute values in an equivalence class, which is defined as a group of records that have the same values for all non-sensitive attributes. I-diversity requires that each equivalence class contain at least 'l' different values for the sensitive attribute, and that the distribution of the sensitive attribute values within each equivalence class be similar to the distribution of the sensitive attribute values in the overall population. For example, let us say we have a dataset of patients, and the sensitive attribute is their disease status. If we want to achieve I-diversity with l = 2, then each equivalence class must contain at least 2 different disease statuses, and the distribution of disease statuses within each equivalence class must be similar to the distribution of disease statuses in the overall population.
- **T-closeness** adds noise to the data in a way that preserves the overall distribution of the data while making it more difficult to identify individuals from the dataset. This is a more sophisticated technique than the previous ones and an improvement over k-anonymity and I-diversity. T-closeness was first proposed in 2007 by Li et al. [96] as a refinement of l-diversity. While I-diversity requires that each equivalence class contain at least l different values for the sensitive attribute, T-closeness extends this by requiring that the distribution of the sensitive attribute values within each equivalence class be close to the distribution of the sensitive attribute values in the overall population. This helps to prevent an adversary from inferring sensitive information about an individual by simply looking at the distribution of sensitive attribute values in their equivalence class. T-closeness has been shown to be more robust to deciphering from background knowledge than l-diversity. It has been used to anonymize medical data, census data, and financial data and has also been used to protect the privacy of individuals in social media data and location data.

2.6.3 Differential Privacy (DP)

Differential Privacy (DP) is a privacy-preserving technique that adds noise to data to prevent individuals from being identified. The amount of noise added is determined by a scientific privacy parameter, which essentially controls the trade-off between privacy and utility. Small changes are done to the individual data so that it cannot be used to infer much about any individual, while ensuring that it does not change the statistical characteristics and data utility. Differential privacy was first introduced in 2006 by Dwork et al. [97]. To preserve data privacy, the authors proposed a generalized methodology for adding noise to data. Their groundbreaking research was recognized with the 2016 TCC Test-of-Time Award as well as the prestigious 2017 Gödel Prize. The main difference between differential privacy and t-closeness or i-diversity is that differential privacy is a mathematically provable guarantee of privacy protection against a wide range of privacy attacks. Differential privacy ensures that an attacker cannot learn anything about an individual's data, even if they have access to the data of all other individuals in the dataset.

Several tools are available for implementing differential privacy:

- RAPPOR library [98]: For differentially private data collection, enabling sensitive data collection without compromising privacy.
- TensorFlow Privacy library [99]: For differentially private machine learning in TensorFlow, allowing model training on sensitive data while maintaining privacy.
- Google's Differential Privacy libraries [100]: Repository offering libraries for generating ε-differential and (ε, δ)-differential private statistics, including Privacy on Beam, an end-to-end differential privacy framework built on Apache Beam.
- Meta's Opacus [101]: PyTorch library for training models with differential privacy.
- OpenDP Smartnoise [102]: Opensource platform providing tools for adding differential privacy to data analysis workflows, supporting Python, R, and Java.
- Diffprivlib [103]: IBM's Python library for adding differential privacy to machine learning models.

2.6.3.1 Differential Privacy—Adoption, Implementation and Applications

Differential privacy has been widely adopted by research communities and is considered one of the most promising privacy-preserving techniques as privacy regulations get enforced globally. However, challenges remain, such as the addition of noise to data that can affect utility, and the computational expenses making it infeasible for some applications. While government agencies, research institutions, and technology giants are at the forefront of adoption, its use remains nascent for many large enterprises. As data generation proliferates and privacy regulations solidify, differential privacy is likely to go mainstream.

Real-world applications of differential privacy include the U.S. Census Bureau protecting individual privacy in the 2020 census, the University of California, Berkeley studying disease spread without identifying patients, Apple implementing it at scale in its system architecture to privatize user data before transmission, and Google exploring it in COVID-19 mobility reports [104], quantifying changes in public place visits and time spent at home.

Readers can refer to the blog by Damien Desfontaines [105] to get the latest updates on differential privacy applications. OpenMined, a non-profit focused on safe and responsible AI, created PyDP [106], a Python wrapper for Google's Differential Privacy project. Startups like Enveil [107], specializing in privacy-preserving technologies including differential privacy, offer solutions for secure data processing and analytics while maintaining privacy.

2.6.4 Multi-party Compute (MPC) and Confidential Compute

Multi-Party Computation (MPC) and Confidential Compute are cryptographic techniques ensuring secure computation and data privacy in collaborative environments. This section explores their history, approaches, ongoing research, current state, and future outlook.

2.6.4.1 Multi-party Compute

Secure multi-party computation (MPC) is a cryptographic technique enabling multiple parties to collectively evaluate a function without revealing their individual inputs. It aims to protect participants' privacy from each other rather than external adversaries. Originating with the development of mental poker in the late 1970s, MPC allows computational tasks over distances without requiring a trusted third party. Unlike traditional cryptography, which conceals content, MPC conceals information about input data while computing with data from multiple sources, producing desired accurate outputs.

Yao's Millionaires' problem is a secure multi-party computation problem introduced in 1982 by world renowned computer scientist and computational theorist Professor Yao [108]. The classic example involves two wealthy individuals, Alice and Bob, who want to determine which one has a higher net worth, but without disclosing their actual financial details. Secure computation was formally introduced in 1982 as a two-party computation (2PC), also referred to as '*Secured Function Evaluation*'. The two-party case was followed by a generalization to multi-party computation.

Various approaches to MPC exist, encompassing two-party settings and privacy-enhancing technologies utilizing cryptographic protocols, secret sharing, and secure multiparty computation algorithms. Historically, MPC faced challenges due to its computation-intensive nature. However, a notable shift can be observed since 2010, with a focus on efficiency improvements tailored for real-world scenarios. Demonstrations of practical efficiency were evident as early as 2008 at the Danish Sugar Beet

Auction [109]. Both theoretical exploration and practical applications are essential for the advancement of MPC, leading to the establishment of the MPC Alliance in 2020 [110]. Comprising of 60 members, including Meta, Alibaba Group, Bosch, and various blockchain startups, the alliance aims to promote awareness, acceptance, and usage of MPC technologies.

2.6.4.2 Confidential Compute

While both multi-party compute (MPC) and confidential compute aim to secure data, they serve distinct purposes. MPC focuses on safeguarding data privacy between collaborating parties by enabling joint computation while keeping individual inputs private. Conversely, confidential compute protects data confidentiality during processing by encrypting data within a trusted execution environment (TEE), preventing unauthorized access. Both technologies enable secure data processing prioritizing privacy and confidentiality. While they serve distinct purposes, they are complementary and often combined to bolster security. For instance, confidential compute enhances the execution environment during MPC. MPC emphasizes privacy among participants and confidential compute safeguards from unauthorized access within a system.

Maintaining data confidentiality '*at rest*' and '*in transit*' are well proven and have established solutions. However, confidential compute addresses the security and privacy challenges when data is '*in use*'. Although the concept has been around for years, it gained prominence recently due to increasing data volumes and regulatory concerns. Coined by Intel in 2016, the term '*Confidential Computing*' is now adopted by industry leaders like Microsoft, IBM, and Google.

Trusted execution environment (TEE) is a tamper-resistant processing environment that executes on a separate kernel. It is a secure area of a processor called an '*enclave*' designed to protect code, data or AI/ML models from unauthorized access, even if the operating system or other software on the system is compromised. Readers are encouraged to dive deeper into confidential compute by reading the survey paper by Salehi et al. [111].

The confidential computing landscape is rapidly evolving. Leading cloud vendors such as Microsoft Azure, Amazon Web Services (AWS), and Google Cloud Platform (GCP) are integrating confidential computing technologies into their offerings. Chip manufacturers like Intel, AMD, and ARM continuously enhance their hardware-based TEEs for improved security and performance. Several software vendors are developing tools and frameworks utilizing confidential computing for secured machine learning. Organizations like the Confidential Computing Consortium (CCC) [112] are establishing standards and best practices, including interoperability.

2.7 AI Trust FEAT (Fairness, Ethics, Accountability, Transparency)

Artificial Intelligence (AI) is increasingly permeating all aspects of our individual lives and society. Questions of fairness, ethics, accountability and transparency have emerged with the underlying question of how to make AI more trustworthy. High profile AI incidents have engulfed the media that were prejudiced, discriminating, on the verge of being illegal and infringing on fundamental rights. Users need to be confident that AI is being developed and used in a responsible and trustworthy manner to get wider acceptance. As a consequence, the study of ethical considerations in artificial intelligence, known as AI trust or responsible AI, has emerged as a crucial research area not just in academia, but also a topic of widespread interest and concern for individuals, organizations, nations, and society as a whole.

The subject of AI trustworthiness and ethics is broad and involves not just technology but various domains of ethics and philosophy and cultural differences that have been debated over generations. This section tries to give an overview of the field and pointers to the readers for further reading, highlighting the problem and ongoing efforts, alongside emerging frameworks and tools. Recently, it has been particularly disconcerting that Generative AI can easily create impersonate videos and phone calls to wreak havoc in the hands of a bad actor. Raging debates are ongoing as Generative AI uses and learns content from creators and generates its own content without acknowledging the original source. Numerous applications, studies, and real-world challenges have helped to identify a plethora of ethical and trust issues, such as lack of transparency, privacy and accountability concerns, bias and discrimination, problems with safety and security, the possibility of criminal and malicious use, etc.

Trust is crucial for the acceptance of AI systems. A global survey by KPMG [113] involving 17,000 respondents across genders, ages, and 17 countries revealed interesting findings highlighting the importance of building trust in AI. While 61% of people were ambivalent or unwilling to trust AI systems, trust levels varied significantly across countries. Less than 25% reported having trust in AI in Finland and Japan, contrasting with majority trust in emerging economies like Brazil, India, China, and South Africa. Nations like Brazil, India, China, and South Africa exhibited optimism about AI, while fears and worries prevailed in Australia, Canada, France, and Japan, with the French being most alarmed. Globally, 73% expressed concerns about AI dangers, including data privacy violations, manipulation, job losses, system failures, human rights deterioration, and biased results. While there was widespread endorsement for ethical and trustworthy AI principles, maintaining public trust hinges on consistently upholding these guiding principles. Notably, 71% of global respondents expected AI to be regulated, with the exception in India, may be because the Indian IT success happened in a relatively light regulatory environment and business-friendly policies.

The recent analysis of LLMs have uncovered many biases. Feng et al. [114] did a comprehensive analysis revealing that LLMs have political biases where GPT-4 leans towards libertarianism, while LLaMA is more authoritarian. In order to investigate these biases, researchers asked questions related to social and economic ideologies. The findings revealed significant biases present in the models, especially when it came to social issues, demonstrating that the nature and composition of the training data as a potential contributing factor. Many AI models have been trained on contemporary web texts such as in the CommonCrawl Dataset [115], a free, open repository of web crawl data that can be used by anyone, which likely might have a liberal undertone. This is a departure from the limitations of older datasets like BookCorpus [116], which some large language models have been trained on, potentially inheriting biases present in those datasets.

2.7.1 Guidelines and Frameworks of AI Trust

While globally there are several ongoing initiatives to establish guidelines and frameworks for trustworthy AI, we highlight some of the prominent efforts across international bodies, academia, industry associations, and companies.

The World Economic Forum's Centre at the Presidio in San Francisco hosted the "Responsible AI Leadership: A Global Summit on Generative AI", in collaboration with AI Commons in April 2023. Over one-hundred AI thought leaders and practitioners gathered to discuss the responsible creation and governance of generative AI systems, resulting in the "Presidio Recommendations" [117], a set of 30 action-oriented guidelines. The Institute for Trustworthy AI in Law and Society (TRAILS) [118], funded by a twenty-million-dollar grant from the National Science Foundation (NSF), focuses on transforming AI practices with ethics and human rights considerations, particularly by incorporating inputs from marginalized communities. UNESCO adopted a recommendation on the ethics of AI in November 2021 [119], highlighting the importance of trustworthiness and integrity across the AI system lifecycle. This high-level "Ethics of Artificial Intelligence" recommendation represents the first global agreement on this topic, endorsed by 193 member states. The European Commission's High-Level Expert Group on Artificial Intelligence (HLEG AI) has released reports on ethics guidelines, an AI ethics assessment framework, policy recommendations, and investment proposals [120]. IBM Research operates a Trustworthy AI portal and offers the AI Fairness 360 opensource library [121, 122], aiding in bias detection and mitigation within machine learning models and datasets.

2.7.2 AI Trustworthiness Approaches

AI is more than just a technology that can replace or augment human tasks and decision-making processes. Unlike other technologies that rely on user input and rules-based programming, AI has more autonomy and latitude. Conceptualizing trust in AI requires interpreting both the technology and its autonomy. When it comes to trusting AI, there are two dimensions to consider: human-like trust and functionality trust. Human-like trust in AI is about the AI's design and the values it reflects, such as fairness and avoiding harm. Functionality trust in AI is about how well the AI works, like being reliable and accurately implementing its assigned tasks. So, we trust AI in two ways, similar to how we trust people based on their character and abilities.

As we were completing the book manuscript, Google's Gemini faced criticism for attempting to be more diverse and inclusive, compromising on facts. The situation escalated when Gemini generated images of the founding fathers of America that included Asians and dark-skinned people, which is factually incorrect. Ethics in AI is a socio-technical challenge demanding the appropriate balance between technology benefits and social norms and values, as highlighted by R. Chatila and John C. Havens in IEEE's Global Initiative on Ethics of Autonomous and Intelligent Systems [123]. The European Commission's High Level Expert Group on AI offers a succinct framework of ethics requirements [120]. Readers are encouraged to read the IEEE paper providing an overview of AI Ethics [124], which lists and categorizes many ethical issues. Jobin et al. [125] published in Nature 'The global landscape of AI ethics guidelines', reviewing 84 ethical guidelines released by national or international organizations from various countries with strong widespread agreement on five key principles: transparency, justice and fairness, non-maleficence, responsibility, and privacy.

2.7.3 AI Trustworthiness and Ethics: Key Principles

AI development and use raise complex ethical questions. Key principles for building trustworthy AI include:

- **Transparency**: Explainable AI (XAI) covered in Sect. 2.3 aids in human comprehension of AI decision-making processes, thereby promoting trust and accountability. It encompasses understanding the AI system's decision-making rationale, development, usage, design choices, and ensuring just processes and outcomes.
- **Fairness and Justice**: AI systems should be unbiased and avoid discrimination against individuals or groups. Tools like IBM's opensource bias detection toolkit [121] can help detect the risks. AI fairness demands unbiased development and use to prevent discriminatory outcomes, an issue highlighted by recent media scrutiny. Mitigating bias is crucial for just and equitable AI, as AI algorithms are not inherently ethical but reflect the social contexts and data they operate in.

- **Responsibility and Accountability**: Stakeholders involved in an AI system's lifecycle should be responsible for its actions and consequences, necessitating clear governance frameworks to ensure accountability as systems become more complex. Ethical AI demands focus on how the system works, the data it uses, and its application to avoid unintended consequences. However, ethical dilemmas arise, such as the trolley problem: an autonomous vehicle facing an unavoidable accident must prioritize passenger safety or minimizing harm to pedestrians. This scenario highlights the challenges of programming ethical decision-making into AI, with no easy answer and varying legal, cultural and ethical implications. Mechanisms for human intervention in critical situations could balance autonomy with ethical considerations. Open dialogue is critical to establish ethical guidelines for AI decision-making, considering diverse perspectives and potential consequences. The trolley problem exemplifies the complexities of assigning responsibility in AI-driven accidents and the dilemmas we will encounter in an AI-driven world.
- **Non-maleficence**: The core principle of "do no harm" applies to AI as well. This means ensuring AI systems and their environments are safe and secure to prevent harm to humans, their dignity, and well-being, as evidenced by concerns surrounding autonomous vehicles and robots. This is like Isaac Asimov First law of Robotics "A robot may not injure a human being or, through inaction, allow a human being to come to harm."
- **AI Privacy**: Responsible AI development necessitates protecting user privacy throughout an AI system's lifecycle through adherence to privacy laws, responsible data collection, and securing data and AI models. Privacy-preserving machine learning and synthetic data techniques as discussed in Sect. 2.5.2 can significantly contribute. Prioritizing data privacy helps build public trust in AI.

Adhering to the basic principles can ensure that AI development and use is ethical, responsible, and beneficial to all. Trustworthy AI requires a collaborative effort from developers, users, and policymakers to ensure ethical and responsible development and use. But as we learnt, AI trustworthiness and ethics is a complex field involving ethics theories involving individual, society and environment.

2.8 Emergence of Opensource in AI Models, Datasets and Benchmarks

The rise of opensource has been a game-changer in the field of AI, democratizing access to powerful models, datasets, and benchmarking efforts. The emergence of opensource can be traced back to 1971, when Professor Richard M. Stallman joined MIT's Artificial Intelligence Lab, where he developed the concept of free software, that laid the groundwork for the modern opensource movement. The movement gained momentum in the 1990s with the rise of the Internet, which facilitated wider sharing of code, championing the principles of collaboration, transparency, and shared knowledge.

At the forefront of today's AI revolution is a diverse and passionate community of researchers, developers, and enthusiasts who believe in the power of open collaboration. This community spans academia, technology giants, startups, and independent contributors, united by a shared vision of advancing AI through open and accessible resources. Notable contributors to the opensource AI ecosystem include product teams and organizations like TensorFlow (Google), PyTorch (Meta), Hugging Face, OpenAI, Anthropic, DeepMind, and countless individual developers and researchers who have generously shared their work on platforms like GitHub, arXiv, and LingHub.

The availability of opensource AI models has been profound, allowing anyone with access to computing resources to leverage AI. Models like BLOOM, Llama, OPT and recently Deepseek have pushed the boundaries of natural language processing and text generation. These models are often released under permissive licenses, allowing for free use, modification, and distribution, fostering an ecosystem of derivative works, fine-tuning, and experimentation. For instance, the Hugging Face Transformers library has become a hub for sharing and accessing pre-trained models for a wide range of tasks. Opensource frameworks like TensorFlow and PyTorch provide essential tools for building and training deep learning models. This democratizes access to AI technology, empowering individuals and organizations to leverage these models in their own applications and research resulting in the super-fast evolution of AI that we are witnessing today.

2.8.1 Opensource AI Models

The opensource movement in AI gained traction with the release of frameworks like TensorFlow by Google in 2015 and PyTorch by Facebook in 2016. These frameworks not only provided tools for building and deploying AI models but also fostered a vibrant community of contributors and users. Several prominent AI models have emerged from this ecosystem. Notable examples include BERT (Bidirectional Encoder Representations from Transformers) [126], a Natural Language Processing (NLP) model introduced by Google AI in 2018, and YOLO (You Only Look Once) [127], an object detection algorithm widely adopted in computer vision applications for its real-time processing capabilities. Opensource AI models are typically released under licenses such as the Apache License, MIT License, and GNU General Public License (GPL), which promote collaboration and innovation while protecting developers' rights. These licenses vary in terms of permissions, restrictions, and obligations, providing flexibility for both individual developers and organizations.

Prior to 2015, only a handful of opensource AI models were available, with the earliest notable model being MOSES (Machine Translation Opensource Engine System) for statistical machine translation in 2003. During the period of 2015–2019, significant number of opensource AI models were released. The period of 2020–2023, witnessed a remarkable surge in opensource AI models driven by the rise of large language models, generative AI models, and multimodal models. The year

Table 2.2 List of Opensource Generative AI models and references

Model	Size parameters	Origin	Opensource version
GPT-2 [128]	1.5 billion	OpenAI	Yes, MIT license
GPT-3 [129]	175 billion	OpenAI	Partial (research) and via APIs
BLOOM [130]	176 billion	BIGSCIENCE	Yes, Open Responsible AI Licenses (OpenRAIL)
LLaMA [131]	7, 13, 33 and 65 billion	Meta AI	Restricted opensource
Falcon [132]	7 and 40 billion	Technology Innovation Institute, Abu Dhabi	Yes, Apache 2.0 license
Mistral-7B [133]	7.3 billion	Mistral AI	Yes, Apache 2.0 license
GPT-NeoX-20B [134]	20 billion	EleutherAI	Yes, Apache 2.0 license
OPT [135]	1.3, 2.7, 6.7, 13 and 30 billion	Meta AI	Yes, Apache 2.0 license
T5 [136]	3, 11 and 24 billion	Google AI	Yes, Apache license
Stable diffusion [68]	890 million to 13 billion	Stability AI, Runway ML	Yes, CreativeML-OpenRail-M license or Bigscience-openrail-M license
Aya [137]	13 billion	Cohere	Yes, Apache 2.0 license

2023 and 2024 alone witnessed an unprecedented surge in the release of opensource AI models in Generative AI, with several new AI models being made available under opensource licenses. Beyond just the number, the AI models were of high quality and diversity, trained in more than 15 languages, and contributed from 13 different countries across four continents.

Table 2.2 lists some of the prominent opensource Generative AI models, their sizes, origins, availability of opensource versions, and their respective links in the references for downloading and learning more about them. It is to be noted that this list is not exhaustive, as the opensource AI landscape is constantly evolving, and new models are being released regularly. Hence the topography of Generative AI opensource models is a snapshot in time. New players will emerge, and existing organizations may shift their strategies, embracing or departing from opensource philosophies. Additionally, the licenses and terms governing the use of these models may change over time, potentially impacting their accessibility and adoption.

Today, the key players within the foundational large-language model space are prominent organizations and research institutes that have dedicated significant resources to developing and releasing these models. OpenAI which has been the leader with its Generative Pre-trained Transformer (GPT) series, a pioneer in this field, has reversed and went proprietary. Anthropic, a relatively newer player, has made waves with its Claude model [138], which has garnered attention for its impressive language understanding and generation capabilities, but they have not made any version of it open yet. Cohere, another AI research company, has contributed the Command and Aya models to the opensource landscape, while tech giants like Google and Meta have also released their own large language models. Meta has opensourced its LLaMA model which is being widely used as a base model for many interesting usecases and applications. Additionally, organizations such as the Technology Innovation Institute (TII) in the United Arab Emirates and Mistral, a French AI research company, have opensourced their respective Falcon and Mistral-7B models. Of these key players, only a few have embraced the true spirit of opensource by releasing their foundational models under permissive licenses that allow for free use, modification, and redistribution. Notably, Meta's LLaMA, TII's Falcon, and Mistral's Mistral-7B models are considered opensource foundation models, accessible to researchers, developers, and enthusiasts worldwide.

2.8.2 *Opensource and Crowdsourced Data*

Opensource and crowdsourced datasets have played a pivotal role in the advancement of AI. These datasets, contributed by researchers, organizations, and individuals from around the world, have democratized access to data, helped compare models across same datasets, fostering innovation and collaboration enabling breakthroughs in various domains.

The origins of opensource and crowdsourced datasets can be traced back to the early days of computer science and AI research. In the 1960 and 1970s, researchers often shared datasets within their academic circles or through personal networks. However, this process was often limited and inefficient, hindering progress and collaboration. In the 1980 and 1990s, with the advent of the internet and the growing popularity of opensource software, the idea of openly sharing datasets gained traction. Initiatives like the University of California Irvine Machine Learning Repository [139], established in 1987, made it easier for researchers to access and contribute datasets for machine learning tasks. The early 2000s saw a significant shift towards crowdsourcing data, leveraging the power of the internet and the collective efforts of individuals worldwide. Projects like the ImageNet [140] dataset, launched in 2009, relied on crowdsourced annotations to create large-scale, labeled datasets for computer vision tasks. Today, opensource and crowdsourced datasets have become integral to the AI and ML ecosystem, spanning various domains such as computer vision, natural language processing, speech recognition, and more.

Needless to say, opensource and crowdsourced datasets offer numerous benefits to the AI and ML community. These datasets are freely available, enabling researchers, developers, and enthusiasts from diverse backgrounds and resource levels to access high-quality data for training and testing AI models. Opensource datasets promote

Table 2.3 Popular opensource and crowdsourced datasets

Dataset	Domain	Description
ImageNet [140]	Computer vision	14.2 million labeled images for object recognition tasks
COCO (Common Objects in Context) [141]	Computer vision	Object detection, segmentation, and captioning dataset with over 330,000 images, 220,000 labelled
MNIST [142]	Computer vision	Handwritten digit recognition dataset with 60,000 training and 10,000 test examples
Open Images [143]	Computer vision	Over 9 million labeled images for object detection, visual relationship detection, and other tasks
WikiText [144]	Natural language processing	Language modeling dataset derived from high-quality Wikipedia articles
LibriSpeech [145]	Speech recognition	Large-scale corpus of read English speech, derived from audiobooks
Mozilla common voice [146]	Speech recognition	Crowdsourced dataset of voice recordings for speech recognition tasks
HuggingFace datasets [147]	Multi-domain	Collection of datasets for various NLP tasks, including text classification, question answering, and more
Kaggle datasets [148]	Multi-domain	Collection of datasets by Kaggle across multiple domains and commercial applications

reproducibility in research, allowing others to validate and build upon existing work, fostering transparency and accountability in the AI ecosystem. Crowdsourcing data leverages the collective knowledge and efforts of individuals worldwide, enabling the creation of large-scale, diverse, and high-quality datasets that would be difficult or impossible for a single entity to create and maintain. Opensource datasets serve as benchmarks for evaluating and comparing the performance of different AI models and algorithms, driving innovation and progress. Table 2.3 showcases some of the most popular opensource and crowdsourced datasets across various facets of AI.

2.8.3 Benchmarking AI Models

In the 1980s, during the personal computer revolution, there was a need for standardized metrics to compare computer system performance, leading to the development of benchmarks like SPEC (Standard Performance Evaluation Corporation). SPEC benchmarks [149] and related tools are widely used to evaluate the performance of computer hardware and software allowing for comparison and benchmarking while the test results were published publicly on the SPEC website.

In the late 2000s, ImageNet [140] emerged as a significant benchmark for computer vision tasks, driving advancements in deep learning vision models. The history of Machine Learning Performance Benchmark (MLPerf) began in 2018 with a series of meetings between engineers and researchers from leading institutions like Baidu, Google and researchers from Stanford, Harvard and Berkeley with a goal to establish common training and inference benchmarks to compare the speed and efficiency of various software frameworks, hardware platforms, and cloud computing platforms for machine learning tasks. By providing a common ground for measurement, MLPerf [150] helps users to make informed decisions when choosing tools and infrastructure for their ML projects. These initial efforts laid the foundation for MLCommons [150], officially established in 2020, which has now grown into a much broader effort encompassing benchmarks, datasets, and best practices.

The field of AI benchmarks has evolved rapidly in recent years, driven by the need to evaluate and compare the capabilities of large language models and other AI systems. These benchmarks span various tasks and domains, including natural language processing, reasoning, and multi-modal understanding. Table 2.4 summarizes some of the top benchmarks in the field, classified by different types.

These benchmarks have played a crucial role in driving the development of more capable AI models and fostering research in various areas of AI. As the field continues to evolve, new benchmarks will emerge to evaluate complex AI systems designed to address challenging tasks.

2.9 AI Regulations

A discussion on AI is incomplete without considering regulation, particularly given the rapid adoption of large language models (LLMs) and generative AI. Readers are encouraged to read the article in Nature on the 'Conflicting Views on AI Regulations' [162] for an overview on how each country or region is proceeding towards regulating AI.

"Regulation of AI is essential", Sam Altman, chief executive of technology firm OpenAI, told US senators during a hearing in May 2023 on AI. Many technology experts and non-experts agree, and the clamor for legal guard rails around AI is rising. Governments worldwide are grappling with the challenge of regulating AI in a way that fosters innovation without compromising safety and ethics. It is noteworthy to mention that this time larger technology giants are voicing strong opinions in favour of AI regulation, but it is very likely to defend their turf as incumbents, as regulations would make it difficult for upcoming startups.

Table 2.4 Benchmarks to compare AI Models across different domains

Benchmark	Type	Description
GLUE and SuperGLUE [151, 152]	Natural language processing	Benchmarks used to assess how well artificial intelligence models understand natural language GLUE is for sentence-level tasks. SUPERGLUE is for more complex tasks requiring reasoning and understanding of longer passages
SQuAD [153]	Question and answer	Stanford Question Answering Dataset, a reading comprehension benchmark where models answer questions based on given passages
ANLI [154]	Natural language inference	Adversarial NLI benchmark is for evaluating natural language models to understand the relationship between two pieces of text
ARC [155]	Reasoning	Abstraction and Reasoning Corpus is a benchmark for evaluating question answering models on questions that require reasoning and combining information
BERTScore [156]	Natural language processing	Not a benchmark, but a metric used within benchmarks to evaluate the performance of natural language generation tasks
VQA [157]	Visual question answering	A benchmark for evaluating models on answering questions about images
NLVR2 [158]	Visual reasoning	Neural Logical Visual Reasoning 2 benchmark for evaluating models on natural language for visual reasoning, to determine if the sentence logically describes the image
BIG-bench [159]	LLM evaluation	Beyond the Imitation Game Benchmark is a collaborative benchmark for evaluating the capabilities of large language models across over 200 tasks
MMLU [160]	LLM evaluation	Massive Multitask Language Understanding benchmark is for evaluating the multi-task capabilities of large LLMs on 57 subjects, spanning STEM, humanities, social sciences etc.
TruthfulQA [161]	LLM evaluation	A benchmark for evaluating the ability of language models to provide truthful and reliable information

The approaches to regulating AI vary considerably across regions. It is no surprise that the European Union (EU) has taken a proactive stance. The EU AI Act [163], passed in December 9, 2023, is the world's first legal framework for AI. It classifies AI systems based on risk, with high-risk applications like facial recognition being subjected to stricter regulations. The EU aims to pass structured AI laws, prioritizing risk categorization and restricting high-risk applications. Conversely, the more market-oriented U.S. is leaning towards industry self-regulation but the approach is more fragmented, as even though there are no overarching federal regulations, some states have enacted specific laws on areas like facial recognition. China, on the other hand is trying to strike a balance between technology advancement with societal health, emphasizing both corporate transparency and content control. Given AI's opacity and varied international approaches, achieving unified regulation appears elusive at present. India had originally planned against all forms of AI regulation at such an early stage of technology and adoption curve. However, a draft framework prepared by the Ministry of Electronics and Information Technology is expected to be released soon.

The varied regulatory approaches will result in a significant cost of compliance for the AI industry. The hope is that all others will follow once a certain regulation becomes well defined, as it has happened in privacy with GDPR (General Data Protection Regulation) and others adopting it with variations. The debate on AI regulation is no more a theoretical topic.

Ongoing Efforts in AI Regulation:

- Global Partnership on Artificial Intelligence (GPAI) is a multi-stakeholder body bringing together governments, industry leaders, and civil society to formulate principles for responsible development and use of AI. GPAI has published several reports and discussion papers on various AI governance topics [164].
- The White House's Blueprint for an AI Bill of Rights outlines a vision for ensuring AI development aligns with American values that includes fairness, non-discrimination, and privacy [165].
- An 'AI Pact' of voluntary behavioral standards is being developed between Google and the EU more of a stop-gap measure to address the AI regulation challenges before the final regulations come into force [166].
- Discussion and efforts are on in the U.S. Congress to establish a federal agency dedicated to AI oversight and to create a Digital Platform Commission (DPC) for regulating digital technology, including AI [167].

Regulating AI presents a complex challenge. Striking the right balance between fostering innovation and mitigating risks will require ongoing dialogue and international cooperation. AI is evolving at a super-fast pace, making it difficult for regulations to keep pace while ensuring adaptability to address unforeseen risks. AI development and deployment transcend national borders and hence international collaboration is crucial to ensure consistent and effective regulations. Lastly, to build public trust, AI systems need to be more transparent in their decision-making processes. It is not just the governments and larger companies that are concerned and want to regulate AI. A recent survey showed that US consumers strongly support government regulation on AI-generated content with over 74% asking for AI to be regulated [168].

2.10 Conclusion

Chapter 1 and all the previous sections of Chap. 2 set the stage of this book entitled 'New Kind of Machine Learning—Cellular Automata Model'. Chapter 1 explained the concept of '*simulated intelligence*' while tracing back the historic and prehistoric perspective of AI. In this chapter went through a comprehensive survey on trends and different challenges faced by AI: compute capability, explainability, security, privacy, the need for reversal of large AI models, non-availability of large data sets for training, how do you develop trust with an AI system, AI regulations and trends of global collaboration with opensource.

The narrative in both chapters begs the question: How do we mimic the most efficient AI system? How can we mimic our brain? Can we do AI cognition in at multiple levels? Can we develop a low-cost lightweight AI/ML platform requiring only a limited set of training data for a specific application domain, running on a resource constrained computing environment? How can we make AI systems more explainable and ensure we address the concerns of security and privacy?

The next Chap. 3 will cover two separate areas—Machine Learning (a subdiscipline of AI) and Cellular Automata (CA). Discussions preceding CA, touches upon a fundamental issue dealing with the emerging behavior of the human cognition system working at multiple levels. A rough guess or estimate at the initial stage, in our view, precedes the final decision arrived at out of the cognition system output. This book explores the possibility of employing the emerging behavior of CA evolution as a tool modeling a physical system. Next chapter touches upon a model employing both CA and ML frameworks to address some the challenges highlighted in this chapter.

References

1. NVIDIA—25 Year Stock Price History. [Online]. Available: https://www.macrotrends.net/stocks/charts/NVDA/nvidia/stock-price-history
2. A. Reuther, P. Michaleas, M. Jones, V. Gadepally, S. Samsi, J. Kepner, AI and ML accelerator survey and trends, in *IEEE High Performance Extreme Computing Conference (HPEC)* (IEEE, 2022), pp. 1–10
3. NVIDIA CUDA platform. [Online]. Available: https://developer.nvidia.com/cuda-zone
4. Syntiant. [Online]. Available: https://www.syntiant.com

5. TinyML Applications with ONNX models. [Online]. Available: https://www.thetinymlbook.com/resources/tinyml-app-with-onnx-models
6. Cerebras Systems. [Online]. Available: https://www.cerebras.net
7. AWS Trainium. [Online]. Available: https://aws.amazon.com/machine-learning/trainium/
8. AWS Inferentia. [Online]. Available: https://aws.amazon.com/machine-learning/inferentia/
9. Sneak peak: Microsoft's Athena AI chip project. [Online]. Available: https://dataconomy.com/2023/11/01/microsofts-athena-chip-project/
10. IIT Mumbai analog Neuromorphic chip. [Online]. Available: https://www.electronicsforu.com/news/whats-new/worlds-first-snn-developed-at-iit-bombay
11. Mythic.ai. [Online]. Available: https://mythic.ai/
12. Analog Inference. [Online]. Available: https://www.analog-inference.com/
13. Carver Mead—the father of Neuromorphic Computing. [Online]. Available: https://en.wikipedia.org/wiki/Carver_Mead
14. Brainchip Akida Platform. [Online]. Available: https://brainchip.com/akida-foundations/
15. C.D. Schuman, T.E. Potok, R.M. Patton, J.D. Birdwell, M.E. Dean, G.S. Rose, J.S. Plank, A Survey of Neuromorphic Computing and Neural Networks in Hardware (2017). arXiv:1705.06963
16. Lightmatter. [Online]. Available: https://lightmatter.co/
17. Luminous Photonics. [Online]. Available: https://www.luminous.com/
18. S.T. Mueller, R.R. Hoffman, W. Clancey, A. Emrey, G. Klein, Explanation in Human-AI Systems: A Literature Meta-Review, Synopsis of Key Ideas and Publications, and Bibliography for Explainable AI (2019). arXiv:1902.01876
19. S.R. Islam, W. Eberle, S.K. Ghafoor, M. Ahmed, Explainable Artificial Intelligence Approaches: A Survey (2021). arXiv:2101.09429
20. Local Interpretable Model-agnostic Explanations (LIME). [Online]. Available: https://www.geeksforgeeks.org/introduction-to-explainable-aixai-using-lime/
21. Top GitHub libraries for building explainable AI models. [Online]. Available: https://analyticsindiamag.com/ai-origins-evolution/top-github-libraries-for-building-explainable-ai-models/
22. Fiddler. [Online]. Available: https://www.fiddler.ai/
23. Abzu. [Online]. Available: https://www.abzu.ai/
24. Howso. [Online]. Available: https://www.howso.com/
25. Aygloo. [Online]. Available: https://aygloo.com/
26. H. Cheng, M. Zhang, J.Q. Shi, A Survey on Deep Neural Network Pruning-taxonomy, Comparison, Analysis, and Recommendations (2023). arXiv:2308.06767
27. E. Bartz, T. Bartz-Beielstein, M. Zaefferer, O. Mersmann, *Hyperparameter Tuning for Machine and Deep Learning with R: A Practical Guide* (Springer Nature, 2023). [Online]. Available: https://library.oapen.org/bitstream/id/240dc394-c1a4-414e-8465-d9dc8824c7e5/978-981-19-5170-1.pdf
28. Y.A. Ali, E.M. Awwad, M. Al-Razgan, A. Maarouf, Hyperparameter search for machine learning algorithms for optimizing the computational complexity. Processes **11**(2) (2023). [Online]. Available: https://www.mdpi.com/2227-9717/11/2/349
29. C. Surianarayanan, J.J. Lawrence, P.R. Chelliah, E. Prakash, C. Hewage, A survey on optimization techniques for edge artificial intelligence (ai). Sensors **23**(3) (2023). [Online]. Available: https://www.mdpi.com/1424-8220/23/3/1279
30. Federated learning: Collaborative machine learning without centralized training data. [Online]. Available: https://research.google/blog/federated-learning-collaborative-machine-learning-without-centralized-training-data/
31. J. Wen, Z. Zhang, Y. Lan, Z. Cui, J. Cai, W. Zhang, A survey on federated learning: challenges and applications. Int. J. Mach. Learn.Cybern. **14**(2), 513–535 (2023). [Online]. Available: https://link.springer.com/article/10.1007/s13042-022-01647-y
32. Q. Li, Z. Wen, Z. Wu, S. Hu, N. Wang, Y. Li, X. Liu, B. He, A survey on federated learning systems: vision, hype and reality for data privacy and protection. IEEE Trans. Knowl. Data Eng. **35**(4), 3347–3366 (2021)

33. Tensorflow Federated. [Online]. Available: https://www.tensorflow.org/federated
34. Pysyft by opensource community. [Online]. Available: https://openmined.github.io/PySyft/index.html
35. Open Federated Learning (openFL). [Online]. Available: https://openfl.readthedocs.io/en/latest/
36. Federated AI Technology Enabler (FATE). [Online]. Available: https://fate.fedai.org/
37. IBM Federated Learning. [Online]. Available: https://ibmfl.res.ibm.com/
38. PaddleFL. [Online]. Available: https://paddlefl.readthedocs.io/en/latest/introduction.html
39. Federated learning powered by NVidia Clara. [Online]. Available: https://developer.nvidia.com/blog/federated-learning-clara/
40. OpenFed. [Online]. Available: https://openfed.readthedocs.io/
41. D. Chen, V.J. Tan, Z. Lu, E. Wu, J. Hu, Openfed: a comprehensive and versatile open-source federated learning framework, in *Proceedings of the IEEE/CVF Conference on Computer Vision and Pattern Recognition* (2023), pp. 5018–5026
42. Substra. [Online]. Available: https://www.owkin.com/substra
43. Sherpa.ai. [Online]. Available: https://sherpa.ai/
44. Owkin. [Online]. Available: https://www.owkin.com/
45. P. Liu, X. Xu, W. Wang, Threats, attacks and defenses to federated learning: issues, taxonomy and perspectives. Cybersecurity **5**(1), 4 (2022)
46. P. Villalobos, J. Sevilla, T. Besiroglu, L. Heim, A. Ho, M. Hobbhahn, Machine learning model sizes and the parameter gap (2022). arXiv:2207.02852
47. Economist article: The bigger-is-better approach to ai is running out of road. [Online]. Available: https://www.economist.com/science-and-technology/2023/06/21/the-bigger-is-better-approach-to-ai-is-running-out-of-road
48. J. Kaplan, S. McCandlish, T. Henighan, T.B. Brown, B. Chess, R. Child, S. Gray, A. Radford, J. Wu, D. Amodei, Scaling laws for neural language models (2020). arXiv:2001.08361
49. Y. Tay, M. Dehghani, S. Abnar, H.W. Chung, W. Fedus, J. Rao, S. Narang, V.Q. Tran, D. Yogatama, D. Metzler, Scaling laws vs model architectures: How does inductive bias influence scaling? (2022). arXiv:2207.10551
50. Med-PaLM 2. [Online]. Available: https://blog.google/technology/health/ai-llm-medpalm-research-thecheckup/
51. Sec-PALM LLM version tuned towards Cybersecurity usecases. [Online]. Available: https://cloud.google.com/security/ai
52. J. Hoffmann, S. Borgeaud, A. Mensch, E. Buchatskaya, T. Cai, E. Rutherford, D. Casas, L. Hendricks, J. Welbl, A. Clark et al., Training compute-optimal large language models, vol. 10 (2022). arXiv:2203.15556
53. When AI's large language models shrink. [Online]. Available: https://spectrum.ieee.org/large-language-models-size
54. Introducing LLaMA: A foundational, 65-billion-parameter large language model. [Online]. Available: https://ai.meta.com/blog/large-language-model-llama-meta-ai/
55. Stanford CRFM Introduces PubMedGPT 2.7B. [Online]. Available: https://hai.stanford.edu/news/stanford-crfm-introduces-pubmedgpt-27b
56. I. Turc, M.-W. Chang, K. Lee, K. Toutanova, Well-read students learn better: On the importance of pre-training compact models (2019). arXiv:1908.08962
57. R. Taori, I. Gulrajani, T. Zhang, Y. Dubois, X. Li, C. Guestrin, P. Liang, T.B. Hashimoto, Alpaca: A strong, replicable instruction-following model, in *Stanford Center for Research on Foundation Models* (2023). [Online]. Available: https://crfm.stanford.edu/2023/03/13/alpaca.html
58. A. Vaswani, N. Shazeer, N. Parmar, J. Uszkoreit, L. Jones, A.N. Gomez, Ł. Kaiser, I. Polosukhin, Attention is all you need, in *Proceedings of the 31st Conference on Neural Information Processing Systems (NIPS 2017)* (2017), pp. 1–11
59. Sakana.ai. [Online]. Available: https://sakana.ai/seed-round/
60. Y. Tay, J. Wei, H.W. Chung, V.Q. Tran, D.R. So, S. Shakeri, X. Garcia, H.S. Zheng, J. Rao, A. Chowdhery et al., Transcending scaling laws with 0.1% extra compute (2022). arXiv:2210.11399

61. J. Wei, M. Bosma, V.Y. Zhao, K. Guu, A.W. Yu, B. Lester, N. Du, A.M. Dai, Q.V. Le, Finetuned language models are zero-shot learners (2021). arXiv:2109.01652
62. Y. Fu, H. Peng, L. Ou, A. Sabharwal, T. Khot, Specializing smaller language models towards multi-step reasoning, in *International Conference on Machine Learning* (PMLR, 2023), pp. 10 421–10 430
63. Tiny LLaMA. [Online]. Available: https://huggingface.co/TinyLlama/TinyLlama-1.1B-step-50K-105b
64. R. Eldan, Y. Li, Tinystories: How small can language models be and still speak coherent english? (2023). arXiv:2305.07759
65. J. Drechsler, A.-C. Haensch, 30 years of synthetic data, 2023. [Online]. Available: https://arxiv.org/abs/2304.02107
66. Google Imagen for Text to Image. [Online]. Available: https://imagen.research.google/
67. Pathways autoregressive text-to-image model (Parti). [Online]. Available: https://sites.research.google/parti/
68. Stable Diffusion. [Online]. Available: https://stablediffusionweb.com/
69. Nvidia GauGAN. [Online]. Available: https://blogs.nvidia.com/blog/what-is-gaugan-ai-art-demo/
70. Unity Engine ProBuilder. [Online]. Available: https://unity.com/features/probuilder
71. Epic games unreal engine metahuman creator. [Online]. Available: https://www.unrealengine.com/en-US/metahuman
72. Open AI Text to Video engine Sora. [Online]. Available: https://openai.com/index/sora/
73. S. Bozinovski, A. Fulgosi, The influence of pattern similarity and transfer learning upon training of a base perceptron b2, in *Proceedings of Symposium Informatica*, vol. 3 (1976), pp. 121–126
74. F. Zhuang, Z. Qi, K. Duan, D. Xi, Y. Zhu, H. Zhu, H. Xiong, Q. He, A comprehensive survey on transfer learning. Proc. IEEE **109**(1), 43–76 (2020)
75. F. Yu, X. Xiu, Y. Li, A survey on deep transfer learning and beyond. Mathematics **10**(19), 3619 (2022)
76. Awesome Domain Adaptation Python Toolbox (ADAPT). [Online]. Available: https://github.com/adapt-python/adapt
77. Transfer Learning Library (TLlib). [Online]. Available: https://github.com/thuml/Transfer-Learning-Library
78. "Domain-Adaptation-Toolbox." [Online]. Available: https://github.com/viggin/domain-adaptation-toolbox
79. Y. Song, T. Wang, P. Cai, S.K. Mondal, J.P. Sahoo, A comprehensive survey of few-shot learning: evolution, applications, challenges, and opportunities. ACM Comput. Surv. **55**(13s), 1–40 (2023)
80. T. Kojima, S.S. Gu, M. Reid, Y. Matsuo, Y. Iwasawa, Large language models are zero-shot reasoners, in *Advances in Neural Information Processing Systems*, vol. 35 (2022), pp. 22 199–22 213
81. Unraveling the power of chain-of-thought prompting in large language models. [Online]. Available: https://www.kdnuggets.com/2023/07/power-chain-thought-prompting-large-language-models.html
82. M. Agrawal, S. Hegselmann, H. Lang, Y. Kim, D. Sontag, Large language models are few-shot clinical information extractors (2022). arXiv:2205.12689
83. Metalearning. [Online]. Available: http://www.scholarpedia.org/article/Metalearning
84. T. Hospedales, A. Antoniou, P. Micaelli, A. Storkey, Meta-learning in neural networks: a survey. IEEE Trans. Pattern Anal. Mach. Intell. **44**(9), 5149–5169 (2021)
85. A. Rafiei, R. Moore, S. Jahromi, F. Hajati, R. Kamaleswaran, Meta-learning in healthcare: a survey (2023). arXiv:2308.02877
86. Y. LeCun, L.D. Jackel, L. Bottou, C. Cortes, J.S. Denker, H. Drucker, I. Guyon, U.A. Muller, E. Sackinger, P. Simard et al., Learning algorithms for classification: a comparison on handwritten digit recognition. Neural Netw. Stat. Mech. Perspect. **261**(276), 2 (1995)

87. Top data augmentation techniques: Ultimate guide for 2024. [Online]. Available: https://research.aimultiple.com/data-augmentation-techniques/
88. X. Zhan, Q. Wang, K.-H. Huang, H. Xiong, D. Dou, A.B. Chan, A comparative survey of deep active learning (2022). arXiv:2203.13450
89. C. Gentry, Fully homomorphic encryption using ideal lattices, in *Proceedings of the Forty-first Annual ACM Symposium on Theory of Computing* (2009), pp. 169–178
90. Microsoft SEAL (Simple Encrypted Arithmetic Library). [Online]. Available: https://en.wikipedia.org/wiki/Microsoft_SEAL
91. OpenFHE. [Online]. Available: https://www.openfhe.org/
92. PALISADE Homomorphic encryption software library. [Online]. Available: https://palisade-crypto.org/
93. TFHE-rs—Zama's variant of Fully Homomorphic Encryption over the Torus (TFHE). [Online]. Available: https://docs.zama.ai/tfhe-rs
94. P. Samarati, L. Sweeney, Protecting privacy when disclosing information: k-anonymity and its enforcement through generalization and suppression (1998)
95. T. Dalenius, Finding a needle in a haystack. J. Official Stat. **2**(3), 329–336 (1986)
96. N. Li, T. Li, S. Venkatasubramanian, t-closeness: privacy beyond k-anonymity and l-diversity, in *IEEE 23rd International Conference on Data Engineering* (IEEE, 2007), pp. 106–115
97. C. Dwork, F. McSherry, K. Nissim, A. Smith, Calibrating noise to sensitivity in private data analysis, in *Theory of Cryptography: Third Theory of Cryptography Conference*, TCC, New York, NY, USA, March 4–7, 2006. Proceedings 3 (Springer, Berlin, 2006), pp. 265–284
98. RAPPOR: Privacy-Preserving Reporting Algorithms library. [Online]. Available: https://github.com/google/rappor
99. Tensorflow privacy library. [Online]. Available: https://www.tensorflow.org/federated/tutorials/federated_learning_with_differential_privacy
100. Google's differential privacy libraries. [Online]. Available: https://github.com/google/differential-privacy
101. Meta's Opacus. [Online]. Available: https://github.com/pytorch/opacus
102. OpenDP Smartnoise. [Online]. Available: https://docs.smartnoise.org
103. IBM differential-privacy-library. [Online]. Available: https://github.com/IBM/differential-privacy-library
104. A. Aktay, S. Bavadekar, G. Cossoul, J. Davis, D. Desfontaines, A. Fabrikant, E. Gabrilovich, K. Gadepalli, B. Gipson, M. Guevara et al., Google covid-19 community mobility reports: anonymization process description (version 1.1) (2020). arXiv:2004.04145
105. Damien Desfontaines' Blog. [Online]. Available: https://desfontain.es/privacy/real-world-differential-privacy.html
106. Openmined differential privacy project. [Online]. Available: https://github.com/OpenMined/PyDP
107. Enveil Privacy Enhancing Technologies (PET). [Online]. Available: https://www.enveil.com/2023-the-year-of-privacy-enhancing-technologies
108. Yao millionaires problem. [Online]. Available: https://en.wikipedia.org/wiki/Yao%27s_Millionaires%27_problem
109. Danish sugar beet auction. [Online]. Available: https://en.wikipedia.org/wiki/Danish_Sugar_Beet_Auction
110. MPC (Multi-Party Compute) Alliance. [Online]. Available: https://www.mpcalliance.org
111. S. Zobaed, M.A. Salehi, Confidential computing across edge-to-cloud for machine learning: a survey study (2023). arXiv:2307.16447
112. Confidential Computing Consortium (CCC). [Online]. Available: https://confidentialcomputing.io/
113. Trust in Artificial Intelligence. [Online]. Available: https://kpmg.com/xx/en/home/insights/2023/09/trust-in-artificial-intelligence.html
114. S. Feng, C.Y. Park, Y. Liu, Y. Tsvetkov, From pretraining data to language models to downstream tasks: tracking the trails of political biases leading to unfair NLP models, in *Proceedings of the 61st Annual Meeting of the Association for Computational Linguistics (Volume*

1: Long Papers), eds. by A. Rogers, J. Boyd-Graber, N. Okazaki (Association for Computational Linguistics, Toronto, Canada, 2023), pp. 11 737–11 762. [Online]. Available: https://aclanthology.org/2023.acl-long.656
115. Common Crawl Dataset. [Online]. Available: https://commoncrawl.org/
116. BookCorpus. [Online]. Available: https://en.wikipedia.org/wiki/BookCorpus
117. The Presidio Recommendations on Responsible Generative AI by World Economic Forum. [Online]. Available: https://www3.weforum.org/docs/WEF_Presidio_Recommendations_on_Responsible_Generative_AI_2023.pdf
118. Institute for Trustworthy AI in Law and Society (TRAILS). [Online]. Available: https://www.trails.umd.edu/
119. UNESCO Ethics of Artificial Intelligence. [Online]. Available: https://www.unesco.org/en/artificial-intelligence/recommendation-ethics
120. High Level Expert Group on Artificial Intelligence (HLEG AI). [Online]. Available: https://digital-strategy.ec.europa.eu/en/policies/expert-group-ai
121. IBM Trustworthy AI. [Online]. Available: https://research.ibm.com/topics/trustworthy-ai
122. IBM Fairness 360. [Online]. Available: https://aif360.res.ibm.com/
123. R. Chatila, J.C. Havens, The IEEE global initiative on ethics of autonomous and intelligent systems, in *Robotics and Well-Being* (2019), pp. 11–16
124. C. Huang, Z. Zhang, B. Mao, X. Yao, An overview of artificial intelligence ethics. IEEE Trans. Artif. Intell. **4**(4), 799–819 (2022)
125. A. Jobin, M. Ienca, E. Vayena, The global landscape of ai ethics guidelines. Nat. Mach. Intell. **1**(9), 389–399 (2019)
126. J. Devlin, M.-W. Chang, K. Lee, K. Toutanova, Bert: pre-training of deep bidirectional transformers for language understanding (2018). arXiv:1810.04805
127. YOLOv9: Advancements in Real-time Object Detection (2024). [Online]. Available: https://viso.ai/computer-vision/yolov9/
128. GPT-2. [Online]. Available: https://openai.com/index/gpt-2-1-5b-release/
129. GPT-3. [Online]. Available: https://community.openai.com/t/gpt-3-model-download/23135
130. BLOOM. [Online]. Available: https://huggingface.co/bigscience/bloom
131. LLaMA. [Online]. Available: https://llama.meta.com/llama2/
132. Falcon. [Online]. Available: https://falconllm.tii.ae/
133. Mistral-7B. [Online]. Available: https://mistral.ai/technology/#models
134. GPT-NeoX-20B. [Online]. Available: https://huggingface.co/EleutherAI/gpt-neox-20b
135. OPT. [Online]. Available: https://huggingface.co/docs/transformers/en/model_doc/opt
136. T5. [Online]. Available: https://huggingface.co/docs/transformers/en/model_doc/t5
137. Cohere Aya. [Online]. Available: https://cohere.com/research/aya
138. Anthropic Claud 3 model. [Online]. Available: https://claude.ai/login?returnTo=%2F%3F
139. University of California Irvine Machine Learning Repository. [Online]. Available: https://archive.ics.uci.edu/
140. ImageNet. [Online]. Available: https://www.image-net.org/
141. COCO (Common Objects in Context). [Online]. Available: https://cocodataset.org/#home
142. MNIST. [Online]. Available: https://www.kaggle.com/datasets/hojjatk/mnist-dataset
143. Open Images. [Online]. Available: https://storage.googleapis.com/openimages/web/index.html
144. WikiText. [Online]. Available: https://huggingface.co/datasets/Salesforce/wikitext
145. LibriSpeech. [Online]. Available: https://www.openslr.org/12
146. Mozilla Common Voice. [Online]. Available: https://commonvoice.mozilla.org/en/datasets
147. HuggingFace Datasets. [Online]. Available: https://huggingface.co/docs/datasets/en/index
148. Kaggle Datasets. [Online]. Available: https://www.kaggle.com/datasets
149. SPEC Benchmarks and tools website. [Online]. Available: https://www.spec.org/benchmarks.html
150. Machine Learning Performance Benchmark (MLPerf) and MLCommons. [Online]. Available: https://mlcommons.org/
151. GLUE. [Online]. Available: https://gluebenchmark.com/

152. SuperGLUE. [Online]. Available: https://super.gluebenchmark.com/
153. SQuAD (Stanford Question Answering Dataset). [Online]. Available: https://github.com/rajpurkar/SQuAD-explorer
154. ANLI (Adversarial Natural Language Inference). [Online]. Available: https://autonlp.ai/datasets/adversarial-nli-(anli)
155. ARC (Abstraction and Reasoning Corpus). [Online]. Available: https://lab42.global/arc/
156. BERTScore. [Online]. Available: https://huggingface.co/spaces/evaluate-metric/bertscore
157. VQA (Visual Question Answering). [Online]. Available: https://allenai.org/
158. NLVR2 (Neural Logical Visual Reasoning 2). [Online]. Available: https://paperswithcode.com/sota/visual-reasoning-on-nlvr2-test
159. Beyond the Imitation Game Benchmark (BIG-bench). [Online]. Available: https://github.com/google/BIG-bench
160. Massive Multitask Language Understanding (MMLU). [Online]. Available: https://paperswithcode.com/sota/multi-task-language-understanding-on-mmlu
161. TruthfulQA. [Online]. Available: https://paperswithcode.com/dataset/truthfulqa
162. M. Hutson, Rules to keep AI in check: nations carve different paths for tech regulation. Nature **620**(7973), 260–263 (2023)
163. European Union AI Act 2023. [Online]. Available: https://www.europarl.europa.eu/topics/en/article/20230601STO93804/eu-ai-act-first-regulation-on-artificial-intelligence
164. The Global Partnership on Artificial Intelligence. [Online]. Available: https://gpai.ai/
165. The Blueprint for AI Bill of Rights. [Online]. Available: https://www.whitehouse.gov/ostp/ai-bill-of-rights/
166. AI Pact between EU and Google. [Online]. Available: https://techcrunch.com/2023/05/24/eu-google-ai-pact/
167. Congress eyes establishing a digital regulator. [Online]. Available: https://www.brookings.edu/articles/congress-eyes-establishing-a-digital-regulator/
168. U.S Consumers strongly support Government Regulation on AI Content: Harrisx Survey. [Online]. Available: https://variety.com/vip/ai-regulation-survey-content-government-harrisx-1235933648/

Chapter 3
Biological Neural Network, Artificial Neural Network and Cellular Automata

"Just as electricity transformed almost everything 100 years ago, today I actually have a hard time thinking of an industry that I don't think AI (Artificial Intelligence) will transform in the next several years"

—Andrew Ng, Computer Scientist and Co-founder of Google Brain

3.1 Introduction

In this chapter is divided into two distinct sections. In the first section we introduce Biological Neural Network (BNN). Knowledge of BNN is not essential these days to work in the field of ML, but it must be remembered from our presentation in Chap. 1 that the pioneers in the field of AI and ML were inspired by BNN. The rudiments of BNN may help to comprehend the existing research still required on BNN and corresponding endeavor required to enhance the Artificial Neural Network (ANN). Hence after we go through BNNs we will delve deeper into ANNs. We have seen in Chap. 1 that Machine learning (ML) is a subset of Artificial Intelligence (AI) that focuses on developing algorithms and statistical models that enable computers to perform tasks without explicit instructions. Instead, these models learn from and make predictions or decisions based on data. Artificial Neural Networks are a type of machine learning model significantly inspired by the structure and functioning of the human brain. They consist of interconnected nodes (neurons) arranged in layers, which process data and learn to perform tasks through training.

© The Author(s), under exclusive license to Springer Nature Singapore Pte Ltd. 2025

P. Pal Chaudhuri et al., *New Kind of Machine Learning—Cellular Automata Model*,
https://doi.org/10.1007/978-981-96-1501-8_3

In Sect. 3.13, we will introduce Cellular Automata. The topics covered in this chapter are listed below.

- 3.2 Biological Neural Networks (BNN)
- 3.3 Communication and Information Processing
- 3.4 Network Organization
- 3.5 Process used by Network to view/store Image: Communication Flow
- 3.6 The Network Effect
- 3.7 Unresolved Questions
- 3.8 Constructing an Artificial Neural Network (ANN)
- 3.9 Activation Functions
- 3.10 Recurrent Neural Network (RNN)
- 3.11 Representation of Neural Network in Matrix Algebra
- 3.12 Convolution Neural Network (CNNs)
- 3.13 History and Origins of Cellular Automata (CA)
- 3.14 Fundamental Procedures of Cellular Automata
- 3.15 Rules of a CA Machine
- 3.16 Method to Represent a Phenomenon using CA
- 3.17 Key Takeaways.

3.2 Biological Neural Networks

Biological Neural Networks (BNN) are the intricate web of interconnected neurons that form the foundation of the nervous system in animals, including humans. These networks orchestrate everything from simple reflexes to complex thoughts and emotions. Here is a simplified breakdown of their key components and functionalities:

Neurons: The Building Blocks

- **Cell Body (Soma)**: The central processing unit of a neuron, containing the nucleus and organelles responsible for maintaining cellular functions.
- **Dendrites**: Branching, tree-like structures that receive signals from other neurons. These signals can be excitatory (increasing the firing probability of the receiving neuron) or inhibitory (decreasing the firing probability).
- **Axon**: A long, thin fiber that transmits electrical signals called action potentials to other neurons or muscles.
- **Synapse**: The junction between the axon of one neuron and the dendrite of another. This is where the magic happens—neurotransmitters, chemical messengers, are released by the presynaptic neuron (the one sending the signal) and received by the postsynaptic neuron (the one receiving the signal). The neurotransmitters bind to receptors on the postsynaptic neuron, influencing its firing behavior.

Figure 3.1 illustrates a neuron, the description above is limited to just a few of its sections, with most of these sections devoted to its structural integrity and metabolism [1].

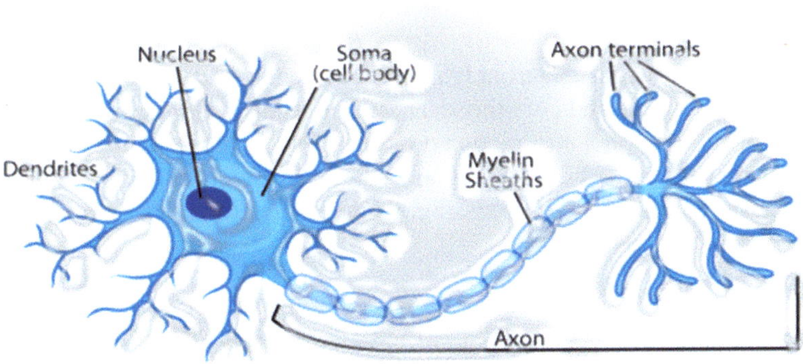

Fig. 3.1 Basic structure of a neuron

3.3 Communication and Information Processing

Information flows through the network of neurons in the form of electrical pulses. The process is described below. When a neuron receives enough excitatory input from other neurons through its dendrites, it reaches a threshold and fires an action potential—a brief electrical impulse that travels down the axon.

- At the axon terminal, the action potential triggers the release of neurotransmitters into the synapse. These neurotransmitters bind to receptors on the dendrites of the postsynaptic neuron.
- Depending on the type of neurotransmitter and receptor involved, the postsynaptic neuron might be excited (more likely to fire) or inhibited (less likely to fire).
- The strength of these connections (synapses) can be modified by experience and learning. This process, called synaptic plasticity, allows the network to adapt and learn from its environment.

Different Types of Neurons

- **Sensory Neurons**: Carry sensory information from the body (touch, sight, smell, etc.) to the Central Nervous System (CNS).
- **Motor Neurons**: Carry signals from the CNS to muscles, controlling movement.
- **Interneurons**: The most abundant type, these neurons connect various parts of the CNS within the brain and spinal cord, integrating information and coordinating complex activities.

3.4 Network Organization

Biological neural networks are strongly interconnected, with a single neuron potentially connecting to thousands of others. These connections form circuits and pathways that allow for complex information processing and behavior. The specific organization of these networks varies depending on the brain region and its function. Some areas may have more localized processing, while others are involved in integrating information from various regions.

Learning and Memory

Biological neural networks are capable of learning and adapting through synaptic plasticity. When a neuron is repeatedly stimulated by another neuron, the connection between them can become stronger, making it more likely for the postsynaptic neuron to fire in response to future stimulation. This process is thought to be the foundation of memory formation.

Beyond the Basics

While this description paints a basic picture of biological neural networks, it is important to understand that they are incredibly complex systems with many intricacies still being unraveled by neuroscientists. These networks involve multiple neurotransmitter types, complex signaling pathways within neurons, and the influence of various neuromodulators that affect overall network activity.

Let us draw an analogy. Imagine a vast network of interconnected cities. Information travels along roads (axons) from one city (neuron) to another. The strength of the connections (roads) between cities (neurons) can change based on traffic flow (neural activity). This allows the network to adapt and become more efficient at moving information (signals) around.

3.5 Process Used by Networks to View/Store Image: Communication Flow

The Communication Flow is as follows.

Information Arrival: Signals from the environment are picked up by sensory neurons and travel to the brain.

1. **Synaptic Dance**: Within the brain, these signals reach the dendrites of other neurons. Here, the strength of the signal determines the next step.

   - **Strong Enough Signal**: If the combined signals from multiple dendrites reach a certain threshold, an electrical impulse called an **action potential** fires in the neuron's cell body.
   - **Not Strong Enough**: If the signal is not strong enough, the neuron does not fire.

2. **Action Potential**: When an action potential fires, it travels rapidly down the axon.
3. **Neurotransmitter Release**: At the end of the axon, the action potential triggers the release of chemicals called **neurotransmitters**.
4. **Synaptic Transmission**: These neurotransmitters travel across the tiny gap (synaptic cleft) and bind to receptors on the dendrites of the next neuron.
5. **Postsynaptic Effect**: Depending on the type of neurotransmitter and receptor involved, the receiving neuron might be:

   - **Excited**: More likely to fire an action potential due to the stimulation.
   - **Inhibited**: Less likely to fire an action potential due to the dampening effect.

By integrating information from various pathways and modifying connections, the network creates a dynamic and constantly evolving system for processing information, generating thoughts, and controlling behavior. When we say 'generating thoughts', we define thoughts as processes caused by spontaneous neural activity which may or may not have a goal, as well as neural processes stimulated by our senses with a goal. These processes may interact at times, which can give rise to the phenomenon of solving problems intuitively.

3.6 The Network Effect

Billions of neurons are (current estimates suggest there are around 100 trillion (10^{14}) synapses, or connections, between neurons in the human brain, forming complex circuits. (order of number of neurons is comparable to the number of estimated stars in our galaxy).

The strength of connections (synapses) can be modified by experience and learning. This process, called **synaptic plasticity**, allows the network to adapt and learn from its environment. By integrating information from various pathways and modifying connections, the network creates a dynamic and constantly evolving system for processing information, controlling behavior [2]. We describe how BNN (Biological Neural Network) stores an image. The exact mechanisms of how biological neural networks retain and remember an image are still being actively researched, but here is what we know so far.

We divide the process into five steps:

1. **Visual Information Capture**: Light enters the eyes and stimulates photoreceptor cells in the retina. These cells convert the light signals into electrical signals.
2. **Signal Transmission**: These electrical signals travel through the optic nerve to the primary visual cortex located at the back of the brain.
3. **Feature Extraction**: In the primary visual cortex, different areas specialize in processing specific visual features of the image, such as edges, lines, colors, and orientations.

4. **Distributed Representation**: The processed information is not stored as a single image in one location but rather distributed across various interconnected neurons throughout the visual cortex and potentially other brain regions like the hippocampus (involved in memory formation). These interconnected neurons may represent different aspects of the image, like its overall shape, color palette, or specific objects within it.
5. **Synaptic Changes**: The specific connections (synapses) between these neurons are believed to play a crucial role in memory formation. When we see an image repeatedly or pay close attention to it, the connections between the neurons ***involved in representing that image*** are strengthened through a process called Long-Term Potentiation (LTP). This strengthening allows the network to more efficiently activate the same pattern of neurons when recalling the image.

Types of Memory

Short-Term Memory: Our initial processing of the image likely involves short-term memory, where the activated neurons hold the information for a brief period.

Long-Term Memory: If the image is important or we focus on it, the synaptic changes mentioned earlier contribute to long-term memory formation. Here, the distributed representation of the image across various brain regions allows us to recall it later.

The context in which we see an image and the emotions it evokes can influence how well we remember it. These factors may trigger additional brain regions to become involved, further strengthening the memory trace.

3.7 Unresolved Questions

While significant research has been conducted and our understanding of biological neural networks continues to improve, we have barely scratched the surface in comprehending such a complex system. Here, we highlight some of the questions for which researchers are still seeking answers.

1. How exactly are different aspects of an image (shape, color, etc.) distributed across the network?
2. How do these distributed representations get "translated" back into a parent image during recall? How do different types of memories (episodic, semantic) differ in terms of their neural representation?

When a neuron fires, or sends an electrical signal, tiny sacs called synaptic vesicles release neurotransmitters into the synaptic cleft, a small gap between the firing neuron and the next neuron it wants to communicate with.

Neurotransmitters float across the synaptic cleft and bind to specific receptor sites on the dendrites (receiving branches) of the neighboring neuron. Depending on the neurotransmitter and the receptor it binds to, the effect on the receiving neuron can be either excitatory (increasing the firing rate) or inhibitory (decreasing the firing rate).

There are many different neurotransmitters, each with its own unique function. Some of the most important neurotransmitters include:

- **Acetylcholine (ACh)**: Involved in muscle movement, memory, and learning.
- **Dopamine (DA)**: Plays a role in reward, motivation, movement, and pleasure.
- **Glutamate (Glu)**: The major excitatory neurotransmitter in the brain, involved in learning and memory.
- **GABA (gamma-aminobutyric acid)**: The major inhibitory neurotransmitter in the brain, helping to calm the nervous system.
- **Serotonin (5-HT)**: Affects mood, sleep, appetite, and digestion.
- **Norepinephrine (NE)**: Involved in alertness, arousal, and mood.
- **Endorphins**: Natural painkillers released by the body in response to pain or stress.

3. **Individual Differences**: Why do people have varying capacities for visual memory? Some may excel at remembering details, while others might focus on the overall gist of the image.
4. **The Role of Other Senses**: How do information from other senses like smell or sound sometimes trigger memories of an image associated with those experiences?
5. **Memory Distortion**: Why and how do memories become distorted or blended with other memories over time?

3.8 Constructing an Artificial Neural Network (ANN)

The biological network of neurons is representing a functional image of what we may call the ***'real universe'***. Just like a child learning to read the word 'flower', she associates it with a picture of a flower and eventually learns to draw it. At some point, the child can imagine painting a flower without actually doing so. She can change its color, even associate a different smell with it, adding or removing properties or features from the flower she was originally taught. We call these activities imagination.

The representation of objects, their functions, and their interrelations with other objects by a neural network initiated a new way to understand, represent, and experiment with data beyond the limits of digital logic. **The construction of Artificial Neural Networks began with the basic principles of a biological neuron.**

1. An **AN** (Artificial Neuron) will have a reservoir which is charged up when it gets an input from outputs of other neurons.
2. A scaling value which will multiply the accumulated inputs.
3. A Bias value to be added.

The main neuron model used is one called the sigmoid neuron. We will get to sigmoid neurons shortly. But to understand why sigmoid neurons are defined the way they are, it is worth taking some time to first understand perceptrons [3, 4].

A perceptron takes several binary inputs, $x_1, x_2, \ldots$, and produces a single binary output. Figure 3.2 shows the perceptron has three inputs x_1, x_2 and x_3.
The neurons output is 0 or 1, determined by the sum:

$$\sum_j w_j x_j$$

where $w_1, w_2, \ldots$ are weights.

- If $\sum_j w_j x_j \leq$ threshold, output = 0
- If $\sum_j w_j x_j >$ threshold, output = 1

That is the basic mathematical model. A way you can think about the perceptron is that it is a device that makes decisions by ***weighing up evidence***. We do it all the time. Suppose we want to drop out from the class if the subject is NOT so important and your friend has invited you for a pizza snack [5].

W1 = Is the weather good, give a value to goodness scale, just good $\cdots$ Excellent.
W2 = Importance of class, boring $\cdots$ very interesting.
W3 = Will your friend pay? Part pay $\cdots$ full pay.

Now, how do we choose the values of these 'Ws', do we hand tune them? The basic perceptron must learn from what range of Ws it can cross the threshold. We will show how adding another layer helps.

In the network shown in Fig. 3.3, the first column of perceptrons—what we will call the first layer of perceptrons—is making three very simple decisions, by weighing

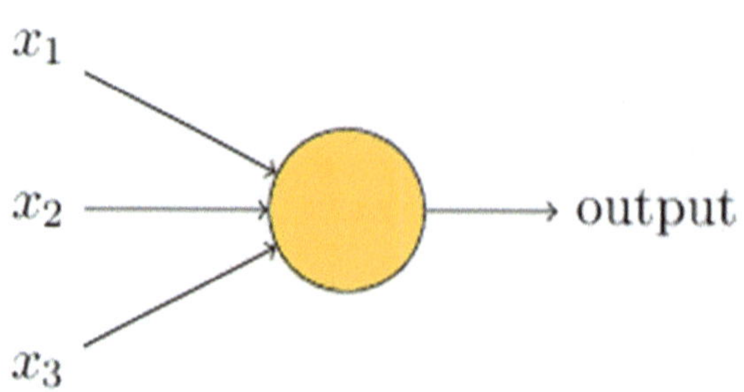

Fig. 3.2 A three-input perceptron

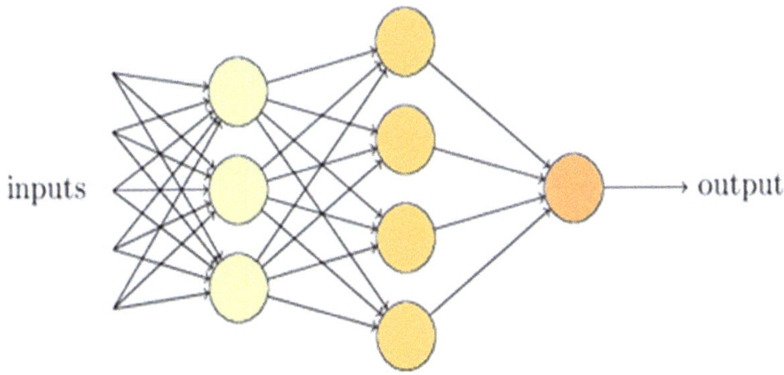

Fig. 3.3 Adding another layer of perceptrons

the **input evidence**. What about the perceptrons in the second layer? Each of those perceptrons is making a decision by weighing up the results from the first layer of decision-making. In this way, a perceptron in the second layer can make a decision at a more complex and more abstract level than perceptrons in the first layer. And even more complex decisions can be made by the perceptron in the third layer. In this way, a multi-layered network of perceptrons can engage in progressively sophisticated decision making.

To simplify the mathematical expression let us write **w** and **x** as vectors and express, the sum as ***dot product***

$$\mathbf{w} \cdot \mathbf{x}$$

whose components are the weights and inputs, respectively. The second change is to move the threshold to the other side of the inequality, and to replace it by what is known as the perceptron's bias, b = threshold. Now the expression becomes:

- **output** = **0** if $\mathbf{w} \cdot \mathbf{x} + \mathbf{b} \leq \mathbf{0}$
- **output** = **1** if $\mathbf{w} \cdot \mathbf{x} + \mathbf{b} > \mathbf{0}$

You can think of the bias as a measure of how easy it is to get the perceptron to output a 1 which is BNN equivalent of a neuron to fire.

But if the bias **b** is very negative, then it is difficult for the perceptron to output a **1 (fire)**. Introduction of the bias refers to a numerical value added to the weighted sum of inputs. This bias term is a **parameter** of the model, and it's essential for the perceptron to learn complex patterns in the data. It doest not inherently represent a prejudice or unfairness.

The bias term allows the perceptron to shift its decision boundary without changing the weights. This flexibility is crucial for accurate classification. By introducing the bias, the perceptron can learn more complex patterns in the data.

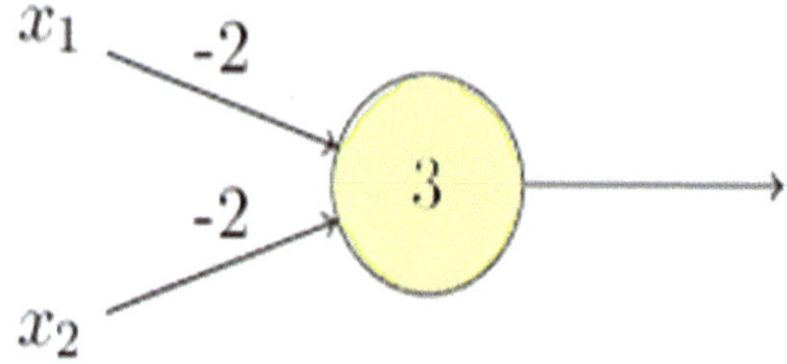

Fig. 3.4 Replicating a NAND gate

For an **AN** to have **0** or **neg** value output means that its output (firing) will **not** contribute to the input of the connected neuron input,

$$X1 \cdot (-2) + X2 \cdot (-2) + 3 = \mathbf{-1}, \text{ if } X1 = X2 = 1 \text{ (no firing)}$$

$$X1 \cdot (-2) + X2 \cdot (-2) + 3 = \mathbf{1}, \text{ if } X1 = 1, X2 = 0 \text{ (firing)}$$

$$X1 \cdot (-2) + X2 \cdot (-2) + 3 = \mathbf{1}, \text{ if } X1 = 0, X2 = 1 \text{ (firing)}$$

$$X1 \cdot (-2) + X2 \cdot (-2) + 3 = \mathbf{3}, \text{ if } X1 = 0, X2 = 0 \text{ (firing)}$$

The NAND example shows that we can use perceptrons to compute simple logical functions. We can use networks of perceptrons to compute any logical function. If we can device a *learning algorithm* then we can automatically tune the ***weights*** and ***biases*** of a network of artificial neurons. This tuning happens in response to external stimuli, without direct intervention by a programmer. These learning algorithms enable us to use artificial neurons in a way more than simple logic gates.

Imagine we have a network of perceptrons, like a tiny artificial brain. We want to train this network to solve a problem, like recognizing handwritten digits from images. The raw pixel data from the image would be fed as inputs to the network. Our goal is for the network to learn the right weights and biases for each connection so that the final output correctly identifies the digit.

To understand how this learning happens, let us say we make a tiny adjustment to a single weight (or bias) within the network. Ideally, this small change should only cause a small shift in the network's output. This is crucial because, if a small weight change causes a drastic output change, it can lead to problems. With many outputs connected in the network, such drastic changes could easily get the network stuck predicting only 0 or 1, preventing it from learning properly (Fig. 3.5).

If it were true that a small change in weight (or bias) causes only a small change in output, then we could use this fact to modify the weights and biases to get our network to behave more in the manner we want. For example, suppose the network was mistakenly classifying an image as an "8" when it should be a "9". We could figure out how to make a small change in the weights and biases so the network

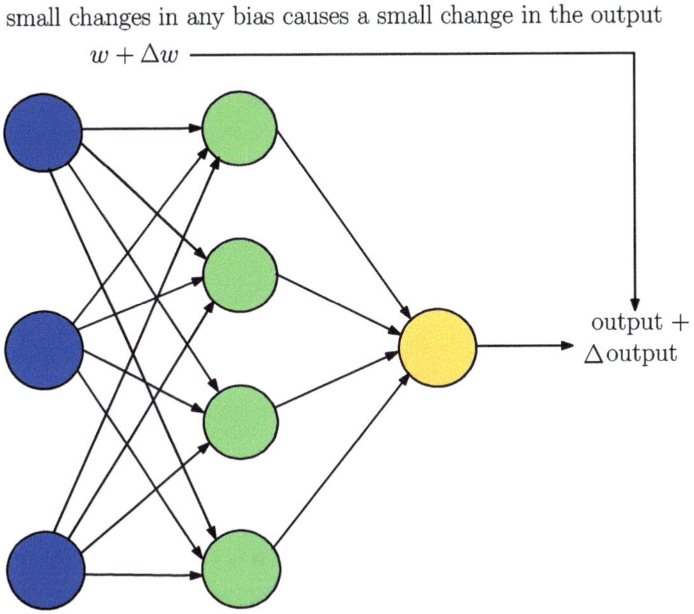

Fig. 3.5 Relationship between input and output

gets a little closer to classifying the image as a "9". And then we would repeat this, changing the weights and biases over and over to produce better and better output, while enabling the network to learn. However, such a procedure is problematic and a solution for this problem follows in the next section.

3.9 Activation Functions

A small change in **bias** may sum to saturation in subsequent connected networks, they may latch to constant firing or unable to fire at all. We can overcome this problem by introducing a new type of artificial neuron called a *sigmoid* neuron. To do that we introduce a function called the sigmoid function:

$$\sigma(z) = 1/(1 + e^{-x})$$

Now we put this function into the sigmoid neuron:

$$1/(1 + exp(-\sum_j w_j x_j - b))$$

suppose $\mathbf{z} = \mathbf{w} \cdot \mathbf{x} + \mathbf{b}$, $\mathbf{z}$ is a large positive number, then $\sigma(z) \approx 1$. In other words, when $\mathbf{z} = \mathbf{w} \cdot \mathbf{x} + \mathbf{b}$, $\mathbf{z}$ is large and positive, the output from the sigmoid neuron is

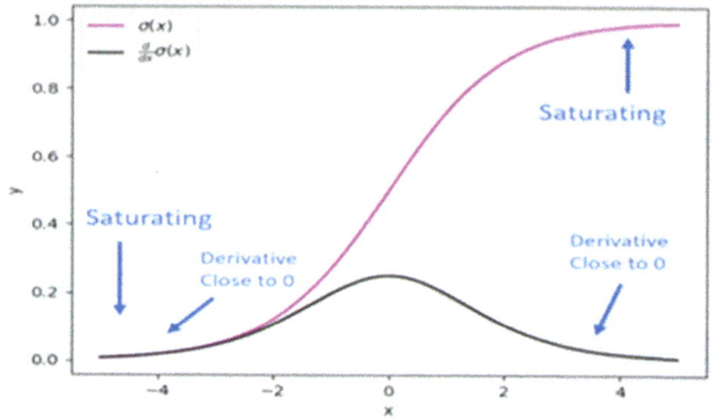

Fig. 3.6 Shape of the sigmoid function and its derivative

approximately 1. Suppose on the other hand that **z** = **w** · **x** + **b**, z is very negative. Then $e - z \to \infty e$ and $\sigma(z) \approx 0$. So, when **z** = **w** · **x** + **b** is very negative, the behavior of a sigmoid neuron also closely approximates a perceptron. It is only when **w** · **x** + **b** is of ***modest size*** that there is much deviation from the perceptron model. If q is the output then the output becomes thus:

$$\Delta q = \sum_j (\delta q / \delta w_j) \Delta x_j + (\delta q / \delta b) \Delta b$$

It is the shape of σ which really matters. We compute those partial derivatives later, using σ will simplify the algebra, simply because exponentials have beautiful properties when differentiated.

Figure 3.6 shows the shape of the sigmoid function; the partial derivative form makes it easier for us when we consider activation function.

As we have already introduced the sigmoid function we mention and introduce some other activation functions here. There are many different activation functions used in neural networks, each with its own properties and applications. Here are some common examples:

- **Sigmoid**: Outputs a value between 0 and 1, often used for binary classification problems.
- **TanH**: Outputs a value between –1 and 1, similar to sigmoid but with a steeper slope around zero.
- **ReLU (Rectified Linear Unit)**: Outputs the input directly if it is positive, otherwise outputs zero. Popular for its efficiency in training.
- **Leaky ReLU**: Similar to ReLU but allows a small non-zero gradient for negative inputs, helping to alleviate the vanishing gradient problem.

Choosing the right activation function depends on the specific task and network architecture.

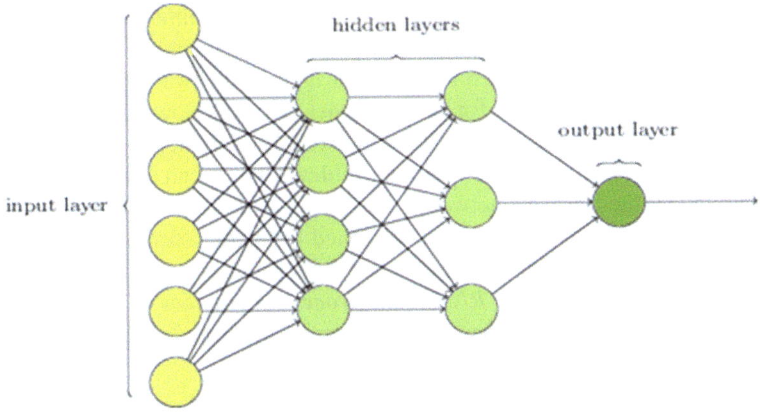

Fig. 3.7 RNN can be implemented anywhere in the hidden layer

In essence, activation functions are the building blocks that enable neural networks to learn complex and nuanced relationships within data, making them a fundamental component of ***deep learning***.

We have mentioned earlier, the leftmost layer in this network is called the input layer. The rightmost or *output* layer contains the *output neurons*, or in this case, a single output neuron. The middle layers are called the *hidden layer*. The network in Fig. 3.7 has two hidden layers. The hidden layers are used to learn distinct broken-down features from the first layer. Say the first hidden layer learns to detect only line segments, the second hidden layer detects tight curves or circles. Neural networks researchers have developed many design heuristics for the hidden layers, which help people get the behavior they want out of their nets. Such heuristics can be used to help determine how to trade off the number of hidden layers against the time required to train the network.

The neural networks where the output from one layer is used as input to the next layer are called *feedforward* neural networks. This means there are no loops in the network—information is always fed forward, never fed back. If we did have loops, we would end up with situations where the input to the σ function depended on the output. That would be hard to make sense of, and so we do not allow such loops.

3.10 Recurrent Neural Network (RNN)

There are other models of artificial neural networks in which feedback loops are possible. These models are called Recurrent Neural Networks (RNN). The idea in these models is to have neurons which fire for some limited duration of time, before becoming quiescent. That firing can stimulate other neurons, which may fire a little later, also for a limited duration. That causes still more neurons to fire, and so over time we get a cascade of neurons firing. Loops do not cause problems in such a model, since a neuron's output only affects its input at some later time, not instantaneously.

Recurrent neural nets have been less popular than feedforward networks, in part because the learning algorithms for recurrent nets are less powerful. But they are much closer in spirit to how our brains work than feedforward networks, it is possible that recurrent networks can solve important problems which can only be solved with great difficulty by feedforward networks. Recurrent neural networks (RNNs) are a special type of artificial neural network designed to handle sequential data, where the order of information matters. Unlike traditional neural networks that process individual inputs independently, ***RNNs can process sequences of information by keeping track of internal memory***. This makes them particularly useful for tasks like:

- **Natural Language Processing (NLP)**: Understanding and generating text, like machine translation, sentiment analysis, and chatbots.
- **Speech Recognition**: Converting spoken language into text.
- **Time Series Forecasting**: Predicting future values based on historical data, such as stock prices or weather patterns.
- **Music Generation**: Creating musical pieces with a specific style.

RNNs have an internal state called the hidden state. This hidden state acts like a memory that stores information about past inputs. As the RNN processes each element in a sequence, it updates its hidden state based on the current input and the previous hidden state. This allows the network to consider the context of the sequence when making predictions. As mentioned earlier, unlike traditional neural networks with a feedforward flow, RNNs have a looping structure where information can flow back into the network. This allows the network to access and utilize past information throughout the processing of the sequence.

There are different variations of RNNs addressing the limitations of the basic structure:

- **Long Short-Term Memory (LSTM)**: LSTMs are specifically designed to address the vanishing gradient problem, which can limit the ability of RNNs to learn long-term dependencies in sequences. LSTMs have internal gates that control the flow of information through the network, allowing them to learn and remember information over longer periods.
- **Gated Recurrent Unit (GRU)**: GRUs are another variant that address the vanishing gradient problem with a simpler architecture compared to LSTMs.

Overall, recurrent neural networks are a powerful tool for dealing with sequential data, enabling them to tackle various tasks that involve understanding and manipulating sequences.

The **vanishing gradient problem** (where gradient becomes too small) is a hurdle encountered during training deep neural networks, especially those with many layers. It affects how efficiently the network learns, particularly for tasks involving long-term dependencies in the data. Neural networks learn by adjusting weights based on the error between their predictions and the actual targets. **Backpropagation** is a technique used to calculate these adjustments by propagating the error backward through the network layer by layer. The adjustments for weights are proportional to the gradients of the error function with respect to each weight. These gradients determine how much each weight should be changed to reduce the error.

Backpropagation is a crucial algorithm used to train artificial neural networks. It is an efficient method for calculating the gradients of a loss function with respect to the weights of the network. These gradients are then used to update the weights and improve the network's performance.

Here is a breakdown of how backpropagation works:

The ultimate goal of training a neural network is ***to minimize the error between its predictions and the actual targets***. Backpropagation helps achieve this by efficiently adjusting the weights of the network based on the calculated error.

Forward Pass: During the forward pass, information flows from the input layer to the output layer. Each neuron performs calculations on the received data (weighted sum) and applies an activation function to generate its output. This output is then passed on to the next layer.

Calculating Error: After the forward pass, the error (loss) between the network's prediction and the actual target value is calculated at the output layer. This error represents how far off the network's guess was.

Error Propagation (Backward Pass): Here is where backpropagation comes in. The error is then propagated backward through the network, layer by layer. This is why it is called "backpropagation".

Gradient Calculation: At each layer, the gradient of the error function with respect to each weight is calculated. This gradient essentially tells us how much a specific weight in that layer contributed to the overall error.

Weight Updates: Finally, the weights in each layer are adjusted based on the calculated gradients and a learning rate. The learning rate controls how much the weights are updated in each step. Here, weights are nudged in a direction that will reduce the error as determined by the gradients.

Efficiency of Backpropagation:

Backpropagation is a clever algorithm because it avoids redundant calculations. It leverages the ***chain rule of calculus*** to efficiently compute the gradients for all weights in a single backward pass through the network. It works efficiently for networks with many layers and weights, making it suitable for deep learning applications.

In deep networks, gradients can become very small or vanish as they propagate backward through many layers. This can hinder learning in earlier layers. Techniques like ReLU activation functions and careful weight initialization can help address this problem. Backpropagation might get stuck in local minima (see Fig. 3.8), where the error is low but not globally optimal. Techniques like momentum and adaptive learning rates can help mitigate this issue.

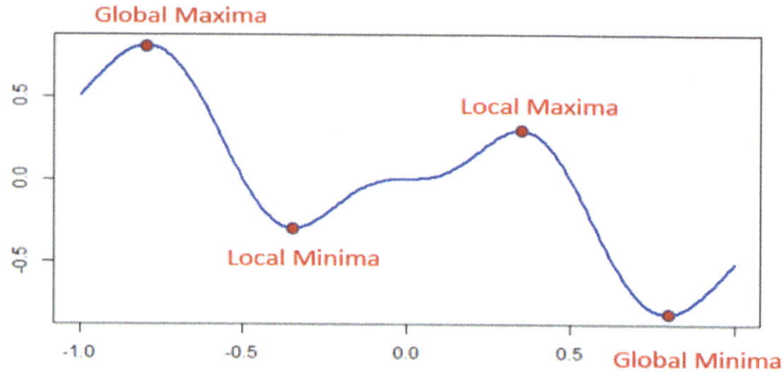

Fig. 3.8 A temporal representation of a sample signal

In the full signal as shown in Fig. 3.8, there can be many local minimums and maximums. Depending on what the signal (or set of data) it may be very difficult to find global minima and maxima.

In some activation functions commonly used in neural networks (like sigmoid and tanh), the gradients tend to become smaller and smaller as they are back propagated through multiple layers. This vanishing effect makes it difficult for the weights in the earlier layers (further from the output) to learn effectively from the error signal. With vanishing gradients, the weights in earlier layers barely change, hindering the network's ability to learn complex relationships, especially for long sequences. In extreme cases, the gradients can become so small that the weights barely change at all, effectively halting the training process. It is obvious why the gradient is important, that is why we introduced the partial derivative form using sigmoid activation function earlier. By understanding and addressing the vanishing gradient problem, we can train deeper and more effective neural networks for various tasks [6].

3.11 Representation of Neural Network in Matrix Algebra

So far, we have depicted the very basic of ANN pictorially. How do we replicate the ANN in a computer? We have seen in Fig. 3.8 the representation of inputs, weights and biases represented as dot product i.e., algebraically. Now, in Fig. 3.9 we show how it is written as matrices.

For four input layers feeding three **AN**s, so we have 4 weights multiplied by 4-element columns, multiplied by a 4-element column matrix of **x** inputs. The result is added with a three-element column matrix containing the bias values.

The result after a suitable activation function gives a three-element column matrix. Now computation can take over. Whether the AN is physically represented by dedicated hardware is a detail one can overlook, what is important at this juncture is that any information is now detected, filtered and represented by a mathematical

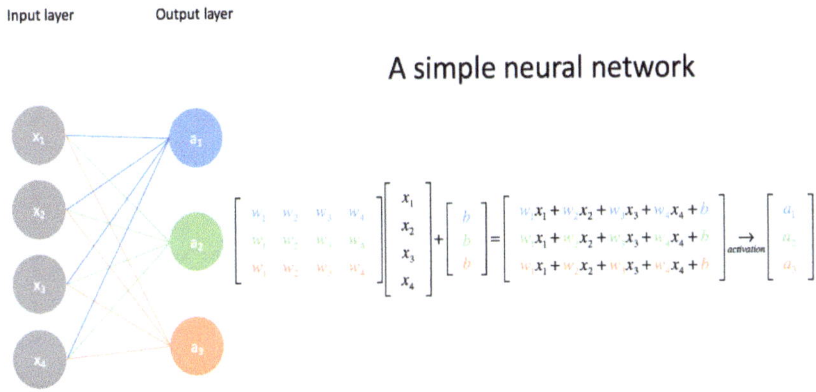

Fig. 3.9 Shows four input layers feeding three ANs

construct. ***It is an approximation of BNN***. Obviously, these ANN need huge computational resources as we have seen in Chap. 2. It needs an enormous amount of power and training data set.

3.12 Convolution Neural Network (CNNs)

At the end of introducing neural network we will touch upon Convolution Neural Network as shown in Fig. 3.10. In Convolutional Neural Networks (CNNs), the convolution layer is the fundamental building block responsible for extracting features from input data, typically images. It acts like a filter that scans the input, identifying and extracting patterns and spatial information.

The convolution layer contains Filters (Kernels) that are small matrices that contain learnable weights. The filter size is typically much smaller than the input image. The output of a convolution layer is called a feature map. It is a new image created by applying the filter to different parts of the input image. Each element in the feature map represents the activation of the filter at a specific location in the input. The filter slides across the input image, one step at a time. At each position, the filter elements are multiplied element-wise with the corresponding elements in a local region of the input image, referred to as the receptive field. The product elements are then summed up, resulting in a single value. This value is passed through an activation function, which introduces non-linearity and helps the network learn complex features [7].

This process of sliding, multiplying, summing, and activating is repeated for every position of the filter across the entire input image. The resulting collection of activations for each filter application throughout the image forms a feature map.

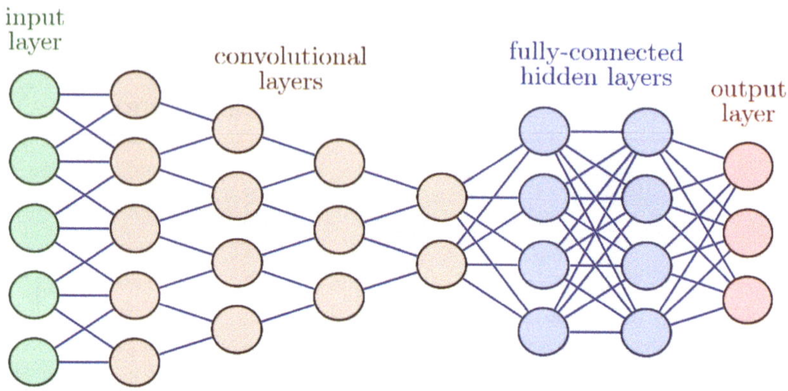

Fig. 3.10 Convolutional neural network

By using different filters, the convolution layer can learn to detect various features in the input image, such as edges, lines, shapes, and even colors. Multiple feature maps are generated, each capturing different aspects of the image. These feature maps become the input for subsequent layers in the CNN, which can then build upon these extracted features for more complex tasks like image recognition or object detection.

Convolution layers are computationally efficient because they share weights across the filter, reducing the number of parameters to learn, incidentally this is very similar to what BNN does. The convolution operation inherently preserves the spatial relationships between pixels in the input image, which is crucial for tasks like object localization. Unlike traditional methods where features are hand-crafted, convolution layers learn features automatically from the data during training.

Near the end of the Sect. 3.1 of this chapter we take a look at energy efficiency comparison between ANN and BNN. It is estimated that Google possesses a massive code dataset containing around 40 trillion tokens, which is four times larger than the dataset used to train GPT-4. A token refers to a unit of text used during the training process. It can be a word, a part of a word, or even a character.

The power consumption required for computer clusters running ANNs is in several kilowatts. We can estimate that. The consumption of Intel's Raptor Lake Architecture CPU goes up to 125 watts. For Matrix arithmetic GPUs are used, Nvidia's H100 GPU has a peak power consumption of $\sim$700 W. So, each CPU+GPU configuration with supporting peripherals will consume 1KW. **ANN** centric computers, clusters use 100 s of such CPU+GPUs [8].

How Artificial Neural Networks Represent Memory

Neural networks represent memory in a fundamentally different way than traditional computers. Rather than storing information in specific memory locations, they encode it in the weights of connections between neurons.

Weights: These are numerical values assigned to the connections between neurons. They determine the strength of the connection and influence the output of the network.

Activation: Neurons in a neural network produce an output based on the weighted sum of its inputs. This output is determined by an activation function.

Learning: The process of adjusting weights to improve the network's performance is called learning or training.

When a neural network is exposed to data, the weights are adjusted through a learning process. Information is encoded in the pattern of weights across the network.

This is analogous to how the human brain stores memories through synaptic connections.

Retrieving Information: When presented with new data, the network activates neurons based on the learned weights. The pattern of activation represents the network's "memory" of similar data. The network can then generate an output based on this internal representation.

Short-term Memory: Represented by the activation state of neurons in the network at a given moment. This is similar to working memory in humans.

Long-term Memory: Encoded in the weights of the network. This is analogous to long-term memory in humans.

Some issues: Neural networks can forget previously learned information when learning new data. Techniques like regularization and continual learning address this issue. The capacity of a neural network to store information is limited by its size and architecture.

At the conclusion of **Sect. 1 of Chap. 3**, we ask a question. ***Can we have any other way of representing phenomena which needs less training, lower resources and lower data set and maybe in the process sacrificing some accuracy? Somehow BNNs does it extremely efficiently. Human brain consumes only 20W in a relaxed condition***.

In this section, we explore the history, development, and fundamentals of Cellular Automata (CA), which is the basic building block of our proposition of creating a light weight machine learning model employing significantly lesser computing resources.

3.13 History and Origins of Cellular Automata (CA)

Cellular Automata (CA) is a captivating computational model that captures complex behavior through remarkably simple rules. Imagine a grid of cells, each following a set of instructions based on the state of its neighbors. This seemingly basic concept has spawned a rich history, fueled groundbreaking discoveries, and continues to hold immense potential across diverse fields.

The concept of Cellular Automata (CA) was originally proposed in the 1940s by Stanislaw Ulam and John von Neumann while they were contemporaries at Los Alamos National Laboratory. Neumann's initial design was based on the notion of a robot building its own copy. This design is known as the kinematic model. As he developed this design, Neumann came to realize the great difficulty of building a self-replicating robot, and of the high cost in providing the robot with a 'sea of parts' from which to build its replica. In 1948 Neumann reported his ideas of self-replicating systems in the paper entitled "The General and Logical Theory of Automata". Ulam was the one who suggested using a *discrete* system for creating a reductionist model of self-replication. Nils Aall Barricelli, a Norwegian-Italian mathematician and geneticist, performed many of the earliest explorations of these models of artificial life supporting self-replication.

> The name of Nils Barricelli is relatively unknown compared to the other giants mentioned here.
>
> The first theoretical biologist who came to the Institute of Advance Studies was Nils Barricelli, who was invited by John von Neumann in 1953 and stayed here for two terms. Using the computer that von Neumann had built at the Institute, Barricelli simulated the evolution of populations of artificial organisms. He observed the phenomena of speciation, parasitism, and predation arising spontaneously in his computer runs. He also observed punctuated equilibrium, the tendency of dominant species to remain static for many generations and then suddenly give way to new dominant species of a different character. He was a pioneer of the new science of artificial life, forty years before it became fashionable.

Researchers like Edward Fredkin and Konrad Zuse recognized the computational capabilities of CA, exploring their potential for universal computation [9].

It was only after publication of John Conway's Game of Life (a two-dimensional cellular automaton) in 1970s, interest in the subject expanded beyond academia. Stephan Wolfram engaged in a systematic study of one-dimensional Cellular Automata; his research assistant Mathew Cook showed that one of these rules is 'Turing Complete'. We suggest readers use the "Conway Game of Life program" to get the initial excitement of CA [10].

Prior to undertaking study of CA, we will take a short discourse on discreteness, computation and computability.

A 'Turing Complete' system means a system in which a program can be written that will find an answer to any problem. There is a closely related Turing equivalence—two computers A and B are called equivalent if B can simulate A and vice versa. Turing completeness is significant in that every real-world design for a computing device can be simulated by a universal Turing machine. Alan Turing, Alanzo Church, and independently in another way, Kurt Gödel went on to prove that there are sets of simple instructions, which, when put together, are able to produce any computation.

We have already devoted some thought on CA in the first chapter as a tentative candidate for a preprocessor for AI/ML systems for providing sets of solutions using less computational resources. We report CA rule design in Chap. 4 followed by the formulation and experimental results on three application domains in Chaps. 5–7 of this book.

3.14 Fundamental Procedures of Cellular Automata

Cellular Automata operate on a discrete grid of cells. Each cell can be in a finite number of states (e.g., alive/dead, on/off). The state of a cell at a given time step depends on a predetermined rule and the states of its neighbors in the previous time step. These rules, often surprisingly simple, govern the overall evolution of the CA. Cellular Automata has found applications in a surprisingly wide range of fields. CAs can simulate fluid flow, crystal growth, and even traffic patterns, providing valuable insights into complex dynamics. Stream ciphers utilize CA-like structures for secure communication. CAs can model the emergence of complex behavior in simple systems, probably offering a glimpse into the origins of life.

Langton's Ant is a captivating example of how simple rules can lead to complex and emergent behavior. It is a two-dimensional model where an ant moves on a grid of black and white squares. It was invented by Chris Langton in 1986.

The ant or turtle moves on a two-dimensional grid made out of squares. It follows a straightforward set of rules, and run in a loop.

If the ant is on a white square:

Turn left 90 °C. Change the color of the square to black.
Move forward one square.

Else If the ant is on a black square:

Turn right 90 °C. Change the color of the square to white.
Move forward one square.

With these simple rules, the ant's behavior over time creates intricate and unpredictable patterns. Initially, the ant's movements might seem random, but as it continues, a structure emerges.

Stephen Wolfram's classification system categorizes Cellular Automata (CA) based on their long-term behavior. It applies specifically to Elementary Cellular Automata (ECA), which are one-dimensional CAs with a simple set of rules governing how cells update based on their own state and the states of their immediate neighbors. Here is a breakdown of the four classes:

- **Class 1: Uniformity**
  - **Behavior**: Cellular Automata in this class eventually reach a homogeneous state where all cells are identical.
  - **Example**: The identity rule, where a cell simply copies the state of its middle neighbor, falls into this class. Regardless of the initial configuration, all cells will eventually become the same.
- **Class 2: Simple Structures**
  - **Behavior**: These CAs exhibit recurring patterns or simple oscillating structures after the initial transient phase.
  - **Example**: The "rule 22" CA, where a cell becomes on if both its neighbors are on or if exactly one neighbor is off, leads to the formation of repeating blocks of alternating on and off cells.
- **Class 3: Chaos**
  - **Behavior**: Class 3 CAs display complex, unpredictable behavior that appears random even though it is deterministic (based on the initial configuration and the CA's rule).
  - **Example**: Rule 30, also known as the "Cook rule" or the "busy beaver" rule, is a famous example in this class. It exhibits highly sensitive dependence on initial conditions, meaning small changes in the initial configuration can lead to drastically different long-term outcomes.
- **Class 4: Universality**
  - **Behavior**: These CAs are the most complex and interesting. They can exhibit a vast range of behaviors, including stable structures, periodic oscillations, and even emulate the behavior of universal Turing machines (theoretical models of computation).
  - **Example**: While not definitively proven, the complex behavior of rule 110 suggests it might be capable of universal computation. This means it could theoretically simulate any other CA, including those from other classes.

The classification system is primarily designed for one dimensional CA employing the same elementary CA rule for each of the cells of a CA that can be referred to as Uniform CA that provides a platform for the theoretical study of CA evolution. As per our evaluation, no real-life application can be designed with Uniform CA.

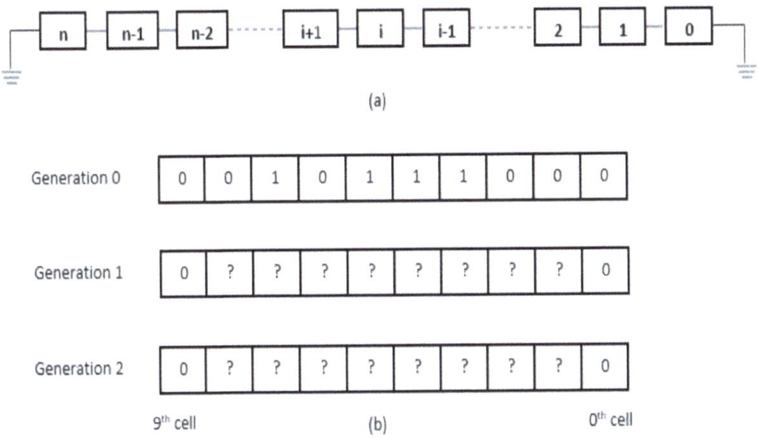

Fig. 3.11 Picture of 10 CA cells evolving with NULL boundaries

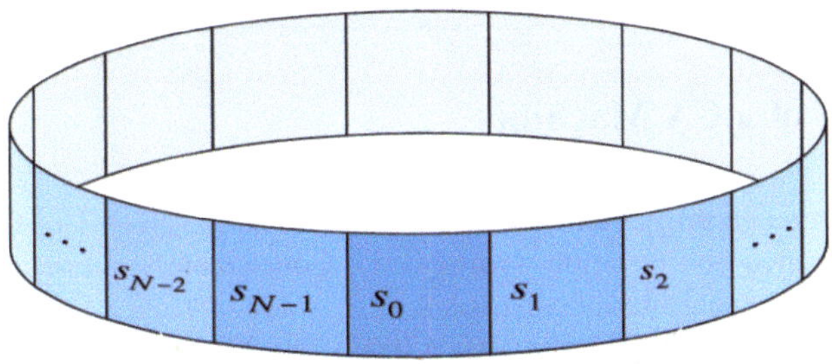

Fig. 3.12 Depiction of CA in periodical boundary

Hence, in the applications we have reported in this book we employ non-Uniform CA, where the cells are configured with any one of 256 elementary CA rules.

Figure 3.11 displays a 10-cell representation numbered from 9 to 0, where the 0 and 9th are pseudo cells representing the CA boundary. For the null boundary these two pseudo cells are permanently set at zero value as shown in Fig. 3.11. Each square block represents a CA cell that can store binary information—'0' or '1'. The information stored is referred to as 'state' of a cell. Let us discuss the simplest CA with two states per cell, three neighborhoods and null boundary. Each cell in Fig. 3.11 has two neighbors—left and right; in addition, the cell itself is assumed as its neighbor, thus making three neighborhoods of a CA cell. Each cell of a CA evolves in discrete time steps—also known as generations. Prior to the evolution of CA cells, each cell is initialized with state '0' or '1'. This binary input string is referred to as 'seed' to initiate CA evolution. The two terminal cells of one-dimensional CA have only two neighbors instead of three—the left most cell has no left neighbor, and the right

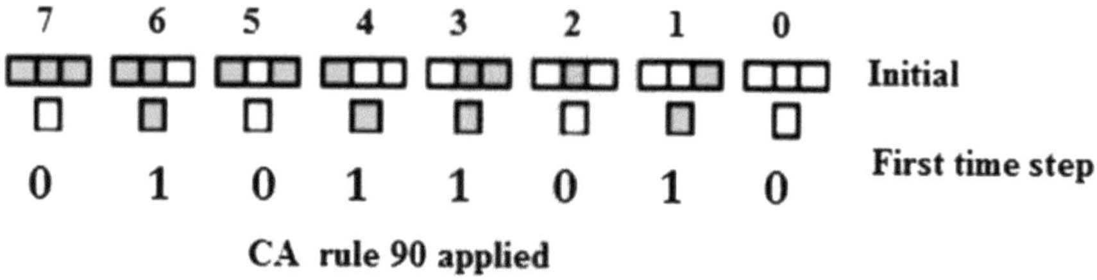

Fig. 3.13 CA rule 90 applied

most cell has no right neighbor. If we assign state 0 (null) for the missing neighbors, the resulting CA is referred to as 'null boundary' CA. The CA is called a periodic boundary (see Fig. 3.12) if the rightmost cell is the neighbor of the leftmost one and vice versa. The CA model proposed in this book only employs periodic boundary CA. In the example above with a periodic boundary the 9th cell does not exist, the 8th cell becomes the right neighbor of the cell zero.

3.15 Rules of a CA Machine

Each ith cell in a cell array can have one of the two state values 1 or 0, sometimes shown as blackened box or empty (white box). Consequently, there can be $2^3 = 8$ combinations of current states of cell triplets $< (i-1)\, i\, (i+1) >$ marked as 7 (111), 6 (110), 5 (101), 4 (100), 3 (011), 2 (010), 1 (001), 0 (000) noted in Fig. 3.13. The last row shows evolution of next state of ith cell for each of the 8 possible combinations of the current states of its neighbors. The decimal counterpart of the 8-bit string of cell next state is referred to as 'CA rule' for the ith cell.

If we work in the same manner for Rule 110, as we did using Rule 90 (see Fig. 3.13) We can justify the value of the central cell (01101110) as shown in Fig. 3.13. As per this rule, for input states <000>, the next state is 0 s, while the output is 1 for input state triplets as <001>, and so on.

The interesting point is the evolution of the 32 cell CA, with rule 110 assigned to each cell. If this CA is operated for 14 steps after initializing with value 1 for 14th cell and 0's for all other cells, we shall arrive at the pattern shown in Fig. 3.14.

CA rules can be categorized as linear or non-linear based on how they determine the next state of a cell. Linear rules are generally simpler and easier to analyze. They often involve basic operations like addition or comparison with a threshold value. The next state of a cell in a linear CA depends linearly on the current states of its neighbors. This means there is no multiplication or complex interactions between neighboring states.

Non-linear rules can lead to more intricate and unpredictable behavior in Cellular Automata. The next state of a cell can be determined by more complex interactions between the states of its neighbors. This might involve multiplication (AND/NAND), logical operations like XOR (exclusive OR), or looking at the combination of multiple

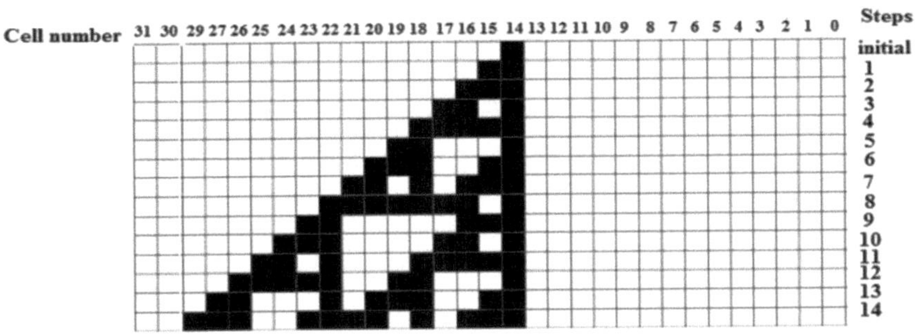

Fig. 3.14 Rule 110 evolution, 14 steps

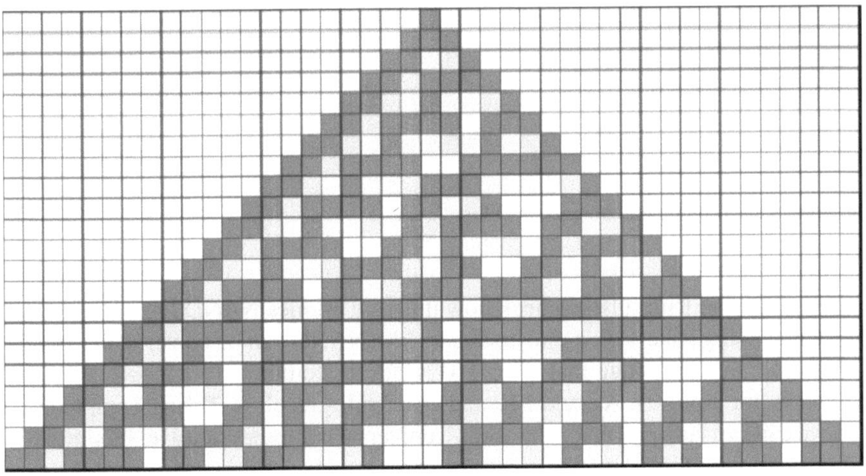

Fig. 3.15 Evolution of CA rule 30

neighbors' states. **Rule 30 (The Cook rule)**: A cell becomes "on" if exactly one of its neighbors is "on" and both are off otherwise. Rule 30 is a non-linear rule. The Evolution of Rule 30, as shown in Fig. 3.15, leads to highly chaotic behavior.

In Chaps. 5 and 6 of this book, we employ non-linear CA rules. Chapter 7 of the book opens up a new direction of CA application, where non-uniform linear CA rules are employed to model a linear function. The motivation of this application is to provide an analytical foundation for the Machine Learning (ML) framework.

Let us present a small example of linking behavior of CA with real world logic. Logic gates are essential parts of digital systems; using logic gates in the correct combination we can perform logical and arithmetic operations. The NAND or NOR logic gates are called 'universal logic' gates, as any other gates can be constructed from them. Let us see the output of a two input NAND gate with inputs A and B and output Q (Table 3.1).

Table 3.1 Two input NAND logic gate

A	B	Q
0	0	1
0	1	1
1	0	1
1	1	0

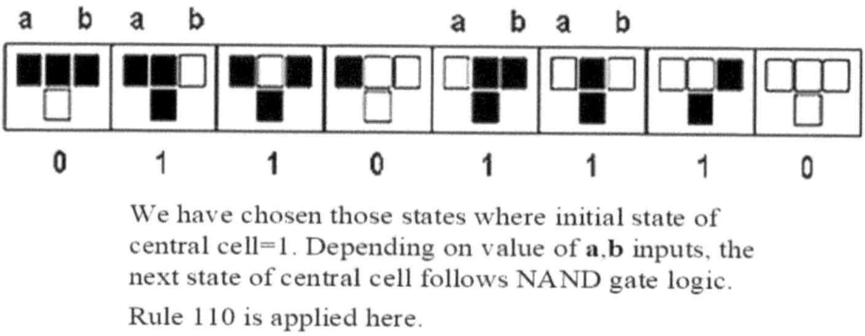

Fig. 3.16 Rule 110 implementing NAND logic

Let us re-visit Rule 110 to check how this rule mimics NAND logic. Figure 3.16 shows that using Rule 110, a universal gate like NAND can be constructed. In other words, we can extrapolate that Rule 110 is Turing complete (obviously, the above method is not a proof). As rule 110 and other rules result in Turing completeness, then we can say 'any problem that needs a universal computer to solve, its simulation can be done with CA'.

In Fig. 3.4 of this chapter we demonstrated how NAND logic can be implemented by ANN.

3.16 Method to Represent a Phenomenon Using CA

As a CA evolves in successive time steps (represented in a vertical scale), a cell will fall in a loop generating the same set of states, that can be viewed as its 'attractor cycle'. If a set of cells evolve, at some point of time, all the evolving cells will fall into loops (cycles). Let the length of loop be referred to as Cycle length (CL). In the process, we will get numbers equal to CLs represented on the vertical axis for each cell location, represented by horizontal axis—that represents a graph referred to as CL (signal) graph. Let us illustrate the phenomenon with reference to the Computational Linguistics application covered in Chap. 6 of this book.

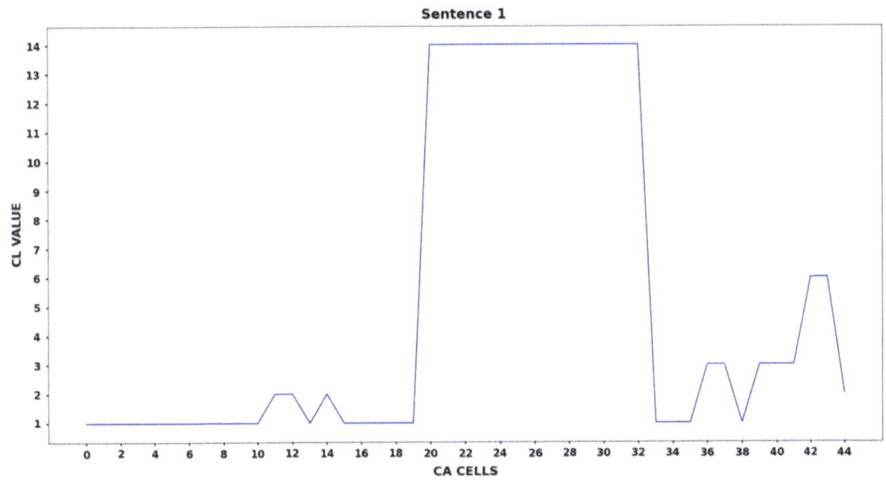

Fig. 3.17 CL graph representing Sentence 1

Let us take two sentences and convert each character of the sentences with CA rule sequence. Next allow the CA to evolve as per each CA rule vector till each CA cell settles down in a cycle. In the process, the sentences get transformed to the CA domain represented by corresponding CL graphs detailed next.

Here are the two sentences:
Sentence 1: *Think it possible you may be making a mistake*

Here is the string of CA rules (Rule Vector) modeling the sentence 1 making up the sentence: [84,104,105,110,107,32,105,32,112,111,115,105,98,108,101,52, 121,111,117, 32,109,97,107,105,110,103,32,97, 32,109,105,115,116,97,107,101]

Figure 3.17 shows the CL graph which is the CA representation of the sentence.

Sentence 2: *Think it possible that you generally make mistakes*

Here are the CA rule vectors making up the sentence: [84,104,105,110,107,32,105, 116,32,112,111,115,98,108,101,32,116,92,121,111,117,32,103,101,110,101,114, 97,108,97,107,32,109,105,115,116,97,107,101,115]

The text of the two sentences has been transformed into the CA domain, which we can think of as being similar to a transformation in BNN or ANN. When we see the sentences and somewhere in our neural network BNN, we understand there is substantial difference of intention (the second one being direct insult). This difference gets reflected in the CL graphs derived for two sentences, shown in Figs. 3.17 and 3.18.

From Chap. 4 onwards in this book this CL graph formation and interpretation has been described in detail. A brief introduction on CAML (CA enhanced/assisted with Machine Learning) model follows.

Architecture of a Light weight ML model using CA (CAML)

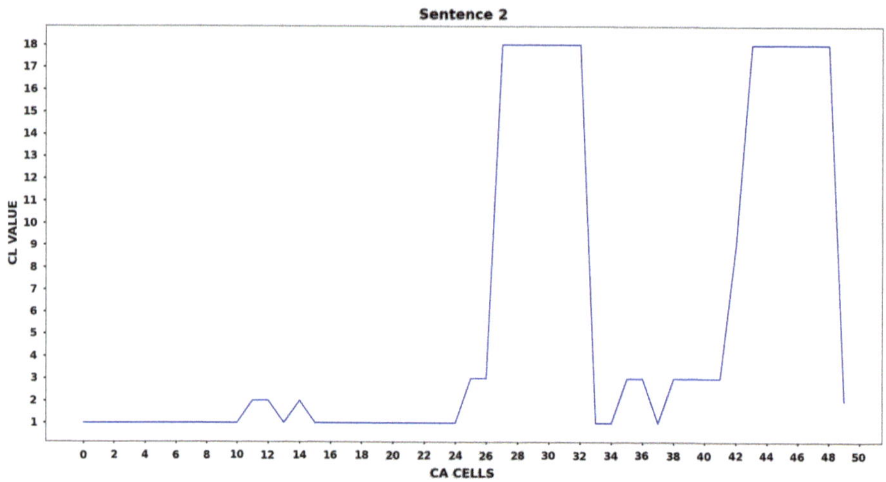

Fig. 3.18 CL graph representing Sentence 2

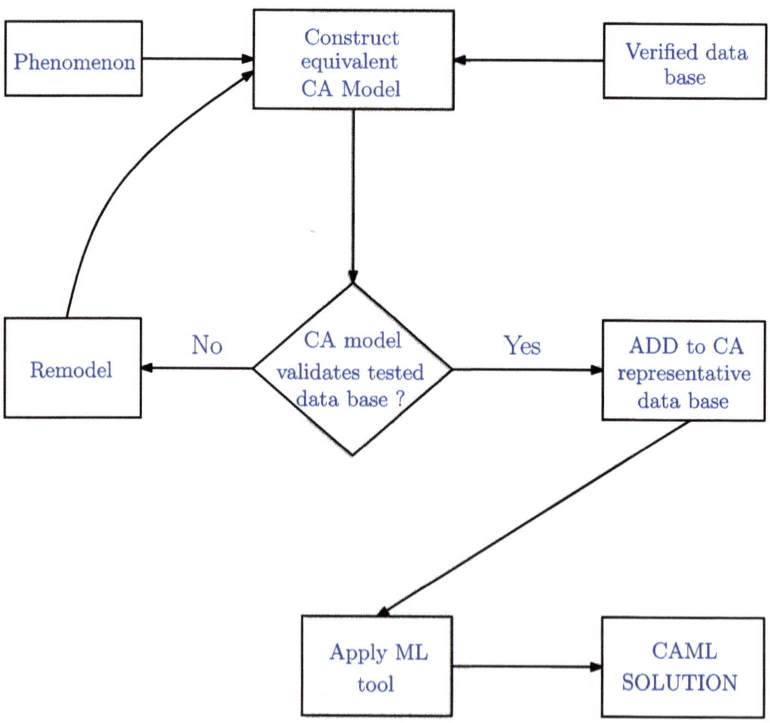

Fig. 3.19 Model of CA (enhanced/assisted with) ML system (CAML)

Figure 3.19 shows a schematic approximating how CA is used employing ML system. It is worth **reemphasizing the fact that characterizing non-linear CA evolution**

is an extremely difficult task. Consequently, we employ ML system to understand non-linear CA evolution that is referred to as CA assisted/enhanced with ML system. In the very first step a physical phenomenon is transformed employing the CA model; the transformed representation is next mapped to the elements of the known database. The mapping is further evaluated in the validation stage. If it passes the validation test, then it is viewed as a CA represented database of the physical phenomenon. ML methods are used on a limited dataset to arrive at the prediction result.

3.17 Conclusion

Both Biological Neural Networks (BNN) and Artificial Neural Networks (ANN) can mimic phenomena, represent objects, and even form their own kind of understanding, similar to Cellular Automata (CA).

The exciting part is BNNs can learn with minimal data, power, and time. They achieve this through a kind of 'educated guess' developed over millions of years of evolution. While CA is not directly related to BNNs, BNNs inspire us to explore how CA can also achieve similar results—rough estimates with limited data and processing power.

From Chap. 4 onwards, we will delve into how this concept can be applied to fields like computational biology [11] and computational linguistics.

References

1. E.R. Kandel, J.H. Schwartz, T.M. Jessell, S. Siegelbaum, A.J. Hudspeth, *Principles of Neural Science*, 5th edn. (McGraw-hill Education, 2013)
2. S.C. Furuta, A.P. Fox, *Neuroscience*, 6th edn. (2009)
3. F. Rosenblatt, The perceptron: a probabilistic model for information storage and organization in the brain. Psychol. Rev. **65**, 386–408 (1958)
4. Stanford encyclopedia of philosophy: Perceptrons. [Online]. Available: https://stanford.edu/~rezab/amdm/notes/lecture9.pdf
5. Neural networks bias and weights. [Online]. Available: https://medium.com/fintechexplained/neural-networks-bias-and-weights-10b53e6285da
6. Local minima in deep learning. [Online]. Available: https://machinelearningmastery.com
7. Convolutional neural networks, course offered by stanford university. [Online]. Available: https://cs231n.stanford.edu/
8. D. Geißler, B. Zhou, M. Liu, S. Suh, P. Lukowicz, The power of training: How different neural network setups influence the energy demand (2014). arXiv:2401.01851
9. S. Wolfram, Computation theory of cellular automata. Commun. Math. Phys. **96**(1), 15–57 (1984)
10. The Game of Life. [Online]. Available: https://en.wikipedia.org/wiki/Conway
11. P.P. Chaudhuri, S. Ghosh, A. Dutta, S.P. Choudhury, *A New Kind of Computational Biology* (Springer, Berlin, 2018)

Chapter 4
CA Rule Design for Proteomics and Linguistics

"The fusion of Cellular Automata and Machine Learning represents a frontier where rule-based systems meet adaptive algorithms, creating models that not only simulate nature but also learn from it"

—Anonymous

4.1 Introduction

Chapters 1, 2, and 3 lay the groundwork of this book entitled 'New Kind of Machine Learning—Cellular Automata Model'. Chapter 1 deals with the concept of 'simulated intelligence' while tracing back the historic and prehistoric perspective of Artificial Intelligence (AI). Chapter 2 reviews the current state of AI along with a comprehensive survey of the challenges encountered in this field. Against this backdrop, Chap. 3 covers two distinct areas—Machine Learning (a sub-discipline of AI) and Cellular Automata (CA). The discussions touch upon the intricacies of the human cognition system that fundamentally operates at multiple levels. An initial rough approximation (or estimation) precedes the final decision derived from the cognition system. As the foundation of AI relies on a comprehensive understanding of the cognition process of the human brain, Chap. 3 explores the potential of analyzing the patterns derived out of CA evolution as an alternative to the initial phase of a multi-layered cognition system.

The fundamental concept of Cellular Automata (CA) is introduced in Chap. 3. Universal appeal of CA as a modeling tool has been highlighted in many publications since the 1960s. CA universality gets demonstrated by the wide varieties of its evolution patterns observed through local interaction of its cells. In 'Nature' we observe

© The Author(s), under exclusive license to Springer Nature Singapore Pte Ltd. 2025
P. Pal Chaudhuri et al., *New Kind of Machine Learning—Cellular Automata Model*,
https://doi.org/10.1007/978-981-96-1501-8_4

evolving patterns out of interaction of local entities of a physical system around us. Further, the growth of human civilization in the last few centuries can be viewed as temporal evolution of relevant facts/patterns in different fields of human society—be it legal system, administrative/political structure, civil society in a country, or international relations among different countries in the world. Consequently, research scholars of diverse disciplines are naturally attracted to develop models based on CA.

Development of an appropriate model for any physical system or phenomenon is a challenging task since the model developer needs to have sound knowledge of both the application domain and characterization of CA evolution patterns. In view of such constraints, we seldom come across relevant industrial or commercial applications leveraging CA. Unless the researchers in the field of Cellular Automata can overcome this bottleneck and develop fruitful applications, it will not be able to serve the human society of twenty-first century, even though CA has enormous potential to build new class of models to address the problems the human society face in today's digital world. In the above context and background, the primary focus of this book is to present applications where CA based solutions hold excellent promise, compared to the contemporary solutions demanding prohibitive computational resources and voluminous 'Big data' corpus as training set, as has been surveyed both in Chaps. 2 and 3. The current book presents two CA applications in the field of Computational Proteomics (a sub-discipline of Computational Biology) and Computational Linguistics in Chaps. 5 and 6.

The focus of Chap. 5 is Computational Proteomics that deals with different aspects of proteins - the workhorse molecule associated with major functions in a living cell of any form of life (animal world, plant kingdom, bacteria). Consequently, Proteomics study has become a major focal point of research in the field of Life Sciences. A protein is a linear chain of 20 common amino acids. CA Rule Design for Amino acids of a Protein Chain is presented in Sect. 4.3 of the current chapter.

The current internetworked human society reports diverse language texts in social media platforms. Automated extraction of relevant information from such a multi-language environment is a challenging task. Since the last decade of last century, the Unicode consortium has been developing Unicode character sets to represent written text of all living languages around the globe. Section 4.4 of Chap. 4 reports the design of CA rules for Unicode character sets derived out of any language text. The driving force is to develop a CA based solution to address the 'sentiment analysis' problem in a multi-language environment, subsequent to conversion of a language text to Unicode text.

We have presented CA rule design for applications in two disparate fields—Computational Proteomics and Computational Linguistics. The application of Machine Learning (ML) framework to model physical systems with CA is highlighted in Sect. 4.5. The background and necessity of ML framework for CA based model development for any application domain is covered in this section entitled 'ML Framework to Model Physical Systems with CA'. As a follow up, Sect. 4.6 presents—'the Iterative Procedure of CA Rule Design for an Application'.

Finally, Sect. 4.7 reports the Cellular Automata (enhanced with) Machine Learning (CAML) model and its differences from the traditional ML models.

The CA preliminaries relevant for two applications covered in this book follows.

4.2 Cellular Automata (CA) Preliminaries

The CA preliminaries are touched upon in Chap. 3. The background necessary to build the CA model for two applications covered in this book are introduced next.

CA is a dynamical system discrete in space and time. The space is represented by a regular lattice in one, two or higher dimensions. Each site on the lattice also referred to as a cell, can be in one of a finite number of states. The next state of a cell depends on the current state of its neighbours and the associated next state function represented as a combinational logic in Fig. 4.1. Neumann [1] proposed the CA model for constructing self-replicating machine employing 2000 cells, each holding 29 states. Subsequently, Wolfram [2] proposed a simpler version of CA with two states per cell and three-neighbourhood. Research of a large number of authors from diverse disciplines has enriched the field of CA [3–7]. The book [7] covers a comprehensive survey of CA theory and wide varieties of applications. Further, the universal appeal of CA model based on local interaction can be ascertained from the materials presented in the book [8] that highlights the effect of local (temporal and physical) changes transforming the human society from pre-historic to modern age.

The CA rule design reported in this section employs simplest CA structure with periodic boundary, three neighborhood, and two state per cell—referred to as 3NCA in the rest of the book. There exist two boundary conditions for a CA—null boundary, where neighborhood of two terminal cells at left and right ends are 0 (null), and periodic boundary where two terminal cells are neighbors of each other. The implementation of an n-cell 3-neighbourhood CA under periodic boundary condition is shown in Fig. 4.1. The middle cell is marked as ith cell while its left and right neighbors are denoted as $(i-1)$th and $(i+1)$th cell respectively. Consequently, $8(2^3)$ combinations exist for the triplet of current state values $< a_{i-1}a_ia_{i+1} >$ of $(i-1)$th,

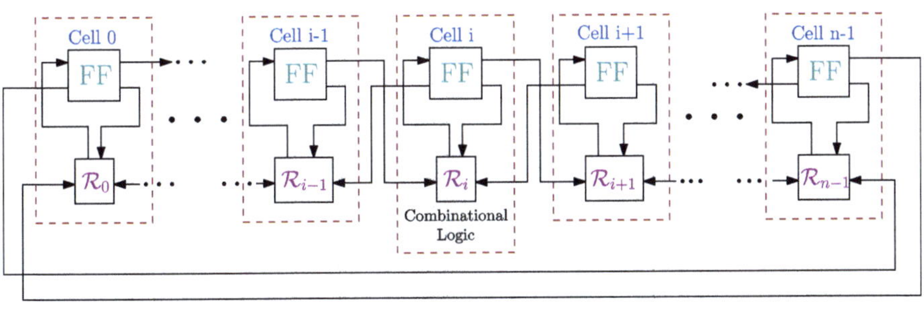

Fig. 4.1 Implementation of an n-cell 3-neighborhood CA under periodic boundary condition

Table 4.1 Look-up table for rule 45 and 105

Present state	111	110	101	100	011	010	001	000	Rule
(RMT)	(7)	(6)	(5)	(4)	(3)	(2)	(1)	(0)	
Next State (b_k)	(b_7)	(b_6)	(b_5)	(b_4)	(b_3)	(b_2)	(b_1)	(b_0)	
(i) Next state	0	0	1	0	1	1	0	1	45
(ii) Next state	0	1	1	0	1	0	0	1	105

ith and $(i+1)$th cells. The next state function of ith ($i = 0, 1, 2, \ldots, (n-1)$) cell is shown in Fig. 4.1 as a combinational logic marked $\mathcal{R}_i$. The decimal value of the 8 bits of cell next state is referred to as 'Rule' of evolution of a CA cell. There are $2^8 = 256$ such rules for three-neighborhood CA. The decimal value derived out of 8 bit string of two CA rules (45) and (105) are illustrated on the rightmost column in Table 4.1 Row 4 and 5. Eight different input combinations of a CA rule is a triplet of binary bits are—111(7), 110(6), 101(5), 100(4), 011(3), 010(2), 001(1), 000(0), noted on row 1 and 2 of Table 4.1. Each of the eight combination, shown on first row, represents the current state of $(i-1)$, i, and $(i+1)$th cells which can be viewed as three binary variables. In Boolean algebra, a combination of binary variables of a combinational logic is referred to as 'minterm'. In subsequent discussions we refer to the combinations of three input variables as Rule Min Terms (RMTs). There are 8 RMTs of the three variable functions. A RMT is referred to by its decimal value that varies from 0 to 7, shown on the second row of Table 4.1 as RMT k. Row 4 and 5 of the table show the cell next as b_k ($b_k = 0$ or 1), for RMT $k = 0$ to 7 for CA rule 45 and 105. By convention, a CA rule is expressed as decimal counterpart of a binary bit string $< b_7b_6b_5b_4b_3b_2b_1b_0 >$. So conventional weight assignment follows for conversion of 8-bit string of a rule to its decimal value with $w_7 = 2^7$, $w_6 = 2^6$ and so on. The decimal rule number 45 (with its binary value as 00101101) is derived from its binary bit string as—$\sum_{k=0}^{7} w_k b_k = 2^5 + 2^3 + 2^2 + 2^0 = 32 + 8 + 4 + 1 = 45$. A CA rule can be viewed as a transform that accepts 3 bit input $k =< a_{i-1}a_ia_{i+1} >$ (noted on first row of Table 4.1 with the corresponding decimal value on second row) to generate single bit output b_k in the next time of evolution of the cell; two CA rules with decimal values 45 and 145 are illustrated in the 8 bit binary format in Table 4.1.

Additive and Non-linear CA

The cells of a 3NCA employs one of the 256 rules (0 to 255). Out of these 255 rules (leaving aside Rule 0), there are 14 rules referred to as Additive CA rules [7] which employ XOR/XNOR logic gates in the 'Combinational Logic' block shown in Fig. 4.1. The remaining 240 rules are referred to as Nonlinear CA rules which employ AND, OR logic gates. A nonlinear CA employs non-linear CA rules. We have used nonlinear CA to model physical entities of two applications covered in this book.

In order to design rules to build CA model for a physical system, it is convenient to use the following format for a rule. We employ this format for design of CA rules for 20 amino acids in the next section.

Table 4.2 Representation of two CA rules 45 and 105 in 1-major and 0-major format

Rule	1-Major RMTs				0-Major RMTs			
	7 (111)	6 (110)	5 (101)	3 (011)	4 (100)	2 (010)	1 (001)	0 (000)
45	0	0	1	1	0	1	0	1
105	0	1	1	1	0	0	0	1

1-major and 0-major (7653 4210) Format: Out of 8 RMTs, the binary string of each of the 4 RMTs (7, 6, 5, 3) has two 1's, while the remaining four RMTs (4, 2, 1, 0) has two 0's—these two classes are referred to as 1-Major and 0-Major RMTs respectively in Table 4.2 that shows rules 45 and 105 in this format.

A physical system can be viewed as a set of interconnected elements that operate in a coordinated manner to realize a specific goal, function or objective. Modeling of two physical systems, addressed in this book, are represented as a linear chain of constituent elements elaborated next.

- The first one is a linear chain of organic molecules of amino acids in a macromolecule referred to as protein, which is the workhorse in any living organism observed on earth. Proteins are associated with nearly every function of a living cell. Study of protein structure, function, and its interaction with other biomolecules of a cell is an integral part of Computational Proteomics (a subdiscipline of Computational Biology) covered in Chap. 5 of this book.
- The second example deals with a linear chain of alphabets in the text of any written language. It is worth noting the fact that since the last decade of the last century, Unicode consortium has initiated the move to design a universal character set to support the written text in all living languages around the world. In the context of the current digital world, processing of multilingual texts available on the internet is a challenging task in Computational Linguistics. This specific problem is addressed in Chap. 6 of this book.

Next two Sects. 4.3 and 4.4 report design of CA rules for two applications covered in this book.

4.3 CA Rule Design for Amino Acids of a Protein Chain

Computational Biology has become an integral part of the discipline of Biology since the last decade of last century. It is an interdisciplinary field encompassing computer science, biology, mathematics, physics, and chemistry. The discipline of Biology covers study of living organisms—human beings, animals, trees, and all life forms observed on earth since the current life form was initiated with unicellular life. 'Origin of life' on earth is a big mystery that could not be adequately addressed till today. The critical roles played by two biomolecules to sustain life on earth are—Nucleic

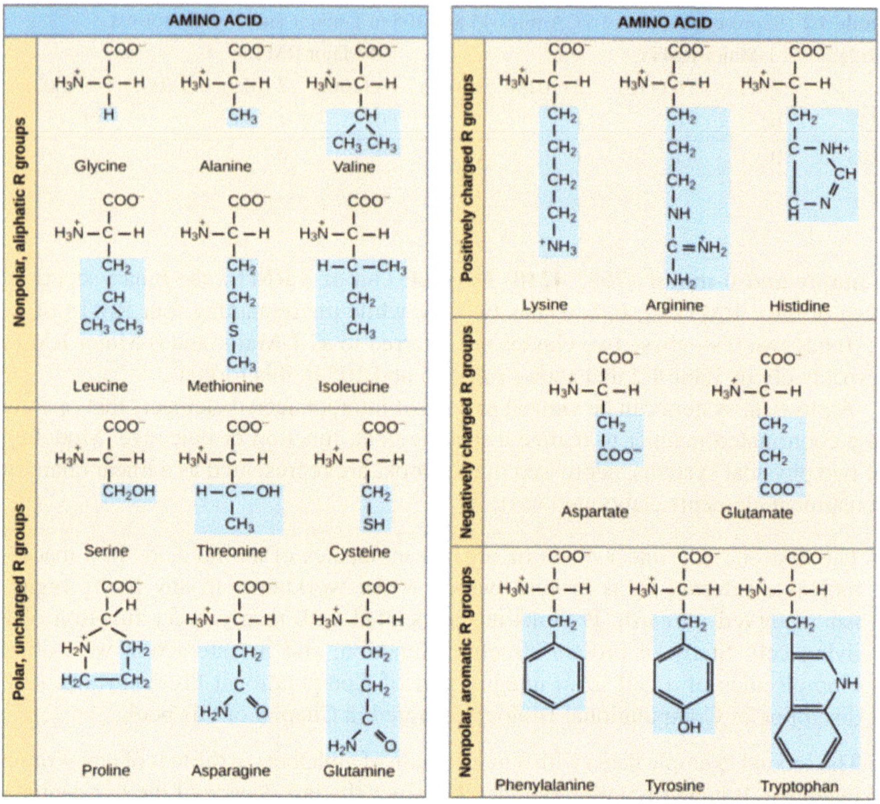

Fig. 4.2 Atomic structure of 20 common Amino Acids (AAs) divided into 5 groups

Acid and Protein. Two types of nucleic acids are DNA (Deoxyribonucleic Acid) and RNA (Ribonucleic Acid). DNA carries genetic information (genetic variation, and heredity in living organisms) to make RNA and proteins in a biological cell. Protein is viewed as the workhorse molecule associated with cell function through interaction with other biomolecules of a cell. DNA/RNA is formed out of a string of nucleotide bases—adenine (A), cytosine (C), guanine (G), thymine (T), and uracil (U). On the other hand, a protein chain consists of a sequence of amino acids connected through a bond referred to as peptide bond. The basic constituents for both amino acids and nucleotide bases are the four atoms—hydrogen (H), carbon (C), oxygen (O), nitrogen (N); in addition to these four, the atom Sulphur (S) is included in the atomic structure of two amino acids. Atomic structures of twenty common amino acids are presented in Fig. 4.2. Rest of this section covers the CA rule design for twenty common amino acids and derivation of the CA rule vector (an ordered sequence of CA rules) for a protein chain.

4.3.1 CA Rule Design for Amino Acids of a Protein

Design of CA model for a physical system involves design of rule for each CA cell. A cell models the smallest component of the system so that the physical domain features of the component get represented in the binary bit pattern of its rule. The CA model for 20 amino acids have been derived from the first principle, by considering the atomic structure of amino acid molecules. Figure 4.2 shows the atomic structure of 20 amino acids divided into 5 different groups based on the property of the side chain referred to as Residue (R). The side chain property—non-polar, polar, positively charged, negatively charged, aromatic—is defined by the structure of interconnected atoms. For the design of CA rules, the atoms are divided into two groups—Hydrogen atom (H) and non-H atom (Carbon C, Nitrogen N, Oxygen O, Sulphur S), each having different proton count in nucleus and electron count in outer shells. The CA model for hydrogen atom H, lightest one in the periodic table elements, treated differently from non-H atoms.

Each amino acid has a common backbone with 9 atoms—5 non-Hydrogen (H) atoms (2 Carbon (C) atoms, 2 oxygen (O) atoms and 1 Nitrogen (N) atom) and 4 Hydrogen (H) atoms. The side chain residues have a widely different number of atoms –1 atom (for Gly - G) to 18 atoms (for Arg - R). The CA rules for an amino acid are designed for the composite module of backbone connected to the side chain. This is a departure from the convention of referring to an amino acid as a residue. In the rest of the book, we refer to an amino acid (AA) as a composite molecule covering both backbone and side chain residue.

4.3.2 Design Methodology

3NCA rules for amino acid molecules are defined as a sequence of rules (decimal value 0 to 255) modeling its atomic structure. On considering the atomic structure of amino acids, it is convenient to design the rules by considering the RMT string <7 6 5 4 3 2 1 0> of a rule in the form of 1-Major and 0-Major RMTs as <7653 4210> (Table 4.2). The count of non-H atoms are assigned as the count of '1' in the next state of 1-major RMTs (7, 6, 5, 3), while count of H-atoms are assigned as count of '1' in the next state of 0-major RMTs (4, 2, 1, 0) of a CA rule. However, we do not populate more than 6 numbers of '1's in the 8-bit pattern of a rule. Hence, rather than a single rule, the design employs a string of rules if the molecule has more than 4 H atoms or non-H atoms.

4.3.3 Design of CA Rule for Amino Acid Backbone

As per this design methodology, a string of two CA rules designed for 9 atom amino acid backbone as <107 99>is reported in Table 4.3, where the first column shows

Table 4.3 Design of CA rule string for amino acid backbone having 9 atoms—two carbon, one nitrogen, two oxygen, and 4 hydrogen atoms

Rules for AA backbone in <7653 4210> format	Number of rules	Number of atoms in (AA) backbone	Rules for AA Backbone in <7 6 5 4 3 2 1 0> format	Rule string for AA backbone in Decimal
<0111 0011> <0110 0011>	2	2C–N–2O–4H(9)	<0110 1011> <0110 0011>	<107 99>

design of two rules expressed in the 1-Major 0-Major format for 9 atoms (4 H atoms and 5 non-H atoms). The fourth column presents two rules in the <7 6 5 4 3 2 1 0> format; finally, column 5 shows the rule string with rules expressed in decimal value. Thus, the amino acid (except Proline) backbone is modelled with a string of two CA rules <107 99>. In view of 5 non-H atoms (2C, 2O, N) and 3 H atoms, for Proline (P), backbone is modelled with CA rules < 105 43 > derived out of 1-major 0-major format < 0111 0001 > and < 0011 0011 > with its normal counterpart as < 0110 1001 > < 0010 1011 > = < 105 43 >.

4.3.4 Design of CA Rule for Amino Acid Side Chain

The atomic structures of 20 amino acids are presented in Fig. 4.2. Following the design methodology presented in Sect. 4.3.1, rule strings for side chains of 20 amino acids are designed and reported in Table 4.4. The first column of the table presents the design of rule string expressed in 1-major 0-major <7653 4210> format with columns 2, 3, 4 respectively showing—number of rules, amino acid name, number of atoms (H and non-H) in the side chain. The rule string is shown in column 5 in the <<7 6 5 4><3 2 1 0>> format and the corresponding decimal value (0–255) in column 6. Design of CA rule string for a composite amino acid, covering backbone and side chain, continues in next subsection.

4.3.5 CA Rule String for Twenty Amino Acids (AAs) Backbone and Side Chain

The composite rule string for an amino acid (AA) with backbone and side chain rule concatenated is reported in column 7 of Table 4.4. For example, the composite Rule string <107 99><63 11 15> in column 7 is designed for the amino acid Ile (I) with 9 atoms for common backbone and 13 atoms for side chain shown in 8th row of the table proceeds as follows. First a string of two rules <107 99> is designed for backbone (Table 4.3). A string of 3 rules is next designed for 13 atoms of side chain with 9 H atoms and 4 non-H atoms. Intermediate columns 5 and 6 show the rules expressed in RMT format <<7 6 5 4><3 2 1 0>> and their decimal counterpart. In the rest of the paper, an amino acid is referred to as AA modeled with 3 to 5 cells configured with a string of 3 to 5 rules. The AAs of a protein chain are serially marked as 0, 1, 2, ... (on excluding met (M)) with the first AA after M as the 0th AA of a protein chain. (Note—‘start codon AUG’ of a protein chain encodes the amino acid M).

Based on the analysis of different amino acids reported in Table 4.4, we note an interesting Observation 4.1 reported next. The observation highlights the characteristics imparted by the CA model for 20 amino acids of a protein chain; the model divides 20 amino acids into three groups. Analysis of CA evolution patterns reported in Chap. 5 for a protein chain, utilizes the result of this observation.

Observation 4.1: Based on the analysis of the rule set for side chains, the amino Acids (reported in Table 4.4) can be divided into the following three groups, where decimal value of CA rule string for AA side chain are noted within symbol pairs < >, with an AA denoted with its single letter code.

Group 1: One Rule side chain for 5 AAs, each designed with single CA rule—each side chain having less than or equal to 6 atoms:
G (<1>), A (<15>), S (<47>), C (<143>), D (<235>).

Group 2: Two Rule side chain for 8 AAs, each designed with two CA rules—each side chain having 8 to 11 atoms:
E (< 11 235>), H (<111 107>), M (<63 47>), N (<11 107>), P (<11 63>), Q (<63 107>), T (<43 15>), V (<59 15>).

Group 3: Three Rule side chain for 7 AAs, each designed with three CA rules—each side chain having greater than or equal to 13 atoms:
L (<47 15 15>), I (<63 11 15>), K (<63 63 15>), R (<63 111 63>), F (<11 107 111>), Y (<11 111 235>), W (<111 239 111>).

While AAs with shorter side chain having less than or equal to 6 atoms, are designed with 1 CA rule (Group 1), the AAs with longer side chain, having greater than or equal to 13 atoms (Group 3), are designed with 3 CA rules. The AAs with medium length side chain having 8 to 11 atoms (Group 2) are designed with 2 CA rules. It is worth pointing out the fact that—there exists a gap of 2 (atoms) between largest number of atoms in a group and least number of atoms in its adjacent earlier group: ((8 − 6) = 2 between Group 1, Group 2, and (13 − 11) = 2 between Group 2, Group 3).

4.3.6 CA Rule Vector for a Protein Chain

Once the rule string design for amino acids is complete, we can model a protein chain with a 3NCA Rule Vector, designed as a string of CA rules (0–255) appended sequentially for each amino acid of the protein chain. Table 4.5 shows Envelope Protein amino acid string for covid virus—(a) CoV-2 (2019)—75 AA, (b) CoV (2003)—76 AA, and (c) Hemoglobin subunit beta HBB gene Protein with 147 AA

Table 4.4 CA rule string for AA residue (R) and Concatenated Composite Rule String (backbone and R) for twenty amino acids (Note—Column 3 of Table 4 shows single letter and three letter code for twenty amino acids)

Rules for AA side chain in <7653 4210> format	No. of rules	Amino acid (AA) name	No. of atoms	Rules for AA side chain in <7 6 5 4 3 2 1 0> format	Rule string for AA side chain in Decimal	Composite Rule String for Amino acid
<0000 0001>	1	Gly(G)	H(1)	<0000 0001>	<1>	<4107 99><1>
<0001 0111>	1	Ala(A)	CH_3(4)	<0000 1111>	<15>	<4107 99><15>
<0011 1111> <0001 0111>	2	Val(V)	C_3H_7(10)	<0011 1111><0000 1111>	<59 15>	<107 99> <59 15>
<0011 0111> <0001 0111> <0001 0111>	3	Leu(L)	C_4H_9(13)	<0010 1111> <0000 1111> <0000 1111>	<47 15 15>	<107 99> <47 15 15>
<0011 1111> <0011 0111>	2	Met(M)	SC_3H_7(11)	<0011 1111> <0011 0111>	<63 47>	<107 99> <463 47>
<0011 1111> <0001 0011> <0001 0111>	3	Ile(I)	C_4H_9(13)	<0011 1111> <40000 1011> <0000 1111>	<63 11 15>	<107 99> <463 11 15>
<0011 0111>	1	Ser(S)	COH_3(5)	<0010 1111>	<47>	<107 99><47>
<0011 0011> <0001 0111>	2	Thr(T)	C_2OH_5(8)	<0010 1011> <0000 1111>	<43 15>	<107 99> <43 15>
<1001 0111>	1	Cys(C)	SCH_3(5)	<1000 1111>	<143>	<107 99><143>
<0001 0011> <0011 1111>	2	Pro(P)	C_3H_6(9)	<0000 1011> <0011 1111>	<11 63>	<105 43> <11 63>
<0001 0011> <0111 0011>	2	Asn(N)	C_2NOH_4(8)	<0000 1011> <0110 1011>	<11 107>	<107 99> <11 107>
<0011 1111> <0111 0011>	2	Gln(Q)	C_3NOH_6(11)	<0011 1111> <0110 1011>	<63 107>	<107 99> <63 107>
<0011 1111> <0011 1111> <0001 0111>	3	Lys(K)	C_4NH_{11}(16)	<0011 1111> <0011 1111> <0000 1111>	<63 63 15>	<107 99> <63 63 15>
<0011 1111> <0111 0111> <0011 1111>	3	Arg(R)	$C_4N_3H_{11}$(18)	<0011 1111> <0110 1111> <0011 1111>	<63 111 63>	<107 99> <63 111 63>
<0111 0111> <0111 0011>	2	His(H)	$C_4N_2H_5$(11)	<0110 1111> <0110 1011>	<111 107>	<107 99> <111 107>
<1111 0011>	1	Asp(D)	$C_2O_2H_2$(6)	<1110 1011>	<235>	<107 99> <235>
<0001 0011> <1111 0011>	2	Glu(E)	$C_3O_2H_4$(9)	<0000 1011> <1110 1011>	<11 235>	<107 99> <11 235>
<0001 0011> <0111 0011> <40111 01114>	3	Phe(F)	C_7H_7(14)	<0000 1011> <0110 1111> <0110 1111>	<11 107 111>	<107 99> <11 107 111>
<0001 0011> <0111 0111> <1111 0011>	3	Tyr(Y)	C_7OH_7(15)	<0000 1011> <0110 1111> <1110 1011>	<411 111 235>	<107 99> <11 111 235>
<0111 0111> <1111 0011> <0111 0111>	3	Trp(W)	C_9NH_8(18)	<0110 1111> <41110 10114> <0110 1111>	<111 239 111>	<107 99> <111 239 111>

Table 4.5 Protein chain with single letter code for amino acids and partial rule vector for (first 6 amino acids excluding Met(M)) rule vector for—(a) Wild CoV-2 (2019)—75 AA, (b) Wild CoV (2003)—76 AA, and (c) Wild Hemoglobin subunit beta—147 AA (Note—single letter code for 20 AAs noted on column 3 of Table 4.4)

CoV-2 (2019)—75 AA	
AA Chain	mysfvseetgtlivnsvllflafvvfllvtlailtalrlcayccnivnvslvkpsfyvysrvknlnssrvpdllv
Partial rule vector	<107, 99, 11, 111, 235, 107, 99, 47, 107, 99, 11, 107, 111, 107, 99, 59, 15, 107, 99, 47, 107, 99, 11, 235, ··· >
CoV (2003)—76 AA	
AA Chain	mysfvseetgtlivnsvllflafvvfllvtlailtalrlcayccnivnvslvkptvyvysrvknlnssegvpdllv
Partial rule vector	<107, 99, 11, 111, 235, 107, 99, 47, 107, 99, 11, 107, 111, 107, 99, 59, 15, 107, 99, 47, 107, 99, 11, 235, ··· >
HBB Hemoglobin Protein—147 AA	
AA Chain	mvhltpeeksavtalwgkvnvdevggealgrllvvypwtqrffesfgdlstpdavmgnpkvkahgkkvlgaf sdglahldnlkgtfatlselhcdklhvdpenfrllgnvlvcvlahhfgkeftppvqaayqkvvagvanalahkyh
Partial rule vector	<107, 99, 59, 15, 107, 99, 111, 107, 107, 99, 47, 15, 15, 107, 99, 43, 15, 105, 43, 11, 63, 107, 99, 11, 235, ··· >

associated with the disease sickle cell anemia. The partial rule vectors for first 6 amino acids for three protein chains are illustrated in the table. The rule vector for an amino acid chain of a protein is designed on concatenating CA rule string for each amino acid.

On completion of rule vector design, a CA evolves at each time step through local interaction of each cell with its neighboring cells—left, self, right (Fig. 4.1). Parameters and Feature Vectors derived out of evolution of CA modeling a protein chain provides the foundation to address the problems of computational proteomics (a sub-discipline of computational biology) presented in Chap. 5.

4.4 CA Rule Vector Design for Any Language Text in Computational Linguistics

Cellular Automata (CA) Model to address the problems in the field of Computational Linguistics is reported in Chap. 6. An input language text is first converted to Unicode text, followed by design of CA rule vector modelling the text. Feature vectors, derived out of CA evolution, lays the foundation to derive solution for a given problem.

Unicode can be viewed as a universal character set. It defines a standard in one platform for all the characters needed for writing most of the living languages in use on computers. It is a superset of all other character sets that have been encoded so far, including ancient scripts like Gothic, Egyptian etc. In addition to character encoding, Unicode supports all the relevant information like character case, alphabetic properties including directionality, to ensure a legible text in any language. The unique initiative taken by Unicode consortium is currently supported by most of the Web architecture and operating systems. To sum it up, Unicode aims to support—generation of valid text encoding characters of any language in use around the globe.

4.4.1 Unicode Standard

As per the Unicode document [9], 'the Unicode Standard specifies a numeric value (code point/position) and a name for each of its characters' in the Unicode Table. The first column of the Unicode table shows the code point position in the format of hex characters and the column 2 specifies the corresponding decimal value derived from the code point position. While the name of the character is specified on column 3, the last column defines the semantic meaning of a character in respect of its identity and alphabetic properties. A concise report in respect the historical background and Unicode development is available in Wikipedia document [10]. Since early 1990 of the last century, Unicode consortium has been developing a standard coding system for all types of character set available in all the living languages. It seems, Unicode development took off with the encoding standard of ASCII character set (0–127) that gets reflected in the first 127 characters encoded in the range—-0 × (0000) to 0 × (007F)—-shown under the name Basic Latin Characters in the Unicode Chart.

4.4.2 Design of CA Rule Pair for Unicode Character

This section reports the design of CA rules for Unicode characters. A Unicode character is represented by the its code point position as noted on column 1 of Unicode Table [9]. While the current version (15.0.0) employs the format 0 × (v1 v2 v3 v4), the earlier versions show the format (v1 v2 v3 v4), where v1, v2, v3, v4 are hex characters.

The decimal value reported on column 2 can be derived for a character as follows: Decimal value = $256^1 \times (16v1 + v2) + 256^0 \times (16v3 + v4)$.

4.4.2.1 CA Rule String to Model a Unicode Character

The rule string for a Unicode character covers a pair of 3NCA rules. The CA rule string with a pair of 3NCA rules for a Unicode character can be expressed as = <r1 r2>, where r1 = (16v1 + v2) and r2 = (16v3 + v4).

The decimal value for the rule pair is derived as = (256r1 + r2). For v1 = v2 = 0, and v3 = 0 to 7, with v4 = 0 to F, the rule pair is: r1 = 0 with r2 = 0 to 127. Thus, for hex digits as v1 = v2 = 0, v3 = 0 to 7, v4 = 0 to F, the Unicode character set is identical to that of 7-bit ASCII code with decimal value 0 to 127, corresponding to hex character range 0000 to 007F.

The CA rule design ensures that, the decimal value derived both for Unicode character and 3NCA rule pair are identical. A few illustrations follow with Unicode character expressed in the format 0 × (v1 v2 v3 v4).

1. **Unicode character 0 × (1023)** = decimal value = $256^1 \times (10 \times 1 + 0) + 256^0 \times (16 \times 2 + 3) = 4131$. The CA rule string for the code = <16 35> with its decimal value = $256 \times 16 + 35 = 4131$.
2. **Cyrillic capital letter O** = 0 × (1054) = decimal value = $256^1 \times (16 \text{x} 1 + 0) + 256^0 \times (5 \times 16 + 4) = 4180$ The CA rule string for the code = <16 84> with its decimal vaue = $256 \times 16 + 84 = 4180$.
3. **Greek small letter NU** = 0 × (03B1) = decimal value = $256^1 = (16 \times 0 + 3) + 256^0 \times (11 \times 16 + 1) = 945$. The CA rule string pair for the code = < 3 177 > with its decimal value = $256 \times 32 + 172 = 945$.
4. **Euro sign €** = 0 × (20AC) = decimal valu = $256^1 \times (16 \times 2 + 0) + 256^0 \times (16 \times 10 + 12) = 8364$. The CA rule string pair for code = <32 172> with its decimal value = $256 \times 32 + 172 = 8364$.
5. **Bengali character** ক = 0 × (0995) = decimal value = $256^1 \times (16 \times 0 + 9) + 256^0 \times (16 \times 9 + 5) = 2453$. The CA rule string for the code = <9 149> with its decimal value = $256 \times 9 + 149 = 2453$.
6. **Character @** = 0 × (FF20) = its decimal value = $256^1 (16 \times 15 + 15) + 256^0 (16 \times 2 + 0) = 256 \times 255 + 32 = 65312$. The CA rule string for the code = <255 32>> with its decimal value = $256 \times 255 + 32 = 65312$.

4.4.3 Converting a Language Text to Unicode Text

A language text is converted to Unicode text employing Unicode character set or Unicode converters available for different languages in websites. Next, we derive CA Rule Vector for Unicode text by employing CA rule pair designed for Unicode character set illustrated in Sect. 4.4.2.1 for 6 Unicode characters. We note below instances of language text in 3 different languages in the format: (Language text, the converted Unicode text, followed by derivation of the CA Rule vector for the Unicode text).

Case 1: (English Language Text—Unicode Text—from https://www.englishtools.org)

English Text: we have taken a number of steps to empower and invest in our employees

Unicode Text employing—https://www.englishtools.org/en/convert-english-to-unicode-and-

\u0057 \u0065 \u0020 \u0068 \u0061 \u0076 \u0065 \u0020 \u0074 \u0061 \u006b \u0065 \u006e \u0020 \u0061 \u0020 \u006e \u0075 \u006d \u0062 \u0065 \u0072 \u0020 \u006f \u0066 \u0020 \u0073 \u0074 \u0065 \u0070 \u0073 \u0020 \u0074

\u006f \u0020 \u0065 \u006d \u0070 \u006f \u0077 \u0065 \u0072 \u0020 \u0061 \u006e \u0064 \u0020 \u0069 \u006e \u0076 \u0065 \u0073 \u0074 \u0020 \u0069 \u006e \u0020 \u006f \u0075 \u0072 \u0020 \u0065 \u006d \u0070 \u006c \u006f \u0079 \u0065 \u0065 \u0073 \u0020

CA Rule Vector for the Unicode Text:

<<0 87><0 101><0 32><0 104><0 96><0 118><0 32><0 116><0 97><0 107><0 32><0 97><0 32><0 110><0 117><0 109><0 98><0 101><0 114><0 32><0 111><0 112><0 102><0 32><0 115><0 116><0 101><0 112><0 115><0 32><0 116><0 111><0 32><0 102><0 32><0 115><0 116><0 101><0 112><0 115><0 32><0 116><0 111><0 32><0 102><0 32><0 115><0 116><0 101><0 112><0 115><0 32><0 116><0 111><0 32><0 102><0 32><0 115><0 116><0 101><0 112><0 115><0 32><0 116><0 111><0 32><0 101><0 109><0 112><0 111><0 119><0 101><0 114><0 32><0 97><0 110><0 100><0 32><0 105><0 110><0 118><0 101><0 115><0 116><0 32><0 105><0 110><0 32><0 111><0 117><0 114><0 32><0 101><0 109><0 112><0 108><0 111><0 121><0 101><0 101><0 115><0 32>>

Case 2: (German Language Text—Unicode Text—CA Rule Vector for the Unicode Text)

German Text: Das wurde auch in der Hauptpflgestelle so gemacht

Unicode Text employing—https://germantools.org>convert-german-text-int

\u0044 \u0061 \u0073 \u0020 \u0077 \u0075 \u0072 \u0064 \u0065 \u0020 \u0061 \u0075 \u0063 \u0068 \u0020 \u0069 \u006e \u0020 \u0064 \u0065 \u0072 \u0020 \u0048 \u0061 \u0075 \u0070 \u0074 \u0070 \u0066 \u006c \u0065 \u0067 \u0065 \u0073 \u0074 \u0065 \u006c \u006c \u0065 \u0020 \u0073 \u006f \u0020 \u0067 \u0065 \u006d \u0061 \u0063 \u0068 \u0074 \u002e

Case 3: (Bangali Language Text—Unicode Text—CA Rule Vector for the Unicode Text)

Bangali Text: আমরা ভাল। তোমরা কেমন আছ।

Unicode Text from—Unicode Block "Bengali"—https://www.compart.com/en/unicode/block/U+0980 (it shows Unicode code for Bengali characters)

\u0986 \u09AE \u09F1 \u09BE \u0020 \u09AD \u09BE \u09B2 \u0020 \u09F7 \u09A4 \u09CB \u09AE \u09B0 \u09BE \u0020 \u0995 \u09C7 \u09AE \u09A8 \u0020 \u0986 \u099B \u0020 \u09F7

CA Rule Vector:

<<9 134><9 174><9 240><9 190><0 32><9 174><9 190><9 178><0 32>
<9 247><9 164>< 203><9 190><9 241><9 190><0 32><9 149><9 199>
<9 174><9 168><0 32><9 134><9 155><0 32><9 247>>

Design Step to Reduce 3NCA Rule Vector Length

As illustrated earlier, CAML model employs a string of two CA rules to represent a Unicode character represented with four hex digits in the format 0 × (v1 v2 v3 v4). In order to reduce the length of CA Rule Vector, we delete CA rule '0' if it exists as the leading rule in the pair. This step is implemented for all our experiments on Computational Linguistics.

Further, for extended Unicode character set expressed with six hex digits in the format 0 × (v1 v2 v3 v4 v5 v6), CAML model employs rule string with three CA rules <r1 r2 r3> for each character. The corresponding decimal value of a rule string is derived as follows: $256^2(16 \times v1 + v2) + 256^1\ (16 \times v3 + v4) + 256^0\ (16 \times v5 + v6)$. For such cases also, the leading '0' rule(s) of the rule string of a Unicode character are deleted.

Once the CA rule vector is designed for a language text expressed with the Unicode character set, the 3NCA modeling the text evolves through interaction of each cell with its neighboring cells. The Feature Vector (FV), derived out of CA evolution, provides the foundation to address the problems of Computational Linguistics in a multi-language environment. Rest of this chapter further elaborates the CA model building steps for twin applications handled in this book.

Designing CA Model for a Physical System—A Key Issue

Development of a model for a physical system demands a close scrutiny in respect of deviation of system characteristics from that of the modeling tool employed. Model developers need to evolve methodologies to mitigate the effect of such deviations. Next section reports the strategies we have adopted to address this challenge.

4.5 ML Framework to Model Physical Systems with CA

Two physical systems modeled with CA are—(i) amino acid chain of a protein, and (ii) Unicode text of a language. Both are linear chains of its constituents with its left and right ends defining a pair of constituent elements. For example, the Unicode text of a language defines a pair of specific alphabets on the end terminals of the text with no correlation between them. On the other hand, the free ends of a protein chain on its left and right terminals, by convention, are referred to as NTD (N Terminal Domain with Nitrogen (N) atom) and CTD (C Terminal Domain with Carbon (C) atom); these two ends are chemically different from one another with no correlation. We have employed periodic boundary 3NCA with non-linear CA rules to model the two physical systems under the assumption that the two terminal ends are neighbors of each other. This gap between CA model and physical systems in respect of two terminal ends, is bridged by employing Machine Learning (ML) framework discussed next.

CA, designed to model a physical system, evolves generating a signal graph. The parameters and Feature Vector, derived out of signal graph of CA evolution, are mapped on to the characteristics extracted from the training set data corpus available in the ML framework for the application domain. This mapping function provides the foundation for design of the prediction algorithm for an application. Availability of training data corpus in the application domain is a prerequisite for CA model development. The underlying reason for this dependence on the training set data corpus of the ML framework stems from the fact that any fruitful characterization of Non-Linear CA (Defined in Sect. 4.2) evolution is an extremely difficult task, if not impossible. Further, the alternative approach of employing null boundary CA, instead of periodic boundary, is not a viable proposition. Because it has been observed that—transfer of the effect of evolution from left to right end of the null boundary CA fails on many occasions. Consequently, we fall back on the ML framework for design and application of CAML model.

Next section elaborates the fact that CA rule design for an application proceeds through an iterative process involving two phases:

Phase 1—Bottom-up design of 3NCA (3 Neighborhood CA) rule for the smallest component of the system being modeled.
Phase 2—Top-down design of Machine Learning (ML) framework for consistent mapping of system characteristics to the Feature Vector (FV) derived out of CA evolution modeling the system.

4.6 Iterative Procedure of CA Rule Design for an Application

The universal appeal of Cellular Automata stems from the fact that its evolution has the capability to model the characteristics of a large variety of physical systems. This capability can be harnessed on implementing the following iterative procedure for an application. It has been assumed that training/testing data corpus is available for the application domain along with the tested/validated output. Further, simplest CA structure with periodic boundary, three neighborhood, two states per cell CA is employed to design the model for an application. The most challenging task is the CA rule design specified in Step 1 undertaken in Phase 1 (bottom-up design of CA rule). Phase 2 is implemented in Step 4.

Input: (1) A system is assumed to be represented by an interconnected set of entities; and (2) the number of iteration cycles to be attempted for design of CA model for an application.

Output: Success/Failure to achieve the desired goal specified as: Design of CA rule vector modeling the system ensures consistent mapping of model parameters/feature vector (extracted from CA evolution) to the physical domain characteristics of the system output reported in the training data corpus.

Step 1: CA Rule design for the smallest entity of the system is modeled such that the design captures the relevant physical parameters of the smallest entity. In the process, the smallest physical entity gets modeled with a set of CA cells, with 3NCA rule specified for each cell.

Step 2: On completion of Step 1, the CA rule vector modeling the system is derived on concatenating CA rules for the cells.

Step 3: Evolution of the CA proceeds as per the rule vector modeling the system. The Parameters and Feature Vector (FV) relevant for the system are extracted out of CA evolution.

Step 4: This step demands consistent mapping of CA Feature Vector (CAFV) to the physical domain characteristics of the validated results of the training/testing set corpus.

Step 5: If the consistent mapping of CAFV to the physical domain characteristics is not realized, go back to Step 1 to refine/redesign the CA rule for the smallest system entity.

Step 6: Stop on specifying 'Success/Failure' to achieve the desired goal of the design within specified iteration cycles noted in Input (2).

The iterative process of Step 1 to Step 5 continues till we arrive at the desired goal of consistent mapping of CA Feature vector to the physical domain characteristics of a system. The CA rule design has proceeded through this iterative process presented in Chaps. 5 and 6. For the sake of illustration of the iterative design process, we briefly highlight one application handled in Chap. 5 in respect of mutational analysis of protein chains. In-vivo/in-vitro/in-silico mutational study of protein chains is a well-studied area with mutations reported for different classes of proteins—virus, cancer etc. The available mutational data is divided into training, validation, and testing data sets. Feature vector derived out of evolution of CA modeling a protein chain is mapped to the occurrence of mutation observed in the proteins of the training data set. Next, mutations predicted out of the CA model are validated against the known results of the validation data set, while introducing refinement, if necessary, for specific protein classes. Finally, prediction quality is ascertained on blind tests on testing data sets. On implementing this process, the CA model predicts Potential Mutational Hot Spot (PMHS) for a protein which may appear in future. Chapter 5 reports the design of an algorithm for prediction of PMHS in a protein chain.

4.7 Cellular Automata (Enhanced With) Machine Learning (CAML) Model

The title of this book is—"The new kind of Machine Learning—Cellular Automata Model". Three motivations that encouraged us to write this book employing both CA (Cellular Automata) and ML (Machine Learning) are as follows.

Motivation 1 (derived out of CA model): Since the middle of last century while J von Neumann first proposed Cellular Automata as a mathematical tool to model physical systems; a large volume of research papers and books are reported by authors of different disciplines. Even though CA has enormous potential to build new classes of models, we hardly find any fruitful industrial/commercial application of CA. Consequently, the main focus of the current book is to lay the foundation that would lead to the development of CA applications of interest for industry and human society.

Motivation 2 (derived out of ML framework): Further, in the context of phenomenal growth of computing power and storage facilities, solutions to problems not addressed in the past are being attempted at present. This is specifically true to solve the problems with the Machine Learning (ML) framework which is employed in this book to characterize non-linear CA evolution. Characterization of non-linear CA evolution for any fruitful application is an extremely difficult task, if not impossible. Hence, we fall back on Machine Learning (ML) framework to characterize and learn the evolution pattern of a non-linear CA modeling a physical system.

Motivation 3 (derived out of the analysis of traditional ML models): CAML model needs significantly reduced computing resources and training data corpus, while achieving acceptable level of prediction quality, as demonstrated in Chaps. 5 and 6. Further, it adequately addresses the security and privacy issue (highlighted in Chap. 2), since CA model operates on input data transformed with CA model. Lastly, it is worthwhile to point out another important issue in respect of CA design. The model employs simple three neighborhood CA with regular, modular, cascadable structure. As a result, hardwired implementation of CAML model will be significantly lesser compared to the currently available models, specifically LLM (Large Language Model).

The emphasis of the book is to develop applications of Cellular Automata model employing Machine Learning (ML) framework and so it is named as Cellular Automata (enhanced with Machine Learning) (CAML) model. The next subsection elaborates two viewpoints of this model.

4.7.1 Light Weight Cellular Automata (Enhanced with) Machine Learning (CAML) Model

The model encompasses the following two viewpoints-

Viewpoint 1: CA enhanced with ML—Characterization of Non-linear CA evolution is a challenging task. Consequently, non-linear CA evolution is characterized by employing Training set data corpus of Machine Learning framework in this viewpoint. Chapters 5 and 6 of this book implement this viewpoint.

Viewpoint 2: CA enhanced ML—This viewpoint reports linear CA evolution modeling Machine Learning applications realizing linear/nonlinear functions. The sole objective is to lay a mathematical foundation for the ML framework enabling 'transparency' in prediction. This viewpoint is implemented in Chap. 7 of this book to realize linear function. Extension of this model employing programmable CA (PCA) [7] has been also projected to realize non-linear functions. Further, CA based implementation will enable design of efficient hardwired implementation of ML framework with locally interconnected modular and cascade-able structure of CA.

Traditional ML models including Deep Learning, employ training data sets to design the algorithms to perform a specific task without any human intervention, followed by prediction of results on testing data sets. In-built learning capability along with explain-ability of prediction results are the desired features of modern ML models.

4.7.2 CAML Model and Traditional ML Framework

The following seven characteristics (marked as C1 to C7) differentiate CAML model from the traditional ML framework:

C1: The input Training data set for CAML model is transformed with CA modeling the physical system and the CAML operates on the transformed data rather than raw input data.
C2: The fully automated prediction algorithms are designed employing Feature Vector (FV) extracted from the parameters derived from evolution of CA modeling a physical system.
C3: Input data set is divided into Training Set (TrS), Validation Set (VaS), and Testing Set (TeS).
C4: The (VaS) is introduced in the CAML model to assess the quality of prediction algorithm designed employing (TrS).
C5: Explain-ability and capability to learn from experience are embedded in CAML framework through program execution on validation Set (VaS) and if necessary, through refinement of the prediction algorithm to enhance prediction quality.

C6: Compared to conventional ML framework, CAML model needs significantly lesser input training corpus data and computational resources registering acceptable prediction quality for specific tasks, as demonstrated in two CAML model applications presented in next two chapters.
C7: Further, the issue of 'Security and Privacy', a major source of concern for current ML models (elaborated in Sect. 2.6 of Chap. 2), gets addressed in CAML model, in view of its execution on CA-transformed data (as noted under point number (1) noted above).

To summarize, the concerns of currently available ML models—'blackbox' approach lacking interpretability of results, extremely large training data corpus, huge computing resources, lack of adequate security and privacy—are addressed in the CAML model.

In view of the above properties, the CAML model is referred to as a 'Light Weight' machine learning model. The CAML characteristics noted above are highlighted in the applications reported in subsequent chapters.

The name CAML model is used in subsequent chapters of the book. Chapters 5 and 6 employ the viewpoint 1—Cellular Automata (enhanced with) Machine Learning, while Chap. 7 deals with the viewpoint 2—Cellular Automata (enhances) Machine Learning, as defined in Sect. 4.7.1.

4.8 Conclusion

This chapter lays the foundation for next two chapters (Chaps. 5 and 6) which present the CAML (Cellular Automata (enhanced with) ML) model applications in the fields of Computational Biology and Computational Linguistics. Subsequent to a brief introduction on CA, the CA rule design for Amino Acids (AAs) and Unicode characters are presented. The generic framework for CA rule design for an application is also reported. The chapter ends with a comparison of Light Weight CAML model with traditional ML frameworks. This comparative study points to the inherent benefits of the model for addressing the concerns of currently available ML models.

References

1. J. Von Neumann, A.W. Burks, *Theory of Self-reproducing Automata* (University of Illinois Press Urbana, 1996)
2. S. Wolfram, Statistical mechanics of cellular automata. Rev. Modern Phys. **55**(3), 601–644 (1983)
3. E.F. Codd, *Cellular Automata* (Academic Press Inc., New York, 1968)
4. J. Conway, *The Game of Life* (Scientific American, 1970)
5. S. Wolfram, *A New Kind of Science* (Wolfram-Media Inc., Champaign, Ilinois, United States, 2002)

6. P.P. Chaudhuri, S. Ghosh, A. Dutta, S.P. Choudhury, *A New Kind of Computational Biology: Cellular Automata Based Models for Genomics and Proteomics* (Springer Nature Singapore, 2018). ISBN 978-981-1-13-163
7. P. Pal Chaudhuri, D. Roy Chowdhury, S. Nandi, S. Chattopadhyay, *Additive Cellular Automata—Theory and Applications*, vol. 1 (IEEE Computer Society Press, Los Alamitos, USA, 1997). ISBN 0-8186-7717-1
8. M. Ridley, *The Evolution of Everything: How Small Changes Transform Our World* (Harper Collins UK, 2015). ISBN 978-0-00-754247-5
9. Unicode 15.0.0. [Online]. Available: https://www.unicode.org/versions/Unicode15.0.0/
10. Wikipedia. [Online]. Available: https://en.wikipedia.org/wiki/Unicode

Chapter 5
CAML Model for Computational Biology

> *"Mutations are the starting point for all evolution, but they also cause many diseases. It's a double-edged sword"*
>
> *—Francis S. Collins*

5.1 Introduction

Motivation for writing this book came from the strong desire of the authors to explore the potential of building a Cellular Automata (CA) model that can be employed to address the problems of interest for industry and human society. The outline of the design of Cellular Automata enhanced with Machine Learning (CAML) model for two application domains is presented in Chap. 4. The current chapter reports CAML model application in the field of Computational Biology.

The field of Computer Science emerged as an independent discipline by the late 1960s. Around the same period, significant growth of storage capacity and computing power was observed with the introduction of LSI/VLSI (Very Large-Scale Integration) technology. Maturity of computer science discipline and growth of computing power continued at an accelerated pace in subsequent decades. Phenomenal growth of computing technology, both in hardware and software, provided excellent support for advancement of research and development in different fields. Solutions of problems which could not be addressed in the past are being attempted at present. This is specifically true for the solution of problems employing Machine Learning (ML) framework processing voluminous and complex data corpus referred to as 'big data'. Researchers of many disciplines came forward to employ computational methods to address the problems of their discipline, particularly in the context of exponential growth of experimental data in respective fields. By the end of 1990s this trend got

© The Author(s), under exclusive license to Springer Nature Singapore Pte Ltd. 2025

P. Pal Chaudhuri et al., *New Kind of Machine Learning—Cellular Automata Model*,
https://doi.org/10.1007/978-981-96-1501-8_5

firmly rooted in the field of Biology, specifically with the initiation of the Human Genome Project.

In the background of this historical development, Computational Biology has become an integral sub-discipline of Biology. It is an interdisciplinary field covering computer science, biology, mathematics, physics, and chemistry. It encompasses study of all the associated areas like genomics, proteomics, bioinformatics, biological systems and processes, including the holistic approach of system biology. Genetic mutation plays an important role in evolution; mutation in coding DNA gets reflected in protein mutation. In view of increasing interest in the study of Life Sciences, the interdisciplinary discipline of Computational Biology has grown in different directions in the last few decades. One major developmental effort of Computational Biology has been directed towards study of proteins which are the workhorses of all living organisms. In-vitro/in-vivo experimental setup to study proteins in living cells is a highly time consuming and costly process. Research in this field got a major boost with the availability of computational models to reduce the cost and time of laboratory experiments to study biological processes associated with protein function and its interaction with other biomolecules.

The focus of the current chapter is Computational Proteomics. Proteins are the most important molecules in a living cell, essential for its survival and growth. A large number of researchers focussed on protein mutational analysis from different perspectives—protein structure, function, interaction with other biomolecules. Recent emphasis has shifted to identify disease causing protein mutations. A brief overview of the topics covered in this chapter is provided in the following three subsections of Sect. 5.1.

5.1.1 Protein Mutational Study

The 'central dogma' of molecular biology specifies the flow of information from DNA (Deoxyribonucleic Acid) to RNA (Ribonucleic Acid), and from RNA to Proteins. The double helix structure of a DNA molecule is formed out of two complementary strands of nucleotide base pairs of Guanine - Cytosine (G - C) and Adenine - Thymine (A - T) held together by hydrogen bonds. Genes, the basic functional unit of heredity, are made up of DNA. Cell division is the biological process through which a living cell generates two daughter cells. A cell duplicates its DNA through the process called DNA replication during cell division so that the daughter cells inherit the same genetic information. There are two types of DNA—coding and non-coding. Proteins are synthesized out of coding DNA through the transcription and translation of codon (triplet of nucleotide bases A, T, C, G) to amino acid. Non-coding DNA controls expression of gene/protein.

Mutation in coding DNA due to changes in its nucleotide sequence, gets carried forward to protein mutation leading to change in the amino acid sequence of a protein chain. The major sources of DNA mutation are—the errors during DNA replication process or due to environmental factors known as mutagens such as radiation, chemicals and infectious agents. Notwithstanding the DNA repair mechanism in place in a cell, accumulation of DNA damage has been observed, specifically with aging. Consequently, mutation in a protein chain is a source of concern. A protein chain without any mutation is referred to as wild type chain that can be observed in nature—that is, in the natural population of an organism.

By convention, the unique part of an amino acid is referred to as a residue, on exclusion of identical backbone common for all amino acids. However, in this book we consider an amino acid as an integrated biomolecule covering the backbone connected to its side chain. The CA rules designed for amino acids reported in Table 4.4 of Chap. 4, are based on the analysis of the atomic structure of both backbone and its side chain. Consequently, throughout this book we shall use the term Amino Acid (AA) rather than the term 'residue' conventionally used. A protein is a chain of interconnected amino acids. Twenty common amino acid molecules exist in nature. Mutation in a protein chain can be referred to as xLx', where original amino acid x at chain location L gets replaced with another amino acid x' different from that of x. Evaluation of the effect of mutation at location L highlights the importance of the amino acid x at location L. Analysis of the effect of protein mutation is crucial for many applications such as protein evolution, evaluation of its structure, function, and interaction with other biomolecules. Some of the protein mutations can be observed to be associated with a disease; these are referred to as disease-causing mutations. In view of its importance, a large volume of research publications on mutational study of important proteins are available in the public domain.

Observation 5.1: During our mutational study of a large number of protein chains, including cancer proteins, it has been observed that compared to other 19 amino acids, the Arginine amino acid (Arg - R) displays the largest number of mutations. In other words, R displayed the highest mutability. The following issues point to a probable cause for this observation.

(i) Polymorphism—There are three amino acids Arg (R), Leu (L), Serine (S), each synthesized out of 6 codons.
(ii) Largest number of atoms in side chain—The side chains of two amino acids Arg (R) and Trp (W) show largest number of atoms—18 atoms. Next amino acid having a number of atoms close to 18 is amino acid Tyrosine (Tyr - Y) has 15 atoms on its side chain.
(iii) Side chain structure—While Trp (W) has a nonpolar aromatic ring, Arg (R) has a positively charged aliphatic chain.

As per the earlier discussions, DNA mutations get carried forward to RNA and next gets mapped to protein mutations. Three issues ((i), (ii), (iii)) listed earlier, point to the possible reasons of highest mutability of Arg (R), reported as the Observation 5.1 and hypothesised as follows.

Hypothesis 5.1: Based on our exhaustive mutational study and the issues listed under Observation 5.1, we hypothesize that—amino acid Arg (R) is likely to have highest mutability.

With respect to amino acid functions, Arg is involved in cell division, one of the crucial steps in cellular process; the malfunction of this process leads to cancer. Probably, that is why highest mutability has been specifically observed for Arg in many proteins implicated for cancer. For example, Database of Curated Mutation (DoCM) [1] reports a total of 212 mutants for p53 protein (with 393 amino acids) encoded by TP53 gene; it is implicated for most of the cancer types. Out of 212 mutants, the highest number of mutations related to Arg is 34 (16.0% = 34/212), while the number of mutations reported for Gly is 14 (6.6% = 14/212).

5.1.2 Design of Light Weight CAML Model for Mutational Analysis of a Protein Chain

The CAML model employs both Cellualr Automata (CA) and Machine Learning (ML). The model is designed in two phases:

Phase 1—Bottom-up design of CA rule based on the atomic structure of common backbone and side chains of twenty common amino acids of a protein. Execution of Phase 1 is reported in Chap. 4.

Phase 2—Top-down design of Machine Learning (ML) framework for mutational study of proteins undertaken in this chapter based on the analysis of data corpus retrieved from in-vivo/in-vitro experimental results available in databases.

On replacing each AA with the 3NCA rule string (reported in Table 4.4 of Chap. 4), we derive the CA rule vector modelling a protein chain. Four generic steps for design of CAML model for protein mutational analysis of Phase 2 follows:

Step 1: Evolution of a CA, modelling a protein chain, generates a graph referred to as Cycle Length (CL) signal graph. CA evolution continues till each CA cell reaches a cycle (also referred to as 'attractor'), where the cell cycles through a set of binary states with 0 and 1 value; the length of the cycle is referred to as CL (Cycle Length). CL signal graph shows the CL value of each CA cell on Y-axis with its X-axis displaying CA cell position $(0, 1, 2, \ldots n-1)$, where n denotes number of cells in the 3NCA modelling the amino acid chain of a protein. Figure 5.1 shown in Sect. 5.2.2 shows the CL signal graph for a protein chain.

Step 2: CL signal graph analytics to derive the parameters relevant for protein mutational analysis.

Step 3: Extraction of Feature Vector (FV) from CAML model parameters for mutational analysis of protein chains.

Step 4: Design of algorithm for consistent mapping of CAML Feature Vector to the physical domain characteristics, relevant for protein mutational study. We have assumed that these characteristics are available in-vivo and/or in-vitro experimental results reported in published literature.

Phase 1 and the four steps of Phase 2 of CAML model design are employed for study of different classes proteins (viral, p53 protein implicated for different types of cancer, and wide varieties of plant proteins) in the remaining sections of Chap. 5.

Notwithstanding some repetition of textual materials for execution of Phase 1 and Phase 2, readers will come across the wide varieties of CA signal graphs out of evolution of CA modelling different classes of proteins analyzed in this book.

It is worth mentioning the point that conventional Machine Learning (ML) models demand a high volume of training set data corpus and huge computing resources. By contrast, CAML model-based prediction algorithms can achieve the goal with significantly reduced training data set and computing resources. Different sections of this chapter validate this claim. The light weight Cellular Automata (enhanced with) Machine Learning (CAML) model can be employed for mutational study of any class of proteins.

5.1.3 *Covid Virus Proteins SARS and MERS*

Human society has faced pandemics in the past due to diseases like the plague, Spanish flu, and HIV. High death tolls, psychological stress, and financial burdens are often associated with such situations, as observed during the COVID-19 pandemic from 2020 to 2022, caused by the SARS-CoV-2 virus. On the other side of the coin, scientific discoveries from intensive research on various aspects of bacteria and viruses have led to the development of drugs and vaccines to combat pandemic situations. The recent development of the COVID-19 vaccine is a notable example. In this context, this introductory section provides a brief overview of the COVID-19 virus.

Seven different virus types, all with crown-like structure associated with coronavirus disease (covid), were identified since 1965 causing common colds in humans. Outbreak of the disease in 2003 in China, followed by the one in the Middle East in 2012, brought the focus on the virus causing severe acute respiratory syndrome and so named as SARS Covid, and MERS Covid. The numbers for the 2003 SARS-CoV outbreak are: 8,000 infections, 774 deaths, across 29 countries. For the 2012 MERS-CoV outbreak, there were 2,500 infections, 876 deaths, across 27 countries. However, the novel virus SARS covid (CoV-2) identified in 2019 has resulted in the pandemic situation in 213 countries. It infected nearly 220 million persons with a death count of more than 4.6 million. High-speed train and air travel have increased significantly in recent decades, facilitating greater global interaction among populations. However, this alone does not explain the dramatic rise in infected individuals—from a few thousand in earlier CoV outbreaks to 220 million with SARS-CoV-2 as of September 2021. The pandemic situation of 2020–2022 motivated us to undertake a thorough analysis of CoV-2 virus protein characteristics with CAML model, while comparing CoV-2 with its predecessors—CoV and MERS. Furthermore, given the ongoing environmental degradation and rapid urbanization, many experts in this field have predicted the potential emergence of future zoonotic viruses that could lead to the next pandemic. Transmission of infection from animal to human being characterizes a typical zoonotic virus. We expect the generic CAML model will provide some guidelines for quick invention of refurbished vaccines for new generations of viruses which may appear in future.

Twin objectives of a living organism are—to survive and replicate. Virus, a cellular parasite, fulfils these objectives by infecting cells of a living organism for its replication and transmission. In order to achieve this goal, a virus typically encodes proteins similar to those of host proteins and/or develop strategy to avail the services of the host cell. Intimate relationship of virus with host and different aspects of viral symbiosis are reported in [2]. A recent survey on human microbiome and CoV-2 relationship is reported in [3]. In the context of the pandemic situation due to SARS CoV-2, it is necessary to decipher structure and function of its four structural proteins (Spike S, Nucleocapsid N, Membrane M, and Envelope E), 16 non-structural proteins (nsps), and 9 accessory proteins (ORFs).

Next three subsections of Chap. 5 report the results derived for three viral proteins of Covid SARS and MERS virus—Envelope protein, non-structural proteins (nsps), and most important CoV-2 spike protein. Analysis of smallest size structural protein (75 and 76 amino acids respectively for CoV-2 and CoV Envelope proteins) will enable readers to comprehend the ease of analysis of protein characteristics with CAML model. Study of nsps with CAML model highlights the interaction of viral proteins with other biomolecules for synthesis of viral proteins within the infected cell; it achieves this goal by hijacking the protein synthesis mechanism of the infected host cell. Viral spike protein facilitates virus entry in the host cell. Evolution of different variants of CoV-2 (Omicron lineage) even in late 2022 was a major concern. In this context we undertake a thorough analysis of CoV-2 spike protein mutational landscape in Sect. 5.4.

Over time, with the spread of viral infection and vaccination of population, the pandemic situation due to a virus subsides, as it happened for CoV-2 by the end of 2022. The major objective of Sects. 5.2, 5.3 and 5.4 is to lay the foundation of the CAML model for viral protein analysis with the focus on protein mutational analysis. Any other protein class can be analogously analysed with the CAML model. While the basic framework has been laid down, identification of CAML model parameters and extraction of Feature Vector (FV) may undergo minor modifications for different protein classes of a new zoonotic virus.

We close the introductory Sect. 5.1 on presenting the organization of the chapter coverage.

5.1.4 Chapter Organization

In view of the 2020–2022 pandemic, we focused on analyzing COVID-19 virus proteins over the past few years. The results are presented in the first three sections of Chap. 5.

- Section 5.2—This section covers the smallest size structural protein referred to as envelope protein.
- Section 5.3—This section covers the non-structural protein (nsp1) detected in coronavirus.
- Section 5.4—Mutational analysis of covid Spike Protein is analysed in this section.

The reason of significantly higher transmissibility of SARS Covid (2019 CoV-2) compared to SARS Covid (2003 CoV) and MERS Covid (2012 MERS) can be attributed to mutations reported in structural proteins, and the role played by non-structural proteins (nsps) and accessory proteins (ORFs) for viral replication, assembly, and shedding. Envelope protein E is one of the four structural proteins of minimum length. Studies on Envelope protein have confirmed critical role played by the protein in the viral life cycle including assembly of virion exported from infected cell for its transmission. However, the determinants of the highly complex viral—host interactions of envelope protein, particularly with host Golgi complex, have not been adequately characterized. Further, the non-structural protein nsp1, referred to as leader protein, hijack the protein synthesis machinery of host cell for synthesis for viral proteins. Finally, all important spike protein plays a key role for entry of virus through interaction with host cell receptor protein.

Beyond the study of covid, the study of viral proteins using the CAML model adds a new direction in the field of virology for the functional classification of biological viruses.

The remaining two Sects. 5.5 and 5.6 focus on the mutational study of proteins associated with the deadly disease cancer. The rate of increase of wide varieties of cancer types, specifically in the aged population, continues to be a major source of concern around the globe. Over the earlier decades, significant improvements can be noticed in cancer treatment. However, there are many unanswered questions with respect to the Probable onset of Cancer (PoC).

- The Sect. 5.5 focuses on the characterization of the p53 protein, which is encoded by the TP53 gene and is implicated in many types of cancer, both directly and indirectly. Since its identification in 1979, research on cancer has advanced significantly. Sect. 5.5.8 of this section presents an outline of the design of Protein Biomarkers (PB) using the CAML model.

Notwithstanding the phenomenal improvement in cancer chemotherapy, search for alternative avenues continues for design of new therapeutic agents to fight cancer. Some of the medicinal plants contain antioxidant, immune-modulatory, and anticancer properties. A few anticancer drugs, such as Paclitexal (Taxol) Taxane, Taxus brevifolia, Vinblastine etc. are derived from extracts of medicinal plants.

- Sect. 5.6—This section reports a machine learning (ML) model that mimics the biochemical pathways for generation of plant-derived anticancer agents, toxic to cancer cell lines. The model employs the CAML framework for analysis of proteins retrieved from medicinal plants listed in UniProtKB [4] and/or NCBI [5]. The focus of this section is to design the CAML model to predict medicinal plants having anticancer property. Prediction is based on the curated knowledge of plant-derived bioactive anti-cancer compounds identified through in-vitro and/or in-vivo experimental study. The results presented in this section will enable the researchers to enlarge the available list of anti-cancer medicinal plants through molecular level study of extracts against cancer cell line.

5.2 Analysis of Coronavirus Envelope Protein with CAML Model

CoV-2 and CoV Envelope proteins of length 75 and 76 amino acids differ in four amino acid locations. Table 5.1 reports the amino acid sequence of CoV-2 (2019) and CoV (2003) with single letter code. The additional amino acid Gly (G) at location 70 makes CoV length 76. The amino acid pair EG at location 69–70 of CoV in place of amino acid R in location 69 of CoV-2, has been identified as a major determining factor in the current investigation. This section concentrates on the design of computational model to compare the structure/function of wild and mutants of CoV-2 with wild and mutants of CoV in the functionally important region of the protein chain pair. We noticed large differences of CAML model parameter of CoV-2 and CoV characterize the deviation in structure and function of envelope proteins in respect of interaction of virus with host Golgi complex (an organelle that packages proteins); this deviation gets reflected in the large difference of their transmissibility.

The surveyed publications highlight two vital issues—(a) entry of virus in host cell through binding of its spike protein with the receptor ACE2 (Angiotensin-converting Enzyme 2), followed by its replication in host cell, and (b) virus assembly/packaging through interaction with host (Golgi complex) prior to shedding. Four structural proteins of the virus are—Spike (S), Membrane (M), Nucleocapsid (N), and Envelope (E). The smallest size envelope protein plays a crucial role in the assembly of virus prior to secretion from infected cells. Some of the publications [6, 7] also pointed to the contribution of Envelope protein for disease severity due to hyperactive cytokine release. Further, some authors [8–11] emphasized the point that—the interaction of

Table 5.1 Amino acid chain and partial (first 6 excluding Met(M)) rule vector for—(a) Wild CoV-2 (2019)—75 AA and (b) Wild CoV (2003)—76 AA

CoV-2 (2019)—75 AA	
AA Chain	mysfvseetgtlivnsvllflafvvfllvtlailtalrlcayccnivnvslvkpsfyvysrvknlnssrvpdllv
Partial rule vector	<107, 99, 11, 111, 235, 107, 99, 47, 107, 99, 11, 107, 111, 107, 99, 59, 15, 107, 99, 47, 107, 99, 11, 235, ··· >
CoV (2003)—76 AA	
AA Chain	mysfvseetgtlivnsvllflafvvfllvtlailtalrlcayccnivnvslvkptvyvysrvknlnssegvpdllv
Partial rule vector	<107, 99, 11, 111, 235, 107, 99, 47, 107, 99, 11, 107, 111, 107, 99, 59, 15, 107, 99, 47, 107, 99, 11, 235, ··· >

envelope protein with host Golgi complex has not been addressed adequately. Consequently, mutational study of envelope protein is a necessity to elucidate the deviation of a mutant from the wild in respect of its structure-function. CoV-2 envelope protein chain has 75 amino acids, while there are 76 amino acids for CoV with difference in four amino acid locations (55, 56, 69, and 70) covered by the C-terminal region. The amino acid pair EG at location 69–70 for CoV is replaced by single amino acid R for CoV-2. Experimental results of mutational study are reported for envelope protein of both CoV-2 (2019) and CoV (2003) with focus on the C-terminal region that covers Golgi complex targeting information [6, 12] and conserved Motif of the chain pair. Comparison of the results shows high difference of CAML parameters of - (i) CoV-2 wild and mutants compared to wild and mutant of CoV, and also (ii) for the mutations inserted in the same amino acid type in the functionally important region of the virus pair. In this background we propose the following hypothesis.

Hypothesis 5.2: Large difference of CAML model parameters of CoV-2 (wild, mutants) with CoV (wild, mutants) has a direct correlation with difference in the structure- function of envelope protein of two viruses. Assembly/packaging of virus prior to its shedding depends on the structure-function of C-terminal domain of envelope protein interacting with host Golgi complex; consequently, difference in structure-function points to the difference of transmissibility of CoV-2 and CoV/MERS.

5.2.1 CA Rule Vector for AA Chain

Rule vector of an AA chain of a protein can be designed by concatenating rule strings of each AA reported in Table 4.4 of Chap. 4. Table 5.1 shows Envelope Protein AA string for—(a) CoV-2 (2019)—75 AA and (b) CoV (2003)—76 AA; partial rule vectors for two AA chains are also illustrated.

Once the CA Rule Vector is designed for a protein, we study the evolution of the CA generating a signal graph referred to as Cycle Length (CL) signal graph.

5.2.2 Generation of CL Signal Graph for AA Chain

The generic steps of execution of Phase 1 and Phase 2 of CAML model design are reported in Step 2, Phase 2 of sub-section 5.1.2 that reports CL graph generation procedure for any protein chain.

CL Signal Graph Analytics for Wild Type AA Chain and Mutants

For the CAML model, signal graph analytics enable extraction of meaningful information from a graph relevant for mutational study of protein. Wild type AA chain refers to the one that can be observed in nature without any mutation. The chain with a mutation is termed as Mutant.

5.2.2.1 CL Signal Graph for Wild Type AA Chain

CL signal graphs for wild type AA chains are shown in Figs. 5.1, 5.2, and 5.3 for CoV-2, CoV, and MERS envelope proteins respectively. In view of the common backbone, the baseline of the CL signal graph has the CL value 3. Signal graph analytics proceeds on identifying mcl (maximum cycle length) and N-mcl (Next to mcl) signals, formally defined next. The mcl signal is the one that covers a number of cells with maximum cycle length value. More than one mcl signal may exist in a CL graph. A signal with CL value less than mcl but greater than y = 6 is referred to as N-mcl. Such an evaluation of N-mcl signals enables avoidance of noisy signals below the CL value 7 for signal graph analytics. The value of the parameter y, in general, will depend on the analysis of low valued signals displayed in CL signal graphs derived for a class of proteins. The left and right ends of a signal graph respectively refer to the NTD (N-Terminal Domain—left terminal) and CTD (C-Terminal Domain—right terminal) of a protein chain. Cycle Length Value Sum (CLVS), as defined in Sect. 5.2.2.3, refers to sum of mcl and N-mcl values of a CL graph; CLVS value can be evaluated for its full length or for a specific region.

Difference in CL Signal graphs of CoV-2 and CoV at CTD—its effect on viral transmissibility

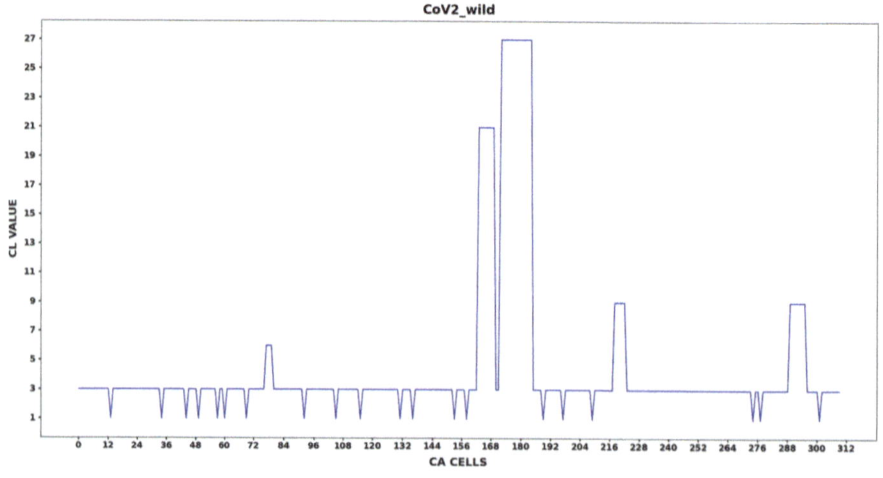

Fig. 5.1 CL signal graph for wild envelope protein of CoV-2 virus AA chain with mcl signal value 27 around location 180 and 3 N-mcl signals—one of value 21 around cell location 165, two signals with each showing CL value 9 around cell locations 220 (with CLVS value = 5 × 9 = 45) and around cell location 290 (with CLVS value = 6 × 9 = 54)

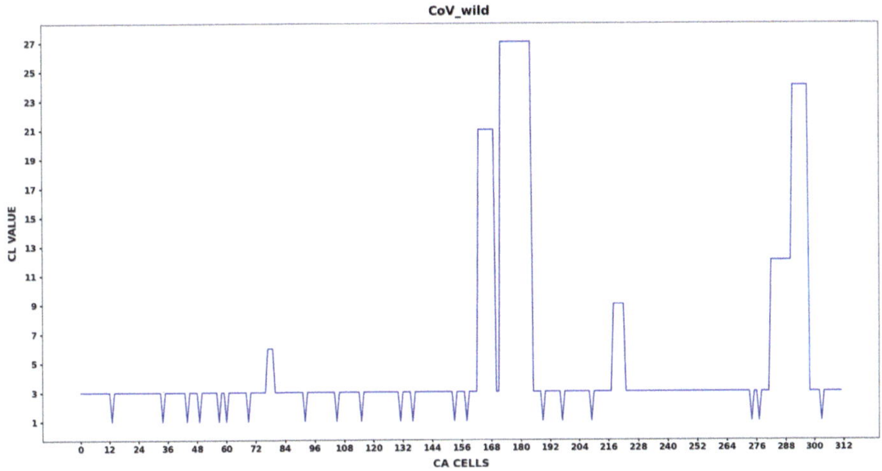

Fig. 5.2 CL signal graph for wild envelope protein of CoV virus AA chain with 1 mcl signal value of 27 around location 180 and 3 N-mcl signals—one of value 21 around cell location 165, 1 of value 9 (at cell loc 216 to 221), and the last one with CL value 12 (cell location 280 to 286), followed by value 24 (from 287 to 292)—the third N-mcl signal of CoV is larger, both in height and width, compared to that of CoV-2 (showing signal value of 9 for 5 cell locations)

It is worthwhile to report the difference in CL signal graphs of CoV-2 and CoV wild (in Figs. 5.1 and 5.2) around cell locations 280 to 290 of C-terminal region.

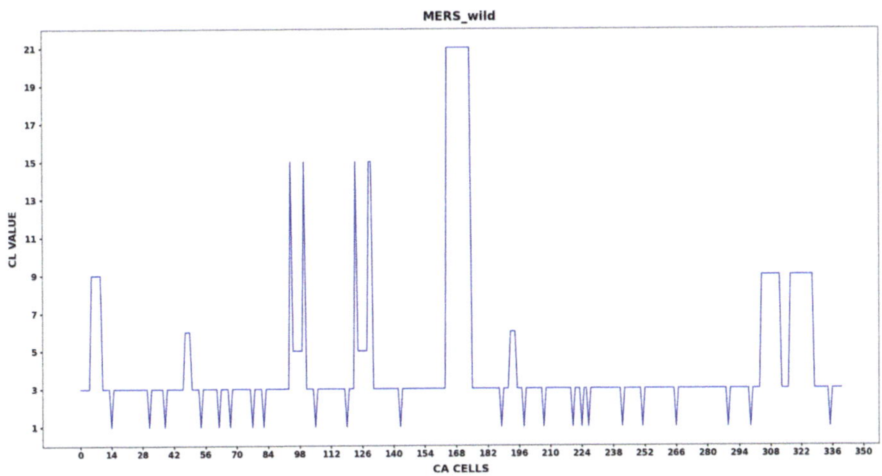

Fig. 5.3 CL signal graph for wild envelope protein of MERS covid Envelope protein AA chain with one mcl signal and two N-mcl signals of value 9 with width 6 and 7 cells in C-terminal domain with CLVS as 6 × 9 (54) and 7 × 9 (63) at C-terminal region (Note—2 split signals around cell locations (93 to 100) and (121 to 129) are excluded for computation of CLVS value for the full length of CL graph)

While CoV shows N-mcl signal of value of 12 followed by value 24 for 13 (7 + 6) cell locations, CoV-2 displays an N-mcl signal of value 9 at cell locations 286 to 290. The area covering cell locations 280 to 292 shows CLVS for CoV higher by the value of 183(228 – 45) than that of CoV-2; while CoV shows CLVS value 228 (144 + 84), CoV-2 shows CLVS as 45. Interaction of CoV envelope protein with host Golgi complex gets adversely affected due to presence of high valued signal at C-terminal Domain. By contrast, absence of high valued signal for CoV-2 ensures higher interaction with host Golgi complex ensuring higher viral transmissibility.

5.2.2.2 CL Signal Graph for Mutant AA Chain

Two sample mutant CL signals graphs for CoV-2 and CoV are presented. CoV mutant show signal value higher than that of CoV-2. Figures 5.4 and 5.5 display CL signal graph for two mutants—(i) P71L (original amino acid Proline (P) at serial location 71 mutated with amino acid Leu (L)) for CoV-2 Envelope Protein AA chain; (ii) P72L (original amino acid Proline (P) at serial location 72 mutated with amino acid Leu (L)) for CoV Envelope Protein AA chain.

5.2.2.3 Evaluation of Difference of CL Value Sum (DCLVS) Between Wild and Mutant AA Chain Signal Graphs

CL Value Sum (CLVS) for a wild is computed considering mcl and Nmcl signals of wild CL graph. Similarly, CLVS is computed out of a mutant CL graph. Next, we derive:

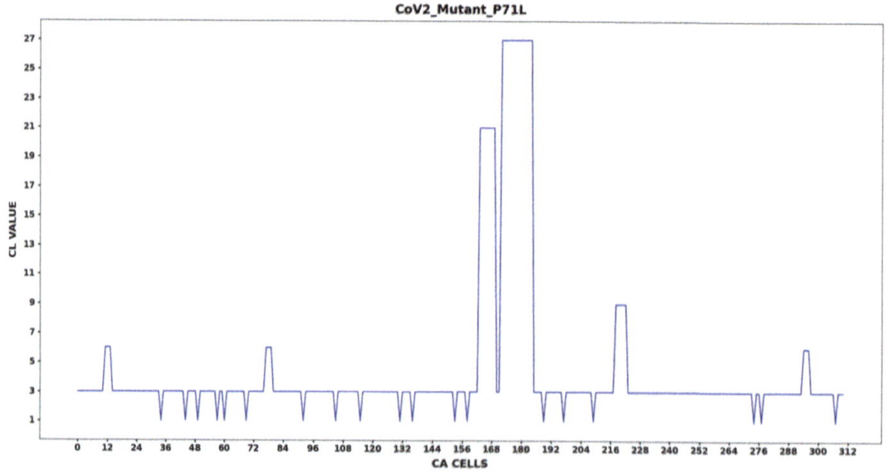

Fig. 5.4 CL Signal graph for mutant P71L for CoV-2 envelope protein (Note: Original amino acid P at location 71 mutated with amino acid L) with CLVS value nil around cell location 220

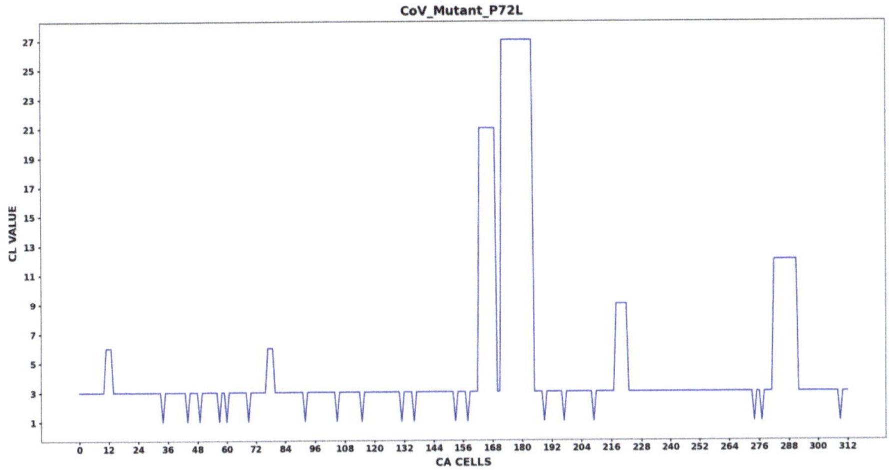

Fig. 5.5 CL Signal graph for mutant P72L for CoV envelope protein (Note: Original amino acid P at location 72 mutated with amino acid L)

$$DCLVS(Difference\,of\,CL\,Value\,Sum) = (CLVS\,of\,mutant - CLVS\,of\,Wild)$$

The CA model parameter DCLVS, is employed to compare difference in structure-function of a pair of envelope proteins of (CoV-2, CoV, MERS with AA count 75, 76, and 82 respectively). The following three categories of cells are excluded for evaluation of CLVS:

(i) Cells not displaying cycle: For a CL signal graph of AA chain, there may exist (say Q cells) which do not reach a cycle; these Q cells are marked with CL(–5) value.

(ii) Cells displaying noise signal with CL value less than (y+1): Signals with CL value less than (y+1) are assumed to be noise in the CL signal graph for AA chain. For the current version (y+1) = 7.

(iii) Cells in a split Nmcl signal: A split Nmcl signal displays multiple peaks with highest CL value and the cells between peaks have CL value less than (y+1) = 7. Figure 5.3 illustrates a CL signal graph displaying two split Nmcl signals at cell locations (93 to 100) and (121 to 129), each with two peaks. Since CL value between two peaks is 5, we ignore such Nmcl signals for computation of CLVS for the CL graph.

5.2.3 *Comparison of Transmissibility of SARS (CoV-2, CoV) and MERS Covid*

For Comparison, we concentrate on the analysis of DCLVS value in CTD (C-Terminal Domain) that interacts with Golgi complex. As discussed earlier, this region of envelope protein affects virus transmissibility.

Deviation of structure—function of a mutant from its wild version gets reflected in the high value (greater than or equal to 50) of CAML model parameter DCLVS. The same framework is also relevant for evaluation of DCLVS for a pair of proteins executing similar function and length (difference less than 10%). First three rows of Table 5.2 compare the DCLVS of a pair of wild envelope proteins of (CoV-2, CoV, MERS). Large difference DCLVS value of 183 between CoV and CoV-2 wild (at C-terminal domain) confirms large difference in transmissibility of CoV-2 compared to CoV. Also, difference of DCLVS value of 72 between MERS and COV-2 implicated higher transmissibility of CoV-2 compared to that of MERS.

The difference in CLVS between CoV and MERS (third row of Table 5.2) is 111 indicating higher transmissibility of MERS covid than that of SARS CoV. Although we have presented the comparison, in view of limited data, comparison of CoV and MERS cannot be adequately addressed with CAML model.

Table 5.2 Comparison of wild pairs of (CoV-2, CoV), (CoV-2, MERS), (CoV, MERS) on first three rows. Fourth row confirms that mutation of CoV with deletion of G at location 70 displays same CL graph as that of CoV-2. Fifth row confirms that CoV wild CL graph is identical with mutated CoV-2 on replacing amino acid R at location 69 with amino acid pair EG at location at 69–70

Pairs of envelop proteins	DCLVS at CTD	Comparison of transmissibility based on envelope proteins
Wild CoV-2 and Wild CoV	$(7 \times 12 + 6 \times 24) - (5 \times 9) = 228 - 45 = 183$ (CoV higher value)	At C-Terminal region CoV display much higher value—that implicates higher transmissibility for CoV-2 than that of CoV
Wild CoV-2 and Wild MERS	$(6 \times 9 + 7 \times 9) - (5 \times 9)117 - 45 = 72$ (MERS higher value)	At C-Terminal region MERS display higher value—that shows higher transmissibility for CoV-2 than that of MERS
Wild CoV and Wild MERS	$(7 \times 12 + 6 \times 24) - (6 \times 9 + 7 \times 9) = 228 - 117 = 111$	At C-Terminal region CoV display higher value than MERS—that shows higher transmissibility for MERS than that of CoV
Wild CoV-2 and CoV mutant with deletion of G at loc 70	0	Same CL graph for CoV-2 and CoV with deletion of Gly (G) at location 70
CoV-2 with R at loc 69 replaced with EG and CoV wild	0	Same CL graph for mutated CoV-2 and CoV wild

5.2.4 *Comparison of Envelope Protein Sequences of CoV-2 and CoV*

The difference in amino acids at the specified locations of CoV-2 and CoV is the determining factor for higher transmissibility of CoV-2 compared to CoV, as established in the subsequent discussions. CoV-2 and CoV Envelope Proteins differ in loc 55, 56 (CoV-2 has S, F in place of T, V for CoV), and location 69, 70 (CoV-2 has R at location 69, while CoV shows E, G). Deletion of amino acid G at location 70 for CoV, makes its length 75. Figure 5.6 shows the CL graph for CoV on deleting the amino acid G. This CoV mutant (with deleted G) shows a large difference of CL signal graph with its wild in the region covering cell locations 280 to 290. As reported on row 4 of Table 5.2, this mutant has zero difference with CoV-2 wild CL graph. The row 5 of Table 5.2 last row compares CoV-2 mutant (with amino acid R replaced with amino acid pair EG) and wild CoV, both having length 76. Figure 5.7 displays the CL signal graph of CoV-2 mutant with amino acid R at location 69 replaced with amino acid pair EG at locations 69–70, making its length 76. This CL graph of CoV-2 mutant matches with that of CoV. These results establish the crucial role of amino acid pair EG at location 69–70 of CoV envelope protein. Replacement of this amino acid pair EG with amino acid R at location 69 of CoV-2 plays as a determining factor for high transmissibility of CoV-2 compared to CoV.

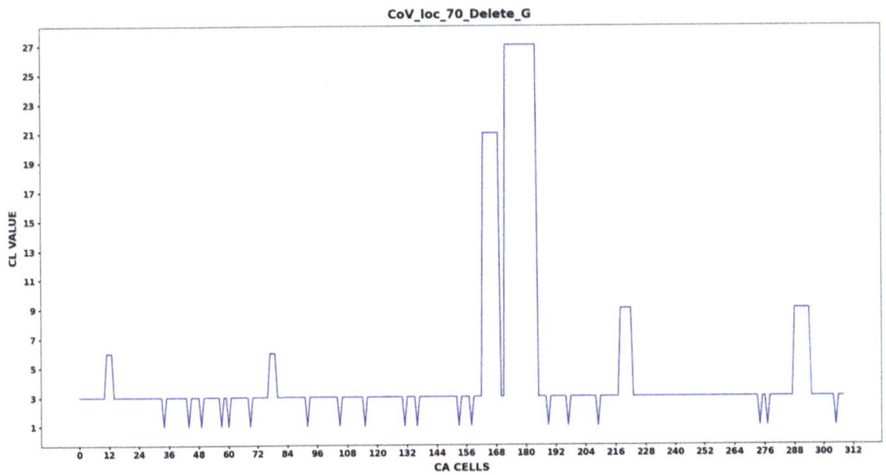

Fig. 5.6 CoV(2003) Envelope Protein CL signal graph on deleting amino acid G at location 70—makes its length 75 (Identical to CL graph for CoV-2 (see Fig. 5.1))

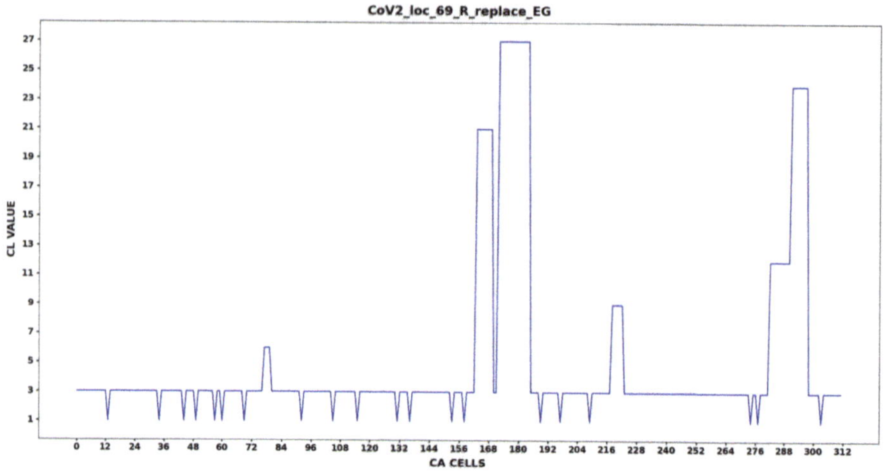

Fig. 5.7 CL graph for mutated CoV-2 with R at location 69 replaced with amino acid pair EG at location 69–70 making length 76; this CL graph of mutated CoV-2 is identical to CoV wild CL graph (see Fig. 5.2)

5.2.5 *Comparison of DCLVS for Mutations Inserted in CoV-2 and CoV*

Table 5.3 rows 2–7 analyzes DCLVS values of mutants for CoV-2 and CoV with mutations inserted in identical amino acid types on the same or adjacent location. The CL signal graphs for mutant S68C on 4th row) for CoV-2 and CoV are shown in Figs. 5.8 and 5.9 showing higher CLVS value of 69 (240–171) for CoV. High DCLVS value between wild SARS CoV-2 and CoV chains and also for their mutants in identical amino acid type establishes large deviation of structure—function of CoV-2 (2019) from that of CoV (2003). The deviation of structure—function gets reflected in the large difference in their transmissibility.

Table 5.3 CoV-2/CoV mutants with mutation inserted on identical or adjacent amino acid locations with same AA type

Mutants CoV-2/Cov	DCLVS—at CTD (C-Terminal Domain)
L37H/L37H	Same difference as of wild CoV-2 and CoV at CTD
L39M/L39M	Same difference as of wild CoV-2 and CoV at CTD
S68C/S68C	CoV higher than Cov-2 by a value = 240 − 171 = 69
S68F/S68F	Same difference as of wild CoV-2 and CoV at CTD
P71L/P72L	Same difference as of wild CoV-2 and CoV at CTD
D72Y/D73Y	Same difference as of wild CoV-2 and CoV at CTD

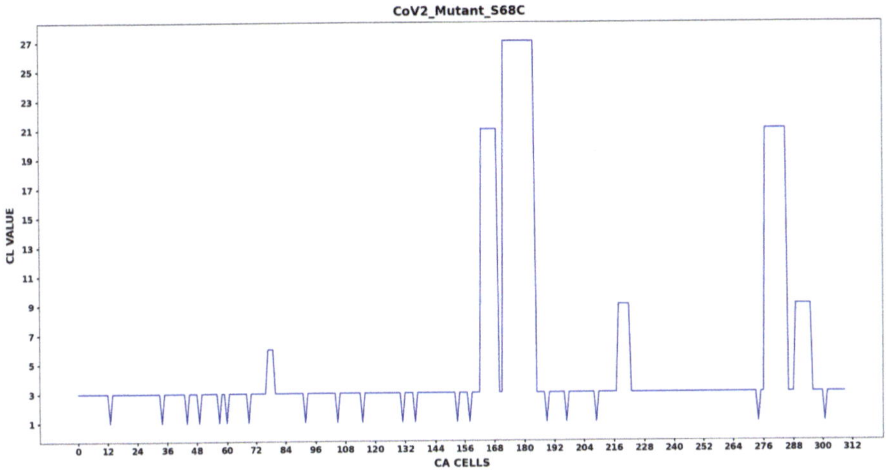

Fig. 5.8 CLVS for CoV-2 mutant S68C at C-terminal region = 21 × 6 + 9 × 5 = 171

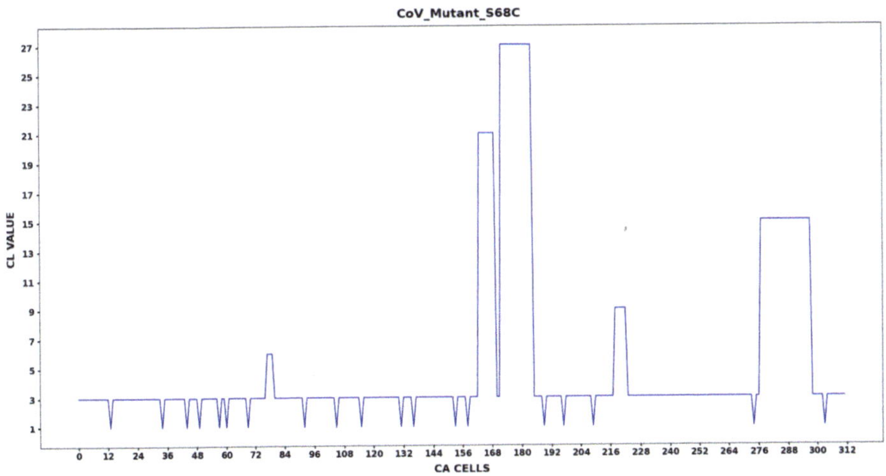

Fig. 5.9 CLVS for CoV mutant S68C at C-terminal domain = 15 × 18 = 240

5.2.6 Conclusion

High transmissibility of CoV-2, as per our analysis, is a combined effect of mutations on structural proteins (Envelope E, Spike S, and Nucleocapsid N) in addition to mutations observed in non-structural proteins (nsps) and accessory proteins (ORFs). Viral life cycle in the host cell is controlled by these proteins for replication and host immune evasion. The Cellular Automata (enhanced with) Machine Learning (CAML) model is presented in this section to investigate the contribution of envelope protein for high transmissibility of SARS CoV-2 compared to that of CoV. CAML model establishes the fact that—difference in the two locations (69–70) of AA sequence of CoV-2 is the main determine factor leading to the difference of higher transmissibility of CoV-2 compared to CoV.

5.3 CAML Model for Non-structural Protein 1 (nsp1)

This section analyses non-structural protein nsp1 of the SARS and MERS covid virus. The analysis establishes higher transmissibility of SARS CoV-2 compared to SARS CoV and MERS CoV. The immune system of a living organism is a complex network evolved to protect a species from invading pathogens—bacteria, vitus etc. Complexity of the human immune system is significantly higher compared to other species. On sensing an invading pathogen, the immune system adjusts its pathways to fight a virus. However, a virus has evolved a strategy for its survival and replication in the host by evading immune system defense. Different aspects of host immune response and viral immune evasion are covered in many publications, as highlighted in the brief survey reported in Sect. 5.3.1.

The non-structural protein nsp1 avails host protein synthesis machinery to initiate viral replication, in addition to neutralization of host immune defence. The key protein out of the 16 nsps, is the non-structural protein nsp1, also known as the leader protein. Nsp1 leads the process of hijacking host resources by blocking host translation. This section concentrates on the analysis of nsp1 of SARS covid (CoV-2, CoV) and MERS covid based on Cellular Automata enhanced Machine Learning (CAML) model developed for study of biological strings. This computational model compares deviation of structure—function of CoV-2 from that of CoV employing CAML model parameters derived out of CA evolution of amino acid chain of nsp1. This comparative analysis points to—(i) higher transmissibility of CoV-2 compared to CoV, and (ii) deviation of MERS covid from SARS CoV in respect to virulence and pathogenesis. A machine learning (ML) framework has been designed to map the CAML model parameters to the physical domain characteristics reported in in-vitro/in-vivo/in-silico experimental studies. The ML framework enables us to learn the permissible range of model parameters derived out of mutational study of nsp1 of three viruses.

A comprehensive survey on nsp1 follows in Sect. 5.3.1. The knowledge curated through this survey enables us to design CAML model for comparative analysis of SARS and MERS nsp1. The survey depicts an astonishing picture that emphasizes the role played by nsp1 of submicron virus particles to survive in its host cell while deactivating host's defence mechanism against the virus.

5.3.1 SARS Covid and MERS Covid nsp1—A Brief Survey

A brief survey on the tasks associated with function of each nsp1 is next presented, while highlighting functionally important amino acids. The CAML model introduces mutation on the amino acids of a protein chain. Derivation of results on employing CAML model for each of the three tasks of nsp1 of SARS covid is reported in Sect. 5.3.5 and nsp1 of MERS covid in Sect. 5.3.6.

5.3.1.1 Tasks Executed by nsp1

In view of its leading position on viral RNA, nsp1 is often referred to as the leader protein. Subsequent to entry in host cell, viral pathogenesis proceeds by executing the following tasks reported in-vivo/in-vitro experimental studies [13–31]. Both CoV-2 and CoV nsp1 have 180 AA, while MERS nsp1 has 193 AA. MERS covid differs significantly from SARS covid in respect of its interaction with other biomolecules. Detailed analysis of MERS nsp1 is reported in [17].

Task Ta1: The very first task of nsp1 of SARS covid (CoV, CoV2) is to hijack host translation machinery to shut off host mRNA translation. Implementation of Ta1 proceeds through binding of nsp1 to ribosomal subunit S40. Details of Ta1 execution has been dealt with by a number of authors [13–22]. Two AAs of KH motif in CTD (K164, H165) of CoV-2 and CoV nsp1 interact with host ribosome to inhibit binding of host mRNA on ribosome necessary for protein synthesis. The amino acid K164 has been reported to be the critical AA of nsp1 for binding with host ribosome [13]. Further, it has been reported that the AA (154 to 160) and (166 to 179) containing two helices are inserted in the entry point of ribosomal RNA. Section 5.3.5 reports the results derived from the CAML model for task Ta1 on comparing CoV-2 and CoV nsp1 covering the critical KH motif (K164, H165). On aligning MERS sequence with that of CoV-2/CoV, a number of authors have pointed to the AA location K181 for host translation shut off through binding of MERS nsp1 on ribosome. Section 5.3.6 reports results derived from the CAML model for execution of task Ta1 of MERS nsp1 and its comparison with that of SARS CoV.

Task Ta2: The next task (referred to as Ta2) of nsp1 is to ensure that nsp1 mediated host translation shut off does not affect viral RNA translation. Uninterrupted viral RNA translation through viral gene expression is ensured through interaction of nsp1 with Stem Loop 1 (SL1) of 5'UTR secondary structure of viral RNA. The overall secondary structure of 5'UTR for SARS CoV-2 and CoV is conserved. Execution of the task Ta2 is covered in many publications [22–27]. Interaction of the 5'UTR with nsp1 through R124 and K125, as reported in [25], is required for evasion of nsp1-mediated translational suppression. MERS covid nsp1 (with 193 amino acids) differs from SARS CoV (with 180 amino acids) in respect of viral RNA recognition. Comparison of different features of MERS covid and SARS covid is covered in [17] both in respect of Ta1 and Ta2. Section 5.3.5 reports results derived out of CAML model on CoV-2 and CoV nsp1 on task Ta2 considering the critical AA of RK motif

(R124, K125). Through successive deletion experiment, the interaction region of MERS nsp1 with 5'UTR has been identified as AA location 11 to 15 [17], while the authors in [17, 23] have also highlighted the importance of amino acid R13 of MERS nsp1 for recognition of RNA 5'UTR.

Task Ta3: The third task (Ta3) of nsp1 is to inhibit/restrict production of host defence immune system components—Interferons (INF-I, INF-gamma, and Interleukin). The task Ta3 can be assumed to be a corollary to Ta1, as the blockage of host mRNA translation stops, synthesis of host proteins necessary to activate immune pathways also stops. Virus also blocks export of mRNA from nucleus of the host cell to cytoplasm where some of the host proteins are made. A number of authors have concentrated on how SARS and MARS covid evade host immune response; a representative set of relevant publications is noted in [27–31]. It has been reported [17, 31] that MERS nsp1 displays host mRNA cleavage function. Two functions of MERS nsp1—(i) host translational shut off, and (ii) host mRNA cleavage is executed by two different regions. While host translational shut off is executed by the CTD AA K179/K181, the task of mRNA cleavage is executed by the AA pair (R146, K147). As a result, the proteins necessary for activation of host immune response are not synthesized leading to compromised host immune response due to MERS nsp1. Section 5.3.5 reports the results derived out of CAML model for execution of task Ta3 of CoV-2 and CoV nsp1, while the results for MERS nsp1 are reported in Sect. 5.3.6.

Table 5.4 AA chain for nsp1 of SARS covid (CoV-2, CoV—each of length 180 AA), MERS covid (193 AA) retrieved from NCBI; partial Rule Vector (RV) for first ten AA (excluding Met (m) encoding start codon) reported following AA chain for three viruses

CoV-2 nsp1 AA sequence—180 AA	
AA Chain	meslvpgfnekthvqlslpvlqvrdvlvrgfgdsveevlsearqhlkdgtcglvevekgvlpqleqpy vfikrsdartaphghvmvelvaelegiqygrsgetlgvlvphvgeipvayrkvllrkngnkgagghs ygadlksfdlgdelgtdpyedfqenwntkhssgvtrelmrelngg
Partial rule vector	<<107, 99, 11, 235>, <107, 99, 47>, <107, 99, 47, 15, 15>, <107, 99, 59, 15>, <105, 43, 11, 63>, <107, 99, 1>, <107, 99, 11, 107, 111>, <107, 99, 11, 107>, <107, 99, 11, 235>, <107, 99, 63, 63, 15>, ⋯>>
CoV nsp1 AA sequence—180 AA	
AA Chain	meslvlgvnekthvqlslpvlqvrdvlvrgfgdsveealsearehlkngtcglvelekgvlpqleqpy vfikrsdalstnhghkvvelvaemdgiqygrsgitlgvlvphvgetpiayrnvllrkngnkgagghsy gidlksydlgdelgtdpiedyeqnwntkhgsgalreltrelngg
Partial rule vector	<<107, 99, 11, 235>, <107, 99, 47>, <107, 99, 47, 15, 15>, <107, 99, 59, 15>, <107, 99, 47, 15, 15>, <107, 99, 1>, <107, 99, 59, 15>, <107, 99, 11, 107>, <107, 99, 11, 235>, <107, 99, 63, 63, 15>, ⋯>>
MERS nsp1 AA sequence—193 AA	
AA Chain	msfvagvtaqgargtyraalnsekhqdhvsltvplcgsgnlveklspwfmdgenayevvkamll kkepllyvpirlaghtrhlpgprvylverliacenpfmvnqlaysssangslvgttlqgkpigmffpy dielvtgkqnillrkygrggyhytpfhyerdntscpewmddfeadpkgkyaqnllkkligg
Partial rule vector	<<107, 99, 47>, <107, 99, 11, 107, 111>, <107, 99, 59, 15>, <107, 99, 15>, <107, 99, 1>, <107, 99, 59, 15>, <107, 99, 43, 15>, <107, 99, 15>, <107, 99, 63, 107>, <107, 99, 1>, ⋯>>

Observation 5.2 – From Analysis of nsp1 sequences and published experimental results: From the analysis of SARS and MERS covid nsp1 and survey of published in vitro/in vivo experimental results, it can be observed that polar positive AAs (Lys K, Arg R, His H) of nsp1, play a prominent role for interaction with host proteins and viral 5'UTR. CAML model results reported in Sects. 5.3.5 and 5.3.6 are derived on employing this key observation on nsp1 AA sequence.

5.3.2 *AA Chain for nsp1 Protein of SARS Covid (CoV-2, CoV) and MERS Covid*

Evaluation of nsps with the CAML model starts with the leader protein nsp1. The AA sequence and partial rule vector for first 10 AAs excluding met (m) encoding Start Codon are presented for CoV-2, CoV, and MERS nsp1 in Table 5.4.

CA rule vector for a protein chain is designed on concatenating 3NCA rules (reported in Table 4.4 of Chapter 4) for each AA of the chain. Once the CA Rule Vector is designed for a protein chain, we study the evolution of the CA generating a signal graph referred to as Cycle Length (CL) signal graph detailed in next subsection.

5.3.3 *CA Evolution Generating CL Signal Graph for a Protein Chain*

The generic steps of execution of Phase 1 and Phase 2 of CAML model design are reported in Sect. 5.1.2 that reports CL graph generation procedure for any protein chain.

5.3.3.1 CL Signal Graph Analytics for Wild Type AA Chain and Mutant

For the CAML model, signal graph analytics enable extraction of meaningful information from a graph relevant for mutational study of protein. Wild type AA chain refers to the one that can be observed in nature without any mutation. The chain with a mutation is termed as Mutant. CL signal graphs for wild type AA chain are shown in Figs. 5.10, 5.11 and 5.12 for SARS covid (CoV-2 and CoV) and MERS covid. In view of the common backbone, the baseline of the CL signal graph has the CL value 3. Signal graph analytics proceeds on identifying mcl (Maximum Cycle Length) and N-mcl (Next to mcl) signals, formally defined next. The mcl signal is the one that covers a number of cells with maximum cycle length value. There may be one or more mcl in a signal graph of an AA chain. A signal with CL value less than mcl but greater than CL value 6. Such an evaluation N-mcl signal enables avoidance of noisy signals below the CL value 7 in a CL signal graph.

CL Signal Graph for Wild Type AA Chain

Figures 5.10, 5.11 and 5.12 report the CL signal graphs for evolution of CA as per Rule Vector for wild type AA chain noted in Table 5.4 for CoV-2, CoV, and MERS nsp1.

CL Signal Graph for Mutant AA Chain

In molecular biology, Ala mutagenesis is usually undertaken to determine the contribution of a specific AA in the function of a given protein. Instead of Ala, CAML model employs Cys mutagenesis to expose the contribution of the AA for protein function. The Property P5 presented in Sect. 5.3.4 reports the reason for such deviation from Ala to Cys; that subsection reports a generic framework of CAML model to compare SARS and MERS nsp1 function.

Figures 5.13, 5.14 and 5.15 display CL signal graph for three mutants—(a) K164C—original amino acid Lys (K) at serial location 164 mutated with amino acid Cys (C) for CoV-2 nsp1 AA chain; (b) K164C—original amino acid Lys (K) at serial location 164 mutated with amino acid Cys (C) for CoV nsp1 AA chain; (c) K179C—original amino acid Lys (K) at serial location 179 mutated with amino acid Cys (C) for MERS nsp1 AA chain. It can be observed that for each of the three mutant CL graphs, an additional signal appears around cell locations 650 corresponding to AA location 164 for CoV-2, CoV in Figs. 5.13 and 5.14. No additional signal in Fig. 5.15 appears around cell location 716 corresponding to AA location 179 of

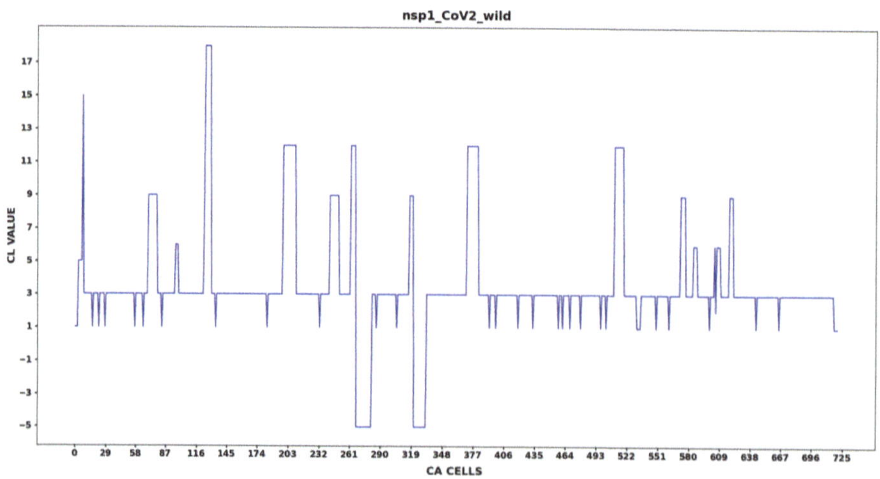

Fig. 5.10 CL signal graph for CoV-2 wild nsp1 AA chain

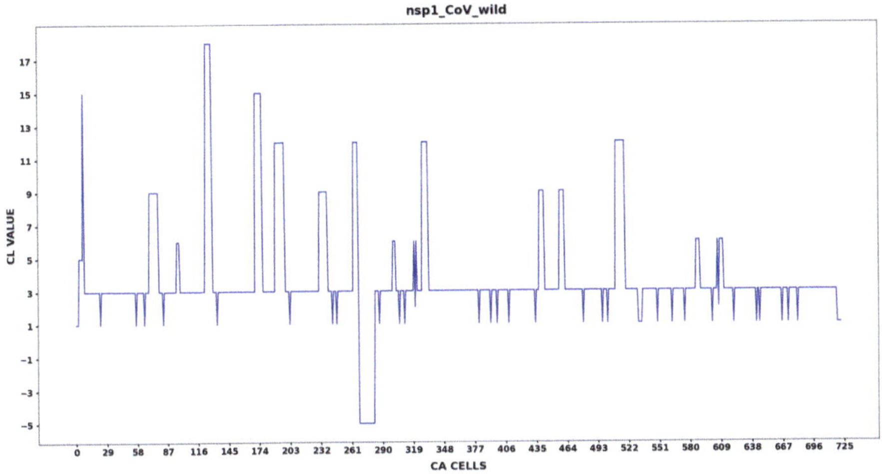

Fig. 5.11 CL signal graph for CoV wild nsp1 AA chain

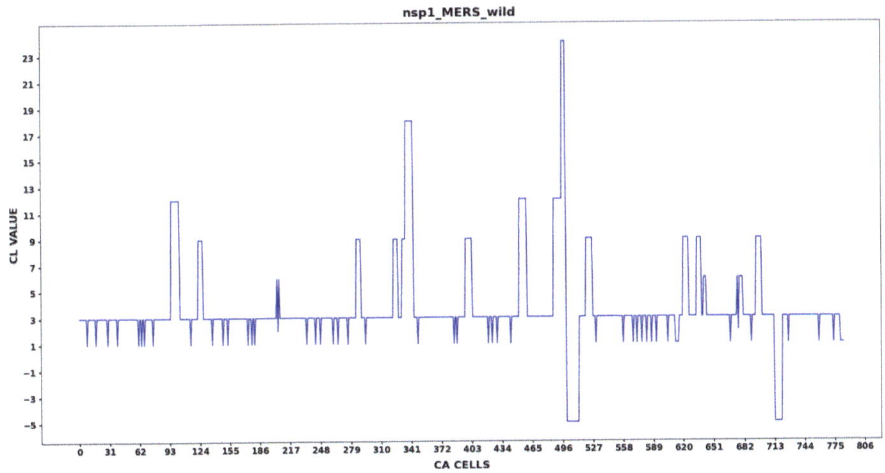

Fig. 5.12 CL signal graph for MERS wild nsp1 AA chain

MERS nsp1 chain. Such additional signals are not present in the CL signal graphs for their wild counterpart.

Evaluation of Difference of CL Value Sum (DCLVS) between Wild and Mutant AA Chain Signal Graphs

CL Value Sum (CLVS) for a wild is computed considering mcl and Nmcl signals of wild CL graph considering CL values greater than 6. Similarly, CLVS is computed out of a mutant CL graph. Next, we derive:

$$DCLVS(Difference\,of\,CL\,Value\,Sum) = CLVS\,of\,mutant - CLVS\,of\,Wild$$

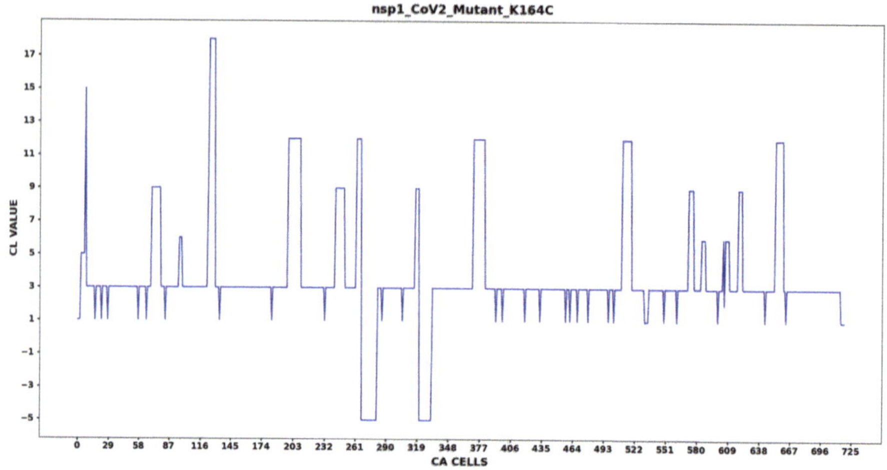

Fig. 5.13 CL Signal graph for mutant K164C for CoV-2 nsp1 (Note: Left and right end of signal graph refers to N Terminal Domain (NTD) and C Terminal Domain (CTD) of the protein)

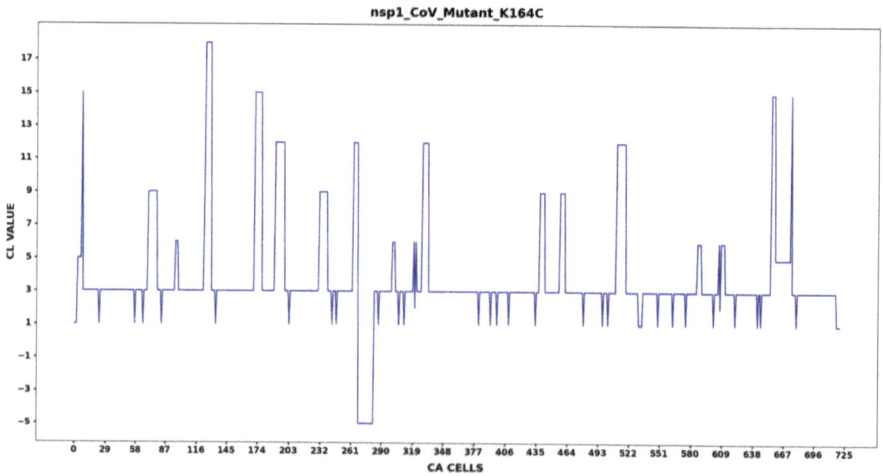

Fig. 5.14 CL Signal graph for mutant K164C for CoV nsp1 (Note: Left and right end of signal graph refers to N Terminal Domain (NTD) and C Terminal Domain (CTD) of the protein)

For evaluating DCLVS, we ignore the cells displaying CL value (–5). For example, Figs. 5.12 and 5.15 display MERS wild and MERS mutant K179C, each with 7 cells having CL value (–5) around cell location 685; such cells are excluded for CLVS evaluation.

A (–ive) DCLVS value indicates that some signal of the wild gets reduced/eliminated in the mutant. While a (+ive) DCLVS value of a mutant indicates the

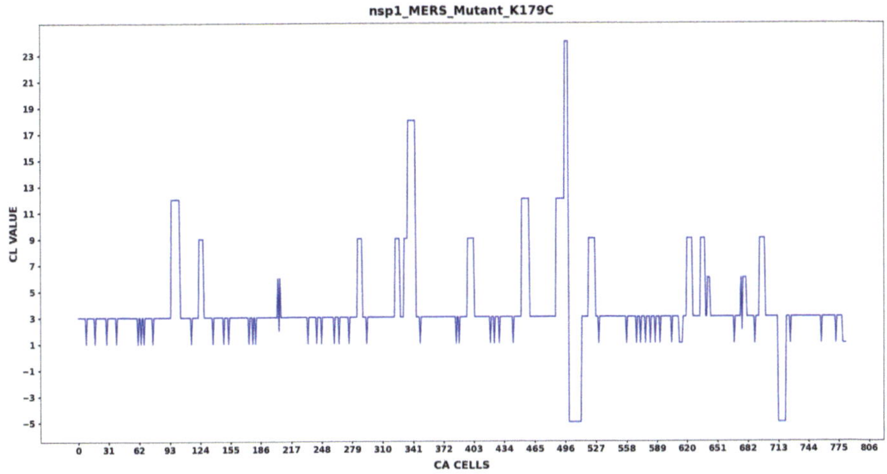

Fig. 5.15 CL Signal graph for mutant K179C for MERS nsp1 (Note: Left and right end of signal graph refers to N Terminal Domain (NTD) and C Terminal Domain (CTD) of the protein)

appearance of some signal in the mutant CL graph that is absent in its wild counterpart. Appearance of such extra signals for a mutant has been found to be associated with the difference in the mutant function compared to that of wild. For example, in the CL signal graphs for two mutants in Figs. 5.13 and 5.14, a signal appears for mutants around the cell location 660 (CoV-2/CoV). Such extra signal in a mutant and absent in wild, represents deviation of mutant function in respect of its interaction with other biomolecules; presence of such a signal inhibits binding of the mutant with the target biomolecule, while no such inhibition in binding exists for the wild counterpart.

The above considerations guide us to design the machine learning framework in the next section.

5.3.4 *ML Framework for CAML Model for SARS and MERS nsp1*

The generic framework of machine learning enables us to map the physical domain features reported in published literature to the CAML model parameter (DCLVS) derived for mutations inserted in a protein chain. Chap. 4 Table 4.4 shows 5 groups of AA (non-polar, polar uncharged, polar +ive, polar –ive, and aromatic ring). In order to identify the AA group that is most critical for structure and function of nsps, CAML model introduces 19 mutations for each AA of nsp chains and evaluate—(i) the count of (-ive) DCLVS and (ii) count of (+ive) valued DCLVS. The polar +ive group AAs displays the highest count (+ive) valued DCLVS across the nsps. Hence, the CAML model assumes that the polar +ive AA group reacts with biomolecules more than other four AA groups. For subsequent discussions, a polar +ive AA is marked as Reactive AA (RAA).

The machine learning framework is designed from the exhaustive study and analysis of

(a) in-vitro/in-vivo/in-silico results reported in published literature, in respect of AAs—(i) interacting with other biomolecules, or (ii) associated with enzymatic function; and
(b) the parameter (DCLVS) derived out of CAML model on inserting Cys-mutation on each functionally relevant AA locations of a nsp, as highlighted under Property P5 elaborated below.

This framework enables us to learn the relationship of (b) and (a).

5.3.4.1 ML Framework Design—Relevant Properties

A few properties (P0 to P6) relevant for the ML framework design are highlighted prior to reporting the algorithmic steps of the design. These properties highlight the underlying principle followed in the ML framework design algorithm reported in this subsection.

P00—CAML model—Mutational Study: The wild CL graph of any protein is derived out of the optimum AA chain for execution of its normal function. The wild AA chain has evolved out of natural evolution of the protein from its DNA/RNA.

P01—CAML Model—Mutational Study: For mutational study of a protein chain, CAML model introduces 19 mutations for each AA of a protein chain to evaluate its deviation from its wild counterpart. This principle is employed for mutational study of CoV-2 spike protein (in Sect. 5.4), p53 protein (in Sect. 5.5), and proteins of medicinal plants (in Sect. 5.6).

However, as reported under property P5, we employ Cys-mutagenesis for comparative analysis of a pair of nsp1 (non-structural proteins of SARS CoV-2, CoV, and MERS) in the current section. Property P5 addresses the question—why we employ Cys-mutagenesis?

P1—The additional signal(s) for a mutant with +ive valued DCLVS confirms inhibition of binding of mutant with a biomolecule, while its wild having no such signal binds with the biomolecule: Appearance of an extra signal for the mutant inhibits the interaction of the mutant with a biomolecule, whereas the CL signal graph of its wild counterpart having no such signal, interacts with the biomolecule. Hence, the relevance of the AA displaying this characteristic gets established in the CAML model in respect of binding of wild with a biomolecule, while the mutant fails to bind.

P2—Importance of Polar +ive AA (Lys (K), Arg (R), and His (H): From analysis of AAs of nsps which interact with other biomolecules, or associated with its enzymatic function, it has been observed that polar +ive AAs are most active. Such an AA is marked as Reactive AA (RAA).

P3—Two adjacent RAA in the nsp1 chain are marked as RAA pairs: A sequence of 5 adjacent AAs covering at least two RAAs is marked as the RAA (Reactive AA) region.

P4—Acceptable range of count of non-0 DCLVS GE 50: From analysis of in vitro/in vivo/in -silico experimental results and DCLVS values of mutants derived with CAML model, the lower acceptable limit of DCLVS is set as greater than or equal to value 50. That is, a DCLVS value less than 50 is viewed as 0 value.

P5—Cys-mutagenesis for CAML model: In order to identify specific AA locations important for protein function, CAML model employs Cys-mutagenesis based on the following consideration. It has been observed that compared to other AA-mutations, Cys-mutation for different AA locations of nsp1, generates the highest count of non-0 (+ive) valued DCLVS with value greater than or equal to 50 across the nsp chains of CoV-2, CoV, and MERS. Higher the DCLVS due to Cys mutation, inserted on an AA, implies higher importance of the AA for the protein function.

P6—Select a sequence of 5 AA as a potential candidate region for binding biomolecules: CAML model assumes that 5 AAs covering a RAA pair (or RAA region) is critical for interaction of nsp1 with a biomolecule (protein or RNA chain). The 5 AAs are assumed to make bonds for binding with a biomolecule. A sequence of 5 AA covering a RAA pair (or RAA region) is identified and the sum of DCLVS values for the sequence is evaluated. The 5 AA sequence with DCLVS sum GE 300 (average value GE 50) and no individual AA having value GE 300 is accepted as a potential candidate region for binding with a biomolecule.

5.3.4.2 Design of ML Framework to Derive CAML Model Results for nsps

The algorithmic steps to design the machine learning framework of CAML model is reported below for an input protein chain of nsp1—(i) on introducing Cys mutation for each AA of a protein chain (Ala mutation if the AA in protein chain is Cys), and evaluating DCLVS (Difference between wild and mutant CLVS).

Algorithm 1 for Comparison of Binding Affinity of nsp1 of SARS and MERS Covid with a bio-molecule

---

Input1: Amino acid (AA) chain of CoV-2, CoV, and MERS nsp1.
Input2: Detailed analysis of published literature, surveyed in Sect. 5.3.1, on in vivo/in vitro/in silico results in respect of—(i) binding of nsp1 with other biomolecule; and (ii) AAs associated with catalytic function of nsp1.

Output: Relative Binding Affinity of a protein pair of SARS and MERS covid with a biomolecule

---

Step 1: Generate CL signal graph for wild and mutants on introducing Cys mutation for each functionally important AA of nsp1 chain; for Cys AA in the sequence, introduce Ala mutation. Note the DCLVS value for each mutant.

Step 2: For enzymatic nsps other than nsp1 and nsp6, go to Step 7.

Step 3(a): Identify a pair of adjacent AAs marked as RAA (Reactive AA—as defined under P2) pair for CoV-2 and CoV AA sequence.

Step 3(b): For MERS, identify a sequence of 5 adjacent AAs in NTD N-terminal Domain) and CTD (C terminal Domain) of nsp1 covering at least two polar positive AAs.

Step 4: Note the sequence of 5 AA around RAA pair for CoV-2 and CoV nsp1 with maximum DCLVS sum for the 5 AAs, in the event of multiple options.

Step 5: Mark the 5 AA sequence (defined under P3) as the binding regions for CoV-2, CoV, and MERS nsp1 with a biomolecule.

Step 6: Compare DCLVS sum for the binding regions identified in Step 5 for CoV-2 and CoV nsp1. Go to Stop.

Step 7: Identify the catalytic domain AA and other functionally important AAs associated with enzymatic function. Introduce Cys mutation for each AA and Ala mutation for a Cys AA in the AA chain in order to ascertain the importance of the AA in respect of interaction of the protein with other biomolecules.

Step 8(a): Note the DCLVS values for each AA of the domain identified in Step 1 for CoV-2, CoV, and MERS to compare DCLVS sum for the functionally important domain(s) of CoV-2 and CoV.

Step 8(b): On comparing the DCLVS values of nsp1 of a pair (of CoV-2, CoV, MERS), the one displaying higher degree of the binding affinity of the wild with the interacting biomolecule can be identified.

Step 9: If majority of the important AAs display (–ive) DCLVS value, compare the CLVS for CoV-2, CoV and MERS wild CL graph to evaluate relative binding affinity.

Step 10: Report comparison of 'Binding Affinity'. Stop.

The results derived for CoV-2, CoV, and MERS nsp1 on executing algorithmic steps are reported in the next two Sects. 5.3.5 and 5.3.6. The leader protein nsp1 stands apart from other nsps in respect of interaction with other biomolecules for viral pathogenesis; results derived for different tasks of nsp1 are next reported.

5.3.5 *Results Derived Out of CAML Model for nsp1 Tasks (CoV-2 and CoV)*

Section 5.3.1 presents a brief survey on nsp1 protein of CoV-2, CoV, and MERS. The tasks associated with execution of functions of nsp1 are reviewed in the survey. Based on the analysis of the results curated from the survey, the CAML model results for nsp1 are reported for three tasks (Ta1, Ta2, Ta3) associated with the nsp1 function. The results are derived on inserting Cys mutation, as noted in Step 1 of the algorithm, for each of the functionally important AAs identified in the survey.

Task Ta1

Results derived out of CAML model in respect of the RAA pair (K164, H165) and the associated 5 AA sequence are reported in Table 5.5. Figures 5.10 and 5.11 show the CL signal graph for wild CoV-2 and CoV, while Figs. 5.16 and 5.17 reports CL signal graphs for two mutants K164C and H165C of CoV-2. Both show a high valued signal

Table 5.5 DCLVS values of two 5 AA sequences showing DCLVS sum for CoV-2 and CoV in respect of Ta1

1st option	DCLVS value for 5 AA					Sum of DCLVS	Average value
	W161	N162	T163	K164	H165		
CoV	0	75	195	75	120	465	465/5 = 93
CoV-2	84	200	270	96	55	705	705/5 = 141
2nd option	DCLVS value for 5 AA						
	K164	H165	S166	S167	G168		
CoV	75	120	0	0	147	342	342/5 = 68.40
CoV-2	96	55	0	0	252	403	404/5 = 80.60

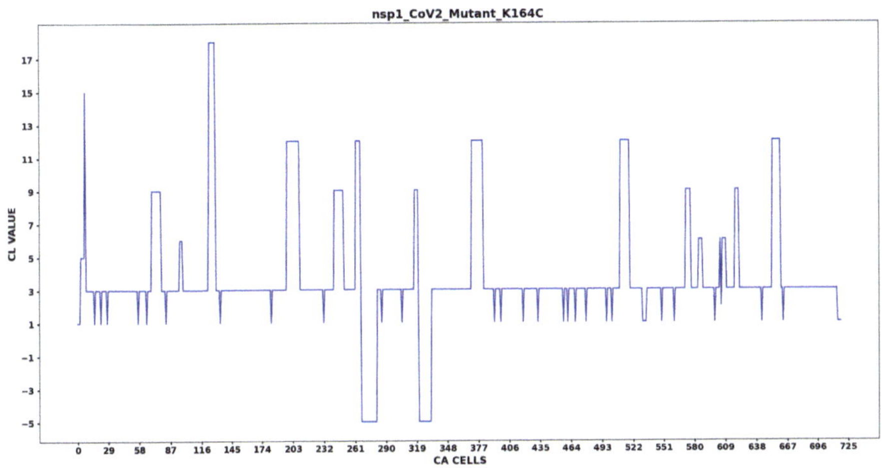

Fig. 5.16 CL signal graph for CoV-2 mutant K164C (reproduced here from Fig. 5.13)

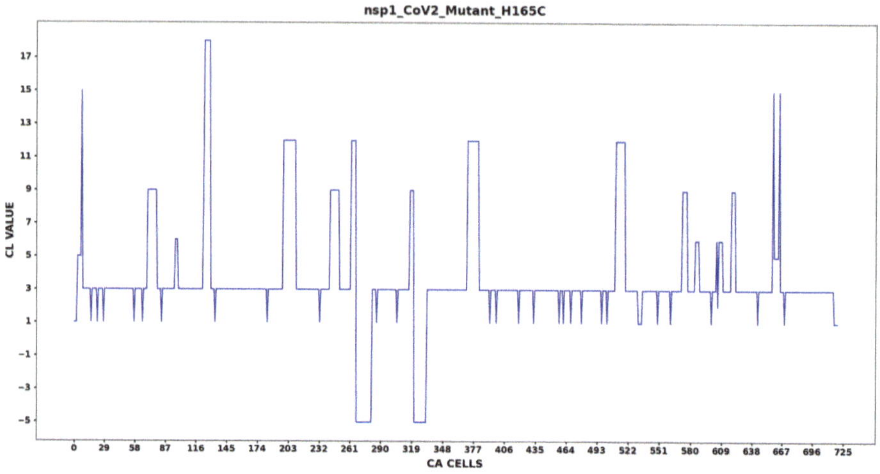

Fig. 5.17 CL signal graph for CoV-2 mutant H165C

at C terminal end of nsp1 around cell location 660 corresponding to AA 164 and 165. Such a signal, as explained earlier, inhibits binding of nsp1 with a biomolecule. Similar results are also derived for CoV mutants K164C and H165C. The wild CL signal graphs of CoV-2 and CoV (Figs. 5.10 and 5.11) do not show such a signal at CTD end; hence wild nsp1 binds on the concerned biomolecule.

As per Property P6, the 5 AA sequence covering RAA (K164, H165), derived in Step 4, is a potential candidate for binding with the biomolecule—host ribosome 40S subunit reported in published literature.

As per Step 4 of the algorithm, there are two options for 5 AA sequence as (R161 to H165) and (K164 to G168). The data for both the options are reported in Table 5.5. The first option is selected, as per Step 4, since it generates higher value sum. It is accepted as the binding region of nsp1 with host ribosome.

Table 5.5 results confirm higher degree of binding affinity for CoV-2 compared to that of CoV for binding with host ribosome. Published experimental results reported in [13–22] match with the result derived out of CAML model.

Task Ta2

Results derived out of CAML model in respect of RAA pair (R124 and K125) and the associated 5 AA sequence are reported in Table 5.6. Figures 5.18 and 5.19 reports CL signal graphs for mutant R124C for CoV-2 and CoV. The 5 AA sequence covering the RAA pair is noted with average DCLVS value as 63 for both CoV-2 and CoV. Hence the 5 AA sequence V121 to K125 is a valid nsp1 candidate 5 AA sequence for binding with a biomolecule (viral 5'UTR Stem Loop SL1). As per the results of Table 5.6, the efficiency of execution of task Ta2 are identical for CoV-2 and CoV.

Task Ta3

As per the Observation 5.2 noted in Sect. 5.3.1 out of nsp1 sequence analysis and published experimental results, a pair of adjacent polar positive AAs (Lys K, Arg

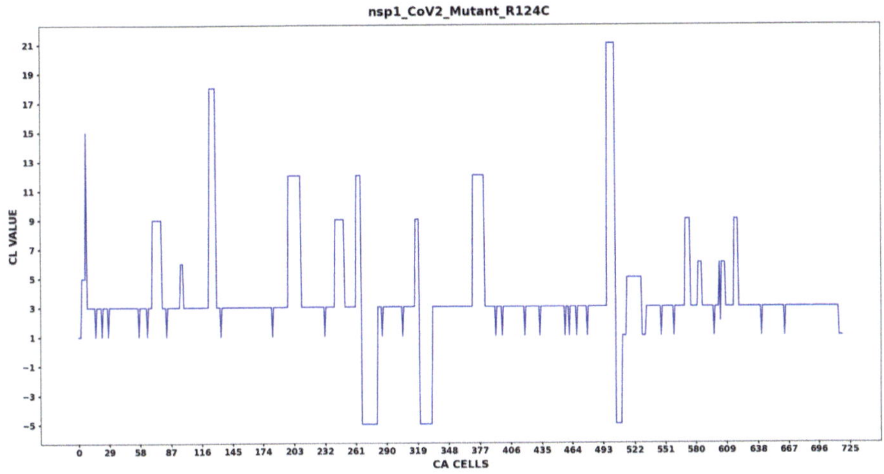

Fig. 5.18 CL signal graph for the mutant R124C of CoV-2

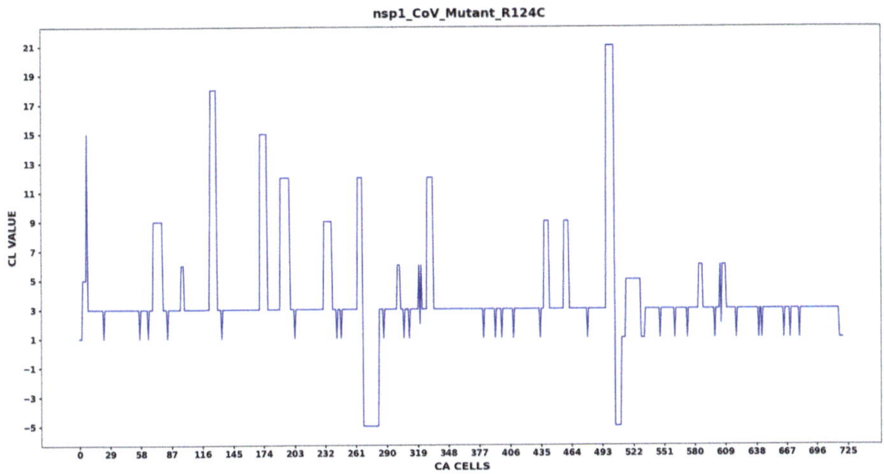

Fig. 5.19 CL signal graph for the mutant R124C of CoV

Table 5.6 DCLVS values of 5 AA sequence showing DCLVS values showing DCLVS sum 63 for CoV-2 and CoV in respect of Ta2

	DCLVS value for 5 AA					Sum of DCLVS	Average value
	V121	L122	L123	R124	K125		
CoV-2	(–78)	65	189	60	(–108)	314	63
CoV	(–102)	65	189	60	(–108)	314	63

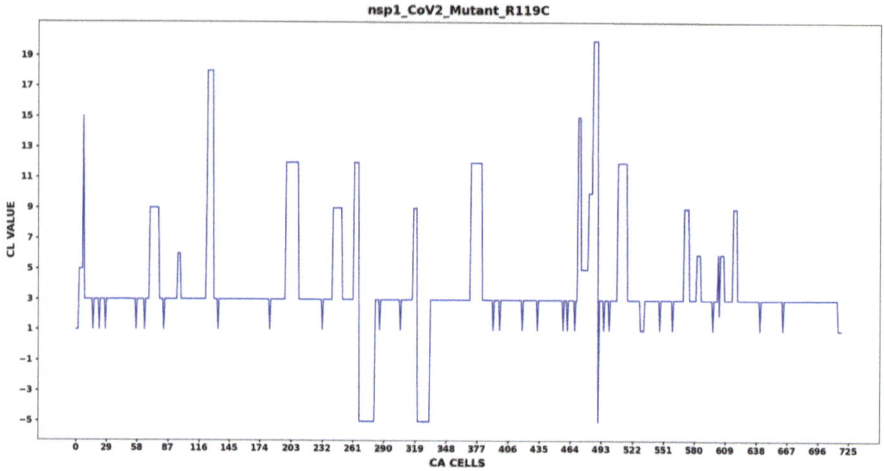

Fig. 5.20 CL signal graph for CoV-2 mutant R119C

R, His H) of nsp1 sequence play critical role for interaction with biomolecules. For example, the RAA pair (K164, H165) and (R124, K125) are associated for interaction with host ribosome and viral 5'UTR, as noted for tasks Ta1 and Ta2. CoV-2 nsp1 displays another RAA pair (R119, K120). Based on the results in [17, 31] in respect of possible cleavage function of CoV-2 and MERS, it has been assumed that 5 AA sequence with RK pair (119, 120) of CoV-2 interact with proteins of host defense immune system to down regulate host immune response.

Results derived out of CAML model in respect of RAA pair (R119, K120) of CoV-2 and the associated 5 AA sequence are reported in Table 5.7. Figures 5.20 and 5.21 show the CL signal graphs for CoV-2 mutants R119C and K120C. While CL graphs of mutant R119C is identical to that of CoV-2 wild (Fig. 5.10), the mutant K120C displays a high valued signal. The 5 AA sequence (119 to 123) covering CoV-2 RAA (R119, K120) displays DCLVS sum as 527 with average value 105. Hence CoV-2 AA sequence (119 to 123) is a potential candidate for binding with a biomolecule. However, this observation is not true for CoV that shows (R119, N120) with 5 AA covering R119 showing total value as 254 and average value 51.

Table 5.7 DCLVS values for 5 AA sequence showing DCLVS sum for CoV-2 and CoV in respect of Ta3

	DCLVS value for 5 AA					Sum of DCLVS	Average value
	R119	K120	V121	L122	L123		
CoV-2	0	273	(–78)	65	189	527	527/5 = 105
	DCLVS value for 5 AA						
	R119	N120	V121	L122	L123		
CoV	0	(–300)	(–102)	65	189	254	254/5 = 51

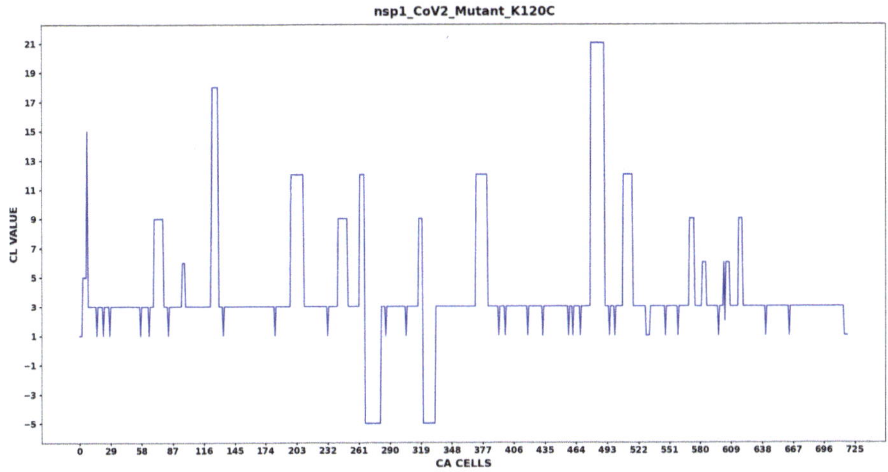

Fig. 5.21 CL signal graph for CoV-2 mutant K120C

CAML model assumes that the 5 AA sequence (119 to 123) of nsp1 around RAA pair (R119, N120) is associated for execution of task Ta3 to inhibit/restrict host immune defense. Table 5.7 results confirm higher efficiency for execution of Ta3 for CoV-2 compared to that of CoV.

Summary of Comparative results derived out CAML model for CoV-2 and CoV

CoV-2 executes the primary task Ta1 (host translation shut off) with higher efficiency compared to CoV, since the average DCLVS values are respectively 141 and 93 for CoV-2 and CoV respectively (50% higher for CoV-2). The higher efficiency of host translational shut off will enable the SARS CoV-2 virus to replicate and transmit with higher efficiency than SARS CoV. Further, this higher transmissibility of CoV-2 gets strengthened due to execution of task Ta3 in respect of better evasion of host immune defence than that of CoV; the respective values are 105 and 51 (100% higher) for CoV-2 than CoV.

Although the focus of this section is primarily on comparison of CoV-2 and CoV nsp1, we also present the results for MERS nsp1 to investigate its differences with CoV nsp1.

5.3.6 CAML Model Results for Comparison of SARS CoV nsp1 and MERS nsp1

For the design of CAML model, a crucial observation is next reported from the analysis of nsp sequences and published experimental results. The observation refers to the key role played by polar positive amino acids in SARS and MERS nsps. In order to execute Step 3(b) of ML algorithm, we identify the polar positive amino acids in MERS nsp1 sequence with maximum distance of 5 between two AAs as: (R13, R17), (K24, H25), (K65, K66), (R146, K147), (K179, K181), (K188, K189). We align 193 AA sequence of MERS with 180 AA of CoV-2/CoV to identify AAs in MERS nsp1 equivalent to AA pair (K168, H169—binding with host ribosome, and R13—for recognition of RNA 5'UTR Stem Loop SL1). In the process we identify—(i) 5 AA sequence L177 to K181 covering two polar +ive AAs (K179, K181) in CTD, and (ii) 5 AA sequence (R13 to R17) covering two polar positive AAs R13, R17 in NTD of MERS nsp1. These two 5 AA sequences are associated with tasks Ta1 and Ta2 of MERS nsp1. For the sake of comparison with CoV, the corresponding average values are copied on the last column from Tables 5.5, 5.6, and 5.7 along with percentage difference of MERS value from CoV.

Task (Ta1) derived out of CAML model for MERS nsp1

The 5 AA sequence (L177 to K181) selected around AA in location (K179, K181) is noted in Table 5.8 with DCLVS value for Cys mutant of each AA. The sum of DCLVS values and average value are 603 and 121. Hence the region of 5 AA sequence (177 to 181) is identified as a potential candidate for binding on a biomolecule. The CL signal graph for mutant K179C is reported in Fig. 5.22. As per Table 5.8 results, 5 AA sequence (177 to 181) is identified as the region of MERS nsp1 binding with

Table 5.8 DCLVS values for AAs associated with execution of task Ta1 for MERS

DCLVS value for 5 AA					Sum of DCLVS	Average value (MERS)	Average value (CoV from Table 5.5)
L177	N178	K179	G180	K181			
168	180	120	135	0	603	121 (23% higher than CoV)	93

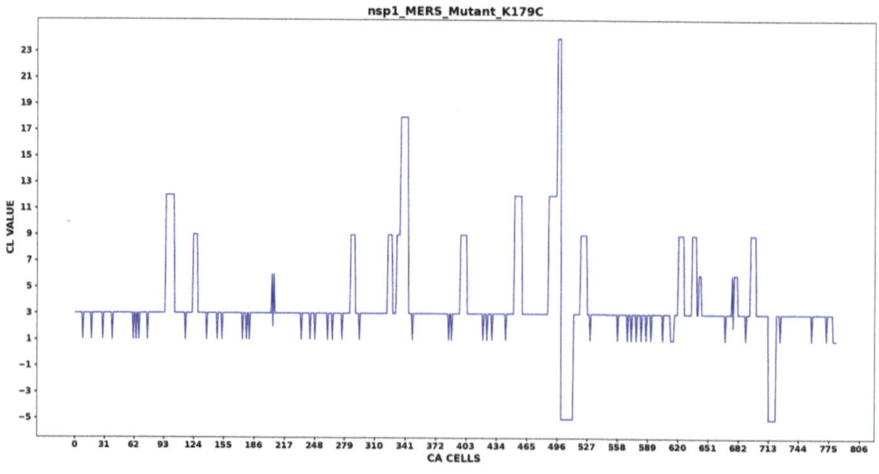

Fig. 5.22 CL signal graph for mutant K179C

host ribosome to shut down host mRNA translation. MERS displays significantly higher DCLVS value than that of CoV.

Task (Ta2) derived out of CAML model for MERS nsp1

The 5 AA sequence (R13 to R17) location covering polar +ive AA (R13, R17) is noted in Table 5.9 with DCLVS value for Cys mutant of each AA. The sum of DCLVS values and average value are 403 and 81. Hence the region of 5 AA (13 to 17) sequence is identified as the potential candidate for binding on 5'UTR of MERS

Table 5.9 DCLVS values for AAs associated with execution of task Ta2 for MERS

DCLVS value for 5 AA					Sum of DCLVS	Average value (MERS)	Average value (CoV from Table 5.6)
R13	G14	T15	Y16	R17			
0	273	65	65	0	403	81 (22% higher than CoV)	63

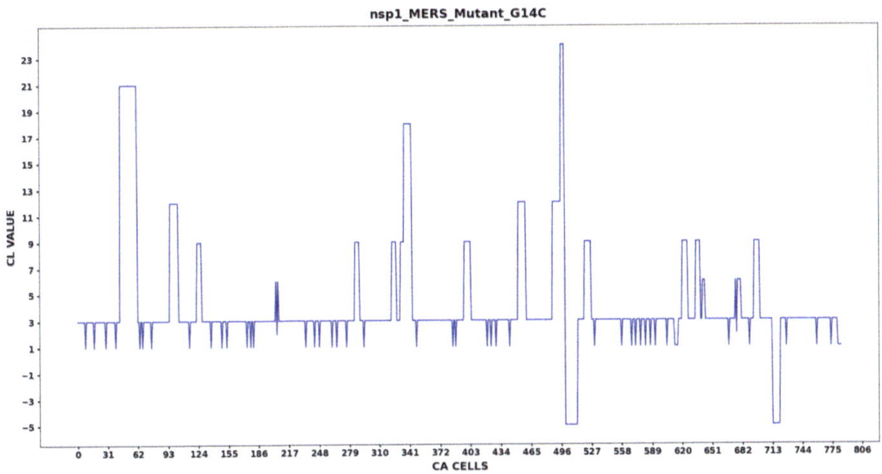

Fig. 5.23 MERS CL signal graph for mutant G14C showing high valued signal around cell location 55 corresponding to G14 for task Ta2

Table 5.10 DCLVS values for AAs associated with execution of task Ta3 for MERS

DCLVS value for 5 AA					Sum of DCLVS	Average value (MERS)	Average value (CoV from Table 5.7)
R146	K147	Y148	G149	R150			
231	144	156	0	0	531	106 (100% higher than CoV)	51

viral RNA. The CL signal graph for mutant G14C is reported in Fig. 5.23 with high valued signal around cell location 55 corresponding to AA location 14.

Task (Ta3) derived out of CAML model for RAA pair (R146, K147)

It has been reported [17, 31] that in addition to host translation shut off, MERS nsp1 displays host RNA cleavage function with AA pair (R146, K147). The 5 AA sequence (R146 to R150) selected around RAA pair (R146, K147) is noted in Table 5.10 with DCLVS value for Cys mutant of each AA. The sum of DCLVS values and average value are 531 and 106. Hence the region of 5 AA sequence (146 to 150) is identified as a potential candidate for binding on a biomolecule. The CL signal graph for mutant R146C and K147C are reported in Figs. 5.24 and 5.25 with high valued signal around

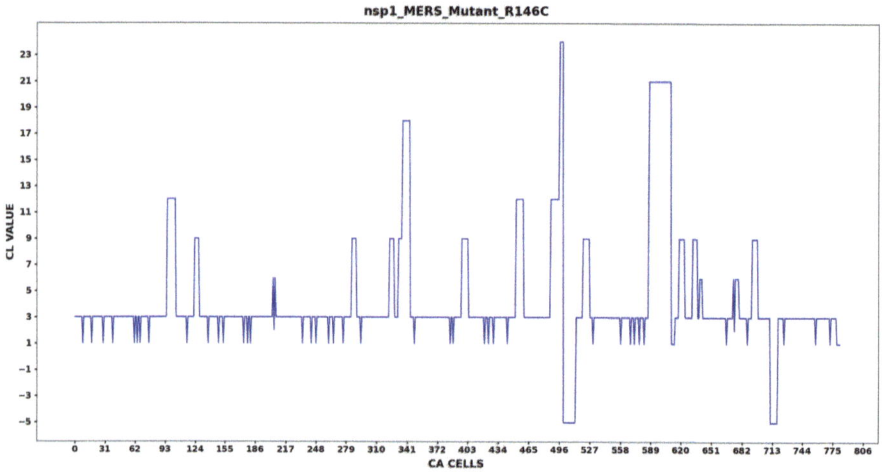

Fig. 5.24 CL signal graph for MERS mutant R146C for task Ta3 displaying high valued signal around cell location 146

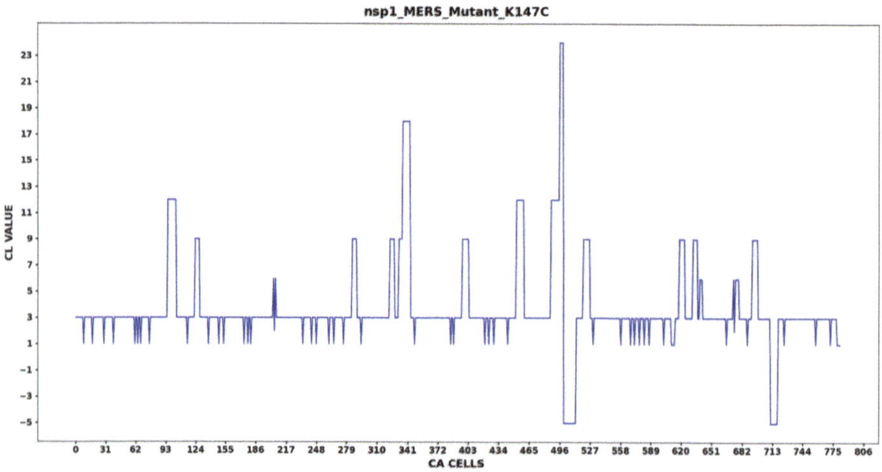

Fig. 5.25 CL signal graph for MERS mutant K147C for task Ta3

cell location 588 corresponding to AA location 146 and 147. The 5 AA sequence (146 to 150) is associated with RNA cleavage activity. As a result, the proteins necessary for activation of host immune response are not synthesized leading to compromised host immune response due to MERS nsp1.

Summary of results derived out of CAML model for comparison of Transmissibility and Virulence of SARS Covid (2003) and MERS covid (2012)

In view of limited data of affected patients (in terms of a few thousands) it is not possible to compare transmissibility of CoV and MERS. However, due to significantly higher (100% higher) value of task Ta3 (in respect of suppression of host immune response), virulence for MERS is likely to be higher than CoV. This results of CAML model gets validated from the historical records reproduced below:

In 2003, the SARS-CoV outbreak impacted 29 countries, infecting approximately 8,000 people and resulting in 774 deaths. In comparison, the 2012 MERS-CoV outbreak affected 27 countries, with 2,500 infections and 876 deaths. The fatality rates for SARS and MERS were 9.6 and 35.0%, respectively. The higher mortality rate of MERS is likely due to greater immune suppression in hosts, which triggers increased virulence in the virus.

5.3.7 Conclusion

Significantly higher transmissibility of SARS CoV-2 (2019) compared to SARS CoV (2003) is an established fact. Section 5.2 employs CAML model for mutational study of envelope protein and establishes higher transmissibility of CoV-2 compared to CoV envelope protein. The current Sect. 5.3 compares the transmissibility factor of CoV-2 and CoV nsp1 to ascertain their contribution towards higher transmissibility of CoV-2. The nsp1 is a major determinant after viral entry in host for—(i) shutting off host translation, while ensuring viral translation and (ii) downregulation of host immune response. Execution of these three tasks (marked as Ta1, Ta2, and Ta3) by CoV2 and CoV are compared to establish that CoV2 nsp1 contributes towards higher transmissibility due to higher efficiency of host translational shut off compared to that of CoV. Further, CoV-2 also adversely affects host immune defence with higher efficiency than CoV. The numerical figures derived out of the CAML model for nsp1 point to higher transmissibility of SARS CoV-2 compared to SARS CoV and MERS covid. This section also analyzes the reason for higher levels of virulence for MERS compared to CoV. We expect the quantitative analysis reported on employing CAML model will provide a platform for design of robust vaccine and therapeutic agents in the context of appearance of new virus strains. Further as many experts apprehend, due to continuous environmental degradation, new types of zoonotic viruses are likely to appear in the near future. CAML platform can help to fight the next pandemic situation for quick design of vaccines and therapeutic agents.

5.4 Prediction of Mutational Hot Spots and Antibody Escape Mutants in SARS CoV-2 Spike Protein

Coronavirus, the sub-microscopic parasite, infects living cells of an organism for its survival and growth. It carries a number of structural and non-structural proteins; the most prominent one is the Spike protein (S). The virus utilizes the spike protein for its entry through binding with host cell surface receptor protein, followed by its replication and subsequent transmission from the infected cell. Last two Sects. 5.2 and 5.3 employ CAML models for analysis of envelope protein and non-structural proteins (nsp1). The model clearly establishes higher transmissibility of SARS CoV-2 (noticed in 2019) compared to CoV (appeared in 2003) and MERS covid (in 2012). However, the pandemic situation of 2020–2022 was due to the inherent capability of CoV-2 virus protein to mutate and mediate immune evasion. Such mutations are mostly concentrated in the Receptor Binding Domain (RBD) of spike protein. The immune network of a living cell fights the virus/pathogens infecting the cell. The novel coronavirus CoV-2 has evolved its strategy to survive in the host cell while evading the onslaught of the cell's immune system. The large size CoV-2 spike protein with 1273 AA is the key player to realize this objective. Detailed mutational analysis of SARS CoV-2 spike protein RBD is undertaken in this section.

5.4.1 Introduction

The spike protein on the virus surface plays a crucial role for its entry in the host cell. The virus mediates its entry into the host cell through binding of its spike protein on the host cell surface receptor, followed by fusion of viral particles with the cell. Consequently, the majority of the CoV-2 vaccine designers have targeted the spike protein to boost up the immune system against the virus. In view of the CoV-2 pandemic situation, a large number of authors have concentrated on in-vitro/in-vivo/in-silico analysis of spike protein. Most of the publications deal with spike protein mutants which mediate escape from neutralizing antibodies. Such mutants belong to the category of Virus Of Concern (VOC).

This subsection concentrates on the analysis of spike protein of SARS CoV-2 based on Cellular Automata (enhanced with) Machine Learning (CAML) model developed for mutational study of biological string of protein amino acid chain. The model introduces nineteen mutations for each amino acid of the spike protein chain RBD (Receptor Binding Domain). Machine Learning (ML) algorithms are designed based on—(i) the analysis of the training set data curated from in vivo/in vitro/in-silico experimental results available in published literature, and (ii) the Feature Vector (FV) derived out of CA model parameters. The parameters are extracted out of CA evolution of wild and mutated versions of spike protein chain. Two algorithms reported in this section enable prediction of Potential Mutational Hot Spots (PMHS) and neutralizing Antibody Escape (nAbE) mutants in spike protein RBD. The CAML model can be extended to predict PMHS and nAbE mutants in the regions of spike protein other than RBD. As discussed earlier, compared to the existing machine learning platforms, the CAML framework employs significantly reduced training set data without sacrificing prediction quality. Also, compared to existing ML models, CAML demands much lesser computing resources. The vaccine designers can utilize this platform to arrive at a quick refurbished vaccine for new class of viruses. The 2020–2022 pandemic highlighted that the quicker a vaccine is available to fight new virus strains, the better the outcome for society.

With the passage of time, a pandemic situation subsides due to rise of infected population (imparting natural immunity against the virus) along with large scale vaccination (imparting acquired immunity), as it happened by the end of 2022 with CoV-2 virus. Nevertheless, the discipline of virology covers detailed analysis of past viruses, particularly those created pandemic situation. In this context, our results present a novel way of tackling a virus epidemic employing CAML model. Specifically, the model provides a platform to fight future pandemic situations that may arise due to new type of zoonotic viruses. The continuous environmental degradation along with large scale urbanization, as some of the experts in the field apprehend, is likely to create a situation that would lead to future zoonotic viruses. Further, CAML model to study viral proteins adds a new direction in the field of virology dealing with structural classification and evolution of biological viruses through interaction with host cell proteins.

The following nomenclature is followed in subsequent discussions. A mutant xLx' refers to change of the amino acid x at location L (in a protein chain) to the amino acid x'. Nineteen mutations are possible for each of the 20 amino acids. An Amino Acid (backbone and its side chain) is referred to as AA. While a mutant is noted as Mut reported in-vivo/in-vitro/in-silico mutational study in published literature, non-Mut is the one where no mutation is reported. Rather than concentrating on an individual mutant, CAML model analyses Mutation site AA (MsAA) where a mutation is reported. The model evaluates the effect of 19 mutations inserted for each MsAA location.

Next section reports a brief survey of papers published in [32–45] dealing with structural and functional details of CoV-2 spike protein interacting with other biomolecules, while emphasizing the mutational landscape of AAs in its RBD (receptor Binding Domain) and their immune evasion. Identification of neutralizing Antibody Escape (nAbE) mutants based on CAML model, is the focus of the Sect. 5.4.

5.4.2 Covid Spike Protein (S)—A Brief Survey

The Spike protein S is the most crucial protein of coronavirus. It is a large trimeric transmembrane glycoprotein supporting glycosylation. It has a unique coronavirus spherical structure with spikes protruding from its surface. The spike protein S of CoV-2 having 1273 AA, consists of two subunits, denoted as S1 (AA location 1 to 681) and S2 (AA location 686 to 1273). The structural details and interaction of different subunits of S are reported in [32–36, 46–49]. The S1 subunit can be divided into three regions—(i) NTD (N-Terminal Domain) from AA 14 to 306, (ii) RBD

(Receptor Binding Domain) from AA 329 to 527 covering the Receptor Binding Motif (RBM at 438 to 506), and (iii) post—RBD domain (marked as Subdomain SD) from AA 528 to 681 [36]. The RBD of S1 is responsible for recognizing host cell surface receptor ACE2 (Angiotensin-Converting Enzyme 2) followed by latching of its spikes on the host cell surface. The S1–S2 interface covers the AA region 681 to 686 followed by subunit S2 (AA location 686 to 1273). The subunit S2 covers the Fusion Peptide (FP) (AA 812 to 855) for fusion of its membrane with the host cell membrane receptor; the FP facilitates virus entry in the host cell. We have marked AA location 686 to 811 of S2 as Pre-FP and AA location 856 to 1273 as post-FP domains. The junction between S1 and S2 (AA 681 to 686) provides the site for effective cleavage by furin and other proteases. In view of its crucial role for virus entry in the host cell, the S protein is the key target for vaccine design. Mutations in the RBD of S1 subunit alter the infection characteristics of mutated virus. A number of authors [33, 50–56] have reported comparative study of structural and functional aspects of spike proteins of SARS covid (CoV-2) with earlier SARS covid (CoV—2003) and MERS (Middle East Respiratory Syndrome) covid (2012). Mutations on non-RBD AAs of spike protein may also directly or indirectly affect spike—receptor binding and viral pathogenesis [57]. Along with the analysis of structure and function, the epidemiological study in respect of fitness, transmissibility, and antibody neutralization of viral mutants are the major focus of the brief survey.

5.4.3 Design of CA Rule Vector for Amino Acid Chain of SARS CoV-2

Chapter 4 reports CA preliminaries and CA rule design for 20 Amino Acids (AAs). Table 4.4 of Chap. 4 reports the CA rule string for twenty amino acids of a protein chain. Observation 4.1 reported in Chap. 4 is relevant for evolution of CA modelling a protein chain. Based on the analysis of the rule set for side chains, amino Acids can be divided into the following three groups: (i) a group of 5 AAs modelled with 1 CA rule; (ii) a group of 8 AAs modelled with two CA rules; (iii) a group of 7 AAs modelled with 3 CA rules. It has been observed in the evolution patterns of CA that the second group covering 8 AAs stand apart from other two groups covering 12 (5 + 7) AAs.

5.4.3.1 Spike Protein 1273 AA Chain

The 1273 amino acid sequence of CoV-2 spike protein is presented in Table 5.11 along with the partial Rule Vector (RV) for the first six AAs of the chain. The Receptor Binding Domain (RBD) of spike protein starts from amino acid F329 (amino acid F at serial number 329) and ends at P527 (shown in bold letter in the AA string).

The rule vector for a protein chain can be derived by concatenating rule strings of each AA. Once the CA Rule Vector is designed for a protein chain, we study the

Table 5.11 SARS CoV-2 Spike protein of length 1273 AA and partial Rule Vector (RV) for first six AA excluding Met (M corresponding to Start codon)

CoV-2 Spike protein—1273 AA	
AA Chain	MFVFLVLLPLVSSQCVNLTTRTQLPPAYTNSFTRGVYYPDKVFRSSVL HSTQDLFLPFFSNVTWFHAIHVSGTNGTKRFDNPVLPFNDGVYFAST EKSNIIRGWIFGTTLDSKTQSLLIVNNATNVVIKVCEFQFCNDPFLGVY YHKNNKSWMESEFRVYSSANNCTFEYVSQPFLMDLEGKQGNFKNLR EFVFKNIDGYFKIYSKHTPINLVRDLPQGFSALEPLVDLPIGINITRFQ TLLALHRSYLTPGDSSSGWTAGAAAYYVGYLQPRTFLLKYNENGTIT DAVDCALDPLSETKCTLKSFTVEKGIYQTSNFRVQPTESIVR**FPNITN** **LCPFGEVFNATRFASVYAWNRKRISNCVADYSVLYNSASFST** **FKCYGVSPTKLNDLCFTNVYADSFVIRGDEVRQIAPGQTGKI** **ADYNYKLPDDFTGCVIAWNSNNLDSKVGGNYNYLYRLFRK** **SNLKPFERDISTEIYQAGSTPCNGVEGFNCYFPLQSYGFQPT** **NGVGYQPYRVVVLSFELLHAPATVCGP**KKSTNLVKNKCVNFNF NGLTGTGVLTESNKKFLPFQQFGRDIADTTDAVRDPQTLEILDITPCS FGGVSVITPGTNTSNQVAVLYQDVNCTEVPVAIHADQLTPTWRVYST GSNVFQTRAGCLIGAEHVNNSYECDIPIGAGICASYQTQTNSPRRARS VASQSIIAYTMSLGAENSVAYSNNSIAIPTNFTISVTTEILPVSMTKTSV DCTMYICGDSTECSNLLLQYGSFCTQLNRALTGIAVEQDKNTQEVFA QVKQIYKTPPIKDFGGFNFSQILPDPSKPSKRSFIEDLLFNKVTLADAG FIKQYGDCLGDIAARDLICAQKFNGLTVLPPLLTDEMIAQYTSALLAG TITSGWTFGAGAALQIPFAMQMAYRFNGIGVTQNVLYENQKLIANQF NSAIGKIQDSLSSTASALGKLQDVVNQNAQALNTLVKQLSSNFGAISSV LNDILSRLDKVEAEVQIDRLITGRLQSLQTYVTQQLIRAAEIRASANLA ATKMSECVLGQSKRVDFCGKGYHLMSFPQSAPHGVVFLHVTYVPAQ EKNFTTAPAICHDGKAHFPREGVFVSNGTHWFVTQRNFYEPQIITTD NTFVSGNCDVVIGIVNNTVYDPLQPELDSFKEELDKYFKNHTSPDVDL GDISGINASVVNIQKEIDRLNEVAKNLNESLIDLQELGKYEQYIKWPW YIWLGFIAGLIAIVMVTIMLCCMTSCCSCLKGCCSCGSCCKFDEDDSE PVLKGVKLHYT
Partial rule vector	<107, 99, 11, 107, 111, 107, 99, 59, 15, 107, 99, 11, 107, 111, 107, 99, 47, 15, 15, 107, 99, 59, 15, 107, 99, 47, 15, 15 ··· >

evolution of the CA generating a signal graph referred to as Cycle Length (CL) signal graph detailed next.

5.4.4 *CA Evolution Generating CL Signal Graph for AA Chain of a Protein*

The generic steps of execution of Phase 1 and Phase 2 of CAML model design are reported in Sect. 5.1.2 that reports CL graph generation procedure for any protein chain.

Figures 5.26 and 5.27 reports the CL signal Graphs for—(a) wild spike protein with 1273 AA for CoV-2, and (b) wild spike protein with 1255 AA for CoV. Figures 5.28, 5.29 and 5.30 shows the CL signal graphs for three CoV-2 mutants—(a) E484K, (b)E484Q and (c) N501Y respectively.

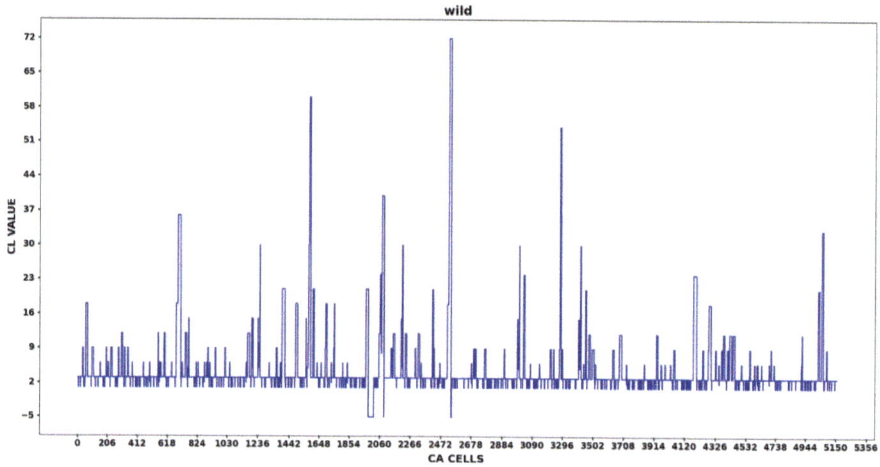

Fig. 5.26 CL signal graph for CoV-2 Spike Protein wild AA chain of length 1273 AA

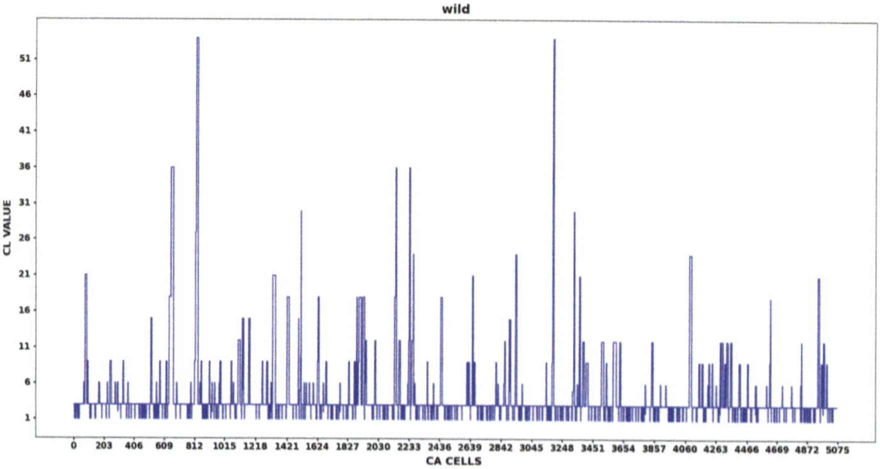

Fig. 5.27 CL signal graph for CoV Spike Protein wild AA chain of length 1255 AA

5.4.5 *CL Signal Graph Analytics for Wild Type and Mutant AA Chain*

For the CAML model, signal graph analytics enable extraction of meaningful information from a graph relevant for mutational study of a protein chain. Wild type AA chain refers to the one that can be observed in nature with normal phenotype/characteristics. The chain with a mutation is termed Mutant referred to as xLx', where the original amino acid x at location L of the protein chain is altered to the amino acid x'.

5.4.5.1 CL Signal Graph for Wild Type AA Chain

Table 5.11 shows the 1273 AA sequence of CoV-2 spike protein and partial rule vector for the first six AAs. Figures 5.26 and 5.27 report the CL signal graphs for evolution of CA as per Rule Vector for wild type AA chain for CoV-2 (1273 AA) and CoV (1255 AA). For the sake of comparison, in addition to the CL signal graph for CoV-2 spike protein, we also report the CL signal graph for CoV spike protein of length 1255 AA. The mcl values for CL graphs for CoV-2 and CoV are respectively 72 and 54. It can be observed that there exists a significant difference in CL signal graphs (wild and mutants) of CoV-2 and CoV.

5.4.5.2 CL Signal Graph for Mutant AA Chain

In Molecular Biology, site directed Ala mutagenesis is usually undertaken to determine the contribution of a specific AA in the function of a given protein. Instead of Ala, CAML model introduces all the 19 mutations for each AA of the spike protein chain followed by analysis of the parameters derived out of CA evolution for wild

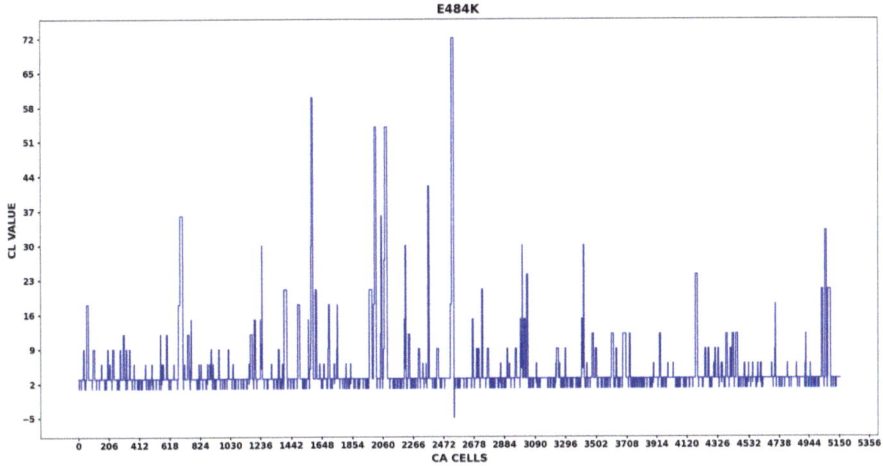

Fig. 5.28 CL Signal graph for mutant E484K of CoV-2 Spike Protein

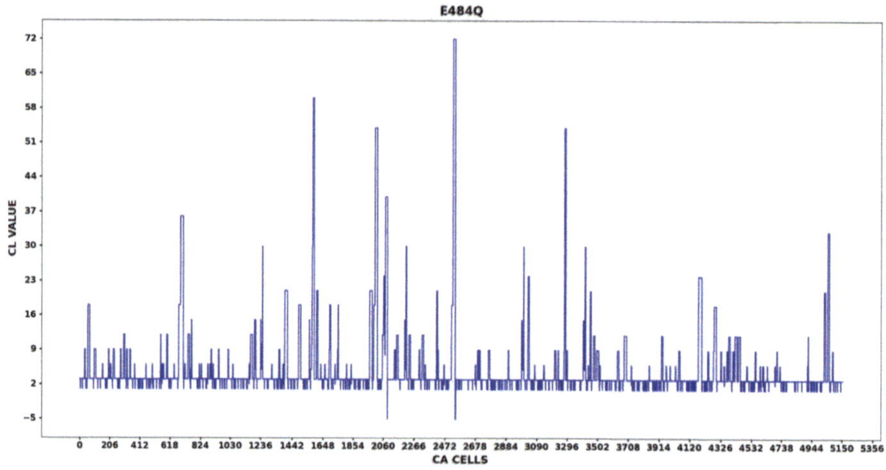

Fig. 5.29 CL Signal Graph for mutant E484Q of CoV-2 Spike Protein

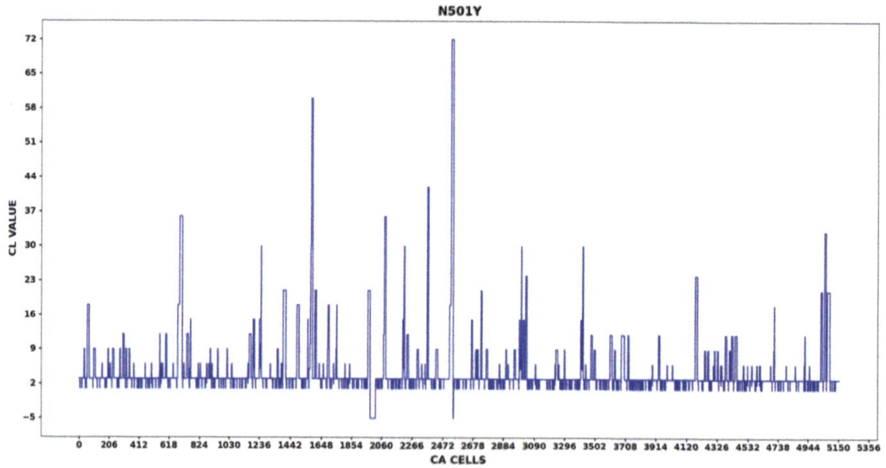

Fig. 5.30 CL Signal graph for mutant N501Y of CoV-2 Spike Protein

and mutated versions of the protein. The survey presented in Sect. 5.4.2 points to the results derived from the specific mutations on spike protein. Researchers have concentrated on mutational study on CoV-2 spike protein Receptor Binding Domain (RBD) AA location 329 to 527 [36]—two such mutants (E484K and N501Y) are marked as VOC (Virus Of Concern) [58]. While the N501Y mutation enhances binding affinity with the ACE2 receptor, the E484K/Q mutations enable the mutated virus to escape neutralizing antibodies through disruption of bonding with antibody epitopes. In this background we report signal graphs for three mutants. Figures 5.28, 5.29 and 5.30 display CL Signal graph for three mutants of CoV-2 spike protein—(a)

E484K—original amino acid Glu (E) at serial location 484 mutated with amino acid Lys(K); (b) E484Q—original amino acid Glu (E) at location 484 mutated with Gln (Q); and (c) N501Y—original amino acid Asn (N) at serial location 501 mutated with amino acid Y (Tyr). The CL graph for the wild version of spike protein is reported in Fig. 5.26.

Table 5.12 reports CL values for Wild and three Mutants—E484K, E484Q, and N501Y for the cell locations 1969 to 2075 (corresponds to approximate AA loc 492 to 519, assuming average 4 cells per AA). The differences between wild and mutant graph CL data are highlighted next.

(i) CL values for Wild and N501Y have identical CL value (CL (–5)) at cell loc 1985 to 2021, while E484K/Q differ from Wild;
(ii) CL values for Wild and three mutants have identical CL values at cell loc 1969 to 1984 with CL value 21;
(iii) CL values for Wild, two mutants E484Q, and N501Y have identical cell values (12 followed by 24) at cell loc 2045 to 2054, while, Mutant E484K differ from Wild and other two Mutants.

Next section analyses the difference of the CL graphs of mutants and Wild, through evaluation of two quantized parameters CLVS (CL Value Sum) and DCLVS (Difference in CLVS) defined next.

CAML model employs three neighbourhood periodic boundary CA. CL signal graphs derived out of periodic boundary CA enables extraction of relevant parameters to compare a mutant with its wild counterpart. Two quantized parameters derived out of CL signal graphs are CLVS and DCLVS.

CL Value Sum (CLVS): CLVS for a wild/mutant is computed considering mcl and Nmcl signal values of—Wild and mutant CL graphs; by definition, only CL values greater than or equal to 7 are considered, while ignoring cells having CL (–5) values. For both (i) wild spike protein CL graph (Fig. 5.26) and (ii) CL graph for mutant N501Y (Fig. 5.30), the cell locations 1985 to 2007 display CL (–5) value, are excluded for CLVS computation.

DCLVS (Difference of CL Value Sum): DCLVS = CLVS (mutant) – CLVS (wild). DCLVS value is assumed to be 0, if the value is less than or equal to the absolute value 50.

Table 5.13 reports the CLVS values for wild and 19 mutants for 10 amino acids F329 to F338 (first 10 AAs of Recptor Binding Domain (RBD) for 1273 spike protein shown in Table 5.11). The DCLVS value for a mutant can be (–ive), (+ive) or 0. The DCLVS value 0 indicates that the CLVS values for the mutant and wild are equal. These three DCLVS values are derived for each AA of a protein chain on introducing 19 mutations. Table 5.13 reports the CLVS values for wild (on Row 2) followed by CLVS for 19 mutants in subsequent 19 Rows for each AA (row 3 to row 21 for amino acid F329, row 22 to row 40 for P330 and so on till amino acid F338 mutants). Column 3 shows the DCLVS values for mutants. Out of 19 rows, the last row for each Lth AA (L = 329, 330, ..., 338) shows data for the mutant xLx', where x = F329, P330, ..., F338, and x' = amino acid W. For example, row 21 Column 2 and 3 reports the CLVS and DCLVS values for amino acid F2W. The same row 21

Table 5.12 Comparison of CL value between Wild and three Mutants E484K, E484Q, N501Y at the region covering cell location 1969 to 2075

Cell Loc	Cell Val-wild	Cell Val—E484K	Cell Val—E484Q	Cell Val—N501Y
1969	21	21	21	21
1970	21	21	21	21
1971	21	21	21	21
1972	21	21	21	21
1973	21	21	21	21
1974	21	21	21	21
1975	21	21	21	21
1976	21	21	21	21
1977	21	21	21	21
1978	21	21	21	21
1979	21	21	21	21
1980	21	21	21	21
1981	21	21	21	21
1982	21	21	21	21
1983	21	21	21	21
1984	21	21	21	21
1985	–5	21	21	–5
1986	–5	21	21	–5
1987	–5	21	3	–5
1988	–5	21	3	–5
1989	–5	3	1	–5
1990	–5	3	3	–5
1991	–5	3	3	–5
1992	–5	3	3	–5
1993	–5	3	3	–5
1994	–5	3	3	–5
1995	–5	3	3	–5
1996	–5	3	3	–5
1997	–5	3	18	–5
1998	–5	18	18	–5
1999	–5	18	18	–5
2000	–5	18	18	–5
2001	–5	18	18	–5
2002	–5	18	18	–5
2003	–5	18	18	–5
2004	–5	18	18	–5
2005	–5	18	54	–5
2006	–5	54	54	–5

(continued)

Table 5.12 (continued)

Cell Loc	Cell Val-wild	Cell Val—E484K	Cell Val—E484Q	Cell Val—N501Y
2007	–5	54	54	–5
2008	–5	54	54	–5
2009	–5	54	54	–5
2010	–5	54	54	–5
2011	–5	54	54	–5
2012	–5	54	54	–5
2013	–5	54	54	–5
2014	–5	54	54	–5
2015	–5	54	54	–5
2016	–5	54	54	–5
2017	–5	54	54	–5
2018	–5	3	54	–5
2019	–5	3	54	–5
2020	–5	3	54	–5
2021	–5	3	54	–5
2022	3	1	3	3
2023	3	3	3	3
2024	3	3	3	3
2025	1	3	1	1
2026	3	3	3	3
2027	3	3	3	3
2028	3	3	3	3
2029	3	3	3	3
2030	3	3	3	3
2031	3	3	3	3
2032	3	3	3	3
2033	3	3	3	3
2034	3	3	3	3
2035	1	3	1	1
2036	3	3	3	3
2037	3	3	3	3
2038	3	3	3	3
2039	3	3	3	3
2040	3	3	3	3
2041	1	3	1	1
2042	3	1	3	3
2043	3	3	3	3
2044	3	3	3	3
2045	1	12	1	1

(continued)

Table 5.12 (continued)

Cell Loc	Cell Val-wild	Cell Val—E484K	Cell Val—E484Q	Cell Val—N501Y
2046	3	12	3	3
2047	3	12	3	3
2048	3	12	3	3
2049	1	12	1	1
2050	3	36	3	3
2051	3	36	3	3
2052	3	36	3	3
2053	3	36	3	3
2054	3	36	3	3
2055	3	3	3	3
2056	12	3	12	3
2057	12	3	12	3
2058	12	3	12	3
2059	12	3	12	3
2060	12	1	12	1
2061	12	3	12	3
2062	12	3	12	3
2063	12	3	12	3
2064	24	3	24	3
2065	24	9	24	3
2066	24	9	24	3
2067	24	9	24	1
2068	24	9	24	3
2069	24	9	24	3
2070	24	9	24	3
2071	24	27	24	3
2072	8	27	8	3
2073	8	27	8	3
2074	8	27	8	3
2075	40	27	40	3

(col 4, 5, 6) reports the total count of (-ive), (+ive), and 0 values (<10 2 7>) for 19 mutations inserted for the amino acid F329. Count of (-ive) and (+ive) values are increased only if the absolute value of numerical difference between mutant and wild is greater than the value 50. That is, the 0 count on column 6 includes all the mutants for which DCLVS value is less than or equal to absolute value 50. This threshold limit of 50 has been set from the analysis of DCLVS values derived out of exhaustive experimentation with CAML model and published experimental results on mutational study of proteins surveyed in Sect. 5.4.2.

Table 5.13 CLVS and DCLVS for ten AA (F329 to F338) for CoV-2

Id	CLVS	DCLVS	(–ve) cnt	(+ve) cnt	0 cnt	Id	CLVS	DCLVS	(–ve) cnt	(+ve) cnt	0 cnt
Wild	13256	0				N334A	13130	–126			
F329A	13193	–63				N334G	13130	–126			
F329G	13193	–63				N334V	13256	0			
F329V	13124	–132				N334L	13130	–126			
F329L	13238	–18				N334M	13256	0			
F329M	13169	–87				N334I	13130	–126			
F329I	13238	–18				N334S	13130	–126			
F329S	13274	18				N334T	13256	0			
F329T	13124	–132				N334C	13247	–9			
F329C	13223	–33				N334P	13256	0			
F329P	13160	–96				N334Q	13256	0			
F329N	13091	–165				N334K	13130	–126			
F329Q	13151	–105				N334R	13130	–126			
F329K	13238	–18				N334H	13316	60			
F329R	13193	–63				N334D	13130	–126			
F329H	13349	93				N334E	13256	0			
F329D	13529	273				N334F	13148	–108			
F329E	13091	–165				N334Y	13130	–126			
F329Y	13217	–39				N334W	13130	–126	11	1	7
F329W	13283	27	10	2	7	L335A	13268	12			
P330A	13079	–177				L335G	13298	42			
P330G	13199	–57				L335V	13160	–96			
P330V	13193	–63				L335M	13172	–84			
P330L	13091	–165				L335I	13256	0			
P330M	13193	–63				L335S	13256	0			
P330I	13091	–165				L335T	13160	–96			
P330S	13079	–177				L335C	13346	90			
P330T	13193	–63				L335P	13238	–18			
P330C	13091	–165				L335N	13196	–60			
P330N	13193	–63				L335Q	13172	–84			
P330Q	13193	–63				L335K	13286	30			
P330K	13079	–177				L335R	13256	0			
P330R	13079	–177				L335H	13232	–24			
P330H	13256	0				L335D	13334	78			
P330D	13124	–132				L335E	13184	–72			
P330E	13205	–51				L335F	13358	102			
P330F	13079	–177				L335Y	13280	24			
P330Y	13079	–177				L335W	13298	42	6	3	10
P330W	13079	–177	18	0	1	C336A	13403	147			
N331A	13142	–114				C336G	13226	–30			
N331G	13376	120				C336V	13100	–156			
N331V	13256	0				C336L	13271	15			
N331L	13130	–126				C336M	13100	–156			

(continued)

Table 5.13 (continued)

Id	CLVS	DCLVS	(–ve) cnt	(+ve) cnt	0 cnt	Id	CLVS	DCLVS	(–ve) cnt	(+ve) cnt	0 cnt
N331M	13256	0				C336I	13271	15			
N331I	13130	–126				C336S	13403	147			
N331S	13142	–114				C336T	13100	–156			
N331T	13256	0				C336P	13181	–75			
N331C	13283	27				C336N	13100	–156			
N331P	13292	36				C336Q	13100	–156			
N331Q	13256	0				C336K	13271	15			
N331K	13142	–114				C336R	13226	–30			
N331R	13142	–114				C336H	13235	–21			
N331H	13256	0				C336D	13226	–30			
N331D	13142	–114				C336E	13100	–156			
N331E	13697	441				C336F	13226	–30			
N331F	13142	–114				C336Y	13226	–30			
N331Y	13142	–114				C336W	13145	–111	8	2	9
N331W	13142	–114	10	2	7	P337A	13100	–156			
I332A	13256	0				P337G	12791	–465			
I332G	13475	219				P337V	13436	180			
I332V	13130	–126				P337L	13289	33			
I332L	13256	0				P337M	13394	138			
I332M	13130	–126				P337I	12908	–348			
I332S	13256	0				P337S	13247	–9			
I332T	13130	–126				P337T	13436	180			
I332C	13256	0				P337C	12719	–537			
I332P	13205	–51				P337N	13238	–18			
I332N	13130	–126				P337Q	13394	138			
I332Q	13130	–126				P337K	13331	75			
I332K	13256	0				P337R	13289	33			
I332R	13256	0				P337H	13346	90			
I332H	13283	27				P337D	12764	–492			
I332D	13280	24				P337E	13226	–30			
I332E	13142	–114				P337F	13100	–156			
I332F	13274	18				P337Y	13100	–156			
I332Y	13256	0				P337W	12845	–411	8	6	5
I332W	13256	0	7	1	11	F338A	12977	–279			
T333A	13130	–126				F338G	13004	–252			
T333G	13130	–126				F338V	12731	–525			
T333V	13256	0				F338L	12977	–279			
T333L	13130	–126				F338M	12749	–507			
T333M	13256	0				F338I	12857	–399			
T333I	13130	–126				F338S	12977	–279			
T333S	13130	–126				F338T	12731	–525			
T333C	13208	–48				F338C	14117	861			
T333P	13301	45				F338P	12905	–351			

(continued)

Table 5.13 (continued)

Id	CLVS	DCLVS	(–ve) cnt	(+ve) cnt	0 cnt	Id	CLVS	DCLVS	(–ve) cnt	(+ve) cnt	0 cnt
T333N	13256	0				F338N	12851	–405			
T333Q	13256	0				F338Q	12851	–405			
T333K	13130	–126				F338K	12977	–279			
T333R	13130	–126				F338R	12977	–279			
T333H	13256	0				F338H	12851	–405			
T333D	13148	–108				F338D	12995	–261			
T333E	13340	84				F338E	13130	–126			
T333F	13130	–126				F338Y	12977	–279			
T333Y	13130	–126				F338W	12857	–399	18	1	0
T333W	13130	–126	11	1	7						

Table 5.14 Pattern Type Triplet (PTT) <(–ve)cnt (+ve)cnt 0 cnt> for CoV-2 amino acid serial location amino acid F329 to amino acid F338

Id	CLVS	DCLVS	(–ve)cnt	(+ve)cnt	0 cnt
Wild	13256	0			
F329	13283	27	10	2	7
P330	13079	–177	18	0	1
N331	13142	–114	10	2	7
I332	13256	0	7	1	11
T333	13130	–126	11	1	7
N334	13130	–126	11	1	7
L335	13298	42	6	3	10
C336	13145	–111	8	2	9
P337	12845	–411	8	6	5
F338	12857	–399	18	1	0

Pattern Type of Triplet (PTT): The PTT refers to the pattern type of triplet <(cnt (–ive)) (cnt (+ive)) cnt (0)> values. These values are derived by inserting 19 mutations for each AA of a protein chain, and next counting the number of instances where DCLVS values are respectively (–ive), (+ive), and (0). Physical significance of these parameters derived out of the CAML model is reported below. Table 5.14 reports the PTT for 10 AAs of CoV-2 (amino acid F329 to F338). Table 5.14 is derived from Table 5.13 column 4, 5, 6 on row 21 (for F329), row 40 (for P330), and so on.

Observation 5.3—PTT characteristics: The PTT of an AA is marked as a Unique-PTT, if it does not match with PTT of any other AA covered by RBD (Receptor Binding Domain (AA location 329 to 507) of Cov-2 spike protein. It plays an important role for prediction of PMHS (Potential Mutational Hot Spot).

Physical Significance of (–ive/+ive) DCLVS value: The (–ive) DCVS value indicates that some signals of wild CL graph get reduced/eliminated in the mutant. While a (+ive) DCLVS value of a mutant indicates the CL value of some signal gets enhanced or there is the appearance of some additional signal in the mutant CL graph that is absent in its wild counterpart. Evaluation of cnt ((–ive), (+ive), and 0) values of DCLVS is illustrated for the CL value data reported in Table 5.12 showing CL values for wild and 3 mutants.

CL values differ for the region covering cell locations (i) 1985 to 2007 and (ii) 2056 to 2072; CL values for all other cell locations other than (i) and (ii) are equal:

(i) Locations (1985 to 2005): DCLVS (E484K) = $(4 \times 21 + 8 \times 18) - 0$ (for wild, since all the cells have CL (–5)) = +288, and DCLVS (N501Y) = 0;
(ii) Locations 2056 to 2070: DCLVS (E484K) = $6 \times 9 - (8 \times 12 + 7 \times 24) = (-210)$, and DCLVS (N501Y) = (assumed to be 0 since less than 50).

Based on the evaluation PTT, we next report the Machine Learning framework for prediction of PMHS in spike protein RBD (Receptor Binding Domain AA location 329 to 527).

PMHS (Potential Mutational Hot Spot): An AA marked as PMHS refers to its location L, where a mutation is likely to occur in the spike protein. The AA location L having the amino acid x may get mutated to another amino acid x' resulting in the mutant (xLx'). PMHS prediction reported in Sect. 5.4.6 specifies the location L.

For mutational study of a protein, CAML model introduces 19 mutations on each amino acid (AA) of a protein chain. Mutation site AA (MsAA) refers to an AA of the chain on which a mutation is reported in published literature out of in-vitro/in-vivo laboratory experiment. Prediction of PMHS is based on the analysis of mutations reported in literature.

5.4.6 *Prediction of Potential Mutational Hot Spot (PMHS) in CoV-2 Spike Protein RBD*

The publications [40–44, 59–68] of 2022 highlight the detection of new mutations on CoV-2 virus proteins. Majority of these mutations belong to different sub lineages of the variant Omicron and are covered in spike protein RBD. Some of the mutants identified in the initial phase of pandemic in 2020–2021, have started reappearing in the omicron mutation list. Consequently, a number of authors [64, 65] have tried to assess the origin of the variant omicron that is dominant in 2022. In this context, evaluation of PMHS in CoV-2 spike protein RBD has attracted major interest in 2022, since there is likelihood of CoV-2 variants with new mutations not observed earlier in spike protein RBD. The CAML framework can be employed to predict PMHS in spike protein RBD and also in other regions of spike protein. Further, the generic CAML framework can be also employed to predict PMHS in any virus which may appear in future. Prediction of PMHS in CAML model is designed from detailed analysis of the following two factors:

(a) CAFV (CA Feature Vector defined below)—It is derived out of the parameter PTT count of <(-ive), (+ive), (0)> DCLVS values (defined earlier) extracted from CAML model on inserting 19 mutations on each AA location of spike protein chain of RBD; and
(b) analysis of the mutants reported in [69] published in 2021.

The CAML framework enables us to learn the relationship of (a) and (b). The set of mutants reported in [69] is viewed as the Training Set (TrS), while the Validation Set (VaS) covers the set of 22 mutations reported in 2022 in [41, 43]. The VaS is employed to refine the prediction algorithm designed based on the TrS. Eight mutants of TrS are covered in VaS. In effect, VaS covers fourteen ($22 - 8 = 14$) independent mutants.

Ten Element CAFV (CA Feature Vector)—The FV <v0 v1 v2 v3 v4 v5 v6 v7 v8 v9> of 10 elements marked as variables v0 to v9 is derived out of PTT of each AA. The CAFV of ith AA specifies the environment of PTTs around each AA by evaluating its 5 neighbours on either end, $(i - 5)$ to $(i + 5)$ excluding the ith AA. Numerical value of each variable spans from 0 to 10. The sequential steps for design of CAFV is reported under ESU2 (Experimental Set Up 2) reported subsequent to next two definitions.

PTT—FV Table—Displays both PTT (Definition 5.9) and 10 element FV (Definition 5.12 (a)) for each AA of a protein chain.

Vector Distance (VD)—A pair of mutants are compared in respect of their Feature Vector <FV>; the Vector Distance (VD) is derived on computing square root of (sum of square of the distance of each pair of elements of 10 element FV). VD = 0 if the vector elements are equal.

Table 5.15 displays PTT and ten element CAFV (both defined earlier) for the AAs of spike protein RBD (F329 to P327) along with some additional AAs on either end.

The Experimental setup, based on which the steps of Algorithm 2 (noted below) have been designed for prediction of PMHS (defined earlier), follows.

Experimental Set-Up (ESU1 to ESU5)—for Prediction PMHS (Potential Mutational Hot Spot) in CoV-2 RBD (AA location 329 to 527).

ESU1: Table 5.15 covers the CoV-2 RBD AA location (329 to 527) which corresponds to approximate cell locations 1316 to 2108 in the CL signal graphs of Figs. 5.26, 5.27, 5.28, 5.29 and 5.30. Table 5.15 columns 2, 3, 4 show the PTT (defined earlier) for the AAs, while column 1 shows the AA type and serial location in CoV-2 spike protein chain. The 10 element FV for each AA is noted on column 5 to 14. ESU2 for the design of FV follows.

ESU2: Design of 10 Element Cellular Automata Feature Vector (CAFV): Ten different Features are extracted for each ith AA of RBD based on the analysis of 10 AAs—$(i - 1)$ to $(i - 5)$ and $(i + 1)$ to $(i + 5)$. The FV <v0 v1 v2 v3 v4 v5 v6 v7 v8 v9> is derived out of the 10 numerical variable v0 to v9 on executing the following two steps:

Table 5.15 The Pattern Type Triplet—Feature Vector (PTT—FV) values for the Recptor Binding Domain (RBD) F329 to P527

AA Loc and type	cnt DCLVS			cnt of PTT										**Mut**(m) [116]	Predict PMHS VaS [145, 152]	Predic rule (Pru1, Pru2)
	(–ive)	(+ive)	val (0)	v0	v1	v2	v3	v4	v5	v6	v7	v8	v9			
T323	11	2	6													
E324	12	0	7													
S325	8	2	9													
I326	8	0	11													
V327	11	0	8													
R328	8	0	11	0	0	0	1	0	0	1	0	8	0			
F329	10	2	7	0	0	0	2	0	0	1	0	7	0			
P330	18	0	1	0	0	0	2	0	0	1	0	7	0			
N331	10	2	7	0	0	0	2	0	0	1	0	7	0			
I332	7	1	11	0	0	0	1	0	0	0	0	9	0			
T333	11	1	7	0	0	0	1	0	0	1	0	8	0			
N334	11	1	7	0	0	0	0	0	1	1	0	8	0			
L335	6	3	10	0	0	0	0	0	2	1	0	7	0			
C336	8	2	9	0	0	0	0	0	2	1	0	7	0			
P337	8	6	5	0	0	0	0	0	2	1	0	7	0			
F338	18	1	0	0	0	0	0	0	2	0	0	8	0			
G339	19	0	0	0	0	0	0	0	1	0	0	9	0		VaS	
E340	19	0	0	0	0	0	0	0	1	0	0	9	0			
V341	16	1	2	0	0	0	1	0	2	0	0	7	0			
F342	11	2	6	0	0	0	2	0	2	0	0	6	0			
N343	11	3	5	0	0	0	3	0	2	0	0	5	0			
A344	9	1	9	0	0	0	3	0	2	0	0	5	0			
T345	11	2	6	0	0	0	3	0	1	0	0	6	0			
R346	8	0	11	0	0	0	3	0	0	0	0	7	0		VaS	
F347	8	0	11	0	0	0	4	0	0	0	0	6	0			
A348	8	0	11	0	0	0	4	0	0	1	0	5	0			
S349	8	1	10	0	0	0	5	0	0	1	0	4	0			
V350	11	2	6	0	0	0	5	0	0	1	0	4	0			
Y351	8	0	11	0	0	0	4	0	0	1	0	5	0			
A352	8	0	11	0	0	0	4	0	0	1	0	5	0			
W353	7	1	11	0	0	0	4	0	0	0	0	6	0			
N354	12	1	6	0	0	0	3	0	0	1	0	6	0			
R355	8	2	9	0	0	0	3	0	0	1	0	6	0			
K356	8	1	10	0	0	0	3	0	1	1	0	5	0			
R357	8	0	11	0	0	0	1	0	1	1	0	7	0			
I358	9	0	10	0	0	0	1	0	1	1	0	7	0			
S359	12	0	7	0	0	0	1	0	1	0	0	8	0			
N360	17	1	1	0	0	0	1	0	1	1	0	7	0		PMHS	Pru1
C361	19	0	0	0	0	0	1	0	0	1	0	8	0			
V362	17	0	2	0	0	0	1	0	1	1	0	7	0		PMHS	Pru1
A363	11	1	7	0	0	0	0	0	1	1	0	8	0			
D364	7	2	10	0	0	0	0	0	1	2	0	7	0			
Y365	7	1	11	0	0	0	0	0	1	1	0	8	0			

(continued)

Table 5.15 (continued)

AA Loc and type	cnt DCLVS			cnt of PTT										**Mut**(m) [116]	Predict PMHS VaS [145, 152]	Predic rule (Pru1, Pru2)
	(–ive)	(+ive)	val (0)	v0	v1	v2	v3	v4	v5	v6	v7	v8	v9			
S366	8	1	10	0	0	0	1	0	1	2	0	6	0			
V367	11	2	6	0	0	0	1	0	0	3	0	6	0			
L368	8	2	9	0	0	0	1	0	0	3	0	6	0			
Y369	7	1	11	0	0	0	1	0	0	2	0	7	0		PMHS	Pru1
N370	12	1	6	0	0	0	2	0	0	3	0	5	0			
S371	8	0	11	0	0	0	1	0	0	2	0	7	0		VaS	
A372	7	1	11	0	0	0	2	0	0	1	0	7	0			
S373	8	1	10	0	0	0	2	0	0	2	0	6	0		VaS	
F374	8	1	10	0	0	0	2	0	1	2	0	5	0			
S375	8	0	11	0	0	0	1	0	1	1	0	7	0		VaS	
T376	12	1	6	0	0	0	2	0	1	1	0	6	0		VaS	
F377	9	1	9	0	0	0	1	0	1	1	0	7	0		PMHS	Pru1
K378	13	4	2	0	0	0	1	0	1	0	0	8	0			
C379	19	0	0	0	0	0	1	0	0	0	0	9	0			
Y380	7	5	7	0	0	0	1	0	1	0	0	8	0			
G381	13	4	2	0	0	0	0	0	1	0	0	9	0			
V382	8	4	7	1	0	0	0	0	1	0	0	8	0			
S383	9	6	4	1	0	0	0	0	1	0	0	8	0			
P384	18	1	0	1	0	0	0	0	1	0	0	8	0			
T385	5	12	2	1	0	0	0	0	0	0	0	9	0			
K386	5	10	4	1	0	0	0	0	0	0	0	9	0			
L387	0	9	10	0	0	0	0	0	0	0	0	10	0			
N388	0	14	5	1	0	0	0	0	0	0	0	9	0			
D389	1	8	10	1	0	1	0	0	0	0	0	8	0			
L390	10	8	1	1	0	2	0	0	0	0	0	7	0			
C391	11	8	0	2	0	2	0	0	0	0	0	6	0			
F392	4	10	5	2	1	2	0	0	0	0	0	5	0			
T393	0	14	5	2	1	2	0	0	0	0	0	5	0			
N394	0	12	7	3	1	1	0	0	0	0	0	5	0			
V395	0	12	7	3	2	1	0	0	0	0	0	4	0			
Y396	0	9	10	2	2	2	0	0	0	0	0	4	0			
A397	0	8	11	4	1	2	0	0	0	0	0	3	0			
D398	0	9	10	3	2	2	0	0	0	0	1	2	0			
S399	0	9	10	3	3	2	0	0	0	0	1	1	0			
F400	0	8	11	5	2	1	0	0	0	0	1	1	0			
V401	0	14	5	5	3	1	0	0	0	0	1	0	0			
I402	0	9	10	3	3	1	0	1	0	0	1	1	0			
R403	0	10	9	4	3	1	0	1	0	0	0	1	0			
G404	0	8	11	3	2	2	0	1	0	0	1	1	0			
D405	0	9	10	2	3	2	0	1	0	0	1	1	0		VaS	
E406	0	12	7	3	2	1	0	1	0	0	1	2	0			
V407	0	13	6	3	2	2	0	0	0	0	1	2	0			
R408	0	8	11	2	1	2	0	1	0	0	1	3	0		VaS	
Q409	0	12	7	2	2	1	0	1	0	0	0	4	0			

(continued)

Table 5.15 (continued)

AA Loc and type	cnt DCLVS			cnt of PTT										**Mut**(m) [116]	Predict PMHS VaS [145, 152]	Predic rule (Pru1, Pru2)
	(–ive)	(+ive)	val (0)	v0	v1	v2	v3	v4	v5	v6	v7	v8	v9			
I410	0	9	10	1	1	2	0	1	0	0	0	5	0		PMHS	Pru2
A411	5	10	4	2	1	2	0	1	0	0	0	4	0			
P412	7	12	0	2	2	1	0	1	0	0	0	4	0			
G413	10	9	0	2	3	1	0	0	0	0	0	4	0			
Q414	1	13	5	2	3	1	0	0	0	0	0	4	0			
T415	0	15	4	3	3	0	0	0	0	0	0	4	0			
G416	0	9	10	1	4	0	0	0	0	0	0	5	0			
K417	0	8	11	2	3	0	0	0	0	0	0	5	0	Mut (m)	VaS	
I418	0	8	11	2	3	0	0	0	0	0	0	5	0		PMHS	Pru1
A419	0	8	11	2	3	0	0	0	0	0	0	5	0		PMHS	Pru1
D420	0	9	10	1	4	0	0	0	0	0	0	5	0			
Y421	0	8	11	2	3	0	0	0	0	0	0	5	0		PMHS	Pru1
N422	2	13	4	1	5	0	0	0	0	0	0	4	0			
Y423	1	9	9	2	4	0	0	0	0	0	0	4	0			
K424	1	9	9	3	3	0	0	0	0	0	0	4	0			
L425	1	8	10	3	2	0	0	0	0	0	0	5	0			
P426	5	12	2	2	2	1	0	0	0	0	0	5	0			
D427	0	8	11	2	1	1	0	0	0	0	0	6	0			
D428	0	9	10	1	2	1	0	1	0	0	0	5	0			
F429	0	9	10	1	3	1	0	1	0	0	0	4	0			
T430	0	14	5	3	3	1	0	1	0	0	0	2	0			
G431	0	12	7	4	3	0	0	1	0	0	0	2	0			
C432	0	8	11	4	2	1	0	2	0	0	0	1	0			
V433	0	13	6	5	2	1	0	1	0	0	0	1	0			
I434	0	8	11	4	1	1	0	3	0	0	0	1	0			
A435	0	9	10	2	2	2	0	3	0	0	0	1	0			
436Y	0	9	10	2	3	2	0	3	0	0	0	0	0			
N437	0	13	6	4	3	1	0	2	0	0	0	0	0			
S438	0	9	10	3	2	2	0	3	0	0	0	0	0			
N439	0	13	6	4	2	2	0	1	0	0	0	1	0	Mut (m)		
N440	0	12	7	4	1	1	0	2	0	0	0	2	0		VaS	
L441	0	8	11	3	0	2	0	2	0	0	0	3	0			
D442	0	9	10	1	1	3	0	2	0	0	0	3	0			
S443	0	12	7	2	1	3	0	1	0	0	0	3	0			
K444	0	14	5	1	2	4	0	1	0	0	0	2	0			
V445	0	16	3	1	2	4	0	1	0	0	0	2	0			
G446	0	11	8	2	2	3	0	1	0	0	0	2	0	Mut (m)	VaS	
G447	0	12	7	3	1	2	0	1	0	0	0	3	0			
N448	0	12	7	3	1	2	0	1	0	0	0	3	0			
Y449	0	8	11	4	0	2	0	1	0	0	0	3	0			
N450	0	13	6	4	2	2	0	0	0	0	0	2	0			
Y451	0	9	10	4	2	2	0	1	0	0	0	1	0		PMHS	Pru1
L452	0	9	10	4	3	2	0	1	0	0	0	0	0	Mut (m)	VaS	
Y453	0	9	10	5	3	1	0	1	0	0	0	0	0	Mut (m)		

(continued)

Table 5.15 (continued)

AA Loc and type	cnt DCLVS			cnt of PTT										**Mut**(m) [116]	Predict PMHS VaS [145, 152]	Predic rule (Pru1, Pru2)
	(–ive)	(+ive)	val (0)	v0	v1	v2	v3	v4	v5	v6	v7	v8	v9			
R454	0	9	10	5	4	0	0	1	0	0	0	0	0			
L455	0	8	11	6	2	1	0	1	0	0	0	0	0	Mut (m)		
F456	0	9	10	5	3	2	0	0	0	0	0	0	0			
R457	0	8	11	5	2	2	0	0	0	0	1	0	0			
K458	0	9	10	3	3	3	0	0	0	0	1	0	0			
S459	0	8	11	4	2	3	0	0	0	0	1	0	0			
N460	0	12	7	3	3	2	0	1	0	0	1	0	0		PMHS	Pru2
L461	0	12	7	3	2	2	0	1	0	0	2	0	0			
K462	0	10	9	2	3	3	0	1	0	0	1	0	0			
P463	0	12	7	3	2	2	0	1	0	0	2	0	0			
F464	0	9	10	2	2	3	0	1	0	0	2	0	0		PMHS	Pru2
E465	0	13	6	3	1	3	0	1	0	0	2	0	0			
R466	0	10	9	3	1	3	0	2	0	0	1	0	0			
D467	0	8	11	3	0	2	0	2	0	0	3	0	0			
I468	0	9	10	3	1	2	0	2	0	0	2	0	0			
S469	0	9	10	3	1	1	0	3	0	0	2	0	0			
T470	0	13	6	3	2	1	0	2	0	0	2	0	0			
E471	0	12	7	4	2	0	0	2	0	0	2	0	0			
I472	0	10	9	4	2	1	0	2	0	0	0	1	0			
Y473	0	9	10	3	1	1	0	3	0	0	1	1	0			
Q474	0	13	6	3	1	1	0	2	0	0	1	2	0			
A475	0	8	11	2	0	1	0	3	0	0	1	3	0			
G476	0	9	10	1	1	1	0	2	0	0	1	4	0	Mut (m)		
S477	0	11	8	2	1	0	0	2	0	0	1	4	0	Mut (m)	VaS	
T478	0	13	6	2	1	0	0	1	0	0	0	6	0	Mut (m)	VaS	
P479	1	18	0	1	1	0	0	2	0	0	0	6	0			
C480	0	19	0	1	1	0	0	1	0	0	0	7	0			
N481	2	16	1	1	0	0	0	1	0	0	0	8	0			
G482	0	19	0	0	0	0	0	1	0	0	0	9	0			
V483	1	17	1	0	0	0	0	1	0	0	0	9	0	Mut (m)		
E484	0	18	1	0	0	0	0	0	0	0	0	10	0	Mut (m)	VaS	
G485	0	19	0	1	0	0	0	0	0	0	0	9	0	Mut (m)		
F486	0	18	1	1	0	1	0	0	0	0	0	8	0		VaS	
N487	0	19	0	1	1	1	0	0	0	0	0	7	0			
C488	0	19	0	1	1	2	0	0	0	0	0	6	0			
Y489	0	18	1	2	1	2	0	0	0	0	0	5	0			
F490	0	9	10	1	1	2	0	0	0	0	1	5	0	Mut (m)	VaS	
P491	0	12	7	3	1	1	0	0	0	0	1	4	0		PMHS	Pru1
L492	0	8	11	3	0	2	0	0	0	0	1	4	0			
Q493	0	12	7	3	1	1	0	0	0	0	1	4	0		VaS	
S494	0	9	10	2	1	2	0	0	0	0	1	4	0	Mut (m)		
Y495	0	10	9	3	1	2	0	0	0		0	4	0			
G496	0	9	10	1	1	2	0	0	0	0	1	5	0		VaS	
F497	2	10	7	2	1	1	0	0	0	0	1	5	0			

(continued)

Table 5.15 (continued)

AA Loc and type	cnt DCLVS			cnt of PTT										**Mut**(m) [116]	Predict PMHS VaS [145, 152]	Predic rule (Pru1, Pru2)
	(−ive)	(+ive)	val (0)	v0	v1	v2	v3	v4	v5	v6	v7	v8	v9			
Q498	1	10	8	2	0	1	0	0	0	0	1	6	0		VaS	
P499	4	2	13	2	0	0	0	0	1	0	1	6	0			
T500	3	0	16	1	0	0	0	0	2	0	1	6	0			
N501	12	0	7	1	0	0	0	0	2	0	0	7	0	Mut (m)	VaS	
G502	14	0	5	0	0	0	0	0	3	0	0	7	0			
V503	18	0	1	0	0	0	0	0	4	0	0	6	0			
G504	19	0	0	0	0	0	0	0	3	0	0	7	0			
Y505	19	0	0	0	0	0	0	0	3	0	0	7	0		VaS	
Q506	17	2	0	0	0	0	0	0	4	0	0	6	0			
P507	19	0	0	0	0	0	0	0	3	0	0	7	0			
Y508	19	0	0	0	0	0	1	0	3	0	0	6	0			
R509	12	5	2	0	0	0	1	0	4	1	0	4	0			
V510	11	3	5	0	0	0	1	0	3	1	0	5	0			
V511	12	0	7	0	0	0	1	0	2	1	0	6	0			
V512	12	0	7	0	0	0	1	0	2	1	0	6	0			
L513	8	0	11	0	0	0	0	0	1	1	0	8	0			
S514	7	1	11	0	0	0	1	0	0	0	0	9	0			
F515	7	2	10	0	0	0	1	0	0	1	0	8	0			
E516	12	2	5	0	0	0	1	0	0	1	0	8	0			
L517	8	2	9	0	0	0	1	0	0	1	0	8	0			
L518	8	4	7	0	0	0	1	0	0	1	0	8	0			
H519	12	0	7	0	0	0	0	0	0	1	0	9	0			
A520	10	1	8	0	0	0	0	0	0	0	0	10	0			
P521	18	0	1	0	0	0	0	0	0	0	0	10	0			
A522	9	3	7	0	0	0	0	0	0	0	0	10	0			
T523	13	0	6	0	0	0	0	0	0	0	0	10	0			
V524	13	2	4	0	0	0	0	0	0	0	0	10	0			
C525	15	1	3	0	0	0	0	0	0	0	0	10	0			
G526	3	8	8	0	0	0	0	0	0	0	0	10	0			
P527	16	1	2	0	0	0	0	0	0	0	0	10	0			
K528	0	3	16	0	0	0	0	0	0	0	0	10	0			
K529	0	1	18													
S530	0	3	16													
T531	0	1	18													
N532	0	1	18													
L533	0	1	18													

(a) Analysis of count of PTTs in RBD—Based on this count analysis (across of RBD of CoV-2 spike protein), eight high count PTTs are selected in non-increasing order: (0-9-10), (0-8-11), (0-12-7), (8-0-11), (0-13-6), (19-0-0), (7-1-11), (0-9-10) of an AA which are marked as variables v0, v1, v2, v3, v4, v5, v6, v7 respectively. The variables are shown on columns 5 to 12 in Table 5.15; the count values of the PTTs across the RBD are respectively 29, 19, 15, 11, 8, 8, 6 for the eight PTTs. Two more variables marked as v8 and v9 (shown on column 13 and 14 of Table 5.15 row 2) are introduced:

v8 = 10 – (v0 + v1 + v2 + v3 + v4 + v5 + v6 + v7)

v9 = 0

The Step 1 of the Algorithm 2 extracts a 10 element Feature Vector (FV) for each AA, as per ESU2.

ESU3: Derivation of Prediction rules (Pru1, Pru2) in Prediction Algorithm 2—These rules are designed based on the analysis of the following parameters—PTT, FV and mutant list reported in Training Set and Validation Set.

(i) PTT and ten element FV.
(ii) The list of 15 mutants, referred to as Training Set (TrS), retrieved from [116] published in 2020–2021, each mutant is marked (as 'Mut') on column 15 of Table 5.15. An AA not marked as 'Mut' is referred to as 'non-Mut'.
(iii) The mutant list covered in Validation Set (VaS), retrieved from [145, 152] published in 2022, noted on column 16 of Table 5.15.

The amino acids predicted as PMHS by Algorithm 2 (reported below) are also reported in column 16.

ESU4: Step 2 of Algorithm 2 implements the prediction rules designed from the following considerations. We employ the mutants reported in [69] published in 2021 as template (marked as 'Mut') for prediction of PMHS, some of which appear in 2022 and noted as Validation Set (VaS). The underlying principle of design of prediction rules Pru1 and Pru2 are next explained.

Pru1: It refers to the evaluation of Vector Distance (VD) of the <FV> of an 'non-Mut' AA from that of an AA (marked as Mut or covered by the VaS (Validation Set)).
Pru2: It is designed based on the analysis of <sub-FV> covering a minimum 4 non-0 variables of FV observed in the AA (marked as 'Mut' or covered by the VaS), with sum of the variables covered by the <sub-FV> is greater than equal to 7.

The next experimental set up ESU5 predicts the set of PMHS out of the AAs covered in the RBD (Receptor Binding Domain) of spike protein; the AAs are listed on column 1 of Table 5.15.

ESU5: CAML machine learning process for prediction of Potential Mutational Hot Spot (PMHS) based on the analysis of the patterns of PTT and ten element FV of AAs -Column 15 of Table 5.15 shows the list mutant (Mut) appeared around the period of 2019–20; the list is retrieved from [69]. This list can be viewed as the Training Set (TrS) of the learning process of CAML model. The set of predicted PMHS is reported on column 16. The list of Mut appeared around the period 2021–2022 is retrieved from [41, 43]; this list of mutants, also reported on column 16, has been considered as the Validation Set (VaS) of CAML learning process. Each of the two

Prediction rules framed in Step 3 and Step 4 of the Algorithm 2 to predict a AA as a PMHS, satisfies the relationship specified under the rules (Pru1 or Pru2)—reported on column 17 of Table 5.15. The PMHS list can be viewed as the Testing Set (TeS) for the CAML model for evaluating nAbE mutants with Algorithm 3 reported in Sect. 5.4.7.

The Input 2 and Input 3 for the algorithm are the list of mutations curated from published literature. In the current section we concentrate on the mutational analysis of CoV-2 spike protein. Same algorithm is adopted in Sect. 5.5 for identification of PMHS in cancer proteins.

As noted in Step 0, the Algorithm 2 is not executed for a protein, if the number of MsAA (Mutation site AA) for the protein chain is more than 5% of its length. Such an instance can be observed for the cancer protein p53 showing 48 MsAAs in its length of 393 AA. The p53 protein is implicated for majority of cancer types and analyzed in Sect. 5.5 of Chap. 5.

Algorithm 2—Predict Potential Mutational Hot Spot (PMHS) in CoV-2 Spike Protein RBD

Input1: Table 5.15 for CoV-2 RBD covering 199 AA, each showing PTT (Pattern Type Triplet on column 2, 3, 4) that represents count of <(–ive), (+ive) , (0)> DCLVS values with columns 5 to 14 showing the 10 element FV.
Input2: The list of AAs reported in 2020–2021 publication [69] marked as Training Set (TrS) reported on column 15 and noted as (Mut) in Table 5.15.
Input3: The list of AAs reported in 2022 publications [41, 43] and marked as Validation Set (VaS) noted on column 16 of Table 5.15.

Output: The set of PMHS (reported on Column 16 of Table 5.15) are identified on execution of the algorithmic steps; column 17 reports the rule (Pru1, Pru2), employed to predict an AA as PMHS.

Step 0: If the number of MsAA is more than 5% of the length of the protein chain, go to Stop.

Step 1: For each ith AA, extract 10 AAs—$(i - 1)$ to $(i - 5)$ and $(i + 1)$ to $(i + 5)$; generate 10 element FV (Feature Vector) on counting the number of specific PTT in these 10 AA around ith AA (as noted under ESU2).

Step 2: An AA and its FV is not considered in subsequent steps, if one of the 10 element of its FV shows a value greater than or equal to 8.

Step 3: Mark an AA as PMHS (Potential Mutational Hot Spot) if the condition specified for the prediction rule Pru1 is valid:

Pru1 (Prediction rule 1): An non-Mut AA is marked as PMHS if its <FV> has Vector Distance (VD) = 0 with an AA having the same <FV> and marked as Mutant (Mut) or it belongs to VaS (Validation Set); this rule is valid if no more than 3 AAs are predicted as PMHS for an instance of this rule.

Step 4: An AA is marked as PMHS if the following rule Pru2 is valid for an AA not predicted as PMHS in Step 3.

Pru2 (Prediction rule 2): An non-Mut AA is marked as PMHS if its <sub-FV> covering minimum of four non-0 variables of <FV> match with an AA having same <sub-FV> of an AA (marked as Mut or belong to VaS); this rule is valid if no more than 3 AAs are predicted as PMHS for an instance of this rule.

Step 5: Stop and report the list of PMHS and MsAAs of the input protein.

Table 5.15 column 16 reports the set of 11 PMHS predicted by Algorithm 2. The Training Set (TrS), Input 2 for Algorithm 2, covers 15 AAs (shown on row 5 to row 29 of Table 5.20). The Validation Set (VaS), input 3 for Algorithm 2, has 22 AAs (shown on row 5 to row 26 of Table 5.21), out of which 8 AAs are covered in (TrS). Thus, 14(22 – 8) new AAs appeared with mutants reported in 2022 which did not appear in 2020–2021. The Algorithm 1 is implemented in Python code and executed on the AAs of CoV-2 RBD (AA location 329 to 527) noted in Table 5.15.

The following eleven AAs are identified as PMHS on execution of Algorithm 2 - (N360, V362, Y369, F377, I418, A419, Y421, Y451, P491) and (N460, F465) - these are reported on Column 17 of Fig. 5.15. First group of 9 PMHS are identified in Step 3 as per prediction rule Pru1. In Step 4, two AAs (N460, F464) are identified and illustrated - (i) N460 shows the same <sub-FV> = <v1 v2 v4 v7> = <3 2 1 1> of D405 marked as VaS; and (ii) F464 shows the same <sub-FV> = <v0 v1 v2 v4> = <2 2 3 1> of G446 marked as Mut (m).

It is worthwhile to point out the following fact. As per the latest report [45], the Omicron variant lineage BF.7 shows “the N460K mutation that has been the most critical factor behind the enhanced neutralization resistance of BF.7”. The CAML model predicts N460 as a PMHS.

Prediction of PMHS can be viewed as one side of the coin. Another side of the coin of major significance is to identify the specific AA of the TrS, VaS, and predicted PMHS set, which may mediate the escape from the neutralization by the antibodies of the infected cells of the affected patients. Next section reports the scheme for prediction of neutralizing Antibody Escape (nAbE) mutants in the Training Set (TrS), Validation Set (VaS), and the Testing Set (TeS); the PHMS set identified with Algorithm 2 is viewed as the TeS.

The PTT-FV table for spike protein RBD is reported in Table 5.15, out of which PMHS set is predicted. Subsequent tables (Tables 5.16, 5.17, 5.18, 5.19, 5.20, 5.21 and 5.22) refer to the next subsection dealing with prediction of nAbE (neutralizing Antibody Escape AAs in spike protein RBD.

Table 5.16 CL values at cell locations 1965 to 2010 for Wild and 19 mutatants for amino acid E484—displays an instance of GM* at cell loc 1996 to 2006 with Wild displaying 0 values (–5 val viewed as 0 value)

Cell no.	Wild	E484																		
		A	C	D	F	G	H	I	K	L	M	N	P	Q	R	S	T	V	W	Y
1965	3	3	3	3	3	3	3	3	3	3	3	3	3	3	3	3	3	3	3	3
1966	3	3	3	3	3	3	3	3	3	3	3	3	3	3	3	3	3	3	3	3
1967	3	3	3	3	3	3	3	3	3	3	3	3	3	3	3	3	3	3	3	3
1968	3	3	3	3	3	3	3	3	3	3	3	3	3	3	3	3	3	3	3	3
1969	21	21	21	21	21	21	21	21	21	21	21	21	21	21	21	21	21	21	21	21
1970	21	21	21	21	21	21	21	21	21	21	21	21	21	21	21	21	21	21	21	21
1971	21	21	21	21	21	21	21	21	21	21	21	21	21	21	21	21	21	21	21	21
1972	21	21	21	21	21	21	21	21	21	21	21	21	21	21	21	21	21	21	21	21
1973	21	21	21	21	21	21	21	21	21	21	21	21	21	21	21	21	21	21	21	21
1974	21	21	21	21	21	21	21	21	21	21	21	21	21	21	21	21	21	21	21	21
1975	21	21	21	21	21	21	21	21	21	21	21	21	21	21	21	21	21	21	21	21
1976	21	21	21	21	21	21	21	21	21	21	21	21	21	21	21	21	21	21	21	21
1977	21	21	21	21	21	21	21	21	21	21	21	21	21	21	21	21	21	21	21	21
1978	21	21	21	21	21	21	21	21	21	21	21	21	21	21	21	21	21	21	21	21
1979	21	21	21	21	21	21	21	21	21	21	21	21	21	21	21	21	21	21	21	21
1980	21	21	21	21	21	21	21	21	21	21	21	21	21	21	21	21	21	21	21	21
1981	21	21	21	21	21	21	21	21	21	21	21	21	21	21	21	21	21	21	21	21
1982	21	21	21	21	21	21	21	21	21	21	21	21	21	21	21	21	21	21	21	21
1983	21	21	21	42	21	21	21	-5	21	21	21	21	42	21	21	21	21	21	21	21
1984	21	21	21	2	21	21	21	-5	21	21	21	21	42	21	21	21	21	21	21	21
1985	21	–5	21	1	21	21	1	-5	21	21	21	21	42	21	21	21	21	21	21	21
1986	–5	–5	21	1	3	–5	1	5	21	21	21	42	42	21	21	21	21	21	21	1
1987	–5	–5	3	1	3	–5	1	5	21	21	21	42	42	21	3	21	3	21	21	3
1988	–5	–5	3	1	3	–5	1	5	21	21	21	42	42	21	3	21	3	21	21	3
1989	–5	–5	3	1	3	–5	3	5	21	3	21	42	42	21	1	21	3	21	21	3
1990	–5	–5	3	1	3	–5	3	5	21	3	21	42	42	21	3	21	3	21	21	3
1991	–5	–5	3	1	3	–5	3	5	21	3	21	42	42	21	3	21	3	21	21	3
1992	-5	-5	3	3	3	–5	3	5	21	3	21	42	42	21	3	21	3	21	21	3
1993	–5	–5	3	3	3	–5	3	–5	21	3	21	–5	–5	-5	6	21	3	–5	–5	3
1994	–5	-5	3	3	3	–5	3	–5	–5	3	–5	-5	–5	–5	6	–5	3	–5	–5	3
1995	–5	–5	3	3	3	–5	3	–5	–5	3	–5	–5	–5	–5	6	–5	3	–5	–5	3
1996	–5	–5	18	18	18	–5	18	–5	–5	3	–5	–5	–5	–5	3	–5	18	–5	–5	3
1997	–5	–5	18	18	18	–5	18	–5	–5	3	–5	–5	–5	–5	18	–5	18	–5	–5	3
1998	–5	-5	18	18	18	–5	18	–5	–5	18	–5	–5	–5	–5	18	–5	18	–5	–5	18 -
1999	–5	–5	18	18	18	–5	18	–5	–5	18	–5	–5	–5	–5	18	–5	18	–5	–5	18
2000	–5	–5	18	18	18	–5	18	–5	–5	18	–5	–5	–5	–5	18	–5	18	–5	–5	18
2001	–5	–5	18	18	18	–5	18	–5	–5	18	–5	–5	–5	–5	18	–5	18	–5	–5	18
2002	–5	–5	18	18	18	–5	18	–5	–5	18	–5	–5	–5	–5	18	–5	18	–5	–5	18
2003	–5	–5	18	18	18	–5	18	–5	–5	18	–5	–5	–5	–5	18	–5	18	–5	–5	18
2004	-5	–5	18	18	18	–5	18	–5	–5	18	–5	–5	–5	–5	18	–5	18	–5	–5	18
2005	–5	–5	18	18	18	–5	18	–5	–5	18	–5	–5	–5	–5	18	–5	18	–5	–5	18

(continued)

Table 5.16 (continued)

Cell no.	Wild	E484																		
		A	C	D	F	G	H	I	K	L	M	N	P	Q	R	S	T	V	W	Y
2006	–5	–5	18	18	18	–5	18	–5	–5	18	–5	–5	–5	–5	18	–5	18	–5	-5	18
2007	–5	–5	3	3	3	–5	3	–5	–5	18	–5	–5	–5	–5	18	–5	3	–5	–5	18
2008	–5	3	3	3	3	–5	3	3	–5	18	–5	3	3	3	3	–5	3	3	3	18
2009	3	3	3	3	3	3	3	3	3	3	3	3	3	3	3	3	3	3	3	3
2010	3	3	3	3	3	3	3	3	3	3	3	3	3	3	3	3	3	3	3	3

Table 5.17 CL values for N501 Wild and 19 mutants at cell loc 2025 to 2075—displays deviation of mutants from Wild at loc 2056–2072

Cell no.	Wild	N501																		
		A	C	D	E	F	G	H	I	K	L	M	P	Q	R	S	T	V	W	Y
2025	1	1	1	1	1	1	1	1	1	1	1	1	1	1	1	1	1	1	1	1
2026	3	3	3	3	3	3	3	3	3	3	3	3	3	3	3	3	3	3	3	3
2027	3	3	3	3	3	3	3	3	3	3	3	3	3	3	3	3	3	3	3	3
2028	3	3	3	3	3	3	3	3	3	3	3	3	3	3	3	3	3	3	3	3
2029	3	3	3	3	3	3	3	3	3	3	3	3	3	3	3	3	3	3	3	3
2030	3	3	3	3	3	3	3	3	3	3	3	3	3	3	3	3	3	3	3	3
2031	12	12	12	12	12	12	12	12	12	12	12	12	12	12	12	12	12	12	12	12
2032	12	12	12	12	12	12	12	12	12	12	12	12	12	12	12	12	12	12	12	12
2033	12	12	12	12	12	12	12	12	12	12	12	12	12	12	12	12	12	12	12	12
2034	12	12	12	12	12	12	12	12	12	12	12	12	12	12	12	12	12	12	12	12
2035	12	12	12	12	12	12	12	12	12	12	12	12	12	12	12	12	12	12	12	12
2036	12	12	12	12	12	12	12	12	12	12	12	12	12	12	12	12	12	12	12	12
2037	12	12	12	12	12	12	12	12	12	12	12	12	12	12	12	12	12	12	12	12
2038	12	12	12	12	12	12	12	12	12	12	12	12	12	12	12	12	12	12	12	12
2039	12	12	12	12	12	12	12	12	12	12	12	12	12	12	12	12	12	12	12	12
2040	12	12	12	12	12	12	12	12	12	12	12	12	12	12	12	12	12	12	12	12
2041	12	12	12	12	12	12	12	12	12	12	12	12	12	12	12	12	12	12	12	12
2042	3	3	3	3	3	3	3	3	3	3	3	3	3	3	3	3	3	3	3	3
2043	3	3	3	3	3	3	3	3	3	3	3	3	3	3	3	3	3	3	3	3
2044	3	3	3	3	3	3	3	3	3	3	3	3	3	3	3	3	3	3	3	3
2045	1	1	1	1	1	1	1	1	1	1	1	1	1	1	1	1	1	1	1	1
2046	3	3	3	3	3	3	3	3	3	3	3	3	3	3	3	3	3	3	3	3
2047	3	3	3	3	3	3	3	3	3	3	3	3	3	3	3	3	3	3	3	3
2048	3	3	3	3	3	3	3	3	3	3	3	3	3	3	3	3	3	3	3	3
2049	1	1	1	1	1	1	1	1	1	1	1	1	1	1	1	1	1	1	1	1
2050	3	3	3	3	3	3	3	3	3	3	3	3	3	3	3	3	3	3	3	3
2051	3	3	3	3	3	3	3	3	3	3	3	3	3	3	3	3	3	3	3	3
2052	3	3	3	3	3	3	3	3	3	3	3	3	3	3	3	3	3	3	3	3
2053	3	3	3	2	3	3	3	3	3	3	3	3	3	3	3	3	3	3	3	3
2054	3	3	3	6	3	3	3	3	3	3	3	3	3	3	3	3	3	3	3	3
2055	3	3	3	3	12	3	1	3	3	3	3	3	3	3	3	3	3	3	3	3
2056	12	3	3	3	12	12	1	3	3	3	3	3	3	12	3	3	3	3	1	12

(continued)

Table 5.17 (continued)

Cell no.	Wild	N501																		
		A	C	D	E	F	G	H	I	K	L	M	P	Q	R	S	T	V	W	Y
2057	12	3	3	3	12	12	1	3	3	3	3	3	3	12	3	3	3	3	7	12
2058	12	1	1	1	12	12	1	3	3	3	3	3	3	12	3	1	3	3	7	12
2059	12	3	3	3	12	12	3	1	3	3	3	3	1	12	3	3	1	1	7	12
2060	12	3	3	3	12	12	3	3	1	1	1	3	3	12	1	3	3	3	7	12
2061	12	3	3	3	12	12	3	3	3	3	3	3	3	12	3	3	3	3	7	12
2062	12	3	3	3	12	12	3	3	3	3	3	3	3	12	3	3	3	3	7	12
2063	12	9	3	9	12	12	9	3	3	3	3	3	3	12	3	9	3	3	7	12
2064	24	9	3	9	12	12	9	3	3	3	3	3	3	24	3	9	3	3	7	12
2065	24	9	1	9	3	24	9	3	3	9	3	3	3	24	9	9	3	3	7	24
2066	24	9	3	9	3	24	9	1	3	9	3	3	1	24	9	9	3	3	7	24
2067	24	9	3	9	3	24	9	3	1	9	1	3	3	24	9	9	3	3	7	24
2068	24	9	3	9	3	24	9	3	3	9	3	3	3	24	9	9	3	3	7	24
2069	24	9	3	9	3	24	9	3	3	9	3	3	3	24	9	9	3	3	7	24
2070	24	9	3	9	3	24	9	3	3	9	3	3	3	24	9	9	3	3	7	24
2071	24	9	3	9	3	24	9	3	6	9	6	3	3	24	9	9	3	3	21	24
2072	24	3	3	3	3	24	3	1	6	9	6	3	1	24	9	3	3	3	21	24
2073	3	3	3	3	3	24	3	3	6	9	6	3	3	3	9	3	3	3	21	24
2074	3	3	3	3	3	3	3	3	3	3	3	3	3	3	3	3	3	3	3	3
2075	3	1	1	1	3	3	1	3	3	3	3	3	3	3	3	1	3	3	3	3

Table 5.18 Wild L455 & 19 mutants (cell loc 2025–2075) for L455—displays a GM* at cell loc 2056 to 2072—with non-0 CL values for wild

Cell no.	Wild	L455																		
		A	C	D	E	F	G	H	I	K	M	N	P	Q	R	S	T	V	W	Y
2025	1	3	3	3	3	1	3	3	1	1	3	3	3	3	1	3	3	3	1	1
2026	3	3	3	3	3	3	3	3	3	3	3	3	3	3	3	3	3	3	3	3
2027	3	3	3	3	3	3	3	3	3	3	3	3	3	3	3	3	3	3	3	3
2028	3	3	3	3	3	3	3	3	3	3	3	3	3	3	3	3	3	3	3	3
2029	3	12	12	12	3	3	12	3	3	3	3	3	3	3	3	12	3	3	3	3
2030	3	12	12	12	12	3	12	12	3	3	12	12	12	12	3	12	12	12	3	3
2031	12	12	12	12	12	12	12	12	12	12	12	12	12	12	12	12	12	12	12	12
2032	12	12	12	12	12	12	12	12	12	12	12	12	12	12	12	12	12	12	12	12
2033	12	12	12	12	12	12	12	12	12	12	12	12	12	12	12	12	12	12	12	12
2034	12	12	12	12	12	12	12	12	12	12	12	12	12	12	12	12	12	12	12	12
2035	12	12	12	12	12	12	12	12	12	12	12	12	12	12	12	12	12	12	12	12
2036	12	12	12	12	12	12	12	12	12	12	12	12	12	12	12	12	12	12	12	12
2037	12	12	12	12	12	12	12	12	12	12	12	12	12	12	12	12	12	12	12	12
2038	12	12	12	12	12	12	12	12	12	12	12	12	12	12	12	12	12	12	12	12
2039	12	12	12	12	12	12	12	12	12	12	12	12	12	12	12	12	12	12	12	12
2040	12	3	3	3	12	12	3	12	12	12	12	12	12	12	12	3	12	12	12	12
2041	12	3	3	3	3	12	3	3	12	12	3	3	3	3	12	3	3	3	12	12

(continued)

Table 5.18 (continued)

Cell no.	Wild	L455																		
		A	C	D	E	F	G	H	I	K	M	N	P	Q	R	S	T	V	W	Y
2042	3	3	3	3	3	3	3	3	3	3	3	3	3	3	3	3	3	3	3	3
2043	3	1	1	1	3	3	1	3	3	3	3	3	3	3	3	1	3	3	3	3
2044	3	3	3	3	3	3	3	3	3	3	3	3	3	3	3	3	3	3	3	3
2045	1	3	3	3	3	1	3	3	1	1	3	3	3	3	1	3	3	3	1	1
2046	3	3	3	3	3	3	3	3	3	3	3	3	3	3	3	3	3	3	3	3
2047	3	1	1	1	3	3	1	3	3	3	3	3	3	3	3	1	3	3	3	3
2048	3	3	3	3	1	3	3	1	3	3	1	1	1	1	3	3	1	1	3	3
2049	1	3	3	3	3	1	3	3	1	1	3	3	3	3	1	3	3	3	1	1
2050	3	3	3	3	3	3	3	3	3	3	3	3	3	3	3	3	3	3	3	3
2051	3	3	3	3	3	3	3	3	3	3	3	3	3	3	3	3	3	3	3	3
2052	3	3	3	3	3	3	3	3	3	3	3	3	3	3	3	3	3	3	3	3
2053	3	3	3	3	3	3	3	3	3	3	3	3	3	3	3	3	3	3	3	3
2054	3	12	12	12	3	3	12	3	3	3	3	3	3	3	3	12	3	3	3	3
2055	3	12	12	12	3	3	12	3	3	3	3	3	3	3	3	12	3	3	3	3
2056	12	12	12	12	3	12	12	3	12	12	3	3	3	3	12	12	3	3	12	12
2057	12	12	12	12	3	12	12	3	12	12	3	3	3	3	12	12	3	3	12	12
2058	12	12	12	12	1	12	12	1	12	12	1	1	1	1	12	12	1	1	12	12
2059	12	12	12	12	3	12	12	3	12	12	3	3	3	3	12	12	3	3	12	12
2060	12	12	12	12	3	12	12	3	12	12	3	3	3	3	12	12	3	3	12	12
2061	12	12	12	12	3	12	12	3	12	12	3	3	3	3	12	12	3	3	12	12
2062	12	24	24	24	3	12	24	3	12	12	3	3	3	3	12	24	3	3	12	12
2063	12	24	24	24	9	12	24	9	12	12	9	9	9	9	12	24	9	9	12	12
2064	24	24	24	24	9	24	24	9	24	24	9	9	9	9	24	24	9	9	24	24
2065	24	24	24	24	9	24	24	9	24	24	9	9	9	9	24	24	9	9	24	24
2066	24	24	24	24	9	24	24	9	24	24	9	9	9	9	24	24	9	9	24	24
2067	24	24	24	24	9	24	24	9	24	24	9	9	9	9	24	24	9	9	24	24
2068	24	24	24	24	9	24	24	9	24	24	9	9	9	9	24	24	9	9	24	24
2069	24	24	24	24	9	24	24	9	24	24	9	9	9	9	24	24	9	9	24	24
2070	24	24	24	24	9	24	24	9	24	24	9	9	9	9	24	24	9	9	24	24
2071	24	3	3	3	9	24	3	9	24	24	9	9	9	9	24	3	9	9	24	24
2072	24	3	3	3	3	24	3	3	24	24	3	3	3	3	24	3	3	3	24	24
2073	3	3	3	3	3	3	3	3	3	3	3	3	3	3	3	3	3	3	3	3
2074	3	3	3	3	3	3	3	3	3	3	3	3	3	3	3	3	3	3	3	3
2075	3	3	3	3	1	3	3	1	3	3	1	1	1	1	3	3	1	1	3	3

5.4.7 Prediction of nAbE-AA (Neutralizing Antibody Escape AA) in Spike Protein RBD

A mutant (Mut), as noted earlier, is referred to as $xLx^{'}$ in the AA chain of a protein, where the original amino acid x at location L is mutated with amino acid $x^{'}$. Generation of CL signal graphs for wild and mutants for CoV-2 RBD is illustrated in Sect. 5.4.4. An nAbE mutant evade the immunogenic response of host cell. The

Table 5.19 Wild and 19 mut for S375 (cell loc 1550–1590)—displays GM** (at cell loc 1566 to 1579)

Cell no.	Wild	S375																		
		A	G	V	L	M	I	T	C	P	N	Q	K	R	H	D	E	F	Y	W
1550	3	3	3	3	3	3	3	3	3	3	3	3	3	3	3	3	3	3	3	3
1551	3	3	3	3	3	3	3	3	3	3	3	3	3	3	3	3	3	3	3	3
1552	3	3	3	3	3	3	3	3	3	3	3	3	3	3	3	3	3	3	3	3
1553	3	3	3	3	3	3	3	3	3	3	3	3	3	3	3	3	3	3	3	3
1554	3	3	3	3	3	3	3	3	3	3	3	3	3	3	3	3	3	3	3	3
1555	3	3	3	1	3	1	3	1	3	1	1	1	3	3	1	3	1	3	3	3
1556	3	3	3	3	3	3	3	3	3	3	3	3	3	3	3	3	3	3	3	3
1557	3	3	3	3	3	3	3	3	3	3	3	3	3	3	3	3	3	3	3	3
1558	3	3	3	3	3	3	3	3	3	3	3	3	3	3	3	3	3	3	3	3
1559	15	15	15	3	3	3	3	3	15	3	3	3	3	3	3	15	3	3	3	3
1560	5	5	5	3	3	3	3	3	5	3	3	3	3	3	3	5	3	3	3	3
1561	5	5	5	3	15	3	15	3	5	3	3	3	15	15	3	5	3	15	15	15
1562	5	5	5	3	5	3	5	3	5	3	3	3	5	5	3	5	3	5	5	5
1563	5	5	5	3	5	3	5	3	5	3	3	3	5	5	3	5	3	5	5	5
1564	5	5	5	3	5	3	5	3	5	3	3	3	5	5	3	5	3	5	5	5
1565	5	5	5	3	5	3	5	3	5	3	3	3	5	5	3	5	3	5	5	5
1566	5	5	5	12	5	12	5	12	5	12	12	12	5	5	12	5	12	5	5	5
1567	5	5	5	12	5	12	5	12	5	12	12	12	5	5	12	5	12	5	5	5
1568	5	5	5	12	5	12	5	12	5	12	12	12	5	5	12	5	12	5	5	5
1569	5	5	5	12	5	12	5	12	5	12	12	12	5	5	12	5	12	5	5	5
1570	5	5	5	12	5	12	5	12	5	12	12	12	5	5	12	5	12	5	5	5
1571	5	5	5	12	5	12	5	12	5	12	12	12	5	5	12	5	12	5	5	5
1572	5	5	5	12	5	12	5	12	5	12	12	12	5	5	12	5	12	5	5	5
1573	5	5	5	12	5	12	5	12	5	12	12	12	5	5	12	5	12	5	5	5
1574	10	10	10	12	5	12	5	12	10	12	12	12	5	5	12	10	12	5	5	5
1575	10	10	10	12	5	12	5	12	10	12	12	12	5	5	12	10	12	5	5	5
1576	10	10	10	3	10	3	10	3	10	3	3	3	10	10	3	10	3	10	10	10
1577	30	30	30	3	10	3	10	3	30	3	3	3	10	10	3	30	3	10	10	10
1578	3	3	3	3	10	3	10	3	3	3	3	3	10	10	3	3	3	10	10	10
1579	3	3	3	3	30	3	30	3	3	3	3	3	30	30	3	3	3	30	30	30
1580	3	3	3	3	3	3	3	3	3	3	3	3	3	3	3	3	3	3	3	3
1581	1	1	1	3	3	3	3	3	1	3	3	3	3	3	3	1	3	3	3	3
1582	3	3	3	1	3	1	3	1	3	1	1	1	3	3	1	3	1	3	3	3
1583	3	3	3	3	1	3	1	3	3	3	3	3	1	1	3	3	3	1	1	1
1584	3	3	3	3	3	3	3	3	3	3	3	3	3	3	3	3	3	3	3	3
1585	3	3	3	3	3	3	3	3	3	3	3	3	3	3	3	3	3	3	3	3
1586	3	3	3	3	3	3	3	3	3	3	3	3	3	3	3	3	3	3	3	3
1587	3	3	3	3	3	3	3	3	3	3	3	3	3	3	3	3	3	3	3	3
1588	3	3	3	3	3	3	3	3	3	3	3	3	3	3	3	3	3	3	3	3
1589	3	3	3	3	3	3	3	3	3	3	3	3	3	3	3	3	3	3	3	3
1590	3	3	3	3	3	3	3	3	3	3	3	3	3	3	3	3	3	3	3	3

Table 5.20 Results derived on execution of Algorithm 3 for prediction of nAbE-AA (neutralising Antibody Escape—amino acids) in the Training Set (TrS)

Variable	v0	v1	v2	v3	v4	v5	v6	v7	v8		
Regions	r0	r1	r2	r3	r4	r5	r6	r7	r8		
CA cells	1358 to 1364	1396 to 1414	1487 to 1501	1574 to 1590	1607 to 1615	1691 to 1702	1749 to 1755	1970 to 1985	2057 to 2090	Reported in [116] and literature	CAML AA class
wild-CLVS	63	399	270	750	189	180	90	336	912		
E484	0	0	0	0	0	0	0	1	1	E484K/Q	nAbE-AA
F490	0	0	0	0	0	0	0	0	0	F490S	non-nAbE
G446	0	0	0	0	0	0	1	1	0	G446V	nAbE-AA
G476	0	0	0	0	0	0	0	0	0	G476S	non-nAbE
G485	0	0	0	0	0	0	0	1	1	G485R	nAbE-AA
K417	0	0	0	0	0	1	1	0	0	K417N/T	nAbE-AA
L452	0	0	0	0	0	0	0	0	0	L452K	non-nAbE
L455	0	0	0	0	0	0	0	0	0	L455F	non-nAbE
N439	0	0	0	0	0	0	0	0	0	N439K	non-nAbE
N501	0	0	0	0	0	0	0	0	1	N501Y	nAbE-AA
S477	0	0	0	0	0	0	0	1	0	S477N	nAbE-AA
S494	0	0	0	0	0	0	0	0	0	S494P	non-nAbE
T478	0	0	0	0	0	0	0	1	1	T478I	nAbE-AA
V483	0	0	0	0	0	0	0	1	1	V483A	nAbE-AA
Y453	0	0	0	0	0	0	1	1	0	Y453F	nAbE-AA
A344	0	0	0	0	0	0	0	0	0	Non-Mut	Non-nAbE
C361	0	0	0	0	0	0	0	0	0	Non-Mut	Non-nAbE
C379	0	0	0	0	0	0	0	0	0	Non-Mut	Non-nAbE
G339	0	0	0	0	0	0	0	0	0	Non-Mut	Non-nAbE
H519	0	0	0	0	0	0	0	0	0	Non-Mut	Non-nAbE
P426	0	0	0	0	0	0	0	0	0	Non-Mut	Non-nAbE
Q409	0	0	0	0	0	0	0	0	0	Non-Mut	Non-nAbE
R457	0	0	0	0	0	0	0	0	0	Non-Mut	Non-nAbE
S494	0	0	0	0	0	0	0	0	0	Non-Mut	Non-nAbE
Y453	0	0	0	0	0	0	0	0	0	Non-Mut	Non-nAbE

CAML model identifies an nAbE mutant through comparison of CL signal graph of mutant with that of its wild counterpart. An nABE AA, formally defined below, covers at least one nAbE mutant.

The CAML model is designed based on the compilation of in-vivo/in-vitro/in-silico experimental results available in published literature [41, 43, 69, 70] reviewed in Sect. 5.4.2 and the CAML features derived on identifying deviation of a Mutant CL graph from that of Wild. Comparative analysis of the patterns in the CL signal graphs of wild and 19 mutants (inserted for each AA of TrS), provides the foundation of the learning process of CAML model. Deviation of CL data of the mutants from the wild are illustrated in Tables 5.17, 5.18, 5.19. Table 5.16 illustrates the CL values for cell locations 1965 to 2010 for the wild and 19 mutants inserted for the amino

Table 5.21 Results derived on execution of Algorithm 3 for prediction of nAbE-AA (neutralising Antibody Escape-AA) in the validation Set (VaS)

Variable	v0	v1	v2	v3	v4	v5	v6	v7	v8		
Regions	r0	r1	r2	r3	r4	r5	r6	r7	r8		
CA cells	1358 to 1364	1396 to 1414	1487 to 1501	1574 to 1590	1607 to 1615	1691 to 1702	1749 to 1755	1970 to 1985	2057 to 2090	Mut reported and [145, 152]	CAML AA class
wild-CLVS	63	399	270	750	189	180	90	336	912		
D405	0	0	0	0	1	1	0	0	0	D405N	nAbE-AA
E484 (TrS)	0	0	0	0	0	0	0	1	1	E484K	nAbE-AA
F486	0	0	0	0	0	0	0	1	1	F486V	nAbE-AA
F490 (TrS)	0	0	0	0	0	0	0	0	0	F490S	non-nAbE
G339	0	1	0	1	1	0	0	0	0	G339D	nAbE-AA
G446 (TrS)	0	0	0	0	0	0	1	1	0	G446V	nAbE-AA
G496	0	0	0	0	0	0	0	0	0	G496S	non-nAbE
K417 (TrS)	0	0	0	0	0	1	1	0	0	K417N	nAbE-AA
L452 (TrS)	0	0	0	0	0	0	0	0	0	L452R	non-nAbE
N440	0	0	0	0	0	0	0	0	0	N440K	non-nAbE
N501 (TrS)	0	0	0	0	0	0	0	0	1	N501Y	nAbE-AA
Q493	0	0	0	0	0	0	0	0	0	Q493R	non-nAbE
Q498	0	0	0	0	0	0	0	0	1	Q498R	nAbE-AA
R346	0	0	0	1	1	0	0	0	0	R346T	nAbE-AA
R408	0	0	0	0	0	0	0	0	0	R408S	non-nAbE
S371	0	0	0	1	1	0	0	0	0	S371F/L	nAbE-AA
S373	0	0	1	1	1	0	0	0	0	S373P	nAbE-AA
S375	0	0	0	1	1	0	0	0	0	S375F	nAbE-AA
S477 (TrS)	0	0	0	0	0	0	0	1	1	S477N	nAbE-AA
T376	0	0	0	1	1	0	0	0	0	T376A	nAbE-AA
T478 (TrS)	0	0	0	0	0	0	0	1	1	T478K	nAbE-AA
Y505	0	0	0	0	0	0	0	0	1	Y505H	nAbE-AA

acid E484. Partial CL value data also reported in Tables 5.17, 5.18 and 5.19—these tables respectively report the CL values of wild and 19 mutants inserted for—(b) N501 cell loc 2025–2075, (c) L455 cell loc 2025–2075, (d) S375 cell loc 1550–1590 (approximate AA loc 387–398). A few definitions and the experimental set up based on which the algorithmic steps have been designed are reported next. The Training Set (TrS) of the experimental set up covers 15 mutants curated from [69] and shown on column 1 rows 5 to 19 of Table 5.20. Ten AAs (noted on rows 20–29) marked as non-Mut are also reported in column 1 of Table 5.20. Column 11 reports the mutants reported in [69]. As per the survey reported in Sect. 5.4.2, no mutations are reported on AAs marked as non-Mut on column 11. Table 5.20 reports the results derived on execution of Algorithm 3 to predict nAbE-AA in 15 AAs of TrS. The prediction algorithm is executed in the background of detailed analysis of CL value data of a large number of non-mutants for which no deviation exists between wild and all the

Table 5.22 The results derived on execution of Algorithm 3 for prediction of nAbE (neutralising Antibody Escape) mutants in the PMHS set identified by Algorithm 2

Variable	v0	v1	v2	v3	v4	v5	v6	v7	v8		
Regions	r0	r1	r2	r3	r4	r5	r6	r7	r8		
CA cells	1358 to 1364	1396 to 1414	1487 to 1501	1574 to 1590	1607 to 1615	1691 to 1702	1749 to 1755	1970 to 1985	2057 to 2090	Reported as PMHS	CAML prediction
Wild-CLVS	63	399	270	750	189	180	90	336	912		
A419	0	0	0	0	0	0	0	0	0	PMHS	Non-nAbE
F377	0	0	1	1	1	0	0	0	0	PMHS	nAbE-AA
F464	0	0	0	0	0	0	0	0	0	PMHS	Non-nAbE
I418	0	0	0	0	0	0	0	0	0	PMHS	Non-nAbE
N360	0	0	1	1	1	0	0	0	0	PMHS	nAbE-AA
N460	0	0	0	0	0	0	0	0	0	PMHS	Non-nAbE
P491	0	0	0	0	0	0	0	0	0	PMHS	Non-nAbE
Y369	0	0	0	1	1	0	0	0	0	PMHS	nAbE-AA
Y421	0	0	0	0	0	1	1	0	0	PMHS	nAbE-AA
Y451	0	0	0	0	0	0	0	0	0	PMHS	Non-nAbE
V362	0	0	1	1	1	0	0	0	0	PMHS	nAbE-AA

19 mutations inserted for each AA of a non-Mutant. Ten of such non-Mut are shown in Table 5.20 rows 20–29.

Three terminologies, defined next, are relevant for nAbE-AA prediction in the CAML model. As highlighted earlier, rather than concentrating on an individual mutant at an AA location, CAML model inserts 19 mutations in an amino acid for nAbE evaluation. The CL values of mutants are compared with that of its wild counterpart. In a specific region, if a mutant CL value differs from that of wild, it is viewed as an nAbE mutant that evades neutralization by cell antibody.

nAbE mutant—A mutant that mediates escape from neutralization by Antibody of infected cell.

nAbE-AA class—This class covers AAs, each of which has at least one nAbE mutant on insertion of 19 mutations. An AA not having any nAbE mutant is referred to as non-nAbE. Column 12 of Table 5.20 illustrates non-nAbE and nAbE-AA.

AA* Class and non-AA* Class: CAML model employs periodic boundary CA (Fig. 4.1 Chap. 4), where the leftmost cell is the neighbour of the rightmost cell and vice versa. In view of evolution of periodic boundary CA modelling a protein chain, the following characteristic of CL signal graph has been observed, with 19 mutations inserted for an AA.

Observation 5.3 with respect of CL values for two group of mutants: On insertion of 19 mutations on each AA of a protein chain, there may exist a region covering a set of CA cells which show equal CL values; this set is of mutants is marked as AA* amino acids. This CL value differs from that of non-AA* class covering other 11 amino acids; each of the non-AA* amino acids display equal CL values for the

CA cells in that region. This observation has been found to be true for any protein chain evaluated with the CAML model.

Table 5.18 reporting CL values for wild and 19 mutants for amino acid L455, cell location 2025 to 2075. This table illustrates the deviation CL values for AA* class (covering 8 AAs—Glu (E), His (H), M (Met), Asn (N), Pro (P), Gln (Q), Thr (T), Val (V)) from that of non-AA* class (covering the remaining 12 AAs) at cell locations 2056 to 2072; row 2 of the table displays 19 mutations inserted.

Group Mutant (GM* and GM) on insertion of 19 mutations**:
(a) GM*—It is a Group Mutant with two groups—AA* and non-AA* class mutants. The AA* class covers 8 AAs Glu (E), His (H), M (Met), Asn (N), Pro (P), Gln (Q), Thr (T), Val (V). CLVS value for each of these 8 AAs is identical and differs from the DCLVS value of other 12 AAs having identical CL values which is referred to as non-AA* class; depending on the group (AA* or non-AA*) an AA belongs, its 19 mutants are grouped as (12 +7) or (11 +8).

(b) GM—each group of mutants display the same CLVS value and the mutant grouping is different from that of GM* (with 2 mutant groups)—it is referred to as a GM. An instance of GM gets illustrated in Table 5.17 for N501 at cell loc 2056–2072 with 5 mutant groups, each group showing the same CL value in the region. Table 5.16 shows CL values for wild and 19 mutants for E484 (cell loc 1965 to 2010) which illustrates an instance of GM at cell location 1983 to 1993 with multiple mutant groupings that is different from GM* (with 2 groups of mutants).

Observation 5.4—CA Rule Design for amino acids in CAML model revisited: The side chain of each of the 8 AAs (E, H, M, N, P, Q, T, V) of AA* Class has 8 to 11 atoms. As reported in Table 4.4 and highlighted in Observation 4.1 in Chap. 4, the side chains of these 8 AAs are designed with 2 CA rules. On the other hand, for 12 (5 + 7) non-AA*, the side chains of 5 AAs having a number of atoms less than equal to 6, are designed with 1 CA rule, and side chains of 7 AAs having 13 to 18 atoms are designed with 3 CA rules.

5.4.7.1 Experimental Set Up for CAML Model to Predict nAbE Mutant

Eight characteristics noted as (a) to (h) guide the design of the Algorithm 3 reported next for identification of nAbE-AA class. Such characteristics are derived on analysis of large number of mutants and non-mutants of different classes of proteins with CAML model. In addition to such analysis, the survey reported in Sect. 5.4.2 for CoV-2 spike protein also provides the guidance for the design of Algorithm 3. Table 5.20 reports nAbE-AA prediction for Training Set (TrS) in RBD of spike protein. The characteristics are illustrated with references to the results reported in Table 5.20.

(a) Identification of neutralizing Antibody escape (nAbE) mutants is a highly complex process involving experimentation with different mutants of an amino acid in spike protein RBD. The results presented in published literature report two main approaches

(i) Approach 1—Experiment employing neutralising antibody titres against CoV-2 strains collected from infected patients.
(ii) Approach 2—Analyses susceptibility of suspected nAbE mutants to the monoclonal Antibodies (mAbs) of different manufacturers.

The results reported for both of these two experimental set-ups vary due to the fact that—patient population and history may vary in Approach 1, while the characteristics of mAbs employed are likely to vary in Approach 2.

(b) Based on the analysis of the wild CL graph of spike protein RBD, 9 different regions marked as r0 to r8 are identified. Each of these regions, (noted on Row 2 of Table 5.20) covers a minimum of 4 adjacent cells with CLVS value greater than 50. Row 4 of Table 5.20 report the CLVS value of each of the 9 regions for wild CL data.

(c) Table 5.20 row 3 column 2 to 10 show the approximate AA locations of each of the regions reported in row 2.

(d) The cell locations in between a pair of regions continues with sequential cell numbering. For example, cells with number 1616 to 1690 exist between region r4 and r5.

(e) A non-Mutant AA is the amino acid location where no mutation is reported in published literature. Ten non-Mut AAs are shown on rows 20–29 of Table 5.20. These non-Mut AAs are selected such that—(i) no deviation exists from wild CL graph other than GM* (Group Mutant) and (ii) each of the 19 mutations inserted for a non-Mut AA show deviation less than or equal to the threshold value 50. The threshold value 50 is set based on the analysis of 19 mutations inserted on non-Mut AAs on different regions of spike protein. Deviations of 19 mutations inserted on spike protein RBD AAs are evaluated in the background of the analysis of non-Mut AAs with CAML.

(f) Nine binary variables (v0, v1, . . ., v7, v8), as reported on row 1 of Table 5.20, are assigned to 9 regions (r0 to r8). Set the binary value of a variable (vx, x = 0 to 8) as '0'. The value is set as '1' for a region rx, if deviation of a mutant is observed for a mutant in the region from its wild counterpart. Step 8 of the Algorithm 3 implements this setting of a variable (v0 to v8). If deviation is observed for an AA in cell location in between a pair of regions (say rx and r(x + 1), x = 0 to 7), then the binary variables for both rx and r(x + 1) are set as 1. If the deviation exists prior to r0, then v0 is set as '1'.

(g) The AA* Class covers 8 amino acids (Glu (E), His (H), M (Met), N (Asn), P (Pro), Q (Gln), Thr (T), Val (V)); the side chain of each of these 8 AAs, as emphasized in Observation 5.4, is designed with 2 CA rules, while the side chains of the remaining 12 AAs are designed with either 1 or 3 CA rules.

(h) Execution of Algorithm 3 generates the results of 9 binary variables (v0 to v8) for each of these AAs reported in Columns 2 to 10 of Table 5.20.

Hypothesis 5.3—CAML model for nAbE-AA class: CAML model introduces 19 mutations for an amino acid in spike protein RBD. By definition, an amino acid in nAbE-AA class has at least one mutant that escapes binding of neutralizing antibody on its epitope [39, 71–73]. We hypothesize that—CAML framework models this physical domain characteristics (escape from binding of antibody on mutant epitope), by the deviation of CL values of a mutant, from its wild counterpart, in a specific region (say rx, x = 0 to 8), represented as non-0 value for the variable vx in the region rx, as shown in Table 5.20 (column 2–10).

5.4.7.2 Algorithm 3 Prediction of nAbE-AA or Non-nAbE in Spike Protein RBD

The Training Set (TrS) retrieved from [69] (published in 2020–2021) has been assumed as the template for design of the algorithm for prediction of nAbE-AA. The algorithmic steps for prediction of nAbE-AA are designed based on the analysis of CAML features derived on comparing 19 mutants with wild for each AA of the TrS. The experimental set up explained under (b) to (h) are formalised in the algorithmic steps. The Python code designed for Algorithm 2 is applied to predict nAbE-AA in—TrS (Training Set), VaS (Validation Set) retrieved from ([41, 43] published in 2022, and PMHS set predicted by Algorithm 2.

Algorithm 3:

Input: The following three sets of AAs of Spike Protein RBD (Receptor Binding Domain) AA loc 329 to 527

(i) Training Set (TrS) covering 25 (15 + 10) AAs reported on Column 1 in Table 5.20; row 20 to 29 shows the ten non-mutants. Column 12 reports the prediction results, while column 11 shows the specific mutation on an AA curated from [69].

(ii) Validation Set (VaS) covering 22 AAs reported on Column 1 of Table 5.21; out of these 22 AAs, 8 are included in (TrS), as noted on column 1. Prediction of nAbE-AA class derived out of CAML model reported on column 12, while column 11 shows the specific mutations on an AA curated from [41, 43].

(iii) 11 AAs predicted as PMHS by Algorithm 2 shown on column 1 of Table 5.22; prediction of nAbE-AA class in the set of PMHS reported on column 12. The PMHS set can be viewed as the Testing Set (TeS) for nAbE-AA prediction framework.

Output: Predicts an AA as an nAbE-AA class or non-nAbE (reported on column 12 of Tables 5.20, 5.21, and 5.22 for Trs, VaS, PMHS set respectively)

Step 1: In addition to 18 AAs covered by the TrS (Training Set), select 10 AAs (marked as non-Mut) displaying the characteristics reported under Experimental set-up (e).

Step 2: Generate CL graphs for wild and 19 mutants, on introducing 19 mutations for each of 28 AAs of TrS (noted on column 1 of Table 5.20).

Step 3: Identify regions where wild CL graph shows CLVS value greater than 50 covering a minimum of 4 adjacent cells. Note the cell locations and AA locations of each region.
(For spike protein RBD, there are 9 regions (r0 to r8 noted on row 2 in Table 5.20; cell locations of each region noted on row 3 of Table 5.20).

Step 4: Assign 9 binary variables v0 to v8 for 9 regions r0 to r8. (Row 1 of Table 5.20 shows the 9 variables).

Step 5: Analyze wild and 19 mutants of each non-Mut for each region. Ensure that no deviation exists for any region other than—(i) group mutant GM* or (ii) DCLVS value (difference with CLVS of wild) greater than 50.

Step 6: Initialize the value of binary variables v0 to v8 to '0' on columns 2–10 (noted on rows 5–29 of Table 5.20 for TrS).

Step 7: Analyse 19 mutants for each AA noted on column 1, rows 5–29 of Table 5.20, and execute Steps 8–10.

Step 8: Set the binary value of the variable (vx, x = 0 to 8) as '1' on the column for rx of an AA, if deviation is observed in respect of—a mutant of the AA in the region from the wild that is different from GM* of group mutants, defined earlier.

Step 9: If deviation for a mutant is observed in the CA cells in between a pair of regions (say rx and r(x + 1), x = 0 to 7), then set the binary variable for both rx and r(x + 1) as 1. If the deviation is prior to r0, then v0 is set as '1'.

Step 10: Predict an AA

(i) as a member of non-nAbE, if v0 to v8 show an all 0's vector with <v0 v1 v2 v3 v4 v5 v6 v7 v8> = <0 0 0 0 0 0 0 0 0>;
(ii) as a member of nAbE-AA Class, if there exists at least one non-0 binary value on column 2–10 for a variable v0 to v8.

Step 11: Repeat the execution of Steps 6–10 for the Input 2 (Validation Set—VaS noted in Table 5.21 column 1) and refine/modify the prediction algorithm, if necessary.

Step 12: Repeat the execution of Steps 1–11 on the Input 3 (PMHS set noted in Table 5.22 column 1). Stop.

The Python code for the Algorithm 3 has been developed. The program is executed to predict nAbE mutants in the Training Set (TrS), Validation Set (VaS), and PMHS set (viewed as TeS).

5.4.8 Results of Prediction of nAbE-AA in Spike Protein RBD

CAML model provides a generic in-silico tool for prediction of nAbE-AA in a protein chain. It achieves the goal—(i) by introducing 19 mutations for each AA of the protein chain, and (ii) comparing the CL signal graphs of 19 mutants with its wild counterpart. It does not specify a mutant, but reports the location of a MsAA(Mutation site AA); a mutant on such a MsAA is likely to mediate escape from antibody neutralization of the infected cell. The CAML model is independent of—(i) patient history, (ii) convalescent sera collected from infected patients, and (iii) varying performance of commercial monoclonal antibodies. These factors, as discussed in the survey reported in Sect. 5.4.2, may vary. Consequently, differences exist in published experimental results identifying nAbE mutants.

The differences between the results predicted with the in-silico tool of CAML model and the published experimental results [41, 43, 69] are discussed in next two subsections.

5.4.8.1 Results of Prediction of nAbE-AA in the Training Set (TrS) Retrieved from [69]

Table 5.20 reports the results of execution of the Algorithm 3 on the (TrS) covering 25 AAs noted on Column 1. Six AAs of TrS are marked as non-nAbE on column 12: (i) F490 on row 6, (ii) G476 on row 8, (iii) L452 on row 11, (iv) L455 on row 12, (v) N439 on row 13, and (vi) S494 on row 16. These are marked as non-nAbE since these AAs show all 0's vectors for v0 to v8. Authors [69] have highlighted the binding affinity and clinical severity of different mutants including F490S, L452R, L455Y, N439K, S494P which are identified in a region/country as nAbE mutants with specific commercial antibody. These five MsAAs are not detected as nAbE-AA with CAML model. Mutation at G476 is not a severe one and reported in a limited number of publications.

The remaining 9 AAs of 15 AAs of TrS are predicted as nAbE-AA Class. As per the Hypothesis 5.3 in respect of binding of neutralizing antibody on mutant epitope, a mutant of these AAs is likely to escape antibody neutralization.

The results derived with the CAML model for the TrS, provides a foundation for prediction of nAbE-AA in the VaS and PMHS set.

5.4.8.2 Results of Prediction of nAbE-AA in the Validation Set (VaS) Retrieved from [145, 152]

While (TrS) MsAAs are retrieved from [69] published in early 2020–2021, the Validation Set (VaS) AAs are retrieved from [41, 43] published in 2022. The (VaS) covers 22 AAs shown on Column 1 of Table 5.21. The set covers 8 AAs (K417, G446, L452, S477, T478, E484, F490, N501) included in the TrS, and indicated in

Column 1 of Table 5.21. Python code for Algorithm 3 is developed and executed for the 14(22 − 8) AAs of (VaS). The prediction results for 14 AAs are shown on Column 12. Columns 2 to 10 of Table 5.21 report the 0/1 value derived for 22 AAs on execution of Algorithm 3.

In addition to F490 (on row 8) and L452 (on row 13), present in TrS, four more AAs are marked as non-nAbE which are—G496 (on row 11), N440 (on row 14), Q493 (on row 16), and R408 (on row 19). These MsAAs are marked as non-nAbE AA since each of these AAs show all 0's vector for <v0 v1 v2 v3 v4 v5 v6 v7 v8>. All the other 16(22 − 6) MsAAs noted on column 1 are predicted to belong to nAbE-AA class. Authors [43] evaluated neutralizing antibody titers against omicron sub-variant mutants reported by the end of 2022 in specific regions/countries. Mutant R408S included in [43] is not covered in [41]. Similar variation of nAbE mutant list can be observed in other contemporary literature which mainly points to variation of patient history.

The prediction results of CAML model on TrS and VaS established the robustness of nAbE-AA prediction algorithm. The Python code has been developed for Algorithm 3 for prediction of nAbE-AA. We next execute the program on the PMHS set identified on Execution of Algorithm 2. The PMHS set is viewed as the Test Set (TeS) for prediction of nAbE-AA.

5.4.8.3 Results of Prediction of nAbE Mutants in the PMHS Set Identified with Algorithm 2 Reported in Sect. 5.4.6

Table 5.22 Column 1 shows the 11 AAs identified as PMHS (Potential Muta- tional Hot Spot) with Algorithm 2 reported in Sect. 5.4.6. Algorithm 3 identifies 6 AAs (F377, N360, N360, Y369, Y421, V362) as nAbE-AA.

Recent publications on mutational analysis of CoV-2 spike RBD points to high mutation propensity in the region covering AA locations 333 to 527.

The remining 6 PMHSs are predicted as non-nAbE with all 0's vector <0 0 0 0 0 0 0 0 0> for 9-elements <v0 v1 v2 v3 v4 v5 v6 v7 v8>; the CL graphs of 19 mutants of these 6 AAs do not show any deviation from wild CL graph.

5.4.9 Conclusion

Cellular Automata enhanced Machine Learning (CAML) model employs both Cellular Automata (CA) and Machine Learning (ML) frameworks. CAML model operates on the input data transformed with CA framework. It achieves acceptable prediction quality on the training set (TrS) and validation set (VaS), that are significantly lesser than the volume of training data corpus necessary for conventional ML systems. The application of CAML model has been reported in earlier two Sects. 5.2 and 5.3 for analysis and comparison of envelope protein and non-structural protein (nsp1) of SARS (CoV-2 and CoV) and MERS covid. The current section concentrates on mutational study of CoV-2 spike protein RBD (Receptor Binding Domain). Higher number of mutations are observed in the spike protein of CoV-2 variants, Omicron and its sub-lineages. The solution lies in prediction of potential mutational hot spots in CoV-2 structural proteins. The machine learning algorithms of CAML model are designed by mapping the Feature Vectors (FV) derived out of CA evolution parameters to in-vivo/in-vitro experimental results available in published literature. The algorithm enables prediction of PMHS (Potential Mutational Hot Spot) and nAbE (neutralizing Antibody Escape) mutants in the TrS (Training Set), VaS (Validation Set) and the PMHS set viewed as the Testing Set (TeS). The major focus of this section is the design of the scheme to predict nAbE-AA class based on introduction of 19 mutations on each AA of a protein chain. This scheme is also implemented in next Sect. 5.5 for analysis of p53 protein implicated for majority of cancer types.

As per the latest report [45], the Omicron variant lineage BF.7 shows "the N460K mutation that has been the most critical factor behind the enhanced neutralization resistance of BF.7". However, as per the report, the adverse effect of N460K mutant was localized mostly in Chin. The CAML model predicts N460 as a PMHS. But the model predicts N460 as a non-nAbE on execution of Algorithm 3 on PMHS set identified by Algorithm 2. The CAML model can be extended to predict PMHS and nAbE mutants in other regions of S1 and S2 partitions of spike protein and other structural proteins of CoV-2. We expect the quantitative analysis, reported in the CAML model, will provide a platform for the design of refurbished vaccines in the event of the appearance of a new class of zoonotic virus. Due to continuous environmental degradation, as many experts have recently predicted [74–77], new types of zoonotic viruses are likely to appear in future. The recent nature brief [75] has highlighted this particular issue. Further, CAML model to study viral proteins adds a new direction in the field of virology dealing with structural classification and evolution of biological viruses.

5.5 Characterization of P53 Protein Encoded by TP53 Gene

The disease cancer is characterized by abnormal/uncontrolled growth of cells leading to formation of tumor that may be benign (non-cancerous) or malignant (cancerous). Biopsy of tumor tissue to detect presence of cancer cells is the very first option of cancer detection. Cancer cells inactivate tumor suppressor gene that inhibits tumor growth. If not treated at an early stage, cancer cells of a malignant tumor invade nearby tissues and travel to other body organs resulting in the growth of new tumours. In medical terminology, such a condition is referred to as Metastasis. The last leg of the journey of a cancer patient's life, particularly with metastasis, is extremely painful.

5.5.1 Introduction

In view of the alarming growth of cancer patients around the globe, study of cancer is a major focal point of medical research. There are more than one hundred types of cancer observed in different organs of the human body. The cells in an organ are equipped to perform their specific role. Cancer originating in a specific body organ is affected by the organ characteristics. Consequently, cancer cell characteristics and their treatment differ for different cancer types. A number of excellent cancer databases are available in public domain which provide a variant of the following details for a specific cancer type—(i) chromosome number and gene name, (ii) gene mutation linked to a specific cancer type, (iii) corresponding mutation in cancer protein encoded by the oncogene, and (iv) the references to the published papers citing the experimental results pointing to the cancer type due to the specific mutation. However, rather than concentrating on analysis of a single mutation on a specific amino acid (AA), the CAML model concentrates on analysis of a MsAA (Mutation site AA) where a mutation is identified through experimental results reported in published literature. Forty-eight MsAAs are identified out of 212 mutations reported in p53 protein. Out of these 48 MsAAs, there are 45 MsAAs which are located within the DNA Binding Domina (DBD) of p53 chain. High concentration of 212 mutations in a protein of length of 393 amino acids is worth detailed investigation in Proteomics study—the focus of the current section.

A mutated gene with potential to cause cancer is referred to as oncogene. One of the most dominant oncogenes is TP53 discovered in 1979. Notwithstanding the excellent advancement of cancer treatment, early detection of the deadly disease is the major focus of recent cancer research. Various alternatives have evolved in recent years. One promising avenue is the design of a non-invasive tool referred to as Protein Biomarker (PB) providing an early indication of Probable onset of Cancer (PoC). An outline of the design of PB with CAML model is included in Sect. 5.5.8 of the current section.

The current Sect. 5.5 concentrates on the analysis of p53 MsAAs based on Cellular Automata (enhanced with) Machine Learning (CAML) model developed for mutational study of protein chains. The model introduces nineteen mutations for each amino acid of p53 protein. Machine learning (ML) algorithms are developed in Chap. 5 on analysing—(i) in vivo/in vitro experimental results curated from published literature on mutational study of different proteins (Viral proteins, proteins observed in animal world, and proteins in plant kingdom), and (ii) the Parameter and Feature Vector (FV) derived out of CAML model for different classes of proteins.

Three algorithms are reported for p53 protein analysis:

1. Based on CAML model parameters, the first algorithm analyses the concentration of mutational hotspots in different regions of p53 chain covering 45 MsAAs in the DNA Binding Domain (DBD) of p53 chain. This protein binds on DNA and is associated with a large number of multifunctional tasks in a cell. The DBD

covers AA locations T102 to K292AA of p53 and this domain is of major interest for cancer research community.
2. The second algorithm evaluates VD (Vector Distance) of the Feature Vector (FV) of a pair of MsAAs to predict their functional proximity in the p53 pathway; the predicted results are validated with the experimental results for the MsAA pair curated from published literature.
3. Immune evasion of a p53 MsAAs are next predicted based on the analysis of deviation of the CL graphs of its mutants from that of the wild type p53.

A concise survey on p53 publications follows in Sect. 5.5.3 subsequent to a brief note on the Landmark Discovery.

5.5.2 A Landmark Discovery

In the history of scientific discovery, there are instances where multiple research groups proceed through independent paths to arrive at the same destination. The epoch-making discovery of the p53 protein encoded by the TP53 gene is such an event. The perspective and background of this discovery are covered in [78–80]; the authors [80] have highlighted the papers of six independent research groups investigating the TP53 gene around the time period of the year 1979. One of these six publications is reproduced in 2019 [81].

Since the discovery of tumor protein p53 in 1979, structural/functional analysis of p53 wild and its mutants have occupied the centre stage of cancer research. The protein p53, encoded by the TP53 gene, plays a dominant role to maintain a wide variety of cellular functions. TP53 gene mutations give rise to stable p53 mutant proteins. The p53 protein controls diverse pathways such as cell cycle division, DNA repair, cell apoptosis (that is, programmed cell death), metabolism etc. That is why p53 is often referred to as 'guardian of the genome'. Mutations in p53 protein encoded by TP 53 gene are implicated directly/indirectly for the majority of cancer types. Deregulation and inactivation of its associated pathways is commonly observed in cancer cells due to p53 mutations. Notwithstanding the enormous progress in p53 research, there are many unanswered questions in respect of the oncogenic effect of p53 mutants. The major challenges are—to understand their influence on cancer phenotype in respect of loss/gain of function and the mechanism of their immune evasion. Rather than analysis of individual p53 mutant, the solution probably lies in the functional classification of p53 Mutation site Amino Acids (MsAAs) affecting tumor malignancy. An MsAA, by definition, refers to an AA on which a mutation has been observed through laboratory experiment reported in published literature.

5.5.3 A Brief Survey on P53 Protein Encoded by TP53 Gene

Subsequent to p53 discovery, cancer research has progressed at a faster pace. The underlying reason for this research focus stems from the fact that p53 mutations have been found to be directly/indirectly linked with the majority of human cancer instances. Consequently, it is one of the most widely studied proteins in cancer research. A concise review of the publications follows.

The progress of p53 research in the last few decades can be ascertained from the publications covered under the Reference list [82–86]. Different aspects of p53 wild and mutants are reported in [87–95]. In this context, it is worth analysing the critical review appeared in [96, 97] in respect of 'cancer hallmark' suggested in [98, 99]. Specific cancer types (breast, skin, colorectal, Melanoma etc.) and their association with p53 are reported in [100–104]. Different approaches of cancer therapy including re-activation of p53 mutants have attracted attention of many researchers [101, 105]. A number of authors [106–108] have pointed to the link between viral infection and cancer. In fact, this link can be traced back to 1979 while the protein p53 was discovered. Five of the six groups, as reported in [78, 80], discovered p53 while it was found to bind with large T-antigen in SV 40 (Siemian Victualing virus 40 found in monkeys and humans). The same protein p53 was also identified through cancer immunological study, while it was found to react with chemically induced mouse sarcoma. A large number of authors [109, 110, 110–115] have covered different aspects of this vital protein in respect of—its structure and function, its isomers and mutants, its binding with DNA (DNA Binding domain—DBD), restoration of p53 mutant function, their temperature sensitivity, zinc binding property [116, 117] etc. Detailed analysis of the impact of individual p53 mutants have been dealt with in [118–126].

The probable reasons for higher mutation rate at specific mutation site amino acids are covered in [127], while the authors in [111, 119] provided the detailed analysis of p53 binding on DNA through the formation of a hydrophobic core with 25 amino acids. Mutation in the p53 amino acids in the DBD (DNA Binding Domain) is likely to lead to non-functional p53 protein. While wild p53 as a druggable target in immunotherapy is explored by many authors, application of mutant p53 based antigen for immunotherapy is reported in [113]. Different aspects of immune evasion of p53 mutants leading to cancer progression are covered in [114, 129].

The major issue on p53 wild and mutant study revolves around the p53 pathway that represents the network of gene products associated with intrinsic and extrinsic stress signals, loss of wild type p53 function, gain of function including switching of function. It is in this context, a natural question has been posed in [130] in respect of meaningful oncogenic effects of p53 mutants, suggesting that—"there could be some underlying feature about p53 mutants that produces real biology but may not be selected for during tumorigenesis". Keeping this point in view, the authors [112] have proposed the 'deployment of multiple hidden Markov Models to computationally classify mutations by functional impact type'.

We introduced a new terminology referred to as MsAA (Mutation site Amino Acid). As defined in earlier sections, a MsAA refers to an AA where single/multiple mutants are reported in published literature out of in-vivo/in-vitro experiments. In the background of the issues highlighted in the brief survey on p53 protein, the present section concentrates on functional classification of p53 MsAAs based on CAML model developed for mutational study of protein chains. Rather than analysis of an individual mutant (xLx', where original amino acid x at site L replaced with amino

Table 5.23 Amino acid chain and partial ((first 10 excluding Met(M))) Rule Vector for p53 protein chain (393 AA)

p53 AA sequence with 393 AA	
AA Chain	MEEPQSDPSVEPPLSQETFSDLWKLLPENNVLSPLPSQAMDDLMLSPDDIEQWFTEDPGP DEAPRMPEAAPPVAPAPAAPTPAAPAPAPSWPLSSSVPSQKTYQGSYGFRLGFLHSGTAK SVTCTYSPALNKMFCQLAKTCPVQLWVDSTPPPGTRVRAMAIYKQSQHMTEVVRRCPHH ERCSDSDGLAPPQHLIRVEGNLRVEYLDDRNTFRHSVVVPYEPPEVGSDCTTIHYNYMCN SSCMGGMNRRPILTIITLEDSSGNLLGRNSFEVRVCACPGRDRRTEEENLRKKGEPHHELP PGSTKRALPNNTSSSPQPKKKPLDGEYFTLQIRGRERFEMFRELNEALELKDAQAGKEPG GSRAHSSHLKSKKGQSTSRHKKLMFKTEGPDSD
Partial rule vector	< 107, 99, 11, 235, 107, 99, 11, 235, 105, 43, 11, 63, 107, 99, 63, 107, 107, 99, 47, 107, 99, 235, 105, 43, 11, 63, 107, 99, 47, 107, 99, 59, 15, 107, 99, 11, 235, ⋯ >

Table 5.24 Forty-eight MSAAs in protein p53 (393 AA, UniProt ID P04637)—212 mutants reported at these Mutation site AAs (MsAAs)—out of 48, the DBD (DNA Binding Domian T102 to K292) covers 45 MsAAs (P47, P72, and R306*—a mutation that leads to premature truncation at amino acid 306)

P47,	P72,	L111,	T125,	K132,	C135,	C141,	Q144,	P151,	Y163,	V173,	R175,
C176,	H179,	H193,	L194,	I195,	R196,	Y205,	R213,	H214,	S215,	V216,	Y220,
Y234,	Y236,	M237,	C238,	N239,	S241,	C242,	G244,	G245,	R248,	R249,	I255,
G266,	F270,	V272,	R273,	V274,	C275,	P278,	R280,	D281,	R282,	E286,	R306*

acid x'), the CAML model concentrates on characterizing MsAAs of p53 protein chain.

The CA preliminaries and CA rules designed for 20 amino acids (AAs) are reported in Chap. 4. The generic steps of execution of Phase 1 and Phase 2 of CAML model design are reported in Sect. 5.1.2 that reports CL graph generation procedure for any protein chain.

5.5.4 Protein p53 AA Chain—Wild and Mutant CL Graphs

The 393 AA sequence of the protein p53 is shown in Table 5.23 and 48 Mutation site AAs (MsAAs) noted in Table 5.24.

CA evolution generating cycle length signal graph (CL Signal Graph) for p53 Protein Chain—wild and mutants

In Molecular Biology, Ala mutagenesis, usually undertaken to determine the contribution of a specific AA in the function of a given protein. Instead of Ala, CAML model introduces all the 19 mutations for each AA of p53 protein chain followed by analysis of the parameters derived out of CA evolution for wild and mutated versions of the protein. Multiple mutations are reported at AA location R175, Y220, D281

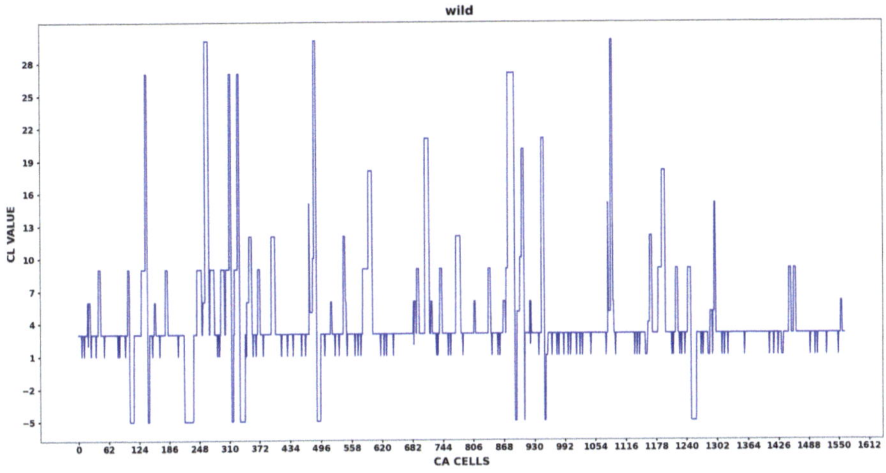

Fig. 5.31 CL signal graph for p53 Protein wild AA chain of length 393 AA

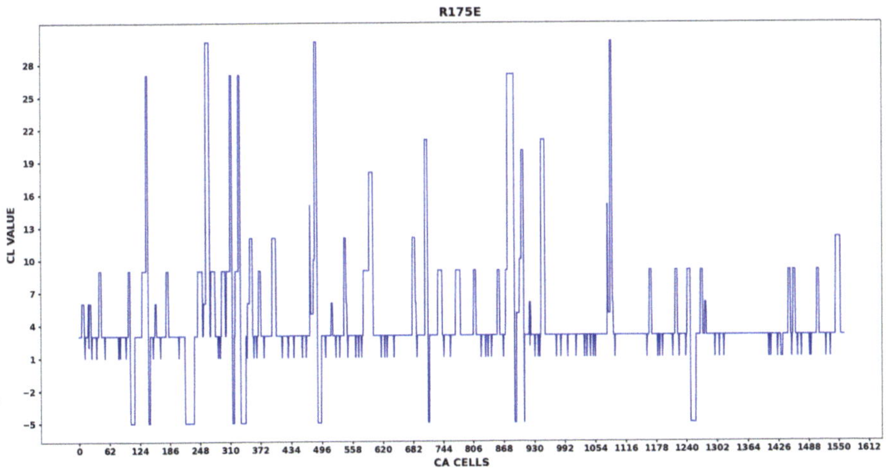

Fig. 5.32 CL signal graph for mutant R175E of p53 protein (the original amino acid R at location 175 is mutated with amino acid E)

of p53 protein chain. While Fig. 5.31 shows the CL signal graph for p53 wild chain, Figs. 5.32, 5.33 and 5.34 report the CL signal graphs for mutant R175E, Y220C, and D281E. In order to illustrate deviation of mutant CL graphs from wild p53, the partial CL data for CA cell locations 680 to 785 is reported in Table 5.25 showing CL value for wild and 19 mutants of the MsAA R175 (a mutational hot spot site in p53 where 3 mutations R175H/G/C are reported).

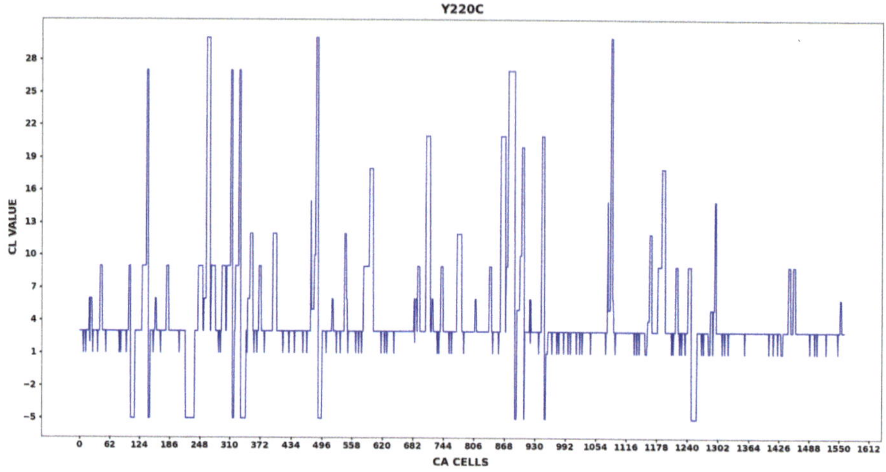

Fig. 5.33 CL signal graph for p53 mutant Y220C of p53 protein (the original amino acid Y at location 220 is mutated with amino acid C)

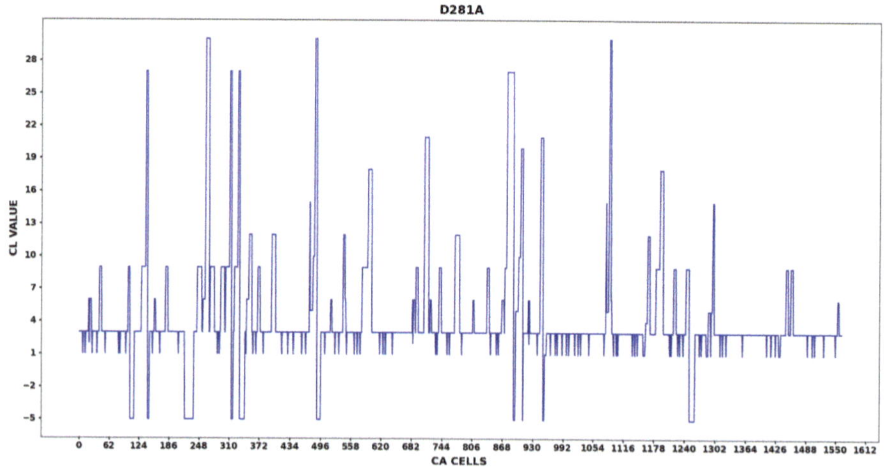

Fig. 5.34 CL signal graph for p53 mutant D281A of p53 protein (the original amino acid D at location 281 is mutated with amino acid A)

CL Signal Graph Analytics for Wild Type and Mutant AA Chain

Table 5.25 Partial CL data (from cell location 680 to 785) for wild and 19 mutant for the MSAA R175 (one of the hot spots in p53 protein chain)

Cell no.	Wild	R175																		
		A	G	V	L	M	I	S	T	C	P	N	Q	K	H	D	E	F	Y	W
680	3	3	3	3	3	3	3	3	3	3	3	3	3	3	3	3	3	3	3	3
681	3	3	3	3	3	3	3	3	3	3	3	3	3	3	1	15	3	3	3	3
682	3	3	3	3	3	3	3	3	3	3	3	3	3	3	3	15	3	3	3	3
683	3	3	3	3	3	3	3	3	3	3	3	18	3	3	3	15	24	3	3	3
684	3	21	3	3	3	18	3	21	3	3	3	18	18	3	3	15	24	3	3	1
685	3	21	3	15	3	18	3	21	15	3	21	18	18	3	3	5	24	3	3	3
686	1	21	3	5	21	18	1	21	5	3	21	18	18	3	3	5	24	3	3	3
687	3	21	3	5	21	18	3	21	5	3	21	18	18	3	3	5	24	3	3	3
688	3	21	3	5	21	18	3	21	5	3	21	18	18	3	3	5	24	3	3	3
689	3	21	3	5	21	18	3	21	5	3	21	18	18	3	3	5	24	3	3	3
690	3	21	3	5	21	18	3	21	5	3	21	18	18	3	3	5	24	3	3	3
691	3	21	3	5	21	18	3	21	5	3	21	18	18	3	3	15	24	3	3	3
692	3	3	3	15	21	18	3	3	15	3	21	18	18	3	1	3	24	3	3	3
693	3	3	3	3	21	3	3	3	3	3	3	3	3	3	3	3	3	3	3	3
694	3	3	3	3	3	3	3	3	3	3	3	3	3	3	3	3	3	3	3	3
695	3	3	3	3	3	3	3	3	3	3	3	3	3	3	3	3	3	3	3	3
696	3	3	3	3	3	3	3	3	3	3	3	3	3	3	3	3	3	3	3	3
697	3	3	3	3	3	3	3	3	3	3	3	3	3	3	3	3	3	3	3	3
698	3	3	3	3	3	3	3	3	3	3	3	3	3	3	3	3	3	3	3	3
699	3	3	3	3	3	3	3	3	3	3	3	3	3	3	3	3	3	3	3	3
700	3	3	3	3	3	3	3	3	3	3	3	3	3	3	3	3	3	3	3	3
701	3	3	3	3	3	3	3	3	3	3	3	3	3	3	3	3	3	3	3	3
702	3	3	3	3	3	3	3	3	3	3	3	3	3	3	3	3	3	3	3	3
703	3	3	3	3	3	3	3	3	3	3	3	3	3	3	3	3	3	3	3	3
704	3	3	3	3	3	3	3	3	3	3	3	3	3	3	3	3	3	3	3	3
705	3	3	3	3	3	3	3	3	3	3	3	3	3	3	3	3	3	3	3	3
706	3	3	3	3	3	3	3	3	3	3	3	3	3	3	3	3	3	3	3	3
707	3	3	3	3	3	3	3	3	3	3	3	3	3	3	3	3	3	3	3	3
708	3	21	21	3	3	3	3	21	3	21	3	3	3	3	3	21	3	3	3	3
709	3	21	21	21	3	21	3	21	21	21	21	21	21	3	21	21	21	3	3	3
710	21	21	21	21	21	21	21	21	21	21	21	21	21	21	21	21	21	21	21	21
711	21	21	21	21	21	21	21	21	21	21	21	21	21	21	21	21	21	21	21	21
712	21	21	21	21	21	21	21	21	21	21	21	21	21	21	21	21	21	21	21	21
713	21	21	21	21	21	21	21	21	21	21	21	21	21	21	21	21	21	21	21	21
714	21	21	21	21	21	21	21	21	21	21	21	21	21	21	21	21	21	21	21	21
715	21	21	21	–5	21	–5	21	21	–5	21	–5	–5	–5	21	–5	21	–5	21	21	21
716	21	21	21	–5	21	–5	21	21	–5	21	–5	–5	–5	21	–5	21	–5	21	21	21
717	21	3	3	–5	21	–5	21	3	–5	3	–5	–5	–5	21	–5	3	–5	21	21	21
718	21	3	3	3	21	3	21	3	3	3	3	3	3	21	3	3	3	21	21	21
719	3	3	3	3	3	3	3	3	3	3	3	3	3	3	3	3	3	3	3	3
720	3	6	6	3	3	3	3	6	3	6	3	3	3	3	3	6	3	3	3	3
721	3	6	6	3	3	3	3	6	3	6	3	3	3	3	3	6	3	3	3	3

(continued)

Table 5.25 (continued)

Cell no.	Wild	R175																		
		A	G	V	L	M	I	S	T	C	P	N	Q	K	H	D	E	F	Y	W
722	6	6	6	3	6	3	6	6	3	6	3	3	3	6	3	6	3	6	6	6
723	6	3	3	3	6	3	6	3	3	3	3	3	3	6	3	3	3	6	6	6
724	6	3	3	3	6	3	6	3	3	3	3	3	3	6	3	3	3	6	6	6
725	3	3	3	3	3	3	3	3	3	3	3	3	3	3	3	3	3	3	3	3
726	3	3	3	1	3	1	3	3	1	3	1	1	1	3	1	3	1	3	3	3
727	3	3	3	3	3	3	3	3	3	3	3	3	3	3	3	3	3	3	3	3
728	3	3	3	3	3	3	3	3	3	3	3	3	3	3	3	3	3	3	3	3
729	3	3	3	3	3	3	3	3	3	3	3	3	3	3	3	3	3	3	3	3
730	3	3	3	3	3	3	3	3	3	3	3	3	3	3	3	3	3	3	3	3
731	3	1	1	3	3	3	3	1	3	1	3	3	3	3	3	1	3	3	3	3
732	3	3	3	3	3	3	3	3	3	3	3	3	3	3	3	3	3	3	3	3
733	1	3	3	3	1	3	1	3	3	3	3	3	3	1	3	3	3	1	1	1
734	3	3	3	3	3	3	3	3	3	3	3	3	3	3	3	3	3	3	3	3
735	3	3	3	3	3	3	3	3	3	3	3	3	3	3	3	3	3	3	3	3
736	3	3	3	3	3	3	3	3	3	3	3	3	3	3	3	3	3	3	3	3
737	3	3	3	3	3	3	3	3	3	3	3	3	3	3	3	3	3	3	3	3
738	3	1	1	3	3	3	3	1	3	1	3	3	3	3	3	1	3	3	3	3
739	3	3	3	1	3	1	3	3	1	3	1	1	1	3	1	3	1	3	3	3
740	1	3	3	3	1	3	1	3	3	3	3	3	3	1	3	3	3	1	1	1
741	3	3	3	3	3	3	3	3	3	3	3	3	3	3	3	3	3	3	3	3
742	3	1	1	3	3	3	3	1	3	1	3	3	3	3	3	1	3	3	3	3
743	3	3	3	1	3	1	3	3	1	3	1	1	1	3	1	3	1	3	3	3
744	1	3	3	3	1	3	1	3	3	3	3	3	3	1	3	3	3	1	1	1
745	3	3	3	3	3	3	3	3	3	3	3	3	3	3	3	3	3	3	3	3
746	3	3	3	3	3	3	3	3	3	3	3	3	3	3	3	3	3	3	3	3
747	3	3	3	3	3	3	3	3	3	3	3	3	3	3	3	3	3	3	3	3
748	3	3	3	3	3	3	3	3	3	3	3	3	3	3	3	3	3	3	3	3
749	3	3	3	3	3	3	3	3	3	3	3	3	3	3	3	3	3	3	3	3
750	3	3	3	3	3	3	3	3	3	3	3	3	3	3	3	3	3	3	3	3
751	3	3	3	3	3	3	3	3	3	3	3	3	3	3	3	3	3	3	3	3
752	3	3	3	3	3	3	3	3	3	3	3	3	3	3	3	3	3	3	3	3
753	3	3	3	3	3	3	3	3	3	3	3	3	3	3	3	3	3	3	3	3
754	3	3	3	3	3	3	3	3	3	3	3	3	3	3	3	3	3	3	3	3
755	3	3	3	3	3	3	3	3	3	3	3	3	3	3	3	3	3	3	3	3
756	3	3	3	3	3	3	3	3	3	3	3	3	3	3	3	3	3	3	3	3
757	3	3	3	3	3	3	3	3	3	3	3	3	3	3	3	3	3	3	3	3
758	3	3	3	3	3	3	3	3	3	3	3	3	3	3	3	3	3	3	3	3
759	3	3	3	3	3	3	3	3	3	3	3	3	3	3	3	3	3	3	3	3
760	3	1	1	3	3	3	3	1	3	1	3	3	3	3	3	1	3	3	3	3
761	3	3	3	1	3	1	3	3	1	3	1	1	1	3	1	3	1	3	3	3
762	1	3	3	3	1	3	1	3	3	3	3	3	3	1	3	3	3	1	1	1
763	3	3	3	3	3	3	3	3	3	3	3	3	3	3	3	3	3	3	3	3
764	3	3	3	3	3	3	3	3	3	3	3	3	3	3	3	3	3	3	3	3

(continued)

Table 5.25 (continued)

Cell no.	Wild	R175																		
		A	G	V	L	M	I	S	T	C	P	N	Q	K	H	D	E	F	Y	W
765	3	3	3	3	3	3	3	3	3	3	3	3	3	3	3	3	3	3	3	3
766	3	3	3	3	3	3	3	3	3	3	3	3	3	3	3	3	3	3	3	3
767	3	3	3	3	3	3	3	3	3	3	3	3	3	3	3	3	3	3	3	3
768	3	3	3	3	3	3	3	3	3	3	3	3	3	3	3	3	3	3	3	3
769	3	3	3	3	3	3	3	3	3	3	3	3	3	3	3	3	3	3	3	3
770	3	3	3	3	3	3	3	3	3	3	3	3	3	3	3	3	3	3	3	3
771	3	12	12	3	3	3	3	12	3	12	3	3	3	3	3	12	3	3	3	3
772	3	12	12	3	3	3	3	12	3	12	3	3	3	3	3	12	3	3	3	3
773	12	12	12	1	12	1	12	12	1	12	1	1	1	12	1	12	1	12	12	12
774	12	12	12	9	12	9	12	12	9	12	9	9	9	12	9	12	9	12	12	12
775	12	12	12	9	12	9	12	12	9	12	9	9	9	12	9	12	9	12	12	12
776	12	12	12	9	12	9	12	12	9	12	9	9	9	12	9	12	9	12	12	12
777	12	12	12	9	12	9	12	12	9	12	9	9	9	12	9	12	9	12	12	12
778	12	12	12	9	12	9	12	12	9	12	9	9	9	12	9	12	9	12	12	12
779	12	12	12	9	12	9	12	12	9	12	9	9	9	12	9	12	9	12	12	12
780	12	12	12	9	12	9	12	12	9	12	9	9	9	12	9	12	9	12	12	12
781	12	3	3	9	12	9	12	3	9	3	9	9	9	12	9	3	9	12	12	12
782	12	3	3	3	12	3	12	3	3	3	3	3	3	12	3	3	3	12	12	12
783	3	3	3	3	3	3	3	3	3	3	3	3	3	3	3	3	3	3	3	3
784	3	3	3	3	3	3	3	3	3	3	3	3	3	3	3	3	3	3	3	3
785	3	3	3	3	3	3	3	3	3	3	3	3	3	3	3	3	3	3	3	3

The parameters and Feature Vector (FV) relevant for signal graph analytics are extracted out of p53 CL signal graphs (Wild and Mutants) and presented next. These are identical to those presented in Sect. 5.4 extracted out of Cov-2 Spike protein CL graphs reported as in Sect. 5.4.5. For ease of readability, we reproduce below the four definitions. The CAML model introduces 19 mutations for each AA of a protein chain. Signal graph analytics enable extraction of meaningful information from a graph relevant for mutational study of a protein chain.

CL Value Sum (CLVS): CLVS for a wild/mutant is computed considering mcl and Nmcl signal (defined in sub-section 5.2.2.1 of Sect. 5.2) values of—Wild and mutant CL graphs; by definition, only CL values greater than or equal to 7 are considered, while ignoring cells having CL(-5) values (defined in subsection 5.2.2.3 of Sect. 5.2).

DCLVS (Difference of CL Value Sum): DCLVS = CLVS (mutant) – CLVS (wild). DCLVS value is assumed to be 0 if the value is less than or equal to absolute value 50, allowing 5% deviation.

Table 5.26 illustrates generation of CLVS and DCLVS values for 10 AAs (T102 to L111 of p53 protein chain). The row 2 shows the CLVS for Wild CL graph. Rows 3–21 reports CLVS and DCLVS values on columns 2 and 3 by introducing 19 mutations at AA location T102. Similarly, rows 22–40 show the CLVS, DCLVS data for AA

Table 5.26 CLVS and DCLVS values for T102 to L111 and PTT values

Id	CLVS	DCLVS	(−ve) cnt	(+ve) cnt	0 cnt	id	CLVS	DCLVS	(−ve) cnt	(+ve) cnt	0 cnt
Wild	3893	0				Y107A	3893	0			
T102A	4004	111				Y107G	3905	12			
T102G	4004	111				Y107V	4181	288			
T102V	3893	0				Y107L	3893	0			
T102L	4004	111				Y107M	4118	225			
T102M	3893	0				Y107I	3893	0			
T102I	4100	207				Y107S	3893	0			
T102S	4004	111				Y107T	4118	225			
T102C	4034	141				Y107C	3893	0			
T102P	3842	−51				Y107P	4400	507			
T102N	3893	0				Y107N	4100	207			
T102Q	3893	0				Y107Q	4208	315			
T102K	4004	111				Y107K	3893	0			
T102R	4004	111				Y107R	3893	0			
T102H	3893	0				Y107H	4088	195			
T102D	4004	111				Y107D	3917	24			
T102E	3893	0				Y107E	4232	339			
T102F	4004	111				Y107F	4013	120			
T102Y	4004	111				Y107W	3893	0	0	9	10
T102W	4004	111	1	12	6	G108A	3911	18			
Y103A	3893	0				G108V	4118	225			
Y103G	3797	−96				G108L	3911	18			
Y103V	4004	111				G108M	4100	207			
Y103L	3893	0				G108I	3893	0			
Y103M	4004	111				G108S	3893	0			
Y103I	3797	−96				G108T	4118	225			
Y103S	3893	0				G108C	3983	90			
Y103T	4004	111				G108P	4100	207			
Y103C	3827	−66				G108N	4112	219			
Y103P	4004	111				G108Q	4100	207			
Y103N	4004	111				G108K	3893	0			
Y103Q	4004	111				G108R	3911	18			
Y103K	3893	0				G108H	4184	291			
Y103R	3893	0				G108D	3893	0			
Y103H	4064	171				G108E	4100	207			
Y103D	3893	0				G108F	3911	18			
Y103E	4004	111				G108Y	3911	18			
Y103F	3911	18				G108W	3893	0	0	9	10
Y103W	3893	0	3	8	8	F109A	3893	0			
Q104A	4004	111				F109G	3893	0			
Q104G	4004	111				F109V	4100	207			
Q104V	3860	−33				F109L	3893	0			
Q104L	4004	111				F109M	4100	207			

(continued)

Table 5.26 (continued)

Id	CLVS	DCLVS	(–ve) cnt	(+ve) cnt	0 cnt	id	CLVS	DCLVS	(–ve) cnt	(+ve) cnt	0 cnt
Q104M	3797	–96				F109I	3893	0			
Q104I	4004	111				F109S	3893	0			
Q104S	4004	111				F109T	4100	207			
Q104T	3860	–33				F109C	3893	0			
Q104C	4004	111				F109P	4100	207			
Q104P	3821	–72				F109N	4100	207			
Q104N	3797	–96				F109Q	4100	207			
Q104K	4004	111				F109K	3893	0			
Q104R	4004	111				F109R	3893	0			
Q104H	3857	–36				F109H	4100	207			
Q104D	4004	111				F109D	3929	36			
Q104E	3905	12				F109E	4100	207			
Q104F	4112	219				F109Y	3893	0			
Q104Y	4004	111				F109W	3893	0	0	8	11
Q104W	4004	111	3	12	4	R110A	3893	0			
G105A	3797	–96				R110G	3893	0			
G105V	4004	111				R110V	4100	207			
G105L	3797	–96				R110L	3893	0			
G105M	4004	111				R110M	4100	207			
G105I	3797	–96				R110I	3893	0			
G105S	3797	–96				R110S	3893	0			
G105T	4004	111				R110T	4100	207			
G105C	3797	–96				R110C	3911	18			
G105P	4064	171				R110P	4145	252			
G105N	4004	111				R110N	4100	207			
G105Q	4004	111				R110Q	4100	207			
G105K	3797	–96				R110K	3893	0			
G105R	3797	–96				R110H	4100	207			
G105H	4058	165				R110D	3938	45			
G105D	3797	–96				R110E	4100	207			
G105E	4004	111				R110F	3893	0			
G105F	3815	–78				R110Y	3911	18			
G105Y	3797	–96				R110W	3893	0	0	8	11
G105W	3797	–96	11	8	0	L111A	3893	0			
S106A	3893	0				L111G	3893	0			
S106G	3797	–96				L111V	4163	270			
S106V	4130	237				L111M	4100	207			
S106L	3917	24				L111I	3893	0			
S106M	4112	219				L111S	3893	0			
S106I	3935	42				L111T	4100	207			
S106T	4130	237				L111C	4019	126			
S106C	3815	–78				L111P	4100	207			
S106P	4112	219				L111N	4082	189			

(continued)

Table 5.26 (continued)

Id	CLVS	DCLVS	(–ve) cnt	(+ve) cnt	0 cnt	id	CLVS	DCLVS	(–ve) cnt	(+ve) cnt	0 cnt
S106N	4004	111				L111Q	4190	297			
S106Q	4112	219				L111K	3893	0			
S106K	4073	180				L111R	3893	0			
S106R	3917	24				L111H	4082	189			
S106H	4112	219				L111D	3893	0			
S106D	3821	–72				L111E	4214	321			
S106E	4049	156				L111F	3893	0			
S106F	3917	24				L111Y	3893	0			
S106Y	4229	336				L111W	3893	0	0	9	10
S106W	3881	–12	3	10	6						

Y103. This methodology continues for generation of CLVS and DCLVS values for each AA of a protein by introducing 19 mutations at each AA location.

Pattern Type of Triplet (PTT): The PTT refers to the pattern type of triplet <cnt (-ive) cnt (+ive) cnt (0)> values. These values are derived by inserting 19 mutations for each AA of a protein chain, and next counting the number of instances where DCLVS values are respectively (–ive), (+ive), and (0). Table 5.26 shows the PTT values on column 4, 5, 6 for AA T102 on row 21. Similarly, row 40 shows PTT values for AA Y103 on columns 4, 5, 6. This procedure continues for generation of PTT for each AA of a protein chain. The number of different PTTs across the full length of the protein chain are next identified. While Table 5.27 reports the PTT table for 10 AAs T102 to L111 of p53 protein, Table 5.28 reports 8 high count PTTs in non-increasing order—with PTTs as <0 9 10>, <0 1 18>, <0 8 11>, <0 12 7>, <0 2 17>, <8 1 10>, <8 0 11>, <12 0 7> displaying count values as (32, 30, 25, 20, 16, 15, 12, 12) respectively; these are marked as variables <v0 v1 v2 v3 v4 v5 v6 v7> in Table 5.29.

Table 5.27 PTT (Pattern Type Triplet) Table for 10 amino acids of p53 protein chain from AA location T102 to L111

Id	(–ve) cnt	(+ve) cnt	0 cnt
T102	1	12	6
Y103	3	8	8
Q104	3	12	4
G105	11	8	0
S106	3	10	6
Y107	0	9	10
G108	0	9	10
F109	0	8	11
R110	0	8	11
L111	0	9	10

Table 5.28 PTT count values across full length (in non-increasing order for first 10 PTT)

PTT	0-9-10	0-1-18	0-8-11	0-12-7	0-2-17	8-1-10	8-0-11	12-0-7	0-10-9	19-0-0
Cnt value	32	30	25	20	16	15	12	12	11	10
Assigned to variable	v0	v1	v2	v3	v4	v5	v6	v7		

Table 5.29 PTT and 10 Element CA Feature Vector (CAFV) across p53 protrin chain—48 MsAAs shown on Column 17 are derived out of 212 mutations

AAs	cnt (−ve)	cnt (+ve)	cnt (0)	v0	v1	v2	v3	v4	v5	v6	v7	v8	v9	48 MsAAs
E2	12	0	7											
E3	12	0	7											
P4	12	1	6											
Q5	12	0	7											
S6	8	1	10											
D7	8	0	11	0	0	0	0	0	1	1	3	5	0	
P8	12	1	6	0	0	0	0	0	1	2	3	4	0	
S9	8	0	11	0	0	0	0	0	1	1	2	6	0	
V10	12	1	6	0	0	0	0	0	2	2	2	4	0	
E11	12	4	3	0	0	0	0	0	2	2	1	5	0	
P12	12	1	6	0	0	0	0	0	1	2	1	6	0	
P13	12	0	7	0	0	0	0	0	1	1	0	8	0	
L14	8	2	9	0	0	0	0	0	2	1	1	6	0	
S15	8	1	10	0	0	0	0	0	1	0	1	8	0	
Q16	12	1	6	0	0	0	0	0	3	0	1	6	0	
E17	12	1	6	0	0	0	0	0	4	0	1	5	0	
T18	12	1	6	0	0	0	0	0	5	0	1	4	0	
F19	8	1	10	0	0	0	0	0	4	1	0	5	0	
S20	8	2	9	0	0	0	0	0	5	2	0	3	0	
D21	8	1	10	0	0	0	0	0	3	2	0	5	0	
L22	8	1	10	0	0	0	0	0	3	2	1	4	0	
23Y	8	1	10	0	0	0	0	0	3	2	1	4	0	
K24	8	0	11	0	0	0	0	0	4	1	1	4	0	
L25	8	0	11	0	0	0	0	0	3	1	1	5	0	
L26	8	3	8	0	0	0	0	0	3	2	2	3	0	
P27	12	0	7	0	0	0	0	0	2	2	1	5	0	
E28	12	1	6	0	0	0	0	0	1	2	2	5	0	
N29	12	5	2	0	0	0	0	0	0	2	2	6	0	
N30	12	1	6	0	0	0	0	0	0	1	3	6	0	
V31	12	0	7	0	0	0	0	0	0	0	2	8	0	
L32	10	1	8	0	0	0	0	0	0	0	3	7	0	
S33	17	0	2	0	0	0	0	0	0	0	3	7	0	
P34	19	0	0	0	0	0	0	0	1	0	3	6	0	
L35	12	0	7	0	0	0	0	0	1	0	2	7	0	
P36	19	0	0	0	0	0	0	0	1	1	3	5	0	
S37	8	3	8	0	0	0	0	0	2	1	2	5	0	
Q38	12	0	7	0	0	0	0	0	3	1	1	5	0	
A39	8	1	10	0	0	0	0	0	2	1	3	4	0	

(continued)

Table 5.29 (continued)

AAs	cnt (−ve)	cnt (+ve)	cnt (0)	v0	v1	v2	v3	v4	v5	v6	v7	v8	v9	48 MsAAs
M40	12	1	6	0	0	0	0	0	4	1	3	2	0	
D41	8	0	11	0	0	0	0	0	4	1	2	3	0	
D42	8	1	10	0	0	0	0	0	3	2	3	2	0	
L43	8	1	10	0	0	0	0	0	3	2	3	2	0	
M44	12	0	7	0	0	0	0	0	5	2	1	2	0	
L45	8	1	10	0	0	0	0	0	3	3	2	2	0	
S46	8	0	11	0	0	0	0	0	4	2	3	1	0	
P47	12	0	7	0	0	0	0	0	4	2	2	2	0	MsAA
D48	8	5	6	0	0	0	0	0	3	3	3	1	0	
D49	8	1	10	0	0	0	0	0	1	4	3	2	0	
I50	8	0	11	0	0	0	0	0	2	3	2	3	0	
E51	12	0	7	0	0	0	0	0	1	4	2	3	0	
Q52	12	1	6	0	0	0	0	0	1	3	3	3	0	
W53	8	0	11	0	0	0	0	0	1	2	2	5	0	
F54	8	0	11	0	0	0	0	0	1	2	2	5	0	
T55	12	4	3	0	0	0	0	0	0	3	3	4	0	
E56	12	0	7	0	0	0	0	0	0	2	2	6	0	
D57	8	6	5	0	0	0	0	0	0	2	2	6	0	
P58	12	2	5	0	0	0	0	0	0	2	2	6	0	
G59	8	3	8	0	0	0	0	0	0	1	2	7	0	
P60	12	0	7	0	0	0	0	0	0	0	1	9	0	
D61	9	1	9	0	0	0	0	0	0	0	2	8	0	
E62	18	0	1	0	0	0	0	0	0	0	1	9	0	
A63	10	0	9	0	0	0	0	0	0	0	1	9	0	
P64	18	0	1	0	0	0	0	0	0	0	1	9	0	
R65	10	1	8	0	0	0	0	0	0	0	1	9	0	
M66	18	0	1	0	0	0	0	0	0	0	0	10	0	
P67	19	0	0	0	0	0	0	0	0	0	0	10	0	
E68	19	0	0	0	0	0	0	0	0	0	0	10	0	
A69	7	6	6	0	0	0	0	0	0	0	0	10	0	
A70	9	2	8	0	0	0	0	0	0	0	0	10	0	
P71	10	3	6	0	0	0	0	0	0	0	0	10	0	
P72	3	4	12	0	0	0	0	0	0	0	0	10	0	MsAA
V73	2	1	16	0	0	0	0	0	0	0	0	10	0	
A74	8	3	8	0	0	0	0	0	0	0	0	10	0	
P75	11	1	7	0	0	0	0	0	0	0	0	10	0	
A76	11	1	7	0	0	0	0	0	0	0	0	10	0	
P77	18	0	1	0	0	0	0	0	0	0	0	10	0	
A78	10	1	8	0	0	0	0	0	0	0	0	10	0	
A79	15	1	3	0	0	0	0	0	0	0	0	10	0	
P80	18	1	0	0	0	0	0	0	0	0	0	10	0	
T81	6	7	6	0	0	0	0	0	0	0	0	10	0	
P82	7	0	12	0	1	0	0	0	0	0	0	9	0	
A83	6	7	6	0	1	0	0	0	0	0	0	9	0	

(continued)

Table 5.29 (continued)

AAs	cnt (−ve)	cnt (+ve)	cnt (0)	v0	v1	v2	v3	v4	v5	v6	v7	v8	v9	48 MsAAs
A84	9	7	3	0	1	0	1	0	0	0	0	8	0	
P85	6	12	1	0	1	1	1	0	0	0	0	7	0	
A86	2	5	12	0	1	1	1	0	0	0	0	7	0	
P87	0	1	18	0	0	1	1	0	0	0	0	8	0	
A88	0	10	9	0	1	1	1	0	0	0	0	7	0	
P89	0	12	7	0	1	2	0	0	0	0	0	7	0	
S90	0	8	11	1	1	1	1	0	0	0	0	6	0	
W91	9	0	10	2	1	2	1	0	0	0	0	4	0	
P92	7	0	12	2	1	2	1	0	0	0	0	4	0	
L93	1	8	10	2	0	2	2	0	0	0	0	4	0	
S94	0	8	11	3	0	1	2	0	0	0	0	4	0	
S95	0	9	10	2	0	2	1	0	0	0	0	5	0	
S96	0	9	10	3	0	1	1	0	0	0	0	5	0	
V97	0	13	6	4	0	1	1	0	0	0	0	4	0	
P98	0	12	7	4	0	1	0	0	0	0	0	5	0	
S99	0	9	10	3	0	1	1	0	0	0	0	5	0	
Q100	1	13	5	4	0	0	1	0	0	0	0	5	0	
K101	0	9	10	2	0	0	1	0	0	0	0	7	0	
T102	1	12	6	3	0	0	1	0	0	0	0	6	0	
Y103	3	8	8	4	0	0	1	0	0	0	0	5	0	
Q104	3	12	4	4	0	1	0	0	0	0	0	5	0	
G105	11	8	0	3	0	2	0	0	0	0	0	5	0	
S106	3	10	6	4	0	2	0	0	0	0	0	4	0	
Y107	0	9	10	3	0	2	0	0	0	0	0	5	0	
G108	0	9	10	3	0	3	0	0	0	0	0	4	0	
F109	0	8	11	4	0	2	0	0	0	0	0	4	0	
R110	0	8	11	4	0	2	1	0	0	0	0	3	0	
L111	0	9	10	3	0	3	1	0	0	0	0	3	0	MsAA
G112	0	9	10	4	0	3	1	0	0	0	0	2	0	
F113	0	8	11	4	0	2	2	0	0	0	0	2	0	
L114	0	14	5	4	0	3	2	0	0	0	0	1	0	
H115	0	12	7	5	0	2	1	0	0	0	0	2	0	
S116	0	10	9	5	0	1	2	0	0	0	0	2	0	
G117	0	9	10	3	0	1	2	0	0	0	0	4	0	
T118	0	12	7	3	0	1	1	0	0	0	0	5	0	
A119	0	9	10	2	0	0	2	0	0	0	0	6	0	
K120	0	9	10	2	0	0	2	0	0	0	0	6	0	
S121	2	6	11	3	0	0	1	0	0	0	0	6	0	
V122	4	9	6	3	0	0	1	0	0	0	0	6	0	
T123	4	10	5	2	0	0	1	0	0	0	0	7	0	
C124	19	0	0	2	0	0	0	0	0	1	0	7	0	
T125	16	1	2	1	0	0	0	0	0	1	0	8	0	MsAA
Y126	15	0	4	0	0	0	0	0	0	1	0	9	0	
S127	10	6	3	0	0	0	0	0	0	1	0	9	0	

(continued)

Table 5.29 (continued)

AAs	cnt (−ve)	cnt (+ve)	cnt (0)	v0	v1	v2	v3	v4	v5	v6	v7	v8	v9	48 MsAAs
P128	11	2	6	0	0	0	0	0	0	1	0	9	0	
A129	8	0	11	0	0	0	0	0	0	0	0	10	0	
L130	7	0	12	0	0	0	0	0	0	1	0	9	0	
N131	11	1	7	0	0	0	0	0	0	1	0	9	0	
K132	8	2	9	0	0	0	0	0	1	1	0	8	0	MsAA
M133	11	0	8	0	0	0	0	0	1	1	0	8	0	
F134	3	11	5	0	0	0	0	0	1	1	0	8	0	
C135	6	0	13	0	0	0	0	0	1	0	0	9	0	MsAA
Q136	11	2	6	0	0	0	0	0	1	0	0	9	0	
L137	8	1	10	0	0	0	0	0	0	0	0	10	0	
A138	7	1	11	0	0	0	0	0	1	0	0	9	0	
K139	6	1	12	0	0	0	0	0	1	0	1	8	0	
T140	10	1	8	0	0	0	0	0	1	0	1	8	0	
C141	11	0	8	0	0	0	0	0	1	0	1	8	0	MsAA
P142	13	2	4	0	0	0	0	0	1	0	1	8	0	
V143	11	1	7	0	0	0	0	0	0	0	1	9	0	
Q144	12	0	7	0	0	0	0	0	0	0	0	10	0	MsAA
L145	7	0	12	0	0	0	0	0	0	0	1	9	0	
146Y	7	1	11	0	0	0	0	0	0	0	1	9	0	
V147	9	2	8	0	0	0	0	0	0	0	1	9	0	
D148	7	0	12	0	0	0	0	0	0	0	1	9	0	
S149	11	1	7	0	0	0	0	0	0	0	1	9	0	
T150	10	2	7	0	0	0	0	0	0	0	0	10	0	
P151	15	0	4	0	0	0	0	0	0	0	0	10	0	MsAA
P152	13	2	4	0	0	0	0	0	0	0	0	10	0	
P153	18	1	0	0	0	0	0	0	0	0	0	10	0	
G154	18	1	0	0	0	0	0	0	1	0	0	9	0	
T155	7	3	9	0	0	0	0	0	1	0	0	9	0	
R156	7	0	12	0	0	0	0	0	1	0	0	9	0	
V157	10	1	8	0	0	0	0	0	1	0	0	9	0	
R158	7	0	12	0	0	0	0	0	1	0	0	9	0	
A159	8	1	10	0	0	0	0	0	0	0	0	10	0	
M160	11	2	6	0	0	0	0	0	1	0	0	9	0	
A161	7	1	11	0	0	0	0	0	2	0	0	8	0	
I162	7	1	11	0	0	0	0	0	2	0	0	8	0	
Y163	5	1	13	0	0	0	0	0	2	0	0	8	0	MsAA
K164	7	1	11	0	0	0	0	0	2	0	0	8	0	
Q165	11	1	7	0	0	0	0	0	1	0	0	9	0	
S166	8	1	10	0	0	0	0	0	0	0	0	10	0	
Q167	3	2	14	0	0	0	0	0	1	0	0	9	0	
H168	8	2	9	0	0	0	0	0	1	0	0	9	0	
M169	10	2	7	0	0	0	0	0	2	0	0	8	0	
T170	11	1	7	0	0	0	0	0	2	0	0	8	0	
E171	11	2	6	0	0	0	0	0	2	0	0	8	0	

(continued)

Table 5.29 (continued)

AAs	cnt (−ve)	cnt (+ve)	cnt (0)	v0	v1	v2	v3	v4	v5	v6	v7	v8	v9	48 MsAAs
V172	9	2	8	0	0	0	0	0	1	0	0	9	0	
V173	11	1	7	0	0	0	0	0	1	0	0	9	0	MsAA
R174	8	1	10	0	0	0	0	0	0	0	0	10	0	
R175	1	1	17	0	0	0	0	0	1	0	0	9	0	MsAA
C176	10	1	8	0	0	0	0	0	1	0	1	8	0	MsAA
P177	5	9	5	0	0	0	0	0	1	0	1	8	0	
H178	14	0	5	0	0	0	0	0	1	0	1	8	0	
H179	11	0	8	0	0	0	0	0	1	0	1	8	0	MsAA
E180	1	1	17	0	0	0	0	0	0	0	1	9	0	
R181	12	0	7	0	0	0	0	0	0	0	0	10	0	
C182	19	0	0	0	0	0	0	1	0	0	1	8	0	
S183	11	0	8	0	0	0	0	1	0	0	1	8	0	
D184	6	2	11	0	0	0	0	1	0	0	1	8	0	
S185	7	1	11	0	0	0	0	1	0	0	1	8	0	
D186	0	4	15	0	0	0	0	1	0	0	1	8	0	
G187	0	2	17	0	0	0	0	0	0	0	0	10	0	
L188	1	0	18	0	0	0	0	2	0	0	0	8	0	
A189	2	5	12	0	1	0	0	2	0	0	0	7	0	
P190	4	1	14	0	2	0	0	2	0	0	0	6	0	
P191	7	1	11	0	2	0	0	2	0	0	0	6	0	
Q192	0	5	14	0	2	0	0	2	0	0	0	6	0	
H193	0	2	17	0	2	0	0	0	0	0	0	8	0	MsAA
L194	0	1	18	0	1	0	0	1	0	0	0	8	0	MsAA
I195	0	1	18	0	1	0	0	1	0	0	0	8	0	MsAA
R196	0	4	15	0	2	0	0	1	0	0	0	7	0	MsAA
V197	2	1	16	0	2	0	0	1	0	0	0	7	0	
E198	15	1	3	0	3	0	0	1	0	0	0	6	0	
G199	17	1	1	0	3	0	0	1	0	0	0	6	0	
N200	2	3	14	0	2	0	0	1	0	0	0	7	0	
L201	0	3	16	0	2	0	0	1	0	0	0	7	0	
R202	0	3	16	0	2	0	0	1	0	0	0	7	0	
V203	0	1	18	0	2	0	0	1	0	0	0	7	0	
E204	0	2	17	0	3	0	0	0	0	0	0	7	0	
Y205	0	3	16	0	4	0	0	1	0	0	0	5	0	MsAA
L206	0	1	18	0	4	0	0	1	0	0	0	5	0	
D207	0	0	19	0	5	0	0	1	0	0	0	4	0	
D208	0	1	18	0	4	0	0	1	0	0	0	5	0	
R209	0	0	19	0	5	0	0	1	0	0	0	4	0	
N210	0	1	18	0	5	0	0	0	0	0	0	5	0	
T211	0	1	18	0	5	0	0	1	0	0	0	4	0	
F212	0	0	19	0	6	0	0	1	0	0	0	3	0	
R213	0	6	13	0	6	0	0	1	0	0	0	3	0	MsAA
H214	0	1	18	0	4	0	0	2	0	0	0	4	0	MsAA
S215	0	1	18	0	4	0	0	2	0	0	0	4	0	MsAA

(continued)

Table 5.29 (continued)

AAs	cnt (−ve)	cnt (+ve)	cnt (0)	v0	v1	v2	v3	v4	v5	v6	v7	v8	v9	48 MsAAs
V216	0	2	17	0	4	0	0	1	0	0	0	5	0	MsAA
V217	0	1	18	0	2	0	0	2	0	0	0	6	0	
V218	0	10	9	0	3	0	0	2	0	0	0	5	0	
P219	0	2	17	0	3	0	0	1	0	0	0	6	0	
Y220	3	1	15	0	2	0	0	2	0	0	0	6	0	MsAA
E221	16	0	3	0	1	0	0	2	0	0	0	7	0	
P222	16	0	3	0	1	0	0	1	0	0	0	8	0	
P223	19	0	0	0	0	0	0	1	0	0	0	9	0	
E224	19	0	0	0	0	0	0	1	0	0	0	9	0	
V225	9	6	4	0	0	0	0	0	0	0	0	10	0	
G226	2	13	4	0	0	0	0	0	0	0	0	10	0	
S227	6	8	5	0	0	0	0	0	0	0	0	10	0	
D228	5	12	2	0	0	0	0	1	0	0	0	9	0	
C229	17	0	2	0	0	0	0	1	0	0	0	9	0	
T230	15	0	4	0	0	0	0	2	0	0	0	8	0	
T231	10	2	7	0	0	0	0	3	0	0	0	7	0	
I232	3	3	13	0	0	0	0	3	0	0	0	7	0	
H233	0	2	17	0	0	0	0	2	0	0	0	8	0	
Y234	0	0	19	0	0	0	0	3	0	0	0	7	0	MsAA
N235	0	2	17	0	0	0	0	2	0	0	0	8	0	
Y236	0	2	17	0	0	0	0	2	0	0	0	8	0	MsAA
M237	0	7	12	0	0	0	0	3	0	0	0	7	0	MsAA
C238	0	0	19	0	0	0	0	3	0	0	0	7	0	MsAA
N239	0	11	8	0	0	0	0	2	0	0	0	8	0	MsAA
S240	2	1	16	0	0	0	0	2	0	0	0	8	0	
S241	9	2	8	0	0	0	0	2	0	0	0	8	0	MsAA
C242	19	0	0	0	0	0	0	2	0	0	0	8	0	MsAA
M243	7	6	6	0	0	0	0	2	0	0	0	8	0	
G244	0	3	16	0	0	0	0	2	0	0	0	8	0	MsAA
G245	0	0	19	0	1	0	0	2	0	0	0	7	0	MsAA
M246	0	2	17	0	1	0	0	1	0	0	0	8	0	
N247	0	2	17	0	1	0	0	2	0	0	0	7	0	
R248	0	6	13	0	2	0	0	3	0	0	0	5	0	MsAA
R249	0	5	14	0	2	0	0	3	0	0	0	5	0	MsAA
P250	0	1	18	0	2	0	0	3	0	0	0	5	0	
I251	0	0	19	0	4	0	0	3	0	0	0	3	0	
L252	0	2	17	0	5	0	0	1	0	0	0	4	0	
T253	0	1	18	0	5	0	0	1	0	0	0	4	0	
I254	0	0	19	0	6	0	0	1	0	0	0	3	0	
I255	0	1	18	0	5	0	0	2	0	0	0	3	0	MsAA
T256	0	1	18	0	4	0	0	2	0	0	0	4	0	
L257	0	1	18	0	4	0	0	3	0	0	0	3	0	
E258	0	1	18	0	4	0	0	2	0	0	0	4	0	
D259	0	4	15	0	5	0	0	2	0	0	0	3	0	

(continued)

Table 5.29 (continued)

AAs	cnt (−ve)	cnt (+ve)	cnt (0)	v0	v1	v2	v3	v4	v5	v6	v7	v8	v9	48 MsAAs
S260	0	2	17	0	5	0	0	1	0	0	0	4	0	
S261	0	5	14	0	5	0	0	2	0	0	0	3	0	
G262	0	2	17	0	4	0	0	2	0	0	0	4	0	
N263	0	0	19	0	4	0	0	3	0	0	0	3	0	
L264	0	1	18	0	3	0	0	3	0	0	0	4	0	
L265	0	5	14	0	4	0	0	4	0	0	0	2	0	
G266	0	1	18	0	4	0	0	3	0	0	0	3	0	MsAA
R267	0	2	17	0	5	0	0	2	0	0	0	3	0	
N268	0	1	18	0	4	0	0	2	0	0	0	4	0	
S269	0	1	18	0	4	0	0	2	1	0	0	3	0	
F270	0	2	17	0	4	0	0	1	1	0	0	4	0	MsAA
E271	0	1	18	0	3	0	0	2	1	1	0	3	0	
V272	0	3	16	0	3	0	0	2	1	1	0	3	0	MsAA
R273	4	0	15	0	3	0	0	1	1	1	0	4	0	MsAA
V274	8	1	10	0	3	0	0	1	0	1	0	5	0	MsAA
C275	19	0	0	0	2	0	0	1	1	1	0	5	0	MsAA
A276	8	0	11	0	3	0	0	0	1	0	0	6	0	
C277	9	9	1	0	3	0	0	0	1	1	0	5	0	
P278	14	2	3	0	3	0	0	0	1	1	0	5	0	MsAA
G279	0	1	18	0	2	0	0	0	1	1	0	6	0	
R280	0	3	16	0	3	0	0	0	0	1	0	6	0	MsAA
D281	0	1	18	0	2	0	0	0	0	1	0	7	0	MsAA
R282	0	1	18	0	3	0	0	0	0	0	0	7	0	MsAA
R283	0	3	16	0	4	0	0	0	0	0	0	6	0	
T284	0	6	13	0	5	0	0	0	0	0	0	5	0	
E285	0	4	15	0	5	0	0	0	0	0	0	5	0	
E286	0	6	13	0	5	0	0	1	0	0	0	4	0	MsAA
E287	0	1	18	0	3	0	0	1	0	0	0	6	0	
N288	0	3	16	0	3	0	0	1	0	1	0	5	0	
L289	0	1	18	0	2	0	0	1	0	1	0	6	0	
R290	0	1	18	0	2	0	0	1	0	1	0	6	0	
K291	0	2	17	0	3	0	0	0	0	1	0	6	0	
K292	2	4	13	0	3	0	0	1	0	1	0	5	0	
G293	8	0	11	0	2	0	0	1	0	0	0	7	0	
E294	3	4	12	0	2	0	0	1	0	1	0	6	0	
P295	2	2	15	0	1	0	0	1	0	1	0	7	0	
H296	4	3	12	0	0	0	0	1	0	1	0	8	0	
H297	1	4	14	0	0	0	0	0	0	1	0	9	0	
E298	0	10	9	0	0	0	0	0	0	1	0	9	0	
L299	3	9	7	0	0	0	1	0	0	0	0	9	0	
P300	6	6	7	0	0	1	1	0	0	0	0	8	0	
P301	3	11	5	0	0	2	1	0	0	0	0	7	0	
G302	10	9	0	1	0	2	1	0	0	0	0	6	0	
S303	2	10	7	1	0	3	1	0	0	0	0	5	0	

(continued)

Table 5.29 (continued)

AAs	cnt (−ve)	cnt (+ve)	cnt (0)	v0	v1	v2	v3	v4	v5	v6	v7	v8	v9	48 MsAAs
T304	0	12	7	1	0	3	1	0	0	0	0	5	0	
K305	0	8	11	1	0	2	2	0	0	0	0	5	0	
R306	0	8	11	1	0	2	3	0	0	0	0	4	0	MsAA
A307	0	9	10	0	0	3	4	0	0	0	0	3	0	
L308	0	8	11	1	0	3	4	0	0	0	0	2	0	
P309	0	12	7	1	0	4	3	0	0	0	0	2	0	
N310	0	13	6	1	0	4	3	0	0	0	0	2	0	
N311	0	12	7	1	0	3	2	0	0	0	0	4	0	
T312	0	12	7	1	0	2	2	0	0	0	0	5	0	
S313	0	8	11	0	0	1	3	0	0	0	0	6	0	
S314	0	11	8	1	0	1	3	0	0	0	0	5	0	
S315	0	11	8	1	0	1	2	0	0	0	0	6	0	
P316	1	12	6	1	0	1	2	0	0	0	0	6	0	
Q317	0	16	3	1	0	1	2	0	0	0	0	6	0	
P318	0	18	1	1	0	2	1	0	0	0	0	6	0	
K319	0	9	10	1	0	1	1	0	0	0	0	7	0	
K320	0	14	5	3	0	1	1	0	0	0	0	5	0	
K321	0	14	5	3	0	1	2	0	0	0	0	4	0	
P322	0	12	7	3	0	1	1	0	0	0	0	5	0	
L323	0	8	11	4	0	0	2	0	0	0	0	4	0	
D324	0	9	10	3	0	1	2	0	0	0	0	4	0	
G325	0	9	10	2	0	2	2	0	0	0	0	4	0	
E326	0	12	7	3	0	2	2	0	0	0	0	3	0	
Y327	0	10	9	3	0	2	3	0	0	0	0	2	0	
F328	0	9	10	2	0	2	2	0	0	0	0	4	0	
T329	0	13	6	4	0	1	2	0	0	0	0	3	0	
L330	0	8	11	3	0	1	2	0	0	0	0	4	0	
Q331	0	12	7	2	0	2	1	0	0	0	0	5	0	
I332	0	10	9	3	0	2	1	0	0	0	0	4	0	
R333	0	10	9	4	0	2	1	0	0	0	0	3	0	
G334	0	9	10	2	0	2	1	0	0	0	0	5	0	
R335	0	8	11	3	0	1	1	0	0	0	0	5	0	
E336	0	13	6	4	0	1	1	0	0	0	0	4	0	
R337	0	9	10	3	0	2	0	0	0	0	0	5	0	
F338	0	9	10	3	0	2	1	0	0	0	0	4	0	
E339	0	14	5	5	0	2	1	0	0	0	0	2	0	
M340	0	13	6	4	0	2	2	0	0	0	0	2	0	
F341	0	9	10	3	0	1	3	0	0	0	0	3	0	
R342	0	8	11	4	0	0	3	0	0	0	0	3	0	
E343	0	12	7	3	0	2	2	0	0	0	0	3	0	
L344	0	9	10	1	0	2	4	0	0	0	0	3	0	
N345	0	12	7	2	0	2	3	0	0	0	0	3	0	
E346	0	12	7	2	0	3	3	0	0	0	0	2	0	
A347	0	10	9	1	0	4	4	0	0	0	0	1	0	
L348	0	8	11	2	0	2	4	0	0	0	0	2	0	

(continued)

Table 5.29 (continued)

AAs	cnt (−ve)	cnt (+ve)	cnt (0)	v0	v1	v2	v3	v4	v5	v6	v7	v8	v9	48 MsAAs
E349	0	12	7	2	0	3	2	0	0	0	0	3	0	
L350	0	10	9	1	0	4	3	0	0	0	0	2	0	
K351	0	8	11	2	0	3	2	0	0	0	0	3	0	
D352	0	8	11	2	0	4	1	0	0	0	0	3	0	
A353	0	9	10	1	0	5	1	0	0	0	0	3	0	
Q354	0	13	6	2	0	4	1	0	0	0	0	3	0	
A355	0	8	11	3	0	3	0	0	0	0	0	4	0	
G356	0	9	10	2	0	5	0	0	0	0	0	3	0	
K357	0	8	11	4	0	3	0	0	0	0	0	3	0	
E358	0	14	5	5	0	3	0	0	0	0	0	2	0	
P359	0	14	5	4	0	3	0	0	0	0	0	3	0	
G360	0	9	10	3	0	3	1	0	0	0	0	3	0	
G361	0	8	11	4	0	1	1	0	0	0	0	4	0	
S362	0	9	10	3	0	2	1	0	0	0	0	4	0	
R363	0	9	10	3	0	1	2	0	0	0	0	4	0	
A364	0	10	9	4	0	2	2	0	0	0	0	2	0	
H365	0	12	7	5	0	2	1	0	0	0	0	2	0	
S366	1	8	10	5	0	2	2	0	0	0	0	1	0	
S367	0	9	10	4	0	2	2	0	0	0	0	2	0	
H368	0	12	7	5	0	2	1	0	0	0	0	2	0	
L369	0	8	11	4	0	2	2	0	0	0	0	2	0	
K370	0	9	10	3	0	3	2	0	0	0	0	2	0	
S371	0	9	10	4	0	3	1	0	0	0	0	2	0	
K372	0	8	11	5	0	2	1	0	0	0	0	2	0	
K373	0	9	10	3	0	4	1	0	0	0	0	2	0	
G374	0	8	11	4	0	3	1	0	0	0	0	2	0	
Q375	0	15	4	4	0	3	2	0	0	0	0	1	0	
S376	0	9	10	3	0	3	2	0	0	0	0	2	0	
T377	0	13	6	3	0	4	2	0	0	0	0	1	0	
S378	0	8	11	3	0	3	2	0	0	0	0	2	0	
R379	0	12	7	2	0	4	2	0	0	0	0	2	0	
H380	0	12	7	2	0	3	2	0	0	0	0	3	0	
K381	0	9	10	1	0	3	3	0	0	0	0	3	0	
K382	0	8	11	1	0	2	3	0	0	0	0	4	0	
L383	0	8	11	1	0	2	3	0	0	0	0	4	0	
M384	0	12	7	1	0	2	2	0	0	0	0	5	0	
F385	0	10	9	1	0	2	2	0	0	0	0	5	0	
K386	0	19	0	1	1	2	1	0	0	0	0	5	0	
T387	0	17	2	0	2	2	1	0	0	0	0	5	0	
E388	0	3	16	0	2	1	1	0	0	0	0	6		
G389	0	7	12											
P390	0	18	1											
D391	0	1	18											
S392	0	1	18											
D393	0	4	15											

Significance of (–ive/+ive) DCLVS value—The (–ive) DCVS value indicates that some signals of the wild get reduced/eliminated in the mutant. While a (+ive) DCLVS value of a mutant indicates the CL values of some signals get enhanced or there is the appearance of some additional signal in the mutant CL graph that is absent in its wild counterpart.

Ten Element CAFV (CA Feature Vector shown in Table 5.29 **for p53)**—The FV <v0 v1 v2 v3 v4 v5 v6 v7 v8 v9> of 10 elements marked as variables v0 to v9 is derived out of PTT of each AA. The CAFV of ith AA specifies the environment of PTTs around the ith AA by evaluating its 5 neighbours on either end, $(i - 5)$ to $(i + 5)$ excluding the ith AA. Numerical value of each variable spans from 0 to 10. Design of CAFV is reported below.

Ten different Features are extracted for each ith AA of a protein chain based on the analysis of 10 AAs—$(i - 1)$ to $(i - 5)$ and $(i + 1)$ to $(i + 5)$. The FV <v0 v1 v2 v3 v4 v5 v6 v7 v8 v9> is derived out of the 10 numerical variable v0 to v9 elaborated next:

(a) Analysis of count of each PTT in the full length of the protein chain (shown in Table 5.28)—Based on this count analysis, eight high count valued PTTs are selected in non-decreasing order: Count of these PTTs of an AA are marked as variables v0, v1, v2, v3, v4, v5, v6, v7 respectively and shown in Table 5.28.
(b) Two more variables marked as v8 and v9 are marked:
v8 = 10 – (v0 + v1 + v2 + v3 + v4 + v5 + v6 + v7) among 10 AAs $(i - 5$ to $i + 5)$ around ith AA, and
v9 = 0.

Based on the earlier discussions, the steps for generation of PTT—FV table for a protein chain can be summarized as follows.

(a) Insert 19 mutations for each AA of the protein chain and generate CLVS, DCLVS values for each of 19 mutants for each AA.
(b) Generate PTT values for each AA.
(c) Generate 8 high count PTTs across the full length of the protein.
(d) Generate 10 element Feature Vector (FV).
(e) Generate PTT—FV table for the protein chain.

Observation 5.5–Significance of PTT-FV: The PTT-FV table derived out of a protein with CAML model inherits certain characteristics of the protein that are employed for protein mutational studies reported in Sects. 5.4, 5.5 and 5.6 of Chap. 5.

The PTT—FV table for p53 protein is reported in Table 5.29; the table shows PTT on column 2, 3, 4, while column 5 to 14 show ten element Feature Vector (FV). Column 1 reports the 392 AAs (E2 to D393), while column 15 shows 48 MsAAs associated with 212 mutants reported in p53 protein chain. For subsequent discussions, the PTT of an AA is viewed as <X Y Z>, where X refers to count of mutants with (–ive) DCLVS value, Y refers to count of mutants with (+ive) DCLVS value, and count of (0) valued DCLVS is represented with Z, for 19 mutants inserted for each amino acid.

5.5.5 Analysis of P53 Protein MsAAs Associated with 212 Mutations

One of the most extensively studied proteins is the p53 which is directly/indirectly implicated for majority of cancer types. This section employs CAML model to identify and analyse the regions of p53 protein displaying 212 mutations reported in published literature. Rather that concentrating analysis of an individual mutant, CAML model evaluates a Mutations site AA (MsAA), each covering at least one mutation.

Study of the mutational landscape of p53 protein is of major interest for the research community. The focus of this subsection is to analyse the regions of p53 chain, particularly its DNA binding domain (DBD covering T102 to K292), showing concentration of mutants reported in published literature. The protein chain has 393 AAs; on exclusion of the start codon Met (M), it has 392 AAs divided into 3 domains: N Terminal Domain (NTD—AA loc 2 to 101), central DNA Binding Domain (DBD—AA loc T102 to K292), and C Terminal Domain (CTD—AA loc 293 to 393). NTD is further subdivided into TAD (Trans Activation Domain) and PRD (Proline Rich Domain). Analysis of these three domains with CAML model follows. While NTD covers 2 MsAAs (both are amino acid Proline at location P47 and P72), the CTD covers one MsAA at S306. The remaining 45 MsAAs are covered by DBD.

In the subsequent discussions, the 3 elements of PTT are viewed as <X Y Z>, where X and Y denotes count of (–ve) and (+ive) valued mutants on introduction of 19 mutations on an amino acid; mutants having DCLVS value 0 is represented by Z. Based on CAML parameter of PTT, different regions of p53 chain are identified employing the 0 and non-0 values of X. Based on CAML parameter of PTT, different regions of p53 chain are identified employing the 0 and non-0 values of X.

Algorithm 4: Analysis of MSAAs in the DBD (Dna Binding Domain) of P53 Protein Chain Covering 45 MsAAs

---

Input1 : PTT List of P53 chain (E2 to M393) reported in Table 5.29 on columns 2, 3, 4 (DBD covers 191 AAs from T102 to K292

Output: Twenty regions (R0 to R19) shown in Table 5.30, each region displaying value of X as either 0 or non-0, for each of the AAs covered by a region; MsAAs are located on non-0 regions and AAs of 0 regions, within a range of 7 AAs from either end of a non-0 region

---

Step 0 : Initialization step—Scan through of PTT input table. Identify isolated instances of an AA displaying value 0 (or 1) for X with complementary value 1 (0 value) for X, prior and after the AA location—these are initialized to 1 (0 value). (As per this step, the 0/1 value of X for the following four AAs are initialized to value 0/1 in Table 5.29: (i) R101 with X = 0 converted to 1, (ii) E298 with X = 0 converted to 1, (iii) P316 with X = 1 converted to 0, (iv) S366 showing X = 1 converted to 0.

Table 5.30 Analysis of 45 MsAAs in twenty regions (R0 to R19) in p53 covering DBD (DNA Binding Domain) from T102 to K292)

Region	From	To	X = non-0/0	Number of MsAA—MsAA Locations
R0	E2	A86	non-0	2—P47, P72
R1	P87	S90	0	0
R2	W91	L93	non-0	0
R3	S94	S99	0	0
R4	Q100	S106	non-0	0
R5	Y107	K120	0	1—L111
R6	S121	S185	non-0	11—T125, K132, C135, C141, Q144, P151, Y163, V173, R175, C176, H179
R7	D186	D187	0	0
R8	L188	P191	non-0	0
R9	Q192	R196	0	4—H193, L194, I195, H196
R10	V197	N200	non-0	0
R11	R201	P219	0	5—Y205, R213, H214, S215, V216
R12	Y220	I232	non-0	1—Y220
R13	H233	N239	0	5—Y234, Y236, M237, C238, N239
R14	S240	C243	non-0	2—S241, C242
R15	G244	V272	0	8—G244, G245, R248, R249, I255, G266, F270, V272
R16	R273	P278	non-0	4—R273, V274, C275, P278
R17	G279	K291	0	4—E280, D281, R282, E286
R18	K292	G303	non-0	0
R19	T304	M393	0	1—S306

Step 1: Scan through PTT input. Identify regions displaying the same value X (0 or non-0) for all the AAs in a region—these are marked as 0 region and non-0 region (as per this step, 20 regions, marked as R0 to R19, are identified and reported in Table 5.30 displaying ten non-0 regions and ten 0 regions).

Step 2 : Note the MsAAs in each non-0 regions; let the location of the terminal AA on either end of a non-0 region be marked as z1 and z2.

Step 3 : MsAAs in 0-region are located within the AA locations—(i) either at (z1–1) to (z1–7) or (ii) (z2 + 1) to (z2 + 7).

Step 4 : Stop

Table 5.30 reports the results derived on execution of Algorithm 4. The p53 chain is divided into 20 regions based on the value of X (count of (-ive) valued DCLVS). Ten non-0 regions cover 18 MsAAs out of total 45 MsAAs present in DBD. Step 3 of the algorithm identifies 25 MsAAs in the ten 0-regions of p53 based on the MsAAs covered by non-0 regions. The algorithm fails to identify two MsAAs at location L111

(Leucine) and I255 (Isoleucine), both having long aliphatic chain with 13 atoms in their side chain.

The following observation is reported based on the analysis of a number of proteins on comparing CAML model PTT values along with the regions of stable secondary structure and unstructured regions reported in published literature (for four CoV-2 structural proteins and a large number of Cancer proteins reported in Uniprot/NCBI).

Observation 5.6: A protein region is intrinsically disordered and unstable, if it covers large number of AAs displaying non-0 count value of X representing count of (-ive) valued DCLVS of PTT.

As per the CAML model, the region covering 85 AAs from location E2 to A86 of NTD, as reported in Table 5.30, is a disordered region. This result, derived with the CAML model for p53 protein chain, can be found to be valid in physical domain [131].

Subsequent observation refers to binding of a protein on its receptor and the corresponding PTT derived out of the protein with CAML model. Viral proteins bind with their receptors. For example, 1273 AA CoV-2 spike protein binds on its receptor ACE2 at the RBD (Receptor Binding Domian at AA location F329 to P527). Similarly, a DNA/RNA binding protein binds on DNA/RNA. For example, Transcription Factor, Histone, p53 etc. bind on DNA and referred to as DBP (DNA Binding Protein), while HuR is a RNA binding protein (RBP). From the analysis of physical binding domain of a protein on its receptor and analysing PTT derived out of the protein with CAML model, we report the next observation.

Observation 5.7: The binding domain of a protein on its receptor is divided into a number of regions, each region covering a set of AAs, with each AA in a region having X value as 0 or non-0 of PTT <X Y Z>, derived out of CAML model for the protein.

It is worth investigating the issue of selective binding of p53 cognate sites with DNA in normal and cancer cells, that is not clearly understood [132]. In this background we report our next observation.

Observation 5.8—The Characteristics of the MsAAs of p53 protein chain in its DBD (DNA Binding Domian) identified with CAML model: Five issues are highlighted under the characteristics C1 to C5 presented next.

C1: The (–ive) DCLVS value indicates that some signals of the wild get reduced/eliminated in the mutant. While a (+ive) DCLVS value of a mutant indicates the CL values of some signals get enhanced or there is the appearance of some additional signal in the mutant CL graph that is absent in its wild counterpart. Thus, we have two situation—(i) Loss of Signal (LoS) for a mutant with (-ive) DCLVS value, and (ii) Gain of Signal (GoS) for a mutant with (+ive) DCLVS value.

C2: Due to GoS, the mutant will fail to interact with other biomolecules, as observed for wild on its pathway. Hence, this would lead to Loss of Function (LoF) for the mutant.

C3: On the other hand, due to LoS, the mutant might interact with biomolecules not observed for its wild counterpart. Thus, LoS (Loss of Signal) may lead to GoF.

C4: Non-0 X valued region of p53, indicates to LoS, resulting in GoF. Hence, insertion of mutation on such a region may enable p53 mutant of a cancer cell for survival and proliferation.

C5: The mutational pressure in non-0 region may get extended to its adjacent 0 region on either end of non-0 region.

The earlier characterization of p53 DBD, derived with the CAML model, may open up new avenues for investigating p53 cognate sites binding with DNA in a cancer cell.

For its growth and survival, a stable p53 mutant of a cancer cell, interacts with different elements of biologically dependant pathways. As noted earlier, rather than a single mutant, we analyse a MsAA that covers at least one mutation. Identification of the relevant functions of a mutant on such pathways, is a highly challenging task. In this context, instead of prediction of function of a single MsAA, we investigate functional proximity of a pair of MsAAs.

5.5.6 CAML Model for Prediction of Functional Proximity of a Pair of MsAAs

Table 5.29 reports 47 MsAAs derived out of 212 mutations reported in published literature. Out of these 47, there are 45 MsAAs covered by the DBD of p53 protein chain. Structural details of p53 mutants in respect of DNA binding are addressed by many authors. The mutants affect wide varieties of cellular function in a complex process [112, 125, 130, 133–135]. The p53 pathway represents the network of gene products associated with intrinsic and extrinsic stress signals, loss of wild type p53 function, gain of function including switching of function. Analysis of the functional impact of an individual mutant on the p53 pathway is a highly challenging task.

In the above context, this section concentrates on comparative analysis of a pair of MsAAs through evaluation of their Functional Proximity. CAML parameter PTT and 10 element Feature Vector (FV) provide the foundation of this analysis. The functional proximity is determined through evaluation of Vector Distance (VD) of FV of a pair of MsAAs computed as:

VD = square root of (sum of square of the distance of each pair of 10 elements of FV).

The CAML model framework has been extensively employed for mutational study of CoV-2 proteins in Sects. 5.2 and 5.3. The same framework is employed for mutational study of CoV-2 Spike protein reported in Sect. 5.4 and wide varieties of cancer proteins retrieved from the databases reported in [1, 136]. Based on such studies, the Machine learning (ML) algorithm is designed to predict functional classification of p53 Mutation site Amino Acids (MsAA), where mutation(s) are reported. In addition to 45 MsAAs identified on p53 protein DBD, if new mutations appear for a new AA site, the corresponding MsAA can be incorporated in this study.

It is worth revisiting the fact that the FV (Feature Vector) of the ith AA is derived on identifying the count of PTTs in the region of 10 AAs (($i - 5$) to ($i + 5$) locations. Thus, FV represents the environment of ith MsAA around 10 AAs (5 AAs preceding the ith AA and 5 AAs following the ith AA). Consequently, on comparing the FV of a pair of MsAAs of different protein classes reported in their respective PTT-FV tables, the following hypothesis is reported.

Observation 5.9—a Hypothesis: Functional proximity of a pair of MsAAs varies directly with the Distance of the Feature Vector (FV) of the pair, referred to as Vector Distance (VD).

This observation/hypothesis gets validated by the results derived on execution of Algorithm 5; the results are tabulated in Table 5.31 for 15 cases with VD = 0, ($\sqrt{2}$), and ($\sqrt{6}$).

Algorithm 5—Predict Functional Proximity of p53 MsAAs

The PTT and FV for 392 AA p53 protein are reported in Table 5.29. The Algorithm 5 concentrates on analysis of VD (Vector Distance) of the FV reported on Table 5.29 for each pair of MsAA of p53 protein. The decimal value of each of the 10 elements of FV varies from 0 to 10, with v9 = 0 for each AA; so, in effect it is a 9-element vector. If the value of an element of FV of an MsAA is greater than 8, it is marked as MsAA*. In view of presence of a high valued element, the effect of all the other elements of an AA* get diluted. Consequently, while evaluating the functional proximity of a pair of MsAAs, the CAML model views such an MsAA* as an aberration and excludes for evaluation of functional proximity. Such MsAA* are noted at locations C135, V173, R175.

Input : Table 5.29—(i) column 1 shows the 392 AAs of p53, (ii) column 2, 3, 4 show the PTT for each AA, (iii) the FV of each AA is reported on column 5–14 for each AA; and (iv) the list of MsAAs are marked as Mut on column 15.

Output:
(i) Table 5.31 Group I covers 7 pairs of MsAAs with VD = 0; a MsAA of the pair has the highest functional proximity with its partner than with any other MsAA. Compared to this group, the MsAA pairs in next group has lesser functional proximity.
(ii) Table 5.31 Group II shows 5 MsAA pairs with VD = $\sqrt{2}$; each MsAA of the pair has higher functional proximity with its partner than with any other MsAA.
(iii) Table 5.31 Group III shows 3 MsAA pair with VD = $\sqrt{6}$; higher the VD between a pair of MsAAs, lesser is their functional proximity.

Step 1 : Generate the 47 × 47 VDM (Vector Distance matrix) showing VD of each of the 45 MsAAs of DBD, with each of the remaining MsAAs.

Table 5.31 Analysis of Functional Proximilty of p53 Mutation site AA (MsAA) Pair—Results for 12 (5 +4 +3) cases

Serial No.	Mutant Pair Sites	Feature Vector (FV)	Vector Distance (VD)	Experimental Results of p53 Mutation site AA (MsAA) Pairs-curated from publications (see Ref of Chapter 5)
	Group I			
1	(a) R248	<0 2 0 0 3 0 0 0 5 0>	0	Mutation at R248 acquire Gain-of-functions (GOFs) that promote tumour progression in CRC (ColoRectal Cancer) [137]
	(b) R249	<0 2 0 0 3 0 0 0 5 0>	0	Mutation at G249 is a hotspot mutationin HCC (Hepato Cellular Carcinoma), with gain-of-funcion reported in [108]
2	(a) C141	<0 0 0 0 0 1 0 1 8 0>	0	[190] predicts Loss of Function (LoF); increased oxidative dissociation compared to wild-type Tp53 in an in vitro assay [189]
	(b) C176	<0 0 0 0 0 1 0 1 8 0>	0	For C176Y, PMID: 26585234 reports in decreased Tp53 activity [188]
3	(a) C176	<0 0 0 0 0 1 0 1 8 0>	0	For C176Y, PMID: 26585234 reports in decreased Tp53 activity [188]
	(b) H179	<0 0 0 0 0 1 0 1 8 0>	0	For H179Q, PMID: 16209708 reports in decreased Tp53 transactivation activity
4	(a) C141	<0 0 0 0 0 1 0 1 8 0>	0	[190] predicts Loss of Function (LoF)
	(b) C179	<0 0 0 0 0 1 0 1 8 0>	0	For H179Q, PMID: 16209708 reports in decreased Tp53 transactivation activity
5	(a) M237	<0 0 0 0 3 0 0 0 7 0>	0	Zinc binding p53 mutation at M237 results in p53 inactivation [162]
	(b) C238	<0 0 0 0 3 0 0 0 7 0>	0	Zinc binding p53 mutation at C238 results in p53 inactivation [162]
6	(a) S215	<0 4 0 0 2 0 0 0 4 0>	0	The mutation affects p53 phosphoralization [175]—leads to cancer progression
	(b) H214	<0 4 0 0 2 0 0 0 4 0>	0	Mutatant H214Y/R are associated with pancreatic acinar cell carcinoma [189]
7	(a) Y205	<0 4 0 0 1 0 0 0 5 0>	0	Y205C leads to increased proliferation, migration in ESCC [190]
	(b) V216	<0 4 0 0 1 0 0 0 5 0>	0	V216G mutation has been noticed in ESCC (Esopheagal Squmous Cell Carcinoma [191])
	Group II			
8	(a) V274	<3 1 0 0 0 0 0 0 6>	$\sqrt{2}$	[190] reports: V274fs (frame shift), a truncation mutation, leads to a loss of p53 protein function
	(b) C275	<2 1 0 0 0 0 0 0 7>	$\sqrt{2}$	ZDHHC1 mediated palmitoylation is a prerequisie for nuclear translocation for p53 function [186]
9	(a) R273	<4 1 0 0 0 0 0 0 5>	$\sqrt{2}$	Mutation at R273 affects DNA binding and consequently associated with caner progression [184]
	(b) V274	<3 1 0 0 0 0 0 0 6>	$\sqrt{2}$	[190] reports: V274fs (frame shift), a truncation mutation, leads to a loss of p53 protein function
10	(a) F270	<0 4 0 0 1 1 0 0 4 0>	$\sqrt{2}$	F270 mutation likely to affect p53 structure
	(b) R273	<0 3 0 0 1 1 1 0 4 0>	$\sqrt{2}$	[190] reports: R273C results in increased proliferation, migration, invasion, and protein stability
11	(a) I255	<0 5 0 0 2 0 0 0 3 0>	$\sqrt{2}$	Both the pair of MsAAs I255 and E286, as reported in [190], lead to Loss of Function
	(b) E286	<0 5 0 0 1 0 0 0 4 0>	$\sqrt{2}$	Due to lower transactivation activity through different pathways

(continued)

Table 5.31 (continued)

Serial No.	Mutant Pair Sites	Feature Vector (FV)	Vector Distance (VD)	Experimental Results of p53 Mutation site AA (MsAA) Pairs-curated from publications (see Ref of Chapter 5)
12	(a) G244	<0 0 0 0 2 0 0 0 8 0>	$\sqrt{2}$	G244S results in a loss of CDKN1A (p21Cip1) transactivation and increased proliferation (PMID: 26818906)
	(b) G245	<0 0 0 0 2 0 0 0 7 0>	$\sqrt{2}$	G245V results in decreased Tp53 transactivation and transrepression activity (PMID: 8001119)
	Group III			
13	(a) Y220	<0 2 0 0 2 0 0 0 6 0>	$\sqrt{6}$	[190] reports: Y220F results in decreased proteasome activity leading to increased Tp53 protein expression
	(b) R280	<0 3 0 0 0 0 1 0 6 0>	$\sqrt{6}$	[190] reports: R280M results in decreased DNA binding and activation of Tp53 target genes and resistance to apoptosis
14	(a) R213	<0 6 0 0 1 0 0 0 3 0>	$\sqrt{6}$	[190] reports Loss of Function for R213Q results in a mild increase in cell proliferation in culture & fails to inhibit tumor
	(b) H214	<0 4 0 0 2 0 0 0 4 0>	$\sqrt{6}$	[190] report Gain of Functions for H214R due to increased proliferation, migration, invasion, and protein stability
15	(a) F270	<0 4 0 0 3 0 0 0 3 0>	$\sqrt{6}$	F270 mutation likely to affect p53 structure and function
	(b) G266	<0 4 0 0 1 1 0 0 4 0>	$\sqrt{6}$	[190] reports: G266V is predicted to lead to loss of function (PMID: 37030635)

Step 2 : Check the 10 element FV of each AA and mark it as MsAA*, if any one of its 10 element FV is greater than 8. (On execution of this step, three MsAAs are * marked at locations C135, V173, R175).

Step 3 : Scan through a column of MsAA of the VDM (excluding MsAA*) marking the MsAA row showing: (I) VD = 0, (II) VD = $\sqrt{2}$ = 1.414214, and (III) VD = $\sqrt{6}$ = 2.44949.

Step 4 : Repeat the Step 3 for each column of VDM.

Step 5 : Generate the output table Group I, II and III—displaying MsAA pairs with VD values as 0, $\sqrt{2}$ and $\sqrt{6}$ respectively. Stop

---

The results derived on execution of Algorithm 5 are reported in Table Group I, II, and III. Column 5 reports the experimental results curated from the published literature for the mutants of a MsAA pair. Such curated results do not necessarily point to the mutant function in the p53 pathway directly affecting tumor malignancy; some mutants may affect the downstream signaling pathway of p53. Functional proximity of MsAA pairs identified with Algorithm 5 get validated with the results reported in Table 5.31. Fifteen instances are reported in Table 5.31, with column 5 reporting experimental results curated from published literature in respect of functional impact of the specific mutation of a pair of MsAAs.

Prediction of functional proximity of a pair of Mutational site AAs (MsAAs) can be viewed as one side of the coin. Another side of the coin of higher significance is to identify the specific AA site, where its mutant(s) mediate the escape from the neutralization by the antibodies of the cancer cell. Next section reports the scheme for identification of neutralizing Antibody Escape (nAbE) mutants in the 45 MsAAs of of the DBD of p53 protein chain.

5.5.7 Prediction of nAbE-AA in P53 Protein

A mutant (Mut), as noted earlier, is referred to as xLx' in the AA chain of a protein, where the original amino acid x at location L is mutated with amino acid x'. The location L is referred to as MsAA (Mutational site AA). The CL signal graphs for wild and mutants of a few AAs of p53 protein are reported in Sect. 5.5.4. The CAML model is designed based on the mutational analysis of different classes of proteins (Covid virus and Cancer). The Machine Learning (ML) algorithm is designed from the analysis of the results derived for prediction of nAbE-AA class for CoV-2 spike protein reported in Sect. 5.4, which can be viewed as the Training set for prediction of nAbE-AA class in p53 protein. The same algorithm is adapted and presented as Algorithm 3 for prediction of nAbE-AA for p53 protein in this subsection following the experimental set up reported next. A few terminologies, observations, and Hypothesis, are reproduced below from Sects. 5.4.7 and 5.4.8 of Sect. 5.4 reporting nAbE prediction for CoV-2 spike protein RBD (Receptor Binding Domain).

Introduction of 19 mutations for an AA of a protein chain, generate different groupings of 19 mutants in respect of deviation of mutant CL graph from that of wild. Classification of mutants into different groups is referred to as Group Mutant (GM) in subsequent discussions.

The Observation 5.4 in respect of grouping of AA* Class and non-AA* Class, reported in Sect. 5.4.7 of Sect. 5.4, is reproduced next.

AA* Class and non-AA* Class: CAML model employs periodic boundary CA (Fig. 4.1 in Chap. 4 on CA Preliminaries), where the leftmost cell is the neighbour of the rightmost cell and vice versa. In view of evolution of periodic boundary CA modelling a protein chain, for a region covering a set of CA cells, the following characteristic of CL signal graph has been observed for 19 mutations inserted for an AA (this Observation is reproduced from earlier section for ease of readability of the subsequent text):

There may exist a region covering a set of CA cells, with amino acid type (marked as AA* class covering 8 amino acids), which show identical deviation of its mutant DCLVS values from that of non-AA* class covering 12 amino acids; each of the non-AA* amino acids display equal CL values for the CA cells in that region. This observation has been found to be true for any protein chain evaluated with the CAML model.

Group Mutant (GM* and GM): CAML introduces 19 mutations on an AA. Depending on the group (AA* or non-AA* class) it belongs to, the 19 mutants can be divided into (8 +11) or (7 +12).

(a) GM*—A Group Mutants referred to as GM* covers two classes of mutants marked as AA* with 8 AAs and non-AA* with 11 AAs for a region. The AA* class covers 8 AAs Glu (E), His (H), M (Met), Asn (N), Pro (P), Gln (Q), Thr (T), Val (V). DCLVS value for each of these 8 AAs, in a region, is identical and differs from the DCLVS value of other 11 AAs which are referred to as non-AA* class; the DCLVS value for each of these 11 non-AA* is identical in that region.

Table 5.25 shows partial CL data (cell location 680 to 785) for 19 mutants of MsAA at R175 of p53 protein chain. It displays a GM* at cell location 773 to 782 with identical DCLVS = 0 for 11 mutants, while each of 8 mutants R175E/H/M/N/P/Q/T/V show DCLVS = $8 \times 9 - 10 \times 12 = (-48)$.

(b) GM—On introduction of 19 mutations on a MsAA, if 19 mutants are divided into multiple groups, each group displaying same DCLVS value and the mutant grouping is different from that of GM*, it is referred to as a GM. (Note—an instance of GM can be observed in Table 5.25 in a region covering CA location 684 to 693).

nAbE mutant, nAbE-AA class and non-nAbE:

(a) nAbE mutant—A mutant that mediates escape from neutralization by Antibody of cancer cells.
(b) nAbE-AA Class—This class covers MsAAs, each of which has at least one nAbE mutant. An MsAAs not having any nAbE mutant is referred to as non-nAbE.

Algorithm for prediction of nAbE-AA class and non-nAbE in the 45 MsAAs in the DBD (DNA Binding Domain) of the p53 protein chain is presented in Algorithm 6 subsequent to reporting the Experimental Setup reported next. The results derived on execution of the Algorithm 6 are shown in Table 5.32. Column 1 row 4 to 48 reports 45 MsAAs and 10 non-mutants are shown on rows 49 to 58.

5.5.7.1 Experimental Set Up for CAML Model to Predict nAbE-AA Class and Non-nAbE in the MsAAs of P53 Protein

Six issues noted under (a) to (f) of the Experimental Set Up are relevant for design of the Algorithm 6.

(a) Identification of neutralizing Antibody escape (nAbE) mutants is a highly complex process involving experimentation with different mutants of an amino acid in p53 protein chain [113, 114, 129]. CAML model inserts 19 mutations for each AA of the p53 chain and identifies nAbE-AA class through comparison of CL graph of wild and 19 mutants; partial data of CL values for wild and 19 mutations (marked on row 3) are reported in Table 5.25 for amino acid R175.

(b) Based on the analysis of the wild CL graph of p53 protein, 21 different regions marked as r0 to r20 are identified. Each of these regions, noted on row 1 of Table 5.32,

Table 5.32 nAbE-AA Prediction Results on Execution of Algorithm 6—the algorithm Identifies 20 MsAAs as nAbE-AA out of total 45 MsAAs in DBD (DNA Binding Domain—T102 to K292)

Region	r0	r1	r2	r3	r4	r5	r6	r7	r8	r9	r10	r11	r12	r13	r14	r15	r16	r17	r18	r19	r20	Label
CA Loc	131 to 143	246 to 255	258 to 270	273 to 281	295 to 302	305 to 316	323 to 333	348 to 358	399 to 406	482 to 489	544 to 549	583 to 602	710 to 718	773 to 782	875 to 892	903 to 911	947 to 952	1088 to 1093	1167 to 1171	1184 to 1198	1245 to 1251	
Variables	v'0	v'1	v'2	v'3	v'4	v'5	v'6	v'7	v'8	v'9	v'10	v'11	v'12	v'13	v'14	v'15	v'16	v'17	v'18	v'19	v'20	
L111	0	0	0	0	0	0	0	0	0	0	0	0	0	0	0	0	0	0	0	0	0	non-nAbE
T125	0	0	0	0	0	0	0	0	0	1	1	0	0	0	0	0	0	0	0	0	0	nAbE-AA
K132	0	0	0	0	0	0	0	0	0	0	0	0	0	0	0	0	0	0	0	0	0	non-nAbE
C135	0	0	0	0	0	0	0	0	0	0	0	0	0	0	0	0	0	0	0	0	0	non-nAbE
C141	0	0	0	0	0	0	0	0	0	0	0	0	0	0	0	0	0	0	0	0	0	non-nAbE
Q144	0	0	0	0	0	0	0	0	0	0	0	0	0	0	0	0	0	0	0	0	0	non-nAbE
P151	0	0	0	0	0	0	0	0	0	0	0	1	0	0	0	0	0	0	0	0	0	nAbE-AA
Y163	0	0	0	0	0	0	0	0	0	0	0	1	1	0	0	0	0	0	0	0	0	nAbE-AA
V173	0	0	0	0	0	0	0	0	0	0	0	0	0	0	0	0	0	0	0	0	0	non-nAbE
R175	0	0	0	0	0	0	0	0	0	0	0	0	0	0	0	0	0	0	0	0	0	non-nAbE
C176	0	0	0	0	0	0	0	0	0	0	0	1	1	0	0	0	0	0	0	0	0	nAbE-AA
H179	0	0	0	0	0	0	0	0	0	0	0	0	0	0	0	0	0	0	0	0	0	non-nAbE
H193	0	0	0	0	0	0	0	0	0	0	0	0	0	0	0	0	0	0	0	0	0	non-nAbE
L194	0	0	0	0	0	0	0	0	0	0	0	0	0	0	0	0	0	0	0	0	0	non-nAbE
I195	0	0	0	0	0	0	0	0	0	0	0	0	0	0	0	0	0	0	0	0	0	non-nAbE
R196	0	0	0	0	0	0	0	0	0	0	0	0	0	0	0	0	0	0	0	0	0	non-nAbE
Y205	0	0	0	0	0	0	0	0	0	0	0	0	0	1	1	0	0	0	0	0	0	nAbE-AA
R213	0	0	0	0	0	0	0	0	0	0	0	0	0	1	1	0	0	0	0	0	0	nAbE-AA

(continued)

Table 5.32 (continued)

Region	r0	r1	r2	r3	r4	r5	r6	r7	r8	r9	r10	r11	r12	r13	r14	r15	r16	r17	r18	r19	r20	Label
CA Loc	131 to 143	246 to 255	258 to 270	273 to 281	295 to 302	305 to 316	323 to 333	348 to 358	399 to 406	482 to 489	544 to 549	583 to 602	710 to 718	773 to 782	875 to 892	903 to 911	947 to 952	1088 to 1093	1167 to 1171	1184 to 1198	1245 to 1251	
Variables	v'0	v'1	v'2	v'3	v'4	v'5	v'6	v'7	v'8	v'9	v'10	v'11	v'12	v'13	v'14	v'15	v'16	v'17	v'18	v'19	v'20	
H214	0	0	0	0	0	0	0	0	0	0	0	0	0	0	0	0	0	0	0	0	0	non-nAbE
S215	0	0	0	0	0	0	0	0	0	0	0	0	0	1	1	0	0	0	0	0	0	nAbE-AA
V216	0	0	0	0	0	0	0	0	0	0	0	0	0	1	1	0	0	0	0	0	0	nAbE-AA
Y220	0	0	0	0	0	0	0	0	0	0	0	0	0	1	1	0	0	0	0	0	0	nAbE-AA
Y234	0	0	0	0	0	0	0	0	0	0	0	0	0	0	0	0	0	0	0	0	0	non-nAbE
Y236	0	0	0	0	0	0	0	0	0	0	0	0	0	0	0	0	0	0	0	0	0	non-nAbE
M237	0	0	0	0	0	0	0	0	0	0	0	0	0	0	0	1	1	0	0	0	0	nAbE-AA
C238	0	0	0	0	0	0	0	0	0	0	0	0	0	0	0	0	0	0	0	0	0	non-nAbE
N239	0	0	0	0	0	0	0	0	0	0	0	0	0	0	0	1	1	0	0	0	0	nAbE-AA
S241	0	0	0	0	0	0	0	0	0	0	0	0	0	0	0	0	0	0	0	0	0	non-nAbE
C242	0	0	0	0	0	0	0	0	0	0	0	0	0	0	0	0	0	0	0	0	0	non-nAbE
G244	0	0	0	0	0	0	0	0	0	0	0	0	0	0	0	0	0	0	0	0	0	non-nAbE
G245	0	0	0	0	0	0	0	0	0	0	0	0	0	0	0	0	0	0	0	0	0	non-nAbE
R248	0	0	0	0	0	0	0	0	0	0	0	0	0	0	0	0	1	1	0	0	0	nAbE-AA
R249	0	0	0	0	0	0	0	0	0	0	0	0	0	0	0	0	1	1	0	0	0	nAbE-AA
I255	0	0	0	0	0	0	0	0	0	0	0	0	0	0	0	0	1	1	0	0	0	nAbE-AA
G266	0	0	0	0	0	0	0	0	0	0	0	0	0	0	0	0	1	1	0	0	0	nAbE-AA
F270	0	0	0	0	0	0	0	0	0	0	0	0	0	0	0	0	1	1	0	0	0	nAbE-AA

(continued)

Table 5.32 (continued)

Region	r0	r1	r2	r3	r4	r5	r6	r7	r8	r9	r10	r11	r12	r13	r14	r15	r16	r17	r18	r19	r20	Label
CA Loc	131 to 143	246 to 255	258 to 270	273 to 281	295 to 302	305 to 316	323 to 333	348 to 358	399 to 406	482 to 489	544 to 549	583 to 602	710 to 718	773 to 782	875 to 892	903 to 911	947 to 952	1088 to 1093	1167 to 1171	1184 to 1198	1245 to 1251	
Variables	v'0	v'1	v'2	v'3	v'4	v'5	v'6	v'7	v'8	v'9	v'10	v'11	v'12	v'13	v'14	v'15	v'16	v'17	v'18	v'19	v'20	
V272	0	0	0	0	0	0	0	0	0	0	0	0	0	0	0	0	1	1	0	0	0	nAbE-AA
R273	0	0	0	0	0	0	0	0	0	0	0	0	0	0	0	0	0	0	0	0	0	non-nAbE
V274	0	0	0	0	0	0	0	0	0	0	0	0	0	0	0	0	1	1	0	0	0	nAbE-AA
C275	0	0	0	0	0	0	0	0	0	0	0	0	0	0	0	0	0	0	0	0	0	non-nAbE
P278	0	0	0	0	0	0	0	0	0	0	0	0	0	0	0	0	0	1	1	0	0	nAbE-AA
R280	0	0	0	0	0	0	0	0	0	0	0	0	0	0	0	0	0	0	0	0	0	non-nAbE
D281	0	0	0	0	0	0	0	0	0	0	0	0	0	0	0	0	0	1	1	0	0	nAbE-AA
R282	0	0	0	0	0	0	0	0	0	0	0	0	0	0	0	0	0	0	0	0	0	non-nAbE
E286	0	0	0	0	0	0	0	0	0	0	0	0	0	0	0	0	0	0	0	0	0	non-nAbE
P71	0	0	0	0	0	0	0	0	0	0	0	0	0	0	0	0	0	0	0	0	0	non-nAbE
A84	0	0	0	0	0	0	0	0	0	0	0	0	0	0	0	0	0	0	0	0	0	non-nAbE
D148	0	0	0	0	0	0	0	0	0	0	0	0	0	0	0	0	0	0	0	0	0	non-nAbE
H164	0	0	0	0	0	0	0	0	0	0	0	0	0	0	0	0	0	0	0	0	0	non-nAbE
E171	0	0	0	0	0	0	0	0	0	0	0	0	0	0	0	0	0	0	0	0	0	non-nAbE
L188	0	0	0	0	0	0	0	0	0	0	0	0	0	0	0	0	0	0	0	0	0	non-nAbE
N200	0	0	0	0	0	0	0	0	0	0	0	0	0	0	0	0	0	0	0	0	0	non-nAbE
R202	0	0	0	0	0	0	0	0	0	0	0	0	0	0	0	0	0	0	0	0	0	non-nAbE
S227	0	0	0	0	0	0	0	0	0	0	0	0	0	0	0	0	0	0	0	0	0	non-nAbE
N263	0	0	0	0	0	0	0	0	0	0	0	0	0	0	0	0	0	0	0	0	0	non-nAbE

covers a minimum of 4 adjacent cells with CLVS value is greater than or equal to 50. The approximate CA cell locations of each of these 21 regions are reported on row 2.

(c) Rows 49–58 of Table 5.32 show ten non-Mut AAs which are not covered by the 47 MsAAs. These non-Mut AAs are selected, where
(i) no deviation exists for any mutant for the cell locations between a pair of regions, with CLVS value greater than the threshold limit of 200; the threshold limit is set based on the analysis of CLVS values for non-Mut at different regions of p53 chain; and

(ii) no deviation exists in any one of 21 regions with instance of a GM (Group Mutant) that is different from Group Mutant (GM*).

(d) Twenty-one binary variables (v'0, v'1, · · · , v'19, v'20), as reported on row 3 of Table 5.32, are assigned to 21 regions marked as r0 to r20. Set the binary value of a variable (v'z, z = 0 to 20) is as '1' if there exists an instance of GM different from GM*; otherwise, the value of the variable v'x is set as '0'. This step is executed in Step 7 of the algorithm.

(e) A mutant may display non-0 CLVS value greater than the value 200 for cell locations not covered by any one of the 21 regions (r0 to r20). If such a deviation exists between a pair of regions (say rz and r(z+1), z = 0 to 20), the binary variables for both rz and r(z+1) are set as 1. If the deviation exists prior to r0, then v'0 is set as '1'. This step is executed in Step 8 of the algorithm.

(f) The AA* Class covers 8 amino acids (Glu (E), His (H), M (Met), N (Asn), P (Pro), Q (Gln), Thr (T), Val (V)); the side chain of each of these 8 AAs is designed with 2 CA rules. Deviation of AA*/non-AA* class Group Mutant (GM*) has been observed for some of the MsAAs in CAML model—hence such deviation is considered normal and not viewed as deviation. However, accept the deviation in a region due to presence of GM different from GM*.

Hypothesis 5.4 (reproduced from Sect. 5.4)**—CAML model for nAbE-AA class:** CAML model introduces 19 mutations for an amino acid in p53 protein. By definition, an amino acid in nAbE-AA class has at least one mutant that escapes binding of neutralizing antibody on its epitope [114, 129]. We hypothesize that—CAML framework models this physical domain characteristics (escape from binding of antibody on mutant epitope), due to the deviation of a mutant, from its wild, in a specific region (say rz, z = 0 to 20); this deviation is represented as non-0 value for the variable v'z in the region rz, as shown in Table 5.32.

Execution of Algorithm 6 generates the results on columns 2 to 22 for 21 binary variables (v'0 to v'20) for each of the MsAAs reported in column 1 of Table 5.32. The algorithmic steps for prediction of nAbE-AA and non-nAbE in the MsAAs of the p53 protein chain are designed based on the experimental set up (b) to (f) noted earlier. In fact, the algorithm steps formalize the issues highlighted in the Experimental Set Up.

Algorithm 6—Prediction of nAbE-AA or non-nAbE in p53 Protein

Input : The list of 45 MsAAs (in the RBD of p53) on column 1 rows 4–48 and 10 non-mutants on row 49–58 of Table 5.32.

Output: Predicts a MsAA as an nAbE-AA or non-nAbE reported on column 1 of Table 5.32.

Step 1 : Generate CL graphs for wild and 19 mutants, on introducing 19 mutations for each of 45 MsAAs (rows 4 to 48), and also 10 non-mutants noted on column 49 to 58 of Table 5.32.

Step 2 : Identify regions where wild CL graph shows CLVS value is greater than or equal to the value of (50) covering a minimum of 4 adjacent cells. Note the cell locations of each region. Based on evaluation of CL graphs of a large number of mutants, the threshold value is set as 50. (For p53 protein, there are 21 regions (r0 to r20 noted on row 2 in Table 5.48; approximate cell locations for each region are noted on row 3 of Table 5.32).

Step 3 : Assign 21 binary variables v'0 to v'20 for 21 regions r0 to r20. (Row 1 of Table 5.32 shows the 21 variables v'0 to v'20).

Step 4 : For non-Mut AAs noted on rows 49 to 58 of Table 5.32—(a) Analyse wild and 19 mutants for each region. (b) Mark a region as GM*, if it exists.

Step 5 : Initialize the value of binary variables v'0 to v'20 to '0' on columns 2–22 (noted on rows 4 to 58 of Table 5.32).

Step 6 : Analyse 19 mutants for each AA noted on column 1, rows 4 to 58 of Table 5.32, and execute Steps 7 to 9.

Step 7 : Set the binary value of the variable (v'z, z = 0 to 20) as '1' if deviation is observed in the region v'z for the set of 19 mutants generating a GM (Group Mutant) that is different from GM*.

Step 8 : If deviation is observed for cell locations in between a pair of regions for a mutant with CLVS value greater than 200, mark the binary variable for both rx and r(x+1) as 1, If the deviation is prior to r0, then v'0 is set as '1'.

Step 9 : Predict a MsAA
(i) as a member of non-nAbE, if v'0 to v'20 show an all 0's vector with <v'0 v'1 ··· v'19 v'20> = <0 0 ··· 0 0>;
(ii) as a member of nAbE-AA Class, if there exists at least one non-0 binary value on column 2 to 22 for a variable v'0 to v'20. Stop.

The Python code for the Algorithm 6 has been developed and the results of 0/1 values are reported on Table 5.32 (rows 4 to 47 on column 2 to 22), on execution of the program. Twenty out of forty-five MsAAs are predicted to belong to nAbE-AA class which are likely to mediate immune evasion.

In addition to p53 protein encoded by TP53 gene, there are a host of other genes, referred to as oncogenes, associated with cancer in different organs of human body. There are more than 100 types of cancer which can be classified according to the organ where the cancer starts; typical illustrations are—breast cancer or lung cancer etc. Next subsection provides an outline of extension of this cancer research based on CAML model.

5.5.8 An Outline of Design of Protein Biomarker (PB) Based on CAML Model

The disease cancer is characterized by abnormal/uncontrolled growth of cells leading to malignant tumours. The rate of increase of wide varieties of cancer continues to be a major source of concern around the globe. The disease is mostly prevalent in the aged population and also among younger generation due to lifestyle risk factors. The second group of cancer patients is a recent phenomenon that has been highlighted by a growing body of clinical research and health news reports. Accumulation of mutations, on coding and non-coding DNA of cancer genes, is implicated as one of the major reasons for cancer development. Higher rate of accumulation of such mutations is more pronounced in the aged population. A mutated gene having the potential to cause cancer is referred to as oncogene. The oncogene mutations linked to specific cancer types in different organs (breast, lung, colon, prostate etc.) are available in databases reporting the mutational landscape of proteins encoded by cancer genes. Notwithstanding the enormous progress in cancer research for treatment of this deadly disease, the reasons for Probable onset of Cancer are not yet clearly understood. A viable solution may evolve out of the design of Protein Biomarker (PB) for early detection of cancer in suspected patients. The non-invasive screening of protein biomarkers in the blood/plasma, urine and other body fluid samples of a patient, may provide an observable flag indicating initiation of the biological process leading to PoC (Probable onset of Cancer). The PoC flag in a suspected cancer patient is not observable in healthy person. A large body of published literature on PB design highlight the benefits, challenges and discovery of different classes of biomarkers. Specific emphasis is reported in respect of extraction, identification, verification of proteins from—cell line of cancerous tissues and/or plasma/body fluids—to be employed as biomarkers.

Genetic mutations being one of the primary reasons of cancer, we concentrate on mutational analysis of proteins derived out of DNA transcripts of cancer genes. While mutations in coding DNA get reflected in a protein, mutation on non-coding DNA affects gene/protein expression. As reported earlier, rather than analysis of a single mutation in an amino acid of a protein chain, this study concentrates on analysis of Mutation site Amino Acids (MsAAs) of such proteins. The MsAAs of a protein cover the amino acid locations on which mutation(s) are observed through in-vivo/in-vitro experimental set up reported in published literature. The MsAA set also covers the amino acids on which mutations are likely to appear in future and is referred to as Potential Mutational Hot Spots (PMHSs). Typical ML (machine

Learning) framework is employed on curating published experimental results divided into Training Set (TrS), Validation Set (VaS). Finally, riding on the learning curve we design algorithm to map physical domain characteristics to CAML model-generated features. Three ML algorithms relevant for PB design are as follows:

(i) prediction of Potential Mutational Hot Spot (PMHS) in a cancer protein.
(ii) prediction of neutralizing Antibody Escape mutants (nAbE-AA) in MsAA (Mutation Site AA) of a cancer protein; a MsAA covers both PMHS and mutations reported in published literature.
(iii) Based on the analysis of parameters derived out of PTT-FV table and nAbE-AA results, Protein Bio-marker is designed.

5.5.9 Conclusion

In view of its implication for wide varieties of cancer types, p53 protein (encoded by TP53 gene) is one of the most widely studied proteins. Notwithstanding the significant progress in research on p53 in the last five decades, there are many unanswered questions. The major challenges are—to understand the influence of p53 mutants on cancer phenotype in respect of loss/gain of function and their immune evasion. While structural aspects of p53 mutants have been dealt with by many authors, the issues associated with p53 mutant function on the p53 pathway demand closer scrutiny. In this context, the major contributions of the current Sect. 5.5 on p53 protein can be summarized as follows. Algorithm 4 identifies 20 regions (marked as R0 to R19 in Table 5.30) in the p53 protein chain based on CAML model parameters. The 20 regions are analysed in respect of the coverage of 45 MsAAs, in the p53 DBD (Dna Binding Domain), where 209 mutations are reported in published literature. Characteristics of P53 binding on DNA are analysed using the CAML model which may open up new avenues for investigating p53 cognate sites binding with DNA in a cancer cell. Next, functional proximity of p53 mutants are evaluated on execution of Algorithm 5. The results derived on employing CAML model Feature Vector (FV), as per Algorithm 5, are validated with the experimental results reported in published literature. It has been hypothesized that—lesser the VD (Vector Distance) of the FV of a pair of MsAAs, higher is the functional proximity of the mutants for the MsAA pair in the p53 pathway. The experimental results curated from published literature for the mutants of MsAAs are noted for the 15 (7 + 5 + 3) pairs with their Vector Distance (VD) respectively as VD = 0, VD = $\sqrt{2}$, and VD = $\sqrt{6}$. Prediction of antibody evasion of p53 mutants is reported on execution of Algorithm 6. Twenty MsAAs out of 45 are identified as nAbE-AA, each covering at least one mutant evading antibody evasion. In continuation of our analysis on p53 protein, we provided a glimpse on Protein Biomarker (PB) design in the last Sect. 5.5.8 of Sect. 5.5 based on CAML model.

5.6 CAML Model to Predict Anti-Cancer Medicinal Plants

Mother Nature has provided us with a voluminous encyclopaedia from where we can discover many therapeutic agents to treat human ailments. The legendary discovery of Penicillin in 1928 by Alexander Fleming from the fungus Penicillium notatum is a glaring example. It is natural to expect that many similar treasures are likely to be available in the plant kingdom. Such a hope stems from the following fact. Evolutionary development of plants, specifically medicinal plants, has imparted them with a widely diverse range of chemical compounds divided into two groups—primary and secondary metabolites, produced during plant metabolism. While primary metabolites are associated with normal function and growth of a plant, the secondary metabolites enable them to survive and protect against environmental stress. Some of these secondary metabolites have toxic effects to deter predators. This specific characteristic of medicinal plants can be exploited to target human diseases including cancer. Laboratory experimental studies have established the fact that many medicinal plants do possess the abilities to kill cancerous cells and also prevent cancer development. For last several centuries, the traditional medicines like Ayurvedic, Herbal, Chinese, Unani etc. are employed for treatment of human diseases based on clinical studies. The ingredients of such medicines are usually derived from medicinal plants. Consequently, since the middle of last century, medicinal chemists have focussed their attention to extract plant-derived compounds to fight cancer. Ten plant-derived anticancer drugs in research/clinical trials or in use as approved drugs, are reported in [137]. Most prominent one in the list is—Paclitaxel (PTX), sold under the brand name Taxol. It is a chemotherapy medication used to treat various cancer types observed in different organs of human body. The history of development of Paclitaxel over a few decades is reported in [138].

5.6.1 *Introduction*

Cancer continues to be one of the deadliest diseases and aggressive killers causing millions of deaths worldwide. A fear-psychosis, in general, exists among the general public in respect of the disease. Notwithstanding the enormous progress of cancer treatment with efficient surgery and targeted chemotherapy, it has certain inherent limitations in terms of associated side effects that vary with the physical condition of the cancer patient. Further, the stage of cancer development in an affected patient plays a crucial role; earlier the detection, better is the prognosis. The cost of cancer treatment is also a point of major concern. Consequently, the cancer research community looks for new, efficacious, and affordable therapeutic strategies to fight cancer with minimal side effects.

For their protection, plants produce bioactive compounds referred to as phytochemicals. Search for plant phytochemical-based 'Green' therapeutic agents having anticancer properties has gained popularity in recent years. The plants out of which anti-cancer agents can be extracted, are referred to as Anti-Cancer Medicinal Plant (referred to as AC plant) in subsequent text. Proteins are the workhorses for living cells of any organism, including plant kingdom. One of the major emphases of this book is to develop CAML model applications on different aspects of Computational Proteomics (a sub-discipline of Computational Biology). The current section of the book undertakes mutational study of medicinal plant proteins; the sole objective is to fight cancer with therapeutic agents extracted from AC Medicinal plants. The pre-requisite for this challenging task is to study medicinal plants for which proteins are listed in Uniport and/or NCBI databases.

Section 5.5 of Chap. 5 report CAML model for mutational study of p53 protein. Employing the light weight CAML model, in Sect. 5.5 we have reported analysis of the different aspects of protein p53, implicated for the majority of cancer types. In Sub-sect 5.5 of Sect. 5.5, we have also proposed an outline of the design of protein biomarkers—a non-invasive tool to predict PoC (Probable onset of Cancer) in a suspected patient. In Sect. 5.6 we continue our search for alternative avenues to fight the deadly disease cancer. Employing the CAML framework, the current section presents a Machine Learning (ML) model to predict whether a given medicinal plant has got some inherent Anti-Cancer (AC) property. The Anti-Cancer property is derived out of some specific medicinal plant extract; the extract, as per laboratory experiment, has been observed to hinder cancer cell growth. In order to achieve this goal, the CAML model needs to mimic the biological pathways generating plant-derived anti-cancer therapeutic agents that are toxic to cancer cell lines. The model foundation is rooted on the following observation.

Published literature has projected different therapeutic properties of bioactive compounds derived from plant secondary metabolites. So far more than 50000 secondary metabolites have been identified and some more are being added every year. Four major classes of secondary metabolites which exert anti-cancer effects are—terpenoids, phenolics, alkaloids, flavonoids with subclasses under each class. In-vitro and in-vivo laboratory experiments have pointed out the fact that the bioactive anti-cancer compounds derived from these metabolites exert direct/indirect toxic effects, along with removal of free radicals, induction of apoptosis, cell cycle arrest etc. Many researchers [139–141] have confirmed the fact that—compared to modern allopathic drugs designed out of synthetic biomolecules, plant derived 'green' anti-cancer therapeutic agents have significantly lesser side effects. However, the major problem that haunts the plant-based drug designer is—how to arrive at the desired bioactive agent displaying anti-cancer effect against cancer cell lines. Proteins are the main workhorses in any living organism, including the plant kingdom. In view of the limited experimental database of plant proteomes and their interactions with bioactive compounds in biological pathways, search for desired anti-cancer agent is an upheaval task in terms of development cost and time. The problem gets further compounded due to paucity of desired volume of the anti-cancer agent extracted from the medicinal plant. Consequently, considerable efforts are directed by biotechnologists to improve yield of the desired anticancer therapeutic agents from medicinal plants.

In the context of earlier background scenarios, this section reports the light weight CAML (Cellular Automata (enhanced with) Machine Learning) model capable of mimicking the biological pathways for generation of plant-derived anti-cancerous products that are toxic to cancer cell lines. The CAML model has been detailed in earlier sections. The characteristics of CAML model enables us to design a two-class classifier—one class covers the medicinal plants having some inherent anti-cancer property, while plants in other class do not display this property. In line with a typical Machine Learning (ML) framework, wc have identified the Training Set (TeS), Validation set (VaS), and Testing Set (TeS) of medicinal plants from the survey reported in this section.

5.6.2 *Medicinal Plants—A Comprehensive Survey*

The survey includes both the classes of plants- Anti-Cancer (AC) and non-Anti-Cancer (non-AC). The knowledge curated from this survey provides the vital input for the design of prediction algorithms for the Training Set (TrS) plants employing the CA model parameters. The prediction algorithm is next validated and refined, if necessary, to ensure correct prediction for the medicinal plants covered by the Validation Set (VaS). Knowledge, derived on traversal on this learning curve, is employed to complete the design of prediction algorithm. Prediction results on AC medicinal plants covered under the Testing Set (TeS) is finally reported.

The surveyed publications are divided into five groups depending on their coverage. The groups are marked as Group 1 (Gr 1) to Group 5 (Gr 5). The papers which mainly add value to the prevailing knowledge based on experimental results, are retrieved and reviewed in the current survey.

Group 1 (Gr 1): Anti-Cancer (AC) Drug from Medicinal Plants—Opportunities and Challenges [140, 142–147]. The Gr 1 publications can be divided into the following three major sub-groups.

Sub-Group 11 (SG11): The first sub-group [142, 144] highlight the benefits derived from use of plant-derived anti-cancer agents having significantly lesser side effect compared to that of conventional drugs synthesized out of synthetic drug molecules. Authors have discussed the challenges faced by plant-derived anti-cancer drug designers along with the excellent opportunities provided by the plant kingdom to design so-called 'Green Drug'.

Sub-Group 12 (SG12): The second subgroup concentrates on analysis of anti-cancer property of medicinal plants available in a specific region such as Sri Lanka, Africa, Himalayan and high-altitude regions. Curated database of Indian medicinal plants is available in IMPPAT [148], while analysis of anticancer agents derived from medicinal plants available in Asian countries is reported in [149].

Sub-Group 13 (SG13): The third sub-groups, the largest one in Gr 1, presents different aspects of the plant-derived anti-cancer agents, including molecular and evidence based mechanistic analysis [140, 143, 147, 150–152]. The term phytochemicals, as

Table 5.33 List of Bio-Active Compounts (BAC) and their function in Medicinal Plants

	Name	BAC Function
1	Acetyl	Participates in many biochemical reaction in protein pathways
2	Actin	Actin is involved in many cellular physiological processes in plants
3	Aldehyde	Metabolize a wide range of compounds
4	Alkaloids**	Have pronounced physiological actions on human
5	Andrographolide	Andrographolide (AGP) is a phytochemical which has anti-cancer properties
6	Cartenoids	Display a range of functions in human health including anti-oxdant effects
7	Flavonoid**	Possess a number of medicinal benefits including anti-cancer
8	Geniposide	Found to be cytotoxic I many cancer cell lines
9	Glyceraldhyde	Glyceraldehyde 3-phosphate occurs as a byproduct in the biosynthesis pathway of tryptophan
10	Glycoside	Participation in the biosynthesis and remodulation of glycans
11	Glycosyltransferase	It is involved in various functions—hormone homeostasis, detoxification etc.
12	Glucosinolates	Plant secondary metabolites with nutritional effects including anti-carcinogenic
13	Heme	Cofactor for various biological processes—oxygen metabolism, transfer etc.
14	Kinase	Kinases regulate the activity, localization, protein-protein interactions
15	Lectin	Act as cancer biomarkers for recognizing the malignant tumor cells
16	Lignan and Lignin	Protects plants against pests and pathogens
17	Lyase	Involved in a range of processes, including amino acid metabolism, and generation of precursors
18	Noscapine	It is identified as an anti-mitotic agent
19	Pectin	Natural pectin is reported to prevent colon cancer as a dietary fiber
20	Quinone and Plastoquinone	Associated with photosynthesis; cytotoxic activity against various cancer cells reported
21	Phenol**	Aromatic ring with multiple functions in plants
22	Phenylpropanoids	Multiple functions in metabolic pathways
23	Protease	The main function of proteases is proteolysis
24	Saponin	Saponins is a toxic plant-derived organic chemicals
25	Synthase	Catalyses a synthesis process
26	Taxadiene	An intermediate in the synthesis of taxol
27	Terpene and Terpenoids**	Play a vital role to repel predators
28	Transcriptional Factor	Regulating biosynthetic pathways
29	Translationally Controlled Tumor Protein (TCTP)	Involved in biological and disese processes
30	Transporter Protein	Translocates ions, solutes, hormones etc. across membrane
31	Tubulin	Perform multiple important cellular functions

reported earlier, refer to Bio-Active Compounds (BAC) produced by plants. Based on the detailed analysis of the publications under this subgroup SG13, we have identified thirty-one major Bio-Active Compounds (BACs) and arrived at the following conclusions:

(i) A general consensus can be observed in respect of anti-cancer activity of four major plant derived BioActive Compounds (BAC)—alkaloids, phenols, terpenoids, flavonoids. Each of these BACs display further subdivision in respect of interaction with specific protein extracted from medicinal plant protein database covered in UniprotKB and NCBI [4, 5].

(ii) The four BACs (reported under (i) with serial number (4, 7, 21, 27) are marked with ** in Table 5.33. The table shows the list of BACs we have compiled based on the analysis of medicinal plants displaying in-vitro, in-vivo anti-cancer properties. The current list covers 31 BACs with diverse functionality. The BAC list covers a subset of plant secondary metabolites reviewed next.

Group 2 (Gr 2): Analysis of Plant Secondary metabolites [153–159]—Plant Primary Metabolites (PMs), in general, govern all the physiological processes associated with normal growth and development of a plant. 'Mother Nature' has provided all living organisms with the inherent support to fight an abnormal and adverse situation for its survival. In this context, the plant kingdom is equipped with the support of the specialized compounds referred to as 'secondary metabolites' (SM) to face environmental stress generated in a plant due to adversarial situations like drought, soil excess-salinity, disease, predator attack etc. Plants generate their SMs out of the PMs in association with their enzymes and gene plasticity observed in medicinal plants [153]; gene plasticity allows plants to produce more than one alternative form. Enhancement of SM production employing molecular biology tools are emphasized in [156, 158], while authors [155] discussed the aspect of their food value in human diet. Some metabolites produce toxins for defense against predators. Drug designers explore—how to use plant derived toxicity against cancer cell lines. For effective use of SMs for drug design, their interaction with proteins extracted from a medicinal plant play an important role; this aspect is surveyed in the next group of publications.

Group 3 (Gr 3): Plant Protein interaction with Secondary Metabolites (SMs) [160–165]—Wide varieties of extracts from different plant proteins through multiple metabolic pathways are focused by authors of many publications [161, 165]. Specifically, derivation of AC (Anti-Cancer) products is highlighted by authors of [160, 164]. Amino acid metabolism, particularly their reprogramming in cancer cell is covered in [163].

Group 4 (Gr 4): Detailed Analysis of Structure and Function of miscellaneous Elements derived from Medicinal Plants—Compounds, Hormones, Enzymes, Proteins etc. [166–174]—Bioactive peptides and proteins derived from plants are covered by the authors in [166, 167]. Different classes of enzymes are detailed in

[170, 175]. The authors in [168] have detailed the compound Myristicin derived from plant named Nutmeg that displays anti-proliferative activity. Analysis of plant hormone Brassinosteroids (BRs) is covered in [169]. Authors [174] have reported the details of the discovery of anti-malarial medicine 'Artemisinin' by Prof Y Tu for which she was awarded Noble prize in 2015. From some old Chinese documents, she got the first-hand information regarding the plant Artemisia annua out of which the antimalarial agent was extracted. Repurposed AC drug out of Artemisinin is reported by authors in [173].

Group 5 (Gr 5): Analysis and interaction of Proteins of specific Medicinal Plant with Bio-Active Compounds (BAC) in the Metabolic Pathway—This group of publications are divided into three sub-groups (SG51, SG52, SG53). Each of the plants covered in this set are analyzed in the context of interaction of the proteins curated from UniProt [4] and/or NCBI [5] with the BAC reported in Table 5.33. Further, we have also consulted the database named as PhytoTypeDB reported in [176].

Sub-Group 51 (SG51): Medicinal plants covered in Training Set (TrS)—The TrS covers total 17 (11 + 6) medicinal plants, with major publications inserted following the plant name: (i) Eleven Medicinal Plants (marked as AC in the referenced publications)—Brassica [137, 177, 178], Taxus brevifolia [137, 179], Podophyllum peltatum [137, 180], Catharanthus roseus [137, 181, 182], Maclura pomifera [137, 183], Catechin [137, 184–186], Combretum caffrum [137, 187], Raphanus sativas [137, 188], Dysoxylum binectariferum [137, 189, 190], Opium poppy [137, 191–193], and Iridaceae [194–197], and (ii) Six Medicinal Plants (marked as non-AC in the referenced publications)—Acacia [198–200], Phyllenthus urinaria [201, 202], Pterocarpus marsupin [198, 203, 204], Curculigo orchioides [198, 205], Mucuna pruriens [198, 206], and Urtica dioica [207–209].

Sub-Group 52 (SG52): Medicinal plants covered in Validation Set (VaS)—The VaS covers the six medicinal plants: Atriplex halimus [210, 211], Centella asiatica [212, 213], Leea genus [149, 214, 215], Limonium species [216, 217], Oryza sativa [218–220], Solanaceae genus [221, 222].

Sub-Group 53 (SG53): Medicinal plants covered in Testing Set (TeS)—The set covers the plants: Artemisia annua [174, 223–225], Taxus chinensis [226–228], Bergenia ligulate [229, 230], Cannabis sativa [231, 232], Clinacanthus nutans [233, 234], Curriculum longa [235–237], Ginseng [238, 239], Momordica cochinchinensis/charantia [165, 240], Moringa oleifera [241, 242], Nigella sativa [243, 244], Citrus genus [141, 245], Neolamarckia cadamba [246, 247], Basil [248, 249].

The Prediction Algorithm presented in Sect. 5.6.5 is designed employing CAML (Cellular Automata model on the plant proteins included in TrS and VaS. The VaS is employed to fine tune the algorithm designed with the TrS. Given any medicinal plant, the prediction algorithm identifies whether any anticancer therapeutic agent can be derived out of the plant to hinder some cancer cell line. In order to test the quality of prediction of the algorithm, we have selected the medicinal plants covered under TeS (Testing Set), while ensuring the fact that—the publications on the plants covered in TeS reports in-vitro and/or in-vivo experimental results clearly establishing their AC (or non-AC) property. This section establishes the fact that CAML algorithm employs significantly lesser training data set and computational resources to achieve the desired level of prediction quality. This goal has been achieved in view of the following characteristics of CAML models marked as C1 to C4.

(C1) CAML model operates on the plant proteins curated from UniProtKB [4] and/or NCBI [5] employing Bio-Active Compounds (BAC listed in Table 5.33) interacting with a protein as its ligand or in its metabolic pathway; both the databases support this search mechanism.

(C2) A protein is modelled with 3-neighborhood Cellular Automata (CA), by representing each amino acid (AA) of a protein with a sequence of 3 neighbourhood CA (3NCA) rules reported in Chap. 4. Next, 19 mutations are inserted for each AA of the protein chain.

(C3) The parameter and Feature Vector (FV) extracted out of evolution of the CA modelling a protein chain (both wild and mutants) identifies specific characteristics of the protein. These characteristics are utilized to design the prediction algorithm to design the 2-class classifier.

(C4) Employing the 2-class classifier, the medicinal plants are classified into two classes—one class, referred to as Anti-Cancer (AC) plants, with plant-derived agent displaying anticancer property against some cancer cell lines, while the plants covered in other class, referred to as non-Anti-Cancer (non-AC), do not cover any such agent displaying anti-cancer property.

5.6.3 *CL Signal Graph Generation for Medicinal Plant Proteins Wild and Mutants*

The generic steps of execution of Phase I and Phase II of CAML model design are reported in Subsect. 5.1.2 that reports CL graph generation procedure for any protein chain.

Table 5.34 shows the amino acid (AA) sequences of four medicinal plant proteins used as illustrative examples for prediction AC (Ant-Cancer) plants reported in Sect. 5.6.5—(a) Tabersonine synthase of length 320 AA of plant Catharanthus roseus [137, 181, 182], (b) Eugenol synthase of length 314 AA of plant Basil [248–251], (c) Dirigent protein of length 212 AA of plant named Brassica [137, 177, 178], and (d) Artemisinic aldehyde delta reductase of length 388 AA of plant Artemesis annua [223–225, 252–255]. Figure 5.35 shows CL signal graph for wild 388 AA of Artemisinic aldehyde, while CL graphs for 3 mutant chains of this protein are reported in Figs. 5.36, 5.37 and 5.38 with mutants P5R, P6R, A11P respectively. A protein mutation, as reported in earlier sections, is noted as xLx', where original amino acid x at location L is replaced with amino acid x'.

Table 5.34 Amino acid (AA) sequence of four medicinal plant proteins—(a) Tabersonine synthase of length 320 AA of medicinal plant Catharanthus roseus, (b) Eugenol synthase of length 314 AA of medicinal plant Basil, (c) Dirigent protein of length 212 AA of medicinal Brassica [256], (d) Artemisinic aldehyde delta reductase of length 388 AA of plant Artemisia annua [173, 174, 223, 224, 252, 253]

(a) Tabersonine synthase of length 320 AA of the plant Catharanthus roseus
MGSSDETIFDLPPYIKVFKDGRVERLHSSPYVPPSLNDPETGGVSWKDVPISSVV SARIYLPKINNHDEKLPIIVYFHGAGFCLESAFKSFFHTYVKHFVAEAKAIAVSVE FRLAPENHLPAAYEDCWEALQWVASHVGLDISSLKTCIDKDPWIINYADFDRLY LWGDSTGANIVHNTLIRSGKEKLNGGKVKILGAILYYPYFLIRTSSKQSDYMENE YRSYWKLAYPDAPGGNDNPMINPTAENAPDLAGYGCSRLLISMVADEARDITLL YIDALEKSGWKGELDVADFDKQYFELFEMETEVAKNMLRRLASFIK
(b) Eugenol synthase of length 314 AA of plant Basil
MEENGMKSKILIFGGTGYIGNHMVKGSLKLGHPTYVFTRPNSSKTTLLDEFQSL GAIIVKGELDEHEKLVELMKKVDVVISALAFPQILDQFKILEAIKVAGNIKRFLPS DFGVEEDRINALPPFEALIERKRMIRRAIEEANIPYTYVSANCFASYFINYLLRPY DPKDEITVYGTGEAKFAMNYEQDIGLYTIKVATDPRALNRVVIYRPSTNIITQLEL ISRWEKKIGKKFKKIHVPEEEIVALTKELPEPENIPIAILHCLFIDGATMSYDFKEN DVEASTLYPELKFTTIDELLDIFVHDPPPPASAAF
(c) Dirigent protein of length 212 AA of plant Brassica
MYFCSLYNTYTHHQRDIKLIPPQSTQMANLILIITSHILLLAAIVSAGKGENFAKNIN RKHFGLRKEKLTFFRVYWHDIQSGTDPSSVVLRPPLSNSSFFGAVTMIDNRLTTGV SVNSTLVGQAQGMYAGAGQHDASALMVMNFAFKTGKYNGSTISILGRNAVMTKV REMPVIGGSGLFRFARGYVEARTKWLNVKTGDATVEYSCYVLHY
(d) Artemisinic aldehyde delta reductase of length 388 AA
MSENPPTLFSAYKMGNFNLSHRVVLAPMTRCRAINAIPNEALVEYYRQRSTAGGF LITEGTMISPSSAGFPHVPGIFTKEQVEGWKKVVDAAHKEGAVIFCQLWHVGRA SHQVYQPGGAAPISSTSKPISKKWEILLPDATYGTYPEPRPLAANEILEVVEDYRV AAINAIEAGFDGIEIHGAHGYLLDQFMKDGINDRTDEYGGSLENRCKFILQVVQA VSAAIATDRVLIRISPAIDHTDAMDSDPRSLGLAVIERLNKLQFKLGSRLAYLHVTQ PRYTADGHGQTEAGANGSEEEVAQLMKTWRGAYVGTFICCGGYTRELGLQAVA QGDADLVAFGRYFVSNPDLVLRLKLNAPLNRYDRATFYTHDPVVGYTDYPSLDK GSLL

5.6.4 CL Signal Graph Analytics

A few related terminologies are next presented. These are employed to characterize the CL signal graph that models the evolution of a protein chain—wild and mutants. These terminologies are reproduced from Sect. 5.4 dealing with CoV-2 spike protein; the same terminologies are also used in Sects. 5.5 and 5.6; sub-sect. 5.2.2.1 of Sect. 5.2.2 defines - mcl and Nmcl signals.

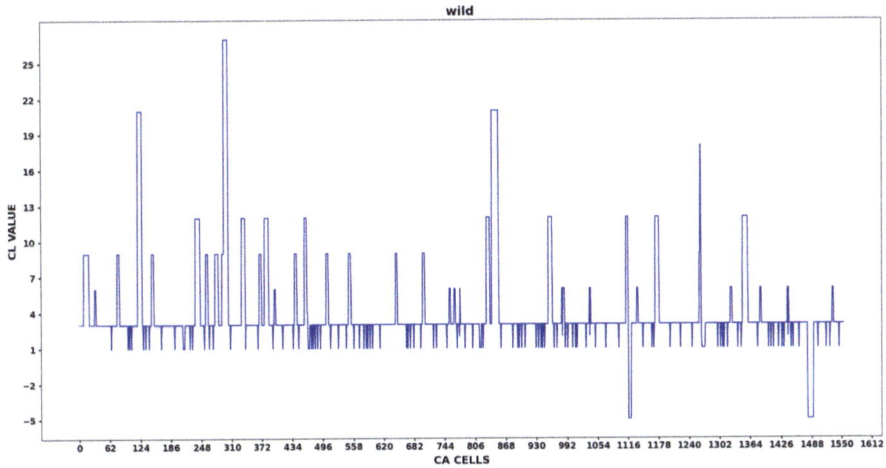

Fig. 5.35 CL Signal Graph for Wild chain of 388 AA of Artemisinic Aldehyde protein

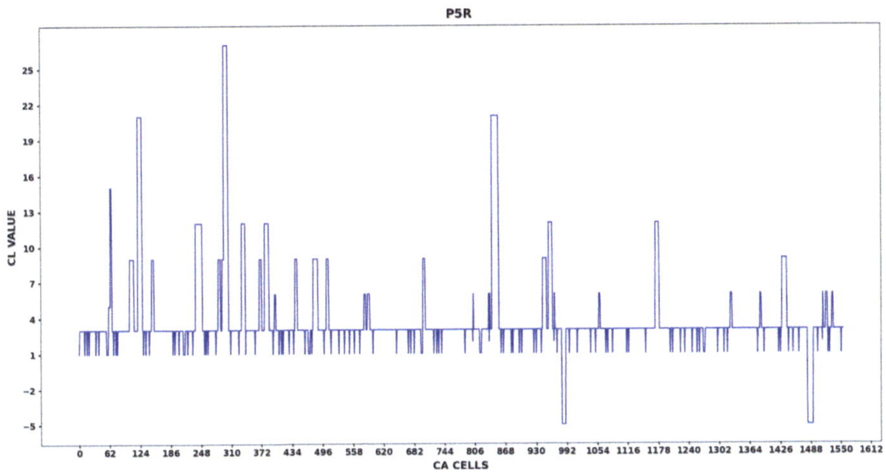

Fig. 5.36 CL Signal Graph of Artemisinic Aldehyde mutant P5R (original amino acid P at location 5 mutated with amino acid R)

CL Signal Graph—The CL signal graph, as illustrated in Fig. 5.35 to Fig. 5.38, refers to the graph showing CL values for each cell on Y-axis, with X-axis displaying serial location of CA cells. A CL Signal graph is also referred to as simply CL graph.

Mapping function (CL signal graph cell location to AA location of protein chain)—The composite AA (its backbone and side chain), as reported in Chap. 4, employs 3 to 5 CA rule string to model an AA. Assuming an average of 4 CA rules for an AA, the approximate cell location for i^{th} AA in a protein chain is ($4 \times i$). For example, Fig. 5.35 shows the CL Signal Graph of approximately 1552 CA cells (4

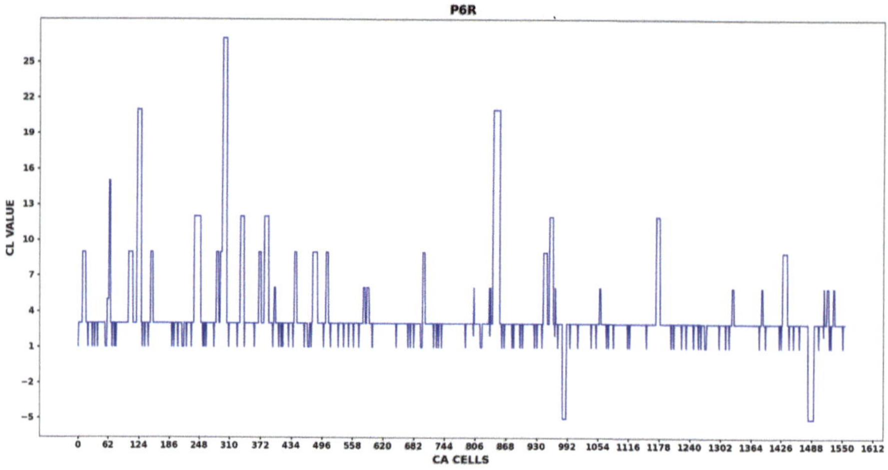

Fig. 5.37 CL Signal Graph of Artemisinic Aldehyde mutant P6R (original amino acid P at location 6 mutated with amino acid R)

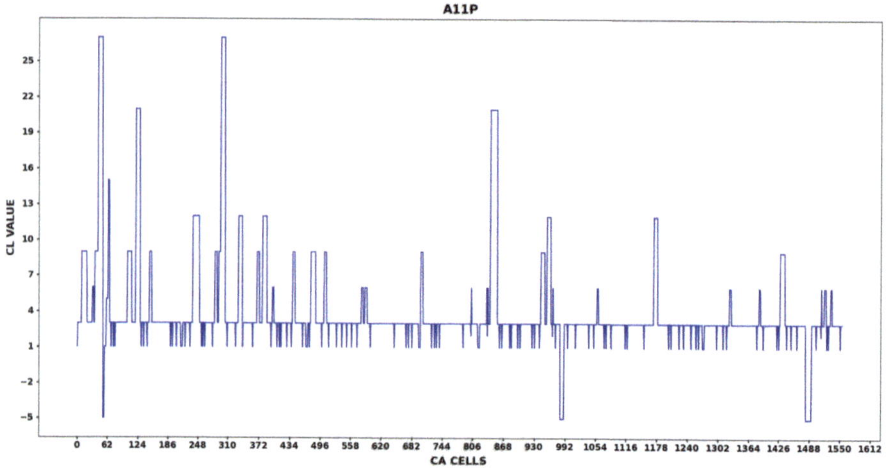

Fig. 5.38 CL Signal Graph of Artemisinic Aldehyde mutant A11P (original amino acid A at location 11 mutated with amino acid P)

$\times$ 388 = 1552) for wild Artemisinic aldehyde protein with 388 amino acids. In view of the common backbone, the baseline of the CL signal graph has the CL value 3. Majority of the signals are low with values ranging from 1 to 6.

Parameters Derived out of CL Signal Graph—CAML model employs three neighbourhood periodic boundary CA. CL signal graphs derived out of periodic boundary CA enables extraction of relevant parameters to compare a mutant with its wild counterpart. Two quantized parameters derived out of CL signal graphs are CLVS and DCLVS.

CL Value Sum (CLVS): CLVS for a wild/mutant is computed considering mcl and Nmcl signal values of Wild and mutant CL graphs; by definition, only CL values greater than or equal to 7 are considered, while ignoring cells having CL (-5) values (defined in earlier sections).

DCLVS (Difference of CL Value Sum): DCLVS = CLVS (mutant) – CLVS (wild). DCLVS value is assumed to be 0 if the value is less than or equal to absolute value 50.

Table 5.35 reports the CLVS values for wild and 19 mutants for each of 7 amino acids S2 to L8 of Artemisinic Aldehyde protein of plant Artemesia annua. The DCLVS value for a mutant can be (–ive), (+ive) or 0. The DCLVS value 0 indicates that the CLVS values for thc mutant and wild are equal. These three DCLVS values are derived for each AA of a protein chain on introducing 19 mutations. Table 5.35 reports the CLVS values for wild (on Row 2) followed by CLVS for 19 mutants in subsequent 19 Rows for each AA on column 2—(row 3 to row 21 for amino acid S2, row 22 to row 40 for E3 and so on till). The column 3 shows the DCLVS values for mutants. Out of 19 rows, the last row for each Lth AA ($L = 2, 3, 4, \cdots, 8$) shows data for the mutant xLx', where x = S2, E3, N4, $\cdots$, L8, and x' = amino acid W. For example, row 21 Column 2 and 3 reports the CLVS and DCLVS values for amino acid S2W. The same row 21 (column 4, 5, 6) reports the total count of (–ive), (+ive), and 0 values (<8 2 9>) for 19 mutants inserted for the amino acid S2. The corresponding value for L8 is <8 1 10> shown on Table 5.35. Count of (-ive) and (+ive) values are increased only if the absolute value of numerical difference between mutant and wild is greater than the value 50. That is, the 0 count of value on column 6 includes all the mutants for which DCLVS value is less than or equal to absolute value 50. This threshold limit of 50 has been set from the analysis of DCLVS values derived out of exhaustive experimentation with CAML model and analysis of published experimental results in respect of mutational study of proteins surveyed in Subsect. 5.6.2.

Pattern Type of Triplet (PTT): The PTT refers to the pattern type of triplet <cnt (–ive) cnt (+ive) cnt (0)> values. These values are derived by inserting 19 mutations for each AA of a protein chain, and next counting the number of instances where DCLVS values are respectively (–ive), (+ive), and (0). Physical significance of these parameters derived out of the CAML model is reported next.

Table 5.36 reports the PTT for the first 7 AAs of the Protein Artemisininc Aldehyde (amino acid S2 to L8). This table is derived from Table 5.35 column 4, 5, 6 on row 21 (for S2), row 40 (for E3), and so on.

Physical Significance of (-ive/+ive) DCLVS value—The (-ive) DCVS value indicates that some signal of the CL graph of the wild chain get reduced/eliminated in the mutant. While a (+ive) DCLVS value of a mutant indicates the CL value of some signal gets enhanced or there is the appearance of some additional signal in the mutant CL graph that is absent in its wild counterpart. Computation of DCLVS values for mutations at AA location P6 are illustrated (Table 5.35): DCLVS (P6R) = mutant CLVS – wild CLVS = 1776–1959 = (–183); on detailed analysis of CL values for the mutant P6R, it can be observed that signals available at cell locations 845 and 1271 of wild CL graph are not present for the mutant CL graph P6R. On the other hand, DCLVS (P6C) = 2049–1959 = (+90) due to additional signal in the mutant CL graph compared to its wild counterpart.

Table 5.35 CLVS & DCLVS for 7 amino acids (S2 to L8) of Artemisinic Aldehyde protein of Plant Artemesia annua

Id	CLVS	DCLVS	(–ve) cnt	(+ve) cnt	0 cnt	Id	CLVS	DCLVS	(–ve) cnt	(+ve) cnt	0 cnt
Wild	1959	0				P5Q	1947	−12			
S2A	1959	0				P5K	1764	−195			
S2G	2031	72				P5R	1764	−195			
S2V	1776	−183				P5H	1947	−12			
S2L	1959	0				P5D	1764	−195			
S2M	1776	−183				P5E	1947	−12			
S2I	1959	0				P5F	1776	−183			
S2T	1776	−183				P5Y	1776	−183			
S2C	2127	168				P5W	1764	−195	12	0	7
S2P	1764	−195				P6A	1776	−183			
S2N	1764	−195				P6G	1776	−183			
S2Q	1764	−195				P6V	1959	0			
S2K	1959	0				P6L	1776	−183			
S2R	1947	−12				P6M	1959	0			
S2H	1764	−195				P6I	1776	−183			
S2D	1959	0				P6S	1776	−183			
S2E	1848	−111				P6T	1959	0			
S2F	1959	0				P6C	2049	90			
S2Y	1959	0				P6N	1959	0			
S2W	1959	0	8	2	9	P6Q	1959	0			
E3A	1764	−195				P6K	1776	−183			
E3G	1764	−195				P6R	1776	−183			
E3V	1947	−12				P6H	1959	0			
E3L	1764	−195				P6D	1776	−183			
E3M	1947	−12				P6E	1977	18			
E3I	1764	−195				P6F	1776	−183			
E3S	1764	−195				P6Y	1776	−183			
E3T	1947	−12				P6W	1776	−183	11	1	7
E3C	1764	−195				T7A	1776	−183			
E3P	1947	−12				T7G	1776	−183			
E3N	1947	−12				T7V	1959	0			
E3Q	1947	−12				T7L	1776	−183			
E3K	1764	−195				T7M	1959	0			
E3R	1764	−195				T7I	1776	−183			
E3H	1947	−12				T7S	1776	−183			
E3D	1764	−195				T7C	1965	6			
E3F	1764	−195				T7P	1959	0			
E3Y	1764	-195				T7N	1959	0			
E3W	1764	−195	12	0	7	T7Q	1959	0			
N4A	1764	−195				T7K	1776	−183			
N4G	1884	−75				T7R	1776	−183			
N4V	1947	−12				T7H	2004	45			
N4L	1764	−195				T7D	1776	−183			

(continued)

Table 5.35 (continued)

Id	CLVS	DCLVS	(−ve) cnt	(+ve) cnt	0 cnt	id	CLVS	DCLVS	(−ve) cnt	(+ve) cnt	0 cnt
N4M	1947	−12				T7E	1977	18			
N4I	1764	−195				T7F	1776	−183			
N4S	1764	−195				T7Y	1776	−183			
N4T	1947	−12				T7W	1776	−183	11	0	8
N4C	2004	45				L8A	1977	18			
N4P	1947	-12				L8G	1959	0			
N4Q	1947	−12				L8V	1794	−165			
N4K	1764	−195				L8M	1776	−183			
N4R	1764	−195				L8I	1959	0			
N4H	2052	93				L8S	1959	0			
N4D	1764	−195				L8T	1794	−165			
N4E	1947	−12				L8C	2019	60			
N4F	1782	−177				L8P	1776	−183			
N4Y	1782	−177				L8N	1776	−183			
N4W	1764	−195	11	1	7	L8Q	1776	−183			
P5A	1776	−183				L8K	1959	0			
P5G	1872	−87				L8R	1977	18			
P5V	1947	−12				L8H	1776	−183			
P5L	1776	−183				L8D	1959	0			
P5M	1947	−12				L8E	1794	−165			
P5I	1764	−195				L8F	1959	0			
P5S	1764	−195				L8Y	1959	0			
P5T	1947	−12				L8W	1959	0	8	1	10
P5C	1764	−195									
P5N	1959	0									

Table 5.36 PTT for 7 AAs (S2 to L8) for protein Artemisininc Aldehyde 388 AA of Plant Artemesia annua

Amino Acid (AA)	cnt (−ve)	cnt (+)	cnt (0)
S2	8	2	9
E3	12	0	7
N4	11	1	7
P5	12	0	7
P6	11	1	7
T7	11	0	8
L8	8	1	10

Ten Element CAFV (CA Feature Vector)—The FV <v0 v1 v2 v3 v4 v5 v6 v7 v8 v9> of 10 elements marked as variables v0 to v9, is derived out of PTT of each AA. The CAFV of ith AA specifies the environment of PTTs around each AA by evaluating its five neighbours on either end, $(i - 5)$ to $(i + 5)$ excluding ith AA. Numerical value of each variable spans from 0 to 10. Design of CAFV is reported below:

(a) Analysis of frequency of PTTs in the full length of the protein chain—Based on this frequency analysis, eight high frequency PTTs are selected in non-decreasing order: Count of these PTTs of an AA are marked as variables v0, v1, v2, v3, v4, v5, v6, v7 respectively and shown on columns 5 to 12 in PTT-FV table (Table 5.37) for the protein Artemisininc Aldehyde.

(b) Two more variables marked as v8 and v9 (shown on column 13 and 14 of PTT-FV table) are marked:

v8 = 10 – (v0 + v1 + v2 + v3 + v4 + v5 + v6 + v7) among 10 AAs $(i - 5$ to $i + 5)$ around ith AA, and

v9 = 0

PTT—FV Table—Displays both PTT and 10 element FV for each AA of a protein chain. Derivation of PTT-FV tables for different protein chains are reported in Sects. 5.3 and 5.4 of Chap. 5 and hence detailed explanation of design of Step (a) and Step (b), noted above, are not repeated in this section.

Based on the earlier formulation, we present three PTT—FV tables for three plant proteins in Table 5.38 for Tabersonine synthase of plant Catharanthus roseus, Tables 5.37 and 5.39 for Artemisinic aldehyde and Dirigent protein of plant Artemesia annua. While the PTT-FV for the full length of AA sequence of Artemisinic aldehyde is reported in Table 5.37, partial PTT-FV data noted for next two proteins in Tables 5.38 and 5.39.

Applications of PTT-FV Table for analysis of a Protein Chain—The PTT- FV table can be generated for any protein chain by inserting 19 mutations for each amino acid of the protein. The PTT-FV table identifies some specific characteristics of a protein chain. Such characteristics can be utilized for multiple applications. Next subsection reports the application of PTT—FV table for prediction of Anti-Cancer (AC) medicinal plant based on two criteria marked as Prediction criteria 1 (PCr1) and Prediction criteria 2 (PCr2) explained under Experimental Set Up (ESU) reported next.

5.6.5 CAML Model to Predict Anti-Cancer (AC) Medicinal Plants

The Experimental Set-Up (ESU1 to ESU4) of CAML model is highlighted prior to presenting the Prediction Algorithm 7. The experimental set up has been designed based on analysis of proteins of a large number of medicinal plants surveyed in Sect. 5.6.2. The terminologies introduced in the set up are relevant for design of the algorithm.

Table 5.37 PTT—FV table for protein Artemisininc Aldehyde (388 AA) of Plant Artemesia annua

AAs	cnt (–ve)	cnt (+ve)	cnt (0)	v0	v1	v2	v3	v4	v5	v6	v7	v8	v9
S2	8	2	9										
E3	12	0	7										
N4	11	1	7										
P5	12	0	7										
P6	11	1	7										
T7	11	0	8	4	1	2	0	0	0	1	0	2	0
L8	8	1	10	3	2	2	1	0	0	0	0	2	0
F9	8	1	10	3	2	1	1	0	0	0	0	3	0
S10	8	0	11	4	2	1	1	0	0	0	0	2	0
A11	8	1	10	3	3	1	1	0	0	0	0	2	0
Y12	8	1	10	3	4	1	1	0	0	0	0	1	0
K13	8	0	11	4	3	2	0	0	0	0	0	1	0
M14	12	2	5	3	4	2	0	0	0	1	0	0	0
G15	8	0	11	3	3	2	0	0	0	1	0	1	0
N16	12	0	7	3	3	1	1	0	0	1	0	1	0
F17	8	0	11	2	3	2	1	0	0	1	0	1	0
N18	12	0	7	1	4	1	1	0	0	1	0	2	0
L19	8	2	9	1	3	2	1	0	1	0	0	2	0
S20	8	1	10	1	3	2	1	0	1	1	0	1	0
H21	11	0	8	3	2	2	0	0	1	1	0	1	0
R22	8	0	11	3	1	2	1	0	1	1	0	1	0
V23	11	1	7	3	1	3	1	0	1	1	0	0	0
V24	12	1	6	3	1	3	1	0	0	1	0	1	0
L25	8	1	10	2	1	3	1	0	1	0	0	2	0
A26	8	1	10	1	1	3	1	0	1	0	0	3	0
P27	12	0	7	2	1	2	0	0	1	0	0	4	0
M28	12	0	7	3	0	2	0	0	1	0	0	4	0
T29	12	0	7	4	0	2	0	0	1	0	0	3	0
R30	15	0	4	4	0	3	1	0	0	0	0	2	0
C31	19	0	0	4	0	3	1	0	0	0	0	2	0
R32	13	1	5	4	0	3	1	0	0	0	0	2	0
A33	8	1	10	3	0	3	1	0	0	0	0	3	0
I34	8	1	10	3	0	2	2	0	0	0	0	3	0
N35	11	0	8	4	0	1	2	0	0	0	0	3	0
A36	8	1	10	3	0	1	3	0	0	1	0	2	0
I37	8	1	10	3	1	1	3	0	0	1	0	1	0
P38	12	0	7	4	1	0	3	0	0	1	0	1	0
N39	11	0	8	3	1	2	2	0	0	1	0	1	0
E40	11	0	8	2	1	2	2	0	0	2	0	1	0
A41	8	2	9	3	1	2	2	0	0	1	0	1	0

(continued)

Table 5.37 (continued)

AAs	cnt (–ve)	cnt (+ve)	cnt (0)	v0	v1	v2	v3	v4	v5	v6	v7	v8	v9
L42	8	0	11	3	0	2	2	0	0	2	0	1	0
V43	11	1	7	2	1	2	3	0	0	2	0	0	0
E44	12	0	7	2	1	0	3	0	0	3	0	1	0
Y45	8	2	9	3	1	1	2	0	0	2	0	1	0
Y46	8	1	10	2	1	1	2	0	0	3	0	1	0
R47	8	1	10	2	1	1	2	0	0	2	0	2	0
Q48	11	0	8	3	0	1	1	0	0	2	0	3	0
R49	8	2	9	3	1	1	2	0	0	1	0	2	0
S50	8	1	10	2	2	0	2	0	0	2	0	2	0
T51	11	0	8	3	2	0	1	0	0	1	0	3	0
A52	8	3	8	3	2	0	2	0	0	1	0	2	0
G53	7	3	9	2	2	1	2	0	0	1	0	2	0
G54	8	0	11	2	1	1	1	0	0	1	0	4	0
F55	8	0	11	2	1	1	1	0	0	0	0	5	0
L56	8	3	8	1	2	1	1	0	1	0	0	4	0
I57	8	1	10	0	2	2	0	0	1	0	0	5	0
T58	12	0	7	2	2	1	0	0	1	0	0	4	0
E59	15	0	4	2	3	2	0	0	1	0	0	2	0
G60	18	1	0	2	2	3	0	0	1	0	0	2	0
T61	12	1	6	3	1	3	0	0	0	0	0	3	0
M62	12	0	7	3	2	2	0	0	1	0	0	2	0
I63	8	1	10	1	2	3	0	0	1	0	0	3	0
S64	8	0	11	3	1	2	0	0	1	0	0	3	0
P65	12	0	7	3	3	1	0	0	1	0	0	2	0
S66	8	1	10	2	3	2	0	0	2	0	0	1	0
S67	8	0	11	3	2	2	0	0	1	0	0	2	0
A68	8	3	8	3	3	1	0	0	2	0	0	1	0
G69	8	1	10	1	3	1	0	0	2	0	0	3	0
F70	8	0	11	3	1	1	0	0	2	0	0	3	0
P71	12	1	6	3	3	0	0	0	1	0	0	3	0
H72	11	1	7	2	4	0	0	0	2	0	0	2	0
V73	12	1	6	2	3	0	0	0	2	0	0	3	0
P74	11	2	6	2	4	0	0	0	3	0	0	1	0
G75	8	1	10	0	4	1	0	0	3	0	0	2	0
I76	8	0	11	1	2	1	0	0	3	0	0	3	0
F77	8	0	11	1	2	2	0	0	2	0	0	3	0
T78	12	1	6	1	3	2	0	0	1	0	0	3	0
K79	8	0	11	1	2	2	0	0	1	0	0	4	0
E80	12	0	7	1	3	1	0	0	1	0	0	4	0
Q81	10	1	8	1	3	2	0	0	1	0	0	3	0

(continued)

Table 5.37 (continued)

AAs	cnt (–ve)	cnt (+ve)	cnt (0)	v0	v1	v2	v3	v4	v5	v6	v7	v8	v9
V82	12	0	7	2	2	1	0	0	1	0	0	4	0
E83	18	0	1	2	1	3	0	0	1	0	0	3	0
G84	18	1	0	2	1	3	0	0	1	0	0	3	0
W85	8	3	8	3	0	3	0	0	1	0	0	3	0
K86	8	1	10	2	1	2	0	0	1	0	0	4	0
K87	8	1	10	3	1	2	0	0	1	0	0	3	0
V88	12	0	7	4	1	1	0	0	1	0	0	3	0
V89	12	1	6	4	2	2	0	0	0	0	0	2	0
D90	8	1	10	3	2	2	0	0	1	0	0	2	0
A91	8	0	11	4	1	2	0	0	1	0	0	2	0
A92	8	1	10	2	2	2	0	0	1	1	0	2	0
H93	12	0	7	2	2	2	0	0	1	1	0	2	0
K94	8	0	11	2	2	2	0	0	1	1	0	2	0
E95	17	0	2	2	3	2	0	0	0	1	0	2	0
G96	18	1	0	2	3	2	0	0	0	1	0	2	0
A97	8	2	9	2	2	2	0	0	0	0	0	4	0
V98	12	0	7	2	2	1	0	0	0	1	0	4	0
I99	8	0	11	2	1	1	0	0	0	1	0	5	0
F100	3	7	9	2	1	1	1	0	0	1	0	4	0
C101	8	1	10	1	1	1	1	0	0	1	0	5	0
Q102	11	1	7	2	2	1	1	0	0	1	0	3	0
L103	8	1	10	1	3	1	1	0	0	0	0	4	0
W104	8	3	8	3	3	0	1	0	0	0	0	3	0
H105	11	0	8	4	2	0	0	0	0	0	0	4	0
V106	12	2	5	4	2	0	2	0	0	0	0	2	0
G107	8	0	11	3	1	1	2	0	0	0	0	3	0
R108	8	0	11	3	1	1	3	0	0	0	0	2	0
A109	8	1	10	1	3	1	3	0	0	0	0	2	0
S110	8	1	10	1	3	1	3	0	1	0	0	1	0
H111	11	0	8	2	3	1	1	0	1	0	0	2	0
Q112	12	0	7	2	3	0	2	0	1	0	0	2	0
V113	11	0	8	2	3	1	1	0	1	0	0	2	0
Y114	8	0	11	2	2	1	2	0	1	0	0	2	0
Q115	12	1	6	2	3	1	2	0	0	0	0	2	0
P116	11	1	7	1	3	1	3	0	1	0	0	1	0
G117	8	3	8	2	3	1	2	0	1	0	0	1	0
G118	8	0	11	3	2	0	2	0	1	0	0	2	0
A119	8	0	11	4	2	0	1	0	1	0	0	2	0
A120	8	1	10	3	2	0	2	0	1	0	0	2	0
P121	11	0	8	5	2	0	1	0	0	0	0	2	0

(continued)

Table 5.37 (continued)

AAs	cnt (–ve)	cnt (+ve)	cnt (0)	v0	v1	v2	v3	v4	v5	v6	v7	v8	v9
I122	8	1	10	5	2	0	2	0	0	0	0	1	0
S123	8	1	10	5	2	1	2	0	0	0	0	0	0
S124	8	1	10	6	1	1	2	0	0	0	0	0	0
T125	11	0	8	7	1	1	1	0	0	0	0	0	0
S126	8	1	10	6	1	1	2	0	0	0	0	0	0
K127	8	1	10	6	2	1	1	0	0	0	0	0	0
P128	12	0	7	6	3	0	1	0	0	0	0	0	0
I129	8	1	10	4	3	2	1	0	0	0	0	0	0
S130	8	0	11	4	2	2	1	0	0	1	0	0	0
K131	8	1	10	4	3	2	0	0	0	1	0	0	0
K132	8	0	11	4	3	2	0	0	0	1	0	0	0
W133	8	0	11	3	3	3	0	0	0	1	0	0	0
E134	12	0	7	3	5	1	0	0	0	1	0	0	0
I135	8	2	9	2	5	2	0	0	0	0	0	1	0
L136	8	1	10	1	4	2	0	0	1	1	0	1	0
L137	8	0	11	1	4	2	0	0	1	1	0	1	0
P138	12	0	7	1	5	1	0	0	1	1	0	1	0
D139	8	0	11	1	3	2	0	0	1	1	0	2	0
A140	8	3	8	2	4	1	0	0	1	1	0	1	0
T141	12	1	6	2	4	1	1	0	0	0	0	2	0
Y142	8	0	11	1	3	2	1	0	1	0	0	2	0
G143	8	0	11	1	2	2	2	0	1	0	0	2	0
T144	11	3	5	1	4	1	2	0	1	0	0	1	0
Y145	8	1	10	0	3	2	2	0	1	0	0	2	0
P146	11	0	8	2	3	2	1	0	1	0	0	1	0
E147	12	0	7	3	3	1	2	0	0	0	0	1	0
P148	11	0	8	3	3	2	1	0	0	0	0	1	0
R149	8	0	11	3	1	2	2	0	0	0	0	2	0
P150	12	0	7	3	2	2	2	0	0	0	0	1	0
L151	8	1	10	1	2	3	2	0	0	1	0	1	0
A152	8	1	10	2	2	3	1	0	0	1	0	1	0
A153	8	0	11	3	1	2	2	0	0	1	0	1	0
N154	11	1	7	3	2	2	1	0	1	1	0	0	0
E155	12	0	7	3	1	1	1	0	2	1	0	1	0
I156	8	2	9	3	1	1	1	0	3	0	0	1	0
L157	8	1	10	1	1	1	1	0	3	2	0	1	0
E158	11	0	8	2	1	1	0	0	3	2	0	1	0
V159	12	1	6	2	1	1	1	0	2	2	0	1	0
V160	12	1	6	2	1	2	1	0	2	2	0	0	0
E161	12	1	6	2	2	1	1	0	2	2	0	0	0

(continued)

Table 5.37 (continued)

AAs	cnt (−ve)	cnt (+ve)	cnt (0)	v0	v1	v2	v3	v4	v5	v6	v7	v8	v9
D162	8	2	9	3	2	1	1	0	3	0	0	0	0
Y163	8	1	10	1	3	1	1	0	3	1	0	0	0
R164	8	0	11	2	2	2	0	0	3	1	0	0	0
V165	12	0	7	2	4	1	0	0	2	1	0	0	0
A166	8	0	11	3	3	2	0	0	1	1	0	0	0
A167	8	1	10	2	4	3	0	0	0	1	0	0	0
I168	8	0	11	3	3	3	0	0	0	1	0	0	0
N169	12	0	7	2	5	2	0	0	0	1	0	0	0
A170	8	0	11	2	4	3	0	0	0	1	0	0	0
I171	8	1	10	2	5	2	0	0	0	1	0	0	0
E172	12	0	7	4	4	1	0	0	0	1	0	0	0
A173	8	2	9	3	5	2	0	0	0	0	0	0	0
G174	8	0	11	3	3	2	0	0	0	1	0	1	0
F175	8	0	11	3	4	1	0	0	0	1	0	1	0
D176	8	1	10	2	4	1	0	0	0	1	0	2	0
G177	8	1	10	2	4	1	0	0	0	1	0	2	0
I178	8	0	11	3	4	0	0	0	0	1	0	2	0
E179	11	1	7	3	5	0	0	0	0	0	0	2	0
I180	8	0	11	4	3	0	0	0	0	0	0	3	0
H181	11	1	7	4	4	0	0	0	0	0	0	2	0
G182	8	1	10	3	4	0	0	0	0	0	0	3	0
A183	8	0	11	3	4	0	0	0	0	0	0	3	0
H184	12	2	5	4	4	0	0	0	0	0	0	2	0
G185	8	1	10	3	4	0	0	0	1	0	0	2	0
Y186	8	0	11	4	2	0	0	0	1	1	0	2	0
L187	8	1	10	3	3	1	0	0	1	1	0	1	0
L188	8	0	11	3	3	1	0	0	1	1	0	1	0
D189	8	1	10	2	3	1	0	0	1	2	0	1	0
Q190	12	1	6	4	3	1	0	0	0	2	0	0	0
F191	8	2	9	3	4	1	0	0	1	1	0	0	0
M192	12	0	7	3	3	0	0	0	2	2	0	0	0
K193	8	0	11	3	2	1	0	0	2	2	0	0	0
D194	8	2	9	3	2	1	0	0	2	2	0	0	0
G195	8	1	10	1	2	1	0	0	3	3	0	0	0
I196	8	0	11	2	1	1	0	0	2	3	0	1	0
N197	12	1	6	2	2	2	0	0	1	2	0	1	0
D198	8	1	10	1	2	1	0	0	2	2	0	2	0
R199	8	2	9	2	1	1	0	0	2	1	0	3	0
T200	12	1	6	2	1	1	0	0	1	1	0	4	0
D201	10	0	9	1	1	1	0	0	2	1	0	4	0

(continued)

Table 5.37 (continued)

AAs	cnt (–ve)	cnt (+ve)	cnt (0)	v0	v1	v2	v3	v4	v5	v6	v7	v8	v9
E202	12	0	7	1	0	0	0	0	2	1	0	6	0
Y203	18	0	1	1	0	1	0	0	1	1	0	6	0
G204	19	0	0	0	0	1	0	0	1	1	0	7	0
G205	9	1	9	0	0	1	0	0	1	0	0	8	0
S206	15	0	4	0	0	1	0	0	0	0	0	9	0
L207	16	1	2	0	0	1	0	0	0	0	0	9	0
E208	19	0	0	0	0	0	0	0	0	0	0	10	0
N209	18	0	1	0	0	0	0	0	0	0	0	10	0
R210	14	0	5	1	0	0	0	0	0	0	0	9	0
C211	19	0	0	1	0	0	0	0	0	0	0	9	0
K212	19	0	0	1	0	1	0	0	0	0	0	8	0
F213	11	1	7	1	0	2	0	0	0	0	0	7	0
I214	9	0	10	1	0	3	0	0	0	0	0	6	0
L215	8	1	10	0	1	3	0	0	0	0	0	6	0
Q216	11	1	7	1	1	3	1	0	0	0	0	4	0
V217	12	0	7	2	1	2	1	0	0	0	0	4	0
V218	12	0	7	3	1	2	1	0	0	0	0	3	0
Q219	12	0	7	4	1	2	1	0	0	0	0	2	0
A220	8	0	11	5	0	3	1	0	0	0	0	1	0
V221	11	0	8	5	1	3	0	0	0	0	0	1	0
S222	8	1	10	4	1	3	1	0	1	0	0	0	0
A223	8	1	10	4	2	2	1	0	1	0	0	0	0
A224	8	1	10	5	2	1	1	0	1	0	0	0	0
I225	8	1	10	5	2	0	2	0	1	0	0	0	0
A226	8	1	10	5	2	0	2	0	1	0	0	0	0
T227	12	1	6	7	2	0	1	0	0	0	0	0	0
D228	8	0	11	7	1	0	1	0	1	0	0	0	0
R229	8	1	10	6	2	0	1	0	1	0	0	0	0
V230	11	0	8	7	2	0	0	0	1	0	0	0	0
L231	8	0	11	6	1	1	1	0	1	0	0	0	0
I232	8	1	10	4	2	1	1	0	2	0	0	0	0
R233	8	1	10	4	2	1	1	0	1	0	0	1	0
I234	8	1	10	4	1	1	1	0	1	0	0	2	0
S235	8	1	10	3	1	1	1	0	1	0	0	3	0
P236	12	0	7	4	1	0	0	0	1	0	0	4	0
A237	12	1	6	4	1	1	0	0	0	0	0	4	0
I238	12	4	3	4	1	1	0	0	1	0	0	3	0
D239	16	0	3	3	1	2	0	0	1	0	0	3	0
H240	19	0	0	3	1	2	0	0	1	0	0	3	0
T241	15	1	3	2	2	2	0	0	1	0	0	3	0

(continued)

Table 5.37 (continued)

AAs	cnt (–ve)	cnt (+ve)	cnt (0)	v0	v1	v2	v3	v4	v5	v6	v7	v8	v9
D242	8	0	11	3	1	1	0	0	1	0	0	4	0
A243	8	1	10	2	2	1	0	0	1	0	0	4	0
M244	12	0	7	4	2	0	0	0	1	0	0	3	0
D245	8	1	10	4	2	1	0	0	1	0	0	2	0
S246	8	0	11	6	1	1	0	0	1	0	0	1	0
D247	8	1	10	6	2	1	0	0	1	0	0	0	0
P248	12	1	6	7	2	1	0	0	0	0	0	0	0
R249	8	1	10	6	2	1	0	0	1	0	0	0	0
S250	8	1	10	6	2	1	0	0	1	0	0	0	0
L251	8	1	10	5	3	1	0	0	1	0	0	0	0
G252	8	1	10	5	2	1	1	0	1	0	0	0	0
L253	8	0	11	5	1	1	1	0	1	1	0	0	0
A254	8	1	10	4	3	1	1	0	0	1	0	0	0
V255	12	0	7	4	3	0	1	0	0	1	0	1	0
I256	8	0	11	4	2	1	1	0	0	1	0	1	0
E257	11	0	8	3	4	1	0	0	0	1	0	1	0
R258	8	2	9	2	4	1	2	0	0	0	0	1	0
L259	8	0	11	2	2	1	2	0	0	2	0	1	0
N260	11	1	7	2	3	1	2	0	0	2	0	0	0
K261	8	1	10	2	3	0	2	0	0	2	0	1	0
L262	8	0	11	4	1	0	2	0	0	2	0	1	0
Q263	11	0	8	4	3	0	0	0	0	2	0	1	0
F264	8	2	9	5	3	0	1	0	0	0	0	1	0
K265	8	1	10	5	2	0	1	0	0	1	0	1	0
L266	8	1	10	6	2	0	1	0	0	1	0	0	0
G267	8	1	10	6	2	0	1	0	0	1	0	0	0
S268	8	0	11	7	0	0	1	0	0	1	0	1	0
R269	8	1	10	6	1	0	1	0	0	1	0	1	0
L270	8	1	10	6	1	1	1	0	0	0	0	1	0
A271	8	1	10	5	1	2	1	0	0	0	0	1	0
Y272	8	1	10	4	1	3	1	0	0	0	0	1	0
L273	8	4	7	4	1	3	2	0	0	0	0	0	0
H274	11	0	8	5	0	3	1	0	0	0	0	1	0
V275	12	0	7	5	0	2	2	0	0	0	0	1	0
T276	12	0	7	4	0	3	2	0	0	0	0	1	0
Q277	12	0	7	3	1	3	2	0	0	0	0	1	0
P278	11	0	8	2	1	4	1	0	0	0	0	2	0
R279	8	1	10	2	1	4	2	0	0	0	0	1	0
Y280	8	1	10	2	1	4	1	0	0	0	0	2	0
T281	12	0	7	4	1	2	1	0	0	0	0	2	0

(continued)

Table 5.37 (continued)

AAs	cnt (–ve)	cnt (+ve)	cnt (0)	v0	v1	v2	v3	v4	v5	v6	v7	v8	v9
A282	8	0	11	4	0	2	1	0	0	0	0	3	0
D283	8	3	8	4	1	2	1	0	0	0	0	2	0
G284	8	1	10	3	1	3	0	0	0	0	0	3	0
H285	12	3	4	3	1	3	0	0	0	0	0	3	0
G286	8	1	10	2	1	3	0	0	0	0	0	4	0
Q287	12	3	4	3	1	2	1	0	0	0	0	3	0
T288	12	0	7	3	0	1	1	0	0	0	0	5	0
E289	12	0	7	3	0	1	1	0	0	0	0	5	0
A290	8	4	7	2	0	2	1	0	0	0	0	5	0
G291	8	1	10	1	0	2	2	0	0	0	0	5	0
A292	11	0	8	1	0	2	1	0	0	0	0	6	0
N293	17	0	2	1	0	2	2	0	0	0	0	5	0
G294	18	1	0	1	0	1	2	0	0	0	0	6	0
S295	15	0	4	1	1	0	2	0	0	0	0	6	0
E296	11	0	8	1	1	1	1	0	0	0	0	6	0
E297	11	1	7	1	1	1	2	0	0	0	0	5	0
E298	11	2	6	1	1	1	2	0	0	0	0	5	0
V299	11	1	7	2	1	1	2	0	0	0	0	4	0
A300	8	0	11	2	0	2	2	0	0	0	0	4	0
Q301	12	0	7	2	2	1	2	0	0	0	0	3	0
L302	8	1	10	1	2	2	1	0	0	1	0	3	0
M303	11	0	8	3	2	2	0	0	0	1	0	2	0
K304	8	1	10	2	3	2	1	0	0	1	0	1	0
T305	12	0	7	3	4	1	1	0	0	1	0	0	0
W306	8	0	11	3	2	2	1	0	0	1	0	1	0
R307	8	2	9	4	3	1	1	0	0	0	0	1	0
G308	8	1	10	2	3	1	1	0	1	1	0	1	0
A309	8	0	11	3	3	1	0	0	1	1	0	1	0
Y310	8	0	11	2	3	1	0	0	1	1	0	2	0
V311	12	3	4	2	4	0	0	0	1	1	0	2	0
G312	8	1	10	1	3	0	0	0	1	1	0	4	0
T313	12	1	6	2	3	0	0	0	0	0	0	5	0
F314	8	0	11	1	2	0	0	0	1	0	0	6	0
I315	9	3	7	1	2	0	0	0	1	0	0	6	0
C316	10	5	4	1	1	0	1	0	1	0	0	6	0
C317	4	9	6	1	2	0	1	0	1	0	0	5	0
G318	10	6	3	0	2	0	1	0	1	0	0	6	0
G319	3	9	7	0	2	0	1	0	0	0	0	7	0
Y320	7	2	10	1	1	0	1	0	0	0	0	7	0
T321	11	0	8	1	2	0	0	0	0	0	0	7	0

(continued)

Table 5.37 (continued)

AAs	cnt (−ve)	cnt (+ve)	cnt (0)	v0	v1	v2	v3	v4	v5	v6	v7	v8	v9
R322	8	0	11	1	1	1	1	0	0	0	0	6	0
E323	11	1	7	1	2	1	1	0	0	1	0	4	0
L324	7	4	8	1	2	1	2	0	0	1	0	3	0
G325	8	1	10	0	3	1	2	0	0	1	0	3	0
L326	8	0	11	1	2	2	2	0	0	1	0	2	0
Q327	12	0	7	1	4	1	1	0	0	1	0	2	0
A328	8	2	9	1	3	2	1	0	0	0	0	3	0
V329	11	0	8	1	3	2	0	0	0	1	0	3	0
A330	8	0	11	2	2	2	1	0	0	1	0	2	0
Q331	12	0	7	2	3	1	1	0	0	1	0	2	0
G332	8	0	11	2	1	2	2	0	0	1	0	2	0
D333	6	9	4	2	2	1	2	0	0	1	0	2	0
A334	7	1	11	2	2	1	2	0	0	0	0	3	0
D335	8	1	10	1	2	1	1	0	0	0	0	5	0
L336	8	1	10	1	1	1	1	0	0	0	0	6	0
V337	11	0	8	2	1	0	0	1	0	0	0	6	0
A338	15	0	4	2	0	0	1	1	0	0	1	5	0
F339	14	0	5	2	0	0	1	1	0	0	2	4	0
G340	19	0	0	2	0	0	1	1	0	0	3	3	0
R341	2	3	14	1	0	0	1	2	0	0	3	3	0
Y342	0	1	18	0	0	0	1	2	0	0	3	4	0
F343	0	0	19	0	0	0	0	4	0	0	2	4	0
V344	0	0	19	0	0	0	0	4	0	0	3	3	0
S345	0	0	19	0	0	0	0	5	0	0	3	2	0
N346	0	1	18	0	0	0	0	4	0	0	5	1	0
P347	0	1	18	0	0	0	0	5	0	0	5	0	0
D348	0	1	18	0	0	0	0	5	0	0	5	0	0
L349	0	0	19	0	0	0	0	7	0	0	3	0	0
V350	0	1	18	0	0	0	0	6	0	0	4	0	0
L351	0	0	19	0	0	0	0	8	0	0	2	0	0
R352	0	1	18	0	0	0	0	7	0	0	3	0	0
L353	0	1	18	0	0	0	0	7	0	0	3	0	0
K354	0	1	18	0	0	0	0	7	0	0	3	0	0
L355	0	0	19	0	0	0	0	9	0	0	1	0	0
N356	0	1	18	0	0	0	0	7	0	0	2	1	0
A357	0	1	18	0	0	0	0	7	0	0	1	2	0
P358	0	1	18	0	0	0	0	6	0	0	1	3	0
L359	0	1	18	0	0	0	0	5	0	0	1	4	0
N360	0	1	18	0	0	0	0	5	0	0	1	4	0
R361	2	1	16	0	0	0	0	7	0	0	0	3	0

(continued)

Table 5.37 (continued)

AAs	cnt (−ve)	cnt (+ve)	cnt (0)	v0	v1	v2	v3	v4	v5	v6	v7	v8	v9
Y362	7	0	12	0	0	0	0	6	0	0	1	3	0
D363	7	1	11	0	0	0	0	5	0	0	2	3	0
R364	1	2	16	0	0	0	0	4	0	0	2	4	0
A365	0	1	18	0	0	0	0	2	0	0	2	6	0
T366	0	1	18	0	0	0	0	1	0	0	2	7	0
F367	0	0	19	0	0	0	0	2	0	0	1	7	0
Y368	0	0	19	0	0	0	0	2	0	0	1	7	0
T369	5	2	12	0	0	0	0	2	0	0	2	6	0
H370	19	0	0	0	0	0	0	3	0	0	2	5	0
D371	18	0	1	0	0	0	0	2	0	0	3	5	0
P372	1	10	8	0	0	0	0	1	0	0	3	6	0
V373	0	11	8	0	0	0	0	1	0	0	3	6	0
V374	0	7	12	0	0	0	0	2	0	0	2	6	0
G375	0	1	18	0	0	0	0	2	0	0	2	6	0
Y376	0	0	19	0	0	0	0	4	0	0	1	5	0
T377	0	2	17	0	0	0	0	4	0	0	3	3	0
D378	0	0	19	0	0	0	0	5	0	0	2	3	0
Y379	0	1	18	0	0	0	0	4	0	0	3	3	0
P380	0	1	18	0	0	0	0	4	0	0	4	2	0
S381	0	1	18	0	0	0	0	3	0	0	5	2	0
L382	0	0	19	0	0	0	0	5	0	0	3	2	0
D383	0	1	18	0	0	0	0	4	0	0	5	1	0
K384	0	5	14										
G385	0	0	19										
S386	0	0	19										
L387	0	1	18										
L388	0	0	19										

Experimental Set Up (ESU):

ESU1: Search in database—The prerequisite for prediction is to derive PTT-FV table for the proteins curated from medicinal plant database in Uniport [4] and/or NCBI [5] with the following two-level search

Level 1 search—with the name of the medicinal plant, the responders are a set of proteins; followed by
Level 2 search—with each element of the BAC (Bio-Active Compound shown in Table 5.33) on the protein set, retrieved out of Level 1 search.

Table 5.38 Partial PTT-FV table for Protein Tabersonine Synthase (320 AA) of Medicinal Plant Ctharanthus roseus

AAs	cnt (–ve)	cnt (+ve)	cnt (0)	v0	v1	v2	v3	v4	v5	v6	v7	v8	v9
G2	7	0	12										
S3	4	0	15										
S4	8	0	11										
D5	8	1	10										
E6	11	1	7										
T7	10	2	7	3	3	0	0	0	2	1	0	1	0
I8	8	0	11	3	2	0	0	0	3	0	0	2	0
F9	8	0	11	4	2	0	0	0	3	0	0	1	0
D10	8	1	10	3	2	0	0	0	3	0	0	2	0
L11	8	1	10	3	2	0	0	0	3	0	0	2	0
P12	11	1	7	4	2	0	1	0	1	0	0	2	0
⋮	⋮	⋮	⋮	⋮	⋮	⋮	⋮	⋮	⋮	⋮	⋮	⋮	⋮
⋮	⋮	⋮	⋮	⋮	⋮	⋮	⋮	⋮	⋮	⋮	⋮	⋮	⋮
N310	0	0	19	0	0	0	0	0	0	0	6	4	0
M311	0	0	19	0	0	0	0	0	0	0	6	4	0
L312	0	1	18	0	0	0	0	0	0	0	4	6	0
R313	0	1	18	0	0	0	0	0	0	0	4	6	0
R314	0	0	19	0	0	0	0	0	0	0	4	6	0
L315	0	1	18	0	0	0	0	0	0	0	3	7	0
A316	0	1	18										
S317	0	0	19										
F318	0	2	17										
I319	0	0	19										
K320	0	5	14										

The responders with Level 2 search are assumed to be a sub-set of proteins associated for interaction with a BAC element on their metabolic pathway. This assumption is based on the information available in Uniprot [4] in respect of plant protein biological functions, and manual search on published results we have curated from the publications surveyed in Sect. 5.6.2. This assumption gets validated from the CAML model-derived results on plant proteins reported in Sects. 5.6.6–5.6.8.

ESU2: Retrieval of proteins from Medicinal Plants—Table 5.40 reports sample set of proteins of six medicinal plants—four covered in the Training Set (TrS) noted under Sub-Group SG51 and two (Basil and Artemesia annua) covered in the Testing Set (TeS) under Sub-Group SG53 of Plant Group GR 5 reported in the survey noted

Table 5.39 Partial PTT—FV table for Dirigent protein (339 AA) of Plant Artemesia annua

AAs	cnt (–ve)	cnt (+ve)	cnt (0)	v0	v1	v2	v3	v4	v5	v6	v7	v8	v9
G2	18	0	1										
A3	12	0	7										
D4	17	0	2										
L5	8	0	11										
M6	12	0	7										
N7	12	0	7	1	2	4	0	1	0	0	0	2	0
E8	12	0	7	2	2	4	0	1	0	0	0	1	0
E9	12	0	7	3	2	3	0	1	0	0	0	1	0
T10	12	1	6	3	2	5	0	0	0	0	0	0	0
R11	8	0	11	3	0	5	0	2	0	0	0	0	0
D12	8	1	10	3	1	4	0	2	0	0	0	0	0
⋮	⋮	⋮	⋮	⋮	⋮	⋮	⋮	⋮	⋮	⋮	⋮	⋮	⋮
⋮	⋮	⋮	⋮	⋮	⋮	⋮	⋮	⋮	⋮	⋮	⋮	⋮	⋮
G329	0	19	0	0	0	0	0	0	0	0	0	10	0
A330	0	17	2	0	0	0	1	0	0	0	0	9	0
G331	0	18	1	0	0	0	1	0	0	0	0	9	0
E332	1	0	18	0	0	0	1	0	0	0	0	9	0
G333	0	5	14	0	0	0	1	0	0	0	0	9	0
S334	0	3	16	0	0	0	1	0	0	0	0	9	0
G335	0	2	17										
G336	4	0	15										
T337	4	0	15										
Q338	1	0	18										
E339	15	0	4										

in Sect. 5.6.2. Explanation of the columns of Table 5.40 follows.

Column 1 and 2—Plant name and whether it belongs to TrS (Training Set) or TeS (Testing Set).
Column 3—Name of the BAC element (shown in Table 5.33) employed for level 2 search on the protein set retrieved with Level 1 search (reported under ESU1). **Column 4**—This column of Table 5.40 reports the proteins retrieved with Level 2 search, only if it satisfies two Prediction Criteria referred to as PCr1 (Prediction Criteria 1 derived out of PTT) and PCr2 (Prediction Criteria 2 derived out of FV) defined below under ESU3. **Column 5**—Shows the number of amino acids (AAs) in the protein chain noted Column 4.

ESU3: Prediction Criteria and Allowable Range—Two Prediction Criteria derived out of PTT (Pattern Type Triplet defined earlier) and FV (Feature Vector) of AC

Table 5.40 Proteins Curated from Medicinal Plant Database—Uniprot [4]/NCBI [5] for prediction of (AC) medicinal plants as per Algorithm 7

Plant name	TrS/TeS	BAC element	Protein satisfies Prediction Criteria PCr1 and PCr2	AA count
Catharanthus roseus	TrS	Alkaloid	Tabersonine synthase	320
Catharanthus roseus	TrS	Alkaloid	Catharanthus synthase	330
Basil	TeS	Synthase	Eugenol Synthase	314
Brassica	TrS	Alkaloids	Dirigent Protein	212
Curculigo orchioides	TrS	Synthase	ATP synthase	498
Acacia	TrS	Phenol	Ubiquinone biosynthesis O-methyltransf	255
Artemisia annua	TeS	Aldehyde	Artemisinic aldehyde Delta reductase	388
Artemisia annua	TeS	Alkaloids	Dirigent Protein	339

medicinal plants are defined next. For evaluation of the PTT-FV table, we exclude the first and last five amino acids (AAs), since no PTT-FV can be generated for these amino acid locations.

Prediction Criteria PCr1—It is derived out of PTT of an AA in a Protein chain—Let the 3 elements PTT be denoted as <X Y Z>, where X and Y refer to count of (–ive) and (+ive) DCLVS value of an amino acid of a protein chain, while Z denotes the count of value 0, with mutant and wild show same CLVS value. PCr1 is defined as -

PCr1 = (Count of X = 0)/ (AA count in the protein chain) (that is, Count of X = 0 across the protein length, expressed as percentage of AA count).

Prediction Criteria PCr2—It is derived out of 10 element FV (Feature Vector) of an AA in a Protein chain and defined as follows

PCr2 = (count of v8 = 0)/ (AA count in the protein chain) (that is, Count of v8 = 0 across the protein length, as percentage of AA count).

Allowable Range of PCr1 and PCr2 from the analysis of (i) PTT—FV tables of a large number of plant proteins included in TrS (Training Set) and VaS (Validation Set) and (ii) study of relevant publications on the related proteins of the medicinal plants reported below:

Allowable range for PCr1 and PCr2 are set as 0% to 24%. If both the criteria of a curated protein of a medicinal plant are satisfied, then the plant is a candidate to be marked as the one having AC (Anti-Cancer) property. The underlying assumption is that—some anti-cancer therapeutic agent may be derived through interaction of the concerned protein with other biomolecules associated on its pathway. In the context of the CAML model, relevance of PCr1 and PCr2 are next highlighted.

Relevance of PCr1 and PCr2 of a protein chain in the context of its interaction with other biomolecules on the metabolic pathway

In Sect. 5.2.5 of Chapt. 5 we have established the fact that, presence of a signal in the CL graph of a protein inhibits its interaction with the associated biomolecule around that cell location, while the signal graph (of another protein not having that signal) allows its interaction with that biomolecule. This characteristic has been observed while comparing wild signal graphs of CoV-2 and CoV Envelope protein, that leads to higher transmissibility of CoV-2 compared to that of CoV. Similarly, Sect. 5.3.3 of Chap. 5 compares wild signal graphs of nsp1 protein of CoV-2 and CoV in Figs. 5.10 and 5.11 to establish the fact that CoV-2 is much more efficient in hijacking protein synthesis machinery of host cell compared to CoV (having additional signals), that results in higher transmissibility of CoV-2 virus.

We have evaluated the PTT-FV tables of a large number of protein chains on inserting 19 mutations on each of its amino acid locations. The PTT-FV table of a protein extracts certain characteristics of the protein. The PTT (pattern Type Triplet), as explained earlier, captures the environment of ith AA around the 10 AAs ((i-5) to (i+5) AAs). The PTT for an AA in a protein is represented as <X Y Z>, where X refers to count of AAs with (-ve) DCLVS (Difference in Cycle Length value Sum), while Y shows the count of AAs with (+ive) DCLVS, and Z shows the count of AAs with 0 DCLVS value. In CAML model, the presence of a signal in a protein mutant shows up as (+ive) DCLVS value compared to its wild counterpart.

In Sect. 5.6.1 we reported the point that, CAML model aims to mimic the biological pathways of a protein out of which the anti-cancer therapeutic agent may be derived. The proteins are identified through two-level search in plant protein database as illustrated in Table 5.40. The AAs of a protein filtered with each of the prediction criteria PCr1 and PCr2, show low (+ive) value of Y, mostly with 0, 1 and 2 values. That is, the MsAAs (Mutation site AAs) of the protein filtered with prediction criteria show CL graph characteristics similar to that of wild. Absence of additional signals in mutant CL graphs allows interaction of the protein chain with other biomolecules on its biological pathways. This observation has been validated in earlier sections of Chap. 5 dealing with virus proteins and cancer protein p53.

The hypothesis noted below is based on the learning curve we have traversed during our study of wide varieties of literature on Medicinal plants displaying Anti-Cancer (AC) property and the relevance of PCr1 and PCr2 derived out of CAML model.

Observation 5.10: A Medicinal Plant having a Protein satisfying the allowable range for PCr1 and PCr2, both in the range of 0.00–24.00%—is marked as the one having AC property, in the sense that—some anti-cancer therapeutic agent may be derived from the plant out of the interaction of the protein with other biomolecules on its biological pathways.

Based on the experimental setup presented earlier, we next present the algorithmic steps for prediction of a medicinal plant having Anti-Cancer (AC) property.

Algorithm 7: CAML Model for Prediction of Anti-Cancer (AC) Medicinal Plants

---

Input : A Medicinal Plant (with its Genus and Species specified); the UniProt [4] and NCBI [5] protein databases

Output: Predicts whether the plant (or its genus) has Anti-Cancer (AC) property
Step 1 : Level 1 search on protein database Uniprot and/or NCBI with the plant name (noted under ESU 1).

Step 2 : If different varieties of proteins with protein count more than 25 are not available, search the database with the name of plant Genus.

Step 3 : If the Step 2 protein count output is less than 50, go to Stop with comment 'no prediction due to insufficient number/varieties of proteins in databases', else proceed with next step.

Step 4 : Level 2 search on proteins retrieved in Step 1, with each element of BAC (Bio-Active Compounds) listed in Table 5.33.

Step 5 : For each of the proteins curated in Step 4, generate its PTT—FV table.

Step 6 : Evaluate two Prediction Criteria PCr1 and PCr2 (noted under Experimental Set UP ESU3) for each protein.

Step 7 : CAML model-derived results—If the allowable range of both PCr1 and PCr2 (0 to 24.00%) for at least one protein of the plant are satisfied, mark the protein as AC (Anti-Cancer), else mark the plant as non-AC.

Step 8 : Compare CAML results with the published results -
Check the publications reported for the medicinal plant with in-vitro and/or in-vivo experimental results in respect of the plant-derived anti-cancer therapeutic agents extracted out of the proteins identified for the plant.

Step 9 : Compare the results evaluated in Step 7 and Step 8. Stop.

5.6.6 Prediction Results for Training Set (TrS) Medicinal Plants

The TrS refers to the Sub-Group SG51 reported in the Survey presented in Sect. 5.6.2. The TrS covers 17 medicinal plants out of which 11 plants, as per published literature, are reported as Anti-Cancer (AC), while 6 are reported as non-AC.

Table 5.41 reports the prediction results derived for medicinal plants covered under TrS on execution of Prediction Algorithm 7. The table displays PCr1 and PCr2 values on columns 5 and 7 for the proteins noted on column 1 for the medicinal plant. Detailed evaluation of PCr1 and PCr2 are presented on columns 8 to 9 and 11 to 12 only for the proteins which satisfy both the criteria PCr1 and PCr2 satisfying the range of 0.00% to 24.00%. The proteins are identified, as reported on columns 3 to 5 of the table, through Level 2 search noted under ESU1 (Experimental Set Up 1) presented in Sect. 5.6.5 and executed in Step 5 and Step 6 of Algorithm 7.

As per the survey in Sect. 5.6.2, Eleven plants are marked as AC—Brassica, Taxus brevifolia, Podyphyllum peltatum, Catharanthus roseus, Macula pomifera, Catechin, Raphanus sativa, Dysoxylum Genus, Opium poppy, Iridaceae, Mucuna pruriens. On the other hand, 6 plants are marked as non-AC—Acacia, Phyllenthus urinaria, Pterocarpus marsupium, Curculigo orchiodes, Macuna Pruriens, Urtica dioica. Out of 17 plants, results for 12 plants derived with CAML model match with that of published results based on experimental evidence against cancer cell lines. The reasons of discrepancy observed for 6 plants are next discussed; these are divided into 4 Case Studies pointing to 4 non-AC plants (Table 5.41).

Case Study 1: The therapeutic agents derived from the plant Mucuna pruriens, as per the authors [198, 206], are used to treat patients with Parkinson's disease, hyperglycaemia, hypo-cholesteric etc. Consequently, this plant is marked as non-AC in the survey reported under SG51 in Sect. 5.6.2. However, as per CAML model this plant is marked as AC. On search of recent published literature, as per Step 9 of the Algorithm, we came across the experimental results against different cancer types reported by authors in [257–259]. Further, dynamics of protein Actin 11 and actin binding proteins are discussed in [260, 261] to fight cancer progression. These published results corroborate the CAML model results identifying Mucuna pruriens as an AC plant.

Case Study 2: Three medicinal plants Acacia, Curculigo orchioides, and Urtica dioica are identified as non-AC as per the survey in Sect. 5.6.2. However, as per CAML model, for each of these three plants, there is at least one protein that satisfies both the criteria PCr1 and PCr2; in fact, the plant Curculigo orchioides show two proteins satisfying both the criteria. On search in recent publications, as per Step 9 of the algorithm, we noticed that the authors [185, 262] reported anti-cancer activity of Acacia on certain cancer cell lines; the protein (Ubiqui biosynt O-methyltransferase) of plant Acacia satisfies both the criteria PCr1 and PCr2. This enzyme methylates many secondary metabolites including Flavonoids, Alkaloids etc. Similarly, in recent publications [263–265] on the plant Curculigo orchioides, authors have highlighted the anti-oxidant, anti-cancer property of the plant. Further, the authors in publications [266–268] have reported anti-cancer property of the extract of the plant Urtica dioica against cell lines of BrC (Breast Cancer), non-small cell lung cancer (NSCLC).

Table 5.41 Prediction results for 17 Training Set (TrS) Medicinal Plants on Execution of Prediction Algorithm 7

Protein	BAC	AA count	Cnt of (–ive) = 0	Criteria PCr1	Cnt of v8 = 0	Criteria PCr2	Prediction Result
1. Plant : Brasicca [137, 177, 178, 271–274]—AC							
Actin	Actin	377		85.94%		33.15%	
Peroxidase P7	Lignin	296		60.47%		5.74%	
Aldehyde Dehydrogenase	Aldehyde	494		45.34%		0.40%	
Chalcone-flavonone	Flavonon	205		31.70%		9.75%	
Dirigent Protein	Alkaloids	212	15/212	7.08%	11/212	5.19%	AC
MYB trans factor	Tran Facto	310		45.16%		16.77%	
Pectin acetylesrase	Pectin	427		27.16%		0.70%	
2. Plant : Taxus brevifolia [137, 179, 275–278]—AC							
Taxadiene Synthase	Synthase	862	132/862	14.26%	275/862	31.90%	
Acetyl-coenzyme A Carboxyl	Acetyl	749	51/749	6.80%	161/749	21.49%	AC
10-dea III-10 acetyl transfera	Acetyl	440		27.27%		3.86%	
ATP Synthase beta sub-unit	Synthase	478	111/478	23.22%	16/478	3.35%	AC
ATP dep Clp protease prot sub	Protease	481		43.03%		1.66%	
3. Plant : Podophyllum peltatum [137, 180, 180, 279]—AC							
Acetyl Coen A trans sub beta	Acetyl	508	13/508	2.56%	61/508	12.00%	AC
ATP dep Clp protease	Protease	202	36/202	17.82%	23/202	11.38%	AC
Corytuberie Synthase	Synthase	510		1.37%		36.86%	
Dirigent Protein	Alkaloids	193		63.21%		9.23%	
Norcod 6-Omethyltrafase	Alkaloids	373		55.22%		3.22%	
Norcoclaurine Synthse	Alkaloids	111	10/111	9.01%	0/111	0.00%	AC
Pluviatolide Synthase	Synthase	489		4.70%		36.40%	
4. Plant : Catharanthus roseus [137, 181, 182, 280, 281]—AC							
Actin	Actin	377		87.00%		33.95%	
Alosonine synthase	Alkaloids	516		39.53%		0.78%	
Chalco-flavonone iso protein	Flavonon	133	15/133	11.28%	22/133	16.54%	AC
Geissoschizene synthase	Alkaloids	364		86.18%		42.31%	
Peroxidase	Lignin	330		53.03%		10.30%	
Tabersonine synthase	Alkaloids	320	36/320	10.90%	23/320	6.97%	AC
Catharanthus synthase	Alkaloids	330	45/330	13.63%	30/330	9.09%	AC
5. Plant : Maclura pomifera [137, 183]—AC							
Agglutinen alpha ch	Lectin	133		83.45%		17.29%	
Glyceraldehyde 3-phospha	Aldehyde	127		90.55%		47.24%	
Glycotransferase	Glycotran	493	19/493	3.85%	105/493	21.29%	AC
MpBBI	Protease	65		40.00%		0.00%	
Ribulose biphos carbo	Lyase	430	26/430	6.04%	30/430	6.97%	AC
Tubulin beta chain	Tubulin	305		30.49%		0.00%	
6. Plant : Catechin [137, 184–186]—non-AC							
Chalcone synthase	Synthase	281		72.59%		12.10%	
Discoidin-1 subunit A	Lectin	253		74.70%		10.67%	
Flavanon 3-hydroxylase	Synthase	251		70.51%		22.71%	
Flavonoid -hydro	Flavonoid	510		48.53%		2.54%	

(continued)

Table 5.41 (continued)

Protein	BAC	AA count	Cnt of (–ive) = 0	Criteria PCr1	Cnt of v8 = 0	Criteria PCr2	Prediction Result
Gallate 1-beta-glucosyltransfe	Glycosyltr	506		50.39%		6.32%	
G-box bind factor	Trans Fact	708		66.05%		20.83%	
BataGlucoside	Glucoside	744		28.53%		9.29%	
Gallate 1-beta-glucosyltransfe	Glucosyltr	517		76.59%		17.98%	
7. Plant : Combretum caffrum [137, 187, 269]—non-AC							
Acety-coe A ca carb beta	Acetyl	488		81.55%		22.74%	
Actin	Actin	167		68.63%		5.32%	
Aldehyde dehydrogenase	Aldehyde	507		82.44%		26.82%	
ATP Synthase sub beta	Synthase	498		33.93%		3.21%	
ATP-dep Clp protease	Protease	196		92.85%		13.77%	
Beta Tubulin	Tubulin	144		70.13%		6.94%	
Ribulo bisph carb large	Lyase	465		50.53%		1.07%	
Transporter	Trans prot	326		45.26%		3.05%	
8. Plant : Raphanus sativas [137, 188]—AC							
Acetyl-coenzyme A carboxyla	Acetyl	491	31/491	6.33%	94/491	19.14%	AC
Aldehyde dehydrogenase	Aldehyde	508		54.24%		4.03%	
Chalcone-flavo isomerase	Flavonoids	247		25.79%		12.86%	
Cyclin-dependent kinsase inhi	kina inhib	211	33/211	15.64%	28/211	13.27%	AC
Dirigent protein	Alkaloids	312		94.21%		23.00%	
L-type lectin-domain recep kin	Lectin	425		81.60%		30.51%	
Peroxidase	Lignin	368		67.85%		26.12%	
9. Plant : Dysoxylum binectariferum [137, 189, 190]—AC							
ATP Synthase sub beta	Synthase	224		67.41%		10.26%	
Beta Tubulin	Tubulin	91		93.40%		60.41%	
Calmodulin	Calmodu	149		91.27%		13.42%	
Chalcone Synthase	Synthase	395		80.25%		29.37%	
Chaperone Protein	from NCBI	308		92.85%		18.83%	
Rubul biphos carb large	Lyase	200		47.00%		4.50%	
Gyrase subunit B	from NCBI	279	56/279	20.07%	52/279	18.66%	AC
10. Plant : Opium poppy [137, 191–193, 282, 283]—AC							
Acetyl-coenzyme A (CoA)	Acetyl	491		35.23%		5.70%	
Aldehyde dehydrogenase	Aldehyde	492		68.09%		23.37%	
Chalco-flavonone isom	Flavonone	237		85.53%		29.95%	
Codeine O-demet	Alkaloids	360		30.55%		1.38%	
Dirigent prot	Alkaloids	407	68/407	16.70%	31/407	7.61%	AC
Noscapine synth	Synthase	348		80.46%		24.14%	
Salutaridine synthase	Phenol	505		60.67%		24.70%	
11. Plant : Iridaceae [194–197]—AC							
Acetyl-coen A carbo	Acetyl	488	22/488	4.51%	60/488	12.29%	AC
Actin	Actin	377		10.61%		27.58%	
Alpha Tubulin	Tubulin	75		37.77%		0.00%	
Beta tubulin	Tubulin	154	15/154	9.74%	6/154	3.89%	AC

(continued)

Table 5.41 (continued)

Protein	BAC	AA count	Cnt of (–ive) = 0	Criteria PCr1	Cnt of v8 = 0	Criteria PCr2	Prediction Result
Mannose-spec lectin 1	Lectin	267		61.80%		0.00%	
Profilin	Actin	131		0.00%		24.42%	
12. Plant : Acacia [198–200, 262, 284]—AC							
Acetyl-coenzyme A carbox	Acetyl	506		49.41%		1.97%	
Aldehyde dehydrogenase	Aldehyde	510		61.76%		19.41%	
ATP synthase subunit beta	Synthase	498		55.62%		2.41%	
Cinnamyl alcohol dehydroge	Lignin	359		26.74%		3.06%	
Lectin	Lectin	225		31.55%		4.88%	
LysR family transcri regul	Flavonoids	349		12.32%		25.78%	
Ribul bisph carbo large chain	Lyase	455		49.67%		3.51%	
Tubulin beta chain	Tubulin	310		31.29%		3.54%	
Ubiqui biosynt O-methyltran	Phenol	255	53/255	20.78%	14/255	5.49%	AC
13. Plant: Phyllenthus urinaria [201, 202]—non-AC							
AccD	Acetyl	284		93.94%		48.62%	
ATP synthase subunit beta	Synthase	501		78.72%		16.07%	
ATP-dep Clp prot prote subunit	Protease	251		57.22%		15.30%	
CcsA	Heme	367		39.75%		14.05%	
DNA-dire RNA polyme sub beta	Trans Fact	771		90.45%		30.75%	
NdhB	Plastoquo	512		89.78%		58.43%	
Phytochrome C	Kinase	193		81.75%		20.88%	
14. Plant: Pterocarpus marsupium [198, 203, 204]—non-AC							
Acetyl coenzyme	Acetyl	501		83.66%		37.84%	
ATP Synthase	Synthase	498		55.51%		3.20%	
ATP-dep Clp Protease	Protease	195		88.75%		65.81%	
ATP synthase subunit beta	Synthase	188		91.49%		53.19%	
DNA-directed RNA polymerase	Trans Facto	331		43.50%		6.64%	
Ribulose biphosphate	Lyase	475		88.63%		17.47%	
15. Plant: Curculigo orchioides [198, 205, 263–265]—AC							
Acetyl Coenzyme	Acetyl	472		48.42%		6.09%	
ATP dependant clp protease	Protease	204	27/204	13.23%	10/204	4.90%	AC
ATP synthase subunit beta	Synthase	498	96/498	19.28%	29/498	5.82%	AC
Ribulos biphos carboxy lar ch	Lyase	488		32.44%		1.89%	
NAD(P)H-quino oxidoreducasr	Plastoquin	363		35.73%		6.00%	
16. Plant: Mucuna pruriens [198, 206, 257–261]—AC							
Cancer related nucl-triph prot	**	191		74.87%		9.42%	
Plastoquinol-plastocyanin redu	Plastoquin	260		35.00%		10.00%	
Actin 11	Actin	420	53/420	12.62%	45/420	10.71%	AC
Tubulin alpha chain	Tubulin	517		83.75%		32.30%	
Tubulin beta chain	Tubulin	433		33.95%		1.61%	
Taxadiene 5-alpha hydroxylase	Taxadiene	494		72.87%		21.45%	
N-alpha acetyltransferase	Acetyl	281		42.35%		3.55%	

(continued)

Table 5.41 (continued)

Protein	BAC	AA count	Cnt of (–ive) = 0	Criteria PCr1	Cnt of v8 = 0	Criteria PCr2	Prediction Result
17. Plant: Urtica dioica [207–209, 266–268] **-AC**							
Agglutinin isolectin	Lectin	113		64.60%		8.84%	
Beta Tubulin	Tubulin	75		90.90%		38.96%	
Lectin endochitinase	Lectin	372		75.53%		3.76%	
Peroxidase	Lignin	337		67.36%		10.97%	
Ribulose bispho carboxylase chain	Lyase	471	113/489	23.99%	1/489	0.21%	AC
Xanthine dehydrogenase	Dehydroge	385		43.11%		6.23%	

Case Study 3: Another discrepancy between CAML results and published reports [137, 187, 269] can be noticed for the plant Combretum caffrum which, as per the survey, marked as an AC plant; we experimented with Combretum genus as per Step 2 of the algorithm, since insufficient number of protein responders is identified. Authors in [137] reported early trial of the plant extract for cancer treatment, and treatment of multiple diseases with this plant extract reported in the review article [269]. Further, authors [187] reported derivation of different medicinal compounds out of the plant Combretum caffrum without any experimental results of the compounds against cancer cells. As per CAML model, Algorithm 7 predicts Combretum genus as non-AC since none of the proteins satisfies both the prediction criteria PCr1 and PCr2. In addition to Combretum Caffrum, two other plants Phyllenthus urinaria and Pterocarpus marsupium are marked as non-AC as per the survey reported in Sect. 5.6.2.

Case Study 4: In respect of Catechin which is a plant product: Catechin is not a plant, but a product available in many plants (notably in green tree). Notwithstanding the published results reported by a large number of authors in respect of its AC property, CAML model identified Catechin as non-AC. This CAML-derived result probably points to the high challenges associated with extraction of AC agent out of Catechin, as highlighted by a number of authors [270].

It is worth highlighting the recent experimental results (in-vitro cyto-toxicity) reported in [189]: authors reported derivation anti-cancer therapeutic agent Rohitukin from leaves of the plant Dysoxylum binectariferum; CAML derived results reported in Table 5.41). The authors [190] reported the importance of gluthathione transporter protein YCF1 (Yeast Cadmium Factor 1) to counter cell stress. Since search in Uniprot resulted in insufficient number of responders, we searched the NCBI database to arrive at the results reported for this plant identifying protein 'Gyrase subunit B'. This protein, as per recently published literature, indirectly affects cancer cell lines - that corroborates the results reported in [189].

Table 5.42 Prediction results for 6 Validation Set (VaS) Plants on Execution of Prediction Algorithm 7

Protein	BAC	AA count	Cnt of (–ive) = 0	Criteria PCr1	Cnt of v8 = 0	Criteria PCr2	Prediction Result
Plant: Atriplex halimus [210, 211, 285, 286, 293]							
Acyl-CoA reduc-NAD aldehy	Aldehyde	460		74.56%		21.08%	
Cell division prot FtsA	Actin	411		82.96%		34.54%	
Cell division prot FtsZ	Tubulin	410		5.12%		37.80%	
Chitinases	Glycoside	394		0.51%		29.44%	
Glycerol kinase	Actin	499	20/499	4.00%	82/499	16.43%	AC
Lectin	Lectin	202		83.74%		36.45%	
NADH-quinone oxidoreductase	Plastoquin	218		89.90%		50.00%	
Riboflavin biosynthes pr RibD	Synthase	360		86.67%		48.89%	
Transporter Protein	Phenol	256		92.58%		50.39%	
Ubiq biosyn O-methyl	phenol	243		81.42%		17.39%	
Plant: Centella asiatica [212, 213, 287, 288]							
Acetyl-coenzyme	Acetyl	488		88.71%		31.93%	
ATP-dep Clp prot	Protease	196		46.15%		5.43%	
Beta-amyrin 28-oxidase	Heme	481		72.50%		26.23%	
Glycerald 3—phosphate	Aldehyde	177	21/177	11.86%	9/177	5.08%	AC
Glycotransferase	Saponin	494		71.60%		14.32%	
Oleanolic acid	Heme	475	27/475	5.68%	37/475	7.79%	AC
Squalene synthase	Terpene	415		85.78%		23.37%	
Plant: Leea Genus [149, 214, 215, 290, 294]							
3-dehydroquinate synthase	Synthase	71	3/71	4.22%	2/71	2.81%	AC
Acetyl-CoA acetyltransferase	Acetyl	431	69/431	16.00%	26/431	6.03%	AC
Aldehyde dehydrogenase	Aldehyde	489	102/489	20.85%	21/489	4.29%	AC
Cell division protein	Tubulin	412		89.78%		68.25%	
Cell division protein	Actin	418		61.39%		7.88%	
Clp protease proteolytic sub	Protease	195		50.00%		1.64%	
Glycoside hydrolase	Glycoside	430		68.30%		17.22%	
Lectin	Lectin	204	36/204	17.56%	6/204	2.92%	AC
Plant: Limonium species [216, 217, 291, 295]							
Acetyl-coenzA carbo carbo	Acetyl	492	13/492	2.64%	84/492	17.07%	AC
Actin	Actin	37	2/37	5.40%	0/37	0.00%	
ATP synthase	Synthase	495		79.96%		14.29%	
ATP-dep Clp protease	Protease	236		39.15%		1.79%	
Class I Chitanase	Glycoside	319	13/319	4.07%	33/319	10.34%	AC
DNA-directed RNA polymeras	Tra Factor	343		85.67%		26.59%	
Lectin	Lectin	221		75.00%		33.49%	
Terpene cyclase	Terpene	342		50.44%		5.76%	
Plant: Oryza sativa [217–220, 291]							
Actin	Actin	377		88.56%		48.77%	
Aldehyde oxygenase	Aldehyde	238		54.85%		11.06%	
Chitinase	Acetyl	326	29/326	8.89%	73/326	22.39%	AC
Dirigent protein	Alkaloids	175	10/175	5.71%	29/175	14.57%	AC

(continued)

Table 5.42 (continued)

Protein	BAC	AA count	Cnt of (–ive) = 0	Criteria PCr1	Cnt of v8 = 0	Criteria PCr2	Prediction Result
Lectin	Lectin	227		27.88%		1.86%	
Peroxidase 2	Lignin	314		27.48%		12.58%	
Terpene synthase	Terpene	610	96/610	15.76%	23/610	3.85%	AC
Plant: Solanaceae genus [221, 221, 222, 292]							
Chalcone -flavonone isomera	Flavonoid	244	0/244	0.00%	43/244	18.03%	AC
Dirigent Protein	Alkaloids	195		68.56%		16.94%	
Flavonol synth flava 3-hydro	Flavonol	348		84.15%		40.70%	
Glucanendoo-1,3 beta glucosi	Glycoside	370		55.01%		9.50%	
Lectin receptor kinase	Lectin	351	79/351	22.50%	10/351	2.85%	AC
Lignin-forming anioni peroxid	Lignin	324	46/324	14.18%	13/324	4.01%	AC
Sesquiterpene synthase 14	Terpene	568		88.51%		35.62%	
Translation control tumor prot	Tum Prot	168		59.28%		16.67%	

5.6.7 *Prediction Results for the Medicinal Plants in the Validation Set (VaS)*

The VaS refers to the Sub-Group SG52 noted in the survey presented in Sect. 5.6.2. Table 5.42 reports the prediction results derived for medicinal plants covered under VaS on execution of Prediction Algorithm 7. The layout and all the details of Table 5.42 is similar to that of Table 5.41 for TrS (Training Set). The proteins are extracted out of Uniport [4] with Level 2 search employing BAC shown on column 2. All the 6 Validation Set (VaS) plants are marked as Anti-Cancer (AC) plants out of which some AC therapeutic agent may be derived. The report of published results on the plants are reviewed next.

The authors [285], have scientifically validated antioxidant and cytotoxic effect of the extract from the leaves of the plant Antriplex halimus, while the authors in [286] reported cytotoxicity on Breast cancer cell line. CAML model identifies the protein Glycerol Kinase (encoded by gene GK) that satisfies both the criteria PCr1 and PCr2. This enzyme plays key role for glycerol metabolism and is involved for synthesis of Triglycerides and Glycerophospholipids. One of the two proteins satisfying, both the criteria PCr1 and PCr2, identified by CAML model for the next plant Centella asiatica [212, 213, 287, 288] is the protein Glycerald 3-phosphate; the other protein Oleanolic acid (a pentacyclic triterpenoid) selected with BAC ‘Heme’ displays anti-oxidant, anti-tumour characteristics; its anti-cancer activity is reported in [287].

For the third plant Leea Genus, CAML model identifies 4 proteins those satisfy both the criteria PCr1 and PCr2; detailed analysis of Aldehyde dehydrogenase, one of those 4 proteins, is reported in [289]. Usage of the plant enzyme to reduce chemoresistance has been dealt with in [290].

While for the fourth plant Limonium having many species, CAML identifies 2 proteins, for each of the last two plants, 3 proteins are identified satisfying both the criteria PCr1 and PCr2. The protein Chitanase of Limonium and Oryza sativa, as per the authors [291], inhibits both breast and Colorectal cancer. Anti-cancer effect of Terpene is reported in [217], it inhibits tumour growth and induce apoptosis. Authors in [218] confirmed derivation of Anti-Cancer agent out of fifth plant Oryza sativa.

The authors in [222] reported the use of extracts from the Solanaceae genus for different diseases, while the survey reported in [221] projected the plant having potential anti-cancer properties in addition to treatment of other diseases like asthma, cholera, bronchitis, fever etc. Further in the recent papers [221, 292], authors have projected the plant family Solanaceae displaying AC (Anti-Cancer) property.

Finally, in the next subsection we report the prediction of AC plants in the list covered under TeS (Testing Set).

5.6.8 Prediction Results for the Medicinal Plants in the Testing Set (TeS)

The TeS refers to the Sub-Group SG53 noted in the Survey reported in Sect. 5.6.2; the set covers 13 plants listed in Table 5.43. The table reports the prediction results derived for 13 medicinal plants covered in Testing Set (TeS) on execution of Prediction Algorithm 7. Layout of Table 5.43 is identical to that of Tables 5.41 and 5.42. The table displays detailed computation for the protein(s) of medicinal plants which satisfy both the prediction criteria—PCr1 and PCr2. The proteins are identified through Level 2 search reported under ESU1 (Experimental Set Up 1) presented in Sect. 5.6.5. Excepting Cannabis sativa, the remaining 12 plants are marked as AC, out of which Anti-Cancer (AC) therapeutic agent may be derived. Explanatory note curated from published literature are inserted below each group of proteins identified for a plant. Published results validate the CAM-derived prediction of AC medicinal plants.

Table 5.43 Prediction of Anti-Cancer (AC) Medicinal Plants on Execution of Algorithm 7 on Testing Set (TeS) covering 13 plants

Protein	BAC	AA count	Cnt of (–ive) = 0	Criteria PCr1	Cnt of v8 = 0	Criteria PCr2	Prediction Result
Plant: Artemesia annua—[173, 223–225, 252–255, 272–274]							
Peroxidase	Lignin	449		89.29%		13.50%	
Peroxidase	Lignin	327		85.93%		17.41%	
Cycline depen kinase inhibitor	Kinase	197		69.39%		14.04%	
Artemisinic aldehy Delta reduct	Aldehyde	388	64/388	16.49%	7/388	1.80%	AC
Dirigent Protein	Alkaloids	339		78.70%		17.43%	
Aldehyde dehydrogenase	Aldehyde	499	2/77	2.61%	83/499	16.63%	AC
Plant: Basil [248–251]							
Cinnamyl alcohol dehydro	Aldehyde	357		43.54%		1.16%	
Flavonoid 7-Omethyltrans	Flavonoid	336		87.46%		35.19%	
Flavonoid 7-Omethyltransf	Flavonoid	340		85.25%		28.66%	
Phenylalnine ammonia Lya	Lyase	693		88.43%		55.39%	
Terpene cyclase family mem	Terpene	765		22.87%		5.75%	AC
Plant: Bergenia ligulate [229, 230]							
Acetyl co-enzyme A Carbo trans	Acetyl	511		53.33%		3.61%	
ATP synthase	Synthase	498		66.80%		17.08%	
ATP-dependent Clp protease	Protease	196		90.26%		19.57%	
Cytocrome c bioge protein	Heme	316		89.84%		17.11%	
DNA-directed RNA polymerase	Trans Fac	337		50.30%		9.85%	
Glycosyltransferase	Glycosyltr	401		25.75%		5.91%	
Glycosyltransferase	Glycosyltr	495		49.19%		1.66%	
Ribulose biphosphate	Lyase	475		0.42%		14.25%	AC
Plant: Cannabis sativa [231, 232]							
Acetyl coenzyme	Acetyl	497		56.63%		8.87%	
Actin	Actin	336		86.87%		39.96%	
Profilin	Actin	131		55.38%		0.00%	
Aldehyde dehydro	Aldehyde	443		67.87%		5.57%	
Clalcone flavonone	Flavonoid	266		71.70%		34.17%	
Dirigent protein	Alkaloids	384		81.46%		37.90%	
Glycoside hydrolase family	Glycoside	286		83.51%		31.75%	
Glycotransferase	Glycosyl	498		2.82%		38.27%	
Lectin	Lectin	348		77.23%		21.13%	
Peroxidase	Lignin	381		32.89%		15.18%	
Terpene synthase	Terpene	551		81.27%		21.34%	
Tubulin beta chain	Tubulin	446		44.49%		3.23%	
Mevalonate kinase	Kinase	416		49.04%		15.31%	
Plant: Citrus genus [141, 245, 296]							
Aromatic prenyltransferase	Alkaloid	421		87.86%		52.08%	
Catalase	Alkaloid	501	30/501	5.99%	47/501	0.02%	AC
Chalcone synthase	Flavonoid	389	16/389	4.11%	41/389	10.54%	AC
Flavonol synthas 3-hydroxylase	Flavonoid	335		8.65%		4.78%	AC

(continued)

Table 5.43 (continued)

Protein	BAC	AA count	Cnt of (–ive) = 0	Criteria PCr1	Cnt of v8 = 0	Criteria PCr2	Prediction Result
Peroxidase	lignin	338		65.88%		15.64%	
Phenol hydroxylase	Phenol	426	0/426	0.00%	83/427	19.44%	AC
Secreted protein	Phenol	375		62.57%		13.22%	
Terpene synthase	Terpene	548		0.10%		24.63%	
Tubulin beta chain	Tubulin	444		70.65%		15.28%	
Tubulin alpha chain	Tubulin	449		5.58%		26.54%	
Plant: Clinacanthus nutans [233, 234]							
Acetyl -coenzyme A carboxy	Acetyl	490		29.65%		11.72%	
ATP synthase subunit beta	Synthase	498		19.28%		9.43%	AC
ATP synthase subunit C, chloro	Synthase	81		86.25%		23.19%	
ATP-dep Clp protease	Protease	196		69.74%		18.48%	
Cytochrome c biogen pro CcsA	Heme	320		1.25%		18.38%	AC
DNA direc RNA polymerase	Trans Fac	337		73.51%		12.00%	
NAD(P)H-quinone oxidor, chlor	Plastoqui	213		44.81%		5.47%	
NADH dehydrogenase subun 4	Plastoqui	484		17.15%		5.37%	AC
Ribulose biphosphate	Lyase	485		78.72%		15.64%	
Plant: Curriculum longa [235–237]							
Atp dep Clp protease	Protease	205	39/205	19.02%	17/205	8.29%	AC
Beta tubulin	Tubulin	88		89.77%		58.44%	
Curcumin synthase 1	Synthase	389	12/389	3.08%	29/389	7.45%	AC
Curcumin synthase 2	Synthase	391	15/391	3.83%	38/391	9.71%	AC
Curcumin synthase 3	Synthase	390		81.23%		30.69%	
DNA directed RNA polymerase	Trans Fac	343	47/343	13.70%	38/343	11.08%	AC
Mannose bind lectin	Lectin	192		87.43%		13.89%	
NADH-plastoquinone oxidored	Plastoqui	470		4.90%		16.80%	AC
Phenylalanine ammo lyase	Lyase	389		88.17%		46.03%	
Plant: Ginseng [238, 239, 297]							
Acetyl coenzyme	Acetyl	487	4/487	0.82%	82/497	16.84%	AC
Actin	Actin	367		10.90%		27.25%	
Beta-amyrin synthase 1	Synthase	141	19/141	13.47%	8/141	5.70%	AC
Betaine aldehyde dehydrogene	Aldehyde	490		86.71%		36.61%	
Chitinese	Glycoside	298		79.80%		16.78%	
Cytochrome 450 CYP82H23	Heme	245		78.28%		35.62%	
Glyceraldehyde-3-phos dehydr	Glycerald	336		69.25%		8.33%	
Interleukin-6	Kinase	212		36.97%		12.00%	
Lectin	Lectin	432		58.70%		2.86%	
Peroxidase	Lignin	354		28.90%		7.89%	
Phenol degradation prot meta	Phenol	299		87.92%		36.24%	
UDP-glucosyltransferase	Glycosylt	442	13/442	2.94%	56/442	12.67%	AC
Plant: Momordica charantia [165, 240]							
Aldehyde dehydrogenase	Aldehyde	478		83.86%		38.63%	

(continued)

Table 5.43 (continued)

Protein	BAC	AA count	Cnt of (–ive) = 0	Criteria PCr1	Cnt of v8 = 0	Criteria PCr2	Prediction Result
Chalcone-flavo iso family prot	Flavonone	279		48.20%		2.62%	
Chitanese	Glycoside	300		80.60%		27.78%	
Dirigent protein	Alkaloids	246	26/246	10.57%	15/246	6.09%	AC
Glycosyltransferase	Glycosyltr	486		72.31%		14.16%	
Multi myeloma tumor-ass prot	tum prot	244	45/244	18.44%	17/244	6.97%	AC
Peroxidase	Heme	324		89.78%		23.40%	
Profilin	Actin	133	0/133	0.00%	22/132	16.67%	AC
Translationally-cont tum prot	tum prot	168		25.75%		6.41%	
Tubulinbeta chain	Tubulin	452	52/452	10.50%	19/452	4.20%	AC
Plant: Moringa oleifera [241, 242, 298]							
2S Albumint	Lectin	163		33.95%		0.00%	
Actin	Actin	283		1.06%		33.24%	
ATP synthase sub beta chloro	Synthase	498		34.00%		1.65%	
Beta tubulin	Tubulin	81	0/81	0.00%	11/81	13.25%	AC
Glyceraldehyde-3-phos dehydr	Aldehyde	80		65.82%		23.59%	
NAD(P)H-quinone oxire chloro	Plastoqui	393		73.47%		16.01%	
Plant: Neolamarckia cadamba [246, 247]							
ATP-dep Clp protease pr subu	Protease	196		85.13%		40.22%	
Cellulose synthase	Tran Fact	242		14.05%		8.23%	AC
Glyceraldehyde-3-phos dehydr	Glycerald	399		41.46%		2.58%	
Phosphoglycerate kinase	Kinase	401		90.50%		33.68%	
S-adenosy decarbo proenzyme	Lyase	360		52.09%		12.36%	
Tubulin alpha chain	Tubulin	451		81.33%		27.11%	
Plant: Nigella sativa [243, 244, 299–302]							
Acetyl-CoA acetyltran chlo	Acetyl	401		74.25%		22.11%	
Alcohol dehydro like, zinc-typ	Aldehyde	360		88.30%		21.84%	
CYC-like protein	Tran Fact	112		100.00%		33.66%	
Glycosyltransferase-like prot	Glycosyltr	345		20.00%		12.28%	
Mevalonate kinase	Kinase	388		62.02%		8.04%	
Monoterpene synthase	Synthase	145		63.45%		23.88%	
NAD(P)H-quinone oxidoredu	Plastoqui	542		30.07%		8.29%	
Phenylalanine ammonia-lyase	Lyase	708		11.60%		22.70%	AC
Squalene monooxygenase	Saponin	521		85.38%		27.31%	
Terpene cyclasemutase fami	Terpene	761		54.74%		16.69%	
Plant: Taxus chinensis [226–228]							
10-deacet III-10-O-acet transfer	Acetyl	440		68.56%		10.75%	
ATP-dependent Clp protease	Protease	375	42/376	11.17%	16/375	4.25%	AC
CYP77F31 (lkaloid/taxol bios)	Flavonoid	508		71.79%		14.11%	
phenylalanind ammo lyase	Lyase	399	3/399	0.75%	42/399	10.27%	AC
Taxadiene 5-alpha hydroxylas	Taxadiene	499		34.74%		2.26%	
Taxadiene synthase	Taxadiene	343		5.26%		29.91%	

5.6.9 Conclusion

Medicinal plants are equipped with the metabolites referred to as Secondary Metabolites (SM) to protect them against environmental stress including deterrent against predators. This property of the plant kingdom opens up a new vista for discovery of therapeutic agents for treatment of human diseases. Consequently, from the middle of last century, medicinal chemists have concentrated their search for plant derived 'green' drugs to treat various diseases including cancer. However, derivation of plant-derived therapeutic agents is an upheaval task in terms of time and cost. Availability of low volume of relevant plant-extracts for laboratory experiments is also a major bottleneck. In this background, this section employs CAML model to investigate whether a given medicinal plant has Anti-Cancer (AC) property or not. The AC therapeutic agent can be derived from plant proteins through their interaction with Bio-Active Compounds (BACs) and other biomolecules. We employ the conventional approach of Machine Learning (ML) for learning the property of known AC plants (marked as Training Set (TrS) and Validation Ser (VaS)), followed by mapping of such properties to CAML parameters. Traversing on this learning curve, we have designed the prediction algorithm. Prediction results, reported for Testing Set (TeS), have been checked against the in-vivo/in-vitro experimental results reported in published literature. The CAML model to predict AC property of a medicinal plant depends on the availability of plant proteins (in protein databases). The proteins are curated from UniprotKB or NCBI databases through Level 2 search, as noted under ESU1 (Experimental Set Up 1) reported in Sect. 5.6.5) with Bio-Active Compounds (BAC) reported in Table 5.33. The CAML model reported in this chapter enables the researchers to enlarge the database of Anti-Cancer (AC) Medicinal Plants. The sole purpose of the current Section is to report a model that can be employed to identify Anti-cancer (AC) medicinal plants in significantly reduced time and cost. The results derived out of this model can be next tested at molecular level through laboratory experiments on cancer lines.

References

1. B.J. Ainscough, M. Griffith, A.C. Coffman, A.H. Wagner, J. Kunisaki, M.N. Choudhary, J.F. McMichael, R.S. Fulton, R.K. Wilson, O.L. Griffith et al., Docm: a database of curated mutations in cancer. Nat. Methods **13**(10), 806–807 (2016)
2. M.J. Roossinck, E.R. Bazán, Symbiosis: viruses as intimate partners. Ann. Rev. Virol. **4**, 123–139 (2017)
3. S. Yamamoto, M. Saito, A. Tamura, D. Prawisuda, T. Mizutani, H. Yotsuyanagi, The human microbiome and covid-19: a systematic review. PloS one **16**(6), e0253293 (2021)
4. Uniprotkb. [Online]. Available: https://www.uniprot.org/
5. National center for biotechnology information (ncbi). [Online]. Available: https://www.ncbi.nlm.nih.gov/
6. E. Petersen, M. Koopmans, U. Go, D.H. Hamer, N. Petrosillo, F. Castelli, M. Storgaard, S. Al Khalili, L. Simonsen, Comparing sars-cov-2 with sars-cov and influenza pandemics. Lancet Infect. Dis. **20**(9), e238–e244 (2020)

7. M. Zheng, R. Karki, E.P. Williams, D. Yang, E. Fitzpatrick, P. Vogel, C.B. Jonsson, T.-D. Kanneganti, Tlr2 senses the sars-cov-2 envelope protein to produce inflammatory cytokines. Nat. Immunol. **22**(7), 829–838 (2021)
8. D. Cabrera-Garcia, R. Bekdash, G.W. Abbott, M. Yazawa, N.L. Harrison, The envelope protein of sars-cov-2 increases intra-golgi ph and forms a cation channel that is regulated by ph. J. Physiol. **599**(11), 2851–2868 (2021)
9. J.R. Cohen, L.D. Lin, C.E. Machamer, Identification of a golgi complex-targeting signal in the cytoplasmic tail of the severe acute respiratory syndrome coronavirus envelope protein. J. Virol. **85**(12), 5794–5803 (2011)
10. D. Schoeman, B.C. Fielding, Coronavirus envelope protein: current knowledge. Virol. J. **16**, 1–22 (2019)
11. J.W. Westerbeck, C.E. Machamer, The infectious bronchitis coronavirus envelope protein alters golgi ph to protect the spike protein and promote the release of infectious virus. J. Virol. **93**(11), e00 015–e00 019 (2019)
12. B.K. Kumar, A. Rohit, K.S. Prithvisagar, P. Rai, I. Karunasagar, I. Karunasagar, Deletion in the c-terminal region of the envelope glycoprotein in some of the indian sars-cov-2 genome. Virus Res. **291**, 198222 (2021)
13. Z. Shen, G. Zhang, Y. Yang, M. Li, S. Yang, G. Peng, Lysine 164 is critical for sars-cov-2 nsp1 inhibition of host gene expression. J. General Virol. **102**(1) (2021)
14. K. Schubert, E.D. Karousis, A. Jomaa, A. Scaiola, B. Echeverria, L.-A. Gurzeler, M. Leibundgut, V. Thiel, O. Mühlemann, N. Ban, Sars-cov-2 nsp1 binds the ribosomal mrna channel to inhibit translation. Nat. Struct. Mole. Biol. **27**(10), 959–966 (2020)
15. K. Nakagawa, S. Makino, Mechanisms of coronavirus nsp1-mediated control of host and viral gene expression. Cells **10**(2), 300 (2021)
16. M. Simeoni, T. Cavinato, D. Rodriguez, D. Gatfield, I (nsp1)ecting sars-cov-2-ribosome interactions. Commun. Biol. **4**(1), 1–5 (2021)
17. Y. Terada, K. Kawachi, Y. Matsuura, W. Kamitani, Mers coronavirus nsp1 participates in an efficient propagation through a specific interaction with viral rna. Virology **511**, 95–105 (2017)
18. F. Benedetti, G.A. Snyder, M. Giovanetti, S. Angeletti, R.C. Gallo, M. Ciccozzi, D. Zella, Emerging of a sars-cov-2 viral strain with a deletion in nsp1. J. Transl. Med. **18**(329), 1–6 (2020)
19. L.K. Clark, T.J. Green, C.M. Petit, Structure of nonstructural protein 1 from sars-cov-2. J. Virol. **95**(4), e02 019–20 (2021)
20. A. Kumar, A. Kumar, P. Kumar, N. Garg, R. Giri, Sars-cov-2 nsp1 c-terminal region (residues 130–180) is an intrinsically disordered region. BioRxiv (2020)
21. A. Tidu, A. Janvier, L. Schaeffer, P. Sosnowski, L. Kuhn, P. Hammann, E. Westhof, G. Eriani, F. Martin, The viral protein nsp1 acts as a ribosome gatekeeper for shutting down host translation and fostering sars-cov-2 translation. RNA **27**(3), 253–264 (2021)
22. N. Vankadari, N.N. Jeyasankar, W.J. Lopes, Structure of the sars-cov-2 nsp1/5'-untranslated region complex and implications for potential therapeutic targets, a vaccine, and virulence. J. Phys. Chem. Lett. **11**(22), 9659–9668 (2020)
23. S. de Breyne, C. Vindry, O. Guillin, L. Condé, F. Mure, H. Gruffat, L. Chavatte, T. Ohlmann, Translational control of coronaviruses. Nucleic Acids Res. **48**(22), 12 502–12 522 (2020)
24. Z. Miao, A. Tidu, G. Eriani, F. Martin, Secondary structure of the sars-cov-2 5'-utr. RNA Biol. **18**(4), 447–456 (2021)
25. T. Tanaka, W. Kamitani, M.L. DeDiego, L. Enjuanes, Y. Matsuura, Severe acute respiratory syndrome coronavirus nsp1 facilitates efficient propagation in cells through a specific translational shutoff of host mrna. J. Virol. **86**(20), 11 128–11 137 (2012)
26. D. Yang, J.L. Leibowitz, The structure and functions of coronavirus genomic 3' and 5' ends. Virus Res. **206**, 120–133 (2015)
27. M. Mohammadi-Dehcheshmeh, S.M. Moghbeli, S. Rahimirad, I.O. Alanazi, Z.S.A. Shehri, E. Ebrahimie, A transcription regulatory sequence in the 5' untranslated region of sars-cov-2 is vital for virus replication with an altered evolutionary pattern against human inhibitory micrornas. Cells **10**(2), 319 (2021)

28. M. Kikkert, Innate immune evasion by human respiratory rna viruses. J. Innate Immun. **12**(1), 4–20 (2020)
29. M. Thoms, R. Buschauer, M. Ameismeier, L. Koepke, T. Denk, M. Hirschenberger, H. Kratzat, M. Hayn, T. Mackens-Kiani, J. Cheng et al., Structural basis for translational shutdown and immune evasion by the nsp1 protein of sars-cov-2. Science **369**, 1249–1255 (2020)
30. N. Taefehshokr, S. Taefehshokr, N. Hemmat, B. Heit, Covid-19: perspectives on innate immune evasion. Front. Immunol. 580641 (2020)
31. K.G. Lokugamage, K. Narayanan, K. Nakagawa, K. Terasaki, S.I. Ramirez, C.-T.K. Tseng, S. Makino, Middle east respiratory syndrome coronavirus nsp1 inhibits host gene expression by selectively targeting mrnas transcribed in the nucleus while sparing mrnas of cytoplasmic origin. J. Virol. **89**(21), 10 970–10 981 (2015)
32. M. Seyran et al., The structural basis of accelerated host cell entry by sars-cov-2. *FEBS J.* **288**, 5010–5020, 9 (2021)
33. F. Li, Structure, function, and evolution of coronavirus spike proteins. Ann. Rev. Virol. **3**(1), 237–261 (2016)
34. G.R. Whittaker, S. Daniel, J.K. Millet, Coronavirus entry: how we arrived at sars-cov-2. Curr. Opin. Virol. **47**, 113–120, 4 (2021)
35. X. Xia, Domains and functions of spike protein in sars-cov-2 in the context of vaccine design. (1) (2021)
36. J. Lan, J. Ge, J. Yu, S. Shan, H. Zhou, S. Fan, Q. Zhang, X. Shi, Q. Wang, L. Zhang, X. Wang, Structure of the sars-cov-2 spike receptor-binding domain bound to the ace2 receptor. Nature **581**, 215–220, 5 (2020)
37. P. Arora, C. Rocha, A. Kempf, I. Nehlmeier, L. Graichen, M.S. Winkler, M. Lier, S. Schulz, H.M. Jäck, A. Cossmann, M.V. Stankov, G.M. Behrens, S.Pöhlmann, M. Hoffmann, The spike protein of sars-cov-2 variant a.30 is heavily mutated and evades vaccine-induced antibodies with high efficiency. Cell. Mole. Immunol. **18**, 2673–2675, 12 (2021)
38. B. Schrörs, P. Riesgo-Ferreiro, P. Sorn, R. Gudimella, T. Bukur, T. Rösler, M. Löwer, U. Sahin, Large-scale analysis of sars-cov-2 spike-glycoprotein mutants demonstrates the need for continuous screening of virus isolates. PLoS ONE **16**, 9 (2021)
39. A.J. Greaney et al., Complete mapping of mutations to the sars-cov-2 spike receptor-binding domain that escape antibody recognition. Cell Host Microbe **29**, 44–57.e9, 1 (2021)
40. C.H.S. da Costa, C.A.B. de Freitas, C.N. Alves, J. Lameira, Assessment of mutations on rbd in the spike protein of sars-cov-2 alpha, delta and omicron variants. Sci. Rep. **12**, 12 (2022)
41. Z. Zhang, J. Zhang, J. Wang, Surface charge changes in spike rbd mutations of sars-cov-2 and its variant strains alter the virus evasiveness via hspgs: a review and mechanistic hypothesis. Front. Public Health **10**, 952916, 8 (2022)
42. C. Yi, X. Sun, J. Ye, L. Ding, M. Liu, Z. Yang, X. Lu, Y. Zhang, L. Ma, W. Gu, A. Qu, J. Xu, Z. Shi, Z. Ling, B. Sun, Key residues of the receptor binding motif in the spike protein of sars-cov-2 that interact with ace2 and neutralizing antibodies. Cell. Mole. Immunol. **17**, 621–630, 6 (2020)
43. N.P. Hachmann, J. Miller, A. ris Y. Collier, D.H. Barouch, Neutralization escape by sars-cov-2 omicron subvariant ba.4.6. New England J. Med. **387**, 1904–1906, 11 (2022)
44. A.S. Peter, E. Grüner, E. Socher, K. Fraedrich, E. Richel, S. Mueller-Schmucker, A. Cordsmeier, A. Ensser, H. Sticht, K. Überla, Characterization of sars-cov-2 escape mutants to a pair of neutralizing antibodies targeting the rbd and the ntd. Int. J. Mole. Sci. **23**, 8 (2022)
45. ABP News Bureau, BF.7 Omicron variant: An Omicron subvariant, BF.7 is highly transmissible. It is derived from the BA.5 subvariant, and is the short term for BA.5.2.1.7. It is responsible for China's COVID surge, 2022. [Online]. Available: https://www.abplive.com/news/bf-7-omicron-variant-an-omicron-subvariant-bf-7-is-highly-transmissible-1570981
46. J. Shang, Y. Wan, C. Luo, G. Ye, Q. Geng, A. Auerbach, F. Li, Cell entry mechanisms of sars-cov-2. **117**, 11 727–11 734 (2020). [Online]. Available: www.pnas.org/cgi/doi/10.1073/pnas.2003138117
47. T. Tang, M. Bidon, J.A. Jaimes, G.R. Whittaker, S. Daniel, Coronavirus membrane fusion mechanism offers a potential target for antiviral development. Antiviral Res. **178**, 6 (2020)

48. Q. Zhang, R. Xiang, S. Huo, Y. Zhou, S. Jiang, Q. Wang, F. Yu, Molecular mechanism of interaction between sars-cov-2 and host cells and interventional therapy. Signal Transduct. Targeted Ther. **6**, 12 (2021)
49. C.B. Jackson, M. Farzan, B. Chen, H. Choe, Mechanisms of sars-cov-2 entry into cells. Nat. Rev. Mole. Cell Biol. **23**, 3–20, 1 (2022)
50. N. Wang, X. Shi, L. Jiang, S. Zhang, D. Wang, P. Tong, D. Guo, L. Fu, Y. Cui, X. Liu, K. C. Arledge, Y.H. Chen, L. Zhang, X. Wang, Structure of mers-cov spike receptor-binding domain complexed with human receptor dpp4. Cell Res. **23**, 986–993, 8 (2013)
51. S. Khare, M. Azevedo, P. Parajuli, K. Gokulan, Conformational changes of the receptor binding domain of sars-cov-2 spike protein and prediction of a b-cell antigenic epitope using structural data. Front. Artif. Intell. **4**, 3 (2021)
52. W. Tai, L. He, X. Zhang, J. Pu, D. Voronin, S. Jiang, Y. Zhou, L. Du, Characterization of the receptor-binding domain (rbd) of 2019 novel coronavirus: implication for development of rbd protein as a viral attachment inhibitor and vaccine. Cell. Mole. Immunol. **17**, 613–620, 6 (2020)
53. G.A. Rossi, O. Sacco, E. Mancino, L. Cristiani, F. Midulla, Differences and similarities between sars-cov and sars-cov-2: spike receptor-binding domain recognition and host cell infection with support of cellular serine proteases. Infection **48**, 665–669, 10 (2020)
54. H. Mou, V.S. Raj, F.J.M. van Kuppeveld, P.J.M. Rottier, B.L. Haagmans, B.J. Bosch, The receptor binding domain of the new middle east respiratory syndrome coronavirus maps to a 231-residue region in the spike protein that efficiently elicits neutralizing antibodies. J. Virol. **87**, 9379–9383, 8 (2013)
55. J. Verma, N. Subbarao, A comparative study of human betacoronavirus spike proteins: structure, function and therapeutics. Arch. Virol. **166**, 697–714, 3 (2021)
56. D. Bojkova, J.E. McGreig, K.M. McLaughlin, S.G. Masterson, M. Antczak, M. Widera, V.K. Hling, S. Ciesek, M.N. Wass, M. Michaelis, J. Cinatl, Differentially conserved amino acid positions may reflect differences in sars-cov-2 and sars-cov behaviour. Bioinformatics **37**, 2282–2288, 8 (2021)
57. D. Ray, L. Le, I. Andricioaei, Distant residues modulate conformational opening in sars-cov-2 spike protein. Biophys. Comput. Biol. **118**, 1–11 (2021). [Online]. Available: https://doi.org/10.1073/pnas.2100943118
58. W.H. Organization, Tracking sars-cov-2 variants. [Online]. Available: https://www.who.int/activities/tracking-SARS-CoV-2-variants
59. O. Ashwaq, P. Manickavasagam, M. Haque, V483a-an emerging mutation hotspot of sars-cov-2, 2020. [Online]. Available: www.preprints.org
60. W.Y. Ching, P. Adhikari, B. Jawad, R. Podgornik, Effect of delta and omicron mutations on the rbd-sd1 domain of the spike protein in sars-cov-2 and the omicron mutations on rbd-ace2 interface complex. Int. J. Mole. Sci. **23**, 9 (2022)
61. Y. Guo, J. Han, Y. Zhang, J. He, W. Yu, X. Zhang, J. Wu, S. Zhang, Y. Kong, Y. Guo, Y. Lin, J. Zhang, Sars-cov-2 omicron variant: Epidemiological features, biological characteristics, and clinical significance. Front. Immunol. **13**, 4 (2022)
62. I.F. Urdaniz, P.J. Steiner, M.B. Kirby, F. Zhao, C.M. Haas, S. Barman, E.R. Rhodes, L. Peng, K.G. Sprenger, J.G. Jardine, T.A. Whitehead, One-shot identification of sars-cov-2 s rbd escape mutants using yeast screening (2021). [Online]. Available: https://doi.org/10.1101/2021.03.15.435309
63. Y. Sixto-López, J. Correa-Basurto, M. Bello, B. Landeros-Rivera, J.A. Garzón-Tiznado, S. Montaño, Structural insights into sars-cov-2 spike protein and its natural mutants found in mexican population. Sci. Rep. **11**, 12 (2021)
64. P. Du, G.F. Gao, Q. Wang, The mysterious origins of the omicron variant of sars-cov-2. Innovation **3**(2) (2022)
65. Y. Sun, W. Lin, W. Dong, J. Xu, Origin and evolutionary analysis of the sars-cov-2 omicron variant. J. Biosaf. Biosecurity **4**(1), 33–37 (2022)
66. R.S. Mahla, L.B. Dustin, Searching for escape-resistant anti-sars-cov-2 neutralizing antibodies. J. Clin. Invest. **132**, 2 (2022)

67. L.-F. Wang et al., Differential escape of neutralizing antibodies by sars-cov-2 omicron and pre-emergent sarbecoviruses. Res. Square **2** (2022). [Online]. Available: http://www.ncbi.nlm.nih.gov/pubmed/35233568 http://www.pubmedcentral.nih.gov/articlerender.fcgi?artid=PMC8887082
68. A. Tuekprakhon et al., Antibody escape of sars-cov-2 omicron ba.4 and ba.5 from vaccine and ba.1 serum. Cell **185**, 2422–2433.e13, 7 (2022)
69. D. Focosi, F. Maggi, Neutralising antibody escape of sars-cov-2 spike protein: Risk assessment for antibody-based covid-19 therapeutics and vaccines. Rev. Med. Virol. **31**, 11 (2021)
70. W. Dejnirattisai et al., Sars-cov-2 omicron-b.1.1.529 leads to widespread escape from neutralizing antibody responses. Cell **185**, 467–484.e15, 2 (2022)
71. V.V. Edara, W.H. Hudson, X. Xie, R. Ahmed, M.S. Suthar, Neutralizing antibodies against sars-cov-2 variants after infection and vaccination. JAMA—J. Am. Med. Assoc. **325**, 1896–1898, 5 (2021)
72. M. Alenquer, F. Ferreira, D. Lousa, M. Valério, M. Medina-Lopes, M.L. Bergman, J. Gonçalves, J. Demengeot, R.B. Leite, J. Lilue, Z. Ning, C. Penha-Gonçalves, H. Soares, C.M. Soares, M.J. Amorim, Signatures in sars-cov-2 spike protein conferring escape to neutralizing antibodies. PLoS Pathog. **17**, 8 (2021)
73. E. Andreano, G. Piccini, D. Licastro, L. Casalino, N.V. Johnson, I. Paciello, S. Dal Monego, E. Pantano, N. Manganaro, A. Manenti, R. Manna, E. Casa, I. Hyseni, L. Benincasa, E. Montomoli, R.E. Amaro, J.S. McLellan, R. Rappuoli, Sars-cov-2 escape from a highly neutralizing covid-19 convalescent plasma. Proc. Natl. Acad. Sci. **118**(36), e2103154118 (2021)
74. World Health Organization, *Imagining the Future of Pandemics and Epidemics: A 2022 Perspective* (World Health Organization, Geneva, 2022)
75. N.M. Vora, L. Hannah, S. Lieberman, M.M. Vale, R.K. Plowright, A.S. Bernstein, Want to prevent pandemics? stop spillovers. Nature **605**, 419–422, 5 (2022). [Online]. Available: https://www.nature.com/articles/d41586-022-01312-y
76. D. Sridhar, Pandemic preparedness outlook: learn from past pandemics. Nature **610**, (2022). COVID-19 shows us how we should prepare for future outbreaks to mount a stronger response
77. S. Makin, Predicting a pandemic: machine learning could help to identify the viruses most likely to spill over from animals to people and cause future pandemics. Outlook **610** (2022)
78. L. Jiang, The discovery of p53 protein," Arizona State University. School of Life Sciences. Center for Biology and ..., Technical Report (2011)
79. C.C. Harris, p53 tumor suppressor gene: from the basic research laboratory to the clinic-an abridged historical perspective. Carcinogenesls **17**(6), 1187–1196 (1996)
80. B. Vogelstein, S. Sur, C. Prives, p53: the most frequently altered gene in human cancers. Nat. Educ. **3**(9), 6 (2010)
81. D. Linzer, The levine laboratory and the discovery of p53. J. Mole. Cell Biol. **11**(7), 534–535 (2019)
82. A.J. Levine, p53: 800 million years of evolution and 40 years of discovery. Nat. Rev. Cancer **20**(8), 471–480 (2020)
83. M. Olivier, A. Petitjean, V. Marcel, A. Petre, M. Mounawar, A. Plymoth, C. De Fromentel, P. Hainaut, Recent advances in p53 research: an interdisciplinary perspective. Cancer Gene Ther. **16**(1), 1–12 (2009)
84. C.L. Brooks, W. Gu, New insights into p53 activation. Cell Res. **20**(6), 614–621 (2010)
85. M. Olivier, M. Hollstein, P. Hainaut, Tp53 mutations in human cancers: origins, consequences, and clinical use. Cold Spring Harbor perspect. Biol. **2**(1), a001008 (2010)
86. S. Di Agostino, G. Fontemaggi, S. Strano, G. Blandino, G. D'Orazi, Targeting mutant p53 in cancer: the latest insights. J. Exp. Clin. Cancer Res. **38**, 1–3 (2019)
87. M. Oren, p53: not just a tumor suppressor. J. Mole. Cell Biol. **11**(7), 539–543 (2019)
88. P. Monti, P. Menichini, A. Speciale, G. Cutrona, F. Fais, E. Taiana, A. Neri, R. Bomben, M. Gentile, V. Gattei et al., Heterogeneity of tp53 mutations and p53 protein residual function in cancer: does it matter? Front. Oncol. **10**, 593383 (2020)
89. A.B. Williams, B. Schumacher, p53 in the dna-damage-repair process. Cold Spring Harbor Perspect. Med. **6**(5), a026070 (2016)

90. A. Carnero, J.D. Hudson, G.J. Hannon, D.H. Beach, Loss-of-function genetics in mammalian cells: the p53 tumor suppressor model. Nucleic Acids Res. **28**(11), 2234–2241 (2000)
91. A. Diaz-Lagares, A.B. Crujeiras, P. Lopez-Serra, M. Soler, F. Setien, A. Goyal, J. Sandoval, Y. Hashimoto, A. Martinez-Cardús, A. Gomez et al., Epigenetic inactivation of the p53-induced long noncoding rna tp53 target 1 in human cancer. Proc. Natl. Acad. Sci. **113**(47), E7535–E7544 (2016)
92. B.J. Aubrey, G.L. Kelly, A. Janic, M.J. Herold, A. Strasser, How does p53 induce apoptosis and how does this relate to p53-mediated tumour suppression? Cell Death Differ. **25**(1), 104–113 (2018)
93. G. Stracquadanio, X. Wang, M.D. Wallace, A.M. Grawenda, P. Zhang, J. Hewitt, J. Zeron-Medina, F. Castro-Giner, I.P. Tomlinson, C.R. Goding et al., The importance of p53 pathway genetics in inherited and somatic cancer genomes. Nat. Rev. Cancer **16**(4), 251–265 (2016)
94. I. Amelio, G. Melino, Context is everything: extrinsic signalling and gain-of-function p53 mutants. Cell Death Discov. **6**(1), 16 (2020)
95. Y. Shi, E. Norberg, H. Vakifahmetoglu-Norberg, Mutant p53 as a regulator and target of autophagy. Front. Oncol. **10**, 607149 (2021)
96. Y. Lazebnik, What are the hallmarks of cancer? Nat. Rev. Cancer **10**(4), 232–233 (2010)
97. C. Sonnenschein, A.M. Soto, The aging of the 2000 and 2011 hallmarks of cancer reviews: a critique. J. Biosci. **38**, 651–663 (2013)
98. D. Hanahan, R.A. Weinberg, Hallmarks of cancer: the next generation. Cell **144**(5), 646–674 (2011)
99. W. Contributors, The hallmarks of cancer. [Online]. Available: https://en.wikipedia.org/wiki/The_Hallmarks_of_Cancer
100. A. Hamilton, D. Larsimont, R. Paridaens, M. Drijkoningen, M. Van de Vijver, P. Bruning, A. Hanby, S. Houston, I. Treilleux, J.P. Guastalla et al., A study of the value of p53, her2, and bcl-2 in the prediction of response to doxorubicin and paclitaxel as single agents in metastatic breast cancer: a companion study to eortc 10923. Clin. Breast Cancer **1**(3), 233–240 (2000)
101. T.P. Berke, S.H. Slight, S.M. Hyder, Role of reactivating mutant p53 protein in suppressing growth and metastasis of triple-negative breast cancer. Onco Targets Ther. 23–30 (2022)
102. M. Molica, C. Mazzone, P. Niscola, P. De Fabritiis, Tp53 mutations in acute myeloid leukemia: still a daunting challenge? Front. Oncol. **10**, 610820 (2021)
103. C.L. Benjamin, H.N. Ananthaswamy, p53 and the pathogenesis of skin cancer. Toxicol. Appl. Pharmacol. **224**(3), 241–248 (2007)
104. T. Zhang, Y. Li, R. Zhu, P. Song, Y. Wei, T. Liang, G. Xu, Transcription factor p53 suppresses tumor growth by prompting pyroptosis in non-small-cell lung cancer. Oxidative Med. Cell. Longevity **2019**(1), 8746895 (2019)
105. H.E. Marei, A. Althani, N. Afifi, A. Hasan, T. Caceci, G. Pozzoli, A. Morrione, A. Giordano, C. Cenciarelli, p53 signaling in cancer progression and therapy. Cancer Cell Int. **21**(1), 703 (2021)
106. G.L. Beatty, W.L. Gladney, Immune escape mechanisms as a guide for cancer immunotherapy. Clin. Cancer Res. **21**(4), 687–692 (2015)
107. D. Benharroch, L. Osyntsov, Infectious diseases are analogous with cancer hypothesis and implications. J. Cancer **3**, 117 (2012)
108. L.K. Vandamme, I.H. de Hingh, J. Fonseca, P.R. Rocha, Similarities between pandemics and cancer in growth and risk models. Sci. Rep. **11**(1), 349 (2021)
109. Y. Li, Y. Zhang, X. Li, S. Yi, J. Xu, Gain-of-function mutations: an emerging advantage for cancer biology. Trends Biochem. Sci. **44**(8), 659–674 (2019)
110. H. Wang, M. Guo, H. Wei, Y. Chen, Targeting p53 pathways: mechanisms, structures, and advances in therapy. Signal Transduct. Targeted Ther. **8**(1), 92 (2023)
111. Y. Wang, M. Reed, P. Wang, J.E. Stenger, G. Mayr, M.E. Anderson, J.F. Schwedes, P. Tegtmeyer, p53 domains: identification and characterization of two autonomous dna-binding regions. Genes Dev. **7**(12b), 2575–2586 (1993)

112. M. Liu, L.T. Watson, L. Zhang, Classification of mutations by functional impact type: Gain of function, loss of function, and switch of function, in *Bioinformatics Research and Applications: 10th International Symposium*, ISBRA, Zhangjiajie, China, June 28–30, 2014. Proceedings 10 (Springer, 2014), pp. 236–242
113. N. Sobhani, A. D'angelo, X. Wang, K.H. Young, D. Generali, Y. Li, Mutant p53 as an antigen in cancer immunotherapy. Int. J. Mole. Sci. **21**(11), 4087 (2020)
114. J. Blagih, M.D. Buck, K.H. Vousden, p53, cancer and the immune response. J. Cell Sci. **133**(5), jcs237453 (2020)
115. M. Ghosh, S. Saha, J. Bettke, R. Nagar, A. Parrales, T. Iwakuma, A.W. van der Velden, L.A. Martinez, Mutant p53 suppresses innate immune signaling to promote tumorigenesis. Cancer Cell **39**(4), 494–508 (2021)
116. H. Li, J. Zhang, J.H.M. Tong, A.W.H. Chan, J. Yu, W. Kang, K.F. To, Targeting the oncogenic p53 mutants in colorectal cancer and other solid tumors. Int. J. Mole. Sci. **20**(23), 5999 (2019)
117. P. Hainaut, K. Mann, Zinc binding and redox control of p53 structure and function. Antioxid. Redox Signal. **3**(4), 611–623 (2001)
118. P.A. Muller, K.H. Vousden, Mutant p53 in cancer: new functions and therapeutic opportunities. Cancer Cell **25**(3), 304–317 (2014)
119. M.G. Lepre, S.I. Omar, G. Grasso, U. Morbiducci, M.A. Deriu, J.A. Tuszynski, Insights into the effect of the g245s single point mutation on the structure of p53 and the binding of the protein to dna. Molecules **22**(8), 1358 (2017)
120. L.J. Warnock, S.A. Raines, J. Milner, Aurora a mediates cross-talk between n-and c-terminal post-translational modifications of p53. Cancer Biol. Ther. **12**(12), 1059–1068 (2011)
121. T. Shukuya, S. Patel, K. Shane-Carson, K. He, E.M. Bertino, K. Shilo, G.A. Otterson, D.P. Carbone, Lung cancer patients with germline mutations detected by next-generation sequencing and/or liquid biopsy. J. Thoracic Oncol. **13**(2), e17–e19 (2018)
122. J.D. Wright, S.Y. Noskov, C. Lim, Factors governing loss and rescue of dna binding upon single and double mutations in the p53 core domain. Nucleic Acids Res. **30**(7), 1563–1574 (2002)
123. C. Grill, K. Bergsteinsdóttir, M.H. Ögmundsdóttir, V. Pogenberg, A. Schepsky, M. Wilmanns, V. Pingault, E. Steingrímsson, Mitf mutations associated with pigment deficiency syndromes and melanoma have different effects on protein function. Human Mole. Genet. **22**(21), 4357–4367 (2013)
124. J.J. McCann, I.A. Vasilevskaya, C. McNair, P. Gallagher, N.P. Neupane, R. de Leeuw, A.A. Shafi, E. Dylgjeri, A.C. Mandigo, M.J. Schiewer et al., Mutant p53 elicits context-dependent pro-tumorigenic phenotypes. Oncogene **41**(3), 444–458 (2022)
125. Y. Tang, H. Song, Z. Wang, S. Xiao, X. Xiang, H. Zhan, L. Wu, J. Wu, Y. Xing, Y. Tan et al., Repurposing antiparasitic antimonials to noncovalently rescue temperature-sensitive p53 mutations. Cell Rep. **39**(2) (2022)
126. J. Tang, W. Peng, Y. Feng, X. Le, K. Wang, Q. Xiang, L. Li, Y. Wang, C. Xu, J. Mu et al., Cancer cells escape p53's tumor suppression through ablation of zdhhc1-mediated p53 palmitoylation. Oncogene **40**(35), 5416–5426 (2021)
127. E.H. Baugh, H. Ke, A.J. Levine, R.A. Bonneau, C.S. Chan, Why are there hotspot mutations in the tp53 gene in human cancers? Cell Death Differ. **25**(1), 154–160 (2018)
128. T.-X. Xie, G. Zhou, M. Zhao, D. Sano, S.A. Jasser, R.G. Brennan, J.N. Myers, Serine substitution of proline at codon 151 of tp53 confers gain of function activity leading to anoikis resistance and tumor progression of head and neck cancer cells. Laryngoscope **123**(6), 1416–1423 (2013)
129. R. Kim, 'Cancer immunoediting: from immune surveillance to immune escape. Cancer Immunother. 9–27 (2007)
130. M.C. Kennedy, S.W. Lowe, Mutant p53: it's not all one and the same. Cell Death Differ. **29**(5), 983–987 (2022)
131. J. Zhao, A. Blayney, X. Liu, L. Gandy, W. Jin, L. Yan, J.-H. Ha, A.J. Canning, M. Connelly, C. Yang et al., Egcg binds intrinsically disordered n-terminal domain of p53 and disrupts p53-mdm2 interaction. Nat. Commun. **12**(1), 986 (2021)

132. F. Bao, P.R. LoVerso, J.N. Fisk, V.B. Zhurkin, F. Cui, p53 binding sites in normal and cancer cells are characterized by distinct chromatin context. Cell Cycle **16**(21), 2073–2085 (2017)
133. O. Degtjarik, D. Golovenko, Y. Diskin-Posner, L. Abrahmsén, H. Rozenberg, Z. Shakked, Structural basis of reactivation of oncogenic p53 mutants by a small molecule: methylene quinuclidinone (mq). Nat. Commun. **12**(1), 7057 (2021)
134. M. Tuna, Z. Ju, K. Yoshihara, C.I. Amos, J.L. Tanyi, G.B. Mills, Clinical relevance of tp53 hotspot mutations in high-grade serous ovarian cancers. Br. J. Cancer **122**(3), 405–412 (2020)
135. S. Ghosh, M. Bhattacharjee, N.K. Jana, Gene regulation by p53 in human cancer system. Asian Pac. J. Cancer Biol. **7**(1), 97–109 (2022)
136. E. Boutet, D. Lieberherr, M. Tognolli, M. Schneider, A. Bairoch, Uniprotkb/swiss-prot: the manually annotated section of the uniprot knowledgebase, in *Plant Bioinformatics: Methods and Protocols* (Springer, Berlin, 2007), pp. 89–112
137. M. Greenwell, P. Rahman, Medicinal plants: their use in anticancer treatment. Int. J. Pharm. Sci. Res. **6**(10), 4103 (2015)
138. T. Meštrović, Paclitaxel history. [Online]. Available: https://www.news-medical.net/health/Paclitaxel-History.aspx
139. C.A. Dehelean, I. Marcovici, C. Soica, M. Mioc, D. Coricovac, S. Iurciuc, O.M. Cretu, I. Pinzaru, Plant-derived anticancer compounds as new perspectives in drug discovery and alternative therapy. Molecules **26**(4), 1109 (2021)
140. A. Rudzińska, P. Juchaniuk, J. Oberda, J. Wiśniewska, W. Wojdan, K. Szklener, S. Mańdziuk, Phytochemicals in cancer treatment and cancer prevention-review on epidemiological data and clinical trials. Nutrients **15**(8), 1896 (2023)
141. S. Cirmi, A. Maugeri, N. Ferlazzo, S. Gangemi, G. Calapai, U. Schumacher, M. Navarra, Anticancer potential of citrus juices and their extracts: a systematic review of both preclinical and clinical studies. Front. Pharmacol. **8**, 420 (2017)
142. A.G. Atanasov, S.B. Zotchev, V.M. Dirsch, C.T. Supuran, Natural products in drug discovery: advances and opportunities. Nat. Rev. Drug Discov. **20**(3), 200–216 (2021)
143. A.G. Desai, G.N. Qazi, R.K. Ganju, M. El-Tamer, J. Singh, A.K. Saxena, Y.S. Bedi, S.C. Taneja, H.K. Bhat, Medicinal plants and cancer chemoprevention. Curr. Drug Metab. **9**(7), 581–591 (2008)
144. G.M. Cragg, D.J. Newman, Natural products: a continuing source of novel drug leads. Biochimica et Biophysica Acta (BBA)-General Subjects **1830**(6), 3670–3695 (2013)
145. H. Regassa, A. Sourirajan, V. Kumar, S. Pandey, D. Kumar, K. Dev, A review of medicinal plants of the himalayas with anti-proliferative activity for the treatment of various cancers. Cancers **14**(16), 3898 (2022)
146. R. Gahtori, A.H. Tripathi, A. Kumari, N. Negi, A. Paliwal, P. Tripathi, P. Joshi, R.C. Rai, S.K. Upadhyay, Anticancer plant-derivatives: deciphering their oncopreventive and therapeutic potential in molecular terms. Future J. Pharm. Sci. **9**(1), 14 (2023)
147. A. Lichota, K. Gwozdzinski, Anticancer activity of natural compounds from plant and marine environment. Int. J. Mole. Sci. **19**(11), 3533 (2018)
148. K. Mohanraj, B.S. Karthikeyan, R. Vivek-Ananth, R.B. Chand, S. Aparna, P. Mangalapandi, A. Samal, Imppat: a curated database of i ndian m edicinal p lants, p hytochemistry a nd t herapeutics. Sci. Rep. **8**(1), 4329 (2018)
149. Y.-Y. Siew, H.-C. Yew, S.-Y. Neo, S.-V. Seow, S.-M. Lew, S.-W. Lim, C.S.E.-S. Lim, Y.-C. Ng, W.-G. Seetoh, A. Ali et al., Evaluation of anti-proliferative activity of medicinal plants used in asian traditional medicine to treat cancer. J. Ethnopharmacol. **235**, 75–87 (2019)
150. J. Iqbal, B.A. Abbasi, T. Mahmood, S. Kanwal, B. Ali, S.A. Shah, A.T. Khalil, Plant-derived anticancer agents: a green anticancer approach. Asian Pac. J. Trop. Biomed. **7**(12), 1129–1150 (2017)
151. M. Shoeb, Anti-cancer agents from medicinal plants. Bangladesh J. Pharmacol. **1**(2), 35–41 (2006)
152. P.S. Sisodiya, Plant derived anticancer agents: a review. Int. J. Res. Dev. Pharm. Life Sci. **2**(2), 293–308 (2013)

153. R.A. Laitinen, Z. Nikoloski, Genetic basis of plasticity in plants. J. Exp. Botany **70**(3), 739–745 (2019)
154. B.M. Twaij, M.N. Hasan, Bioactive secondary metabolites from plant sources: types, synthesis, and their therapeutic uses. Int. J. Plant Biol. **13**(1), 4–14 (2022)
155. D.M. Pott, S. Osorio, J.G. Vallarino, From central to specialized metabolism: an overview of some secondary compounds derived from the primary metabolism for their role in conferring nutritional and organoleptic characteristics to fruit. Front. Plant Sci. **10**, 835 (2019)
156. M.A. Fazili, I. Bashir, M. Ahmad, U. Yaqoob, S.N. Geelani, In vitro strategies for the enhancement of secondary metabolite production in plants: a review. Bull. Natl. Res. Centre **46**(1), 35 (2022)
157. R.A. Hussein, A.A. El-Anssary, Plants secondary metabolites: the key drivers of the pharmacological actions of medicinal plants. Herbal Med. **1**(3), 11–30 (2019)
158. T. Isah, Stress and defense responses in plant secondary metabolites production. Biol. Res. **52** (2019)
159. Y. Li, D. Kong, Y. Fu, M.R. Sussman, H. Wu, The effect of developmental and environmental factors on secondary metabolites in medicinal plants. Plant Physiol. Biochem. **148**, 80–89 (2020)
160. A. Ahamed, A. Panneerselvam, A. Alaklabi, I.A. Arif, V. Ambikapathy, N. Thajuddin, Molecular perspective and anticancer activity of medicinal plants. Saudi J. Biol. Sci. **27**(2), 666–675 (2020)
161. A. Hashiguchi, J. Tian, S. Komatsu, Proteomic contributions to medicinal plant research: from plant metabolism to pharmacological action. Proteomes **5**(4), 35 (2017)
162. F. Rasheed, J. Markgren, M. Hedenqvist, E. Johansson, Modeling to understand plant protein structure-function relationships-implications for seed storage proteins. Molecules **25**(4), 873 (2020)
163. Q. Yang, D. Zhao, Q. Liu, Connections between amino acid metabolisms in plants: lysine as an example. Front. Plant Sci. **11**, 928 (2020)
164. S. Bhukta, P. Gopinath, R. Dandela, Target identification of anticancer natural products using a chemical proteomics approach. RSC Adv. **11**(45), 27 950–27 964 (2021)
165. Z.-W. Cai, T. Ye, P.-W. Jiang, Y.-J. Liao, L. Wang, Q.-L. Zhang, W.-Q. Du, M. Huang, P. Yang, M.-H. Li, Mapk cascade signaling is involved in α-mmc induced growth inhibition of multiple myeloma mm. 1s cells via g2 arrest and mitochondrial-pathway-dependent apoptosis in vitro. Pharmaceuticals **16**(1), 124 (2023)
166. A.A. Zaky, J.-H. Shim, A. Abd El-Aty, A review on extraction, characterization, and applications of bioactive peptides from pressed black cumin seed cake. Front. Nutr. **8**, 743909 (2021)
167. B. Ranty, D. Aldon, J.-P. Galaud, Plant calmodulins and calmodulin-related proteins: multifaceted relays to decode calcium signals. Plant Signal. Behav. **1**(3), 96–104 (2006)
168. E.F. Seneme, D.C. Dos Santos, C.A. de Lima, Í.A.M. Zelioli, J.M. Sciani, G.B. Longato, Effects of myristicin in association with chemotherapies on the reversal of the multidrug resistance (mdr) mechanism in cancer. Pharmaceuticals **15**(10), 1233 (2022)
169. L. Wang, J. Liu, Y. Shen, R. Pu, M. Hou, Q. Wei, X. Zhang, G. Li, H. Ren, G. Wu, Brassinosteroids synthesised by cyp85a/a1 but not cyp85a2 function via a bri1-like receptor but not via bri1 in picea abies. J. Exp. Botany **72**(5), 1748–1763 (2021)
170. S. Ye, D. Yin, X. Sun, Q. Chen, T. Min, H. Wang, L. Wang, Molecular cloning, expression, and functional analysis of glycosyltransferase (tbuggt) gene from trapa bispinosa roxb. Molecules **27**(23), 8374 (2022)
171. T. Pei, M. Yan, Y. Huang, Y. Wei, C. Martin, Q. Zhao, Specific flavonoids and their biosynthetic pathway in scutellaria baicalensis. Front. Plant Sci. **13**, 866282 (2022)
172. Y. Qu, M.L. Easson, J. Froese, R. Simionescu, T. Hudlicky, V. De Luca, Completion of the seven-step pathway from tabersonine to the anticancer drug precursor vindoline and its assembly in yeast. Proc. Natl. Acad. Sci. **112**(19), 6224–6229 (2015)
173. Z. Ma, C.Y.-N. Woon, C.-G. Liu, J.-T. Cheng, M. You, G. Sethi, A.L.-A. Wong, P.C.-L. Ho, D. Zhang, P. Ong et al., Repurposing artemisinin and its derivatives as anticancer drugs: a chance or challenge? Front. Pharmacol. **12**, 828856 (2021)

174. X.-Z. Su, L.H. Miller, The discovery of artemisinin and the nobel prize in physiology or medicine (2015)
175. J.-Y. Zhang, F. Zhang, C.-Q. Hong, A.E. Giuliano, X.-J. Cui, G.-J. Zhou, G.-J. Zhang, Y.-K. Cui, Critical protein gapdh and its regulatory mechanisms in cancer cells. Cancer Biol. Med. **12**(1), 10 (2015)
176. M. Necci, D. Piovesan, D. Micheletti, L. Paladin, A. Cestaro, S.C. Tosatto, Phytotypedb: a database of plant protein inter-cultivar variability and function. Database **2018**, bay125 (2018)
177. S.A. Jan, Z.K. Shinwari, M. Malik, M. Ilyas, Antioxidant and anticancer activities of brassica rapa: a review. MOJ Biol. Med. **3**(4), 175–178 (2018)
178. Y. Kwak, J. Lee, J. Ju, Anti-cancer activities of brassica juncea leaves in vitro. EXCLI J. **15**, 699 (2016)
179. C. Temple, A. Lopez, Fatal ingestion of taxus brevifolia (pacific yew): a case report. Toxicol. Commun. **7**(1), 2220532 (2023)
180. G. Yoon, M.-H. Lee, A.-W. Kwak, H.-N. Oh, S.-S. Cho, J.-S. Choi, K. Liu, J.-I. Chae, J.-H. Shim, Podophyllotoxin isolated from podophyllum peltatum induces g2/m phase arrest and mitochondrial-mediated apoptosis in esophageal squamous cell carcinoma cells. Forests **11**(1), 8 (2019)
181. L. Sheeba, M. Selvanayaki, M. Harshini, Anticancer activity of catharanthus roseus and murraya koenigii. **7**(8), 1841–1851 (2020)
182. H.N.T. Pham, Q.V. Vuong, M.C. Bowyer, C.J. Scarlett, Phytochemicals derived from catharanthus roseus and their health benefits. Technologies **8**(4), 80 (2020)
183. C. Fernández-Ponce, N. Geribaldi-Doldán, I. Sánchez-Gomar, R. Navarro Quiroz, L. Atencio Ibarra, L. Gomez Escorcia, R. Fernández-Cisnal, G. Aroca Martinez, F. García-Cózar, E. Navarro Quiroz, The role of glycosyltransferases in colorectal cancer. Int. J. Mole. Sci. **22**(11), 5822 (2021)
184. J.-W. Oh, M. Muthu, S.S.C. Pushparaj, J. Gopal, Anticancer therapeutic effects of green tea catechins (gtcs) when integrated with antioxidant natural components. Molecules **28**(5), 2151 (2023)
185. S. Xiong, S. Tan, P. Huang, Y. Li, J.E. Chung, M. Kurisawa, D. Zink, J.Y. Ying, Toxicity and efficacy of green tea catechin derivative-based micellar nanocomplexes for anticancer protein delivery. Biomater. Sci. **11**(13), 4675–4683 (2023)
186. X.-X. Li, C. Liu, S.-L. Dong, C.-S. Ou, J.-L. Lu, J.-H. Ye, Y.-R. Liang, X.-Q. Zheng, Anticarcinogenic potentials of tea catechins. Front. Nutr. **9**, 1060783 (2022)
187. N.T.H. Thu, P.T.H. Hoa, N.T. Dat, P.N.K. Tuyen, Triterpenoids, steroid, and aromatic compounds from combretum indicum leaves. Vietnam J. Chem. **60**(5), 629–635 (2022)
188. O.M. Noman, F.A. Nasr, A.S. Alqahtani, M. Al-Zharani, M.A.W. Cordero, A.A. Alotaibi, A. Bepari, S. Alarifi, A. Daoud, Comparative study of antioxidant and anticancer activities and hptlc quantification of rutin in white radish (raphanus sativus l.) leaves and root extracts grown in saudi arabia. Open Chem. **19**(1), 408–416 (2021)
189. V. Kumar, S.K. Guru, S.K. Jain, P. Joshi, S.G. Gandhi, S.B. Bharate, S. Bhushan, S.S. Bharate, R.A. Vishwakarma, A chromatography-free isolation of rohitukine from leaves of dysoxylum binectariferum: evaluation for in vitro cytotoxicity, cdk inhibition and physicochemical properties. Bioorg. Med. Chem. Lett. **26**(15), 3457–3463 (2016)
190. N.K. Khandelwal, C.R. Millan, S.I. Zangari, S. Avila, D. Williams, T.M. Thaker, T.M. Tomasiak, The structural basis for regulation of the glutathione transporter ycf1 by regulatory domain phosphorylation. Nat. Commun. **13**(1), 1278 (2022)
191. Y. Li, S. Li, K. Thodey, I. Trenchard, A. Cravens, C.D. Smolke, Complete biosynthesis of noscapine and halogenated alkaloids in yeast. Proc. Natl. Acad. Sci. **115**(17), E3922–E3931 (2018)
192. A. Vadhel, S. Bashir, A.H. Mir, M. Girdhar, D. Kumar, A. Kumar, A. Mohan, T. Malik, A. Mohan, Opium alkaloids, biosynthesis, pharmacology and association with cancer occurrence. Open Biol. **13**(5), 220355 (2023)
193. K. Ye, Y. Ke, N. Keshava, J. Shanks, J.A. Kapp, R.R. Tekmal, J. Petros, H.C. Joshi, Opium alkaloid noscapine is an antitumor agent that arrests metaphase and induces apoptosis in dividing cells. Proc. Natl. Acad. Sci. **95**(4), 1601–1606 (1998)

194. A.N.B. Singab, I.M. Ayoub, M. El-Shazly, M. Korinek, T.-Y. Wu, Y.-B. Cheng, F.-R. Chang, Y.-C. Wu, Shedding the light on iridaceae: ethnobotany, phytochemistry and biological activity. Ind. Crops Prod. **92**, 308–335 (2016)
195. O. Mykhailenko, R. Lesyk, N. Finiuk, R. Stoika, T. Yushchenko, A. Ocheretniuk, V. Vaschuk, V. Mishchenko, V. Georgiyants, In vitro anticancer activity screening of iridaceae plant extracts. J. Appl. Pharm. Sci. **10**(7), 059–063 (2020)
196. V. Jiménez-González, G. Benítez, J.E. Pastor, M. López-Lázaro, J.M. Calderón-Montaño, Evaluation of anticancer activity of 76 plant species collected in andalusia (spain) against lung cancer cells. Plants **12**(18), 3275 (2023)
197. A.L. Parker, M. Kavallaris, J.A. McCarroll, Microtubules and their role in cellular stress in cancer. Front. Oncol. **4**, 153 (2014)
198. V. Gulati, I.H. Harding, E.A. Palombo, Enzyme inhibitory and antioxidant activities of traditional medicinal plants: potential application in the management of hyperglycemia. Bmc Complement. Altern. Med. **12**, 1–9 (2012)
199. G.E.-S. Batiha, N. Akhtar, A.A. Alsayegh, W.F. Abusudah, N.H. Almohmadi, H.M. Shaheen, T.G. Singh, M. De Waard, Bioactive compounds, pharmacological actions, and pharmacokinetics of genus acacia. Molecules **27**(21), 7340 (2022)
200. A. Atiya, T. Majrashi, S. Akhtar, A.A. Khan, A.M.S. Asiri, H.J. Al-Zahrania, R.S. Alnami, S.A. Alsharif, T. Amer, Z.A. Faiz et al., The value of genus acacia in arid and semi-arid environments for the treatment of chronic inflammatory diseases. Phytomed. Plus **2**(3), 100315 (2022)
201. C.-M. Yang, H.-Y. Cheng, T.-C. Lin, L.-C. Chiang, C.-C. Lin, The in vitro activity of geraniin and 1, 3, 4, 6-tetra-o-galloyl-β-d-glucose isolated from phyllanthus urinaria against herpes simplex virus type 1 and type 2 infection. J. Ethnopharmacol. **110**(3), 555–558 (2007)
202. M. Geethangili, S.-T. Ding, A review of the phytochemistry and pharmacology of phyllanthus urinaria l. Front. Pharmacol. **9**, 1109 (2018)
203. M. Irfan Dar, M.I. Qureshi, S. Zahiruddin, S. Abass, B. Jan, A. Sultan, S. Ahmad, In silico analysis of ptp1b inhibitors and tlc-ms bioautography-based identification of free radical scavenging and α-amylase inhibitory compounds from heartwood extract of pterocarpus marsupium. ACS Omega **7**(50), 46 156–46 173 (2022)
204. S. Mekala, S.S.S. Mchenga et al., Antidiabetic effect of pterocarpus marsupium seed extract in gabapentin induced diabetic rats. Int. J. Basic Clin. Pharmacol. **9**(3), 371–377 (2020)
205. S. Kushalan, A.S. Khyahrii, S. Kini, S. Hegde, Curculigo orchioides gaertn.: an overview of its effects on human health. J. Health Allied Sci. NU **13**(02), 153–160 (2023)
206. N. Kamkaen, C. Chittasupho, S. Vorarat, S. Tadtong, W. Phrompittayarat, S. Okonogi, P. Kwankhao, Mucuna pruriens seed aqueous extract improved neuroprotective and acetylcholinesterase inhibitory effects compared with synthetic l-dopa. Molecules **27**(10), 3131 (2022)
207. G. Nafeh, M. Abi Akl, J. Samarani, R. Bahous, G. Al Kari, M. Younes, R. Sarkis, S. Rizk, Urtica dioica leaf infusion enhances the sensitivity of triple-negative breast cancer cells to cisplatin treatment. Pharmaceuticals **16**(6), 780 (2023)
208. Y. Taheri, C. Quispe, J. Herrera-Bravo, J. Sharifi-Rad, S.M. Ezzat, R.M. Merghany, S. Shaheen, L. Azmi, A. Prakash Mishra, B. Sener et al., Urtica dioica-derived phytochemicals for pharmacological and therapeutic applications. Evid. Based Complement. Altern. Med. **2022**(1), 4024331 (2022)
209. C. Sens-Albert, S. Weisenburger, B.C. König, S.F. Melcher, U.A. Scheyhing, K. Rollet, P. Lluel, E. Koch, M.D. Lehner, M.C. Michel, Effects of a proprietary mixture of extracts from sabal serrulata fruits and urtica dioica roots (ws® 1541) on prostate hyperplasia and inflammation in rats and human cells. Front. Pharmacol. **15**, 1379456 (2024)
210. N.K. Al-Senosy, A. Abou-Eisha, E.S. Ahmad, In vitro antiproliferation effect of atriplex halimus l. crude extract on human cell lines by induction of apoptosis and g2/m phase arrest. Egypt. Acad. J. Biol. Sci. C, Physiol. Mole. Biol. **10**(1), 115–126 (2018)
211. I. Chikhi, H. Allali, M.E.A. Dib, H. Medjdoub, B. Tabti, Antidiabetic activity of aqueous leaf extract of atriplex halimus l. (chenopodiaceae) in streptozotocin-induced diabetic rats. Asian Pac. J. Trop. Dis. **4**(3), 181–184 (2014)

212. K.J. Gohil, J.A. Patel, A.K. Gajjar, Pharmacological review on centella asiatica: a potential herbal cure-all. Indian J. Pharm. Sci. **72**(5), 546 (2010)
213. S. Pantia, T. Kangsamaksin, T. Janvilisri, W. Komyod, Asiatic acid inhibits nasopharyngeal carcinoma cell viability and migration via suppressing stat3 and claudin-1. Pharmaceuticals **16**(6), 902 (2023)
214. A.A. Patel, A.A. Amin, A.H. Patwari, M.B. Shah, Validated high performance thin layer chromatography method for simultaneous determination of quercetin and gallic acid in leea indica. Revista Brasileira de Farmacognosia **27**, 50–53 (2017)
215. S.-Y. Neo, Y.-Y. Siew, H.-C. Yew, Y. He, K.-L. Poh, Y.-C. Tsai, S.-L. Ng, W.-X. Tan, T.-I. Chong, C.S.E.-S. Lim et al., Effects of leea indica leaf extracts and its phytoconstituents on natural killer cell-mediated cytotoxicity in human ovarian cancer. BMC Complement. Med. Ther. **23**(1), 79 (2023)
216. N.C. Gancedo, R. Isolani, N.C. de Oliveira, C.V. Nakamura, D.C. de Medeiros Araujo, A.C.C. Sanches, F.S. Tonin, F. Fernandez-Llimos, D. Chierrito, J.C.P. de Mello, Chemical constituents, anticancer and anti-proliferative potential of limonium species: a systematic review. Pharmaceuticals **16**(2), 293 (2023)
217. P. Wróblewska-Łuczka, J. Cabaj, J. Bargieł, J.J. Łuszczki, Anticancer effect of terpenes: focus on malignant melanoma. Pharmacol. Rep. **75**(5), 1115–1125 (2023)
218. F.K. Hartati, A.B. Djauhari, Potential of black rice (oryza sativa l.) as anticancer through mortalin-p53 complex inhibitors. Biointerface Res. Appl. Chem. **10**(5), 6174–6181 (2020)
219. P. Leenutaphong, S. Tancharoen, K. Kikuchi, T. Nararatwanchai, C. Phruksaniyom, S. Chaichalotornkul, Downregulation of tumor promotor genes in oryza sativa linn.-induced antiproliferative activity of human squamous carcinoma cells. Asian Pac. J. Cancer Prev. APJCP **24**(7), 2431 (2023)
220. W.H. Talib, A.I. Mahmod, D. Awajan, R.A. Hamed, I.H. Al-Yasari, Immunomodulatory, anticancer, and antimicrobial effects of rice bran grown in iraq: an in vitro and in vivo study. Pharmaceuticals **15**(12), 1502 (2022)
221. T. Kowalczyk, A. Merecz-Sadowska, P. Rijo, M. Mori, S. Hatziantoniou, K. Gorski, J. Szemraj, J. Piekarski, T. Śliwiński, M. Bijak et al., Hidden in plants-a review of the anticancer potential of the solanaceae family in in vitro and in vivo studies. Cancers **14**(6), 1455 (2022)
222. K. Chidambaram, T. Alqahtani, Y. Alghazwani, A. Aldahish, S. Annadurai, K. Venkatesan, K. Dhandapani, E. Thilagam, K. Venkatesan, P. Paulsamy et al., Medicinal plants of solanum species: the promising sources of phyto-insecticidal compounds. J. Trop. Med. **2022**(1), 4952221 (2022)
223. H. Forouhandeh, V. Tarhriz, M. Zadehkamand, P. Asgharian, Anti-proliferative activity of artemisia marschalliana on cancerous cell lines. BMC Complement. Med. Ther. **23**(1), 119 (2023)
224. Y. Augustin, H.M. Staines, S. Krishna, Artemisinins as a novel anti-cancer therapy: targeting a global cancer pandemic through drug repurposing. Pharmacol. Ther. **216**, 107706 (2020)
225. A.-M. Rydén, Identification, characterization and expression of early biosynthetic genes from artemisia annua (2010)
226. L. Sun, S. Ding, Q. Luo, P. Wang, X. Yang, L. Wu, Y. Chen, X. Zheng, H. Zhang, L. Yuan et al., Taxus wallichiana var. chinensis (pilg.) florin aqueous extract suppresses the proliferation and metastasis in lung carcinoma via jak/stat3 signaling pathway. Front. Pharmacol. **12**, 736442 (2021)
227. G. Zhang, S. Dai, Y. Chen, H. Wang, T. Chen, Q. Shu, S. Chen, L. Shou, X. Cai, Aqueous extract of taxus chinensis var. mairei regulates the hippo-yap pathway and promotes apoptosis of non-small cell lung cancer via atf3 in vivo and in vitro. Biomed. Pharmacother. **138**, 111506 (2021)
228. Q. Shu, M. Shen, B. Wang, Q. Cui, X. Zhou, L. Zhu, Aqueous extract of taxus chinensis (pilger) rehd inhibits lung carcinoma a549 cells through the epidermal growth factor receptor/mitogen-activated protein kinase pathway in vitro and in vivo. J. Tradit. Chin. Med. **34**(3), 293–301 (2014)

229. M.S. Khan, W. Khan, W. Ahmad, M. Singh, S. Ahmad, Bergenin determination in different extracts by high-performance thin-layer chromatographic densitometry. J. Pharm. Bioallied Sci. **7**(4), 272–274 (2015)
230. Y. Gan, X. Li, S. Han, L. Zhou, W. Li, Targeting mcl-1 degradation by bergenin inhibits tumorigenesis of colorectal cancer cells. Pharmaceuticals **16**(2), 241 (2023)
231. E. Assadpour, A. Rezaei, S.S. Das, B.V. Krishna Rao, S.K. Singh, M.S. Kharazmi, N.K. Jha, S.K. Jha, M.A. Prieto, S.M. Jafari, Cannabidiol-loaded nanocarriers and their therapeutic applications. Pharmaceuticals **16**(4), 487 (2023)
232. B. Hinz, R. Ramer, Cannabinoids as anticancer drugs: current status of preclinical research. Br. J. Cancer **127**(1), 1–13 (2022)
233. L.-W. Hii, S.-H.E. Lim, C.-O. Leong, S.-Y. Chin, N.-P. Tan, K.-S. Lai, C.-W. Mai, The synergism of clinacanthus nutans lindau extracts with gemcitabine: downregulation of anti-apoptotic markers in squamous pancreatic ductal adenocarcinoma. BMC Complement. Altern. Med. **19**, 1–13 (2019)
234. S.Y. Fong, D. Wimalasiri, T. Piva, C. Dekiwadia, S. Urban, T. Huynh, Evaluation of cytotoxic and apoptotic activities of clinacanthus nutans (burm. f.) lindau leaves against d24 human melanoma cells. J. Herbal Med. **17**, 100285 (2019)
235. R. Wilken, M.S. Veena, M.B. Wang, E.S. Srivatsan, Curcumin: a review of anti-cancer properties and therapeutic activity in head and neck squamous cell carcinoma. Mole. Cancer **10**, 1–19 (2011)
236. C. Porro, M.A. Panaro, Recent progress in understanding the health benefits of curcumin. Molecules **28**(5), 2418 (2023)
237. P. Paradkar, A. Juvekar, M. Barkume, A. Amonkar, J. Joshi, G. Soman, A. Vaidya, In vitro and in vivo evaluation of a standardized curcuma longa linn formulation in cervical cancer. J. Ayurveda Integrative Med. **12**(4), 616–622 (2021)
238. S.A. Nag, J.-J. Qin, W. Wang, M.-H. Wang, H. Wang, R. Zhang, Ginsenosides as anticancer agents: in vitro and in vivo activities, structure-activity relationships, and molecular mechanisms of action. Front. Pharmacol. **3**, 25 (2012)
239. H. Hong, D. Baatar, S.G. Hwang, Anticancer activities of ginsenosides, the main active components of ginseng. Evid. Based Complement. Altern. Med. **2021**(1), 8858006 (2021)
240. D. Nguyen, J. Holien, C. Dekiwadia, T. Thrimawithana, T. Piva, T. Huynh, Momordica cochinchinensis (gấc) seed extracts induce apoptosis and necrosis in melanoma cells. Pharmaceuticals **16**(1), 100 (2023)
241. K. Bhadresha, V. Thakore, J. Brahmbhatt, V. Upadhyay, N. Jain, R. Rawal, Anticancer effect of moringa oleifera leaves extract against lung cancer cell line via induction of apoptosis. Adv. Cancer Biol. Metastasis **6**, 100072 (2022)
242. A.K. Al-Asmari, S.M. Albalawi, M.T. Athar, A.Q. Khan, H. Al-Shahrani, M. Islam, Moringa oleifera as an anti-cancer agent against breast and colorectal cancer cell lines. PloS one **10**(8), e0135814 (2015)
243. A. Khan, H.C. Chen, M. Tania, D.Z. Zhang, Anticancer activities of nigella sativa (black cumin). Afr. J. Tradit. Complement. Altern. Med. **8**(5S) (2011)
244. S. Das, A. Ghosh, P. Upadhyay, S. Sarker, M. Bhattacharjee, P. Gupta, S. Chattopadhyay, S. Ghosh, P. Dhar, A. Adhikary, A mechanistic insight into the potential anti-cancerous property of nigella sativa on breast cancer through micro-rna regulation: an in vitro and in vivo study. Fitoterapia **169**, 105601 (2023)
245. A.S. Brah, F.A. Armah, C. Obuah, S.A. Akwetey, C.K. Adokoh, Toxicity and therapeutic applications of citrus essential oils (ceos): a review. Int. J. Food Prop. **26**(1), 301–326 (2023)
246. S. Razali, A.Y. Firus Khan, A. Khatib, Q.U. Ahmed, R. Abdul Wahab, Z.A. Zakaria, An in vitro anticancer activity evaluation of neolamarckia cadamba (roxb.) bosser leaves' extract and its metabolite profile. Front. Pharmacol. **12**, 741683 (2021)
247. M. Nie, J. Huang, J. Huang, Z. Chen, L. Lin, F. Luo, X. Zhang, S. Xiao, Differences in the components of neolamarckia cadamba from different provenance and the drug resistance reversal activity of characteristic alkaloid. Ind. Crops Prod. **186**, 115145 (2022)

248. S.N. Begum, A.S. Ray, C.H. Rahaman, A comprehensive and systematic review on potential anticancer activities of eugenol: From pre-clinical evidence to molecular mechanisms of action. Phytomedicine **107**, 154456 (2022)
249. I. Padhy, P. Paul, T. Sharma, S. Banerjee, A. Mondal, Molecular mechanisms of action of eugenol in cancer: recent trends and advancement. Life **12**(11), 1795 (2022)
250. A. Hussain, A. Priyani, L. Sadrieh, K. Brahmbhatt, M. Ahmed, C. Sharma, Concurrent sulforaphane and eugenol induces differential effects on human cervical cancer cells. Integr. Cancer Ther. **11**(2), 154–165 (2012)
251. A.T. Zari, T.A. Zari, K.R. Hakeem, Anticancer properties of eugenol: a review. Molecules **26**(23), 7407 (2021)
252. K.S. Allemailem, Aqueous extract of artemisia annua shows in vitro antimicrobial activity and an in vivo chemopreventive effect in a small-cell lung cancer model. Plants **11**(23), 3341 (2022)
253. S. Krishna, L. Bustamante, R.K. Haynes, H.M. Staines, Artemisinins: their growing importance in medicine. Trends Pharmacol. Sci. **29**(10), 520–527 (2008)
254. S. Slezáková, J. Ruda-Kucerova, Anticancer activity of artemisinin and its derivatives. Anticancer Res. **37**(11), 5995–6003 (2017)
255. A.N. Khan, E. Dilshad, Enhanced antioxidant and anticancer potential of artemisia carvifolia buch transformed with rol a gene. Metabolites **13**(3), 351 (2023)
256. M.G. Distler, A.A. Palmer, Role of glyoxalase 1 (glo1) and methylglyoxal (mg) in behavior: recent advances and mechanistic insights. Front. Genet. **3**, 250 (2012)
257. S. Seetharamaiah, V.S. Muddappa, M.B. Krishnaswamy, R.K. Vasappa, Antineoplastic effects of mucuna pruriens against human colorectal adenocarcinoma. Appl. Biochem. Biotechnol. **196**(3), 1350–1364 (2024)
258. S.F. Taghizadeh, M. Azizi, J. Asili, F.S. Madarshahi, H. Rakhshandeh, Y. Fujii, Therapeutic peptides of mucuna pruriens l.: anti-genotoxic molecules against human hepatocellular carcinoma and hepatitis c virus. Food Sci. Nutr. **9**(6), 2908–2914 (2021)
259. S. Sinha, S. Sharma, J. Vora, H. Shah, A. Srivastava, N. Shrivastava, Mucuna pruriens (l.) dc chemo sensitize human breast cancer cells via downregulation of prolactin-mediated jak2/stat5a signaling. J. Ethnopharmacol. **217**, 23–35 (2018)
260. M. Izdebska, W. Zielińska, D. Grzanka, M. Gagat, The role of actin dynamics and actin-binding proteins expression in epithelial-to-mesenchymal transition and its association with cancer progression and evaluation of possible therapeutic targets. BioMed Res. Int. **2018**(1), 4578373 (2018)
261. B. Xuan, D. Ghosh, E.M. Cheney, E.M. Clifton, M.R. Dawson, Dysregulation in actin cytoskeletal organization drives increased stiffness and migratory persistence in polyploidal giant cancer cells. Sci. Rep. **8**(1), 11935 (2018)
262. K.A. Diab, M.A. Fahmy, E.M. Hassan, S.A. El-Toumy, Evaluation of the cytotoxic, anticancer, and genotoxic activities of acacia nilotica flowers and their effects on n-methyl-n-nitrosourea-induced genotoxicity in mice. Mole. Biol. Rep. **49**(9), 8439–8448 (2022)
263. P. Bhukta, S.K. Ranajit, P.K. Sahu, D. Rath, Phytochemistry and pharmacology of curculigo orchioides gaertn: a review. J. Appl. Pharm. Sci. **13**(10), 083–091 (2023)
264. Y. Wang, J. Li, N. Li, Phytochemistry and pharmacological activity of plants of genus curculigo: an updated review since 2013. Molecules **26**(11), 3396 (2021)
265. I.I. Hejazi, R. Khanam, S.H. Mehdi, A.R. Bhat, M.M.A. Rizvi, S.C. Thakur, F. Athar, Antioxidative and anti-proliferative potential of curculigo orchioides gaertn in oxidative stress induced cytotoxicity: in vitro, ex vivo and in silico studies. Food Chem. Toxicol. **115**, 244–259 (2018)
266. B. D'Abrosca, V. Ciaramella, V. Graziani, F. Papaccio, C.M. Della Corte, N. Potenza, A. Fiorentino, F. Ciardiello, F. Morgillo, Urtica dioica l. inhibits proliferation and enhances cisplatin cytotoxicity in nsclc cells via endoplasmic reticulum-stress mediated apoptosis. Sci. Rep. **9**(1), 4986 (2019)
267. P. Karakol, S.U. Saraydin, M. Bozkurt, C. Hepokur, Z.D.S. Inan, M. Turan, Anticancer effects of urtica dioica in breast cancer. Asian Pac. J. Cancer Prevent. APJCP **23**(2), 673 (2022)

268. S. Esposito, A. Bianco, R. Russo, A. Di Maro, C. Isernia, P.V. Pedone, Therapeutic perspectives of molecules from urtica dioica extracts for cancer treatment. Molecules **24**(15), 2753 (2019)
269. S.D. Umoh, G. Bojase, I.B. Masesane, D. Loeto, R.T. Majinda, A comprehensive review of combretum flavonoids and their biological activities: an update between 1990 and 2022. Biochem. Syst. Ecol. **108**, 104644 (2023)
270. O. Cioanca, I.-I. Lungu, I. Mita-Baciu, S. Robu, A.F. Burlec, M. Hancianu, F. Crivoi, Extraction and purification of catechins from tea leaves: An overview of methods, advantages, and disadvantages. Separations **11**(6), 171 (2024)
271. G.T. Belachew, M.A. Mazlomi, G.A. Kardar, G.T. Belachew, M.H. Seyedzadeh, Z. Pourpak, G.A. Kardar, M. Javanmardi, K. Mokhtarian, R. Falak, Immunochemical characterization of licorice root proteins and assessment of their effects on proliferation of cancer cells. Biomed. J. Sci. Tech. Res. **17**(1), 12 611–12 617 (2019)
272. C. Paniagua, A. Bilkova, P. Jackson, S. Dabravolski, W. Riber, V. Didi, J. Houser, N. Gigli-Bisceglia, M. Wimmerova, E. Budínská et al., Dirigent proteins in plants: modulating cell wall metabolism during abiotic and biotic stress exposure. J. Exp. Botany **68**(13), 3287–3301 (2017)
273. L. Li, W. Sun, P. Zhou, H. Wei, P. Wang, H. Li, S. Rehman, D. Li, Q. Zhuge, Genome-wide characterization of dirigent proteins in populus: gene expression variation and expression pattern in response to marssonina brunnea and phytohormones. Forests **12**(4), 507 (2021)
274. R. Gasper, I. Effenberger, P. Kolesinski, B. Terlecka, E. Hofmann, A. Schaller, Dirigent protein mode of action revealed by the crystal structure of atdir6. Plant Physiol. **172**(4), 2165–2175 (2016)
275. T. Wang, L. Li, W. Zhuang, F. Zhang, X. Shu, N. Wang, Z. Wang, Recent research progress in taxol biosynthetic pathway and acylation reactions mediated by taxus acyltransferases. Molecules **26**(10), 2855 (2021)
276. J. Wu, F. Ji, W. Di, H. Chen, Y. Wan, Activation of acetyl-coenzyme a carboxylase is involved in taxol-induced ovarian cancer cell death. Oncol. Lett. **2**(3), 543–547 (2011)
277. C. Loncaric, E. Merriweather, K.D. Walker, Profiling a taxol pathway 10β-acetyltransferase: assessment of the specificity and the production of baccatin iii by in vivo acetylation in e. coli. Chem. Biol. **13**(3), 309–317 (2006)
278. J. Gallego-Jara, G. Lozano-Terol, R.A. Sola-Martínez, M. Cánovas-Díaz, T. de Diego Puente, A compressive review about taxol®: history and future challenges. Molecules **25**(24), 5986 (2020)
279. S. Motyka, K. Jafernik, H. Ekiert, J. Sharifi-Rad, D. Calina, B. Al-Omari, A. Szopa, W.C. Cho, Podophyllotoxin and its derivatives: potential anticancer agents of natural origin in cancer chemotherapy. Biomed. Pharmacother. **158**, 114145 (2023)
280. L. Almagro, F. Fernández-Pérez, M.A. Pedreño, Indole alkaloids from catharanthus roseus: bioproduction and their effect on human health. Molecules **20**(2), 2973–3000 (2015)
281. J. Gao, Y. Zuo, F. Xiao, Y. Wang, D. Li, J. Xu, C. Ye, L. Feng, L. Jiang, T. Liu et al., Biosynthesis of catharanthine in engineered pichia pastoris. Nat. Synth. **2**(3), 231–242 (2023)
282. M. Schneider, L. Lane, E. Boutet, D. Lieberherr, M. Tognolli, L. Bougueleret, A. Bairoch, The uniprotkb/swiss-prot knowledgebase and its plant proteome annotation program. J. Proteomics **72**(3), 567–573 (2009)
283. G. Chen, B. Bao, Y. Cheng, M. Tian, J. Song, L. Zheng, Q. Tong, Acetyl-coa metabolism as a therapeutic target for cancer. Biomed. Pharmacother. **168**, 115741 (2023)
284. H.F. Bakheit, S. Taurin, E.M. Elamin, M. Bakhiet, Acacia nilotica pod extract has an anticancer effect on the u937 cell line. Pharmacognosy Res. **15**(4) (2023)
285. M. Roubi, A. Elbouzidi, M. Dalli, S.-E. Azizi, M. Aherkou, M. Taibi, B. El Guerrouj, M. Addi, N. Gseyra, Phytochemical, antioxidant, and anticancer assessments of atriplex halimus extracts: in silico and in vitro studies. Sci. Afr. **22**, e01959 (2023)
286. A. Elbouzidi, H. Ouassou, M. Aherkou, L. Kharchoufa, N. Meskali, A. Baraich, H. Mechchate, M. Bouhrim, A. Idir, C. Hano et al., Lc–ms/ms phytochemical profiling, antioxidant activity, and cytotoxicity of the ethanolic extract of atriplex halimus l. against breast cancer cell lines: computational studies and experimental validation. Pharmaceuticals **15**(9), 1156 (2022)

287. Z.-Y. Tang, Y. Li, Y.-T. Tang, X.-D. Ma, Z.-Y. Tang, Anticancer activity of oleanolic acid and its derivatives: recent advances in evidence, target profiling and mechanisms of action. Biomed. Pharmacother. **145**, 112397 (2022)
288. R.K. Yadav, M. Singh, S. Sarkar, S. Maity, S. Saha, Cytotoxicity of different extracts of mucuna pruriens seeds on hepatoma cells but not on normal hepatic cells. Pharmacognosy Commun. **5**(1) (2015)
289. A.J. Tola, A. Jaballi, H. Germain, T.D. Missihoun, Recent development on plant aldehyde dehydrogenase enzymes and their functions in plant development and stress signaling. Genes **12**(1), 51 (2020)
290. D.W. Clark, K. Palle, Aldehyde dehydrogenases in cancer stem cells: potential as therapeutic targets. Ann. Transl. Med. **4**(24) (2016)
291. S.R. Kabir, M.R. Karim, M.T. Alam, Chitinase inhibits growth of human breast and colorectal cancer cells in vitro and ehrlich ascites carcinoma cells in vivo. Arab. J. Chem. **15**(11), 104264 (2022)
292. D.O. Nkwe, B. Lotshwao, G. Rantong, J. Matshwele, T.E. Kwape, K. Masisi, G. Gaobotse, K. Hefferon, A. Makhzoum, Anticancer mechanisms of bioactive compounds from solanaceae: an update. Cancers **13**(19), 4989 (2021)
293. A.H. Alhamadani, A.N. Al-Waheeb et al., New phytochemical investigation of atriplex halimus l. and evaluation of its cytotoxic and anticancer effect on human pancreas cancer cells. J. Pharm. Negative Results 2155–2168 (2022)
294. D. Singh, Y.-Y. Siew, T.-I. Chong, H.-C. Yew, S.S.-W. Ho, C.S. E.-S. Lim, W.-X. Tan, S.-Y. Neo, H.-L. Koh, Identification of phytoconstituents in leea indica (burm. f.) merr. leaves by high performance liquid chromatography micro time-of-flight mass spectrometry. Molecules **24**(4), 714 (2019)
295. M.H. Sultan, R. Bedair, O.G. Ragab, E. Abd-ELShafy, A.Y. Mahfouz, G.E. Daigham, Biological activities and ecological aspects of limonium pruinosum (l.) collected from wadi hof eastern desert, Egypt, as a promising attempt for potential medical applications. Biomass Convers. Biorefinery 1–21 (2023)
296. S. Jongrungraungchok, F. Madaka, T. Wunnakup, T. Sudsai, C. Pongphaew, T. Songsak, N. Pradubyat, In vitro antioxidant, anti-inflammatory, and anticancer activities of mixture thai medicinal plants. BMC Complement. Med. Ther. **23**(1), 43 (2023)
297. Y. Wang, G. Li, T. Chen, W. Wu, Z. Yan, X. Li, Anticancer effect and molecular mechanism of ginsenoside rg3 in various cancer types. Intell. Pharm. **1**(2), 52–63 (2023)
298. R. Sultan, A. Ahmed, L. Wei, H. Saeed, M. Islam, M. Ishaq, The anticancer potential of chemical constituents of moringa oleifera targeting cdk-2 inhibition in estrogen receptor positive breast cancer using in-silico and in vitro approches. BMC Complement. Med. Ther. **23**(1), 396 (2023)
299. B. Rathi, S. Devanesan, M.S. AlSalhi, A.J.R. Singh, In-vitro free radical scavenging effect and cytotoxic analysis of black cummins and honey formulation. Saudi J. Biol. Sci. **28**(3), 1576–1581 (2021)
300. I. Zafar, A. Safder, H. Imran Afridi, S. Riaz, R. ur Rehman, A. Unar, F. Un Nisa, A.-R.Z. Gaafar, M. Bourhia, G.F. Wondmie et al., In silico and in vitro study of bioactive compounds of nigella sativa for targeting neuropilins in breast cancer. Front. Chem. **11**, 1273149 (2023)
301. V.S. Periasamy, J. Athinarayanan, A.A. Alshatwi, Anticancer activity of an ultrasonic nanoemulsion formulation of nigella sativa l. essential oil on human breast cancer cells. Ultrason. Sonochem. **31**, 449–455 (2016)
302. K. Saravanakumar, S. Shin, A. Sathiyaseelan, M.-H. Wang, Cytotoxicity of black cumin (nigella sativa l.) seed sprout extract mediated titanium oxide (tio2) nanoparticles in human lung cancer cells. Mater. Lett. **338**, 134000 (2023)

Chapter 6
CAML Model for Computational Linguistics

"The central task of computational linguistic is to encode a theory of natural language that is both testable and computationally effective"

—Martin Kay

6.1 Introduction

Computational linguistics is a multidisciplinary field that combines aspects of computer science and linguistics to develop computational models and algorithms for analysis, understanding, and generation of human language. It sits at the intersection of linguistics, computer science, artificial intelligence. In addition, computational linguistics also encompasses the field of cognitive science that aims to enable machines to interpret and understand human language text in a meaningful way.

Chapter 4 of this book report the light weight Cellular Automata (enhanced with) Machine Learning (CAML) model that employs both Cellular Automata (CA) and Machine Learning (ML) frameworks. It provides an outline of two applications of the model in the fields of Computational Linguistics and Computational Proteomics (a sub-discipline of Computational Biology). Chapter 5 reports the application of CAML model for mutational study of protein chains. The current chapter presents the application of this CAML framework in the field of Sentiment Analysis covered under the discipline of Computational Linguistics. It presents the results of sentiment analysis in a multi-language environment. A few key aspects and components of computational linguistics are listed below.

© The Author(s), under exclusive license to Springer Nature Singapore Pte Ltd. 2025

P. Pal Chaudhuri et al., *New Kind of Machine Learning—Cellular Automata Model*,
https://doi.org/10.1007/978-981-96-1501-8_6

- *Natural Language Processing (NLP)*: NLP is a subfield of computational linguistics that focuses on the interaction between computers and human (natural) languages. It involves the development of algorithms and models to enable computers to understand, interpret, and generate human language.
- *Speech Recognition*: This involves the development of systems that can convert spoken language into written text. Speech recognition is crucial for applications such as voice assistants, transcription services, and hands-free device control.
- *Text Mining and Information Retrieval*: Text mining involves extracting valuable information and patterns from large volumes of textual data. Information retrieval focuses on retrieving relevant documents or information from a collection based on user queries. Both are essential for tasks like search engines and data analysis.
- *Machine Translation*: Machine translation involves developing algorithms to automatically translate text or speech from one language to another. This area has gained significant attention with the rise of globalization and the need for effective communication across different languages.
- *Syntax and Semantics*: Computational linguistics deals with the development of models that can analyze and understand the structure (syntax) and meaning (semantics) of sentences. This is crucial for tasks like parsing, sentiment analysis, and understanding context.
- *Named Entity Recognition (NER)*: NER involves identifying and classifying entities (such as names of people, organizations, locations) within a text. It is essential for information extraction and knowledge base construction.
- *Dialog Systems and Conversational Agents*: The development of systems capable of engaging in natural language conversations. Chatbots and virtual assistants are examples of applications that utilize dialog systems to interact with users in a conversational mode.
- *Cognitive Computing*: Computational linguistics draws inspiration from cognitive science to model human language processing. This includes understanding how humans comprehend and produce language, with the goal of building more human-like language models.

6.1.1 The Inherent Challenges

There are a few inherent challenges in computational linguistics such as ambiguity, variability, and context understanding. Human language may be ambiguous, with words having multiple meanings depending on context. Resolving ambiguity is a persistent challenge in computational linguistics. Further, language usage varies across regions, cultures, and individuals. Adapting models to handle this variability is a complex task, especially in multilingual and diverse linguistic contexts. Capturing and understanding context is crucial for accurate language processing. Developing models that can effectively consider context in language understanding will continue as an ongoing challenge in the decades to come.

Computational linguistics finds applications in a wide range of fields, including information retrieval, sentiment analysis, language translation, speech recognition, and virtual assistants. In recent times, the surge in user-generated data across various languages on social media platforms has generated significant interest in sentiment analysis research. Next two subsections present an overview of the application of two models (LLM and CAML) on sentiment analysis task.

6.1.2 LLM Model on Sentiment Analysis

In recent time (2022 onwards), the advent of Large Language Models (LLMs) and Generative AI (GenAI) has indeed revolutionized the field of computational linguistics. LLMs, such as GPT-4, achieve state-of-the-art results in many Natural Language Processing (NLP) tasks, including sentiment analysis. Their ability to understand complex language patterns allows them to make more accurate predictions compared to traditional models. LLMs excel at understanding the context in which words and phrases are used. This enables them to capture nuances and infer sentiment more accurately, even in complex or ambiguous sentences. LLMs are pre-trained on vast datasets and can be fine-tuned on specific tasks like sentiment analysis.

Large Language Models (LLMs) like GPT-4 are powerful tools, but they come with certain disadvantages when applied to sentiment analysis tasks, specifically in a multi-language environment. LLMs can sometimes memorize and overfit to specific patterns in their training data, which might lead to biased or overly confident predictions that do not generalize well to unseen data. Sentiment analysis often requires understanding subtle nuances in text, like sarcasm, irony, or context-dependent sentiment. LLMs may struggle with these subtleties, leading to incorrect sentiment classification. Further, running large models requires significant computational resources, making them expensive and less practical for deployment in real-time or on devices with limited computational resources. LLMs may perform well in languages they were predominantly trained on, such as English, but might struggle with less commonly represented languages. The quality of sentiment analysis can vary significantly across different languages due to the unequal representation of languages in the training data. For low-resource languages, where large annotated datasets are scarce, LLMs may not have enough data to learn the nuances of sentiment, leading to poor performance in these languages.

6.1.3 CAML Model on Sentiment Analysis

In this chapter, we elaborate on the design of CAML model equipped with the capability for analysis of sentiment in a multi-language environment. We do not take into account any pre-trained models, and the proposed model results demonstrates more than 70% accuracy even when trained with a limited dataset. The model is language independent and capable of analyzing sentiments expressed in multi-language texts.

As we start our journey on this chapter, we provide a brief historical sketch of the problem of sentiment analysis in Sect. 6.2. We discuss how the solutions for sentiment analysis problems evolved with time, employing different machine learning and deep learning models. We also report different levels of sentiment analysis and a few applications. In Sect. 6.3, we present a comprehensive survey of the available literature on sentiment analysis in two Asian languages, namely Hindi and Arabic, as well as in three European languages, English, Greek and Georgian.

In order to establish the fact that our scheme can handle sentiment analysis task with small training set corpus, we have concentrated on sentiment analysis in languages with limited data source. Our objective is to create a machine-learning model without relying on pre-trained language models. We employed Cellular Automata (CA) to transform the text into vectorized format, enabling us to apply a rule-based approach for classifier design and development. The proposed model is language-agnostic, and does not rely on linguistic information and language dictionaries from the corpora. The very first step of the proposed solution demands conversion of a given text to Unicode text. Each Unicode character is modelled with a sequence of CA rules. In the process, a text in any language is modelled with a CA rule vector. Once CA rule vector is designed for an input text, we analyze evolution of the CA modeling the text. CA evolves in successive time steps as per the rule vector to generate a graph referred to as CL (Cycle Length) signal graph. Multiple features are next extracted from the signal graph to design the machine learning algorithm. The proposed CAML model is presented in Sect. 6.4, subsequent to providing background of sentiment analysis problem in Sect. 6.2 followed by survey of associated literature in Sect. 6.3. The quality of prediction derived out of the model is subsequently assessed on testing data set, while employing the specified performance metrics for evaluation. The results we achieved exhibit notable performance compared to state-of-the-art models identified during our literature review. Our traversal on the 'Learning Curve' and performance analysis of the model is reported in Sect. 6.5.

6.2 Sentiment Analysis

Sentiment analysis has come a long way since it was introduced as a natural language processing task nearly twenty years back. Sentiment analysis aims to extract the underlying attitudes and opinions toward an entity. It has become a powerful tool used by governments, businesses, healthcare administrators, marketing executives, and others. The traditional sentiment analysis model focuses mainly on text content. However, technological advances have allowed people to express their opinions and feelings through audio, image and video channels.

6.2.1 *Brief History of Sentiment Analysis*

The history of sentiment analysis, also known as opinion mining, can be traced back to the early 2000s, with its roots in natural language processing and computational linguistics. The primary objective of sentiment analysis is to determine the sentiment expressed in a piece of text, whether it be positive, negative, or neutral.

1. Early Developments (2000–2010): Sentiment analysis gained momentum in the early 2000s as researchers began exploring techniques to automatically classify opinions in text. Initial approaches were rule-based and relied on linguistic patterns to identify sentiment. Researchers focused on sentiment lexicons, lists of words associated with positive or negative sentiment.
2. Machine Learning Era (2010–2015): The advent of machine learning techniques, particularly supervised learning, marked a significant shift in sentiment analysis. Researchers started using labeled datasets to train models, employing algorithms such as Support Vector Machines (SVM), Naive Bayes, followed by more complex models like Recurrent Neural Networks (RNN) and Long Short-Term Memory (LSTM) networks.
3. Social Media Influence (2010 onwards): The rise of social media platforms played a crucial role in the evolution of sentiment analysis. The vast amount of user-generated content on platforms like Twitter, Facebook, and others provided a rich source for sentiment data. Researchers adapted their models to handle the informal language and character limitations common in social media posts.
4. Deep Learning Dominance (2015 onwards): Deep learning techniques, particularly neural networks, have become the predominant force in sentiment analysis. Convolutional Neural Networks (CNNs) and Transformer models, like BERT and GPT, have demonstrated state-of-the-art performance in understanding context and nuances in sentiment-laden text.
5. Aspect-Based Sentiment Analysis (2018 onwards): Recent advancements in sentiment analysis have focused on aspect-based sentiment analysis, which involves identifying the sentiment towards specific aspects or entities within a given text. This approach provides a more granular understanding of opinions, making it valuable for businesses and decision-makers.
6. Large Language Models Era (2022 onwards): Sentiment analysis with Large Language Models (LLMs) has seen significant advancements post-2022, driven by improvements in model architectures, training methodologies, and the availability of larger and more diverse datasets. LLMs released after 2022, like GPT-4, have shown substantial improvements in understanding complex linguistic patterns and context.

6.2.2 *Levels of Sentiment Analysis*

Sentiment analysis has been explored across various levels, primarily focusing on document-level, sentence-level, and aspect-level detection [1, 2]. Figure 6.1 illustrates the tiers of sentiment analysis, with the initial two levels posing significant interest and challenges. The third level, however, presents a heightened difficulty as it involves a meticulous examination [3] of text. Enhanced performance can be achieved by combining two or more levels instead of conducting sentiment analysis solely at a single level. A succinct overview of each level is provided below:

6.2.2.1 Aspect-Level Sentiment Analysis

This level conducts a detailed analysis, focusing on discerning sentiments related to the specific attributes of entities. For example, consider the following sentence, "*The sound quality of Sony Xperia 10 V phone is exceptional*". The review is on "*sound quality*" which is an aspect of the entity "*Sony Xperia 10 V phone*", and the review is positive. Hence, the objective at this stage is to precisely identify people's preferences or dislikes [5]. It concentrates on the specific attributes of entities, such as product features, rather than determining the sentiment of entire paragraphs or sentences.

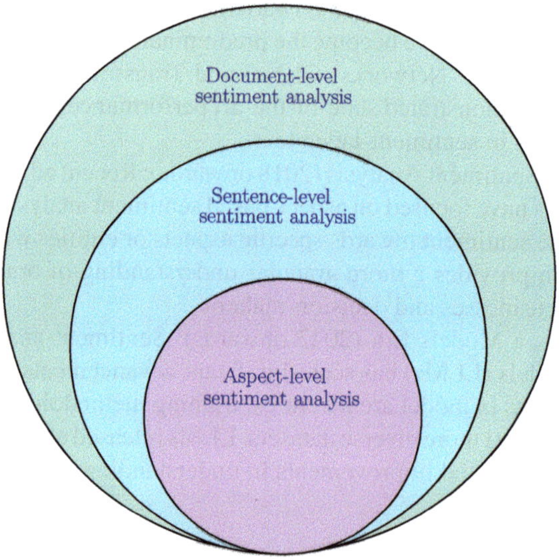

Fig. 6.1 Levels of sentiment analysis [4]

6.2.2.2 Sentence-Level Sentiment Analysis

This level concentrates on the sentence, aiming to ascertain whether it conveys a positive, negative, or neutral opinion. To achieve this objective, the sentence must be classified as either objective, conveying factual information, or subjective, expressing views and opinions. Numerous approaches have been employed to address this level of analysis [6].

6.2.2.3 Document-Level Sentiment Analysis

At this level, the objective is to classify whether an entire document conveys a negative or positive sentiment or opinion. Each document is categorized according to the overall sentiment expressed by the opinion holder regarding a singular entity. Document-level classification is most effective when a document is authored by a single person and may not be suitable for documents evaluating or comparing multiple entities. Various approaches have been suggested for document-level sentiment analysis [7].

6.2.3 Applications of Sentiment Analysis

Sentiment analysis proves highly valuable across diverse application domains, spanning from discerning customer opinions [8, 9] to monitoring mental health through the analysis of patients' social media posts [10]. The advent of emerging technologies like Big Data, Cloud Computing, and Blockchain has significantly expanded the scope of applications, offering sentiment analysis boundless opportunities for implementation across nearly every domain. Subsequent subsections elaborate on some common application domains of sentiment analysis.

6.2.3.1 Business Intelligence

Sentiment analysis in Business Intelligence involves the utilization of natural language processing and machine learning techniques to analyze and interpret the sentiments expressed in textual data relevant to business operations. This approach aims to extract valuable insights from customer feedback, reviews, social media interactions, and other textual sources as input to the business decision-making processes. By understanding the sentiments associated with products, services, or brands, organizations can gain a deeper understanding of customer satisfaction, identify emerging trends, and proactively respond to the associated issues.

In Business Intelligence, sentiment analysis can be integrated into dashboards, reports, and analytics tools to provide a comprehensive view of customer sentiment across various channels. This enables businesses to make data-driven decisions, enhance customer experiences, and adjust strategies based on real-time feedback. Sentiment analysis in Business Intelligence contributes to a more holistic understanding of market dynamics, competitive landscapes, and overall brand perception, empowering organizations to stay agile and responsive in a rapidly evolving business environment.

6.2.3.2 Recommendation System

Sentiment analysis plays a valuable role in recommendation systems by enhancing the understanding of user preferences and opinions. In a recommendation system, the goal is to provide personalized suggestions to users based on their preferences and historical interactions. Sentiment analysis can be integrated into these systems to analyze textual data, such as reviews, comments, or feedback, associated with items or products.

Here is how sentiment analysis contributes to recommendation systems:

- **User Feedback Analysis**: Sentiment analysis helps in understanding the sentiments expressed in user reviews and feedback. This information can be used to assess the overall satisfaction or dissatisfaction with specific items.
- **Fine-Tuning Recommendations**: By incorporating sentiment analysis, recommendation algorithms can adjust their suggestions based on the sentiment of reviews. For example, if a user expresses positive sentiments towards a particular genre of movies, the system can recommend more items from that genre.
- **Handling Negative Feedback**: Sentiment analysis can identify negative sentiments in user feedback. This information can be used to improve the recommendations by avoiding items that have received consistently negative reviews.
- **Dynamic Adaptation**: Sentiment analysis allows recommendation systems to adapt dynamically to changing user sentiments. For instance, if a previously well-received product starts receiving negative sentiments, the system can adjust its recommendations accordingly.
- **Improved User Experience**: Understanding the sentiments associated with recommended items helps in providing a more personalized and satisfactory user experience. Users are more likely to engage with a recommendation system that aligns with their preferences and sentiments.

Incorporating sentiment analysis into recommendation systems enhances the system's ability to offer personalized and context-aware suggestions, ultimately leading to improved user satisfaction and engagement.

6.2.3.3 Government Intelligence

Sentiment analysis in government intelligence involves the application of natural language processing and data analytics techniques to analyze public opinions, social media content, news articles, and other textual data relevant to government activities. This form of analysis provides valuable insights into public sentiments, concerns, and attitudes, assisting government agencies in decision-making, policy formulation, and crisis management. We next outline some of the ways, the sentiment analysis can be used in government intelligence:

- **Public Opinion Monitoring**: Analyzes social media and news to gauge public sentiment on policies and political decisions.
- **Crisis Management**: Assesses public response during emergencies to identify concerns and guide timely actions.
- **Policy Evaluation**: Evaluates public reactions to policies, aiding informed decision-making and adjustments.
- **Security and Threat Monitoring**: Detects potential threats by analyzing online sentiments related to unrest or extremist activities.
- **Election Monitoring**: Gauges public opinions on candidates and issues to inform campaign strategies.
- **Emergency Response**: Assesses sentiment during disasters to identify urgent needs and coordinate responses effectively.
- **Community Engagement**: Enhances communication strategies by understanding public sentiments and fostering transparency.

It is important to note that while sentiment analysis in government intelligence offers valuable insights, it also raises ethical considerations related to privacy, surveillance, and the responsible use of public data. Striking a balance between leveraging technology for public benefit and safeguarding individual rights is crucial in the implementation of sentiment analysis in government intelligence.

6.2.3.4 Healthcare and Medical Intelligence

Sentiment analysis in the healthcare and medical domain involves the application of natural language processing and machine learning techniques to analyze and understand sentiments expressed in textual data related to healthcare services, medical treatments, patient experiences, and healthcare professionals. Noted below are some key aspects of sentiment analysis in this domain:

- **Patient Feedback and Experience**: Analyzes reviews to assess satisfaction and identify areas for improvement in healthcare.
- **Clinical Trial Feedback**: Evaluates patient sentiments during trails to understand treatment impacts and experiences.
- **Healthcare Provider Performance**: Assesses reviews of providers to gauge the performance of hospitals and professionals.

- **Public Health Monitoring**: Tracks social media sentiments to identify public concerns on health issues and policies for better interventions.
- **Telehealth and Remote Patient Monitoring**: Evaluates patient feedback on telehealth services to enhance satisfaction and service delivery.
- **Mental Health Monitoring**: Analyzes sentiments in communication on monitor conditions and customize treatment plans.
- **Compliance and Adherence Monitoring**: Examines patient communication on medication adherence to identify challenges and provides support.
- **Health Information on Social Media:** Gauges public sentiments on health topics for awareness campaigns and to combat misinformation.

Integrating sentiment analysis in the healthcare and medical domain contributes to improving patient care, optimizing healthcare services, and enhancing overall healthcare outcomes. However, it is crucial to ensure patient privacy, data security, and ethical considerations when implementing sentiment analysis in healthcare settings.

6.3 Related Literature Review

Sentiment analysis models have been developed in many languages with different variations such as aspect-based sentiment analysis [11, 12], fine-grained sentiment analysis, intent-based sentiment analysis, and emotion detection covering lexicon-level [13, 14], sentence-level [15, 16], and document-level [17–20]. In Aspect-Based Sentiment Analysis (ABSA), we need to identify specific aspects of a product or business, aspects of healthcare enterprises, or aspects of a company's culture people are talking about. For example, the quality of a product, its design, price of a product, employee's job satisfaction, medications in healthcare, quality of care, etc., are some specific aspects that are liked or disliked by customers. In the context of fine-grained sentiment analysis [21], the objective is to ascertain the underlying polarity of sentiment (positive or negative) expressed in customer reviews. This method employs a lexicon-based approach to comprehensively explore the emotions and sentiments conveyed within a provided textual content based on intensity, emotions, and target. Intent-based sentiment analysis [22, 23] determines the consumer's intent and emotions. Emotion detection focuses on discerning distinct emotions of a text, including happiness, frustration, shock, fear, worry, panic, anger, grief, etc. This type of analysis typically uses lexicons to identify emotions. Carrying out analyses at the document-level and aspect-based levels is a demanding endeavor, primarily due to the formidable challenge posed by the extensive range of document categories and potential aspects that come into play. Sentiment analysis can be approached from different language perspectives:

- Monolingual sentiment analysis is the most common form of sentiment analysis. It involves analyzing the sentiment of text in a single language. For example, you might perform sentiment analysis on English text to determine whether it is positive, negative, or neutral.

- Bilingual sentiment analysis involves analyzing sentiment in text written in two languages. This can be useful when dealing with multilingual communities or text data that contains a mix of languages. The sentiment of each language is typically analyzed separately.
- Multilingual sentiment analysis involves analyzing sentiment in text written in multiple languages within a single analysis. This is more complex than bilingual sentiment analysis, as it requires handling multiple languages simultaneously. Models and techniques that support multiple languages are essential for this approach.
- Cross-lingual sentiment analysis goes a step further and involves analyzing sentiment in text across different languages while maintaining a unified sentiment scale. This requires the ability to understand the sentiment expressed in one language and map it to a standard sentiment scale across all languages. The goal of a unified sentiment scale is to ensure that sentiment scores or labels are comparable and consistent, even when analyzing text in diverse contexts. It can be particularly challenging due to linguistic and cultural differences.

Overall, the choice of which type of sentiment analysis to use depends on the researcher's specific use case, the languages involved, and the available tools and resources. Monolingual sentiment analysis is the most straightforward, while multilingual and cross-lingual sentiment analysis tasks are more complex but necessary when dealing with diverse linguistic data. In the current survey, we focus our analysis on monolingual sentiment analysis. Extensive research has been conducted in the field of sentiment analysis within the English language. However, the amount of research dedicated to sentiment analysis in low-resource languages is notably limited [24]. A multilingual language-specific XLM-T model [25] was developed in 2022 using a unified dataset of almost 200M tweets in 8 languages for Twitter sentiment analysis. Another model XLM-RoBERTa (XLM-R), was developed for low-resource language understanding by Conneau et al. [26], which outperforms mBERT [27] by up to 23% accuracy. The results of monolingual cases are shown in Table 6.1 indicating the F1 score, explained in the Eq. 6.6, under Step 7 of Algorithm 1 reported in Sect. 6.5. The referenced publications out of which the results are curated are noted.

Recently, there has been significant progress in the development of large language models (LLMs) such as GPT-3, PaLM, Flan-UL2, LLaMA, and ChatGPT. Initial efforts have been made to evaluate the performance of LLMs in sentiment analysis tasks. For example, Zhong et al. [28] found that the zero-shot performance of LLMs is comparable to fine-tuned BERT models. Wang et al. [29] conducted a preliminary study with ChatGPT, focusing on its ability to handle polarity shifts, open-domain scenarios, and sentiment inference challenges. Additionally, Zhao et al. [30] investigated ChatGPT's capacity for generating emotional responses, indicating promising results in emotional conversations. Deng et al. [31] explored fine-tuning a smaller student model using an LLM to generate weak labels, achieving perfor-

Table 6.1 Sentiment analysis F1 score results on different Asian and European languages

Languages	FT [25]	XLM-R [25]	XLM-T [25]	BERT_Wiki [26]	BERT_CC [26]
Hindi	37.08	36.60	40.29	–	–
Arabic	45.98	63.56	67.67		–
English	50.85	68.18	66.89	84.5	86.7
French	54.82	71.98	68.19	78.6	81.2
German	59.56	73.61	76.13	80	81.2
Chinese	–	–	–	77.7	79.5
Russian	–	–	–	75.5	78.2
Italian	54.65	71.47	70.91	–	–
Portuguese	55.05	67.11	75.98	–	–
Spanish	50.06	65.87	68.52	–	–
Urdu	–	–	–	57.3	65.1
Swahili	–	–	–	60.1	70.8
Greek	–	–	–	60.1	70.8

mance on par with existing supervised models. However, despite these efforts, the scope of these studies is often limited to specific tasks, involving different datasets and experimental designs. The full potential of LLMs for sentiment analysis remains uncertain [32].

6.3.1 Study Related to Arabic Text Sentiment Analysis

The research work carried out on Arabic sentiment analysis is typically performed using rule-based classifiers and machine-learning classifiers. The proposed analysis explores sentiments at different levels—sentence level, document level, and also the aspect level. The Arabic language exhibits many variations, including Classical Arabic, Modern Standard Arabic, and various dialects. Oueslati et al. [33] conducted a comprehensive survey on Arabic sentiment analysis and concluded that, according to their findings, sentiment analysis in Arabic is at an early stage of development when compared to the English language. In 2020, the six-level framework for Arabic sentiment analysis was explained by Alsayat et al. [34]. We can categorize the prior studies under three types, such as rule-based, lexicon-based, and machine-learning based approaches.

In 2014, a lexicon-based study [35] was reported for morphological analysis and disambiguation of the Arabic language by combining two systems: MADA (Morphological Analysis and Disambiguation of Arabic) [36] and AMIRA [37]. MADA produces morphological features of the word and its interpretation. AMIRA is a shallow syntactic parser, that can be used as a toolkit for tokenizing and for finding base phrases of words. In 2014, Abdul-Mageed et al. [38] developed a subjectivity and sentiment analysis - SSA system for social media data to handle lexical information and Arabic dialects. A three-class sentiment analysis problem was solved by Al-Ayyoub et al. [39] in 2015 using lexical information and they got 86.89% of accuracy. In 2021, Touahri et al. utilized an extensive collection of lexical resources, including words, stems, lemmas, and semantic classes, for the purpose of Arabic sentiment classification, as detailed in their study [40]. The HTL corpus demonstrated notably high accuracy, reaching approximately 93% across all combinations of lexical resources. In contrast, the accuracy for the other three corpora, MOV (Movie Scripts Corpus), PROD (Product Reviews Corpus), and RES (Research Articles Corpus) which are typically refer to different types of datasets used in linguistic or natural language processing research, was observed to be around 85%.

There are a number of studies using deep learning techniques for the Arabic language. Nabil et al. [41] employed a variety of machine learning algorithms, including KNN (K-Nearest Neighbors), SVM (Support Vector Machine), SGD (Stochastic Gradient Descent), MNB (Multinomial Naive Bayes), BNB (Bernoulli Naive Bayes), Logistic Regression, and Linear Perceptron, for the task of classifying Arabic sentiments, as documented in their study [41]. Among these algorithms, SVM demonstrated the highest performance, achieving a maximum accuracy of 62% on the Arabic Sentiment Tweets Dataset (ASTD). An ensemble model was developed by Heikal et al. [42] by combining CNN and LSTM models. They achieved an F1-score of 64.46%. In 2019, Al-Ayyoub et al. [43] made an effort to categorize articles related to sentiment analysis tasks in Arabic language. On the other hand, Badaro et al. [44] presented a comprehensive survey encompassing recent advancements in Arabic opinion mining systems, tools for Arabic Natural Language Processing (NLP), sentiment resources in Arabic, and classification models tailored for Arabic sentiment analysis.

6.3.2 *Study Related to Hindi Text Sentiment Analysis*

In 2010, Joshi et al. [45] presented machine-translated-based Hindi sentiment analysis using Google Translate API. In 2012, Balamurali et al. [46] presented a sense-based approach for cross-lingual SA using WordNet synset identifiers and they got 72% of accuracy for Hindi language. Bakliwal et al. [47] proposed a model for Amazon product review classification in Hindi using Google Translate. A graph-based method is used for generating Hindi subjectivity lexicons and they achieved 79% accuracy. In 2015, Sharma et al. [48], had proposed an unsupervised lexicon method for classification. Patra et al. [49] developed a model for classifying Hindi Tweets; the authors reported 55.67% of accuracy. In 2016, the sentiment analysis task was done using Hindi-English code-mixed data [50] in which subword-LSTM architecture was used for learning, which produced an F1 score of 65.8%.

Many prior works were Aspect Based Sentiment Analysis (ABSA) in Hindi language. Akhtar et al. [51] discuss ABSA and multi-labelled aspect category detection in Hindi language using 'MEKA' software. Their proposed model reports F1 scores for sentiment analysis as 54.48, 47.95, 65.20, and 91.62% in electronics, mobile apps, travel, and movies domains respectively. Garg et al. [52] proposed an ABSA method using negation handling and conjunction handling techniques. Yadav et al. (2021) conducted an e-commerce review classification with a focus on aspect-based information. Their study covered analysis of data in the home appliances domain and they achieved a maximum accuracy of 79.23%. However, in the movie domain, the accuracy dropped significantly to 39.23%, and the precision value during cross-validation was 54.05%. In the paper by Pathak et al. [53], the authors proposed transfer learning-based methods for ABSA. Specifically, they presented two models: mBERT-E-MV and mBERT-E-AS. In the mBERT-E-MV model, auxiliary sentences were constructed using aspect information, and a sentence-pair classification task was fine-tuned with the pre-trained mBERT. The mBERT-E-AS model differed from the mBERT-E-MV model in that the former made final label predictions by averaging the output softmax scores of four mBERT models, while the latter based its prediction on the majority. The results obtained on various domains are summarized in Table 6.2. In 2020, Shrivastava et al. [54] proposed a Genetic Algorithm-Gated Recurrent Unit (GA-GRU) model for solving sentiment classification problems using the Hindi movie review dataset. They used FastText pre-trained vectors as input to GRU for enhancing the text representation quality. Their model produced an F1 score of 88%. In 2022, Hindi Bengali joint dual input learning architecture with Self-Attention mechanism was introduced by Khan et al. [55]. They developed a single network for Hindi and Bengali binary classification that helps to avoid overfitting problems. In 2023, Kumari et al. [56] used several LSTM models such as Traditional LSTM, Bidirectional LSTM, and Attention-based LSTM for classifying medical reviews in Asian Hindi languages. Attention-based LSTM model performs better with the ReLU activation function and produces an F1 score of 81%.

Table 6.2 Evaluation results for IIT-Patna Hindi reviews [53]

Methods used	Domain	Precision	Recall	F1 score
mBERT-QA-M	Electronics	80.71	67.11	73.28
mBERT-E-MV	Electronics	84.39	66.31	74.26
mBERT-E-AS	Electronics	84.53	64.82	73.38
mBERT-QA-M	Mobile Apps	72.22	31.70	44.06
mBERT-E-MV	Mobile Apps	76.92	48.78	59.70
mBERT-E-AS	Mobile Apps	70.83	41.46	52.31
mBERT-NLI-M	Travel	73.91	48.11	58.28
mBERT-E-MV	Travel	76.32	54.72	63.74
mBERT-E-AS	Travel	78.46	48.11	59.65
mBERT-NLI-M	Movise	77.09	77.52	77.31
mBERT-E-MV	Movies	80.70	77.53	79.08
mBERT-E-AS	Movies	80.95	76.40	78.61

6.3.3 Study Related to English Text Sentiment Analysis

In view of wide use of the language, a large number of authors have reported results of sentiment analysis in English language. Gautam et al. [57] used the Naive-Bayes and Maximum-Entropy algorithms along with the 'semantic orientation based wordNet', in which the similarity of synonyms in the feature list is calculated for finding adjective_score and polarity of the reviews; they reports semantic analysis of tweeter data (19,340 reviews). The accuracy rates for their Naive-Bayes and Maximum-Entropy models are 88.2 and 83.8%, respectively, obtained by extracting adjectives from the phrases. However, retrieving adjectives was not the best method for feature extraction since occasionally even adjectives have their own descriptions. A dataset of 14000 tweets was used by Singh et al. [58] with Support Vector Machine (SVM), Random Forest (RF), and Decision Tree (DT) for bi-polar classification. The Decision tree method, out of these three, yields the best accuracy, 88.51%, but they got very little F1-measure on 14000 tweets collected from KFC and McDonald's datasets. The RoBERTa-LSTM model of Tan et al. [59] effectively encodes the words into word embedding while LSTM excels at capturing the long-distance relationships, and performed well on the Sentiment140 dataset with 1.6 million reviews. Naive Bayes with W-WSD embedding was used by Hasan et al. [60] to create a model, and they achieved an accuracy of 79% on sentiment tweets.

A decision tree algorithm with a classification approach was proposed by Adnan et al. [61] for sentiment analysis on restaurant reviews, which they had collected in real-time by crawling data using WebHarvy. They used Decision Tree-J48 of WEKA software for classifying the reviews. Unfortunately, it produces a very less accuracy of 45.60% and the issue that we analyzed is that a slight change in the polarity level of a query led to a significant change in the context as a whole. They processed only 64 documents. Govindarajan [62] proposed a hybrid model using three base algorithms: Naïve Bayes (NB), Support Vector Machine (SVM), and Genetic Algorithm (GA), to predict class labels. With the help of a genetic algorithm, they got an accuracy of 92.44% for Restaurant Reviews. For sentiment analysis, Basiri et al. [63] proposed a deep architecture with the help of CNN bidirectional LSTM and the GRU attention mechanism. The proposed model is tested with different word embedding such as word2vec, BERT, and FastText on IMDB movie reviews. The best F1 score is 89.8% for BERT with CNN-LSTM. Hossain et al. [64] worked on restaurant reviews using the Bidirectional-LSTM approach and Sazzed [65] proposed a hybrid model of opinion mining to solve sentiment analysis problem.

6.3.4 Study Related to Greek Text Sentiment Analysis

The Greek language is one of the low-resource European languages, classified as a lower-density language with limited linguistic resources and knowledge bases dedicated to essential text mining and NLP activities. In contrast, publicly accessible resources have demonstrated their effectiveness in state-of-the-art sentiment analysis and related tasks in English, but their development and evaluation for the Greek language have been significantly less comprehensive. In 2016, Spatiotis et al. [66] used 11156 user-generated comments to perform opinion analysis using supervised machine learning algorithms such as the J48 algorithm, Multilayer Perceptron_N_500, and RBFKernel_C_1 and RBFKernel_C_10. They classified the users' comments into five main categories: very negative, negative, neutral, positive, and very positive, using annotated data. They got 56% of accuracy with the J48 algorithm. Markopoulos et al. [67] used a lexicon-based unigram approach for classifying hotel reviews using SVM. They used a TF-IDF weighting scheme for generating feature vectors. Many research efforts in sentiment analysis for Greek rely on manually crafted sentiment lexicons. For instance, in a study [68], researchers created an emotional sentiment lexicon for a Twitter dataset in Greek. They collected the sentiment lexicon's entries by mining the electronic version of the Greek dictionary by Triantafyllides (Dictionary of Standard Modern Greek).

In 2021, Alexandridis et al. [24] conducted a survey focused on sentiment analysis and opinion mining within Greek Social Media. Their work delves into various aspects, including NLP models, Greek embeddings, and annotated corpora. They also provide insights into the classification performance of various pre-trained language models. Notably, the study reports that GreekBERT [69], PaloBERT [24], and Greek-SocialBERT [24] achieved average F1 scores of 78.45, 79.80, and 80.17, respectively, for sentiment analysis on Greek social media. Antypas et al. [70] performed a multifaceted sentiment analysis by collecting large-scale tweets from members of parliament in multiple languages to explore the correlations between sentiment and the virality of tweets.

They used multiple transformer-based language models such as XLM-T, XLM-T-Sent, XLM-R, RoBERTa-Base, TweetEval-Sent, Bertweet-Sent, SVM, LSTM, and VADER for sentiment analysis in Greek language. The best one is XLM-T-Sent, which produces 75% F1_score. Athanasiou et al. [71] applied gradient-boosting machines to demonstrate efficiency in handling high-dimensional data using a corpus of Greek tokens, and they achieved an accuracy of 84.2%.

6.3.5 Study Related to Georgian Text Sentiment Analysis

The Georgian language, considered a low-resource language, has its roots in the Caucasus region. It is spoken by approximately 3.7 million people worldwide [72]. There is limited information available on linguistic resources and NLP tools for the Georgian language. Kapanadze et al. [73] described how to develop a syntactic parser using vanilla CFG to improve the computational processing of the Georgian language text. They contributed treebank-related resources as knowledge sources for linguistic applications of the Georgian language. Few works related to morphologically-tagged corpus were discussed in papers [74, 75]. The morphological analyzer was developed using finite state automata using parts of speech lexicons and rules [75]. Commonly used lexicons include nouns, pronouns, verbal nouns, verbs, adverbs, adjectives, numerals, conjunctions, particles, postpositions, participles, punctuations, and abbreviations. Kardava et al. [74] developed a software for getting all word forms from the unchanged part of the word and getting morphological categories. The first attempt at Georgian language-based text classification in the medical field was discussed in paper [76]. They used SVM and k-nearest neighbor (KNN) algorithms for ultrasonography, endoscopy, and X-ray document classification. The average F1 scores obtained for ultrasonography, endoscopy, and X-ray documents using SVM are 77, 86, and 88% respectively. But for KNN, the F1 scores obtained were comparatively less, that is, 68, 72, and 83%. Soselia et al. [77] proposed a parallel network structure to avoid 'catastrophic forgetting' in the LSTM architecture that helps for continual learning by weight freezing and modification mechanism.

Barbieri et al. [25] have done work on Semantic Evaluation during the 13th International Workshop in the USA and also provide information on the use of cross-lingual sentiment classification with bilingual document representation learning. It also discusses the evaluation and experimental results of the XLM-T model for sentiment analysis on Twitter data. The document provides information about the distribution of languages in the dataset used for training the Twitter-based language model. Referring to Fig. 1 [25], it is evident that Uighur, Dhivehi, Lao, and Georgian are the least prevalent languages, with the number of tweets corresponding to those languages being less than/equal to 1000 out of a total of 198 million tweets. In the paper, [78] Table 1 shows the language distribution in which there are only 16 tweets in Georgian. This makes up a very small fraction of the total tweets, with a fraction of 0.0000017. The fractions represent the proportion of tweets in each language compared to the total number of tweets in the dataset. The overall accuracy and AUC score for the mono-lingual and multi-lingual classification tasks hover around 70%. Stefanovitch et al. [72] explored different machine learning models such as LR, SVM, and transformer-based models using annotated datasets for sentiment classification in Georgian language. They got the best overall results for the transformer-based approach is 75.6 and 75.2% of weighted and macro F1 score respectively using the GSS corpus for training and evaluation.

Literature study reveals that there have been numerous approaches for handling sentiment analysis in textual data, in recent years. These methods have ranged from the utilization of sentiment lexicons [79, 80] to the employment of linear machine-learning models [81]. More recently, there has been a shift towards employing transformer models such as BERT [82] for this task. Most of the work surveyed are language-dependent and accomplished the reported results employing pre-trained language models or dictionaries. In this chapter, we proposed a language-independent classifier for sentiment analysis tasks of any language. In order to achieve this goal, we have used Unicode standards to represent written text in five different languages surveyed in earlier Sects. 6.3.1–6.3.5.

6.3.6 *Evolution of Unicode Standard*

The evolution of the Unicode standard represents a remarkable journey in the field of digital communication and computing. Unicode, a character encoding standard, serves as the backbone for representing text in almost all modern software systems, including operating systems, programming languages, web browsers, and mobile devices. Its history is a testament to the challenges and triumphs in the quest for universal text representation for all the living languages around the globe.

6.3.6.1 Origins and Early Challenges (1980–1990s)

The need for a universal character encoding standard became apparent as computers began to connect globally. In the early days, various encoding systems like ASCII (American Standard Code for Information Interchange) were used, but they lacked support for non-Latin scripts and characters. This led to interoperability issues and made it difficult to handle multilingual text. Unicode emerged as a solution to this problem.

6.3.6.2 Unicode Consortium Formation (1987)

The Unicode consortium was formed with the goal of developing a single, universal character encoding standard. The consortium included major technology companies, academic institutions, and experts in the field. Their collaboration was crucial in driving the development and adoption of Unicode.

6.3.6.3 Unicode 1.0 (1991)

The first version of the Unicode standard, Unicode 1.0, was released in October 1991. It aimed to provide a consistent way of representing text across different platforms, languages, and scripts. Unicode 1.0 initially encoded 7,161 characters, including basic Latin letters, common punctuation marks, and various symbols.

6.3.6.4 Expansion and Standardization (1990–2000s)

Over the following years, Unicode continued to expand to encompass more scripts and characters of languages used around the globe. This expansion was a collaborative effort involving input from linguists, scholars, and experts in the specific language. Unicode 2.0, released in 1996, included support for additional scripts such as Cyrillic, Greek, and Han ideographs. Subsequent versions further expanded the standard to cover a wide range of languages and writing systems.

6.3.6.5 Unicode Transformation Format (UTF)

Alongside the Unicode Standard, several encoding schemes were developed to efficiently represent Unicode characters in binary form. UTF-8, UTF-16, and UTF-32 are the most commonly used encoding formats, offering various trade-offs between compatibility, efficiency, and storage requirements.

6.3.6.6 Emoji Revolution (2000s Present)

One of the most significant developments in recent years has been the widespread adoption of emoji, small pictorial icons used to express emotions, ideas, and concepts. Unicode has incorporated thousands of emoji characters into its standard, facilitating their use across different platforms and devices. The inclusion of emoji reflects Unicode's adaptability to evolving communication trends and its commitment to inclusivity.

6.3.6.7 Ongoing Development and Challenges

The Unicode consortium continues to work on refining and expanding the Unicode standard to address emerging needs and challenges. This includes encoding additional characters, improving support for complex scripts, and ensuring compatibility with evolving technology standards. Challenges such as backward compatibility, font rendering, and the need for regular updates to accommodate new characters and symbols remain ongoing concerns.

The evolution of the Unicode standard represents a remarkable achievement in the history of computing and communication. From its humble beginnings to the de-facto standard for text encoding, Unicode has played a crucial role in enabling global digital communication and fostering linguistic diversity. As technology continues to advance and communication methods evolve, Unicode will undoubtedly remain at the forefront, ensuring that people around the world can communicate effectively across linguistic and cultural barriers. Unicode's notable accomplishment lies in its extensive scope, capable of theoretically accommodating over a million distinct characters, adequate for encompassing all known character sets, including emojis.

6.4 Methodology for Sentiment Analysis Employing CAML Model

The proposed methodology employs the Cellular Automata based Machine Learning model for addressing the problems of sentiment analysis for any language text. An input language text is first converted to Unicode text. CAML model assigns a rule

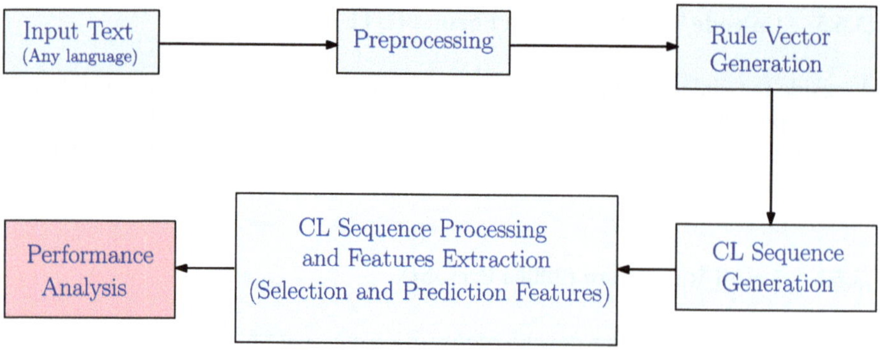

Fig. 6.2 Architecture of the proposed cellular automata-based machine learning approach

sequence for each Unicode character; on concatenating the rule sequence of each character of Unicode text, we generate a sequence of CA rules referred to as Rule Vector. In the process, the input text is modelled with a CA Rule Vector. Essentially the text get transformed to a CA model. Evolution of the CA proceeds as per the CA rule Vector generating a graph referred to as CL (Cycle Length) signal graph. CL sequence is next extracted out of CL signal graph. Thus, the model employs CA based vectorization technique for an input language text. The model features are subsequently extracted on processing the CL sequence. Figure 6.2 presents the model architecture showing the interconnected blocks. Functions of the four major blocks of Fig. 6.2 are elaborated in next four subsections. These four major blocks are : (i) Preprocessing of text (ii) Generation of CA rule vector (iii) CL graph generation (iv) Feature extraction from CL Graph.

6.4.1 Preprocessing (Conversion of Input Language Text to Unicode Text)

The Unicode standard is the global character encoding platform created to allow exchange, processing, and provision of a visual representation of written texts created in different languages. Unicode database contains Unicode charts. A list of character names and their corresponding character codes of different languages are reported in the Unicode table [83]. In the preprocessing step, the alphabets of input language text are replaced with Unicode character/code assigned for the language characters. In the process, the input text gets transformed to Unicode text. Code converters from one language text to Unicode text are available in different websites.

6.4.2 Generation of CA Rule Vector (on Inserting Rule Sequence for Each Character of Unicode Text)

Unicode assigns a unique code point to each of the characters, allowing them to be represented digitally and enabling interoperability across different systems and platforms. CAML model assigns a sequence of CA rules for each Unicode character. In order to cover the entire set of Unicode characters, minimum of one to maximum of three CA rules is necessary.

Following two steps are executed for generation of CA Rule Vector for the input language text, converted to Unicode text in the preprocessing phase:

- From the Unicode chart and table, identify the position for an unicode character representing an alphabet in a language.
- If the position is noted in the format: 0x (v1 v2 v3 v4), where v1, v2, v3, v4 are hexa-decimal characters, then the decimal value derived for the character in that position is $256^1(16v1 + v2) + 256^0(16v3 + v4)$. The corresponding CA rule can be calculated using the expression: <(16v1 + v2), (16v3 + v4)>. If v1 and v2 both are 0 then the corresponding CA rule calculated using the expression is : <(16v3 + v4)>. In case a Unicode character is encoded with six hexa-decimal characters, it will need three CA rules to represent that character.

A few illustrations are noted below:

1. The Unicode position for the Greek small letter α is 0x(03B1); its CA rule sequence will be <3 177> which is obtained from the expression: <(16 * 0 + 3) (16 * 11 + 1)>.
2. The Unicode position for the character @ is 0x(FF20); its CA rule sequence will be <255 32> which is obtained from the expression:<(16 * 15 + 15), (16 * 2 +0)>.
3. The Unicode for character # is 0x(0023); its CA rule sequence <0 35> is represented as <35> on excluding rule 0 of the sequence obtained from the expression : <(16 * 2 +3)>. That is, while generating CA rule sequence for a Unicode character, we delete the leading 0 rule of the generated sequence.
4. The Unicode position for space character is 0x0020; its CA rule sequence will be < 0 32 >. In case of English language, all the characters are represent by single rule, so for the English text we used CA rule < 32 > to represent space character.

6.4.2.1 Rule Vectors for the English Language Text

English language, being one of the most widely spoken languages globally, has naturally played a major role in the initial phase of design of the Unicode standard. Unicode includes all the characters that can be encoded in ASCII (American Standard Code for Information Interchange), in addition to many more language characters.

Within the Unicode standard, the English language characters are primarily represented using the Basic Latin block (U+0000 to U+007F); the CA rule sequence is noted as <127> for the control (C0) character 'unit separator' code U+007F. This block includes the standard English alphabet (both uppercase and lowercase letters), digits (0–9), punctuation marks, and other symbols commonly used in English writing. The CA rule sequence for all the English alphabets and digits are shown in Table 6.3. Unicode extends the rage to U+00FF to support extended ASCII characters; the CA rule sequence for the last character in the list 'Latin Small Letter Y with diaeresis' is <255>. Using Table 6.3, any English language text can be converted to CA rule vector. For example, a text can be vectorized using the rules noted in Table 6.3 as shown below :

English Text: "I would appreciate an apology from both of you but I can see that is unlikely."

CA Rule Vectors for English Text: [73, 32, 119, 111, 117, 108, 100, 32, 97, 112, 112, 114, 101, 99, 105, 97, 116, 101, 32, 97, 110, 32, 97, 112, 111, 108, 111, 103, 121, 32, 102, 114, 111, 109, 32, 98, 111, 116, 104, 32, 111, 102, 32, 121, 111, 117, 32, 98, 117, 116, 32, 73, 32, 99, 97, 110, 32, 115, 101, 101, 32, 116, 104, 97, 116, 32, 105, 115, 32, 117, 110, 108, 105, 107, 101, 108, 121, 46].

6.4.2.2 Rule Vectors for the Arabic Language Text

Arabic Unicode encompasses a vast array of characters, symbols, and diacritics used to write the Arabic script, one of the most widely used writing systems in the world. Unicode, being a universal character encoding standard, includes comprehensive support for Arabic script characters to facilitate digital communication, text processing, and localization efforts across various platforms and devices. Within the Unicode standard, the Arabic language is primarily represented using the Basic Arabic Block (U+0600 to U+06FF). This block includes the core Arabic alphabet, which consists of 28 letters. Additionally, this block contains Arabic punctuation marks, mathematical symbols, and other characters essential for Arabic script text. The CA rules for all the importance Arabic alphabets are shown in Table 6.4. Using this table, any Arabic text can be converted to CA rule vector. For example, a text can be vectorized using the rules noted in Table 6.4 as shown below:

Arabic Text : افلام الرعب تاثر اطفالنا

(English Translation: "Horror movies affect our children") *CA Rule Vector for the Arabic Text*: [6, 39, 6, 65, 6, 68, 6, 39, 6, 69, 0, 32, 6, 39, 6, 68, 6, 49, 6, 57, 6, 40, 0, 32, 6, 42, 6, 39, 6, 43, 6, 49, 0, 32, 6, 39, 6, 55, 6, 65, 6, 39, 6, 68, 6, 70, 6, 39]

Table 6.3 CA Rules for English alphabets and digits

Alphabet	Rules	Alphabet	Rules	Alphabet	Rules	Alphabet	Rules
	<32>	8	<56>	P	<80>	h	<104>
!	<33>	9	<57>	Q	<81>	i	<105>
"	<34>	:	<58>	R	<82>	j	<106>
#	<35>	;	<59>	S	<83>	k	<107>
$	<36>	<	<60>	T	<84>	l	<108>
%	<37>	=	<61>	U	<85>	m	<109>
&	<38>	>	<62>	V	<86>	n	<110>
'	<39>	?	<63>	W	<87>	o	<111>
(	<40>	@	<64>	X	<88>	p	<112>
)	<41>	A	<65>	Y	<89>	q	<113>
*	<42>	B	<66>	Z	<90>	r	<114>
+	<43>	C	<67>	[	<91>	s	<115>
,	<44>	D	<68>	\	<92>	t	<116>
-	<45>	E	<69>	]	<93>	u	<117>
.	<46>	F	<70>	^	<94>	v	<118>
/	<47>	G	<71>	_	<95>	w	<119>
0	<48>	H	<72>	`	<96>	x	<120>
1	<49>	I	<73>	a	<97>	y	<121>
2	<50>	J	<74>	b	<98>	z	<122>
3	<51>	K	<75>	c	<99>	{	<123>
4	<52>	L	<76>	d	<100>	|	<124>
5	<53>	M	<77>	e	<101>	}	<125>
6	<54>	N	<78>	f	<102>	~	<126>
7	<55>	O	<79>	g	<103>		

Table 6.4 Rules generated for extended Arabic letters and digits

Alphabet	Rules	Alphabet	Rules	Alphabet	Rules	Alphabet	Rules	Alphabet	Rules
؀	<6, 0>	ش	<6, 52>	٨	<6, 104>	ڜ	<6, 156>	ې	<6, 208>
؁	<6, 1>	ص	<6, 53>	٩	<6, 105>	ڝ	<6, 157>	ۑ	<6, 209>
؂	<6, 2>	ض	<6, 54>	٪	<6, 106>	ڞ	<6, 158>	ے	<6, 210>
؃	<6, 3>	ط	<6, 55>	٫	<6, 107>	ڟ	<6, 159>	ۓ	<6, 211>
؄	<6, 4>	ظ	<6, 56>	٬	<6, 108>	ڠ	<6, 160>	۔	<6, 212>
	<6, 5>	ع	<6, 57>	٭	<6, 109>	ڡ	<6, 161>	ە	<6, 213>
؆	<6, 6>	غ	<6, 58>	ٮ	<6, 110>	ڢ	<6, 162>	◌ۖ	<6, 214>
؇	<6, 7>	ػ	<6, 59>	ٯ	<6, 111>	ڣ	<6, 163>	◌ۗ	<6, 215>
؈	<6, 8>	ؼ	<6, 60>	◌ٰ	<6, 112>	ڤ	<6, 164>	◌ۘ	<6, 216>
؉	<6, 9>	ؽ	<6, 61>	ٱ	<6, 113>	ڥ	<6, 165>	◌ۙ	<6, 217>
؊	<6, 10>	ؾ	<6, 62>	ٲ	<6, 114>	ڦ	<6, 166>	◌ۚ	<6, 218>
؋	<6, 11>	ؿ	<6, 63>	ٳ	<6, 115>	ڧ	<6, 167>	◌ۛ	<6, 219>
،	<6, 12>	ـ	<6, 64>	ٴ	<6, 116>	ڨ	<6, 168>	◌ۜ	<6, 220>
؍	<6, 13>	ف	<6, 65>	ٵ	<6, 117>	ک	<6, 169>	۝	<6, 221>
؎	<6, 14>	ق	<6, 66>	ٶ	<6, 118>	ڪ	<6, 170>	۞	<6, 222>
؏	<6, 15>	ك	<6, 67>	ٷ	<6, 119>	ګ	<6, 171>	◌۟	<6, 223>
◌ؐ	<6, 16>	ل	<6, 68>	ٸ	<6, 120>	ڬ	<6, 172>	◌۠	<6, 224>
◌ؑ	<6, 17>	م	<6, 69>	ٹ	<6, 121>	ڭ	<6, 173>	◌ۡ	<6, 225>
◌ؒ	<6, 18>	ن	<6, 70>	ٺ	<6, 122>	ڮ	<6, 174>	◌ۢ	<6, 226>
◌ؓ	<6, 19>	ه	<6, 71>	ٻ	<6, 123>	گ	<6, 175>	◌ۣ	<6, 227>
◌ؔ	<6, 20>	و	<6, 72>	ټ	<6, 124>	ڰ	<6, 176>	◌ۤ	<6, 228>
◌ؕ	<6, 21>	ى	<6, 73>	ٽ	<6, 125>	ڱ	<6, 177>	ۥ	<6, 229>
ؖ	<6, 22>	ي	<6, 74>	پ	<6, 126>	ڲ	<6, 178>	ۦ	<6, 230>
ؗ	<6, 23>	◌ً	<6, 75>	ٿ	<6, 127>	ڳ	<6, 179>	◌ۧ	<6, 231>
ؘ	<6, 24>	◌ٌ	<6, 76>	ڀ	<6, 128>	ڴ	<6, 180>	◌ۨ	<6, 232>
ؙ	<6, 25>	◌ٍ	<6, 77>	ځ	<6, 129>	ڵ	<6, 181>	۩	<6, 233>
ؚ	<6, 26>	◌َ	<6, 78>	ڂ	<6, 130>	ڶ	<6, 182>	◌۪	<6, 234>
؛	<6, 27>	◌ُ	<6, 79>	ڃ	<6, 131>	ڷ	<6, 183>	◌۫	<6, 235>
	<6, 28>	◌ِ	<6, 80>	ڄ	<6, 132>	ڸ	<6, 184>	◌۬	<6, 236>
□	<6, 29>	◌ّ	<6, 81>	څ	<6, 133>	ڹ	<6, 185>	◌ۭ	<6, 237>
؞	<6, 30>	◌ْ	<6, 82>	چ	<6, 134>	ں	<6, 186>	ۮ	<6, 238>
؟	<6, 31>	◌ٓ	<6, 83>	ڇ	<6, 135>	ڻ	<6, 187>	ۯ	<6, 239>
ؠ	<6, 32>	◌ٔ	<6, 84>	ڈ	<6, 136>	ڼ	<6, 188>	۰	<6, 240>
ء	<6, 33>	◌ٕ	<6, 85>	ډ	<6, 137>	ڽ	<6, 189>	۱	<6, 241>
آ	<6, 34>	◌ٖ	<6, 86>	ڊ	<6, 138>	ھ	<6, 190>	۲	<6, 242>
أ	<6, 35>	◌ٗ	<6, 87>	ڋ	<6, 139>	ڿ	<6, 191>	۳	<6, 243>
ؤ	<6, 36>	◌٘	<6, 88>	ڌ	<6, 140>	ۀ	<6, 192>	۴	<6, 244>
إ	<6, 37>	◌ٙ	<6, 89>	ڍ	<6, 141>	ہ	<6, 193>	۵	<6, 245>
ئ	<6, 38>	◌ٚ	<6, 90>	ڎ	<6, 142>	ۂ	<6, 194>	۶	<6, 246>
ا	<6, 39>	◌ٛ	<6, 91>	ڏ	<6, 143>	ۃ	<6, 195>	۷	<6, 247>
ب	<6, 40>	◌ٜ	<6, 92>	ڐ	<6, 144>	ۄ	<6, 196>	۸	<6, 248>
ة	<6, 41>	◌ٝ	<6, 93>	ڑ	<6, 145>	ۅ	<6, 197>	۹	<6, 249>
ت	<6, 42>	◌ٞ	<6, 94>	ڒ	<6, 146>	ۆ	<6, 198>	ۺ	<6, 250>
ث	<6, 43>	◌ٟ	<6, 95>	ړ	<6, 147>	ۇ	<6, 199>	ۻ	<6, 251>
ج	<6, 44>	٠	<6, 96>	ڔ	<6, 148>	ۈ	<6, 200>	ۼ	<6, 252>
ح	<6, 45>	١	<6, 97>	ڕ	<6, 149>	ۉ	<6, 201>	۽	<6, 253>
خ	<6, 46>	٢	<6, 98>	ږ	<6, 150>	ۊ	<6, 202>	۾	<6, 254>
د	<6, 47>	٣	<6, 99>	ڗ	<6, 151>	ۋ	<6, 203>	ۿ	<6, 255>
ذ	<6, 48>	٤	<6, 100>	ژ	<6, 152>	ی	<6, 204>		
ر	<6, 49>	٥	<6, 101>	ڙ	<6, 153>	ۍ	<6, 205>		
ز	<6, 50>	٦	<6, 102>	ښ	<6, 154>	ێ	<6, 206>		
س	<6, 51>	٧	<6, 103>	ڛ	<6, 155>	ۏ	<6, 207>		

6.4.2.3 Rule Vectors for the Hindi Language Text

Among the multitude of languages, Hindi, one of the most widely spoken languages globally, has its own Unicode standard. Hindi Unicode plays a crucial role in enabling digital communication, content creation, and accessibility for millions of Hindi speakers worldwide. Hindi Unicode includes characters used in Devanagari script, which is the primary script used for writing Hindi. Devanagari Unicode stands as a cornerstone in the digital representation of Indic scripts, serving as the standardized encoding system for the Devanagari script and its variants. With its roots deeply entrenched in the rich cultural and linguistic heritage of the Indian subcontinent, Devanagari Unicode plays a pivotal role in preserving and propagating Indic languages. Devanagari script covers a wide range of characters, including consonants, vowels, diacritics, and other symbols used in Hindi writing. The Unicode range for Devanagari script starts from U+0900 to U+097F. This range includes characters for Hindi and other languages that use Devanagari script, such as Marathi, Nepali, and Sanskrit. The CA rules for all the importance Hindi alphabets are shown in Table 6.5. Using this table, any Hindi text can be converted to CA rule vector. An example for Hindi text conversion using Table 6.5 is reported below :

Hindi Text: "मकिी वाइरस पूरी तरह से मनीष पॉल की फलि्म है और फलि्म में उनकी इमेज के हसिाब से ही दृश्य और स्थतियिां रची गई थीं "

(English Translation: "Mickey Virus" is completely Manish Paul's film, and the scenes and situations in the film were created according to his image.)

CA Rule Vector for Hindi Text: [9, 46, 9, 63, 9, 21, 9, 64, 0, 32, 9, 53, 9, 62, 9, 7, 9, 48, 9, 56, 0, 32, 9, 42, 9, 66, 9, 48, 9, 64, 0, 32, 9, 36, 9, 48, 9, 57, 0, 32, 9, 56, 9, 71, 0, 32, 9, 46, 9, 40, 9, 64, 9, 55, 0, 32, 9, 42, 9, 73, 9, 50, 0, 32, 9, 21, 9, 64, 0, 32, 9, 43, 9, 63, 9, 50, 9, 77, 9, 46, 0, 32, 9, 57, 9, 72, 0, 32, 9, 20, 9, 48, 0, 32, 9, 43, 9, 63, 9, 50, 9, 77, 9, 46, 0, 32, 9, 46, 9, 71, 9, 2, 0, 32, 9, 9, 9, 40, 9, 21, 9, 64, 0, 32, 9, 7, 9, 46, 9, 71, 9, 28, 0, 32, 9, 21, 9, 71, 0, 32, 9, 57, 9, 63, 9, 56, 9, 62, 9, 44, 0, 32, 9, 56, 9, 71, 0, 32, 9, 57, 9, 64, 0, 32, 9, 38, 9, 67, 9, 54, 9, 77, 9, 47, 0, 32, 9, 20, 9, 48, 0, 32, 9, 56, 9, 77, 9, 37, 9, 63, 9, 36, 9, 63, 9, 47, 9, 62, 9, 2, 0, 32, 9, 48, 9, 26, 9, 64, 0, 32, 9, 23, 9, 8, 0, 32, 9, 37, 9, 64, 9, 2].

6.4.2.4 Rule Vectors for the Greek Language Text

The Greek Unicode standard is an essential component of digital communication and text processing, enabling the representation of the Greek language and its characters across various digital platforms. The Greek Unicode standard encompasses a wide range of characters, including the Greek alphabet, diacritics, punctuation marks, and additional symbols used in the Greek language and its historical scripts. The Greek alphabet, which originated in ancient Greece and has been in use for over 2,500 years, serves as the foundation of the Greek Unicode standard. It consists of 24 letters, both uppercase and lowercase, each represented by a unique Unicode code point. The Unicode range for Greek characters spans from U+0391 to U+03C9 for the basic Greek

Table 6.5 Rules generated for Devanagari script

Alphabet	Rules	Alphabet	Rules	Alphabet	Rules	Alphabet	Rules
ँ	<9, 0>	ठ	<9, 32>	ँ	<9, 64>	ॠ	<9, 96>
ँ	<9, 1>	ड	<9, 33>	ँ	<9, 65>	ॡ	<9, 97>
ँ	<9, 2>	ढ	<9, 34>	ँ	<9, 66>	ँ	<9, 98>
ँ	<9, 3>	ण	<9, 35>	ँ	<9, 67>	ँ	<9, 99>
ऄ	<9, 4>	त	<9, 36>	ँ	<9, 68>	।	<9, 100>
अ	<9, 5>	थ	<9, 37>	ँ	<9, 69>	॥	<9, 101>
आ	<9, 6>	द	<9, 38>	ँ	<9, 70>	०	<9, 102>
इ	<9, 7>	ध	<9, 39>	ँ	<9, 71>	१	<9, 103>
ई	<9, 8>	न	<9, 40>	ँ	<9, 72>	२	<9, 104>
उ	<9, 9>	ऩ	<9, 41>	ँ	<9, 73>	३	<9, 105>
ऊ	<9, 10>	प	<9, 42>	ँ	<9, 74>	४	<9, 106>
ऋ	<9, 11>	फ	<9, 43>	ँ	<9, 75>	५	<9, 107>
ऌ	<9, 12>	ब	<9, 44>	ँ	<9, 76>	६	<9, 108>
ऍ	<9, 13>	भ	<9, 45>	ँ	<9, 77>	७	<9, 109>
ऎ	<9, 14>	म	<9, 46>	ि	<9, 78>	८	<9, 110>
ए	<9, 15>	य	<9, 47>	ँ	<9, 79>	९	<9, 111>
ऐ	<9, 16>	र	<9, 48>	ॐ	<9, 80>	॰	<9, 112>
ऑ	<9, 17>	ऱ	<9, 49>	ँ	<9, 81>	·	<9, 113>
ऒ	<9, 18>	ल	<9, 50>	ँ	<9, 82>	ॲ	<9, 114>
ओ	<9, 19>	ळ	<9, 51>	`	<9, 83>	ॳ	<9, 115>
औ	<9, 20>	ऴ	<9, 52>	´	<9, 84>	ॴ	<9, 116>
क	<9, 21>	व	<9, 53>	ँ	<9, 85>	ॵ	<9, 117>
ख	<9, 22>	श	<9, 54>	ँ	<9, 86>	ॶ	<9, 118>
ग	<9, 23>	ष	<9, 55>	ँ	<9, 87>	ॷ	<9, 119>
घ	<9, 24>	स	<9, 56>	क़	<9, 88>	ॸ	<9, 120>
ङ	<9, 25>	ह	<9, 57>	ख़	<9, 89>	ॹ	<9, 121>
च	<9, 26>	ँ	<9, 58>	ग़	<9, 90>	ॺ	<9, 122>
छ	<9, 27>	ँ	<9, 59>	ज़	<9, 91>	ॻ	<9, 123>
ज	<9, 28>	ँ	<9, 60>	ड़	<9, 92>	ॼ	<9, 124>
झ	<9, 29>	ऽ	<9, 61>	ढ़	<9, 93>	?	<9, 126>
ञ	<9, 30>	ँ	<9, 62>	फ़	<9, 94>	ॿ	<9, 127>
ट	<9, 31>	ॉ	<9, 63>	य़	<9, 95>		

alphabet. In addition to the basic alphabets, the Greek Unicode standard also incorporates diacritics, which are marks or accents added to letters to indicate pronunciation or modify their meaning. Diacritics commonly used in Greek include accents (acute, grave, and circumflex), breathings (rough and smooth), and diaeresis. These diacritical marks are assigned specific Unicode code points, allowing for their accurate representation and combination with Greek letters. Furthermore, the Greek Unicode standard includes a variety of punctuation marks, numerals, mathematical symbols, and other characters used in Greek texts. The CA rules for all the importance Greek alphabets are shown in Table 6.6. Using this table, any Greek text can be converted to CA rule vector. An example for Greek text conversion using Table 6.6 is given below :

Greek Text: " **Δεν έλαβα από πότε ενημέρωση για τη εξέλιξη της παραγγελίας μου και εμφανίζεται ακόμα σε αναμονή έχω στείλει μέιλ και καμιά απαντηση** "

(English Translation: "I haven't received any updates on the progress of my order since when it still appears as pending. I have sent an email but haven't received any response.") *CA Rule Vector for Greek Text*: [3, 148, 3, 181, 3, 189, 0, 32, 3, 173, 3, 187, 3, 177, 3, 178, 3, 177, 0, 32, 3, 177, 3, 192, 3, 204, 0, 32, 0, 32, 3, 192, 3, 204, 3, 196, 3, 181, 0, 32, 3, 181, 3, 189, 3, 183, 3, 188, 3, 173, 3, 193, 3, 201, 3, 195, 3, 183, 0, 32, 3, 179, 3, 185, 3, 177, 0, 32, 3, 196, 3, 183, 0, 32, 3, 181, 3, 190, 3, 173, 3, 187, 3, 185, 3, 190, 3, 183, 0, 32, 3, 196, 3, 183, 3, 194, 0, 32, 3, 192, 3, 177, 3, 193, 3, 177, 3, 179, 3, 179, 3, 181, 3, 187, 3, 175, 3, 177, 3, 194, 0, 32, 3, 188, 3, 191, 3, 197, 0, 32, 3, 186, 3, 177, 3, 185, 0, 32, 3, 181, 3, 188, 3, 198, 3, 177, 3, 189, 3, 175, 3, 182, 3, 181, 3, 196, 3, 177, 3, 185, 0, 32, 3, 177, 3, 186, 3, 204, 3, 188, 3, 177, 0, 32, 3, 195, 3, 181, 0, 32, 3, 177, 3, 189, 3, 177, 3, 188, 3, 191, 3, 189, 3, 174, 0, 32, 3, 173, 3, 199, 3, 201, 0, 32, 3, 195, 3, 196, 3, 181, 3, 175, 3, 187, 3, 181, 3, 185, 0, 32, 3, 188, 3, 173, 3, 185, 3, 187, 0, 32, 3, 186, 3, 177, 3, 185, 0, 32, 3, 186, 3, 177, 3, 188, 3, 185, 3, 172, 0, 32, 3, 177, 3, 192, 3, 177, 3, 189, 3, 196, 3, 183, 3, 195, 3, 183].

6.4.2.5 Rule Vectors for the Georgian Language Text

Georgian Unicode plays a fundamental role in the digital representation and communication of the Georgian language, providing a standardized encoding system for Georgian characters across various digital platforms and devices. The Georgian Unicode standard encompasses a range of characters used in the Georgian alphabet, as well as additional symbols and punctuation marks specific to the Georgian language. These characters are assigned specific Unicode code points, allowing for their accurate representation and handling in digital environments. The Georgian alphabet, also known as Mkhedruli, is the modern script used for writing the Georgian language. It consists of 33 letters, both uppercase and lowercase, each represented by a unique Unicode code point. The Unicode range for Georgian characters spans from U+10D0 to U+10FF. In addition to the basic alphabet, the Georgian Unicode standard also incorporates diacritics and additional characters used in Georgian texts. The CA rules for all the importance Georgian alphabets are shown in Table 6.7. Using this table, any Georgian text can be converted to CA rule vector. An example of Georgian text conversion using the rules given in Table 6.7 is presented below :

Georgian text: "**კომპანიას უკვე მეორე დღეა თავის Facebookის გვერდზე უამრავი შეურაც ხმყოფელი კომენტარით ამკობენ გაბრაზებული გულშემატკივრები**"

(English Translation: "The company has already been gathering numerous disapproving comments on its Facebook page for the second day in a row.")

Table 6.6 Rule table for Greek letters

Alphabet	Rules	Alphabet	Rules	Alphabet	Rules	Alphabet	Rules
Ͱ	<3, 112>	Κ	<3, 154>	ν	<3, 189>	ϟ	<3, 223>
ͱ	<3, 113>	Λ	<3, 155>	ξ	<3, 190>	Ϡ	<3, 224>
Ͳ	<3, 114>	Μ	<3, 156>	ο	<3, 191>	ϡ	<3, 225>
ͳ	<3, 115>	Ν	<3, 157>	π	<3, 192>	Ϣ	<3, 226>
ʹ	<3, 116>	Ξ	<3, 158>	ρ	<3, 193>	ϣ	<3, 227>
͵	<3, 117>	Ο	<3, 159>	ς	<3, 194>	Ϥ	<3, 228>
Ͷ	<3, 118>	Π	<3, 160>	σ	<3, 195>	ϥ	<3, 229>
ͷ	<3, 119>	Ρ	<3, 161>	τ	<3, 196>	Ϧ	<3, 230>
ͺ	<3, 122>	Σ	<3, 163>	υ	<3, 197>	ϧ	<3, 231>
ͻ	<3, 123>	Τ	<3, 164>	φ	<3, 198>	Ϩ	<3, 232>
ͼ	<3, 124>	Υ	<3, 165>	χ	<3, 199>	ϩ	<3, 233>
ͽ	<3, 125>	Φ	<3, 166>	ψ	<3, 200>	Ϫ	<3, 234>
;	<3, 126>	Χ	<3, 167>	ω	<3, 201>	ϫ	<3, 235>
Ϳ	<3, 127>	Ψ	<3, 168>	ϊ	<3, 202>	Ϭ	<3, 236>
΄	<3, 132>	Ω	<3, 169>	ϋ	<3, 203>	ϭ	<3, 237>
΅	<3, 133>	Ϊ	<3, 170>	ό	<3, 204>	Ϯ	<3, 238>
Ά	<3, 134>	Ϋ	<3, 171>	ύ	<3, 205>	ϯ	<3, 239>
·	<3, 135>	ά	<3, 172>	ώ	<3, 206>	ϰ	<3, 240>
Έ	<3, 136>	έ	<3, 173>	Ϗ	<3, 207>	ϱ	<3, 241>
Ή	<3, 137>	ή	<3, 174>	ϐ	<3, 208>	ϲ	<3, 242>
Ί	<3, 138>	ί	<3, 175>	ϑ	<3, 209>	ϳ	<3, 243>
Ό	<3, 140>	ΰ	<3, 176>	ϒ	<3, 210>	ϴ	<3, 244>
Ύ	<3, 142>	α	<3, 177>	ϓ	<3, 211>	ϵ	<3, 245>
Ώ	<3, 143>	β	<3, 178>	ϔ	<3, 212>	϶	<3, 246>
Ï	<3, 144>	γ	<3, 179>	ϕ	<3, 213>	Ϸ	<3, 247>
Α	<3, 145>	δ	<3, 180>	ϖ	<3, 214>	ϸ	<3, 248>
Β	<3, 146>	ε	<3, 181>	ϗ	<3, 215>	Ϲ	<3, 249>
Γ	<3, 147>	ζ	<3, 182>	Ϙ	<3, 216>	Ϻ	<3, 250>
Δ	<3, 148>	η	<3, 183>	ϙ	<3, 217>	ϻ	<3, 251>
Ε	<3, 149>	θ	<3, 184>	Ϛ	<3, 218>	ϼ	<3, 252>
Ζ	<3, 150>	ι	<3, 185>	ϛ	<3, 219>	Ͻ	<3, 253>
Η	<3, 151>	κ	<3, 186>	Ϝ	<3, 220>	Ͼ	<3, 254>
Θ	<3, 152>	λ	<3, 187>	ϝ	<3, 221>	Ͽ	<3, 255>
Ι	<3, 153>	μ	<3, 188>	Ϟ	<3, 222>		

Table 6.7 Rule table for Georgian letters

Alphabet	Rules	Alphabet	Rules	Alphabet	Rules	Alphabet	Rules
Ⴀ	<16, 160>	Ⴖ	<16, 182>	ე	<16, 212>	ც	<16, 234>
Ⴁ	<16, 161>	Ⴗ	<16, 183>	ვ	<16, 213>	ძ	<16, 235>
Ⴂ	<16, 162>	Ⴘ	<16, 184>	ზ	<16, 214>	წ	<16, 236>
Ⴃ	<16, 163>	Ⴙ	<16, 185>	თ	<16, 215>	ჭ	<16, 237>
Ⴄ	<16, 164>	Ⴚ	<16, 186>	ი	<16, 216>	ხ	<16, 238>
Ⴅ	<16, 165>	Ⴛ	<16, 187>	კ	<16, 217>	ჯ	<16, 239>
Ⴆ	<16, 166>	Ⴜ	<16, 188>	ლ	<16, 218>	ჰ	<16, 240>
Ⴇ	<16, 167>	Ⴝ	<16, 189>	მ	<16, 219>	ჱ	<16, 241>
Ⴈ	<16, 168>	Ⴞ	<16, 190>	ნ	<16, 220>	ჲ	<16, 242>
Ⴉ	<16, 169>	Ⴟ	<16, 191>	ო	<16, 221>	ჳ	<16, 243>
Ⴊ	<16, 170>	Ⴠ	<16, 192>	პ	<16, 222>	ჴ	<16, 244>
Ⴋ	<16, 171>	Ⴡ	<16, 193>	ჟ	<16, 223>	ჵ	<16, 245>
Ⴌ	<16, 172>	Ⴢ	<16, 194>	რ	<16, 224>	ჶ	<16, 246>
Ⴍ	<16, 173>	Ⴣ	<16, 195>	ს	<16, 225>	ჷ	<16, 247>
Ⴎ	<16, 174>	Ⴤ	<16, 196>	ტ	<16, 226>	ჸ	<16, 248>
Ⴏ	<16, 175>	Ⴥ	<16, 197>	უ	<16, 227>	ჹ	<16, 249>
Ⴐ	<16, 176>	Ⴧ	<16, 199>	ფ	<16, 228>	ჺ	<16, 250>
Ⴑ	<16, 177>	Ⴭ	<16, 205>	ქ	<16, 229>	჻	<16, 251>
Ⴒ	<16, 178>	ა	<16, 208>	ღ	<16, 230>		
Ⴓ	<16, 179>	ბ	<16, 209>	ყ	<16, 231>		
Ⴔ	<16, 180>	გ	<16, 210>	შ	<16, 232>		
Ⴕ	<16, 181>	დ	<16, 211>	ჩ	<16, 233>		

CA Rule Vector for Georgian Text: [16, 217, 16, 221, 16, 219, 16, 222, 16, 208, 16, 220, 16, 216, 16, 208, 16, 225, 0, 32, 16, 227, 16, 217, 16, 213, 16, 212, 0, 32, 16, 219, 16, 212, 16, 221, 16, 224, 16, 212, 0, 32, 16, 211, 16, 230, 16, 212, 16, 208, 0, 32, 16, 215, 16, 208, 16, 213, 16, 216, 16, 225, 0, 32, 16, 216, 16, 225, 0, 32, 16, 210, 16, 213, 16, 212, 16, 224, 16, 211, 16, 214, 16, 212, 0, 32, 16, 227, 16, 208, 16, 219, 16, 224, 16, 208, 16, 213, 16, 216, 0, 32, 16, 232, 16, 212, 16, 227, 16, 224, 16, 208, 16, 234, 16, 238, 16, 219, 16, 231, 16, 221, 16, 228, 16, 212, 16, 218, 16, 216, 0, 32, 16, 217, 16, 221, 16, 219, 16, 212, 16, 220, 16, 226, 16, 208, 16, 224, 16, 216, 16, 215, 0, 32, 16, 208, 16, 219, 16, 217, 16, 221, 16, 209, 16, 212, 16, 220, 0, 32, 16, 210, 16, 208, 16, 209, 16, 224, 16, 208, 16, 214, 16, 212, 16, 209, 16, 227, 16, 218, 16, 216, 0, 32, 16, 210, 16, 227, 16, 218, 16, 232, 16, 212, 16, 219, 16, 208, 16, 226, 16, 217, 16, 216, 16, 213, 16, 224, 16, 212, 16, 209, 16, 216].

....	1	0	1	0	1	0	1	0	....
....	0	1	0	1	0	1	1	0	....
....	1	0	1	0	1	1	1	0	....
....	1	0	0	1	0	0	1	1	....
....	0	0	1	0	0	1	1	1	....
....	1	1	0	1	1	0	1	0	....
....	1	1	0	0	1	0	0	0	....
....	0	0	0	1	1	0	0	1	....
....	1	1	0	0	0	1	1	0	....
....	1	0	0	1	1	0	0	0	....
....	0	1	1	0	0	0	0	0	....
....	1	0	0	1	0	0	0	0	....
....	1	0	0	0	0	1	0	1	....
....	⋮	⋮	⋮	⋮	⋮	⋮	⋮	⋮	....

Fig. 6.3 CA evolution

6.4.3 CL Graph Generation and Extraction of CL Sequence

The CA evolution proceeds as per the CA rule vector generated for an input text. The evolution generates Cycle Length (CL) signal graph. The CA begins with an initial configuration for the cells, consisting alternating sequence of 1's and 0's. The length of this initial sequence matches the size of the rule vector showing the CA rule assigned for each cell.

The next state of the current cell is evaluated based on the states of neighboring cells and the rule number specified for the cell in the rule vector. The CA evolves a minimum of 1000 iterations in our experiment for an input text modelled by the CA rule vector. If the length of the CA exceeds 2000, then half of the length of the CA is considered as evaluation steps. While Fig. 6.3 illustrates sample CA evolution, Fig. 6.4 reports CL signal graph generated for an English language text. On the other hand, Fig. 6.5 illustrates generation of CL signal graph out of CA evolution for an Arabic language text. After a certain period of time, a pattern begins to emerge on each CA cell; the length of the pattern is referred to as Cycle length. Thus, the CL value characterizes the length of the recurring pattern during CA evolution. If a specific pattern recurs at least 32 times, we designate this count as the CL value for that particular CA cell. The choice of 32 times, serves as a threshold value; altering it does not affect performance, since CL values represent the length of the repeated pattern. In cases where no repeated patterns are discerned in the CA cell, we assign a '–5' value to that cell. Alternatively, zero or any negative value can be considered

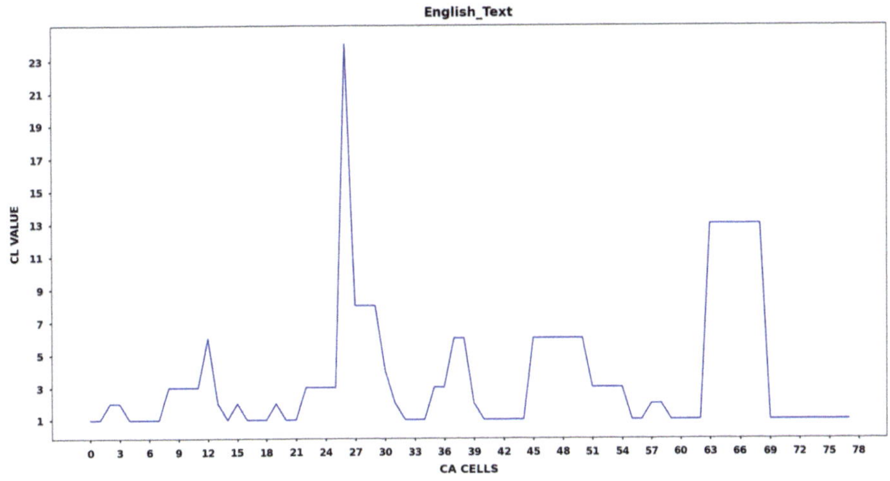

Fig. 6.4 CL graph of English text

instead of '–5'. The underlying phenomenon of Cycle Length is elaborated further with reference to Fig. 6.3.

Figure 6.3 depicts the partial sequence of binary patterns evolved out of a CA evolution. The figure depicts repetition of the sequence '011011' on the first column; the repetition of patterns of lesser length can be also observed on 4th and 6th columns (all noted in bold). Examples 6.1–6.5 (noted below) report the sequence of patterns of decimal values. The CL sequences are derived out of CL signal graphs generated by the CA modelling five language texts illustrated earlier (in Sect. 6.4.2 under Sects. 6.4.2.1, 6.4.2.2, 6.4.2.3, 6.4.2.4 and 6.4.2.5 for English, Arabic, Hindi, Greek, and Georgian respectively). The generated CL sequences are copied below in five examples. The corresponding CL signal graphs are presented in Figs. 6.4, 6.5, 6.6, 6.7 and Fig. 6.8 respectively.

Example 6.1 The list of CL values obtained for English Text is noted below. The graph for the CL sequence is illustrated in Fig. 6.4.
CL sequence generated for English Text: [1, 1, 2, 2, 1, 1, 1, 1, 3, 3, 3, 3, 6, 2, 1, 2, 1, 1, 1, 2, 1, 1, 3, 3, 3, 3, 24, 8, 8, 8, 4, 2, 1, 1, 1, 3, 3, 6, 6, 2, 1, 1, 1, 1, 1, 6, 6, 6, 6, 6, 6, 3, 3, 3, 3, 1, 1, 2, 2, 1, 1, 1, 1, 13, 13, 13, 13, 13, 13, 1, 1, 1, 1, 1, 1, 1, 1, 1].

Example 6.2 The list of CL values obtained for Arabic Text is given below. The graph for the CL sequence is illustrated in Fig. 6.5.
CL sequence generated for Arabic Text: [3, 3, 1, 1, 1, 1, 5, 5, 5, 1, 1, 1, 3, 3, 1, 1, 4, 2, 1, 2, 1, 1, 1, 1, 10, 10, 10, 10, 10, 10, 10, 2, 1, 1, 20, 20, 20, 20, 20, 20, 4, 4, 1, 1, 1, 1, 6, 6].

Example 6.3 The list of CL values obtained for Hindi Text is given below. The graph for the CL sequence is illustrated in Fig. 6.6.

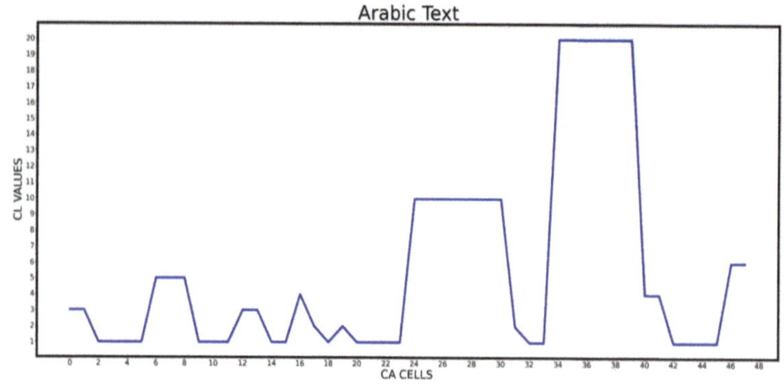

Fig. 6.5 CL graph of Arabic text

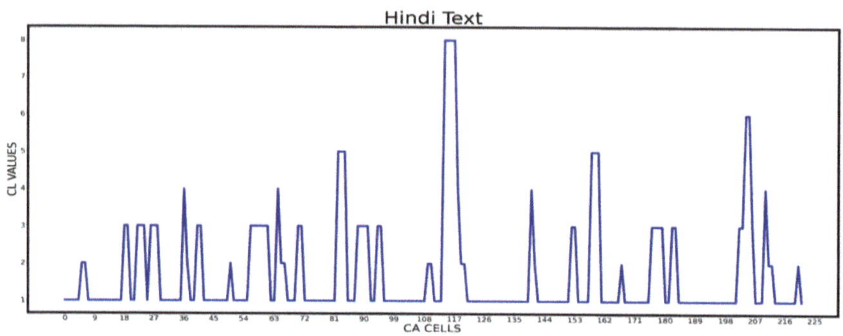

Fig. 6.6 CL graph of Hindi text

CL sequence generated for Hindi Text: [1, 1, 1, 1, 1, 2, 2, 1, 1, 1, 1, 1, 1, 1, 1, 1, 1, 1, 3, 3, 1, 1, 3, 3, 3, 1, 3, 3, 3, 1, 1, 1, 1, 1, 1, 1, 4, 2, 1, 1, 3, 3, 1, 1, 1, 1, 1, 1, 1, 1, 2, 1, 1, 1, 1, 1, 3, 3, 3, 3, 3, 3, 1, 1, 4, 2, 2, 1, 1, 1, 3, 3, 1, 1, 1, 1, 1, 1, 1, 1, 1, 1, 5, 5, 5, 1, 1, 1, 3, 3, 3, 3, 1, 1, 3, 3, 1, 1, 1, 1, 1, 1, 1, 1, 1, 1, 1, 1, 2, 2, 1, 1, 1, 8, 8, 8, 8, 4, 2, 2, 1, 1, 1, 1, 1, 1, 1, 1, 1, 1, 1, 1, 1, 1, 1, 1, 1, 1, 4, 2, 1, 1, 1, 1, 1, 1, 1, 1, 1, 1, 3, 3, 1, 1, 1, 1, 5, 5, 5, 1, 1, 1, 1, 1, 1, 2, 1, 1, 1, 1, 1, 1, 1, 1, 3, 3, 3, 3, 1, 1, 3, 3, 1, 1, 1, 1, 1, 1, 1, 1, 1, 1, 1, 1, 1, 1, 1, 1, 1, 1, 3, 3, 6, 6, 3, 1, 1, 1, 4, 2, 2, 1, 1, 1, 1, 1, 1, 1, 2, 1].

Example 6.4 The list of CL values obtained for Greek Text is given below. The graph for the CL sequence is illustrated in Fig. 6.7.
CL sequence generated for Greek Text: [16, 16, 2, 4, 4, 4, 1, 1, 2, 4, 4, 3, 3, 3, 3, 3, 3, 2, 1, 1, 2, 2, 2, 1, 2, 1, 1, 1, 1, 1, 2, 1, 2, 1, 2, 1, 2, 2, 1, 1, 2, 4, 4, 4, 4, 8, 8, 8, 8, 8, 8, 8, 2, 1, 2, 4, 4, 4, 1, 1, 2, 2, 2, 3, 3, 2, 1, 1, 2, 1, 2, 2, 1, 1, 2, 4, 4, 4, 4, 4, 4, 3, 3, 3, 3, 3, 3, 3, 1, 1, 2, 1, 2, 4, 4, 1, 1, 1, 2, 1, 2, 2, 2, 1, 2, 2, 2, 2, 2, 2, 2, 4, 4, 3, 3, 3, 3, 3,

3, 1, 1, 1, 2, 4, 4, 4, 4, 1, 1, 1, 2, 6, 3, 3, 3, 2, 1, 1, 2, 4, 4, 8, 8, 1, 1, 2, 2, 4, 4, 4, 4, 4, 4, 8, 8, 1, 2, 2, 2, 2, 1, 1, 2, 2, 2, 6, 3, 1, 2, 4, 4, 2, 1, 1, 2, 4, 4, 4, 1, 1, 2, 2, 2, 4, 4, 2, 2, 4, 4, 4, 4, 4, 4, 1, 1, 1, 2, 4, 4, 1, 1, 2, 1, 1, 2, 4, 4, 1, 2, 4, 4, 4, 4, 3, 3, 9, 9, 2, 1, 1, 2, 4, 4, 4, 4, 3, 3, 2, 1, 1, 2, 6, 3, 3, 3, 2, 1, 1, 2, 6, 3, 3, 3, 6, 6, 3, 3, 1, 1, 1, 2, 2, 2, 1, 2, 2, 2, 4, 4, 1, 2, 4, 4, 8, 8, 16].

Example 6.5 The list of CL values obtained for Georgian Text is given below. The graph for the CL sequence is illustrated in Fig. 6.8.
CL sequence generated for Georgian Text: [3, 3, 1, 1, 3, 3, 1, 1, 3, 3, 1, 1, 3, 3, 3, 3, 3, 3, 1, 1, 1, 2, 1, 2, 1, 1, 1, 1, 1, 1, 2, 1, 1, 1, 1, 2, 1, 1, 1, 1, 1, 1, 2, 2, 1, 1, 1, 1, 1, 1, 1, 1, 3, 3, 3, 3, 3, 3, 3, 3, 3, 1, 1, 1, 1, 1, 2, 1, 1, 1, 1, 1, 4, 4, 4, 4, 1, 1, 2, 1, 1, 1, 1, 1, 1, 1, 2, 4, 4, 4, 4, 2, 1, 1, 1, 1, 3, 3, 3, 1, 1, 1, 1, 1, 1, 1, 2, 2, 1, 1, 1, 1, 1, 1, 1, 3, 3, 1, 1, 1, 1, 2, 1, 1, 1, 1, 1, 1, 1, 1, 1, 2, 1, 1, 3, 3, 1, 1, 1, 1, 2, 1, 1, 1, 1, 1, 1, 1, 1, 1, 1, 1, 1, 1, 1, 2, 1, 2, 1, 1, 3, 3, 1, 1, 1, 1, 1, 1, 1, 1, 1, 1, 1, 3, 3, 1, 1, 1, 1, 1, 1, 1, 1, 3, 3, 3, 3, 3, 3, 3, 1, 1, 1, 1, 1, 2, 1, 2, 2, 1, 1, 1, 1, 2, 4, 4, 4, 1, 1, 3, 3, 3, 1, 3, 3, 1, 1, 1, 1, 3, 3, 3].

6.4.4 *Feature Extraction from CL Graphs*

We have identified two sets of features. The first set of features is used for the selection/filtering process. The second set is used for the prediction process. These sets of features are extracted from the CL-graph of a language text of sentiment analysis.

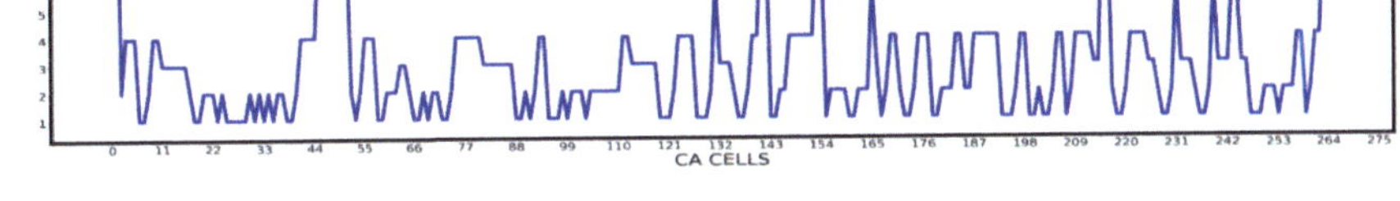

Fig. 6.7 CL graph of Greek text

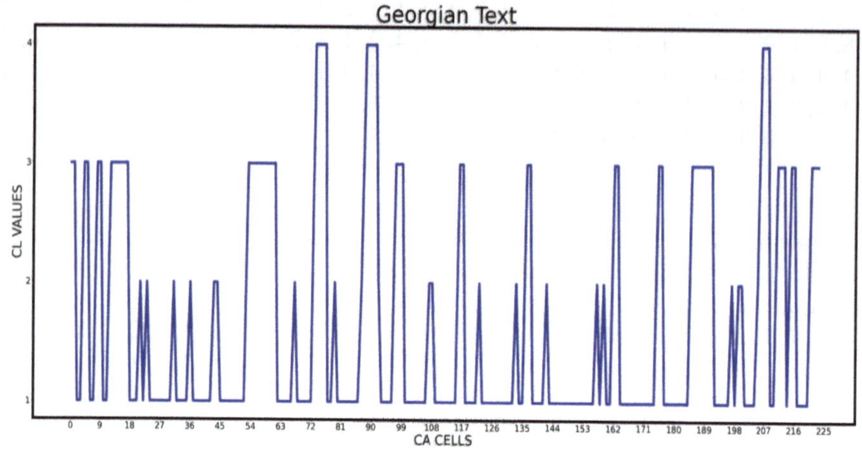

Fig. 6.8 CL graph of Georgian text

6.4.4.1 Features for Selection Process

The following eight features are extracted from CL graphs—(i) Maximum Cycle Length (MCL), (ii) MCL count, (iii) a signal with value next to MCL (NMCL), (iv) MCL Signal location Vector (SLV), (v) Signal Distance Vector (SDV), (vi) MCL signal pattern characteristics, (vii) CL(-5) signal, (viii) CL graph Group value. These features are identified based on detailed analysis of large number of training set data corpus in different language texts. These selection features/parameters are used to choose appropriate training data by matching the parameter value of test data with training data. Appropriate selection of training data, as per our evaluation, pushes up quality of prediction for test data set. Prediction parameters are calculated based on filtered training data set. Using these prediction parameters, the CAML model predict the level/class of test data.

The eight features, used for selection/filtering, lay the foundation for design of Prediction algorithm in next Sect. 6.5. Explanation of each feature follows:

(i) MCL: An MCL is the peak point of the CL graph. For example, the MCL value of English language text CL graph (see Fig. 6.4) is 24. While for Hindi language text CL graph (see Fig. 6.6) show MCL value as 8. The MCl value for Greek text CL graph (see Fig. 6.7) is 16 and for Georgian language text CL graph (see Fig. 6.8) is 4.

(ii) MCL count: The number of MCL peaks in the CL graph is taken as MCL Count. The MCL count for the Figs. 6.4, 6.5, 6.6, 6.7 and 6.8 are 1, 1, 1, 2 and 3 respectively.

(iii) NMCL Values: All values less than MCL and greater than a specified threshold limit, are considered as NMCL signals. The NMCL values for the earlier graphs are listed below:

NMCL values for Fig. 6.5: [5, 4, 10, 6]
NMCL values for Fig. 6.6: [4, 4, 5, 4, 5, 6, 4]
NMCL values for Fig. 6.7: [8, 6, 8, 8, 6, 9, 6, 6]
NMCL values for Fig. 6.8: [3, 3, 3, 3, 3, 3, 3, 3, 3, 3, 3, 3, 3, 3]
Based on the analysis of CL graphs derived for wide varieties of language texts in different languages, the threshold value is set as '3'. So, the values greater than '3' and less than 'MCL' are included in the NMCL list for Figs. 6.5 and 6.6. The MCL value of the CL graph guides the selection of this threshold limit. If the MCL value is low (e.g. Fig. 6.8 shows MCL value as 4), then the threshold limit is set as equal to 3, instead of greater than 3 (set for CL graphs of Figs. 6.5 and 6.6). On the other hand, the MCL value for graph of Fig. 6.7 is 16 and hence the threshold limit is set as greater than 4 instead of greater than 3 (as noted for Figs. 6.5 and 6.6).

(iv) MCL Signal Location Vectors (SLV): The locations of MCL and NMCL signals on the CL graph are taken into account. For each MCL, a signal location vector is created, encompassing all NMCL locations and MCL locations, excluding the current location, in the event of presence of multiple MCL locations.
(a) For the Arabic CL graph (see Fig. 6.5), the NMCL locations are [8, 17, 28, 47] of NMCL values [5, 4, 10, 6] and its MCL location is [37]. So, Signal Location Vectors (SLV) for this CL graph is $< 8, 17, 28, 47 >$.
(b) For the Hindi CL graph (see Fig. 6.6), the NMCL locations are [37, 65, 84, 141, 160, 205, 211] of NMCL values [4, 4, 5, 4, 5, 6, 4] and its MCL location is [116]. Hence, the Signal Location Vector of the graph is $< 37, 65, 84, 141, 160, 205, 211 >$.
(c) For the Greek CL graph (see Fig. 6.7), the NMCL locations are [49, 132, 142, 154, 166, 216, 232, 244] of NMCL values [8, 6, 8, 8, 6, 9, 6, 6] and its MCL locations are [1, 266]. Therefore, its Signal Location Vectors are $< 49, 132, 142, 154, 166, 216, 232, 244, 266 >$ and $< 1, 49, 132, 142, 154, 166, 216, 232, 244 >$.
(d) For the Georgian CL graph (see Fig. 6.8), the NMCL locations are [1, 5, 9, 15, 58, 99, 117, 137, 163, 176, 189, 213, 216, 223] of NMCL values [3, 3, 3, 3, 3, 3, 3, 3, 3, 3, 3, 3, 3, 3] and its MCL location is [75, 90, 208]. Therefore, there Signal Location Vectors are $< 1, 5, 9, 15, 58, 90, 99, 117, 137, 163, 176, 189, 208, 213, 216, 223 >$, $< 1, 5, 9, 15, 58, 75, 99, 117, 137, 163, 176, 189, 208, 213, 216, 223 >$ and $< 1, 5, 9, 15, 58, 75, 90, 99, 117, 137, 163, 176, 189, 213, 216, 223 >$.

(v) Signal Distance Vectors (SDV): The distance from the current MCL location to every other signal location is computed as Signal Location Vector (SLV). The examples derived out of each language CL graphs are illustrated below:
(a) For the Arabic CL graph (Fig. 6.5), the MCL location is [37] and its signal location vector is [8, 17, 28, 47]. Therefore, SDV is $< 29, 20, 9, 10 >$.
(b) For the Hindi CL graph (Fig. 6.6), the MCL location is [116] and its signal location vectors is $< 37, 65, 84, 141, 160, 205, 211 >$. Therefore, SDV is $< 79, 51, 32, 25, 44, 89, 95 >$.
(c) For the Greek CL graph (Fig. 6.7), the MCL location are [1, 265] and

its signal location vectors are $< 49, 132, 142, 154, 166, 216, 232, 244, 266 >$ and $< 1, 49, 132, 142, 154, 166, 216, 232, 244 >$. Therefore, SDV are $< 48, 131, 141, 153, 165, 215, 231, 243, 265 >$ and $< 265, 217, 134, 124, 112, 100, 50, 34, 22 >$ respectively.
(d) For the Georgian CL graph (Fig. 6.8), the MCL location are [75, 90, 208] and its signal location vectors are $< 1, 5, 9, 15, 58, 90, 99, 117, 137, 163, 176, 189, 208, 213, 216, 223 >$, $< 1, 5, 9, 15, 58, 75, 99, 117, 137, 163, 176, 189, 208, 213, 216, 223 >$ and $< 1, 5, 9, 15, 58, 75, 90, 99, 117, 137, 163, 176, 189, 213, 216, 223 >$. Therefore, three SDV are $< 74, 70, 66, 60, 17, 15, 24, 42, 62, 88, 101, 114, 133, 138, 141, 148 >$, $< 89, 85, 81, 75, 32, 15, 9, 27, 47, 73, 86, 99, 118, 123, 126, 133 >$ and $< 207, 203, 199, 193, 150, 133, 118, 109, 91, 71, 45, 32, 19, 5, 8, 15 >$ respectively.

The Signal Distance Vector is split into two segments: the Left Signal Distance Vector (LSDV) and the Right Signal Distance Vector (RSDV). Specifically, all the values located to the left of an MCL location within its respective SDV constitute the LSDV, while all the values situated to the right of an MCL location in its corresponding SDV form the RSDV.

The examples of CL graph for each language are illustrated below:
(a) For the Arabic CL graph (Fig. 6.5), the SDV is $< 29, 20, 9, 10 >$. Therefore, the LSDV = $< 29, 20, 9 >$ and RSDV = $< 10 >$.
(b) For the Hindi CL graph (Fig. 6.6), the SDV is $< 79, 51, 32, 25, 44, 89, 95 >$. Therefore, the LSDV = $< 79, 51, 32 >$ and RSDV = $< 25, 44, 89, 95 >$.
(c) For the Greek CL graph (Fig. 6.7 with two MCL signals), the SDV is $< 48, 131, 141, 153, 165, 215, 231, 243, 265 >$ and $< 265, 217, 134, 124, 112, 100, 50, 34, 22 >, < 100, 49, 34, 26, 21, 1 >>$. Therefore, the LSDV= $<<>, < 265, 217, 134, 124, 112, 100, 50, 34, 22 >>$ and RSDV= $<< 48, 131, 141, 153, 165, 215, 231, 243, 265 >, <>>$.
(d) For the Georgian CL graph (Fig. 6.8 with three MCL signals), the SDV is $<< 74, 70, 66, 60, 17, 15, 24, 42, 62, 88, 101, 114, 133, 138, 141, 148 >$, $< 89, 85, 81, 75, 32, 15, 9, 27, 47, 73, 86, 99, 118, 123, 126, 133 >$, $< 207, 203, 199, 193, 150, 133, 118, 109, 91, 71, 45, 32, 19, 5, 8, 15 >>$. Therefore, the LSDV= $<< 74, 70, 66, 60, 17 >, < 89, 85, 81, 75, 32, 15 >$ $, < 207, 203, 199, 193, 150, 133, 118, 109, 91, 71, 45, 32, 19 >>$ and RSDV = $<< 15, 24, 42, 62, 88, 101, 114, 133, 138, 141, 148 >$, $< 9, 27, 47, 73, 86, 99, 118, 123, 126, 133 >, < 5, 8, 15 >>$.

(vi) MCL Signal Characteristics- RightStep, LeftStep, RightFork, and LeftFork flags: Different MCL shapes in the CL-graphs are associated with the introduction of various parameters, including Right Step Signal (RSS), Left Step Signal (LSS), Right Fork (RF), and Left Fork (LF) flags. These parameters are set to '1' based on the specific characteristics of the MCL signal up and down slope. For instance, when a Right Step is observed in the MCL signal curve, the RSS flag is set to 1; otherwise,

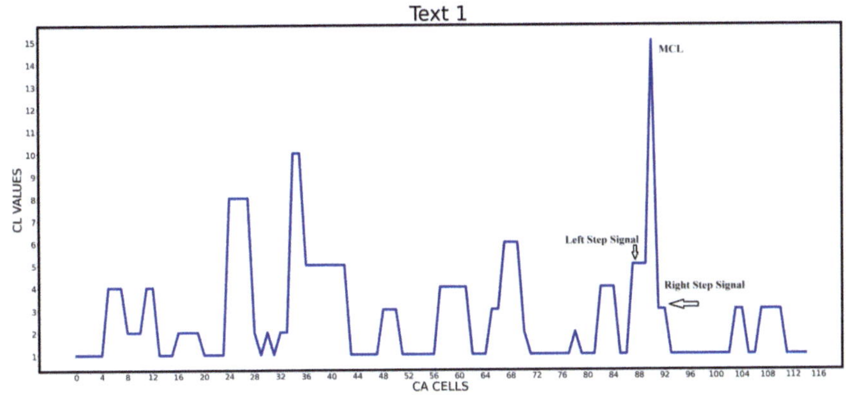

Fig. 6.9 Presence of a left step signal and right step signal

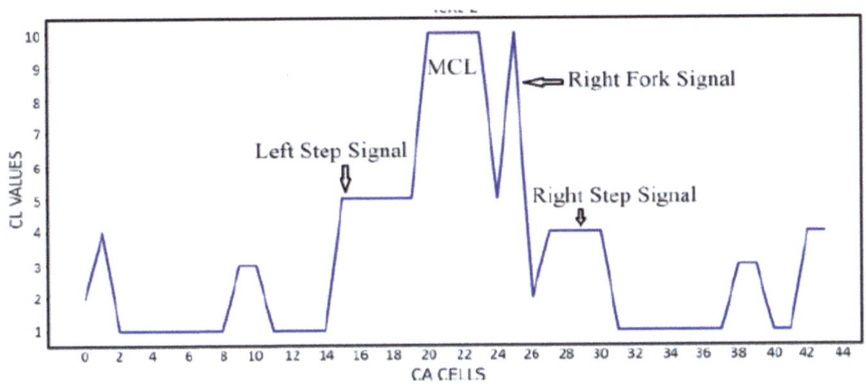

Fig. 6.10 Presence of a left step signal and right step signal

it is set to 0. Similarly, the values of the remaining flags are determined according to the shape of the MCL curve.

For example, in Fig. 6.9, both LSS and RSS flag values are set to 1 because there is a left and right step signal present on both sides of the MCL signal at location 90. Similarly, in Fig. 6.10, LSS, RSS and RF flag values are set to 1 as both the steps signal and right fork signal present in MCL signal. A fork in a MCL signal refers to the situation where the signal value goes down from MCL value and next gets restored (Fig. 6.10).

(vii) CL(-5) Flag: This flag is set to '1' if the CL sequence contains '–5'.

(viii) Group Value: Each comment in the dataset is categorized into various groups based on the following conditions:

(a) *Group 0*: If $MCL - max(NMCL) \leq 20\%\ of\ MCL$
(b) *Group 1*: If Number of MCL count = 1
(c) *Group 2*: If Number of MCL count >1

All the features mentioned above are used for the filtering process. These features help to identify the relevant training set data points to be considered for prediction of result for a particular test data.

6.4.4.2 Features for Prediction Process

For prediction, we have used three different features, which are also extracted from the CL-graph.

1. Cosine Similarity Index (CSI):
The similarity index serves as a metric of likeness, computed using CL values in accordance with Eq. 6.1. It represents the cosine angle between the CL signals of each test data point and all the train data signals. A measurement of one indicates a high degree of similarity between the signals, signifying that they closely resemble each other.

$$CSI = (< test, train > /||test||.||train||) \tag{6.1}$$

2. Euclidean Distance:
This measurement is computed to discern the distinctions between the CL values of the testing and training data, as described by Eq. 6.2.

$$d(p, q) = \sqrt{\sum_{i=1}^{n} (q_i - p_i)^2} \tag{6.2}$$

3. R-value:
The relationship is determined for each testing data point with reference to each training data point, by calculating the ratio of Match Signal Pair (MSP) to Mismatch Count (MMC).

Match Signal Pair(MSP): To establish a Match Signal Pair (MSP) for each distance (d1) in the LSDV or RSDV of training data and each distance (d2) in the LSDV or RSDV of testing data, a predefined set of conditions must be met. The final MSP value for a specific pair of testing and training data is the sum of MSP for the LSDV and the RSDV. The conditions for a pair (d1, d2) to be considered an MSP are as follows: If the value of q, calculated as $q = d1/d2$, is greater than or equal to 0.85, then the output is set to 1.

Mis Match Count (MMC): If any LSDV (or RSDV) of the training data does not form a matching pair with any LSDV (or RSDV) of the testing data, the mismatch count

(MMC) is incremented by one. If the value of MMC is 0, then we assign MMC = 1. Finally, we can calculate the R-value as $r = MSP/MMC$.

We utilize the earlier three features in the design of prediction algorithm reported in next subsection. These features are identified based on details analysis of CL signal graphs of training and test data corpus sets.

6.5 Learning Process and Performance Analysis

The training and testing processes are executed using the following Algorithm 1. Step 1 of the algorithm divides the available input data corpus into certain ratio (say, $80:20$ or $70:30$) as Training and Testing data set. The features extracted from CL signal graphs, reported in Sect. 6.4.4.1, play key role, as reported in Step 5 of the algorithm. During this learning process, particular training data, which exhibit higher similarity to the testing data, are chosen based on the extracted parameters. This selection is achieved through a rule-based approach, where a set of rules guide the prediction process. The prediction is subsequently made using prediction parameters, including CSI (Cosine Similarity Index), Euclidean distance, and R (relation)-values. The predicted class labels for each testing data point are next compared with the actual labels to find the accuracy of the proposed classifier.

Different data sets on which we evaluated the prediction quality on executing Algorithm 1 are reported in next subsection.

Algorithm 1 Sentiment Prediction algorithm

INPUT: Sentiment Reviews
OUTPUT: Predicted class labels for each data in the testing set.

1: (a) Pre-process each review text to remove ambiguity and unnecessary characters from the text.
(b) Divide the data corpus into Training and Testing set with certain ratio.
2: Convert pre-processed data into rule vectors using rule tables.
3: Perform CA evolution process for generating CL-graphs.
4: Extract the data selection features and prediction features from the CL-graph.
5: Apply those features for training the model using the training dataset.
6: Predict the class labels of testing data using the prediction parameters.
7: Calculate precision, recall, accuracy, and F1 Score using the following formulae:

$$Precision = TP/(TP + FP) \quad (6.3)$$

$$Recall = TP/(TP + FN) \quad (6.4)$$

$$Accuracy = (TP + TN)/total\ \#\ of\ comments \quad (6.5)$$

$$F1\ Score = (2 * precision * recall)/(precision + recall) \quad (6.6)$$

6.5.1 Dataset Details

In this work, we used different datasets of five languages available in public domain. A brief discussion on the data sets of different languages follows:

1. Arabic dataset [84] For Arabic sentiment analysis, we used the Arabic Jordanian General Tweets (AJGT) Corpus, consisting of 1,800 tweets classified as positive and negative. A few examples are given in Table 6.8.
2. Hindi datasets:
    a. Hindi Twitter Dataset [85] : This dataset contains Twitter Hindi tweets. We have taken 4691 reviews. Out of which 2281 are negative and the rest of 2409 are positive reviews.
    b. Hindi movie reviews [86] : The Hindi movie reviews dataset contains a total of 1000 Hindi movie reviews for Sentiment Analysis. After preprocessing, there are 995 sentiments. Out of 995, 502 reviews are positive and the rest 493 are negative reviews.
3. English datasets:
    a. Restaurant Reviews [87]: It is a small dataset of 1000 reviews which includes 500 positive reviews and 500 negative reviews.
    b. Twitter Sentiment [88]: contains 10,715 tweets distributed into 8402 positive and 2313 negative reviews.
    c. The SST-Binary dataset [89]: This movie review contains 4963 positive reviews and 4650 negative reviews, with approximately 50% data corpus in either group. We have observed that correct prediction of results for such corpus is a challenging task for a language-independent model like CAML.
    d. Amazon Alexa Reviews [90]: Amazon customer reviews of 3066 statements (2828 positive reviews and 238 negative reviews).

Table 6.8 Few samples of Arabic dataset entries

Reviews	Labels
سوف صادقه كانت ونيتك عليه وتوكلت بالله استعنت اذا ربى ?احبكابدا يخزلك ولن بجوارك الله يقف	Positive
يكرمك ربنا بجد رائع كله	Positive
معو والا هو خام وتمثيلو بيمثل انو واضح الاخير اجل	Negative
مهستر واحد اخر	Negative

Table 6.9 Few samples of Greek dataset entries

Reviews	Labels
Γρήγορη παραλαβή και φιλική εξυπηρέτηση.	Positive
Πολύ ευχαριστημένη με την παράδοση. Επικοινωνία πριν για το πότε θα παραλάβω την παραγγελία μου. Το εμπόρευμα σε άριστη προσεγμένη συσκευασία.	Positive
καθυστέρηση στην αποστολή καμία ενημέρωση για την αποστολή πολύ καλή τιμή.	Negative
Έγκαιρη παραλαβή ωστόσο η συσκευασία του προϊόντος ηρθε με πολλες ζημιές . Κακή εικόνα για δώρο	Negative

4. Greek datasets:
   a. Skroutz Greek dataset [91]: This dataset comprises shop reviews in Greek sourced from the Skroutz website, intended for sentiment analysis. It consists of a total of 6,549 reviews, evenly split into two categories: 3,276 positive reviews and 3,273 negative reviews. The dataset is structured with two columns, namely "review", and "label". A few examples are given in Table 6.9.
   b. Greek hotel reviews: We gathered real-time hotel reviews from the Greek edition of TripAdvisor, a renowned global travel website (www.tripadvisor.com.gr). Our dataset comprises 200 reviews, evenly split between 100 positive and 100 negative ones. Only meaningful comments regarding hotels are taken into account.
5. Georgian Dataset [92]: This dataset contains 2182 reviews. Out of which 1417 are negative and the rest of 765 are positive reviews.

Next section reports the matrices employed to evaluate the prediction quality on executing Algorithm 1.

6.5.2 *Matrices Used for Evaluation*

A confusion matrix (illustrated in Fig. 6.11) is a performance measurement tool for classification algorithms. It is particularly useful in assessing the performance of predictive models, especially in scenarios where the classes are imbalanced. Here is a breakdown of its components:

(i) *True Positive (TP)*: These are the cases where the model correctly predicts the positive class.

(ii) *True Negative (TN)*: These are the cases where the model correctly predicts the negative class.

		Predicted		
		Positive	Negative	
Actual	Positive	True Positive (TP)	False Positive (FP) Type I Error	**Recall** TP/(TP+FN)
	Negative	False Negative (FN) Type II Error	True Negative (TN)	**Specificity** TN/(TN+FP)
		Precision TP/(TP+FP)	**Negative Predictive Value** TN/(TN+FN)	**Accuracy** (TP+TN)/ (TP+TN+FP+FN)
		F1_Score = 2 x (Precision x Recall)/ (Precision + Recall)		

Fig. 6.11 Confusion matrix with advanced classification metrics

(iii) *False Positive (FP)*: These are the cases where the model incorrectly predicts the positive class when the actual class is negative. Also known as Type I error.

(iv) *False Negative (FN)*: These are the cases where the model incorrectly predicts the negative class when the actual class is positive. Also known as Type II error.

From the confusion matrix, various performance metrics can be derived, including:

(a) *Precision*: The proportion of true positive predictions out of all positive predictions made by the model. It's calculated as TP / (TP + FP).

(b) *Recall (Sensitivity)*: The proportion of true positive predictions out of all actual positives. It's calculated as TP / (TP + FN).

(c) *Specificity*: The proportion of true negative predictions out of all actual negatives. It's calculated as TN / (TN + FP).

(d) *Accuracy*: The proportion of correctly classified instances among the total instances. It's calculated as (TP + TN) / (TP + TN + FP + FN).

(e) *F1_Score*: The harmonic mean of precision and recall. It is calculated as 2 * ((Precision * Recall) / (Precision + Recall)).

All the advanced classification metrics are presented in the Fig. 6.11. These metrics provide insights into different aspects of model performance. For instance, accuracy gives an overall view, while precision and recall are particularly useful when dealing with imbalanced datasets.

Table 6.10 Results of various datasets with the proposed model

Dataset	Accuracy (%)	Precision (%)	Recall (%)	F1 Score (%)
Sentiment Tweets [88]	92.44	95.49	94.81	95.14
Restaurant reviews [87]	81.50	89.21	77.77	83.09
Amazon Alexa reviews [90]	91.53	92.26	99.11	95.56
SST-Binary[89]	68.00	80.38	61.86	69.91

6.5.3 *Results and Comparative Analysis*

In order to evaluate performance of CAML model, we have curated ten different datasets in five languages—English, Arabic, Hindi, Greek, and Georgian. Each dataset is divided into testing and training sets with 80:20 and also 70:30 ratio. The results derived employing CAML model are compared with the results reported in published literature for a few state-of-the-art models. The results of different schemes used for comparison divides the input data sets with 80:20 ratio for training and testing sets. We have included results derived out of CAML model in Sect. 6.5.3.6 on dividing dataset with 70:30 ratio for training and testing sets. Since the volume of data corpus, we have employed is low, reduction of training data set is unlikely to capture the associated underlying features. As a result, the prediction quality achieved with 70:30 ratio is bound to be inferior to that achieved with 80.20 ratio. This is normally expected for any ML framework, and CAML model is no exception to this phenomenon.

6.5.3.1 Results Derived for English Dataset

In view of its wide usage, a large number of research groups have concentrated on Sentiment Analysis in English language datasets. The performance analysis of the cellular automata-based ML model is done using four data sets i.e., Sentiment Tweets (10715 tweets), Restaurant Reviews (1000 reviews), Amazon Alexa Reviews (3066 review) and SST-Binary (9613 review). To obtain the results from the proposed model, we have divided the datasets into testing and training sets with a 1:4 ratio. That is, 80% of the data is used for the training process and 20% of the data for the testing process. On testing our model, we have got the accuracy that is summarized in Table 6.10. Figure 6.12 shows samples of a few confusion metrics for the Restaurant Reviews dataset and Amazon Alexa dataset.

We next compare CAML model-derived results with other state-of-art classification approaches. The comparative analysis is reported in Table 6.11 for four different data sets—Sentiment tweets, Amazon Alexa, Restaurant data and SST-Binary with

80% of training data and 20% of testing data. The baselines selected for text classification are based on the datasets used. We can infer from Table 6.11 that the proposed CAML model is capable in determining whether a text conveys a favourable or unfavourable view expressed in a sentence. The results derived with SVM model for 14000 tweets is reported on third row of the first block of result table in Table 6.11. The CAML model, independent of language analysis, performs better than SVM model that predicts the class labels based on prior analysis of input text employing statistical learning framework.

In the case of sentiment tweets, the RoBERTa-LSTM model proposed by Tan et al. [59] in 2022 currently stands as one of the top-performing models. However, our proposed model surpasses this benchmark by achieving even higher levels of accuracy and F1_score. CNN with Glove model [93] produces the best results in the case of Amazon Alexa reviews. The proposed CAML model produces a higher F1_score than the existing model. In 2021, the Naive Bayes ML model is used on 68 online restaurant reviews producing 73.54% of F1_score, while the CAML model produces more than 83% of F1_score. While for first three case studies on Sentiment Tweets, Amazon Alexa, Restaurant data, CAML model performs better than other models, it fails on the fourth case study on SST-binary reviews. The CAML model on the SST-Binary dataset produces only an accuracy of 68% and F1_score of 69.91%. For this class of dataset, further investigations and analysis are in progress to improve the results employing on CAML model. The recent research models and comparative study are summarized in Table 6.11.

6.5.3.2 Results Obtained for Arabic Dataset

The performance of the CAML model is evaluated using AJGT Corpus consisting of 1,800 tweets for the Arabic language. The results obtained are illustrated in Fig. 6.13. The comparative analysis is shown in Table 6.12. From Fig. 6.13, it is evident that the

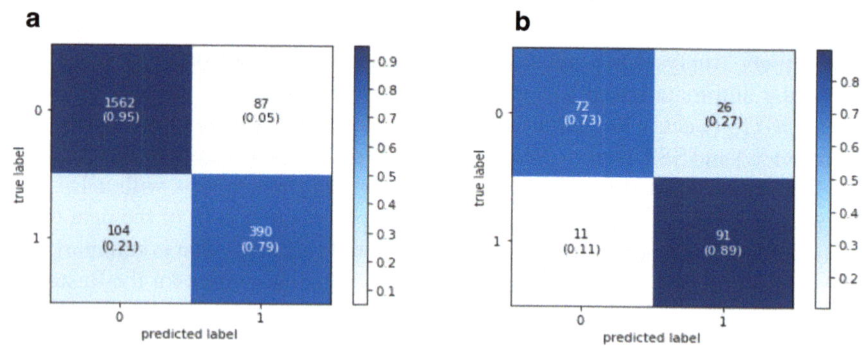

Fig. 6.12 Confusion metrics (a). Sentiment Tweets dataset (b). Restaurant review dataset

Table 6.11 Comparison of CAML model with other baseline models for English Text

Models	Acc.	Prec.	Recall	F1_Score
Sentiment Tweets(10,715 tweets)				
RoBERTa-LSTM on Sentiment140 (1.6 million tweets) (2022) [59]	89.70	90	90	90
Decision tree on 14000 tweets (2021) [58]	88.51	79.62	84.88	55.57
SVM on 14000 tweets (2021) [58]	87.71	80.66	85.73	73.02
Attention-based Bi-CNN-RNN(2021) on Airline tweets [63]	92.75	89.44	88.43	88.77
ABCDM(2021) on Sentiment140 [63]	81.82	82.77	82.31	81.99
Domain attention model on Sanders 5513 tweets (2018) [94]	87.69	–	–	–
GloVe-DCNN on 3326 Sentiment Strength Twitter data (2018) [95]	81.36	80.61	80.86	80.72
Proposed CAML Model	**92.44**	**95.49**	**94.81**	**95.14**
Amazon Alexa (3066 reviews)				
CNN with Glove (2019) using 21k unbalanced data [93]	92.73	92	92	92
CNN with Glove (2019) using balanced data [93]	76.51	76	76	76
Domain attention model for multi-domain sentiments of	84.38	–	–	–
8000 reviews (2018) [94]				
Proposed CAML Model	**91.53**	**92.26**	**99.11**	**95.56**

(continued)

Table 6.11 (continued)

Models	Acc.	Prec.	Recall	F1_Score
		Restaurant data (1k reviews)		
Naïve Bayes on 68 online restaurant reviews(2021) [96]	73.00	68	80.07	73.54
Naive Bayes on 337 restaurant customer reviews (2019) [97]	72.06	71.43	73.53	72.46
Text Blob on 337 restaurant customer reviews (2019) [97]	69.12	64.15	94.45	76.41
Decision Tree J48(2019) [61]	45.20	48.7	36.8	41.92
Naïve Bayesian Classifier(2019) [98]	72.2	71.29	64.58	67.76
Proposed CAML Model	**81.50**	**89.21**	**77.77**	**83.09**
		SST-Binary (9613 reviews)		
Dual Contrastive Learning with RoBERTa (2022) [99]	94.91	–	–	–
Contextual sentiment embeddings with Bi-GRU model (2022) [100]	89.80	–	–	–
CNN with word2 vec (2021) [101]	86.61	–	–	–
MUPPET Roberta Large (2021) [102]	97.40	-	–	–
SMART with RoBERTa on SST-2 (67k)(2020) [17]	97.50	–	–	–
BERT with Distillation Approach (2019) [103]	90.70	–	–	–
Capsule Networks with DR (2018) [104]	86.80	–	–	–
LR with Emo2vec and GLove (2018) [105]	81.20			
Proposed CAML Model	**68.00**	**80.38**	**61.86**	**69.91**

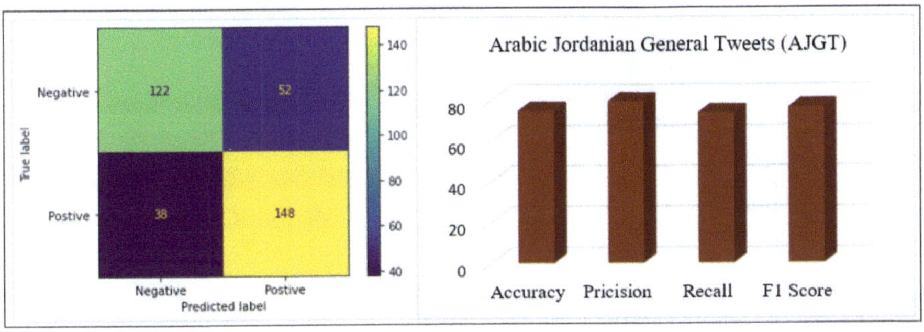

Fig. 6.13 Results obtained for Arabic Twitter tweets

Table 6.12 Comparative study of Arabic sentiment analysis

Model used	Accuracy	Precision	Recall	F1_Score
XLM-Twitter (2022) [25]	–	–	–	67.67
XLM-R (2022) [25]	–	–	–	63.56
NileTMRG (2017) [106]	76.81	–	76.71	77.01
ELiRF-UPV (2017) [106]	72.12	–	72.42	73.42
Ensemble model(2018) [42]	65.05	–	–	64.46
DziriBERT (2023) [107]	–	–	–	74.20
Proposed CAML model	**75.0**	**79.57**	**74.0**	**76.68**

model performs effectively for the AJGT corpus. It produces an F1 score of 76.68%. The model demonstrates a strong overall performance with balanced precision and recall.

6.5.3.3 Results Obtained for Hindi Datasets

The results obtained for Hindi Twitter and movie reviews are shown in Figs. 6.14 and 6.15. On comparing the outcomes with the models presented in Table 6.13, it becomes apparent that the results derived from various transformer-based models yield a range between 70 and 80%. Notably, the CAML model also generates outcomes within the similar range. The proposed system does not depend on the size of the dataset and it generated good performance with balanced precision and recall for Hindi datasets. The comparative analysis is reported in Table 6.13.

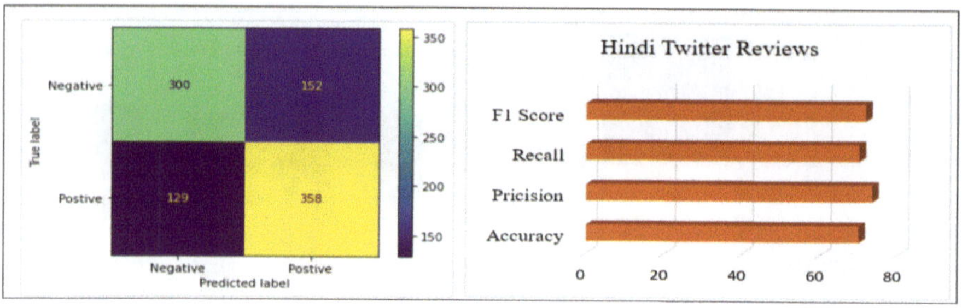

Fig. 6.14 Results obtained for Hindi Twitter reviews

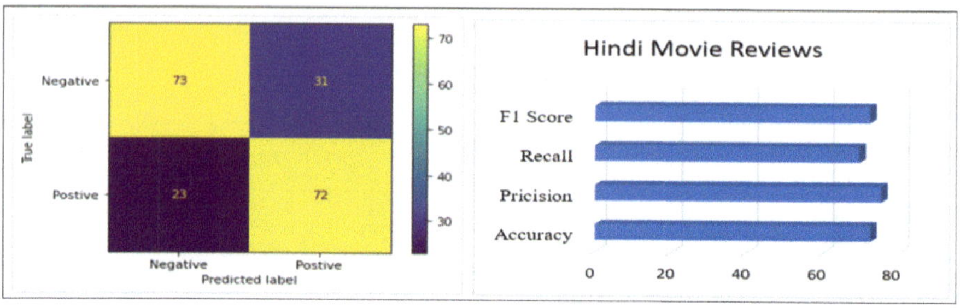

Fig. 6.15 Results obtained for Hindi movie reviews

Table 6.13 Comparative analysis of Hindi reviews with other state-of-the-art models

Methods used	Accuracy	Precision	Recall	F1 score
BiLSTM-Hindi (2022) [55]	76.00	76.00	76.00	76.00
mBERT-E-MV (2021) [53]	–	84.39	66.31	74.26
mBERT-E-MV (2021) [53]	–	76.32	54.72	63.74
mBERT-E-MV (2021) [53]	–	80.70	77.53	79.08
SVM with TF-IDF (2022) [108]	–	79.517	96.11	87.03
SVM with count vectorizer (2022) [108]	–	77.91	90.77	84.85
Proposed CAML Classifier	**72.86**	**75.78**	**69.90**	**72.72**

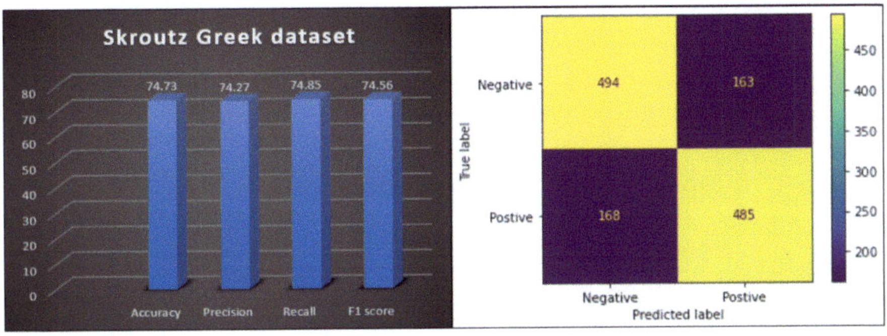

Fig. 6.16 The results of the proposed CAML model in terms of accuracy, precision, recall, and F1_Score using Skroutz Greek dataset

6.5.3.4 Results Obtained for Greek Datasets

We have divided the Skroutz Greek dataset into training and testing with an 80:20 ratio. The confusion matrices and results are reported in Fig. 6.16. CAML model generated 74.56% of F1 score and 74.73% of accuracy for the Skroutz Greek dataset.

Further, the accuracy, precision, recall, and F1 score of the Greek hotel reviews are 85.00, 76.19, 94.12, and 84.21%, respectively (Table 6.14). The F1 score for hotel review analysis is 84.21% indicating approximately 10% of improvement with the CAML based classifier. The ROC curve and AUC score are shown in Fig. 6.17. Here we used a very small number of real-time hotel reviews, and we got good scores compared to state-of-the-art models. We can conclude that the model produces overall accuracy for the Greek dataset, which is approximately 0.85 if we consider the results of the two datasets. The hit rate of the model is 85%. That is, the ratio of correctly identified positive data points to all actual positive data points. In simpler terms, a higher True Positive Rate (TPR) implies that fewer positive data points will be missed. So the CAML model based classifier performs well for all sets of data. When we compute the False-Positive rate (FPR) of the model, it stands at 0.26, indicating that few negative data points are misclassified. To combine the FPR and the TPR into a single metric, we calculated the AUC score of the proposed classifier, which is 0.85, as shown in Fig. 6.17.

To perform a comparative study of Greek sentiment analysis, we have curated the prediction results of different machine learning and deep learning models that are summarized in Table 6.14. As per this analysis, CAML model achieved comparatively better results in terms of accuracy and F1 score.

6.5.3.5 Results Derived for Georgian Datasets

For the Georgian language, we used the GSS dataset with an 80:20 split ratio. The training set contains 1745 tweets that are used for the learning process. Then the

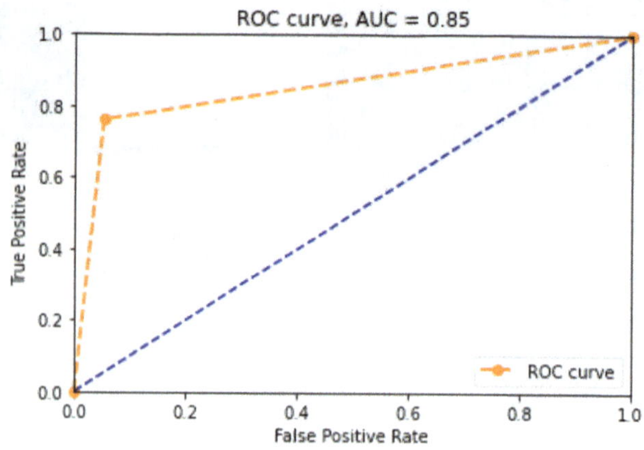

Fig. 6.17 ROC Curve and AUC score of Greek hotel reviews

Table 6.14 Comparative study of different models for the Greek language with the proposed model

Dataset	Accuracy (%)	Precision (%)	Recall (%)	F1 score (%)
J48 algorithm (2016)[66]	56	–	–	–
Decision Trees (2017) [71]	68.42	67.44	72.2	69.26
SVM (2017) [71]	77.82	79.65	77.5	78.56
Naive Bayes (2017) [71]	69.12	67.35	68.4	67.87
Deep Learning (2017) [71]	72.00	74.95	76.4	75.66
GBM (2017) [71]	84.20	84.35	83.10	83.72
GreekBERT (2020) [69]	–	71.68	58.03	78.45
BERT_CC (2020) [26]	–	–	–	70.8
BERT_Wiki (2020) [26]	–	–	–	60.1
GreekSocialBERT (2021) [24]	–	73.63	54.91	80.17
PaloBERT (2021) [24]	–	80.45	50.89	79.80
XLM-T-Sent (2023) [70]	–	–	–	75
Proposed Model	**85.00**	**76.19**	**94.12**	**84.21**

Table 6.15 Comparative analysis for sentiment classification of Georgian language [72]

Model used	Accuracy	Precision	Recall	F1 score
Logistic regression	–	64.8	68.3	66.1
SVM	–	65.3	68.0	66.3
XLM-Roberta-based model	–	76.8	75.0	75.2
Proposed CAML model	**83.75**	**73.29**	**76.98**	**75.09**

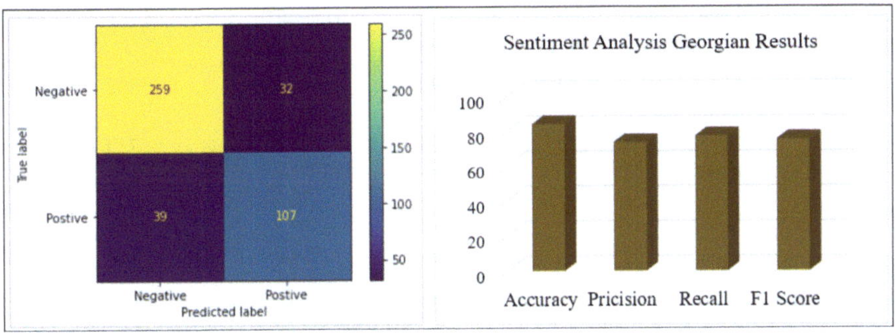

Fig. 6.18 Results obtained for Georgian datasets

model is evaluated using 437 tweets as a testing set. As per Table 6.15, the XLM-Roberta-based model is performing best with 75.2% of the F1 score. A few dictionary-based approaches are discussed in [72], in which the maximum F1 scores obtained are in the range of 45–60%. However, the proposed CAML model has produced prediction results with 83.75% of accuracy without any analysis of the characteristics of the Georgian language. The results in terms of accuracy, precision, recall, and F1 score, are shown in Fig. 6.18. The comparative analysis is summarized in Table 6.15. When assessing the best sentiment analysis classifier for our particular use case, it became evident that our CAML model stands out as the most fitting choice for sentiment analysis tasks in a multi-language environment. As per the results obtained, our evaluation consistently illustrates the superiority of the proposed CAML model over most of the lexicon-based methods and traditional machine-learning models.

6.5.3.6 Results Derived Out of CAML Model on Dividing Input Dataset with 70:30 Ratio for Training and Testing Sets

Performance of the CAML model is also analysed considering 70% data as training data and 30% data as testing data. Given the already small dataset, we believe it may negatively affect the results. However, we are still interested in evaluating how well

Table 6.16 Results of various datasets for CAML model using 70% data as training data and 30% data as testing data

Language	Datasets	Accuracy	Recall	Precision	F1 Score
English	Sentiment Tweets [88]	91.38	82.41	79.87	81.10
	Restaurant reviews [87]	78.00	70.44	85.49	77.20
	Amazon Alexa [90]	90.55	90.79	90.52	95.00
	SST-Binary [89]	68.34	63.59	71.66	67.40
Hindi	Twitter Dataset [85]	61.50	61.63	66.57	64.01
Arabic	AJGT [84]	59.26	58.08	63.30	60.57
Georgian	Georgian Dataset [92]	62.44	43.07	38.35	40.57
Greek	Skroutz Greek dataset [91]	71.60	72.75	71.01	71.87

the model perform, particularly since CAML model is designed to handle smaller datasets and limited resources. For this experiment, we have used eight datasets in five languages—English, Arabic, Hindi, Greek, and Georgian. On testing the model, we have got the accuracy that is summarized in Table 6.16.

It is well known that, higher the training set data volume, better will be prediction results. Further, if training data set count falls below a threshold limit, it fails to capture the variability and the associated characteristics of input data, that would result in inferior prediction results. CAML model is no exception to such a phenomenon. Relevant data, extracted from Table 6.16 and tabulated in Table 6.17, displays this fact. The first row with highest training data count (7500 for English Sentiment tweet) achieves the best performance with (Accuracy and F1 Score) as (91.38 and 81.10). Two weak performers are the Arabic and Georgian language texts. Compared to English language tweeter training data points of 7500, Arabic and Georgian language texts are trained with very low number of data points of 1260 and 1527 respectively.

6.5.3.7 Interpretability of CAML Model-Derived Results

The following discussions establish the issue of interpretability of results derived out of CAML model. In this context, we next look for the answer for the question noted below while comparing CAML model derived results for English language Amazon Alexa (third row of Table 6.17) and Greek language (last row of Table 6.17):

> Notwithstanding lesser number of training datapoints of 2146 of English language Amazon Alexa compared to 4584 of Greek language—why the CAML model derived results (Accu-

Table 6.17 Summary of CAML model derived results with 70:30 division for training and testing data

Language	Dataset	Total data point count	70% of Total cnt (used for training)	Comments
English	Sentiment Tweets [88]	10715	7500	Best performance
English	Amazon Alexa [90]	3066	2146	Better result even with low training data cnt
Hindi	Twitter Dataset [85]	4691	3283	–
Arabic	AJGT [84]	1800	1260	–
Georgian	Georgian Dataset [92]	2182	1527	–
Greek	Skroutz Greek dataset [91]	6549	4584	Inferior results, with training data set not-so-low

racy of 90.55 and F1 Score of 95.00) for English language is significantly better than that of Greek language (71.60 and 71.87)?

In order to get answer for the above question, we analyze the effect of bias in training data corpus in the CAML model that employs the Unicode platform to handle multi-language environment. As per the Unicode chart, the English language text uses the basic Latin character set and are encoded by Unicode block 0000 to 007F, while Greek language alphabets are encoded by Unicode block 0370 to 03FF. For both English and Greek alphabets, CAML model employs two 3NCA rules. However, as reported in Sect. 6.4.2, 'while generating CA rule sequence for a Unicode character, we delete the leading 0 rule of the generated sequence'. Consequently, while Greek language basic alphabets are represented with two CA rules, the corresponding alphabets of English language basic alphabets are represented with one CA rule. This is true, since each character in English text in Unicode block 0000 to 007F is encoded with two CA rules with leading 0 rule that is deleted. Let us compare CA rule vector size and number of CA cells for English and Greek language text with n alphabets each. While Greek language text is modelled with $2n$ cell CA, the English language text is modelled with n cell CA. In view of CL graph for English language text being half the length of Greek language text, the features extracted out CL graph, as reported in Sect. 6.4.4.1, will be better tuned for training and prediction for English language texts than that of Greek language text of same size.

While designing the CAML model for Computational Linguistics, we noticed this inherent bias of the model towards English Language. However, we planned to continue with this bias, in view of the widest use of the language around the globe.

Earlier discussions establish the explainability and interpretability of CAML model-derived results. This characteristics of CAML model gets further strengthened from the following discussions explaining - why CAML model performed so poorly for English language text on SST-Binary reviews (the last block of Table 6.11), while for all other datasets CAML displayed superior performance compared to other models surveyed in this chapter on five different languages. The answer to this specific issue lies on the following observation:

Section 6.5 dealing with 'Learning Process and Performance Analysis' we have reported the fact that - during this learning process, the particular training data, which exhibit higher similarity to the testing data, are chosen based on the extracted parameters. In this context, we undertook a detailed analysis of the final and intermediate results derived out of CAML model on SST-Binary datasets. We observed that the parameters used to select the training set work well for all datasets excepts the SST-Binary data. As a result, due to the unique characteristics of this dataset, a new selection rule needs to be incorporated into the CAML model for the parameter selection process.

6.6 Conclusion

One of the major motivations for writing this book is to develop CAML models which can be employed to address the problems of interest for industry and society. The current chapter reports an application in the field of 'Computational Linguistics'. The application deals with 'sentiment analysis' of textual data expressed in multi-language environment. While traditional approach is based on analysis of language structure and semantics, the recent solution methodologies employ deep learning models that demand voluminous training set data corpus and large computing resources. By contrast, the CAML model provides a solution for this problem in a multi-language environment with low computing resources and low volume of training data corpus. CAML model derived results are reported on textual data expressed in five languages—two Asian languages (Hindi and Arabic) and three European languages (English, Greek, Georgian). The results derived with CAML model are compared with those derived with state-of-art schemes reported in published literature. The CAML model derived results consistently outperform various lexicon-based methods and machine learning models. Twin issues which have enabled CAML model to achieve this height are—use of Unicode text and analysis of CL graph derived out of evolution Cellular Automata (CA) modelling the textual data. We also establish the point that—for any ML platform, prediction quality gets affected, if the training data set is below a threshold limit and CAML model is no exception to this phenomenon.

References

1. H.H. Do, P.W. Prasad, A. Maag, A. Alsadoon, Deep learning for aspect-based sentiment analysis: a comparative review. Expert Syst. Appl. **118**, 272–299 (2019)
2. S. Behdenna, F. Barigou, G. Belalem, Sentiment analysis at document level, in *Smart Trends in Information Technology and Computer Communications: First International Conference*, SmartCom, Jaipur, India, August 6–7, 2016, Revised Selected Papers 1 (Springer, Berlin, 2016), pp. 159–168
3. E. Cambria, D. Das, S. Bandyopadhyay, A. Feraco et al., *A Practical Guide to Sentiment Analysis*, vol. 5 (Springer, Berlin, 2017)
4. M. Birjali, M. Kasri, A. Beni-Hssane, A comprehensive survey on sentiment analysis: approaches, challenges and trends. Knowl.-Based Syst. **226**, 107134 (2021)
5. N. Indurkhya, F.J. Damerau, *Handbook of Natural Language Processing*, vol. 2 (CRC Press, 2010)
6. T. Chen, R. Xu, Y. He, X. Wang, Improving sentiment analysis via sentence type classification using bilstm-crf and cnn. Expert Syst. Appl. **72**, 221–230 (2017)
7. Z. Zhao, G. Rao, Z. Feng, Dfds: a domain-independent framework for document-level sentiment analysis based on rst, in *Web and Big Data: First International Joint Conference*, APWeb-WAIM, Beijing, China, July 7–9, 2017, Proceedings, Part I 1 (Springer, Berlin, 2017), pp. 297–310
8. S. Kumar, M. Yadava, P.P. Roy, Fusion of eeg response and sentiment analysis of products review to predict customer satisfaction. Inf. Fusion **52**, 41–52 (2019)
9. R. Bose, R.K. Dey, S. Roy, D. Sarddar, Sentiment analysis on online product reviews, in *Information and Communication Technology for Sustainable Development: Proceedings of ICT4SD 2018* (Springer, Berlin, 2020), pp. 559–569
10. A. Rajput, Natural language processing, sentiment analysis, and clinical analytics, in *Innovation in Health Informatics* (Elsevier, 2020), pp. 79–97
11. M. Mitroi, C.-O. Truică, E.-S. Apostol, A.M. Florea, Sentiment analysis using topic-document embeddings, in *2020 IEEE 16th International Conference on Intelligent Computer Communication and Processing (ICCP)* (IEEE, 2020), pp. 75–82
12. Ł. Augustyniak, T. Kajdanowicz, P. Kazienko, Comprehensive analysis of aspect term extraction methods using various text embeddings, in *Computer Speech and Language*, vol. 69 (2021), p. 101217
13. R. Catelli, S. Pelosi, C. Comito, C. Pizzuti, M. Esposito, Lexicon-based sentiment analysis to detect opinions and attitude towards covid-19 vaccines on twitter in italy. Comput. Biol. Med. **158**, 106876 (2023)
14. M. Naldi, S. Petroni, A testset-based method to analyse the negation-detection performance of lexicon-based sentiment analysis tools. Computers **12**(1) (2023)
15. A. Altaf, M.W. Anwar, M.H. Jamal, U.I. Bajwa, Exploiting linguistic features for effective sentence-level sentiment analysis in urdu language. Multimed. Tools Appl. 1–27 (2023)
16. J. Su, Q. Chen, Y. Wang, L. Zhang, W. Pan, Z. Li, Sentence-level sentiment analysis based on supervised gradual machine learning. Sci. Rep. **13**(1), 14500 (2023)
17. H. Jiang, P. He, W. Chen, X. Liu, J. Gao, T. Zhao, SMART: Robust and efficient fine-tuning for pre-trained natural language models through principled regularized optimization, in *Proceedings of the 58th Annual Meeting of the Association for Computational Linguistics* Online: Association for Computational Linguistics (2020), pp. 2177–2190
18. C. Raffel, N. Shazeer, A. Roberts, K. Lee, S. Narang, M. Matena, Y. Zhou, W. Li, P.J. Liu, Exploring the limits of transfer learning with a unified text-to-text transformer. J. Mach. Learn. Res. **21**(1), 5485–5551 (2020)
19. Z. Lan, M. Chen, S. Goodman, K. Gimpel, P. Sharma, R. Soricut, Albert: a lite bert for self-supervised learning of language representations. CoRR (2019). arXiv:abs/1909.11942
20. M. Elizabeth, A.K. Panda, P.P. Chaudhuri, R. Hazari, Cellular automata-based sentiment analysis, in *Proceedings of Second Asian Symposium on Cellular Automata Technology: ASCAT 2023* (Springer, Berlin, 2023), pp. 53–64

21. R. Zhong, S. Shao, K. McKeown, Fine-grained sentiment analysis with faithful attention (2019). arXiv:1908.06870
22. S. Agarwal, A. Sureka, Characterizing linguistic attributes for automatic classification of intent based racist/radicalized posts on tumblr micro-blogging website (2017). arXiv:1701.04931
23. J.L. Lavado, I. Cantador, M.E. Cortés-Cediel, M. Fernández, Automatic intent-based classification of citizen-to-government tweets. in *EGOV-CeDEM-ePart-** (2021), pp. 47–55
24. G. Alexandridis, I. Varlamis, K. Korovesis, G. Caridakis, P. Tsantilas, A survey on sentiment analysis and opinion mining in greek social media. Information 12(8) (2021). [Online]. Available: https://www.mdpi.com/2078-2489/12/8/331
25. F. Barbieri, L. Espinosa Anke, J. Camacho-Collados, XLM-T: Multilingual language models in Twitter for sentiment analysis and beyond, in *Proceedings of the Thirteenth Language Resources and Evaluation Conference* (European Language Resources Association, Marseille, France), pp. 258–266. [Online]. Available: https://aclanthology.org/2022.lrec-1.27
26. A. Conneau, K. Khandelwal, N. Goyal, V. Chaudhary, G. Wenzek, F. Guzmán, E. Grave, M. Ott, L. Zettlemoyer, V. Stoyanov, Unsupervised cross-lingual representation learning at scale, in *Proceedings of the 58th Annual Meeting of the Association for Computational Linguistics*. Online: Association for Computational Linguistics (2020), pp. 8440–8451. [Online]. Available: https://aclanthology.org/2020.acl-main.747
27. J. Devlin, M.-W. Chang, K. Lee, K. Toutanova, BERT: Pre-training of deep bidirectional transformers for language understanding, in *Proceedings of the 2019 Conference of the North American Chapter of the Association for Computational Linguistics: Human Language Technologies, Volume 1 (Long and Short Papers)* (Association for Computational Linguistics, Minneapolis, Minnesota, 2019), pp. 4171–4186. [Online]. Available: https://aclanthology.org/N19-1423
28. Q. Zhong, L. Ding, J. Liu, B. Du, D. Tao, Can chatgpt understand too? a comparative study on chatgpt and fine-tuned bert (2023). arXiv:2302.10198
29. Z. Wang, Q. Xie, Y. Feng, Z. Ding, Z. Yang, R. Xia, Is chatgpt a good sentiment analyzer? a preliminary study (2023). arXiv:2304.04339
30. W. Zhao, Y. Zhao, X. Lu, S. Wang, Y. Tong, B. Qin, Is chatgpt equipped with emotional dialogue capabilities? (2023). arXiv:2304.09582
31. X. Deng, V. Bashlovkina, F. Han, S. Baumgartner, M. Bendersky, Llms to the moon? reddit market sentiment analysis with large language models, in *Companion Proceedings of the ACM Web Conference* (2023), pp. 1014–1019
32. W. Zhang, Y. Deng, B. Liu, S. Pan, L. Bing, Sentiment analysis in the era of large language models: a reality check, in *Findings of the Association for Computational Linguistics: NAACL 2024*, eds. by K. Duh, H. Gomez, S. Bethard (Association for Computational Linguistics, Mexico City, Mexico, 2024), pp. 3881–3906. [Online]. Available: https://aclanthology.org/2024.findings-naacl.246
33. O. Oueslati, E. Cambria, M.B. HajHmida, H. Ounelli, A review of sentiment analysis research in arabic language. Future Gener. Comput. Syst. **112**, 408–430 (2020)
34. A. Alsayat, N. Elmitwally, A comprehensive study for arabic sentiment analysis (challenges and applications). Egypt. Inform. J. **21**(1), 7–12 (2020)
35. A. Pasha, M. Al-Badrashiny, M.T. Diab, A. El Kholy, R. Eskander, N. Habash, M. Pooleery, O. Rambow, R. Roth, Madamira: a fast, comprehensive tool for morphological analysis and disambiguation of arabic. Lrec **14**(2014), 1094–1101 (2014)
36. N. Habash, R. Roth, O. Rambow, R. Eskander, N. Tomeh, Morphological analysis and disambiguation for dialectal Arabic, in *Proceedings of the 2013 Conference of the North American Chapter of the Association for Computational Linguistics: Human Language Technologies*, eds. bt L. Vanderwende, H. Daumé III, K. Kirchhoff (Association for Computational Linguistics, Atlanta, Georgia, 2013), pp. 426–432
37. M. Diab, Second generation amira tools for arabic processing: fast and robust tokenization, pos tagging, and base phrase chunking," in *2nd International Conference on Arabic Language Resources and Tools*, vol. 110 (2009), p. 198

38. M. Abdul-Mageed, M. Diab, S. Kübler, Samar: subjectivity and sentiment analysis for arabic social media. Comput. Speech Lang. **28**(1), 20–37 (2014)
39. M. Al-Ayyoub, S.B. Essa, I. Alsmadi, Lexicon-based sentiment analysis of arabic tweets. Int. J. Soc. Netw. Mining **2**(2), 101–114 (2015)
40. I. Touahri, A. Mazroui, Studying the effect of characteristic vector alteration on arabic sentiment classification. J. King Saud Univ. Comput. Inf. Sci. **33**(7), 890–898 (2021)
41. M. Nabil, M. Aly, A. Atiya, ASTD: Arabic sentiment tweets dataset,in *Proceedings of the 2015 Conference on Empirical Methods in Natural Language Processing* (Association for Computational Linguistics, Lisbon, Portugal, 2015), pp. 2515–2519
42. M. Heikal, M. Torki, N. El-Makky, Sentiment analysis of arabic tweets using deep learning. Procedia Comput. Sci. **142**, 114–122 (2018)
43. M. Al-Ayyoub, A.A. Khamaiseh, Y. Jararweh, M.N. Al-Kabi, A comprehensive survey of arabic sentiment analysis. Inf. Process. Manag. **56**(2), 320–342 (2019)
44. G. Badaro, R. Baly, H. Hajj, W. El-Hajj, K.B. Shaban, N. Habash, A. Al-Sallab, A. Hamdi, A survey of opinion mining in arabic: A comprehensive system perspective covering challenges and advances in tools, resources, models, applications, and visualizations. ACM Trans. Asian Low-Resour. Lang. Inf. Process.(TALLIP) **18**(3), 1–52 (2019)
45. A. Joshi, A. Balamurali, P. Bhattacharyya et al., A fall-back strategy for sentiment analysis in hindi: a case study, in *Proceedings of the 8th ICON* (2010)
46. A. Balamurali, A. Joshi, P. Bhattacharyya, Cross-lingual sentiment analysis for indian languages using linked wordnets, in *Proceedings of COLING 2012: Posters* (2012), pp. 73–82
47. A. Bakliwal, P. Arora, V. Varma, Hindi subjective lexicon: a lexical resource for hindi adjective polarity classification, in *International Conference on Language Resources and Evaluation* (2012). [Online]. Available: https://api.semanticscholar.org/CorpusID:1657748
48. Y. Sharma, V. Mangat, M. Kaur, A practical approach to sentiment analysis of hindi tweets, in *2015 1st International Conference on Next Generation Computing Technologies (NGCT)* (2015), pp. 677–680
49. B.G. Patra, D. Das, A. Das, R. Prasath, Shared task on sentiment analysis in Indian languages (sail) tweets—an overview, vol. 9468 (Springer, Berlin, 2015), pp. 650–655
50. A. Joshi, A. Prabhu, M. Shrivastava, V. Varma, Towards sub-word level compositions for sentiment analysis of hindi-english code mixed text, in *Proceedings of COLING 2016, the 26th International Conference on Computational Linguistics: Technical Papers* (2016), pp. 2482–2491
51. M.S. Akhtar, A. Ekbal, P. Bhattacharyya, Aspect based sentiment analysis: category detection and sentiment classification for hindi, in *Computational Linguistics and Intelligent Text Processing*. ed. by A. Gelbukh (Springer International Publishing, Cham, 2018), pp.246–257
52. K. Garg, P. kaur Buttar, Aspect based sentiment analysis of hindi text review. Int. J. Adv. Res. Comput. Sci. **8**, 831–836, 8 (2017). [Online]. Available: http://ijarcs.info/index.php/Ijarcs/article/view/4503
53. A. Pathak, S. Kumar, P.P. Roy, B.G. Kim, Aspect-based sentiment analysis in hindi language by ensembling pre-trained mbert models. Electronics (Switzerland) **10**, 11 (2021)
54. K. Shrivastava, S. Kumar, A sentiment analysis system for the hindi language by integrating gated recurrent unit with genetic algorithm. Int. Arab J. Inf. Technol. **17**, 954–964, 11 (2020)
55. S. Khan, M. Shahid, Hindi/bengali sentiment analysis using transfer learning and joint dual input learning with self attention. BOHR Int. J. Comput. Sci. **1**, 31–36, 2 (2022)
56. R. kumari, D.K. Sah, K. Cengiz, N. Ivković, P. Balaji, Automatic graph construction and exploring different types of lstms for asian hindi languages for medical review sentiment analysis. ACM Trans. Asian Low-Resour. Lang. Inf. Process. (2023)
57. G. Gautam, D. Yadav, Sentiment analysis of twitter data using machine learning approaches and semantic analysis, in *2014 Seventh International Conference on Contemporary Computing (IC3)* (IEEE, 2014), pp. 437–442
58. J. Singh, P. Tripathi, Sentiment analysis of twitter data by making use of svm, random forest and decision tree algorithm, in *2021 10th IEEE International Conference on Communication Systems and Network Technologies (CSNT)* (IEEE, 2021), pp. 193–198

59. K.L. Tan, C.P. Lee, K.S.M. Anbananthen, K.M. Lim, Roberta-lstm: a hybrid model for sentiment analysis with transformers and recurrent neural network. *IEEE Access* **10**, 21 517–21 525 (2022)
60. A. Hasan, S. Moin, A. Karim, S. Shamshirband, Machine learning-based sentiment analysis for twitter accounts. Math. Comput. Appl. **23**(1), 11 (2018)
61. M. Adnan, R. Sarno, K.R. Sungkono, Sentiment analysis of restaurant review with classification approach in the decision tree-j48 algorithm, in *Proceedings—2019 International Seminar on Application for Technology of Information and Communication: Industry 4.0: Retrospect, Prospect, and Challenges, iSemantic 2019* (2019), pp. 121–126
62. M. Govindarajan, Sentiment analysis of restaurant reviews using hybrid classification method. Int. J. Soft Comput. Artif. Intell. **2**(1), 17–23 (2014)
63. M.E. Basiri, S. Nemati, M. Abdar, E. Cambria, U.R. Acharya, Abcdm: An attention-based bidirectional cnn-rnn deep model for sentiment analysis. Future Gener. Comput. Syst. **115**, 279–294 (2021)
64. E. Hossain, O. Sharif, M.M. Hoque, I.H. Sarker, Sentilstm: a deep learning approach for sentiment analysis of restaurant reviews, in *International Conference on Hybrid Intelligent Systems* (Springer, Berlin, 2021), pp. 193–203
65. S. Sazzed, A hybrid approach of opinion mining and comparative linguistic analysis of restaurant reviews, in *Proceedings of the International Conference on Recent Advances in Natural Language Processing (RANLP 2021)* (2021), pp. 1281–1288
66. N. Spatiotis, I. Mporas, M. Paraskevas, I. Perikos, Sentiment analysis for the greek language. Assoc. Comput. Mach. **11** (2016)
67. G. Markopoulos, G. Mikros, A. Iliadi, M. Liontos, Sentiment analysis of hotel reviews in greek: a comparison of unigram features, in *Cultural Tourism in a Digital Era*, ed. by V. Katsoni (Springer International Publishing, Cham, 2015), pp. 373–383
68. G. Kalamatianos, D. Mallis, S. Symeonidis, A. Arampatzis, Sentiment analysis of greek tweets and hashtags using a sentiment lexicon, in *Proceedings of the 19th Panhellenic Conference on Informatics*, ser. PCI '15 (Association for Computing Machinery, New York, NY, USA, 2015), pp. 63–68. [Online]. Available: https://doi.org/10.1145/2801948.2802010
69. J. Koutsikakis, I. Chalkidis, P. Malakasiotis, I. Androutsopoulos, Greek-bert: the greeks visiting sesame street, in *11th Hellenic Conference on Artificial Intelligence*, ser. SETN 2020 (Association for Computing Machinery, New York, NY, USA, 2020), pp. 110–117
70. D. Antypas, A. Preece, J. Camacho-Collados, Negativity spreads faster: a large-scale multilingual twitter analysis on the role of sentiment in political communication. Online Soc. Netw. Media **33**, 100242 (2023). [Online]. Available: https://www.sciencedirect.com/science/article/pii/S2468696423000010
71. V. Athanasiou, M. Maragoudakis, A novel, gradient boosting framework for sentiment analysis in languages where nlp resources are not plentiful: a case study for modern greek. Algorithms **10**, 34 (2017). [Online]. Available: https://api.semanticscholar.org/CorpusID:7263511
72. N. Stefanovitch, J. Piskorski, S. Kharazi, Resources and experiments on sentiment classification for georgian, in *Proceedings of the Thirteenth Language Resources and Evaluation Conference* (2022), pp. 1613–1621
73. O. Kapanadze, G. Kotzé, T. Hanneforth, Building resources for georgian treebanking-based nlp, in *Language, Logic, and Computation*, ed. by A. Özgün, Y. Zinova (Springer International Publishing, Cham, 2022), pp. 60–78
74. I. Kardava, N. Gulua, J. Antidze, B. Toklikishvili, Morphological synthesis and analysis of georgian words (2019)
75. N. Doborjginidze, Corpus of the georgian language (2016), pp. 328–334. [Online]. Available: http://corpora.iliauni.edu.ge/
76. M. Khachidze, M. Tsintsadze, M. Archuadze et al., Natural language processing based instrument for classification of free text medical records. BioMed Res. Int. **2016** (2016)
77. D. Soselia, L. Shugliashvili, S. Amashukeli, I. Koberidze, G. Chelidze, Freezing networks: weight preservation procedure for continual learning

78. J. Lampert, C.H. Lampert, Overcoming rare-language discrimination in multi-lingual sentiment analysis, in *2021 IEEE International Conference on Big Data (Big Data)* (IEEE, 2021), pp. 5185–5192
79. C. Banea, R. Mihalcea, J. Wiebe, A bootstrapping method for building subjectivity lexicons for languages with scarce resources. LREC **8**, 2–764 (2008)
80. M. Taboada, J. Brooke, M. Tofiloski, K. Voll, M. Stede, Lexicon-based methods for sentiment analysis. Comput. Linguist. **37**(2), 267–307 (2011)
81. M. Ahmad, S. Aftab, I. Ali, Sentiment analysis of tweets using svm. Int. J. Comput. Appl **177**(5), 25–29 (2017)
82. J. Devlin, M.-W. Chang, K. Lee, K. Toutanova, Bert: pre-training of deep bidirectional transformers for language understanding (2018). arXiv:1810.04805
83. Unicode 15.0 character code charts. [Online]. Available: https://unicode.org/charts/
84. K.M. Alomari, H.M. ElSherif, K. Shaalan, Arabic tweets sentimental analysis using machine learning, in *Advances in Artificial Intelligence: From Theory to Practice*, eds. by S. Benferhat, K. Tabia, M. Ali (Springer International Publishing, Cham, 2017), pp. 602–610
85. N. Choudhary, R. Singh, A.R. Vijjini, M. Shrivastava, Twitter corpus of resource-scarce languages for sentiment analysis and multilingual emoji prediction," in *International Conference on Computational Linguistics* (Association for Computational Linguistics, Santa Fe, New Mexico, USA, 2018), pp. 1570–1577
86. Gaurav, Hindi movie reviews dataset, 2019. [Online]. Available: https://www.kaggle.com/datasets/disisbig/hindi-movie-reviews-dataset
87. Restaurant reviews | kaggle. [Online]. Available: https://kaggle.com/datasets/d4rklucif3r/restaurant-reviews
88. Sentimental analysis for tweets | kaggle. [Online]. Available: https://kaggle.com/datasets/gargmanas/sentimental-analysis-for-tweets
89. R. Socher, A. Perelygin, J. Wu, J. Chuang, C.D. Manning, A.Y. Ng, C. Potts, Recursive deep models for semantic compositionality over a sentiment treebank, in *Proceedings of the 2013 Conference on Empirical Methods in Natural Language Processing* (2013), pp. 1631–1642
90. Amazon alexa reviews | kaggle. [Online]. Available: https://kaggle.com/datasets/sid321axn/amazon-alexa-reviews
91. N. Fragkis, Skroutz shops greek reviews, sentiment analysis. [Online]. Available: https://kaggle.com/datasets/nikosfragkis/skroutz-shop-reviews-sentiment-analysis/data
92. J.K.S. Stefanovitch, N. Piskorski, Sentiment_analysis_georgian, 2023. [Online]. Available: https://jeodpp.jrc.ec.europa.eu/ftp/jrc-opendata/LANGUAGE-TECHNOLOGY/
93. S.A. Aljuhani, N.S. Alghamdi, A comparison of sentiment analysis methods on amazon reviews of mobile phones. Int. J. Adv. Comput. Sci. Appl. **10**, 608–617 (2019)
94. Z. Yuan, S. Wu, F. Wu, J. Liu, Y. Huang, Domain attention model for multi-domain sentiment classification. Knowl.-Based Syst. **155**, 1–10 (2018)
95. Z. Jianqiang, G. Xiaolin, Z. Xuejun, Deep convolution neural networks for twitter sentiment analysis. IEEE Access **6**, 23 253–23 260 (2018)
96. M.M. Hamad, M.A. Salih, R.A. Jaleel, Sentiment analysis of restaurant reviews in social media using naïve bayes. Appl. Model. Simul. **5**, 166–172 (2021)
97. R.A. Laksono, K.R. Sungkono, R. Sarno, C.S. Wahyuni, Sentiment analysis of restaurant customer reviews on tripadvisor using naïve bayes, in *Proceedings of 2019 International Conference on Information and Communication Technology and Systems, ICTS 2019* (2019), pp. 49–54
98. R. Rajasekaran, U. Kanumuri, M. Siddhardha Kumar, S. Ramasubbareddy, S. Ashok, Sentiment analysis of restaurant reviews," in *Smart Intelligent Computing and Applications*, eds. by S.C. Satapathy, V. Bhateja, S. Das (Springer Singapore, Singapore, 2019), pp. 383–390
99. Q. Chen, R. Zhang, Y. Zheng, Y. Mao, Dual contrastive learning: text classification via label-aware data augmentation. CoRR (2022). arXiv:abs/2201.08702
100. J. Wang, Y. Zhang, L.C. Yu, X. Zhang, Contextual sentiment embeddings via bi-directional gru language model. Knowl.-Based Syst. **235**, 107663 (2022)

101. A. Deniz, M. Angin, P. Angin, Sentiment and context-refined word embeddings for sentiment analysis, in *2021 IEEE International Conference on Systems, Man, and Cybernetics (SMC)* (2021), pp. 927–932
102. A. Aghajanyan, A. Gupta, A. Shrivastava, X. Chen, L. Zettlemoyer, S. Gupta, Muppet: Massive multi-task representations with pre-finetuning, in *Proceedings of the 2021 Conference on Empirical Methods in Natural Language Processing* (Association for Computational Linguistics, Online and Punta Cana, Dominican Republic, 2021), pp. 5799–5811
103. R. Tang, Y. Lu, L. Liu, L. Mou, O. Vechtomova, J. Lin, Distilling task-specific knowledge from BERT into simple neural networks. CoRR (2019). arXiv:abs/1903.12136
104. W. Zhao, J. Ye, M. Yang, Z. Lei, S. Zhang, Z. Zhao, Investigating capsule networks with dynamic routing for text classification. CoRR (2018). arXiv:abs/1804.00538
105. P. Xu, A. Madotto, C.-S. Wu, J.H. Park, P. Fung, Emo2Vec: Learning generalized emotion representation by multi-task training, in *Proceedings of the 9th Workshop on Computational Approaches to Subjectivity, Sentiment and Social Media Analysis* (Association for Computational Linguistics, 2018), pp. 292–298
106. S. Rosenthal, N. Farra, P. Nakov, SemEval-2017 task 4: sentiment analysis in Twitter, in *Proceedings of the 11th International Workshop on Semantic Evaluation (SemEval-2017)* (Association for Computational Linguistics, Vancouver, Canada, 2017), pp. 502–518
107. A. Benlahbib, A. Boumhidi, NLP-LISAC at SemEval-2023 task 12: sentiment analysis for tweets expressed in African languages via transformer-based models," in *Proceedings of the 17th International Workshop on Semantic Evaluation (SemEval-2023)*. (Association for Computational Linguistics, Toronto, Canada, 2023), pp. 199–204
108. A. Gupta, U. Sharma, Machine learning based sentiment analysis of hindi data with TF-IDF and count vectorization (Institute of Electrical and Electronics Engineers Inc., 2022)

Chapter 7
Cellular Automata Based Binarized Machine Learning Model

> *"If I can't make it through one door, I'll go through another door or I'll make a door. Something terrific will come no matter how dark the present."*
>
> *—Rabindranath Tagore*

7.1 Introduction

Machine learning has emerged as a pivotal technique for developing analytical models through inductive reasoning, especially in extracting meaningful information and patterns from large volumes of raw datasets. This process demands extensive resources, including computational power, storage capacity, programmability, and efficient data movement capabilities. Consequently, there is a continuous need to advance machine-level architectures to keep pace with the increasing demands in this field. The introduction of new machine learning models has been facilitated by advancements in computational power, the utilization of GPU-based systems, and expanded memory capacities. The current research is getting increasingly focused on developing methods that maintain or improve performance while reducing computational costs and memory requirements. One such innovation is Binarized Neural Networks (BNNs), introduced by Hubara [1]. In BNNs, binary weights, and activations replace real-valued gradients during the training phase, akin to operations in Convolutional Neural Networks that reduce memory usage and access time. In the current scenario, this chapter presents a new design for a cost-effective machine learning model with reduced memory and computation requirements by leveraging the computational model of Cellular Automata (CA).

© The Author(s), under exclusive license to Springer Nature Singapore Pte Ltd. 2025

P. Pal Chaudhuri et al., *New Kind of Machine Learning—Cellular Automata Model*,
https://doi.org/10.1007/978-981-96-1501-8_7

A Machine Learning Model, in general, is concerned with the issues like Input Data, associated Parameters, and the derived Feature Vector (FV), in addition to the Objective Function, and Optimization Algorithm operating on the model architecture in order to arrive at the desired performance. Machine Learning algorithms span a spectrum of complexity, directly impacting their resource requirements. While Linear Regression, Support Vector Machines, and Decision Trees introduce moderate complexity in terms of their design, significantly higher complexity is associated with Neural Networks, Deep Neural Networks, Recurrent Networks, and Generative Adversarial Networks. As the complexity increases, so does the need for optimized hardware solutions to handle the resource-intensive nature of advanced machine learning tasks.

Historically, Cellular Automata (CA) has proven effective in various computing applications. The regular, modular, cascadable structure of CA with an analytical framework have been exploited in numerous applications, starting from VLSI circuit testing, error correcting codes, pattern recognition to cryptography. In this chapter, we explore the potential of CA for the design of efficient Machine Learning (ML) model. The ML algorithm is designed with CA framework employing linear CA rules. Our initial focus is to model the Linear Regression using Cellular Automata, that is to de-construct the Linear Regression followed by its reconstruction with an innovative model employing CA framework. We use various heuristics to do the parameter optimization and test the formulations of this proposed model using binary datasets to evaluate the accuracy and conduct an analytical study. The insights gained from this study will be extended in future for general applications covering non-linear functions. We anticipate that this research will pave the way for new advancements in binarized machine learning models and expand the theoretical and practical applications of cellular automata.

7.1.1 Why Yet Another Machine Learning Model

Machine learning fundamentally relies on mathematical and probabilistic models that require extensive computations. Training these models typically demands significant computational power, and without the appropriate hardware, the process can be frustrating. This highlights the need for specialized hardware that optimally supports various machine learning models. Although there is a wealth of literature on machine learning algorithms, models, their applications, and theoretical foundations, there is a notable lack of attention given to the underlying infrastructure - especially the hardware models that power these algorithms. This oversight is particularly concerning in light of the growing complexity and resource demands of modern machine learning techniques. Against this backdrop, two key motivations for the study presented in this chapter are outlined.

- **Need of a Binary-Level Machine Learning Model suited for Hardware**
In the realm of machine learning and data science, most traditional and applied models rely on real-valued inputs and outputs, employing real-valued mathematical frameworks. While this approach has proven successful, it highlights an interesting gap in exploring machine learning with binary-level data. By converting an input data into a binary form, it becomes easier to identify and extract relevant features, which can be used as inputs to a machine-learning model. With the binary data. it also becomes more consistent and easier to compare across different samples. Binarization can be used to simplify the classification process by reducing the number of possible output values. This can make it easier to train a machine learning model, as well as improve the accuracy of the model. Moreover, binary data, governed by basic functions such as AND, OR, and XOR, plays a crucial role in computing and digital systems. It is important to note that all machine learning data and operations ultimately need to be converted to binary form for the final computations to take place, and in particular if the application needs to be implemented in hardware.
- **Potential of Cellular Automata as Hardware for Binarized Machine-Learning Model**
Traditionally, machine learning frameworks are constructed as mathematical models, which are then converted into programming models and ultimately compiled into binary code for execution. This process of compiling complex binary models before execution introduces unnecessary computational overhead, which could be mitigated if machine learning models could be directly translated into machine-level binary formats. A review of the existing literature emphasizes this potential, revealing that, while hardware is crucial for the efficiency and scalability of machine learning, research discussions tend to focus more on algorithmic advancements, often neglecting the hardware foundation with high computational power. In recent years, machine learning workloads are becoming increasingly complex, demanding the use of specialized hardware accelerators like GPUs or TPUs and custom hardware solutions. Companies are developing Application-Specific Integrated Circuits (ASICs) tailored for specific deep learning tasks, achieving higher performance and energy efficiency. 2023 marks a significant year in AI advancements, highlighting the importance of choosing the dedicated machine learning hardware [2, 3]. This chapter introduces Cellular Automata (CA) as one such dedicated machine learning hardware.
The Cellular Automata framework reports de-construction of traditional machine learning model, followed by analysis and reconstruction of the model. This process initiates a new research avenue exploring the application of Cellular Automata in machine learning. To achieve this, our first objective is to develop a functional and executable binary machine learning model based on a pre-existing linear regression model, utilizing the computational framework of linear Cellular Automata.

The use of Cellular Automata (CA) as a computing model is a largely unexplored avenue in the context of machine learning and design of its associated hardware. CA provide computation models composed of a grid of cells where the state of each cell evolves over discrete time steps according to a set of rules. Each cell can be realized in hardware with a combinational logic and a 1-bit memory element, forming an abstract mathematical model with simple hardware construction. This very simple model has proved to be a very powerful tool and has shown promise in emulating complex behavior and information processing. Consequently, regular structure of CA can be viewed as the most desirable candidate for hardware design of binarized machine learning model. Design of specialized hardware for LLM (Large Language Model) employing matrix operations on real numbers are excluded in the earlier discussions. So, we briefly touch upon the impact of its associated issues.

The hardware design of currently available LLM models can impact the real-world variables to a significant extent. The most important variable is the cost of infrastructure for hardware.

7.1.2 Overview of the Binarized ML Model with Cellular Automata

In this chapter, the computational model of Cellular Automata has been presented to explore the applicability in the domain of machine learning, in particular, to replace the real-valued computational model of machine learning with the binary level Cellular Automata model. The approach and the experiments presented in this chapter are highlighted below.

- Study and deconstruct the Cellular Automata (CA) model at the very basic level in order to draw similarities and analogies with machine learning. In order to realize this objective, based on certain characteristics and features of the Cellular Automata model, we narrow down the choices to linear regression.
- Deconstruct the basic model of linear regression, we redefine and transform the data inputs, features, model architecture, parameters, objective function, and optimization algorithm into Cellular Automata model. The above features are analyzed and transformed in order to assimilate into the CA construct. Execution of such initial steps enable us to formulate an efficient CA-based model for linear regression problems.
- Perform certain test runs of the modified linear regression on the self-generated binary datasets in order to test the executability of the formulated linear regression model. We next perform an analysis of the test runs and the nature of the results in order to improve the parameter space design.
- Analyze the proposed model by varying factors to study and address the erratic nature of of the algorithm convergence due to complex parameter space. The analysis helps to modify and accelerate the speed of successful convergence by studying the parameter space on self-generated datasets and plotting the objective function curve followed by its detailed analysis.
- Modify and optimize the parameter space in the model to formulate a more efficient objective function curve in order to optimize the convergence of the algorithm.

1. Based on the nature of the objective function curve, modification of the parameters to include different rules of CA in the system.
2. Modification of the optimization algorithm to account for the problem of getting stuck in the local minima of the space.
3. Modifying the CA encoding rules into the Transition Vector (TRV) string to change the parameter space of the TRV.
4. Improvement of the optimization algorithm by addressing the issue of convergence into local minima.
5. Employment of certain heuristics based on momentum-based gradient descent in the system in order to get a better-minima of the system.

- Propose certain modifications and possibilities that can form the basis of further research work in this field.

This chapter is organized as follows. Section 7.1, as noted earlier, presents a brief introduction to machine learning with the focus on its hardware limitations. This section also reports the motivation to undertake the research work in the field of binarized machine learning model, followed by projection of the potential of Cellular Automata as a viable candidate for the same. In Sect. 7.2, a theoretical background is provided for the linear regression model and the recapitulation of Cellular Automata fundamentals. The Sect. 7.3, justifies the selection of CA for developing a machine learning model using Cellular Automata. In Sect. 7.4, an analytical deconstruction is reported for both the machine learning Model of linear regression and the computational model of Cellular Automata in order to finally formulate a binary CA model for linear regression. Also, a preliminary experiment is set which is used to check the veracity of the model and to analyze the model to establish the scope of further improvement. In Sect. 7.5, an insight into the experimental results are provided. The Sect. 7.6 gives an outline of hardware design for CA based binarized ML model. Finally, Sect. 7.7 reports the scope of future work in the field of binarized machine learning models for nonlinear functions.

7.2 Background

This section reports the background information in respect of linear model out of which linear regression is chosen based on certain observations; the section also covers a brief introduction on Cellular Automata (CA). Based on these two inputs, the formulation of a new model is presented in next subsection.

7.2.1 *Machine Learning and Linear Regression Model*

The basic work of the learning system is to improve its performance at a task with experience. Therefore, the very basic essence of machine learning is embodied in the following four aspects.

1. System: The model design
2. Task: The task assigned for the system
3. Performance: The measurement metric of how good a system is at its task
4. Experience: The aspect using which the system improves its task.

A learning scheme at its core is a model that primarily relies on inductive reasoning to infer an analytical function. This function extracts meaningful information and patterns from large unprocessed datasets and utilizes experience in order to improve its performance. For the present case, the inference that is drawn from inductive reasoning is achieved through experience which is established through basically three means.

1. Supervised learning: Models trained with labeled data
2. Unsupervised learning: Models trained with non-labelled data
3. Reinforcement learning: Models learning to make sequential decisions by interactions with an environment without any labeled data.

Linear regression becomes the best choice for the initial step for the formulation of the new binary Cellular Automata model for the following pivotal reasons.

1. Linear regression being a linear model is comparatively easier to assimilate in the Cellular Automata domain as the simplest Cellular Automata also relies on linear binary operations.
2. Linear regression being a supervised model is easy to set up and validate due to the presence of labeled data which makes it easier to check for error metrics.
3. The simple construct of the linear regression model makes it a viable and excellent candidate for the initiation of the study of the implementation of machine learning models on a hardware level.

The aim is to employ Cellular Automata to redefine a pre-existing machine-learning model in order to formulate a new model. For the experimentation, as discussed earlier, linear regression is chosen as the preexisting model for its simplicity and also linear nature of the task which can be modeled conveniently employing linear Cellular Automata.

Linear Regression is a very basic machine learning algorithm that is primarily employed to infer a relationship between two variables—a dependent variable and an independent variable—using a certain set of assumptions and a hypothesis function. The model aims to find and learn the best-fitting linear function among the search space of the hypothesis function. Linear regression, in a nutshell, can be defined as a type of ML algorithm, supervised in nature, whose purpose is to compute a linear relationship between the independent variable and one or more dependent variables.

Consider a Model with an Equation like -

$$Y = f(x_1, x_2, \ldots, x_{n-1}, x_n) \tag{7.1}$$

Where,

$$\begin{aligned} Y &= \text{Independent Variable.} \\ x_1, x_2, \cdots, x_{n-1}, x_n &= \text{Dependent Variables.} \\ f &= \text{The function which is being learned through} \\ &\quad \text{experience or training.} \end{aligned}$$

7.2.2 Basic Aspects of Linear Regression

The key components of Linear Regression that come under the focus while formulating a new model can be categorized as follows.

A. Data and Features

The major purpose of Linear regression model is to derive a linear relation between two sets of variables—dependent variable (predicted variable) and one or more independent variables (predictor variable).

The nature of the data depends on the problem statement and available dataset, and can be of various types such as numerical or categorial data. Generally, any data that can be converted into ordered numeric form is acceptable in the linear regression model.

In the case of the linear regression, certain assumptions are pre-established in the model for the dataset in order for the model to work. Such assumptions can be listed as follows.

(a) **Supervised Learning**—The set of data utilized for learning is labeled; the data is a combination of dependent and independent variables.
(b) **Linearity**—The assumption of linearity pertains to independent and dependent variables that can actually be related using a linear function.
(c) **Independence**—The assumption of independence pertains to the observations in the dataset that are independent of each other.
(d) **Homoscedasticity**—The homoscedasticity assumption is based on the assumption that across all the different levels of independent variables, the variance of errors is constant. This assumption mainly describes a scenario where the term of error (that is, the random disturbance between the independent variables and the dependent variable) is the same across all the values of the range of the independent variables.

(e) **Normality**—Errors in the model are assumed to be normally distributed across the range of independent variables.
(f) **No Multicollinearity**—It is assumed that there is no high degree of correlation between the independent variables.

B. Model Architecture and Parameters
The model of linear regression seeks to infer, using inductive reasoning (using special cases to deduce a general case) a linear equation in the form of

- $y_i \in Y \quad (i = 1, 2, \ldots, n)$; labels to data (supervised learning)
- $x_i \in X \quad (i = 1, 2, \ldots, n)$; independent training data
- $\hat{y}_i \in Y \quad (i = 1, 2, \ldots, n)$; the predicted values

Assumptions:

(a) **Hypothesis Function**—For the case of linear regression, on one independent and one dependent variable, linear function is taken wherein it is assumed to fit the model because of the linearity assumption

$$\hat{Y} = \theta_2 X + \theta_1$$

$$\begin{aligned} \theta_1 &: \text{ intercept} \\ \theta_2 &: \text{ coefficient of } x \\ Y &: \text{ Dependent Variable set} \\ X &: \text{ Independent Variable set} \\ \hat{Y} &: \text{ Predicted Variable set} \end{aligned}$$

(b) **Parameter Space**—In general linear regression, the parameter space is essentially a set of real numbers R, which may or may not have any constraints. The task of the linear regression construct is to provide a model that can actually start from an assumed parameter or hypothesis function and find an optimal hypothesis function.

Optimal Hypothesis Function:
The linear regression algorithm is tasked with finding the best possible relation between the set of independent and dependent variables and based on the template of the definition of the function, the algorithm tries to identify the best function in the space of all linear functions. All the possible functions lie in the hypothesis function space defined by the parameters and the best-fitting function is called the optimal hypothesis function. In searching for the optimal function, we require two items.

- A **Metric to Quantify** how good is the fitness of a particular hypothesis function.
- A **Guiding Quantity** to update the parameter to optimally steer towards the desired Optimal Function.

C. Objective Function and Optimization Algorithm:

The metric required to evaluate how good a particular hypothesis function is for a given set of parameters and a given dataset is called the Objective Function.

Quantification of the Goodness of Hypothesis Function:

In the case of linear regression, it is measured using a form of cumulative error metrics like Mean Squared Error or Absolute Error which takes the current hypothesis function, predicts the dependent variable for all datasets, and evaluates the cumulative distance measure (error) among all the labeled independent variable and predicted ones.

Residuals—The cost function is a function of the distance between the predicted variable and the labelled independent variable. This value is called the residuals which is essentially the difference between the actual and predicted values.

Types of cost functions are

a. **R2 Score**—Evaluation using the values of residuals with a score from 0 to 1

$$R^2 = 1 - \frac{RSS}{TSS} \quad \text{Where} \quad RSS = \sum (y_i - \hat{y}_i)^2 \quad TSS = \sum (y_i - \bar{y}_i)^2$$

b. **Mean Absolute Error(MAE)**—The MAE is simply defined as the summation of all the residuals for all the datasets averaged over all the datasets.

$$MAE = \frac{1}{N} \sum |y_i - \hat{y}_i|$$

c. **Mean Squared Error(MSE)**—The MSE is defined as the summation of the square of all the residuals for the dataset averaged over all the datasets.

$$MSE = \frac{1}{n} \sum \underbrace{(y_i - \hat{y}_i)}^2$$

7.2.3 *Algorithm to Guide the Model to Optimal Hypothesis Function*

An optimization algorithm is tasked with the function to update the model parameters to minimize the objective function in order to reach the optimal hypothesis function.

Objective Function

The objective function is a mathematical expression that gives a quantification to the performance/quality of the model with respect to the ability to make predictions on a given dataset. The objective function is representative of the objective that the machine learning algorithm is aimed to optimize during the training process. Further, the Objective function acts as a means to optimize a certain problem based

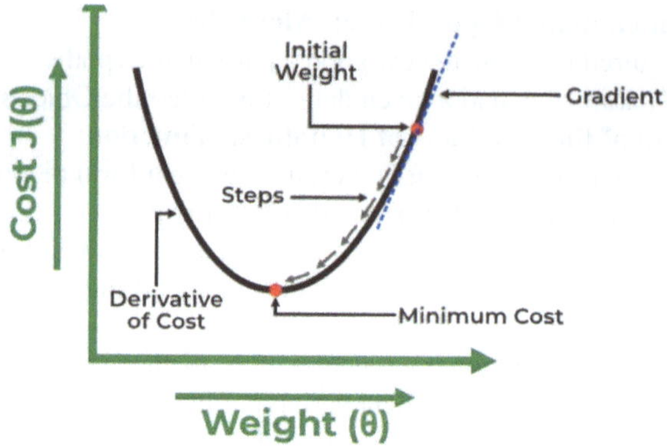

Fig. 7.1 Objective function minima search

on certain constraints; especially in the present case, the objective function needs to be minimized in order to reach the optimal solution.

The objective function is expressed as a function of model parameters and thus its minima can be searched by varying the parameters and thus consequently finding the optimal function. The choice of the objective function in the case of linear regression can be any of the error functions, Mean Absolute Error, Mean Squared Error, or R2 Score.

Gradient Descent

The basic aim is to find the minima of the objective function as highlighted in Fig. 7.1, and by the basic calculus theory we can find a means to

1. Locate the Minima—Derivative = 0
2. Derive direction of Minima—The slope of the curve gives the direction

So, finally the linear regression model can be trained using the optimization algorithm of gradient descent based on the above two factors by iteratively modifying the model's parameter to reduce the objective function of the model on the labeled training dataset.

1. **Location of the Minima using Derivative**

   To achieve the above mathematically, we can employ the use of the derivative function

$$
\begin{aligned}
J'_{\theta_1} &= \frac{\partial J(\theta_1, \theta_2)}{\partial \theta_1} \\
&= \frac{\partial}{\partial \theta_1}\left[\frac{1}{n}\sum(\hat{y}_i - y_i)^2\right] \\
&= \frac{1}{n}\left[\sum 2(\hat{y}_i - y_i)\left(\frac{\partial}{\partial \theta_1}(\hat{y}_i - y_i)\right)\right]
\end{aligned}
$$

$$
\begin{aligned}
&= \frac{1}{n}\left[\sum 2(\hat{y}_i - y_i)\left(\frac{\partial}{\partial \theta_1}(\theta_1 + \theta_2 x_i - y_i)\right)\right] \\
&= \frac{1}{n}\left[\sum 2(\hat{y}_i - y_i)(1 + 0 - 0)\right] \\
&= \frac{2}{n}\left[\sum (\hat{y}_i - y_i)\right] \\
&= \frac{2}{n}\sum (\hat{y}_i - y_i)
\end{aligned}
$$

$$
\begin{aligned}
J'_{\theta_2} &= \frac{\partial J(\theta_1, \theta_2)}{\partial \theta_2} \\
&= \frac{\partial}{\partial \theta_2}\left[\frac{1}{n}\sum (\hat{y}_i - y_i)^2\right] \\
&= \frac{1}{n}\left[\sum 2(\hat{y}_i - y_i)\left(\frac{\partial}{\partial \theta_2}(\hat{y}_i - y_i)\right)\right] \\
&= \frac{1}{n}\left[\sum 2(\hat{y}_i - y_i)\left(\frac{\partial}{\partial \theta_2}(\theta_1 + \theta_2 x_i - y_i)\right)\right] \\
&= \frac{1}{n}\left[\sum 2(\hat{y}_i - y_i)(0 + x_i - 0)\right] \\
&= \frac{1}{n}\left[\sum (\hat{y}_i - y_i) \cdot 2x_i\right] \\
&= \frac{2}{n}\sum (\hat{y}_i - y_i) \cdot x_i
\end{aligned}
$$

2. **Movement/Updation in the direction of Minima**
   The parameters can be updated using various update policies but for the formulation of a newer model we stick with the most simple update policy. Update Policy—where α = Learning Parameter = How much to update in the current direction provided by the derivative function.

$$
\begin{aligned}
\theta_1 &= \theta_1 - \alpha\left(J'_{\theta_1}\right) \\
&= \theta_1 - \alpha\left(\frac{2}{n}\sum_{i=1}^{n}(\hat{y}_i - y_i)\right)
\end{aligned}
$$

$$
\begin{aligned}
\theta_2 &= \theta_2 - \alpha\left(J'_{\theta_2}\right) \\
&= \theta_2 - \alpha\left(\frac{2}{n}\sum_{i=1}^{n}(\hat{y}_i - y_i) \cdot x_i\right)
\end{aligned}
$$

7.2.4 Cellular Automata Model

Chapter 3 introduces Cellular Automata (CA) fundamentals. For ease of reference, this subsection recapitulates a few relevant issues on linear CA.
Cellular Automata is a class of mathematical and computational model which at the simplest level consist of a grid or an array of cells that comprise of a finite number of states that evolve in time steps. The evolutions are based on the function of the states of the neighboring cells. The real power of the CA is that it can be used to simulate various real-world processes as well as to model computational constructs and models.

While the CA is defined at length in Chap. 4, we summarize some basic tents of CA for the purpose of this chapter.

1. The Cellular Automata is a 1-Dimensional Array of cells (1-D Cellular Automata).
2. The Cellular Automata has a 3-neighborhood space that is a cell has only 2 neighboring cells stacked against it like a linear array of cells.
3. Each cell has only 2 states—Binary Model—0/1, $Q = state = 0/1$.
4. The Next state - $Q_i(t+1)$ of a cell is the function of 3 parameters-

   a. The Previous State of the cell—$Q_i(t)$
   b. The Previous state of left cell—$Q_{i-1}(t)$
   c. The Previous state of right cell—$Q_{i-1}(t)$

   In the case of the above equation

   a. N—The Length of the Binary Strings in the CA-N-bit.
   b. i—position index of the bit in the Binary String.
   c. $Q_i(t+1)$—Bit Value/State of the ith cell.

The CA function that applies on each bit of the binary string, takes the given index and its immediate neighbors $i-1$ and $i+1$ and returns a value for the $Q_i(t+1)$ as the output string

$$Q_i(t+1) = f_{CA}\left[Q_{i-1}(t), Q_i(t), Q_{i+1}(t)\right]$$

In this case, as mentioned in Chap. 3, a combination of CA rules can be selected. Since there are N bits therefore at one time of instance, the number of rules acting on that string will be N. Therefore, we can represent the CA function as a transition vector of N rules that act on N-bit Strings to give a result

$$T =< f_1, f_2, f_3, f_4, \ldots, f_n >$$

The Transition vector is a vector representing the set of rules acting on the binary string where each f_i in the Transition Vector (TRV) has a choice of functions from the functions defined in the table below

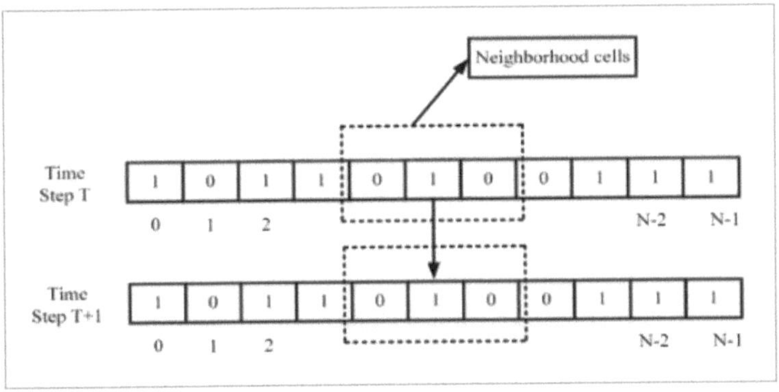

Fig. 7.2 State transition of 3-neighbourhood CA

Hence if for all f_i-
Number of Choices $= p$
Number of bits required to represent said number of choices $= \gamma$
Then each f_i can be represented by a sub-string of length

$$\gamma = \lceil \log_2(p) \rceil$$

Hence, based on the number of choices of functions allocated to each f_i of the TRV, we can have TRV of length

$$Length(TRV) = \beta = N \times \gamma$$

Therefore, the rule vector can be denoted as a tuple of functions. Based on the availability of the various binary functions, we can have various rules that can be encoded for the sake of the formulation as (Fig. 7.2).

Linear Cellular Automata is a special class of Cellular Automata whose transition function is comprised only of linear binary rules employing XOR/XNOR logic functions. The transition function of the linear CA can be characterized using a linear matrix wherein

- $S[t] =$ a $N \times 1$ matrix to represent the present state of the CA.
- $T =$ a $N \times N$ matrix to represent the transition rule of the CA.

It has been established in the book [4] that the Cellular Automata transition function can be characterized by the following linear equation

$$S(t+1) = f_{CA}(< TRV >, S(t))$$

The linear nature of the Cellular Automata transition rule can be extrapolated to the linear regression model and can be used to model a learning algorithm in the binary space using CA transitions (Table 7.1).

Table 7.1 Transition functions

Rule no.	Next state function with XOR logic	Rule no.	Next state function with XNOR logic
Rule 60	$q_i(t+1) = q_{i-1}(t) \oplus q_i(t)$	Rule 195	$q_i(t+1) = q_{i-1}(t) \oplus q_i(t)$
Rule 90	$q_i(t+1) = q_i(t) \oplus q_{i+1}(t)$	Rule 165	$q_i(t+1) = q_i(t) \oplus q_{i+1}(t)$
Rule 102	$q_i(t+1) = q_i(t) \oplus q_{i+1}(t)$	Rule 153	$q_i(t+1) = q_i(t) \oplus q_{i+1}(t)$
Rule 150	$q_i(t+1) = q_{i-1}(t) \oplus q_i(t) \oplus q_{i+1}(t)$	Rule 105	$q_i(t+1) = q_{i-1}(t) \oplus q_i(t) \oplus q_{i+1}(t)$
Rule 170	$q_i(t+1) = q_{i+1}(t)$	Rule 85	$q_i(t+1) = q_{i+1}(t)$
Rule 204	$q_i(t+1) = q_i(t)$	Rule 51	$q_i(t+1) = q_i(t)$
Rule 240	$q_i(t+1) = q_{i-1}(t)$	Rule 15	$q_i(t+1) = q_{i-1}(t)$

7.3 Cellular Automata and Machine Learning

Cellular Automata has emerged as one of the most versatile, robust, and successful computational tools in the field of computer science which offers a unique mix of simplicity and complexity [5]. The capability of the Cellular Automata model to be able to capture and model intricate behavior from the very basic fundamental local rules has always sparked interest in diverse fields, including binary systems and machine learning [6].

Binary system, the fundamental layer of digital computing, relies on the manipulation of the bits, 0 and 1. The early work on CA by researchers like von Neumann [7] and Toffoli [8, 9] established CA as a theoretical framework for studying complex behavior arising from very simple local rules in the binary system. Beyond theoretical explorations, CA has found practical applications in binary systems [4]. The researchers have also successfully designed CA rules in creating successful models of fundamental binary operations like Addition, Subtraction and Multiplication [10, 11]. This allows for the simulation of logic gates and the application of basic arithmetic circuits in digital systems. The versatility of CA extends far beyond the ability to successfully model the binary systems. The CA has an inherent capability to capture spatial and temporal dependencies and patterns within data which makes them a well-suited candidate for various tasks within the realm of machine learning. Extracting meaningful features from the data is a crucial step in many machine learning tasks. For example, Tangsakul et al. [12] demonstrates the effectiveness of using CA to extract features from images for image classification task. CA has also been employed to reduce dimensions in the machine learning data and compress complex data into a lower dimensional representation suitable for machine learning; such an application is reported in Sfairopoulos et al. [13]. A novel CA model is integrated with deep learning to model the dynamics of Land Use Change LUC [14]. Recurrent Neural Networks (RNN) are powerful machine learning architectures for tasks involving sequential data but the training of RNNs are computationally expensive and hence CA have been used to act as a substrate for such tasks [15].

The above work of application of CA in the field of Binary Systems and Machine Learning presents a good testament to how CA can be utilized in various different forms. Such applications provide the incentive to apply CA in a way where it can be applied both in the domain of Binary Systems and Machine Learning to develop a Binary Machine Learning System—an area not adequately explored.

7.3.1 Congruity Between Linear Regression and Linear Cellular Automata

This subsection elaborates the major reason to initiate our current research of building CA based binarized machine learning model for Linear Regression. There exist various congruities between the characteristics and architecture of linear regression and the computational characteristics of the Cellular Automata. This makes the task of modeling, especially the part of taking each aspect of the linear regression model, deconstructing them and redefining it in the domain of CA, more intuitive and easier.

The basic congruities that can be observed between both models are listed below

1. **Structure—Linearity**
   The linear regression model is based on the linear relationship between the input features/independent variables and the output/dependent variables and therefore the model architecture can be mathematically represented by a linear equation

$$Y = \theta_m \cdot X_m + \theta_{m-1} \cdot X_{m-1} + \cdots + \theta_1 \cdot X_1 + \theta_0$$

   where m = Number of features/independent variables.
   The Cellular Automata computation model, in case of the constraint applied on the choice of functions for the transition functions to only be linear functions (XOR-based functions), ends up making the Cellular Automata model a linear model. In work [4], it has been established that XOR-based transition functions can make the Cellular Automata function linear in nature

$$S(t+1) = f_{CA}(< T >, S(t))$$

   – The CA function when applied using the linear rules gives rise to the linear function.
   – The incorporation of a bias term will finally make the CA function the form of a linear function.

$$S(t+1) = f_{CA}(< TRV >, S(t)) + b(t)$$

The linear nature of both the regression model and CA can be used to extrapolate the linear regression model into the domain of the CA.

$$Y = \theta_m \cdot X_m + \theta_{m-1} \cdot X_{m-1} + \cdots + \theta_1 \cdot X_1 + \theta_0$$

$$S(t+1) = TRV_m \cdot S_m(t) + TRV_{m-1} \cdot S_{m-1}(t) + \cdots + TRV_1 \cdot S_1(t) + b(t)$$

2. **Computation—Simplicity**
   Linear regression model uses a simple linear equation model as its basis and this once again means the mathematical computations involved in the linear regression are rather computationally simple and therefore easy to translate in the domain of Cellular Automata.

   Linear Function → CA Function
   Addition Subtraction → Binary Addition Subtraction
   Product → Binary Product

   The rest of the mathematical computation involved in the linear regression model and algorithm can be generated using the basic functions as defined above in the machine level binary space. Thus, this simple translation of the fundamental functions of linear regression as well as the availability of some other gate level functions like AND, OR, XOR, etc. also helps in the formulation of the model detailed in next section.

7.4 Cellular Automata-Based Linear Regression Model

The basic approach to achieve a Cellular Automata-based linear regression model is to deconstruct the structure of the already pre-existing linear regression model and redefine it in terms of the tools and functions that the Cellular Automata support. In order to avail this support, first the computation data is formulated wherein the variable types of linear regression are modified into CA binary space domain generating a binary dataset along with dependent and independent variables. Simultaneously, we need to formulate the model architecture enabling modification of linear function into CA transition rule, defining parameter search space. Finally, we need to design the optimization algorithm employing heuristics to complete the design of machine learning algorithm.

7.4.1 Developing CA Based Model

After the initial development of a workable model through refinement of the linear regression aspects, the model is analyzed based on the variable factors related to data types, architecture, parameter space, and optimization algorithm. The analysis of the various factors related to all of the above aspects of the model is done and the model is improved to achieve a better working model for the CA domain.

The development of such a model is of prime importance in the field of both computational hardware and machine learning algorithms.

1. **Parallel Processing Power**—Cellular Automata has the capability of performing parallel computation because of its grid structure where each cell in the grid can execute some function in parallel.
2. **Efficiency Boost**—A dedicated hardware for the Machine Learning Algorithm along with newer computational models like CA, significantly optimizes the efficient utilization of the given resources compared to general-purpose CPU and GPU.
3. **Reduced Power Consumption**—The specialized hardware is designed to be more energy efficient for machine learning compared to the CPU.
4. **Enhanced Scalability**—Dedicated hardware is easier and more efficient and easier to scale in comparison to general-purpose CPU and GPU.

The Cellular Automata, with the potential advantages that it offers with its application, also confronts the designers with some challenges which can be summarized as follows.
Cost vs Performance Trade-offs—Development and deployment of the dedicated hardware for machine learning can be significantly more expensive if the complexity of the basic computation is not handled efficiently.
Programming Complexity—The programming of such hardware will require low-level coding skills to harness the full power the CA based hardware; this will lead to increased complexity for its application design.
Limited Re-usability—Balancing Efficiency and Flexibility—An appropriate trade off in this regard is a necessity for efficient use of the model.

7.4.2 Problem Formulation

The problem is to redefine the Data Input, Model Architecture, Objective Function, and Optimization Algorithm of the linear regression model of machine learning to formulate the new binary model based on the linear Cellular Automata.

The formulation of any machine learning model requires a well-defined description of every aspect. To that end, we list below all the aspects of the linear regression model that are the focus of this work.

1. Data Input and Input Features
2. Model Architecture and Parameters
3. Objective Function and Optimization Algorithm.

Starting Point: The basic foundation on which the modification of the linear regression into a binary-level cellular Automata model lies is the commonality in the linear nature of the analytic function of both models.

Linear Regression	Cellular Automata
$Y = \theta_2 \cdot X + \theta_1$	$(t+1) = f_{CA}([T], S(t)) + b(t)$

The commonality in the linear nature of the function as well as the fact that both models share the analytic function of the same nature means that.

1. this commonality can be extracted and extrapolated in the system to extrapolate the model
2. this provides a starting point for us to work on the extrapolation which can be extended to multiple features in the system.

Extrapolation: The first basic extrapolation based on the provided function can be realized as follows

Linear Regression	Cellular Automata
1. Dependent Variable—Y	$\longrightarrow S(t+1)$—The Next state of CA
2. Independent Variable—X	$\longrightarrow S(t)$—The previous state of CA
3. Parameter (slope)—θ_2	$\longrightarrow T$—Transition Vector of CA
4. Parameter (Intercept)—θ_1	$\longrightarrow b$—a constant valued bias CA array of values

In this formulation, the concept of time steps is disregarded and hence the CA arrays simply become the representation of data values in regard to the Linear regression model.

The transition matrix can be formulated as an N × N matrix or as a Transition N-tuple.

7.4.3 *Model Formulation*

Given a linear regression model, our aim is to frame a binary machine learning Cellular Automata model that can perform linear regression using the computational model of Cellular Automata. Given a dataset of an independent variable Y, and dependent variable $X_1, X_2, \ldots, X_m$ the Cellular Automata model is as follows

$$Y = \theta_m \cdot X_m + \theta_{m-1} \cdot X_{m-1} + \cdots + \theta_1 \cdot X_1 + \theta_0$$

The linear regression modelling in the domain of Cellular Automata can be done by redefining the constituents of linear regression into Cellular Automata domain.

Data Input and Features

In order to take advantage of the computational model of CA we need to define the data on which the model is going to work in a way that it is compatible with the CA model and hence all the data utilized in the linear regression needs to be redefined. The linear regression model has the following main types of data on which it works. Such data types will have to be constrained in the CA domain for its compatibility. Independent variables / input feature and dependent variable can be real numbers in the model but any data being manipulated in the CA domain are essentially binary strings since CA work on the binary strings.

1. **Data**
   – Independent variable :
   Real number ⇒ Whole numbers ⇒ Binary numbers
   – Dependent variable :
   Real number ⇒ Whole numbers ⇒ Binary numbers
2. **Function**
   The Hypothesis Function of the linear regression is modelled using the Cellular Automata function where the
   – Multiplication ⇒ f_{CA} – Addition ⇒ binary addition
3. **Parameter Space**
   A machine learning requires a hypothesis function—point 2 above—and the hypothesis function fits the data and the fitting is done by searching for the optimal parameters in the parameter space. For searching the parameter, we require
   – A well modelled parameter space
   – A well modelled search algorithm

The parameters in case of CA are the strings of rules, or Transition Rule Vector which has the same number of rules, in order, as the number of bits in the input X. Wherein all f are CA rules that act on a single bit. The n-bit CA acts on the input as follows:

$$\begin{aligned} f_{CA} = &\ \langle f_1, f_2, f_3, \ldots, f_n \rangle \\ X :&\ n - \text{bit binary number} \\ f_i :&\ n - \text{bit linear CA with rules 90 and 150} \\ b :&\ n - \text{bit binary number} \\ Y :&\ n - \text{bit binary number} \end{aligned}$$

In order to search the optimal parameter, the parameter space has to be designed with the two features, ordering and distance. Ordering guides the search algorithm to move forward or backward in the order to go to newer parameters in a analytical fashion without missing any parameters. Distance between parameters is defined so that the quantification of how much to move in a direction of parameters space is possible so that searching the parameter is feasible.

The rules in the Transition Vector has to be encoded into a data type so that they are represented in binary and must have an ordering and a formulation of distance.

The encoded rules can be ordered in the lexicographic order in such that all the combinations of the choice of the rules can be included in the given order from the smallest binary string to the largest string in binary. For example, if we consider only rule 90 and rule 150 (R 90 = 0 and R 150 = 1), the ordering that is parameter space, plotted will be defined as follows

$$\begin{array}{cccc} < R90R90\cdots R90R90R90 > & < R90R90\cdots R90R90R150 > & \cdots\cdots & < R150R150\cdots R150R150R150 > \\ \Downarrow & \Downarrow & & \Downarrow \\ < 00\cdots 000 > & < 00\cdots 001 > & \cdots\cdots & < 11\cdots 111 > \end{array}$$

The distance metric can be defined as the binary difference i.e. XOR of two binary string representing the rules.

Sketch of Algorithm: binarized_CA_based_ML

1. **Input** the dataset:

   a. Dependent variable set: Y
   b. Independent variable sets: $X_1, X_2, \ldots, X_m$

   Based on the range of values in sets $Y, X_1, X_2, \ldots, X_m$ input the bit-length n of the Cellular Automata is chosen in such that the largest values of the inputs can be accommodated.
2. **Pre-process** the dataset into the domain of Cellular Automata model, the inputs, both independent and dependent variables are assumed as non-negative whole numbers.
3. **Binarize** the dataset to convert it into binary strings of bit-length n.
4. **Initialize Randomly all** the parameters $\theta_1, \theta_2, \ldots, \theta_m$, the n-bit CA rule sets for all X_i's. The algorithm requires initial values of parameters from where it can start the update process and that is done using random initialization that gives the first initial value of the objective function. Next, the algorithm explores the parameter space using the values of Objective Function at the neighboring values of the parameters and then updating the parameter accordingly.
5. **Set** a value $p(= \Delta\theta)$ and select the two CA rules $\theta - \Delta\theta$ and $\theta + \Delta\theta$ for a parameter θ. Find a number m by some pre-processing where m determines the number of cycles to run the CA to determine the distance. The values of p and m together determine the direction.
6. **Calculate** the value of objective function J for neighboring values of θ i.e. $\theta - \Delta\theta$ and $\theta + \Delta\theta$ for parameter θ while keeping all the other parameters constant at the current values, i.e. $f_1(\theta)$, $f_2(\theta - \Delta\theta)$ and $f_3(\theta + \Delta\theta)$. Here, f_1, f_2, f_3 are transition functions of three different CA rules at points (θ), $(\theta - \Delta\theta)$ and $(\theta + \Delta\theta)$ respectively.
   Determine the direction of the update parameter (refer Fig. 7.3). Here, the notions slope left and slope right are denoted as SL and SR and defined as:

$$SL = \frac{f(\theta_1, \theta_2, \ldots, \theta_i, \ldots, \theta_n) - f(\theta_1, \theta_2, \ldots, \theta_i - \delta\theta_i, \ldots, \theta_n)}{\delta\theta_i}$$

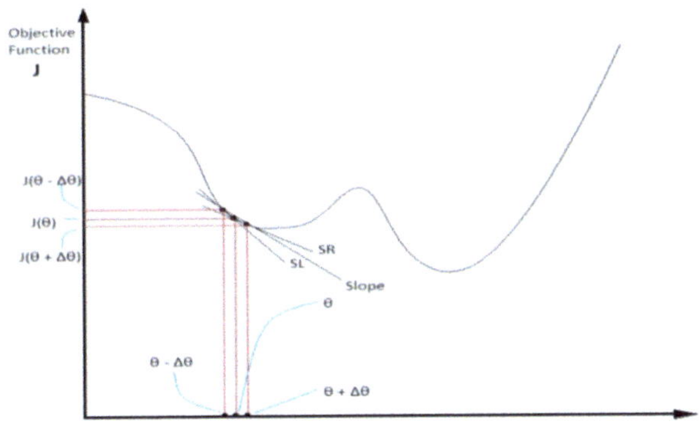

Fig. 7.3 Reaching towards the Minima of the Objective Function

$$SR = \frac{f(\theta_1, \theta_2, \ldots, \theta_i + \delta\theta_i, \ldots, \theta_n) - f(\theta_1, \theta_2, \ldots, \theta_i, \ldots, \theta_n)}{\delta\theta_i}$$

Update using the value with more downward slope value among SL and SR and all the update metrics are applied to update the complete set of parameters. Finally, the minima is achieved when $J(\theta - \Delta\theta) > J(\theta) < J(\theta + \Delta\theta)$.

7. **Repeat** the running of the updates, the model is evaluated using the testing-dataset and the final error-metrics calculated.

7.5 Experiments and Results

In the previous section, a new model of binarized machine learning based on Cellular Automata for linear regression is proposed. The model still poses some challenges regarding its convergence and accuracy. The design of the parameter and the parameter search space play a pivotal role in determining how good and accurate, the model is going to perform.

In the case of the binarized machine learning model proposed above, the CA transition rules are encoded as binary strings and it is necessary to impose ordering on such strings. This encoding of rules as binary strings makes the parameter space complex in nature and therefore, the way of encoding the CA rules is very important. Another important issue is the selection of optimization algorithm. The algorithm should be designed in such that it must be consistent on the convergence of the model and have some rules for way out where convergence gets stuck. Also, the algorithm should have some rules of improvements in order to reduce the time of optimization.

In this section, we perform very basic experiments and analysis to find the merits of the new CA based binarized machine learning model. Based on the results, different changes to achieve an improved version of the model may further be explored. The study focuses on two basic fronts

1. Input data and parameter search space
2. The optimization algorithm.

7.5.1 Input Data and Parameter Search Space

The input data, used in the experiment, is generated using Python library scikit-learn and are defined as n-bit binary strings. Certain linear transformations are performed and with different noise in the data generated to get the desired binary dataset required for the experimentation in the system. To use dataset, available in public domain, it is required to create binary data to be used for the experimental setup in the current CA model. The following three datasets, D1 (see Fig. 7.4), D2 (see Fig. 7.5) and D3 (see Fig. 7.6) are generated and used in the experiment.

Datasets—D1,D2,D3
The improvement in the parameter space design lies in the analysis of the objective function. In machine learning, parameter design has a significant impact on the complexity of the objective function curve. Parameter design significantly influences whether the model converges to the global minimum or gets stuck in a local one.

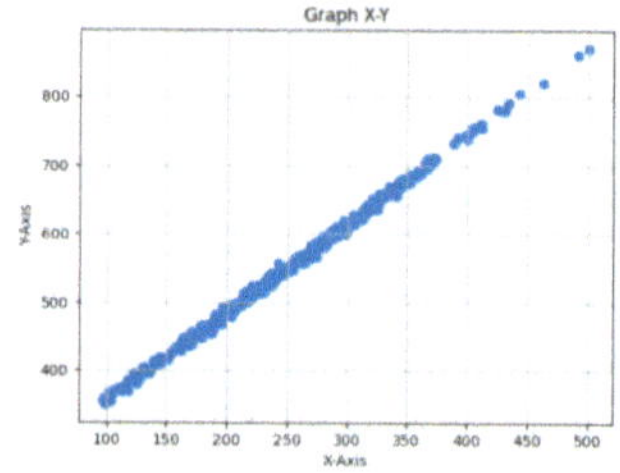

Fig. 7.4 D1-Noise 0.08

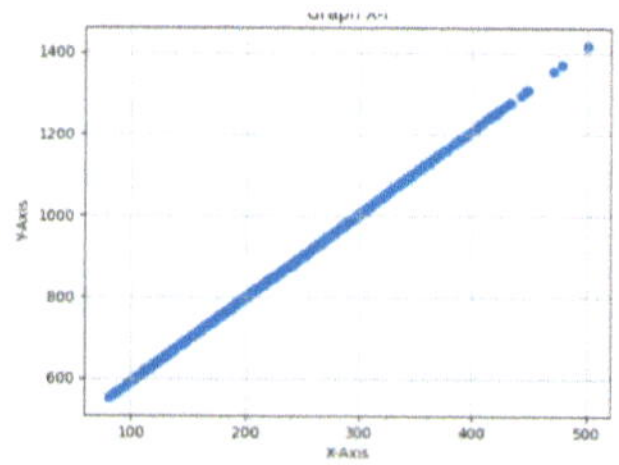

Fig. 7.5 D2-Noise 0.5

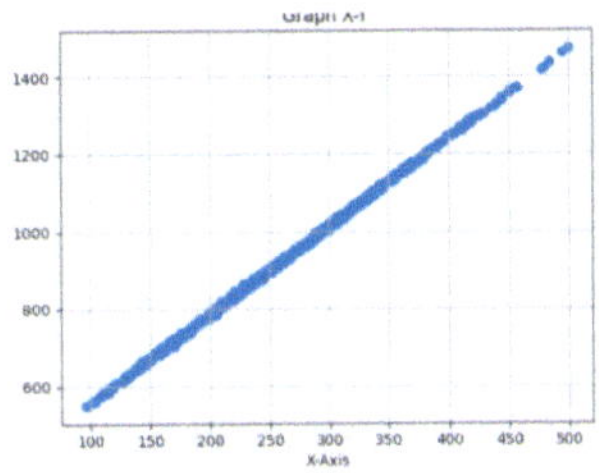

Fig. 7.6 D3-Noise 4.00

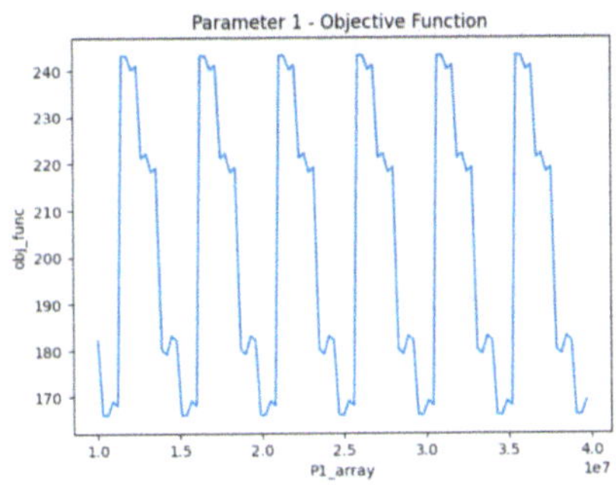

Fig. 7.7 Parameter Space: P1

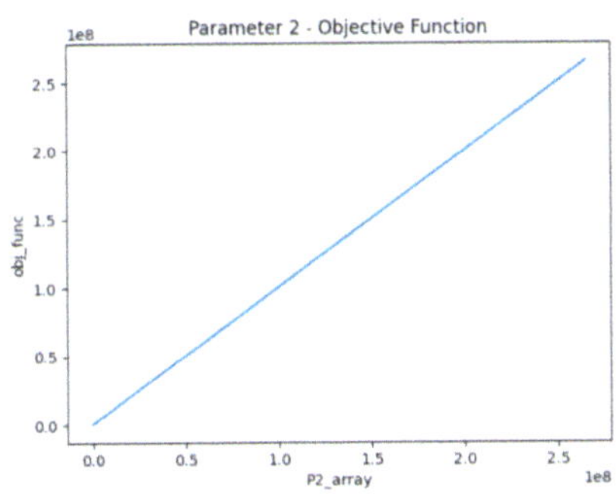

Fig. 7.8 Parameter Space: P2

The objective function curve for parameter 1 of the CA-based linear regression model is a recurring curve with multiple minima and the objective function curve of parameter 2 of the CA model is a linear curve. By using the concept of propagation of the errors, approximately we can get an idea of the complete objective function curve in two dimensions wherein Parameter 1 (Fig. 7.7) will be a periodic curve but Parameter 2 (Fig. 7.8) will create a linearly increasing curve, thus the complete curve will not be a periodic curve and will have a certain global minimum.

Table 7.2 Rules

0	Rule 90
1	Rule 150

Parameter engineering is a crucial step in machine learning that involves transforming the raw data into informative features. These features act as the building blocks for the model's learning process and significantly impact the complexity of the objective function curve. Strategically, initializing parameter values can influence the optimization process. Techniques like pre-training or initializing with values based on prior knowledge can steer the model towards a region with a simpler objective function landscape.

7.5.2 Optimization Algorithms

Optimization algorithms are the workhorses of machine learning, tirelessly searching for the best parameter configurations that minimize the objective function and lead to optimal model performance.

The convergence of the optimization algorithm lies on the design of the objective function curve. Hence, experiments have been done with objective function curves with different encoding. The results of convergence with generated datasets, as mentioned in the previous sub-section are presented with different encoding strategies.

- Objective Function Curve with Encoding—1 [Rules—90, 150]: The first approach wherein only the rules 90 and 150 are utilized (Table 7.2). The CA rule set with 90 and 150 is treated as universal set [4] and the structure becomes hardware friendly because of the ease of implementation of 90–150 with programmable CA. The objective function curve of parameter of periodic and linear nature are shown in Figs. 7.7 and 7.8 respectively. The results of Mean Absolute Error (MAE) and R2 Score for datasets D1, D2 and D3 are shown in Figs. 7.9, 7.10 and 7.11.

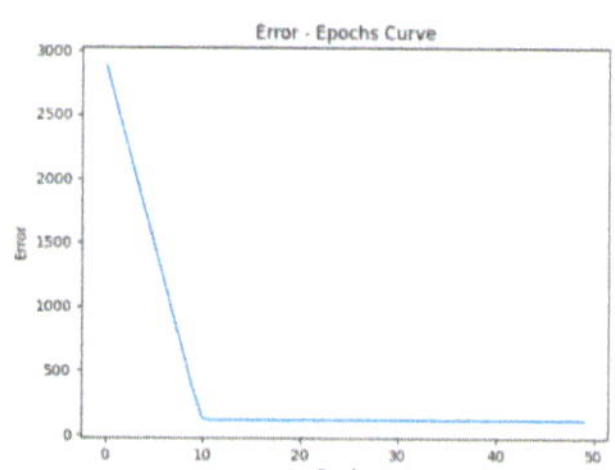

Fig. 7.9 MAE = 120; R2 = 0.01

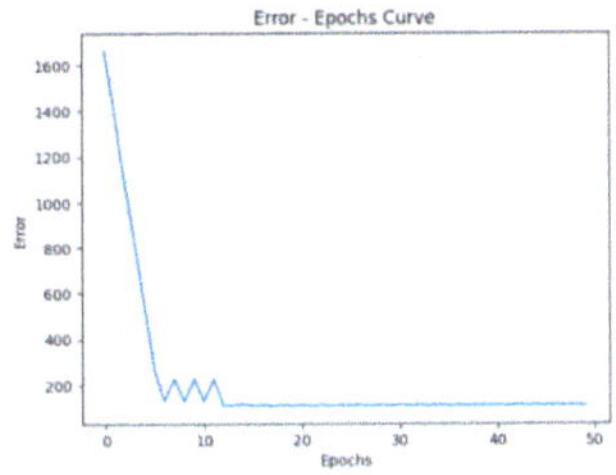

Fig. 7.10 MAE = 126; R2 = –5.97

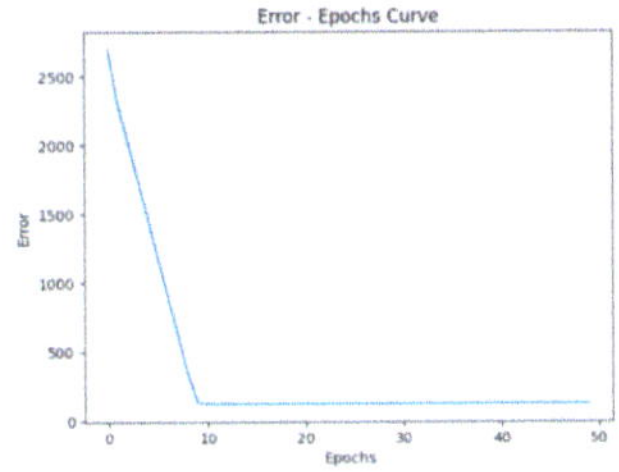

Fig. 7.11 MAE = 133; R2 = –0.10

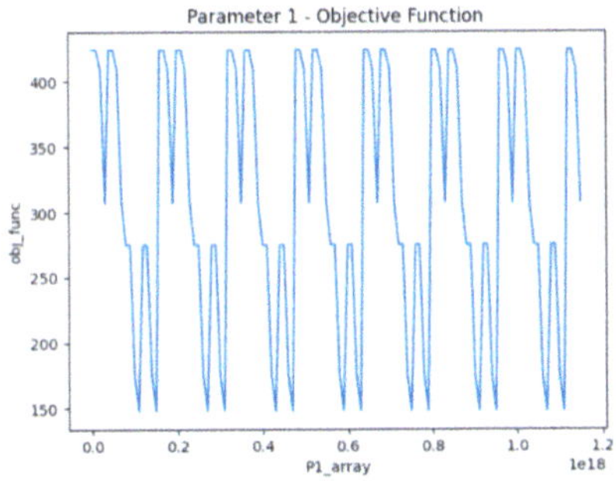

Fig. 7.12 Parameter Space: P1

Table 7.3 Rules

00	Rule 204
01	Rule 90
10	Rule 150
11	Rule 204

- Objective Function Curve with Encoding—2 [Rules—90, 150, 204]: Table 7.3 shows the 2-bit binary encoding. Including rule 204 along with rule 90 and 150 in the encoding creates no change to the input features. Rule 204 does not change the state of the bit, it is applied upon. So, framing the ruleset with rule

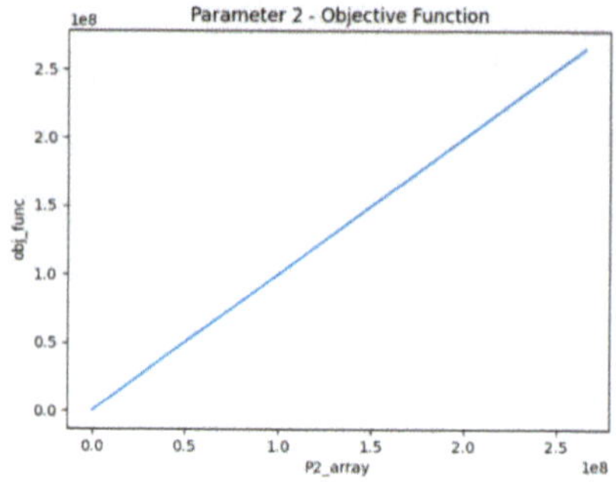

Fig. 7.13 Parameter Space: P2

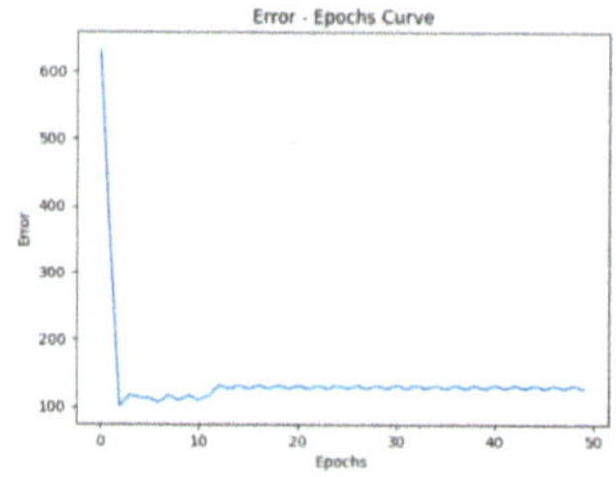

Fig. 7.14 MAE = 64; R2 = 0.74

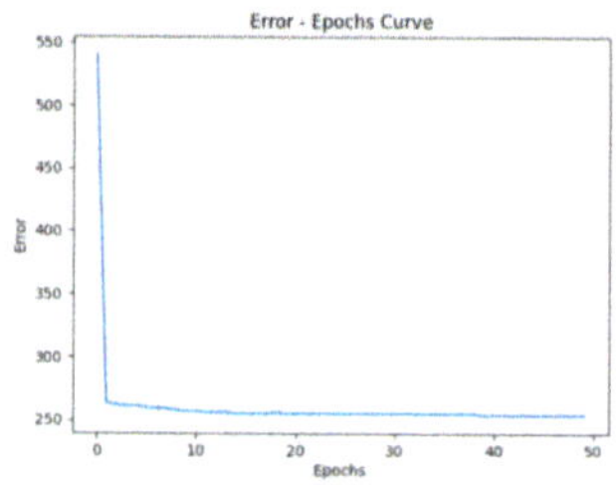

Fig. 7.15 MAE = 245; R2 = –0.1

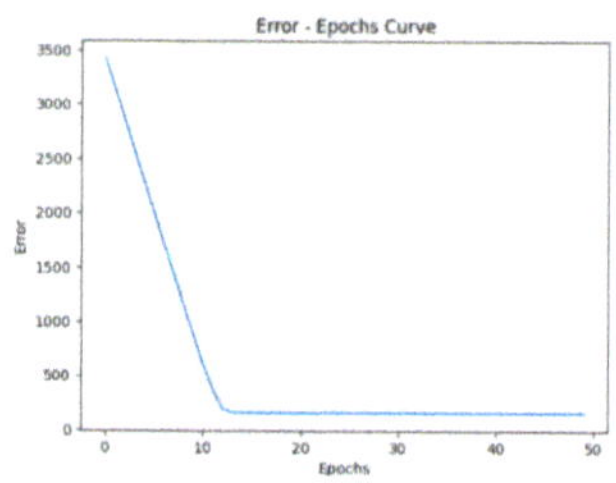

Fig. 7.16 MAE = 19; R2 = 0.44

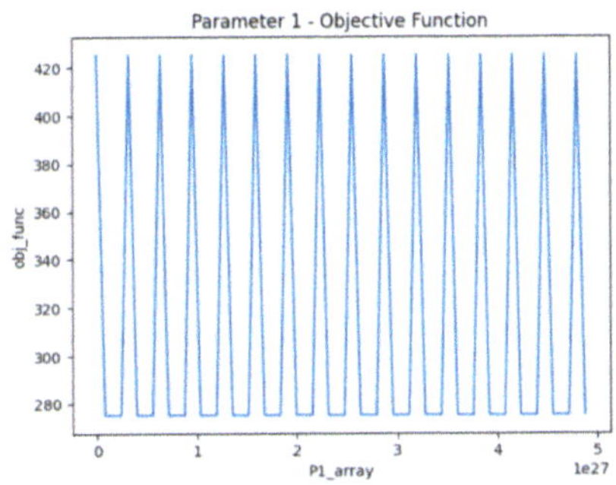

Fig. 7.17 Parameter Space: P1

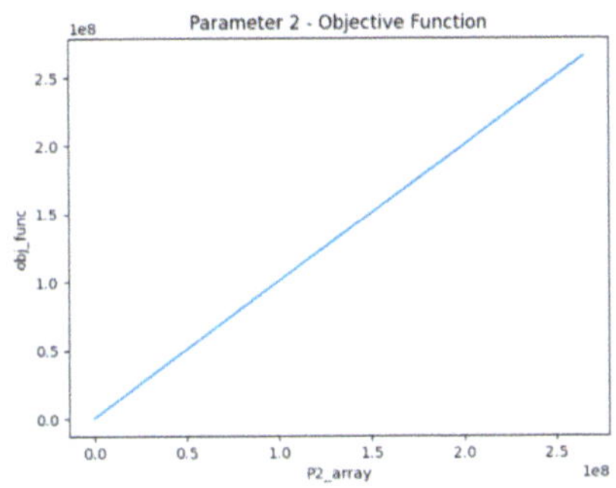

Fig. 7.18 Parameter Space: P2

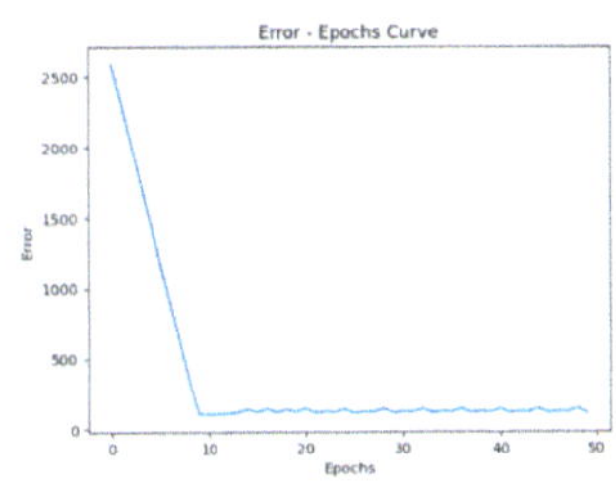

Fig. 7.19 MAE = 220; R2 = –20.56

204 at two extreme edges keep the changes in the middle only. Figures 7.12 and 7.13 show the parameter space. The results of MAE and R2 score are shown in Figs. 7.14, 7.15 and 7.16.

- Objective Function Curve with Encoding—3 [Rules—60, 90, 102, 150, 170 204, 240]: Table 7.4 shows the 3-bit encoding for seven rules. To verify if the inclusion of all the rules can provide a better parameter design and consequently, a better Objective Function Curve since finally the convergence of the optimization algorithm rests on the design of the Objective Function curve. The parameter space P1

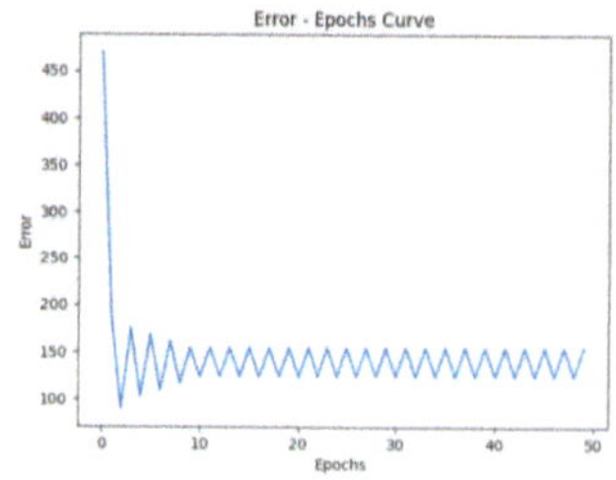

Fig. 7.20 MAE = 200; R2 = −10.78

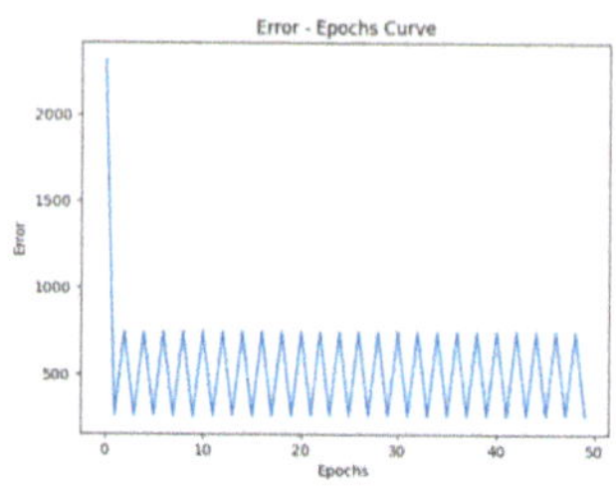

Fig. 7.21 MAE = 828; R2 = −25

Table 7.4 Rules

000	Rule 204
001	Rule 240
010	Rule 170
011	Rule 60
100	Rule 102
101	Rule 90
110	Rule 150
111	Rule 150

and P2 are given in Figs. 7.17 and 7.18. The MAE value and R2 score are shown in Figs. 7.19, 7.20 and 7.21 respectively.

In the above study of the Objective Function in different cases of encoding of the system, the following observations can be drawn.

In Encoding-1, the values of Minima encounter are very high and thus the performance of the given model is not very good since the parameter design does not embody better domain intricacies. In the case of Encoding-1 the convergence is fast because of the simpler model but the convergence is always in the non-optimal minima and thus the model performance is lower.

In Encoding-2, three rules are used, 90, 150 and 204. The addition of Rule 204 creates a more complex objective function curve but at the same time provides a better minima since inclusion of more rules means a better incorporation of the domain knowledge. In case of Encoding 2, the convergence is optimal amongst the given options and the score of the system is also optimal in the given context. Encoding 2 is preferred based on the score of the model.

In Encoding-3, a complete set of linear CA rules are added in the system, which on one hand, will completely incorporate the domain knowledge into the system but on the other hand leads to a complex system and gives a compromised performance in the current algorithm, In the case of Encoding 3 the convergence becomes oscillatory in nature as shown in the objective function curve.

The computational complexity of the model increases as the incorporation of more rules increases in the system since the parameter search space increases.

7.6 Outline of Hardware Design for CA Based Binarized ML Model

In order to provide an outline of the proposed hardware for CA based Binarized ML, we refer to Fig. 4.1 of Chap. 4 of this book that is reproduced as Fig. 7.22, inserted below. It refers to a three neighborhood n cell CA with ith cell having three neighbors, $(i-1)$th cell, ith cell, and $(i+1)$th cell. The combinational logic R_i receives the current state value (0 or 1) from its three neighbors (as indicated with directed link), to generate the next state of the ith cell; this binary data movement is indicated with a directed link from R_i to the ith cell. The combinational logic of R_i, in the present case, implements XOR logic function. The ith cell is referred to as Cell i Flip Flop (FF) storing 0 or 1, a basic memory element. On inserting three on/off switches on the three incoming links to combinational logic block of R_i, it can implement any one of the transition rules noted in Table 7.4 that reports seven different linear CA rules (60, 90, 108, 150, 170, 204, 240). The control logic for each switch can be easily implemented with a one-bit memory element. Further, in view of serial evaluation of each cell, we need an n bit intermediate memory array to store the next state of each cell after each time step (say, Qth). The binary data from this n bit memory is fed back to n FFs of n cell CA prior to evolution of the CA in next time step $(Q+1)$. The implementation of this simple hardware has been detailed in [4].

The three CA rules we have used to implement the proposed CA based ML model are 90, 150 and 204. While to implement rule 204, all the switches are set 'off', for rule 150, all the switches are set 'on'. Implementation of rule 90 demands left and right link stitches 'on' with middle link switch 'off'. Thus, to implement the ML scheme on n binary bits, the hardware cost is the n cell CA noted in Fig. 7.22, in addition to $4n$ bit memory (n for intermediate memory and $3n$ for three switches of each cell). The hardware operates for say k successive steps if operation of CA is necessary for k time steps to reach at the optimum cost point of the objective function curve (Fig. 7.1).

Further, let us evaluate the hardware implementation with T matrix operation, presented in Sect. 7.2.4 as

- $S[t]$ = a $N \times 1$ matrix to represent the present state of the Cellular Automata
- T = a $N \times N$ matrix to represent the transition rule of the Cellular Automata, where T is a binary 0–1 matrix to implement Encoding scheme 1 employing only 90 and 150 rules.

If through emulation of CA hardware for experimentation with a specific data type employing the Encoding-1 scheme, the value of k can be identified, we can evaluate 0–1 binary T^k matrix. For such an implementation we can evaluate next state of the CA in 1 time step instead of k time steps without any extra hardware cost. In Fig. 3.5 of our previous book [4], we had proposed the simple hardwired implementation of rule pair (90, 150) for each cell of an n-cell CA that demands n control bits. Each control bit operates a switch in the link between ith cell output to ith cell logic. Other two inputs from two neighbouring cells are connected to ith cell logic without any switch. While for implementing the rule 150 for a cell, the switch is in *on* state and for rule 90, the switch is in *off* state.

7.7 Conclusion and Future Work

Machine Learning models are continuously being used in real-world applications with increasing pressure on the computation resources available at the hardware level. In order to meet the constraints of the computation resources, the research discourse continuously moves towards the optimization of the algorithms of machine learning models without paying due attention on the optimization of the hardware of the system on which ML model operates. This scenario points to the necessity of developing hardware to support efficient implementation of ML models. While this necessity is fulfilled with the design of specialized hardware chip set for LLM applications, no such move is visible for non-LLM applications employing conventional ML models. The current chapter of this book aims to bridge this gap. The computational model of Cellular Automata is proposed as the Binary Level Machine Learning

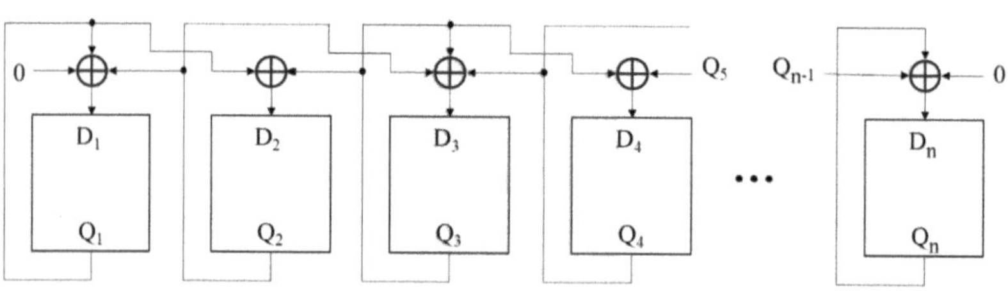

Fig. 7.22 Hardware of an n-cell three neighborhood CA

model that can work with significantly lesser computing resources, as outlined in the earlier section. The formulation of the binary model has been proposed imposing a number of constraints and assumptions for study of the model in its simplest form to arrive at the optimal heuristics for linear regression task. However, search for efficient heuristics for different input datasets will continue to guide the future work.

In view of the choice of the parameter space, the proposed CA model tends to have an objective function with a multiplicity of minima. Consequently, search for efficient heuristics for different datasets will continue in future. Further, the proposed model may generate inflection points in the data and hence new heuristics may be needed. The inflection point may be identified through detection change in sign of the second derivative on the objective function curve (illustrated in Fig. 7.3).

The scope of the future work can be broadly classified as follows

1. **Work on the Formulation of the Cellular Automata Function**
   In order to better capture the relationship between the independent and dependent variables we can expand from 3-neighbourhood CA to higher-neighborhood CA. However, as per our exhaustive analysis of building CA models for different real-life applications (reported in Chaps. 5 and 6), we notice that higher neighborhood does not lead to better results. It is worth investigating whether this experience is valid for CA based ML model employing higher neighborhood.
2. **Work to improve the optimization algorithm**
   In order to improve the optimization algorithm, we can utilize certain heuristics like Simulated Annealing.
3. **Work to accommodate non-linear functions**
   In order to accommodate nonlinear functions, we can use the nonlinear CA rules or to employ the concept of piecewise linear function (linear CA rules) of the proposed CA model in order to fit the model to solve the nonlinear functions. Such an approach is proposed in our previous book [4].

References

1. I. Hubara, M. Courbariaux, D. Soudry, R. El-Yaniv, Y. Bengio, Binarized neural networks, in *Advances in Neural Information Processing Systems 29: Annual Conference on Neural Information Processing Systems* (Barcelona, Spain, 2016), pp. 4107–4115
2. V. Sze, Y. Chen, J.S. Einer, A. Suleiman, Z. Zhang, Hardware for machine learning: challenges and opportunities, in *IEEE Custom Integrated Circuits Conference, CICC 2017* (IEEE, Austin, TX, USA, 2017), pp. 1–8
3. K. Berggren, Q. Xia, K.K. Likharev, D.B. Strukov, H. Jiang, T. Mikolajick, D. Querlioz, M. Salinga, J.R. Erickson, S. Pi et al., Roadmap on emerging hardware and technology for machine learning. Nanotechnology **32**(1), 012002 (2020)
4. P.P. Chaudhuri, D.R. Chowdhury, S. Nandi, S. Chattopadhyay, *Additive Cellular Automata: Theory and Applications, Volume 1*, vol. 43 (Wiley, New York, 1997)
5. S. Wolfram, *A New Kind of Science* (Wolfram-Media, 2002)
6. P. Povalej, P. Kokol, T. Welzer-Druzovec, B. Stiglic, Machine-learning with cellular automata, in *Advances in Intelligent Data Analysis VI, 6th International Symposium on Intelligent Data Analysis, IDA 2005, Madrid, Spain, September 8-10, 2005, Proceedings*, ser. Lecture Notes

in Computer Science, eds. by A.F. Famili, J.N. Kok, J.M.P. Sánchez, A. Siebes, A.J. Feelders, vol. 3646 (Springer, Berlin, 2005), pp. 305–315. [Online]. Available: https://doi.org/10.1007/11552253_28

7. J. Von Neumann, A.W. Burks, *Theory of Self-Reproducing Automata* (University of Illinois press Urbana and London, 1966)
8. T. Toffoli, N. Margolus, *Cellular Automata Machines—A New Environment for Modeling, Ser* (MIT Press series in Scientific Computation, MIT Press, 1987)
9. T. Toffoli, N.H. Margolus, Invertible cellular automata: a review. Physica D: Nonlinear Phenomena **45**(1–3), 229–253 (1990)
10. E. Petraglio, J. Henry, G. Tempesti, Arithmetic operations on self-replicating cellular automata, in *Advances in Artificial Life, 5th European Conference, ECAL'99, Lausanne, Switzerland, September 13-17, 1999, Proceedings*, ser. Lecture Notes in Computer Science, eds. by D. Floreano, J. Nicoud, F. Mondada, vol. 1674 (Springer, Berlin, 1999), pp. 447–456. [Online]. Available: https://doi.org/10.1007/3-540-48304-7_62
11. E. Sapin, O. Bailleux, J.-J. Chabrier, Research of a cellular automaton simulating logic gates by evolutionary algorithms, in *EuroGP 2003, LNCS 2610*, ed. by C. Ryan et al. (Springer, Berlin Heidelberg, 2003), pp. 414–423
12. S. Tangsakul, S. Wongthanavasu, Deep cellular automata-based feature extraction for classification of the breast cancer image. Appl. Sci. **13**(10), 6081 (2023)
13. K. Sfairopoulos, L. Causer, J.F. Mair, J.P. Garrahan, Cellular automata in d dimensions and ground states of spin models in $(d + 1)$ dimensions (2023). arXiv:2309.08059
14. W. Xing, Y. Qian, X. Guan, T. Yang, H. Wu, A novel cellular automata model integrated with deep learning for dynamic spatio-temporal land use change simulation. Comput. Geosci. **137**, 104430 (2020). [Online]. Available: https://doi.org/10.1016/j.cageo.2020.104430
15. S. Nichele, A. Molund, Deep learning with cellular automaton-based reservoir computing. Complex Syst. **26**(4) (2017). [Online]. Available: https://doi.org/10.25088/complexsystems.26.4.319

Appendix
Epilogue and Looking Forward

The current book is entitled 'New Kind of Machine Learning—Cellular Automata Model'. It is 'new' in the sense, the book proposes a new computational model employing both Cellular Automata (CA) and Machine Learning (ML). The underlying driving force to design this new model is to lay the foundation that would lead to development of CA applications of interest for industry and human society. Two orthogonal viewpoints of the model are reported.

Viewpoint 1: CA (enhanced with) ML—Chaps. 5 and 6 of this book employ non-linear CA. Analysis of Non-linear CA evolution is a highly challenging task, if not impossible. Consequently, non-linear CA evolution is characterized by employing the Training set data corpus of Machine Learning framework, followed by design of computational algorithms to predict results for testing sets.

Viewpoint 2: CA (enhances) ML—Chap. 7 of this book employs linear CA to model ML framework realizing linear functions. The sole objective is to lay an analytical foundation for ML ensuring 'transparency' and 'interpretability' of the results derived out of the prediction process. Extension of this CAML model employing programmable CA (PCA) [ISBN - 13-978-0818677175] has been also projected to model the ML framework realizing nonlinear functions.

Traditional ML models including Deep Learning employ black-box approach. The models demand 'big data sets' for training and very large computing resources for prediction of results on Testing data sets. The following characteristics differentiate CAML model from the traditional ML framework:

1. The input Training data set for CAML model is transformed with CA modelling the physical system and the CAML operates on the transformed data rather than raw input data.
2. The fully automated prediction algorithms are designed employing Feature Vector (FV) extracted from the parameters derived from evolution of CA modelling a physical system.

© The Editor(s) (if applicable) and The Author(s), under exclusive license to Springer Nature Singapore Pte Ltd. 2025

P. P. Chaudhuri et al., *New Kind of Machine Learning—Cellular Automata Model*,
https://doi.org/10.1007/978-981-96-1501-8

3. Input data set is divided into Training Set (TrS), Validation Set (VaS), and Testing Set (TeS).
4. The (VaS) is introduced in the CAML model to assess the quality of prediction algorithms designed employing (TrS).
5. Explain-ability and capability to learn from experience are embedded in CAML framework through program execution on validation Set (VaS) and if necessary, refinement of the prediction algorithm to enhance prediction quality.
6. Compared to conventional ML framework, CAML model needs significantly lesser input training corpus data and much lesser computational resources for prediction of results without sacrificing quality.

In view of the last characteristics, the CAML model is referred to as a 'Light Weight' machine learning model. The CAML model characteristics noted above are highlighted in the CA applications formulated in Chaps. 5, 6, and 7.

The prerequisite for formulation of CA application is—to design CA rules for the set of interconnected entities of a physical system being modelled with a CA. Chapter 4 reports the generic approach of CA rule design for an entity. The generic design approach is illustrated for two application domains. The first application in the field of Computational Biology, covered in Chap. 5, deals with mutational study of the amino acid chain of a protein. CA rule design for twenty amino acids, the entities of a protein chain, is reported in Sect. 4.2.5 of Chap. 4. On the other hand, the entities of a language text are the language alphabets. The second application in the field of Computational Linguistics, covered in Chap. 6, presents a solution for the problem of 'Sentiment Analysis' in a multi-language environment. The proposed solution demands transformation of the input text of a language to Unicode text. CA rule design for Unicode character set is reported in Sect. 4.3 of Chap. 4 of the book.

Chapters 1, 2, and 3 of the book provide a state-of-art review on the discipline of AI/ML. In the context of the historical and current perspective of Artificial Intelligence (AI), we have presented our view point on 'Intelligence' in Sect. 1.6 of Chap. 1. We have discussed the issues associated with the term 'meta recognition', a deep-seated aptitude to 'think on the thinking process' of the human mind. Developing meta recognition skills can lead to more effective and efficient thinking and learning - two basic ingredients of intelligence. In the context of the expanding horizon of AI/ML applications, the review presented in Chap. 2, makes the interested readers aware of the upcoming challenges in the field including the associated ethical issues. Chapter 3 addresses a key issue associated with Machine Learning (ML), a sub-discipline of AI. How are human beings able to make some sense out of the huge volume of data acquired through sensory organs and stored in memory? In all probability, human beings possess a multi-stage decision-making process. An initial guess, in earlier stages, is made in a comparatively lesser time, to correlate the filtered-out data points and come up with a solution. In this context, we hypothesise that a variant of 'light weight ML model' exists in the human mind to implement the so-called 'initial guess' of the decision-making process.

The hypothesis of Chap. 3 laid the foundation of this book and motivated us to develop the Light Weight CAML model to address some real-life problems in remaining Chapters. As we conclude the epilogue, let us look forward to the next step we plan to embark on, based on the foundation laid in the current book. Chapter 5 of this book reports the results derived out of mutational study on—(i) proteins of CoV-2 virus, (ii) proteins implicated for different types of cancer, and (iii) proteins of medicinal plants out of which anti-cancer therapeutic agents may be derived in association with other biomolecules. Subsequent discussions highlight the importance of large-scale proteomics study.

If we look back to the recent past, we can observe the adverse effect of large-scale urbanization and continuous degradation of environmental conditions around the globe. The accumulated effect of such a situation leads to—global warming, unpredictable weather conditions, rising sea level due to melting of ice in north/south poles etc. The pandemic situation in 2020–2022 is a glaring example. Possibility of future pandemic situation, experts apprehend, exists due to new types of zoonotic viruses. Two major casualties of such a situation are—human health hazard and dwindling agricultural production. Consequently, medical sciences and agricultural sciences are likely to dominate the research scenario in the coming decades of the current century, with emphasis on study on Genomics and Proteomics.

Proteins are responsible to execute the majority of the tasks in a living cell. The sub-discipline of Computational Proteomics covers the computational methods, algorithms, databases and methodologies used to process, manage, analyse and interpret the large volume of data generated out of proteomics experiments. As per 2024 report, uniprot database covers nearly 250 million proteins of different organisms. There are identical proteins observed in all life forms - bacteria, animal kingdom, plant world. It is worth investigating—how the function and interaction of the same protein differ in different life forms. For example, Calmodulin protein can be observed in animals (Homo sapiens, Mus Musculus, Bovine etc.), and also in model plant Arabidopsis thaliana, Fungus (Saccharomyces cerevisiae).

Notwithstanding significant advances in mass spectrometry for large scale study of Proteins, it is extremely difficult to correlate the functional characteristics of millions of proteins available in protein databases across the species and organisms. So, new kinds of Computational models are necessary with focussed attention on Comparative Proteomics. In this background, our next step will be—to employ the Light Weight CAML model for Comparative Proteomics, within and across different organisms. In our next book, we propose to deal with four contemporary areas of Comparative Proteomics—Expression Proteomics, Functional Proteomics, Protein-Protein interaction under Structural Proteomics, and Proteomics related to Human and Plant diseases. This project, no doubt, is extremely challenging. However, a little progress in this direction will make a significant impact in the field of Medical Sciences and Agricultural Sciences.

MIX
Papier aus verantwortungsvollen Quellen
Paper from responsible sources
FSC® C105338

If you have any concerns about our products,
you can contact us on
ProductSafety@springernature.com

In case Publisher is established outside the EU,
the EU authorized representative is:
Springer Nature Customer Service Center GmbH
Europaplatz 3, 69115 Heidelberg, Germany

Printed by Libri Plureos GmbH
in Hamburg, Germany